D1613807

Women Rulers
throughout the Ages

throughout the Ages

An Illustrated Guide

Guida M. Jackson

ABC-CLIO

Library of Congress Cataloging-in-Publication Data
Jackson-Laufer, Guida M. (Guida Myrl)
    Women rulers throughout the ages : an illustrated guide / Guida M. Jackson.
        p.   cm.
    ISBN 1-57607-091-3
    1. Women heads of state—Biography Dictionaries.   2. Queens—Biography Dictionaries.   I. Title.
    D107.J32   1999
    940'.099—dc21   99-22705
                                                                 CIP

ABC-CLIO, Inc.
130 Cremona Drive, P.O. Box 1911
Santa Barbara, California 93116-1911

This book is printed on acid-free paper∞.

Manufactured in the United States of America

For my husband, William H. Laufer

Contents

Geographical Chronology of Entries, xv
Preface, xxxi
Introduction, xxxv

Women Rulers throughout the Ages

Absh Khatun, 1
Ada, 1
Adame, Mama, 2
Addagoppe of Harran, 3
Adela, 4
Adelaide, 5
Adelaide of Salona, 6
Adele, 7
Aelfgifu of Northumbria, 7
Aelfwyn, 8
Aethelflaed, 8
Afua Koba, 9
Agnes de Dampierre, 10
Agnes de Nevers, 10
Agnes of Dunbar, 11
Agnes of Poitou, 11
Ahhotpe I, 12
Ahmose-Nofretari, 12
Aissa Koli, 13
Alaghai-bäki, 14
Alam al-Malika, 15
Alexandra, 15
Alexandra, 16
Alice, 17
Aline Sitoe, 18
Alix of Anjou, 19
Alix of Vergy, 19
Amalswinthe, 20

Amanishakhete, 20
Amina, 21
Ankhesenamun, 22
Ankhnesneferibre, 24
Ankyeaa Nyame, 24
Anna Anachoutlou, 24
Anna Dalassena, 25
Anna Leopoldovna, 25
Anna of Savoy, 26
Anna Palaeologina, 27
Anna Palaeologina-
    Cantacuzena, 27
Anne, 28
Anne, 28
Anne, 30
Anne-Marie-Louise
    d'Orléans, 31
Anne of Austria, 31
Anne of England, 32
Anne of France, 33
Anula, 34
Apumatec, 34
Aquino, María Corazon, 34
Arsinde, 36
Arsinoë II, 37
Artemisia I, 38
Artemisia II, 38
'Arwa Bint Ahmad al-Sulayhiyya, 39

Asa, 40
Asma Bint Shihab
  al-Sulayhiyya, 41
Athaliah, 41
Awura Pokou, 42
Āzarmēdukht, 43
Bailor-Caulker, Honoraria, 45
Balkis, 46
Balthild, 48
Bandaranaike, Sirimavo Ratevatte
  Dias, 48
Barbara, Agatha, 49
Barrow, Ruth Nita, 50
Beatrice, 51
Beatrice, 52
Beatrice, 52
Beatrice, Countess, 52
Béatrix de Bourgogne, 53
Béatrix Wilhelmina Armgard, 53
Bendjou, Empress, 54
Berenice, 55
Berenice III, 56
Berenice IV, 57
Bergmann-Pohl, Sabine, 57
Bhutto, Benazir, 58
Bianca, 61
Bianca Maria, 61
Bjerregaard, Ritt, 62
Blanca, Doña, 63
Blanche of Castile, 64
Bona of Savoy, 64
Bōrān, 65
Boraqchin, Khatum, 65
Boudicca, 66
Brigantia, 66
Brundtland, Gro Harlem, 67
Brunhilde, 68
Busignani, Patricia, 70
Campbell, Kim, 71
Candace, 72
Cartimandua, 73
Catalinda d' Albret, 73

Caterina Sforza, 74
Catherine, 75
Catherine I, 76
Catherine II the Great, 77
Catherine Cornaro, 79
Catherine de Médicis, 80
Catherine of Aragon, 82
Catherine of Braganza, 83
Catherine of Valois, 83
Ceccoli, Edda, 84
Chamorro, Violeta
  Barrios de, 84
Charles, Mary Eugenia, 86
Charlotte, 88
Charlotte, 88
Cheng-Chun, 89
Chindók Yówang, 90
Chinsóng Yówang, 91
Christina, 92
Christine of France, 93
Çiller, Tansu, 94
Cixi, 95
Claude, 97
Claudine, 97
Cleopatra I, 97
Cleopatra II, 98
Cleopatra III, 99
Cleopatra VI Tryphaena, 99
Cleopatra VII, 99
Cleopatra of Cyrene, 102
Cleopatra Thea, 103
Constance, 103
Constance, 105
Constance, 106
Constance, 107
Cresson, Edith, 108
da Lourdes-Pintasilgo, María, 111
Daura, Queen of, 112
Dawlat Khatun, 113
Deborah, 113
Deidameia, 115
Diane of Poitiers, 115

Didda, 116
Dido, 116
Dola, 118
Domitien, Élisabeth, 118
Drahomira, 119
Dreifuss, Ruth, 120
Durgavati, 120
Dzeliwe Shongwe, 121
Ebuskun, 123
Eji, 123
Eleanor, 124
Eleanor of Aquitaine, 125
Eleanor of Arborea, 127
Elisa Bonaparte, 127
Elizabeth, 129
Elizabeth, 130
Elizabeth I, 131
Elizabeth I, 132
Elizabeth II, 134
Elizabeth of Görlitz, 135
Elizabeth of Poland, 136
Emma, 137
Erato, 138
Ermengarde, 138
Ermengarde, 139
Ermensinde, 139
Eschiva of Ibelin, Lady, 140
Eudocia Macrembolitissa, 140
Eudoxia, 142
Eugénie-Marie, 143
Euphrosine, 144
Euphrosyne, 145
Fatima, 147
Fatima, 147
Finnbogadóttir, Vigdis, 148
Fredegund, 150
Gandhi, Indira, 153
Gemmei-tennō, 155
Genshō-tennō, 156
Gordon, Minita, 156
Go-Sakuramachi-tennō, 157
Grey, Lady Jane, 157

Gulama, Madame, 158
Gwamile Mdluli, 159
Gyda, 160
Hatshepsut, 161
Hazrat Mahal, Begum, 163
Hedwig, Saint, 164
Helena Lecapena, 165
Henriette de Cleves, 166
Hetepheres I, 167
Himnechildis, 168
Hind al-Hīrah, 168
Hinematioro, 168
Hodierna of Jerusalem, 169
Hoho, 170
Homāy, 171
Hortense de Beauharnais, 171
Hsiao-shih, 173
Hu, 173
Ide d'Alsace, 175
'Inayat Shah Zakiyyat
    al-Din Shah, 175
Indzhova, Renata, 175
Irene, 176
Irene Godunova, 178
Irene Palaeologina, Empress, 178
Isabel, 179
Isabella, 180
Isabella, 180
Isabella I the Catholic, 180
Isabella II, 182
Isabella Clara Eugenia
    of Austria, 183
Isabella d'Este, 184
Isabella Farnesio of Parma, 185
Isabella of Bavaria, 186
Isabella of Cyprus, 186
Isabelle, 187
Isabelle, 187
Jacqueline, 189
Jadwiga, 190
Jagan, Janet, 191
Jayaram, Jayalalitha, 193

Jeanne I, 194

Jeanne II, 194

Jeanne d'Albret, 195

Jeanne de Castile, 196

Jeanne de Chatillon, 196

Jeanne de Nemours, 196

Jeanne de Penthièvre, 197

Jindan, 197

Jingō-kōgū, 198

Jitō-tennō, 199

Joan I, 199

Joan II, 200

Joanna I, 200

Joanna II, 201

Joanna of Austria, 202

Johanna, 202

Johanna, 203

Jolanthe, 203

Juana I, 204

Juana II, 204

Juana la Loca, 205

Judith, 205

Julia Avita Mammaea, 207

Julia Domna, 207

Julia Maesa, 208

Juliana, 209

Jumper, Betty Mae, 210

Kaahumanu, Queen, 213

Kahina, Al-, 214

Kalyānavati, 215

Kamalat Shah, Zaynt
  al-Din, 215

Kanal-Ikal, Lady, 215

Kassi, 216

Khadija, 217

Khentkaues, 217

Kinigi, Sylvie, 218

Kirum, 219

Kōgyoku-tennō, 219

Kōken-tennō, 220

Kossamak, 221

Ku-Baba, 222

Kumaratunga, Chandrika, 223

Kutlugh Khatun, 224

Lakshmi Bāī, 227

Laodicé, 228

Leonora Telles, 228

Liang, 229

Lilavati, 229

Liliuokalani, 230

Louise de Savoy, 231

Louise Hippolyte, 232

Lucia of Antioch, 232

Lucienne, 233

Ludmila, 234

Lü Hou, 234

Luisa, 235

Luisa María de Guzmán, 236

Luise-Marie, 236

Maham Anga, 237

Mahaut, 238

Mahaut I, 238

Mahaut II de Dampierre, 238

Mahaut de Boulogne, 239

Mahaut de Courtenay, 239

Mahaut de Dammartin, 240

Mamochisane, 240

Mandughai, 240

Mankiller, Wilma T., 241

Mansarico, 243

Mantantisi, 244

Margaret, 245

Margaret, 245

Margaret II, 246

Margaret III, 247

Margaret of Anjou, 247

Margaret of Antioch-Lusignan, 249

Margaret of Austria, 249

Margaret of Austria, 250

Margaret of Brabant, 251

Margaret of Navarre, 251

Margaret of Norway, 252

Margaret Tudor, 253

Margareta, 253

Margaretha, 254
Margrethe II, 254
Marguerite, 255
Marguerite de Thouars, 256
Maria, 256
María I of Braganza, 256
Maria II da Gloria, 257
Maria Adélaïde, 258
María Ana Victoria of Spain, 259
Maria Anna of Austria, 259
Maria Carolina, 260
Maria Christina, 261
Maria Christina of Austria, 262
María Cristina I of Naples, 263
María de la Mercedes, 263
Maria of Anjou, 264
Maria of Austria, 265
Maria Theresa, 266
Marie, 267
Marie, 267
Marie, 267
Marie de Bourbon, 268
Marie de Bourbon Montpensier, 268
Marie de Chatillon, 268
Marie de Médicis, 269
Marie-Louise, 270
Marozia Crescentii, 271
Martha, 272
Mary, 272
Mary, 273
Mary I, 274
Mary II, 275
Mary Bosomworth, 276
Mary of Antioch, 276
Mary of Guise, 277
Mary Stuart, 278
Mathilde, 279
Matilda, 279
Matilda, 280
Matilda, 281
Matilda of Flanders, 282
Matilda of Tuscany, 282

Mavia, 284
Mawa, 284
McAleese, Mary, 285
Mei, 286
Meir, Golda, 287
Melisende, 288
Mentewab, 289
Meryit-Net, 290
Mfalma Fatima, 290
Min, 291
Mnkabayi, 292
Mo-ki-lien, Khatun of, 293
Mother of the King of Kongo, 293
Mout, 294
Mujaji I, II, III, IV, 295
Munjŏng, Queen Dowager, 296
Myōjō-tennō, 296
Myriam, 297
Nandi, 299
Naqi'a, 300
Naryshkina, Natalya Kirillovna, 301
Nefrusobek, 302
Nicole, 303
Nitocris, 303
Ntombe Twala, 304
Ntsusa, 305
Nur al-'Alam Nakiyyat
     al-Din Shah, 306
Nūr Jahān, 306
Nyakaima, 307
Nyamazana, 308
Nzinga Mbandi, 308
Oghul Qamish, 313
Olga, 314
Olga, Saint, 314
Olympias, 315
Orghana, 316
Padishah Khatun, 319
Pandit, Vijaya Lakshmi, 320
Pāndyan Queen, 321
Pao-Ssŭ, 321
Parysatis, 321

Pascal-Trouillot, Ertha, 322
Pauline, 324
Pedini-Angelini, Maria Lea, 325
Pemba, Queen of, 325
Perón, Isabel, 326
Perry, Ruth, 327
Petronilla, 328
Pheretima, 329
Pimiku, 330
Placidia, Galla, 331
Plaisance of Antioch, 331
Plavsic, Biljana, 332
Plectrudis, 334
Pomare IV, 334
Pomare V, 334
Prabhāvatī Gupta, 335
Prunskiene, Kazimiera-Daniute, 335
Pu-abi, 336
Puduhepa, 336
Pulcheria, 337
Purea, 338
Radiyya, Sultana, 341
Ranavalona I, 343
Ranavalona II, 344
Ranavalona III, 345
Ranocchini, Glorianna, 345
Rasoherina, 346
Robinson, Mary, 346
Russudan, 348
Rweej, 349
Sada Kaur, 351
Salote Tupou III, 351
Samsia, 352
Sancha, Queen, 353
Sarraounia, 354
Sati Beg, 355
Sauvé, Jeanne Mathilde, 355
Saw, 356
Seaxburh, 357
Shagshag, 357

Shajar Al Durr, 358
Shammu-ramat, 359
Shibtu, 360
Shipley, Jenny, 360
Shu-lü Shih, 362
Sibylla, 362
Sibylle, 363
Sinqobile Bahle Mabhena, 364
Sirikit, 364
Sitt al-Mulk, 366
Sivali, 367
Sofya Alekseyevna, 368
Sóndók Yówang, 369
Soong Ch'ing-ling, Madame, 370
Suchocka, Hanna, 371
Sugandha, 372
Suiko-tennō, 373
Sung, 373
Sung, 374
Susanne de Bourbon, 374
Tadj al-'Alam Safiyyat
    al-Din Shah, 377
Taitu, 377
Tamara, 378
Ta-pu-yen, 379
Tārā Bāī, 380
Tejada, Lidia Gueiler, 380
Teng, 381
Teresa of Castile, 381
Teuta, 382
Thatcher, Margaret, 383
Thecla, 385
Theodolinda, 386
Theodora, 387
Theodora, 388
Theodora, 389
Theodora, 390
Theophano, 391
Theophano, 391
Tindu, 392
Tiy, 393

Tizard, Dame Catherine, 394
Tomyris, 395
Töregene, 396
Tou Hsien, 397
Tribhuvana, 398
Trieu Au, 398
Trung Nhi and Trung Trac, 398
Tuckabatchee, Queen of, 399
Turunku Bakwa, 399
Twosret, 400
Tz'u-an, 400
Udham Bāī, 403
Uicab, María, 404
Ulrica Eleanora, 404
Urraca, Doña, 405
Uwilingiyimana, Agathe, 405
Vaekehu, 407
Victoria, 407
Vittoria, 409
Wac-Chanil-Ahau, Lady, 411
Wajed, Hasina, 412
Werleigh, Claudette, 413

Wilhelmina, 414
Wu Hou, 415
Yaa Akyaa, 417
Yaa Asantewaa, 419
Yelena Glinskaya, 421
Ye-lü Shih, 422
Yoko, Madame, 422
Yolanda, 423
Yolande, 424
Yolande de Bourgogne, 425
Yüan Yu, 425
Ywahoo, Dhyani, 425
Zabel, 427
Zabibi, 428
Zac-Kuk, Lady, 429
Zainab al-Nafzawiyya, 430
Zauditu, 431
Zenobia, 432
Zia, Begum Khaleda, 433
Zoë, 434
Zungu, Dr. Sibongile, 436

Bibliography, 437
Index, 453
About the Author, 471

Geographical Chronology of Entries

Abyssinia
See Ethiopia

Achaea
See Crusader States

African Tribes
amaRharhabe / Ngqika
Ntsusa (18th c.)
Asante Empire
Afua Koba (19th c.)
Yaa Akyaa, Asantehemaa tribe
  (19th c.)
Yaa Asantewaa, Asante Edweso
  tribe (20th c.)
Azna Kingdom
Sarraounia (19th c.)
baTlokwa
Mantantisi (19th c.)
Baule
Awura Pokou (18th c.)
Berber
Kahina, Al- (7th–8th c.)
Bunyoro
Nyakaima (ca. 16th c.)
Daura
Daura, Queen of (10th c.)
Diola
Aline Sitoe (20th c.)
The Gambia
Adame, Mama (n.d.)
Itsekiri
Dola (19th c.)

Kanuri Empire
Aissa Koli (16th c.)
Khoi
Hoho (18th c.)
Kololo
Mamochisane (19th c.)
Kongo
Mother of the King of Kongo
  (ca. 12th c.)
Kpa Mende Confederacy
Yoko, Madame (19th–20th c.)
Kumasi
Ankyeaa Nyame (ca. 17th c.)
Lovedu
Mujaji I, II, III, IV (19th–20th c.)
Lunda
Rweej (16th c.)
Madlebe
Zungu, Dr. Sibongile (20th c.)
Mali Empire
Kassi (13th c.)
Bendjou, Empress (14th c.)
Mani
Mansarico (16th c.)
Matamba
Nzinga Mbandi (also ruler of
  Mbundu and Ndongo)
  (17th c.)
Mbundu
Nzinga Mbandi (also ruler of
  Matamba and Ndongo) 17th c.)
Mende
Gulama, Madame (20th c.)

Ndebele
Sinqobile Bahle Mabhena
   (20th c.)
Ndongo
Nzinga Mbandi (also ruler of
   Matamba and Mbundu) (17th c.)
Ngoni
Nyamazana (19th c.)
Shenge
Bailor-Caulker, Honoraria (20th c.)
Zaria, Hausaland
Turunku Bakwa (16th c.)
Amina (15th or 16th c.)
Zulu
Mnkabayi (18th c.)
Nandi (19th c.)
Mawa (19th c.)

Arabia, Southern
Samsia (8th c. B.C.)
Zabibi (8th c.B.C.)

Argentina
Perón, Isabel (20th c.)

Armenia
Erato (1st c.)
Lesser Armenia
Zabel (13th c.)

Assyria
See Babylonia

Austria
Maria Theresa (also empress of
   Hapsburg empire, queen of
   Bohemia and Hungary, ruler
   of Luxembourg) (18th c.)

Axum
Balkis (10th c. B.C.)

Babylonia
Assyria
Shammu-ramat (9th c. B.C.)
Addagoppe of Harran
   (ca. 6th c. B.C.)
Naqi'a (ca. 7th c. B.C.)
Kingdom of Kish
Ku-Baba (24th c. B.C.)

Bangladesh
Zia, Begum Khaleda (20th c.)
Wajed, Hasina (20th c.)

Barbados
Barrow, Ruth Nita (20th c.)

Belgium
Brabant
Marie (13th c.)
Johanna (14th–15th c.)
Flanders
Margareta (12th c.)
Johanna (13th c.)
Margaret II (also ruler of Hainault)
   (13th c.)
Margaret III (14th–15th c.)
Gelderland and Zutphen
Margaretha (13th c.)

Belize
Gordon, Minita (20th c.)

Bohemia
See Czechoslovakia

Bolivia
Tejada, Lidia Gueiler (20th c.)

Bosnian Serb Republic
Plavsic, Biljana (20th c.)

Brabant
See Belgium

Brazil
Brazilian Empire
María I of Braganza (18th c.)
Isabel (19th c.)

Bulgaria
Indzhova, Renata (20th c.)

Burgundy
See France

Burma
Pagan
Saw (13th c.)

Burundi
Kinigi, Sylvie (20th c.)

Byzantine Empire (Eastern Roman Empire)
Eudoxia (5th c.)
Pulcheria (5th c.)
Theodora (6th c.)
Irene (8th, 9th. c.)
Thecla (9th c.)
Theodora (9th c.)
Helena Lecapena (10th c.)
Theophano (10th c.)
Eudocia Macrembolitissa (11th c.)
Anna Dalassena (11th c.)
Zoë (11th c.)
Theodora (11th c.)
Mary of Antioch (12th c.)
Euphrosyne (12th–13th c.)
Catherine of Valois (14th c.)
Anna of Savoy (14th c.)
Latin Empire
Yolande (13th c.)

Cambodia
Mei (19th c.)
Kossamak (20th c.)

Canada
Sauvé, Jeanne Mathilde (20th c.)
Campbell, Kim (20th c.)

Cappadocia
Laodicé (2d. c. B.C.)

Caria
Ada (4th c. B.C.)
Artemisia II (4th c. B.C.)

Carthage
Dido (9th c. B.C.)

Central African Republic
Domitien, Élisabeth (20th c.)

Ceylon
See Sri Lanka

China (also see Mongol Empire)
Pao-Ssŭ (ca. 3rd c. B.C.)
Lü Hou (2d. c. B.C.)
Wu Hou (7th–8th c. A.D.)
Cheng-Chun (1st c. B.C.–
    1st c. A.D.)
Tou Hsien (1st c.)
Teng (2d c.)
Liang (2d c.)
Yüan Yu (11th c.)
Sung (11th c.)
Sung (13th c.)
Tz'u-an (19th c.)
Cixi (19th–20th c.)
The People's Republic of China
Soong Ch'ing-ling, Madame
    (20th c.)

Chosōn
See Korea

Croatia
Elizabeth (also regent of Hungary)
    (14th c.)
Maria of Anjou (also "king" of
    Hungary) (14th c.)

Crusader States
Achaea
Isabelle (13th, 14th c.)
Matilda (14th c.)
Marie de Bourbon (14th c.)
Antioch
Alice (12th c.)
Constance (12th c.)
Lucia of Antioch (also titular ruler
    of Tripoli) (13th c.)
Lucienne (13th c.)
Beirut
Isabella (13th c.)
Eschiva of Ibelin, Lady (13th c.)
Cyprus
Isabella (13th c.)
Plaisance of Antioch (also regent
    of Jerusalem) (13th c.)
Charlotte (15th c.)
Catherine Cornaro (15th c.)
Edessa
Beatrice (12th c.)
Jerusalem
Melisende (12th c.)
Sibylla (12th c.)
Marie (13th c.)
Yolanda (13th c.)
Plaisance of Antioch (also regent
    of Cyprus) (13th c.)
Tripoli
Hodierna of Jerusalem (12th c.)

Lucia of Antioch (also princess of
    Antioch) (13th c.)
Sibylle (13th c.)
Lucienne (also regent of Antioch)
    (13th c.)
Tyre
Margaret of Antioch-Lusignan
    (13th c.)

Cyrene
Cleopatra of Cyrene (1st c. B.C.)
Pheretima (ca. 6th c.)

Czechoslovakia
Bohemia
Ludmila (10th c.)
Drahomira (10th c.)
Maria Theresa (also empress of
    Hapsburg empire, queen of
    Hungary, archduchess of Austria,
    ruler of Luxembourg) (18th c.)

Denmark
Margaret (also queen of Norway
    and regent of Sweden)
    (14th–15th c.)
Margrethe II (20th c.)
Bjerregaard, Ritt (20th c.)

Dominica
Charles, Mary Eugenia (20th c.)

Edessa
See Crusader States

Egypt
Hetepheres I (ca. 27th c. B.C.)
Khentkaues (ca. 25th c. B.C.)
Nitocris (ca. 25th c. B.C.)
Nefrusobek (18th c. B.C.)
Ahhotpe I (16th c. B.C.)
Ahmose-Nofretari (16th c. B.C.)

Hatshepsut (16th–15th c. B.C.)
Tiy (ca. 14th c. B.C.)
Eji (14th c. B.C.)
Ankhesenamun (14th c. B.C.)
Twosret (13th c. B.C.)
Ankhnesneferibre (6th c. B.C.)
Meryit-Net (4th c. B.C.)
Arsinoë II (3d c. B.C.)
Cleopatra I (2d c. B.C.)
Cleopatra II (2d. c. B.C.)
Cleopatra III (2d. c. B.C.)
Berenice III (2d–1st c. B.C.)
Cleopatra VI Tryphaena (1st c. B.C.)
Berenice IV (1st c. B.C.)
Cleopatra VII (1st c. B.C.)
Sudan
Mout (8th c. B.C.)
Islamic Egypt
Sitt al-Mulk (11th c.)
Shajar Al Durr (13th c.)

Eire
See Irish Republic

England
See Great Britain

Epirus
Deidameia (3d c. B.C.)
Anna Palaeologina-Cantacuzena
  (13th–14th c.)
Anna Palaeologina (14th c.)

Ethiopia (Abyssinia)
Candace (1st c.)
Judith (10th c.)
Mentewab (18th c.)
Taitu (20th c.)
Zauditu (20th c.)

Flanders
See Belgium

France
Frankish Kingdoms
Brunhilde (Austrasia) (also regent
  of Burgundy) (6th–7th c.)
Fredegund (Neustria) (6th c.)
Balthild (Neustria) (7th c.)
Himnechildis (Austrasia) (7th c.)
Plectrudis (Austrasia and Neustria)
  (8th c.)
Kingdom of France
Eleanor of Aquitaine (also regent
  of England, queen of England,
  duchess of Aquitaine, countess
  of Poitiers) (12th c.)
Blanche of Castile (13th c.)
Isabella of Bavaria (14th–15th c.)
Anne of France (15th c.)
Louise de Savoy (16th c.)
Catherine de Médicis (16th c.)
Diane of Poitiers (16th c.)
Anne of Austria (also governor
  of Brittany) (17th c.)
Marie de Médicis (also governor
  of Normandy) (17th c.)
The First Empire
Marie-Louise (also duchess of
  Parma) (19th c.)
The Second Empire
Eugénie-Marie (19th c.)
Fifth French Republic
Cresson, Edith (20th c.)
Aquitaine
Eleanor of Aquitaine (also regent
  of England, queen of England,
  queen of France, countess of
  Poitiers) (12th c.)
Artois
Mahaut (14th c.)
Joan I (14th c.)
Margaret of Brabant (14th c.)
Joan II (14th c.)

France *(continued)*

Auvergne

Marie de Bourbon Montpensier
  (17th c.)
Anne-Marie-Louise d'Orléans
  (17th c.)

Blois

Adela (also countess of Chartres)
  (11th–12th c.)
Marguerite (13th c.)
Marie de Chatillon (13th c.)
Jeanne de Chatillon (13th c.)

Boulogne

Mahaut de Boulogne (12th c.)
Marie (12th c.)
Ide d'Alsace (12th–13th c.)
Mahaut de Dammartin (13th c.)

Bourbon

Mahaut I (12th c.)
Béatrix de Bourgogne (13th c.)
Mahaut II de Dampierre (also ruler
  of Nevers) (13th c.)
Agnes de Dampierre (13th c.)
Susanne de Bourbon (16th c.)

Brittany

Constance (12th c.)
Alix of Anjou (13th c.)
Jeanne de Penthièvre (14th c.)
Anne (15th–16th c.)
Claude (16th c.)
Anne of Austria (also regent of
  France) (17th c.)

Burgundy

Brunhilde (also regent for
  Austrasia) (6th–7th c.)
Alix of Vergy (13th c.)
Mary (also ruler of Luxembourg)
  (15th c.)

Carcassonne

Arsinde (10th c.)
Ermengarde (11th c.)

Champagne

Juana I (also queen of Navarre)
  (13th–14th c.)

Chartres

Adela (also countess of Blois)
  (11th–12th c.)

Dreux

Jeanne I (14th c.)
Jeanne II (14th c.)
Marguerite de Thouars (14th c.)

Foix

Isabella (14th–15th c.)

Lorraine

Jolanthe (15th c.)
Isabelle (Upper Lorraine)
  (15th c.)
Nicole (17th c.)

Narbonne

Ermengarde (12th c.)

Nevers

Mathilde (10th–11th c.)
Agnes de Nevers (12th c.)
Mahaut de Courtenay (12th–
  13th c.)
Mahaut II de Dampierre (also ruler
  of Bourbon) (13th c.)
Yolande de Bourgogne (13th c.)
Margaret III, also ruler of Belgium
  (14th–15th c.)
Henriette de Cleves (16th–
  17th c.)

Normandy

Matilda of Flanders (11th c.)
Matilda (also queen regent of
  England) (12th c.)
Marie de Médicis (also regent of
  France) (17th c.)

Poitiers

Eleanor of Aquitaine (also
  duchess of Aquitaine, regent
  of England, queen of England,
  queen of France) (12th c.)

Provence
Beatrice, Countess (13th c.)
Joanna I (also queen of Naples)
   (14th c.)
Vendôme
Adele (11th c.)
Euphrosine (11th–12th c.)
Jeanne de Castile (14th c.)
Catherine (14th–15th c.)

Georgia
Mary (11th c.)
Tamara (12th–13th c.)
Russudan (13th c.)

Germany (also see Roman Empire[s])
Bavaria
Agnes of Poitou (also regent
   of Holy Roman Empire)
   (11th c.)
Jacqueline (also countess of
   Ostrevant, ruler of Zeeland
   and Hainault) (15th c.)
Carinthia
Margaret (also countess of Tirol)
   (14th c.)
German Democratic Republic (East Germany)
Bergmann-Pohl, Sabine
   (20th c.)
German Empire
Adelaide (also queen of
   Non-Carolingian Italy)
   (10th c.)
Matilda (10th c.)
Theophano (10th c.)
Ostrevant
Jacqueline (also countess of
   Bavaria, ruler of Zeeland and
   Hainault) (15th c.)

Silesia
Hedwig, Saint (13th c.)
Tirol
Margaret (also duchess of
   Carinthia) (14th c.)

Great Britain
Brigantia
Brigantia (1st c.)
Cartimandua (1st c.)
Iceni in East Anglia
Boudicca (1st c.)
England, Mercia
Aelfwyn (10th c.)
Aethelflaed (10th c.)
England, unspecified jarldom
Gyda (10th c.)
Kingdom of Wessex (West Saxons)
Seaxburh (7th c.)
England, Kingdom
Matilda (also duchess of
   Normandy) (12th c.)
Eleanor of Aquitaine (also duchess
   of Aquitaine, queen of France,
   countess of Poitiers) (12th c.)
Margaret of Anjou (15th c.)
Grey, Lady Jane (16th c.)
Catherine of Aragon (16th c.)
Mary I (16th c.)
Elizabeth I (16th–17th c.)
Mary II (17th c.)
Anne (also queen of Scotland)
   (18th c.)
Victoria (19th–20th c.)
Great Britain
Elizabeth II (20th c.)
Thatcher, Margaret (20th c.)
Scotland
Margaret of Norway (13th c.)
Mary Stuart (16th c.)
Mary of Guise (16th c.)

Great Britain *(continued)*
Margaret Tudor (16th c.)
Anne (also queen of England)
  (18th c.)
Scotland, Dunbar
Agnes of Dunbar (14th c.)

Greece (also see Macedonia)
Olga (20th c.)

Guyana
Jagan, Janet (20th c.)

Hainault
See The Netherlands

Haiti
Werleigh, Claudette (20th c.)
Pascal-Trouillot, Ertha (20th c.)

Halicarnassus and Cos
Artemisia I (5th c. B.C.)

Hapsburg Empire
Maria Theresa (also queen of
  Bohemia and Hungary,
  archduchess of Austria, ruler
  of Luxembourg) (18th c.)

Hawaii
Kaahumanu, Queen (19th c.)
Liliuokalani (19th c.)

Hittites
Puduhepa (13th c. B.C.)

Holland
See The Netherlands

Holy Roman Empire
See Roman Empire(s)

Hungary
Maria of Anjou (also queen of
  Croatia) (14th c.)
Elizabeth of Poland (also regent of
  Poland) (14th c.)
Elizabeth (also regent of Croatia)
  (14th c.)
Elizabeth (15th c.)
Maria Theresa (also archduchess
  of Austria, Hapsburg empress,
  queen of Bohemia, ruler of
  Luxembourg) (18th c.)

Iceland
Finnbogadóttir, Vigdis
  (20th c.)

Il-Khan Empire
See Iran; Iraq

Illyria
Teuta (3d c. B.C.)

India
Delhi
Radiyya, Sultana (13th c.)
Gondwana
Durgavati (16th c.)
Jhānsi (Uttar Pradesh)
Lakshmi Bāī (19th c.)
Kashmir
Sugandha (10th c.)
Didda (10th c.)
Marāthā State of the Deccan
Tārā Bāī (18th c.)
Oudh
Hazrat Mahal, Begum (19th c.)
Pāndya
Pāndyan Queen (2d. c. B.C.)
Punjab
Jindan (19th c.)

Tamil Nadu
Jayaram, Jayalalitha (20th c.)
Vākātakas of the Deccan
Prabhāvatī Gupta (4th–5th c.)
Mughal Empire
Maham Anga (16th c.)
Nūr Jahān (17th c.)
Udham Bāī (18th c.)
Republic of India
Gandhi, Indira (20th c.)

Indonesia
Atjeh
'Inayat Shah Zakiyyat al-Din Shah
    (17th c.)
Kamalat Shah, Zaynt al-Din (17th c.)
Nur al-'Alam Nakiyyat al-Din Shah
    (17th c.)
Tadj al-'Alam Safiyyat al-Din Shah
    (17th c.)
Java
Tribhuvana (14th c.)

Iran
Luristan
Dawlat Khatun (14th c.)
Massagetae
Tomyris (6th c. B.C.)
Persia
Homāy
Parysatis (5th c. B.C.)
Absh Khatun (13th c.)
Kutlugh Khatun (13th c.)
Padishah Khatun (13th c.)
Sati Beg (14th c.)
Sasanid Empire
Bōrān (7th c.)
Āzarmēdukht (7th c.)

Iraq
Tindu (15th c.)

Irish Republic
Robinson, Mary (20th c.)
McAleese, Mary (20th c.)
Israel
Deborah (13th–12th c. B.C.)
Judah (or Judaea)
Athaliah (9th c. B.C.)
Berenice (1st c.)
Maccabees
Alexandra (1st c. B.C.)
Modern Israel
Meir, Golda (20th c.)

**Italy (also see Roman
    Empire[s])**
Kingdom of Etruria
Luisa (also duchess of Lucca)
    (19th c.)
Forli and Imola
Caterina Sforza (15th–16th c.)
Guastalla
Pauline (19th c.)
Lombards
Theodolinda (6th, 7th c.)
Lucca
Elisa Bonaparte (also duchess
    of Tuscany and princess of
    Piombino) (19th c.)
Luisa (also regent of Etruria)
    (19th c.)
Mantua
Isabella d'Este (15th, 16th c.)
Milan
Bianca Maria (15th c.)
Bona of Savoy (15th c.)
Naples
Joanna I (also countess of
    Provence) (14th c.)
Joanna II (15th c.)
Juana II (as Giovanna III) (also
    queen of Spain and, as Queen
    Jan, queen of Sicily) (16th c.)

Italy *(continued)*

Maria Carolina (also de facto ruler of Sicily) (18th, 19th c.)

Non-Carolingian Kingdom

Adelaide (also regent, German Empire) (10th c.)

Parma

Margaret of Austria (also governor general of The Netherlands) (16th c.)

Marie-Louise (also regent of France) (19th c.)

Parma and Piacenza

Luise-Marie (19th c.)

Piombino

Elisa Bonaparte (also duchess of Tuscany and duchess of Lucca) (19th c.)

Rome

Marozia Crescentii (10th c.)

Sardinia

Eleanor of Arborea (14th–15th c.)

Sicily, Kingdom of

Margaret of Navarre (12th c.)

Adelaide of Salona (12th c.)

Constance (also regent of Germany) (12th c.)

Constance (13th–14th c.)

Maria (14th–15th c.)

Bianca (15th c.)

Maria Carolina (also de facto ruler of Naples) (18th, 19th c.)

Tuscany

Beatrice (11th c.)

Matilda of Tuscany (11th c.)

Elisa Bonaparte (also duchess of Lucca and princess of Piombino) (19th c.)

Urbino

Vittoria (17th c.)

Japan

Pimiku (2d–3d c.)

Jingō-kōgū (3d c.)

Suiko-tennō (6th–7th c.)

Kōgyoku-tennō (7th c.)

Jitō-tennō (7th c.)

Gemmei-tennō (8th c.)

Genshō-tennō (8th c.)

Kōken-tennō (8th c.)

Myōjō-tennō (17th c.)

Go-Sakuramachi-tennō (18th c.)

Kara-Khitai Empire

See Turkestan

Korea

Chosōn

Munjōng, Queen Dowager (16th c.)

Min (19th c.)

Silla

Sóndók Yówang (7th c.)

Chindók Yówang (7th c.)

Chinsóng Yówang (9th c.)

Kush

Amanishakhete (1st c. B.C.)

Lagash

Shagshag (3d millennium B.C.)

Lakhm

Hind al-Hīrah (6th c.)

Liberia

Perry, Ruth (20th c.)

Lithuania

Prunskiene, Kazimiera-Daniute (20th c.)

Lombard
See Italy

Lorraine
See France

Luxembourg
Ermensinde (12th–13th c.)
Elizabeth of Görlitz (15th c.)
Mary (also ruler of Burgundy)
    (15th c.)
Maria Theresa (also empress of
    Hapsburg Empire, queen of
    Bohemia and Hungary,
    archduchess of Austria) (18th c.)
Maria Adélaïde (20th c.)
Charlotte (20th c.)

Macedonia (also see Greece)
Olympias (4th c. B.C.)

Madagascar
Ranavalona I (19th c.)
Rasoherina (19th c.)
Ranavalona II (19th c.)
Ranavalona III (19th c.)

Maldive Islands
Khadija (14th c.)
Myriam (14th c.)
Fatima (14th c.)

Malta
Barbara, Agatha (20th c.)

Mari
Shibtu (18th c. B.C.)
Ilansura
Kirum (18th c. B.C.)

Marquesas Islands
Taiohae Tribe
Vaekehu (19th c.)

Maya
Wac-Chanil-Ahau, Lady (Naranjo)
    (7th c.)
Kanal-Ikal, Lady (Palenque)
    (6th–7th c.)
Zac-Kuk, Lady (Palenque) (7th c.)
Uicab, María (19th c.)

Mesopotamia
See Babylonia, Assyria, Seleucid
    Empire

Monaco
Claudine (15th c.)
Louise Hippolyte (18th c.)

**Mongol Empire (also see
    Turkestan)**
Oghul Qamish (13th c.)
Alaghai-bäki (13th c.)
Khita
Hsiao-shih (10th c.)
Kipchak
Boraqchin, Khatum (13th c.)
Mongolia
Mo-ki-lien, Khatun of (8th c.)
Shu-lü Shih (10th c.)
Töregene (13th c.)
Mandughai (15th c.)

Morocco
Zainab al-Nafzawiyya (11th c.)

**Native North American Tribal
    Chiefs (also see Maya)**
Apumatec (17th c.)
Mary Bosomworth (18th c.)
Tuckabatchee, Queen of (18th c.)
Jumper, Betty Mae (Seminole)
    (20th c.)
Ywahoo, Dhyani (Cherokee)
    (20th c.)

Native North American Tribal Chiefs *(continued)*
Mankiller, Wilma T. (Cherokee) (20th c.)

Navarre
See Spain

The Netherlands
Dutch Republic
Anne of England (18th c.)
Holland (Bonapartist)
Hortense de Beauharnais (19th c.)
Kingdom of The Netherlands
Emma (19th c.)
Wilhelmina (19th–20th c.)
Juliana (20th c.)
Béatrix Wilhelmina Armgard (20th c.)
Holland, County of
Jacqueline (also ruler of Zeeland and Hainault) (15th c.)
Burgundian Netherlands, Holy Roman Empire
Margaret of Austria (also duchess of Savoy) (16th c.)
Margaret of Austria (also duchess of Parma) (16th c.)
Maria of Austria (16th c.)
Austrian Netherlands
Maria Christina (18th c.)
Spanish Netherlands
Isabella Clara Eugenia of Austria (16th–17th c.)
Hainault
Margaret II (also ruler of Flanders) (13th c.)
Jacqueline (also ruler of Holland and Zeeland) (15th c.)

Zeeland
Jacqueline (also ruler of Holland and Hainault) (15th c.)

New Zealand
Tizard, Dame Catherine (20th c.)
Shipley, Jenny (20th c.)
Maori Ngati Porou
Hinematioro (17th or 18th c.)

Nicaragua
Chamorro, Violeta Barrios de (20th c.)

Norway
Asa (9th c.)
Aelfgifu of Northumbria (11th c.)
Margaret (also queen of Denmark, regent of Sweden) (14th–15th c.)
Brundtland, Gro Harlem (20th c.)

Pakistan
Bhutto, Benazir (20th c.)
Śukerchakīās
Sada Kaur (18th–19th c.)

Palmyra (Syria)
Zenobia (3d c.)

Pate
Mfalma Fatima (18th c.)

Pemba
Pemba, Queen of (17th c.)

Persia
See Iran

The Philippines
Aquino, María Corazon (20th c.)

Poland

Kingdom of Poland

Jadwiga (4th c.)

Elizabeth of Poland (also queen of Hungary) (14th c.)

The People's Republic of Poland

Suchocka, Hanna (20th c.)

Portugal

Teresa of Castile (12th c.)

Beatrice (14th c.)

Leonora Telles (14th c.)

Joanna of Austria (16th c.)

Luisa María de Guzmán (17th c.)

Catherine of Braganza (18th c.)

María Ana Victoria of Spain (18th c.)

María I of Braganza (18th–19th c.)

Maria II da Gloria (19th c.)

da Lourdes-Pintasilgo, María (20th c.)

Roman Empire(s)

Julia Domna (3d c.)

Julia Maesa (3d c.)

Julia Avita Mammaea (3d c.)

Placidia, Galla (5th c.)

Ostrogoths

Amalswinthe (6th c.)

Holy Roman Empire

Agnes of Poitou (11th c.)

Constance (also queen of Sicily) (12th c.)

Latin Emperors

Yolande (13th c.)

Rwanda

Uwilingiyimana, Agathe (20th c.)

Russia

Olga, Saint (10th c.)

Yelena Glinskaya (16th c.)

Irene Godunova (16th c.)

Martha (17th c.)

Sofya Alekseyevna (17th c.)

Naryshkina, Natalya Kirillovna (17th c.)

Catherine I (18th c.)

Anne (18th c.)

Anna Leopoldovna (18th c.)

Elizabeth I (18th c.)

Catherine II the Great (18th c.)

Alexandra (20th c.)

San Marino

Pedini-Angelini, Maria Lea (20th c.)

Busignani, Patricia (20th c.)

Ranocchini, Glorianna (20th c.)

Ceccoli, Edda (20th c.)

Saracens (Sinai)

Mavia (4th c.)

Sardinia

See Italy

Sasanid Empire

See Iran

Savoy

Margaret of Austria (also regent of The Netherlands) (16th c.)

Christine of France (17th c.)

Jeanne de Nemours (17th c.)

Scotland

See Great Britain

Seleucid Empire

Cleopatra Thea (2d c. B.C.)

Sicily
See Italy

Sierra Leone
Bailor-Caulker, Honoraria (Shenge)
(20th c.)
Gulama, Madame (Mende)
(20th c.)

Spain
Aragon
Petronilla (12th c.)
Juana la Loca (also queen of
Castile) (16th c.)
*Kingdom of Castile and León
(united)*
Urraca, Doña (also queen of León)
(12th c.)
Juana la Loca (also queen of
Aragon) (16th c.)
Isabella I the Catholic (also queen
of Spain) (15th–16th c.)
Kingdom of León
Sancha, Queen (11th c.)
Kingdom of Navarre
Juana I (also countess of Cham-
pagne) (13th–14th c.)
Juana II (14th c.)
Blanca, Doña (15th c.)
Eleanor (15th c.)
Catalinda d' Albret (15th–16th c.)
Jeanne d'Albret (16th c.)
Kingdom of Spain
Isabella I the Catholic (also queen
of Castile and León) (15th c.)
Juana la Loca (16th c.)
Maria Anna of Austria (17th c.)
Isabella Farnesio of Parma
(18th c.)
Isabella II (19th c.)
María Cristina I of Naples
(19th c.)

María de la Mercedes (19th c.)
Maria Christina of Austria
(19th–20th c.)

Sri Lanka (Ceylon)
Anula (1st c. B.C.)
Sivali (1st c.)
Lilavati (13th c.)
Kalyānavati (13th c.)
Bandaranaike, Sirimavo Ratevatte
Dias (20th c.)
Kumaratunga, Chandrika (20th c.)

Swaziland
Gwamile Mdluli (19th–20th c.)
Dzeliwe Shongwe (20th c.)
Ntombe Twala (20th c.)

Sweden
Margaret (also queen of Denmark
and Norway) (14th–15th c.)
Christina (17th c.)
Ulrica Eleanora (18th c.)

Switzerland
Dreifuss, Ruth (20th c.)

Tahiti
Purea (18th c.)
Pomare V (19th c.)

Thailand
Sirikit (20th c.)

Toba
Hu (6th c.)

Tonga
Pomare IV (ca. 19th c.)
Salote Tupou III (20th c.)

Trebizond
Theodora (13th c.)
Irene Palaeologina, Empress
    (14th c.)
Anna Anachoutlou (14th c.)

Turkestan
Ebuskun (13th c.)
Orghana (13th c.)
Kara-Khitai Empire
Ta-pu-yen (12th c.)
Ye-lü Shih (12th c.)

Turkey (also see Hittites)
Çiller, Tansu (20th c.)

**United Nations General
    Assembly**
Pandit, Vijaya Lakshmi (20th c.)

Ur, Sumeria
Pu-abi (ca. 26th c. B.C.)

Vietnam
Trung Nhi and Trung Trac (1st c.)
Hill People
Trieu Au (3d c.)

Yemen
'Arwa Bint Ahmad al-Sulayhiyya
    (11th–12th c.)
Asma Bint Shihab al-Sulayhiyya
    (11th c.)
Zubayd
Alam al-Malika (12th c.)

Zanzibar
Fatima (17th c.)

Zeeland
See The Netherlands

—

This book has at its core the original *Women Who Ruled,* although half again as many completely new biographical entries have been added for this second edition. These include not only women rulers who have come upon the scene in the decade since the publication of the original work, but many more culled from historical records by dedicated researchers and from oral tradition by translators and field anthropologists. In addition, many entries in the original work have been revised, expanded, and updated. The result is a biographical listing of every known ruling queen, empress, prime minister, president, regent ruler, de facto ruler, constitutional monarch, and verifiable ruler who was female, from the oral tradition and written history of the world's kingdoms, islands, empires, nations, and tribes down to present time. The entries are arranged alphabetically according to rulers' names and supported by bibliographic sources. A country-by-country geographical index arranged chronologically by centuries is provided for the reader's overall orientation.

The name of each woman ruler is followed by a title or titles and, in parentheses, the year(s) during which she ruled. In the case of entries that give more than one title, the additional title will distinguish that ruler from other women in history with similar names, designate either a title different from that which the ruler held while ruling or a title that was not the usual one held by a ruler of that particular place, or clarify for the reader the type of title used in a certain time and place.

Such a history could not solely be compiled from original research of primary sources in their hundreds of languages; it must rather be gathered from secondary sources, from the works of others from many cultures. As such, if it cannot be an original scientific work, it carries an added obligation that a history does not, and that is to provide information in some cases even beyond so-called historical fact.

Since gray areas are inherent in a categorization as broad as "women rulers," there will be questions about certain inclusions or exclusions. In broad terms, I have sought to include the name (or when the name has not survived, the identifying clan, dynasty, or even locale) of any woman who held the reins of power, regardless of the extent to which she exercised that power and regardless of her official sanction to do so. To include only those who presided from a recognized seat of government would omit certain tribal leaders. Yet there is a difference between "leaders" and "rulers." On the one hand, Joan of Arc, certainly a leader, did not preside from a recognized seat of government and would not be termed a ruler. On the other hand, Trieu Au, another leader who did not preside from any recognized seat of government, is included because she clearly ruled over the Vietnamese hill people whom she led into battle, who had no other ruler.

Far more open to controversy is my inclusion of certain women behind the throne, such as Diane de Poitiers, and exclusion of others like Marie Antoinette and Eva Perón, both of whom no doubt influenced history to a greater degree. My inclination has been to omit these powers behind the throne unless history indicates that they dominated the designated rulers completely.

In addition, with some ambivalence, I have included the names of a few legendary rulers about whom no firm historical or archaeological evidence survives, whose embroidered histories may—or may not—have been based on the lives of actual (albeit far less colorful) persons. These leaders are clearly labeled as legendary and are included because of the unique information that their stories provide, which in some cases may link the historical to the legendary or may contain some elements that coincide with known historical data. There are others, such as Herodotus's two "queens" named Nitocris whom no historical data confirm, that I feel a responsibility to include, if only to clear up confusion and to present the possibilities as to the historical counterpart of one of these women. Historians sometimes disagree as to the authenticity of a person—for example, Dido. My stance is that exclusion of such a controversial legendary figure would imply closure of such a matter without corroborating evidence.

Diacritics, particularly in accounts of rulers of recent times, have been kept to a minimum for the sake of fluidity; however, in the case of certain of the more exotic and distantly removed entries, where names have not been Anglicized by current usage, the use of diacritics seems preferable and even unavoidable.

In this ongoing endeavor, I am indebted to those who brought newly elected rulers to my attention, who lent or located research materials, and who offered editing assistance, inspiration, and encouragement: William H. Laufer, James Tucker Jackson, Mary Winzig, William A. Jackson, Mary Gillis, Jeffrey A. Jackson, Linda Johnson, Annabeth Davis, Leland Davis, Glenda Miller, Davis Lowery, Joyce Harlow, R. Daniel Ramos, Julia Mercedes Castilla de Gomez-Rivas, Ida H. Luttrell, Gregory A. Jackson, Jeana Kendrick, Jeff Kendrick, Ashley D. Ramos, Chichi Layor Okoye, Elizabeth A. Jackson, Patsy Ward Burk, Jan Tickner, Jackie Pelham, Mary Zimmeth Schomaker, Louise Gaylord, Mattie R. Jackson, Mel McKinney, Troy B.

Lowery, Ann Anderson, Christopher Michael Ramos, Irene Bond, Charles Lowrie, Bobbi Sissel, Eleanor Frances Jackson, Stephanie L. Gray, David Bumgardner, Betty Joffrion, Jack Crumpler, Linda Helman, Colleen Thompson, Ruby Tolliver, Jan Matlock, Rance J. Lowery, Olivia Orfield, Gloria Wahlen, Carol Rowe DeBender, Joyce Pounds Hardy McDonald, Donn Taylor, James Husum, and Omar Pound.

I am grateful for the help and support of my acquisitions editor, Todd Hallman; developmental editor, Kevin Downing; production editor, Melanie Stafford; copy editor, Libby Barstow; and permissions editor, Liz Kincaid, who obtained the illustrations.

Guida M. Jackson
The Woodlands, Texas

Introduction

Women rulers, what pitifully few there have been in our long recorded history, have only rarely come to power through the front door. True, some have been born inside the walls or inherited the scepter by divine right, but still more arrived via the alley door or over the basement transom, as queen mothers, regents, widows, even concubines. A handful of the most daring have been gate crashers, usurpers who took their lives in their hands in their lust for power. Some of those have been assassinated for their trouble. Many have been allowed to share authority with another, usually a spouse. Others were summoned to fill a void by machinators who expected them to behave like puppets, but sometimes the puppets cut their own strings. In recent years a growing number have knocked politely on the portals of power and have been invited in via the front entrance by an ever more tolerant electorate.

Much as we would like to fantasize that at some time in the peaceful idyllic past, vast numbers of matriarchs presided over happy, bucolic subjects, there is no anthropological evidence to prove a universal prehistoric matriarchy (Lerner 1986, 31), although there was a time when women were held in awe for their magical ability to bleed and not die, to reproduce seemingly at will, and to manufacture food from their bodies. Mother-goddesses abounded, and no doubt women had much more bargaining power, but evidence that they used it to rule is scant.

There were isolated exceptions, however; some west African nations at one time had only women rulers. The Baule tribe came into being under the rule of a woman (Awura Pokou), as did Zaria (Turunku Bakwa). At least three women in a row ruled the Hausa state of Zaria in its prime, and one of them in fact gave the tribe her name. The late Jomo Kenyatta, founder of Kenya, related the origin of the Gikuyu clans, originally named for daughters of the founder and all ruled by women. While holding a superior position in the community, the women practiced polyandry and became domineering and ruthless. Men were put to death for committing adultery or for minor infractions of the civil law. Finally, the men plotted, overthrew the women, and took command, becoming for the first time the heads of their families. This event probably coincided with realization of their role in procreation. Immediately the men took steps to abolish polyandry and establish polygamy. They planned to change the clan names as well, but the women, infuriated by this ultimate insult, threatened that they would bear no children if the clan names, which stood as proof that women were their founders, were changed. The men backed down, and the female clan names stand today (Kenyatta 1965, 8).

On the east African islands of Zanzibar, Pate, and their neighbors, as recently as the eighteenth century there was a tradition of women rulers, many called Fatima, but few of whose birth names remain on record. Since only the names of outstanding leaders have survived, it is not known how many African tribes may have been matriarchal for at least some period.

Appearance of a number of queens in a row does not necessarily indicate existence of a matriarchy, but it might. The Lovedu of South Africa were ruled by at least four women who carried the dynastic title of Mujaji. On the South Pacific island of Tonga, there were at least four ruling queens who took the name of Pomare and at least one by that name on Tahiti.

Many matrilineal societies have existed, particularly near forested areas where domesticated animals were not present. However, matrilinearity, polyandry, or matrilocality also do not necessarily indicate the existence of a matriarchy (Lerner 1986, 30). In Buganda, for example, among the Babito people, the kings perpetuated the long-held custom of adopting the clan of their mothers. Mothers were honored, but men ruled.

In ancient Egypt, full-blooded consanguineous marriage (or marriage between siblings) among royalty became common during the late seventeenth century B.C. or early sixteenth century B.C. This practice reflected the belief in divine rule, but in addition, Egyptian kings married their royal sisters because they wished to partake of the family inheritance that often passed from mother to daughter. The Greek historian Diodorus Siculus, writing in the first century B.C., described the matriarchal character of the Egyptian royal family. His *Bibliotheca historica* was compiled from earlier works that have not survived. Although every royal Egyptian princess bore the titles and dignities of the office from birth, a man only acquired them at his coronation and could do so only by becoming the consort of a royal princess.

The queen of Egypt bore the title "God's Wife of Amon." Even after the practice of full-blooded consanguineous marriage was abandoned in the mid-sixteenth century B.C., the title of God's Wife remained. It was bestowed in childhood upon the pharaoh's legitimate heiress. The incoming pharaoh, to secure his right to the throne, generally—but not always—married the God's Wife. Some variations of this tradition have been practiced in many other parts of the world. Often these unions resulted in co-rule by both king and queen; other times certain duties were assigned to each. In the case of Cleopatra II, when she was divorced by Eurgetes in favor of her daughter, Cleopatra III, the cast-aside queen revolted and in 130 B.C. became queen of parts of Upper Egypt on her own, ruling it alone until 118 B.C. There is at least one instance in which the queen (Arsinoë II) ruled the land while the king (Ptolemy II) engaged in cultural pursuits.

In addition to establishing a precedent on the African continent for the occasional sole woman ruler, Egypt is credited with the concept of an "official woman" within the government, a model followed through to recent times in some African kingdoms. This office carries in some instances the weight of vice-ruler, in others that of prime minister or secretary of state.

Elsewhere, in ancient Anatolia, a similar system prevailed among the Indo-European Hatti people who flourished prior to the Hittite's Old Kingdom, somewhere from ca. 2000 to 1700 B.C. Following the model of an older culture of the Middle Minoan III–Late Minoan II at Knosses, Phaistos, and Hagia Triada, in which women held a privileged position in society, in Hattian government the right of succession rested with the Tawannanna, a priestess and the sister to the crown prince. The Hatti also practiced consanguineous marriage, the king-to-be (Labarna) marrying the Tawannanna. As priestess, the Tawannanna had the right to levy and collect taxes from cities. She wielded a king-sized amount of political clout as well. Even after brother-sister marriage was outlawed, the Tawannanna continued to hold the right of succession, to function as priestess, and to occupy a strong position of power. These privileges were hers by divine right (Kinder and Hilgemann 1974, 35; Lerner 1986, 155).

A similar system also existed in the Sumerian Dynasty I of Ur (ca. 2500 B.C.). Queens shared not only power and wealth with their husbands but divinity as well. In one record that survives, in ca. 2350 B.C. King Lugalanda of Lagash seized control of the temples from the priestesses and appointed his wife, Baranamtarra, as administrator, along with other relatives. Queen Baranamtarra managed her own private estates and those of the temple of the goddess Bau. She bought and sold slaves and sent diplomatic missions to neighboring states (Kinder and Hilgemann 1974, 62).

Divine right, then, if held by a woman, often amounted to co-rule, as exemplified by, but not confined to, ancient Egypt. This model spanned the globe and lasted until medieval times. Medieval traveler Ibn Battuta, a devout Moroccan Muslim theologian, expressed utter dismay at the behavior of women at court during his visit to Central Asia in 1334. In Mongol states, he found women sharing openly in governing, being awarded apanages, or landed properties, along with their male siblings. These royal princesses, *khatuns* in their own right, ruled and taxed their own fiefs separately from the state domain. Completely independent of the *khan,* they signed decrees and made major administrative decisions, a situation that

Ibn Battuta considered not only scandalous but ungodly. This pious man, it might be recalled, liked to travel with slave girls. He also thought nothing of taking sustenance from the mouths of starving subjects of whom he was a guest. Arriving in Muslim India during a famine, he was granted the crops from five destitute villages—and later two more. He stayed there for seven years, frequently complaining to the ruler of Delhi about the skimpiness of his gifts (Naipul 1999, 12–16).

Ibn Battuta had also found the custom of joint rule odious in Islamic Mali, where, to show obeisance to and acceptance of the queen, the noble women of the court would throw earth on their heads—a practice to honor the queen still found in parts of Africa in the recent past. In Mali it was the custom for the empress to be crowned with the Mansa and to share the imperial power. However, her ability to rule depended upon this vote of confidence from the other women of the court. Empress Bendjou, for example, receiving no such homage, went after blood. Among the Mossi the queen was also crowned and shared in a joint rule.

During feudal times in Europe, the right of female succession boosted the number of female rulers, but many of these were forced to share power with a spouse, often the ruler of a neighboring kingdom. Some queens, like "King" Jadwiga of Poland, exercised little or no authority. Many duchies and smaller states fell to the care of women. During Jadwiga's time, there was not much that the papacy did that was not first sanctioned by the powerful Matilda of Tuscany.

Governing by divine right was not the sole province of the queens of Europe, although Elizabeth I, Anne of England and Scotland, Victoria, Mary Stuart (Queen of Scots), Catherine II the Great, Maria Theresa, and Margrete (Margaret) of Denmark come naturally to the western mind. Between A.D. 592 and 770, half the rulers of Japan were queens by divine right. The Chinese historical *Wei* records, describing Japan as "queen country," gives a list of provinces over which the Japanese queen ruled. At least three women ruled by divine right in Korea, and at least three divine right queens have been discovered in the Western hemisphere, in Maya societies. Lady Kanal-Ikal and Lady Zac Kuk were both called "king of Palenque" and the activities of Lady Wac-Chanil-Ahau, another legitimate Mayan queen of Naranjo, are well documented in glyphs (Schele and Freide, 1990, 221–225, 227–228, 268–278).

Divine right was occasionally visited upon a daughter by alteration in the law. Certain kings, whose dream of establishing a dynasty to perpetuate their names seemed doomed by the absence of a male heir, simply changed the law and named their daughters to succeed them in the hopes that in another generation a male would come to the throne to carry on the name. There was no prohibition against the succession of a female when there was no male heir in England, Scotland, Scandinavia, Angevin Naples, Navarre, Georgia, Portugal, Byzantium, the Crusader states, Japan, Madagascar, Spain (prior to 1713), and many South Pacific islands. In France, the Salic Law of Succession was established from the end of the Capetian Dynasty in the fourteenth century onward, excluding women from succession to the throne. At the same time it was agreed that descent from the daughter of a French king did not constitute a legitimate claim to the throne.

In Confucian China in times of famine, baby girls were sacrificed. A woman had no property rights except for a dowry. But when she became a mother-in-law, all rules changed; she could—and often did—become autocratic and domineering. During the middle years of the eastern Han Dynasty, the rebellion of the "yellow turbans" (A.D. 184) was triggered by the power of dowager empresses and their eunuchs. For sheer wanton bloodthirsty mayhem, few could equal Empress Wu Hou (or Wu Chao), who began by having two of her rivals killed and followed quickly with killing her own baby just after birth (Bloodworth and Bloodworth 1976, 214–215).

Queen-mothers have wielded power since the kingdoms of ancient Egypt as well. In the Asante (Ashanti) Empire of west Africa, British conquerors found it necessary to exile both the king, Agyeman, and the queen-mother, Yaa Akyaa, since she was considered as powerful and influential as he. In Swaziland at least one queen-mother, Gwamile Mdluli, ruled until her son came of age. Among the Babito kings of Kitara, there might be as many as sixty royal princesses, one of whom would be elected Rubaga, or official Queen-Sister. She would have an official position and a seat on the king's council. In Kitara the queen-mother was also an indispensable figure, in some ways more pivotal than the king. Her subjects greeted her in the same manner as they greeted the king: "You who are better than all the men in this village" or "The savior of the people in the country" (Nyakatura 1973, 191).

In Sudan the preeminent offices were nearly always those of the queen-mother, the queen-sister, and a limited number of titled "great wives" of the ruler. Sole power to rule unhindered was denied these women, but there are countless other instances where widows or grand-mothers have come to power upon the death of a king—in Europe, Turko-Mongolia, the Middle East, and China. Even excluding Byzantium, several other Middle East kingdoms that frequently fell into the hands of women were actually European anomalies. The kingdoms of Jerusalem and Cyprus and the Principality of Antioch were guided by Crusaders but frequently were governed by women, usually a titular heir whose ruling consort had died or the mother of a minor legal heir.

Women regents have provided an uncommon amount of vigor to history. Among the Merovingians, for example, the seventh century became a period of boy-kings and female rulers. It was not uncommon for these regents of boy-kings to usurp power entirely and go to any length to maintain it. The notoriety of the bloodthirsty Fredegund is rivaled only by the aforementioned Chinese regent, Wu Hou, who killed off rivals by the thousands, including her own baby. From an account of Fredegund's crimes, it is barely conceivable that she had time to rule or to think of anything other than methods of revenge against her arch rival, Queen Brunhilde.

Few have gone to the lengths of Byzantine Empress Irene, who, after her own abdication, still so lusted for power that she finally had her own son blinded and deposed so that she could be sole ruler; or of Athaliah, who seized the throne of Judah and had all her grandsons put to death— save one, who was spirited away.

There are few recorded acquisitive women rulers. Women fought to defend their realm against invaders or usurpers or to avenge a death but generally not to acquire new territory or bring new populations under subjection. Bloodthirsty performances like those of Queen Nzinga Mbandi were aimed at discouraging challenges to the queen's authority. A crusty Turko-Mongol dowager, the widow of A-Pao-ki (d. 926), supposedly ruled "with" her son but in fact held sole power. Her manner of dealing with recalcitrant ministers was to send them to the land of the departed, delivering "news of her to her late husband." The story goes that when one wily old Chinese thus sentenced to die coyly suggested that such a high honor should go to her instead, the queen expressed regrets that she couldn't oblige, but she lopped off one of her own hands and sent it along with the condemned man to be buried in her husband's tomb as a remembrance (Grousset 1970, 129).

Despite the forceful example set for Jenghiz-khan by his own mother, Oelun-eke, this founder of the Mongolian Empire, who liked nothing better than "to cut my enemies to pieces . . . seize their possessions, witness the tears of those dear to them, and embrace their wives and daughters!" (Grousset 1970, 249), could not have envisioned how soon his empire would fall into the hands of his daughters-in-law and his granddaughters. Nor would he have sanctioned the overbearing influence upon their men of other of his progeny's wives: Sorqhaqtani, for example, was called the directing spirit of the house of Tolui (Jenghiz-khan's fourth son). Another son, Hulägu, married a Kerayit princess, Doquz-khatun, who was a Nestorian Christian with a mind of her own. When he sacked Baghdad, she interceded to save the lives of all the Christians, a great bother to the khan, who nevertheless obliged. The great khan Mongka also respected her wisdom and advised Hulägu that he would do well to consult her in all his affairs. This could not have set well with the son of the great Jenghiz-khan; nevertheless, to please his queen, Hulägu heaped favors upon the Christians, and new churches sprang up all over his realm (Grousset 1970, 356–357). Jenghiz-khan owed to another widow queen, Mandughai, twice the head of the Mongol army, the fifteenth-century renaissance of his all-but-defunct empire.

Nor were Mongolian queens the only battling women. It was a warrior queen, Tomyris, who ended the life of Cyrus the Great, founder of the Persian Empire. The last Asante war against the British invaders is called the Yaa Asantewaa War after the feisty Ohemaa of Edweso, Yaa Asantewaa, who at the age of fifty led the futile fight.

Among most social classes throughout world history, the preference for a son has emphasized the inferior status of women, but exceptional women, usually of the upper class, continued to grab the reins of government intended for their husbands or sons. Among the most notable usurpers in ancient Egypt was the famed Hatshepsut, who was only supposed to assume the regency for Thutmose III, the son by one of her late husband's other wives. But she soon wrested the throne from him and had herself crowned pharaoh, even adopting a beard for state occasions. In 1741 Elizabeth I, tsarina of Russia, headed a coup d'état ousting the infant emperor Ivan and his regent-mother, Anna Leopoldovna. But whereas Elizabeth stole into the palace quarters herself, in Bohemia, Queen Drahomira is thought only to have instigated the plot whereby her followers broke into Tetin Castle and strangled Queen-mother Ludmila, Wenceslas's regent-grandmother. Queen Drahomira then took her mother-in-law's place as regent.

India had been scoured and desecrated by Muslim invaders for more than 600 years before the British drove them out and took over themselves. The dispirited state of Indian men, even among royalty, was dwarfed only by the misery of the women. Yet even women maintained that spark of human dignity that ignited from time to time in mutiny. Nūr Jahān issued her edicts and even rode into battle on her elephant litter, firing her rifle through a slit in her tent without ever leaving the confines of purdah. Durgavati, during the time of the great Moghuls, and Lakshmi Bāī and Hazrat Mahal, during the Sepoy War two centuries later, were not so circumspect.

In the aftermath of the Sepoy War, at least one ex-leader's wife turned outlaw: The bloodstained rani of Tulsipur, apparently a widow who had escaped with only her life, vented her outrage by joining a band headed by Babu Ram Babhsh, the taluqdor of Dhundiakhera. This rebel took advantage of the power vacuum in 1858 to ravage and plunder everything in his path. The enraged rani of Tulsipur, who refused to give up without a fight, escaped capture by the British only to die of exposure or disease in the wilds of northern Oudh or southern Nepal, a fate she may have preferred to slavery (Pemble 1977, 237).

A woman scorned, belittled, or dishonored has always meant trouble. In ca. A.D. 39, after the murder of a Vietnamese nobleman and the rape of his widow Trung Trac, guerrilla Vietnamese tribes under the leadership of this woman and her sister attacked Chinese strongholds and massacred the Chinese, replacing their kingdom with a Vietnamese one. The kingdom established by these rebels was ruled by the sisters as co-queens, one of the few examples in history where two women shared power. In A.D. 695, in North Africa, Berber tribes of the Aures Mountains united under the leadership of priestess-queen Al-Kahina (or Dahiya al-Kahina) to sweep down in repeated raids on Arabs who had taken Carthage from Byzantine forces. Saracen Queen Mawia led raids against the Romans and later even chilled the blood of the barbarous Goths. Ghaliyya al-Wahhabiyya was a Bedouin amira al-umara (generalissimo) in the early eighteenth century, an Arab tribeswoman from Tarba, near Ta'if, just southeast of Mecca. At the beginning of the century, when foreign Muslims attempted to take control of Mecca, Ghaliyya formed and led a military resistance movement to defend Mecca. Legend grew among her battlefield adversaries that she possessed the magical ability to render the Wahhibi forces invisible. Certainly ascribing magic power to a woman was preferable than admitting that she defeated them fair and square. In Angola, the aforementioned Nzinga Mbandi, who first undertook diplomatic missions for her brother the king, later inherited leadership of the Mbundu at a time when the Dutch and Portuguese vied for the slave trade. She dealt with the foreign invaders in a language that needed no diplomatic translation: She put on a gory dance display across the river from the camp of a Dutch captain, designed to keep him at a distance. By one account, for her first humiliating audience with the arrogant Portuguese overlord who refused her the courtesy of a chair, she sat on her own slave, then hacked him to death when she had finished with him as proof that she didn't have to use the same seat twice. In this century, a young Senegalese queen, Aline Sitoe, mounted such a revolt against the French that she had to be deported after her capture to keep her from continuing her fight from prison.

During the second half of the twentieth century, women have attained positions of leadership through less violent means: usually by election, even in tribal societies. Dr. Sibongile Zungu was elected chief of the Madlebe tribe of South Africa in 1993. In Sierra Leone at least two female tribal chiefs have served: Honoraria Bailor-Caulker of the Shenge and Madam Gulama of the Mende. Madam Gulama gained much of her power from arranging marriages between men in positions of authority and graduates of her famed Sande Bush, a female society whose students are instructed in strategies of leadership. The school is so renowned that mothers vie for acceptance of their daughters into its program. A comparable system for training young women for leadership roles does not exist on any other continent.

The official organ of the African National Congress of South Africa most succinctly describes African women: "African women are not fragile flowers" (Pannikar 1963, 162). A case in point: During the turbulent six years of the bloody Liberian civil war, when many lawmakers and private citizens fled to neighboring countries for safety, Ruth Perry (b. 1939), legislator and later senator, remained in the country. In 1996 she was elected president of Liberia, heading a six-member collective governing body charged with bringing order to the war-ravaged land. She assured the electorate that, although she had the "touch of velvet," she could be "as hard as steel." Perry's principle of exploring nonviolent means for conflict resolution was adopted by a United Nations–sponsored conference of some sixty women involved in government in various African countries.

This gift for reconciliation and tolerance may be women's best contribution to our history, and it did not begin with elected rulers in the twentieth century. The reign of Elizabeth I of England ushered in a respite from the religious turmoil of the reigns of Mary and James I, and "Merry Olde England" enjoyed an era of peace and prosperity. Catholic Catherine de Médicis, appalled by the hatred of Catholics for Protestant Hugenots, which resulted in the Massacre of Vassy that left hundreds of men, women, and children dead, urged parliament to call for restraint. The result was her Edicts of Toleration. Unfortunately, her son did away with them when he came to power.

Religious restraints lingering into the twentieth century notwithstanding, Hindu India is famous for prime minister Indira Gandhi, but it was Buddhist Sri Lanka that provided the world's first woman prime minister, Sirimavo Bandaranaike. Later Bandaranaike's daughter, Chandrika Kumaratunga, was also elected prime minister. Bangladesh has had two women prime ministers, Khaleda Zia and Hasina Wajed, and in Pakistan Benazir Bhutto, a Muslim, has twice held the post of prime minister. In 1993 Agathe Uwilingiyimana was elected prime minister of Rwanda, but she was assassinated the following year. In nearby Burundi, Sylvie Kinigi was elected prime minister in 1993, but Élisabeth Domitien was Africa's first woman prime minister in 1975. By the closing decades of the twentieth century, Europe has seen ten women prime ministers: Margaret Thatcher, Gro Harlem Brundtland, Edith Cresson, Hanna Suchocka, María da Lourdes-Pintasilgo, Biljana Plavsik, Renata Indzhova, Sabine Bergman-Pohl, Kazimiera-Daniute Prunskiene, and Ritt Bjerregaard. Canada, Dominica, and Haiti had each elected one: Kim Campbell, Mary Eugenia

Charles, and Claudette Werleigh. In Myanmar (formerly Burma), Aung San Suu Kyi should have been elevated to prime minister when her National League for Democracy won a landslide victory in 1990, but at the time she was being held a political prisoner by the ruling military junta, which refused to honor the election results. In 1991, while still a prisoner, she won the Nobel Peace Prize for her attempts to bring democracy to Myanmar.

The People's Republic of China, frequently cited for its poor record on human rights, had a woman acting head of state for two years in the late 1970s—Madame Soong Ch'ing-ling, widow of revolutionary leader Sun Yat-sen.

In the Pacific, the closing decades of the twentieth century saw the election of Corazon Aquino as president of the Philippines and Jenny Shipley as prime minister of New Zealand, along with the appointment of Dame Catherine Tizard as governor-general of New Zealand.

In the twentieth century, Europe can boast of having the first woman to be elected president in her own right, Vigdis Finnebogadóttir, who was also the longest-serving president. Europe has had four other elected presidents—Mary Robinson, Mary McAleese, Ruth Dreifuss, and Agatha Barbara—and several co-captains-regent of San Marino, and yet it has still maintained ties to the past by having four "divine right" queens—Elizabeth II, Margrethe, Juliana, and Béatrix. In the Western hemisphere, there have been five women presidents—Lidia Tejada, Isabel Perón, Janet Jagan, Violeta Chamorro, and Ertha Pascal-Trouillot—and four female governors-general—Jeanne Sauvé of Canada, Nita Barrow of Barbados, Calliopa Pearlette Louisy of Saint Lucia, and Minita Gordon of Bolivia. In the 1980s, two large tribal nations, the Seminoles and Cherokees, were headed by women—Betty Mae Jumper and Wilma Mankiller—and history records at least four others. By the close of the twentieth century, many Native American tribes and clans had begun electing presidents, chairpersons, or governors instead of chiefs. About 150 of these, too many to list here, are women. Their names can be found on the Internet.

The duties of these chiefs, presidents, governors, and chairpersons are usually primarily concerned with promoting the tribe's economic betterment and maintaining what few sovereign rights remain to the tribe. For example, the focus of Evelyn James's administration, as president of the Southern Paiutes, was to obtain from the neighboring Navajo tribe by peaceful means Paiute lands the U.S. government assigned to the Navajo when it expanded the Navajos' reservation in the 1930s (Kelley 1998, 23A). Cherokee Ani Yunwiwa clan chief Dhyani Ywahoo is the spiritual leader of her tribe, charged with the mission to pass on the traditions of her ancestors. Chief Ywahoo maintains her own website at sunray@sover.net.

The mention of offspring in the account of a woman's life is essential, particularly any woman born prior to this century, because along with whatever else she was doing, the bearing of children did not stop until she could have them no longer. Women managed because they are accustomed to stirring many pots at once. Today's rulers, while neglecting neither their political responsibilities nor motherhood, even find time to demonstrate their creative versatility: Queen Margrethe is a renowned illustrator whose best known work accompanies *The Lord of the Rings;* her other work is respected as well—she also wrote a book with her husband. Gro Harlem Brundtland is a doctor; Queen Béatrix, a sculptor. Queen Liliuokalani wrote a song recognized worldwide, "Aloha Oe." Nor does leadership diminish a woman's capacity for compassion. During her administration, Irish president Mary Robinson found time to undertake missions to impoverished African countries to call the world's attention to the plight of starving children, victims of widespread famine. An extremely popular leader, she voluntarily left her presidential office at the end of her term, declining to run for reelection, opting instead to accept a post as head of the United Nations Commission on Human Rights. This motivation to serve rather than be served is characteristic of many if not most modern women's terms.

Compassion, reconciliation, and the characteristic socialization of women often carry over into their method of governing. Elizabeth I's "wait and see" attitude often drove her ministers to distraction, but her reluctance for rash confrontation often resulted in a problem's resolution without drastic aggressive action. In Iceland, where a woman president was backed by a parliament of more women than men, the all-women political party did not have a leader. Instead, the women formed groups to work out a consensus on each issue. In Canada, where a large number of women worked nationwide for only one year to accomplish the passage of the Women's Equality Clause 28 (passed in 1981), the conference that led to its passage was headed not by a charismatic leader, as is the case in most social reform movements, but by a team of three women. In conducting the affairs of the shrinking global village, there will be little room for large egos and great need for leaders from individual nations adept at working by consensus for the welfare of all.

The twenty-first century may call for leaders with wide-ranging capabilities, none of which are military in nature. Some situations will be best addressed by goal-oriented linear thinking, while others will require a holistic approach. Throughout history, men have been the changers, women the adapters. More so than men, women have for millennia had to adapt to changing conditions that were beyond their power to alter. Adaptability and the willingness to change course must be added to the ability to work harmoniously with others without demanding star billing as necessary attributes for tomorrow's leaders. Since the time of early gathering societies, women have maintained a strong connection with the earth. With the realizations that the resources of our fragile planet are finite and that war has become unthinkable, more of the skills that have lent women versatility will be paramount among the qualities needed by our future leaders, whatever their gender.

References

Bloodworth, Dennis, and Ching Ping Bloodworth. *The Chinese Machiavelli, 3000 Years of Chinese Statecraft.* New York: Farrar, Straus and Giroux, 1976.

Grousset, René. *The Empire of the Steppes, a History of Central Asia.* trans. Naomi Walford. New Brunswick, NJ: Rutgers University Press, 1970.

Kelley, Matt. "Land Agreement Would Give Tribe Their Own Land." *Houston Chronicle,* 11 January 1998: 23A.

Kenyatta, Jomo. *Facing Mount Kenya.* New York: Vintage Books, 1965.

Kinder, Hermann, and Werner Hilgemann. *The Anchor Atlas of World History,* 2 vols. trans. Ernest A. Menze. Garden City, NY: Anchor/Doubleday, 1974.

Lerner, Gerda. *The Creation of Patriarchy.* New York: Oxford University Press, 1986.

Naipul, V. S. "The Writer and India." *New York Review.* 4 March 1999.

Nyakatura, J. W. *Anatomy of an African Kingdom, A History of Bunyoro-Kitara.* Garden City, NY: Anchor/Doubleday, 1973.

Pannikar, K. Madhu. *The Serpent and the Crescent, A History of the Negro Empires of West Africa.* Bombay: Asia Publishing House, 1963.

Pemble, John. *The Raj, The Indian Mutiny and the Kingdom of Oudh 1801–1859.* Rutherford, NJ: Fairleigh Dickinson University Press, 1977.

Schele, Linda, and David Freidel. *A Forest of Kings, The Untold Story of the Ancient Maya.* New York: Quill/William Morrow, 1990.

Women Rulers
throughout the Ages

A

Absh Khatun
Queen of Persia (1263–1287)

Absh Khatun was the daughter of Bibi Khatun, one of the daughters of Kirman queen Turkhan Khatun, and niece of Padishah Khatun, ruler of Kirman from 1291 to 1295. Absh Khatun was married very young to Manku Timur, one of the sons of the great Turko-Mongolian Khan Hulägu. The couple was living in Urdu, the Ilkhan capital, when Hulägu, displeased at the way things were going in his Persian realm, sent an army to kill Seljuk Shah. Hulägu then dispatched his daughter-in-law, Absh Khatun, to Shiraz, the capital of her native country, to become head of state in 1263. She was received with great pomp, and coins were struck in her name. She was the ninth and last sovereign of the Persian dynasty of Atabeks, which was known as the Sulghurid dynasty after the Turkoman chief Sulghur who had migrated with his tribe to Iran a century earlier. She reigned until 1287.

References
Mernissi, Fatima. *The Forgotten Queens of Islam.* Trans. Mary Jo Lakeland. Minneapolis: University of Minnesota Press, 1993. p. 104.

Uçok Un, Badriye. *Al-nisa' al-hakimat fi tarikh.* Trans. I. Daquqi. Baghdad: Matba'a al-Sa'dun, 1973. pp. 101ff.

Ada
Queen of Caria (344–341 B.C. and 334–? B.C.)

Caria was a separate Persian satrapy belonging to the Delian League. It was located in southern Turkey. Ada was the wife-sister of Idrieus (or Hidreus), who ruled from 351 to 344 B.C. After his death, Ada ruled Halicarnassus (modern-day Bodrum) for three years until her younger brother, Pixadarus (or Pixodarus, r. 341–335 B.C.), expelled her. She moved to the strong fortress of Alinda, southwest of Alabanda, where she held out for several years. When her brother Pixadarus died in 335 B.C., his son-in-law Orontobates claimed the throne, but Ada quickly disputed his claim. On the road she had met Alexander (the Great), who was preparing to attack Halicarnassus. She made him her adopted son, thus assuring him her throne. Alexander soon destroyed Halicarnassus and left 3,000 mercenaries to garrison Caria, which he granted to Ada with the title of queen (ca. 334 B.C.). Soon after, Ada brought about the surrender of the Persians in the citadel of Myndus, which Alexander had been unable to accomplish earlier.

References
Hammond, N.G.L. *A History of Greece to 322 B.C.* Oxford: Clarendon Press, 1986. pp. 607, 621.
Olmstead, A. R. *History of the Persian Empire.* Chicago: University of Chicago Press, 1948. pp. 436, 483, 499.
Peters, F. E. *The Harvest of Hellenism.* New York: Barnes & Noble Books, 1996. p. 48.

Adame, Mama
Mansa (Ruler) of Niumi Bato at Bakindiki, West Africa

The history of Niumi Bato, occupied by a Mandika-speaking people in the northern coastal regions of Niumi in the Lower Gambia, is still passed down by *griots* (oral historians). Although great kingdoms had arisen in west Africa as early as the twelfth and thirteenth centuries, many villages were ruled by local kings or queens. South of the Gambia the country had been under the control of the Mandika since early times, but no accurate dates can be assigned to their leaders. Oral tradition as recounted by current *griots* mentions that when the Sonko people first came from Fulbe to the Gambia, the Jammeh people were already there. The Sonka found a woman ruling in the village of Bakindiki. This same tradition names Mama Adame as the first woman *mansa* there, although at the time women had been *mansa* in other villages. At that time, when a woman ruled, "the men slept behind the women." At the time of the arrival of the Sonko, the Jammeh were fighting against the people of Saloum, who were "tricksters and good fighters." The queen lodged the Sonko newcomers, who said to her, "Since these people are fighting against you, we wish to help you." She answered, "Thank you, but before you help us, wait until they have almost finished us off." The Sonko disagreed: "No, that is not safe. Unity is not a bad thing. But if we should overcome them we could intermarry, but that is not enough. We must share your position— that is, we must rotate *mansaya*." Thereafter the Janneh, the Sonko, and another tribe that arrived from Kabu, the Manneh, all rotated the rule peacefully. However, Mama Adame decided that no more women should rule. She said, "Underwear is not strong, but trousers are."

References

Wright, Donald R. *Oral Traditions from the Gambia*. Vol. 2. Athens: Ohio University Center for International Studies, 1980. pp. 76–79.

Addagoppe of Harran

Priestess, Probable Regent of Babylon (ca. 522 B.C.)

Addagoppe, also known as Adda-Guppi, was born in 445 B.C. in Harran and became a priestess of the god Sin. Nitocris is a possible misnomer for this queen. According to Herodotus, writing of Nitocris, she was married to an Assyrian king named Labynetus and had a son of the same name. According to Olmstead, based on datable historical facts in Herodotus's account, the son Labynetus corresponds to the ruler Nabonidus, or Nabu-naid. The true history of Addagoppe is known from a stele (found in 1956) preserved in a paving stone inscription side down in the Great Mosque at Harran. Her remarkable career spanned the whole Neo-Babylonian Dynasty down to the ninth year of its last king. She came to Babylon from Harran and managed to obtain a responsible position for her son at court. Nabu-naid eventually became king of Babylon (r. 556–539 B.C.), although he spent little actual time in Babylon. Herodotus refers to the king's mother as "Queen Nitocris" and says that in order to strengthen the security of Babylon, she altered the course of the Euphrates, constructed tall embankments on each side, and built a foot bridge across the river that could be removed at night. In great but erroneous detail, Herodotus describes her "grim practical joke": She placed her own tomb above one of the main gates of the city and inscribed on it: "If any king of Babylon hereafter is short of money, let him open my tomb and take as much as he likes. But this must be done only in case of need. Whoever opens my tomb under any other circumstances will get no good of it." The tomb was untouched until the reign of Darius, who opened it to find only the queen's body and the message: "If you had not been insatiably greedy and eager to get money by the most despicable means, you would never have opened the tomb of the dead." Legends abound about illustrious persons, especially those who were particularly long lived. There is no historical verification of Herodotus's tales, but it is a historical fact that when Addagoppe died (ca. 543/547 B.C.) at the age of 104, she was buried in Harran with all the honors reserved for a queen. It is possible that, when Nabu-naid left Babylon in ca. 552 to reside in Taima (northeastern Asia), leaving his son Belshar-usur (Belshazzar in the book of Daniel) in charge, he also left his mother. It is even likely that, during Belshazzar's absences, Addagoppe would serve as regent, which would explain her being honored as a queen at death. Nabu-naid did not return to Babylon until 542 B.C., so she may have been honored by her grandson and not her son, or her death might have been the occasion of her son's belated return. After his mother's death, Nabu-naid named his daughter high priestess of the god Sin.

References

Herodotus. *The Histories.* Trans. Aubrey de Sélincourt. New York: Viking Penguin, 1988. pp. 115–117.

Olmstead, A. T. *History of the Persian Empire.* Chicago: University of Chicago Press, 1948. pp. 55, 115, 321–322.

Adela
Countess of Blois and Chartres, Regent (ca. 1097–1109)

The daughter of William I the Conqueror of England, Adela (B.C. 1062) inherited his strong will and an interest in politics. She married Count Stephen of Blois and Chartres and governed alone when her husband left for the Holy Land on the First Crusade, c. 1097. In the spring of 1098, Stephen became discouraged and decided to return home. On his way, he met Byzantine Emperor Alexius and convinced him that the attempt to take Antioch was hopeless, so Alexius also turned back. Steven's advice was to cause Alexius difficulties later, for when the remaining crusaders learned he had turned back, they felt no obligation to return Antioch to him. Stephen's return without fulfilling his crusading vows was a source of great humiliation to Adela, reared in the tradition of the great William the Conqueror. It was said that behind the doors of their bedchamber she shamed him for his cowardice and urged him to redeem his honor. Stephen could not argue that he was needed to rule Blois, for Adela had always actually ruled. Against his own better judgment, Steven set out on another expedition in 1101. This time he survived the seige of Antioch and continued the pilgrimage to Jerusalem. The crusaders' ship was blown ashore off Jaffa, where, under the command of Jerusalem's King Baldwin, they planned to attack the approaching Egyptian army, believing it to be much smaller than it was. Stephen saw the proposed attack as precipitous, but his comrades, remembering his past cowardice, ignored his advice. Too late, they realized their mistake, but they went into battle bravely. Stephen redeemed his honor but lost his life (1102). After his death Adela continued to serve as regent until 1109, when her oldest son, Theobald, reached majority, and she had him made count. During the years of her regency she worked to strengthen her fiefdom so that her son would have an increasingly important role to play in European affairs. It was due to her efforts, through her friend the bishop St. Ives of Chartres, that her younger brother, King Henry I of England, was able to reach a compromise with the archbishop of Canterbury over the lay investiture of churchmen. The schoolmaster Hildebert of Lavardin (1056–1133), who became archbishop of Tours, earned the ardent admiration of Adela because of his classical Latin poetry. She addressed many love songs to him, as did the empress Matilda. Adela's third son, Stephen, became king of England, based on her claim of inheritance following Henry's death. She died in 1137.

References

Heer, Friedrich. *The Medieval World.* Trans. Janet Sondheimer. New York: The New American Library, Mentor Books, 1962. p. 124.

Runciman, Steven. *A History of the Crusades.* Vol. 2, *The Kingdom of Jerusalem and the Frankish East.* Cambridge: Cambridge University Press, 1952, 1987. pp. 20, 48, 78.

Adelaide
Queen of Italy, Regent of German Empire (983–995)

Adelaide was born in 931, the daughter of King Rudolph II of Burgundy and Bertha of Swabia. She married King Lothair of Italy in 947, at about age sixteen. Lothair died only three years later and Adelaide ruled alone, briefly. However, the following year, her kingdom was threatened with siege by Berengar of Pavia. Adelaide was imprisoned, but because she was a beautiful woman of strong character, she found many willing to help her. She managed to escape after a confinement of four months. She offered her hand in marriage as reward for helping her regain her Italian throne. Several nobles sought to intervene, but it was Otto (Otto the Great, Saxon emperor of the German Empire) who stepped in to the rescue. Seeing an opportunity to expand his holdings, he came to Adelaide's aid, defeated Berengar's forces, and declared himself king of the Franks and Lombards. Adelaide, glad to have Otto's protection and envisioning for herself a larger kingdom, married him and ceded Italy to Berengar in exchange for Istria, Friuli, and Verona, which became part of Bavaria. Otto and Adelaide were crowned emperor and empress of the Western German Empire in 962. Their son, Otto II, succeeded to the throne upon his father's death in 973. Only ten years later, three-year-old Otto III, son of Otto II and Theophano, inherited the throne. Adelaide, his grandmother, served as co-regent, sharing the duties with her daughter-in-law from 983 to 991, when Theophano died. Adelaide then governed alone until Otto came of age in 995. After his coronation, she devoted herself to found-

Adelaide, Queen of Italy (Archive Photos)

ing churches and monastaries. She died in 999 at the age of sixty-eight and was buried in Seltz, Alsace, where miracles were reported to have occurred. She was made a saint of the Catholic Church; her feast day is December 16.

References

Kinder, Hermann, and Werner Hilgemann. *Atlas of World History.* Trans. Ernest Menze. Garden City, NY: Anchor/Doubleday, 1982. p. 143.

Previté-Orton, C. W. *The Shorter Cambridge Medieval History.* Vol. 1, *The Later Roman Empire to the Twelfth Century.* Cambridge: Cambridge University Press, 1952, 1982. pp. 436–437.

Adelaide of Salona
Countess, Regent of Sicily (1101–1112)

Adelaide was the daughter of the Marquis Manfred and the niece of Boniface of Salona (or Savona). She married the great Count Roger I of Sicily in 1089, becoming his third wife. When Roger died two years later, she assumed the regency for his brother Simon, who died in 1105, and thereafter for her son Roger II, who went on to become one of the most remarkable rulers of the Middle Ages. Countess-Dowager Adelaide's immense wealth attracted the attention of the Frankish king Baldwin I of Jerusalem, who had cast aside his dowerless second wife and was looking for a new wealthier queen. Adelaide had just retired from more than a decade of her regency and was looking for a new husband. Baldwin sent word, asking for her hand; Adelaide accepted, providing the king would agree to the terms of her contract: that if no baby was born of the union—and the ages of both suggested little possibility—the crown of Jerusalem would pass to her son, Roger II. Her terms accepted, Adelaide sailed the Mediterranean in an elegant splendor reminiscent of Cleopatra, with a fleet of gold- and silver-trimmed ships carrying all her personal treasure. Baldwin met her with equal pomp and ordered all his kingdom adorned for her arrival. However, once he had spent her dowry to pay off his debts, his ardor cooled, as did hers, when she found that Jerusalem was a far cry from her luxurious Palermo palace. In 1117 Baldwin fell seriously ill, and his confessors reminded him that he might die in a state of sin, since he had never legally divorced his second wife. When he recovered, he announced the annulment of his marriage to Adelaide. Now alone, scorned, stripped of her wealth, Adelaide sailed back to Sicily in humiliation. Baldwin's insult would cost the kingdom of Jerusalem dearly in the ensuing years, but Adelaide's marriage contract would be the basis for her son's claim upon the lands of Jerusalem. Roger II never forgot Baldwin's humiliation of his mother. In 1117, two lunar eclipses and the appearance of the aurora borealis were taken as foretelling the death of princes. In the following months, in 1118, King Baldwin, his patriarch Arnulf, Pope Paschal, Iranian sultan Mohammed, Baghdad caliph Mustazhir, and ex-queen Adelaide all died.

References

Runciman, Steven. *A History of the Crusades.* Vol. 2, *The Kingdom of Jerusalem and the Frankish East.* Cambridge: Cambridge University Press, 1952, 1987. pp. 102–105, 199, 207, 251–252.

Smith, Dennis Mack. *A History of Sicily.* Vol. 1. New York: Dorset Press, 1968. p. 24.

Adele
Co-ruler of Vendôme (ca. 1017–1031)

Adele was the wife of Bouchard I, count of Vendôme, Paril, and Corbeil, ruler of Vendôme from 958 to 1012. The couple had three sons, Renaud (bishop of Paril), Bouchard II, and Foulques d'Oison. When Bouchard I died in 1012, the oldest son ruled for four years. Following his death in 1016, a nephew, Eudes, son of Landry, count of Nevers, ruled briefly because Bouchard II was too young and quite possibly Adele was again pregnant. Bouchard II assumed the rule sometime after 1016 with his mother, but apparently he died soon after. The youngest child, Foulques d'Oison, then ruled with his mother until 1031, when Adele, in financial straits, sold the duchy to Foulques's uncle, Geoffri Martel, count of Anjou.

References

Egan, Edward W., Constance B. Hintz, and L. F. Wise, eds. *Kings, Rulers, and Statesmen.* New York: Sterling Publishing, 1976. p. 162.

Aelfgifu of Northumbria
Regent of Norway (ca. 1029–1035)

Aelfgifu (or Eligifu) was the daughter of an ealdorman of Northumbria who in 1006 had been murdered at the order of King Aethelred II. In ca. 1013 she met and became the mistress of Canute (the Great), son of Danish king Sven I Fork Beard, who invaded England that year. Canute became king of Denmark when his father died in 1014, was elected king of England in 1016, and became king of Norway in 1028. Aelfgifu bore two sons, Sven (Sweyn) and Harold (Harefoot). However, in 1017, to bolster English support in case of an attack by Aethelred, Canute married Emma, the mother of exiled King Aethelred's sons. Emma was also sister of Duke Richard II. After Canute became king of Norway, he assigned Haakon as his regent; however, Haakon soon died. He then put Norway in the hands of Aelfgifu as regent for their son Sven. The two, Aelfgifu and Sven, remained in Norway for some six years before they were driven out. They escaped to Denmark, where Canute had put his legitimate son by Emma, Harthacnute (Hardecanute), in charge (1035). Canute died the same year, and Aelfgifu returned to England to champion the cause of her second son, Harold I Harefoot, as king. He ruled as regent from 1035 until his death in 1040, when his half brother ascended to the throne.

References

Derry, T. K. *A History of Scandinavia.* Minneapolis: University of Minnesota Press, 1979. p. 39.

Langer, William L., ed. *World History.* Boston: Houghton Mifflin, 1940, 1980. pp. 182–183.

Aelfwyn
Queen of Mercia (918–919)

The daughter of Aethelred II, who ruled from 879 to 911, and Queen Aethelflaed, who ruled following his death until 918, Aelfwyn briefly ascended to the throne upon her mother's death. She was deposed in 919 when Mercia was annexed to West Saxony.

References

Morby, John. *Dynasties of the World.* Oxford: Oxford University Press, 1989. p. 66.

Aethelflaed
Queen of Mercia (ca. 910–918)

Mercia was an Anglo-Saxon kingdom located in central England. Originally consisting of the border areas of what is now Derbyshire, Staffordshire, and northern Warwickshire, Mercia eventually encompassed an area bounded on the north by the River Humber, on the east by East Anglia, on the south by the Thames, and on the west by Wales. Aethelflaed (also known as Ethelfleda) was the daughter of Alfred the Great. She married Aethelred, ealdorman of the Mercians, and became the effective ruler in his stead long before he died. When Aethelred died in 911, she anomalously succeeded him, having already become firmly established as ruler. She became known as the Lady of the Mercians. She rivaled her brother Edward the Elder, ruler of West Saxony (899–924), in both war and organization, and she assisted him in overcoming the Danish armies that controlled great portions of eastern England. While Edward spent six years (910–916) fortifying the southeastern midlands, Aethelflaed was doing the same for Mercia. In 913 she erected the great earthen mound near present-day Warwick Castle as a fortress. By 917 the two of them had amassed large forces for a joint assault against the Danes. She captured Derby easily and went on to occupy Leicester in 918. She had already extended her boundaries into Wales on the west and Northumberland on the north. She gained a promise of submission from the Danes in Northumberland; however, before she could gain complete victory, she died (918) in Tamworth, now in Staffordshire, leaving Edward to win the final victory against the Danes. With his sister gone, Edward claimed her lands, and thus nearly all of what is present-day England was united under his control.

References

Grun, Bernard. *The Timetables of History.* New York: Simon & Schuster, 1979. p. 913.

Previté-Orton, C. W. *The Shorter Cambridge Medieval History.* Vol. 1, *The Later Roman Empire to the Twelfth Century.* Cambridge: Cambridge University Press, 1952, 1987. pp. 385–389.

Whitelock, Dorothy. *The Pelican History of England.* Vol. 2: *The Beginnings of English Society.* Harmondsworth, Middlesex: Penguin Books, 1952, 1976. pp. 76–77.

Afua Koba

Asantehemaa, Queen Mother of the Asante Empire (ca. 1834–1884)

The Asante Empire comprised at that time most of the present-day west African nations of Ghana and Togo and portions of Ivory Coast and Dahomey. The office of *asantehemaa,* or queen mother, was an elected position of great importance and influence. The holder of this office nominated the *asantehene,* or leader of the chiefs, and in some cases she served during several administrations. Accession to the Golden Stool, or throne, was matrilineal. Afua Koba, whose second husband, Boakye Tenten, occupied the Boakye Yam Panin *okeyeame* stool, was the mother of Kofi Kakari, occupant of the Golden Stool from 1867 to 1874, and Mensa Bonsu, occupant of the Golden Stool from 1874 to 1883. She was a powerful and influential figure in a troubled period in the history of Asante. During the reign of her first son, a British general asked Kofi Kakari, as a condition of the general's not advancing to his city, to send the queen mother and Prince Mensa, next heir to the throne, to him as hostages. The general did not understand that in the eyes of the Asante, these were the most important persons in the kingdom, and it was not within Kofi Kakari's power to surrender them, even if he had been so inclined. In 1881, Afua Koba's intervention in the interest of peace with the British invaders was instrumental in preventing bloodshed for a time. She held the office of queen mother during the reign of several of her royal family members. In 1884, after Kwaku Dua was poisoned and the governmental system was in disarray with several outlying areas threatening to secede, she put forth, as candidate for the office of Golden Stool, an unpopular candidate, Kwasi Kisi, who she knew had no chance of winning. This nomination was a gesture to win British assistance and to bring the outlying rulers into the capital for council deliberations. The ploy was unpopular; she was deposed in late 1884 and was succeeded by Yaa Akyaa.

References

Balmer, W. T. *A Brief History of the Akan Peoples.* New York: Atlantis Press, 1925. p. 167.

Lewin, Thomas J. *Asante Before the British.* Lawrence: Regents Press of Kansas, 1978. pp. 49, 74, 82.

Agnes de Dampierre
Baroness, Ruler of Bourbon (1262–1287)

Agnes ruled Bourbon during that period in French history in which so-called feudal anarchy existed. The French kings actually ruled a small area around Paris and Orleans while the heads of the great duchies and baronies maintained their independence. Agnes was the daughter of Dame Mahaut I and Gui II de Dampierre and the sister of Baroness Mahaut II, who ruled from 1249 to 1262. Mahaut II married Eudes de Bourgogne and Agnes married his brother, Jean de Bourgogne. She succeeded to the barony when her sister died in 1262.

References

Egan, Edward W., Constance B. Hintz, and L. F. Wise, eds. *Kings, Rulers, and Statesmen.* New York: Sterling Publishing, 1976. p. 153.

Agnes de Nevers
Countess, Ruler of Nevers (1181–1192)

Nevers was located in the modern-day Departement of Nievre in central France, south-southeast of Paris. Agnes succeeded Count Guillaume V, who ruled from 1175 to 1181. She married Pierre de

Courtenay, and they had a daughter, Mahaut, who succeeded her mother in 1192.

References

Egan, Edward W., Constance B. Hintz, and L. F. Wise, eds. *Kings, Rulers, and Statesmen.* New York: Sterling Publishing, 1976. p. 159.

Agnes of Dunbar
Countess of March, Ruler of Dunbar (ca. 1338)

Agnes of Dunbar (Black Agnes) was the daughter of the great Randolph, earl of Moray, who had been fighting off the British for years. In 1338 the English troops of Edward III attacked Dunbar castle; Edward had never been happy about the Treaty of Northampton (1028) making Scotland an independent realm, and he intended to bring it back under English control. Agnes held out triumphantly for five months, successfully defending the castle until the English retreated. Fortunately for the Scots, Edward, attempting also to gain the French throne, took his army to France.

References

Mackie, J. D. *A History of Scotland.* Harmondsworth, Middlesex: Penguin Books, 1984. p. 80.

Agnes of Poitou
Duchess of Bavaria (1056–1061), Regent for Holy Roman Emperor Henry IV (1056–1062)

Agnes of Poitou was born ca. 1024, the daughter of William V the Pious, duke of Aquitaine, a descendant of the kings of Italy and Burgundy. She married Henry III on November 1, 1043, becoming the second wife of the Holy Roman emperor and forming an allegiance cementing the empire's relations with its neighbors to its west. She and Henry III had a son, Henry IV, for whom Agnes assumed the regency when her husband died in 1056. However, although she was descended from kings both of Italy and Burgundy, she had no talent for leadership; she was, in fact, characterized as being pious and colorless. She gave away the duchies of Bavaria, Swabia, and Carinthia to relatives. An opponent of church reform, she allied herself with Italian dissidents and helped elect Cadalus as Antipope Honorarius II to oppose Pope Alexander II, elected by the reformers. In 1062 Archbishop Anno of Cologne, with the help of several princes, succeeded in kidnapping the young king and bringing him to Cologne, out of his mother's grasp. He jumped overboard but was rescued and recaptured. As ransom for her son, Agnes resigned as regent, and Anno took her place. She spent the remainder of her life in a convent.

References

Previté-Orton, C. W. *The Shorter Cambridge Medieval History.* Vol. 1, *The Later Roman Empire to the Twelfth Century.* Cambridge: Cambridge University Press, 1952, 1987. p. 460.

Ahhotpe I
Queen of Thebes (ca.1570–ca.1548 B.C.)

Ahhotpe was the wife of Seqenenre Ta'a II ("the Brave") and the mother of Egyptian king Kamose (d. ca. 1570 B.C.); king Ahmose I (r. c. 1570–1546 B.C.), who succeeded him and who is generally given credit for founding the Eighteenth Dynasty in Egypt; and Ahmose-Nofretari, their younger sister, whom Ahmose I married. On the doorway at Buhen an inscription alludes to Ahhopte I and Ahmose I in such a manner as to suggest a co-regency existed during the early years of Ahmose's reign when he was too young to rule alone. Later, while Ahmose I was driving the Hyksos kings out of Egypt, Ahhotpe ran the government in Thebes, which is near modern-day Luxor. Her achievements are commemorated on King Ahmose's stele in the temple of Amon-Re at Karnak. She is given credit for having "taken care of Egypt," of having "watched over her troops and protected them," of having "pacified Upper Egypt and hunted down rebels." The latter refers to the fact that she helped to quell an uprising until her son could arrive with reinforcements. Her efforts, added to his, reunited Egypt under one rule. She died ca. 1548 B.C.

References

The Cambridge Ancient History. 3d. ed. Vol. 1. Cambridge: Cambridge University Press, 1970–1971. pp. 40, 62.

Carpenter, Clive. *The Guinness Book of Kings, Rulers & Statesmen.* Enfield, Middlesex; Guinness Superlatives, 1978. p. 68.

Grimal, Nicolas. *A History of Ancient Egypt.* Trans. Basil Blackwell Ltd. New York: Barnes & Noble Books, 1997. pp. 190, 200, 201.

Ahmose-Nofretari
Queen, Co-ruler of Egypt (ca. 1552–1546 B.C.)

During the Second Intermediate Period of Egyptian history (ca.1674–1553 B.C.), which was characterized by turbulence and regional rulers, the Hyksos, from Asia, invaded. Ahmose I, Nofretari's brother and husband, continued the fight against the invaders that his brother King Kamose had begun, eventually defeating the Hyksos and founding the Eighteenth Dynasty. He married his sister, Ahmose-Nofretari, who, in Ahmose's sixteenth or twenty-second year of reign, renounced the title of second prophet and received instead the title of God's Wife of Amon, through which the matrilineal dynasty would succeed. She was the first queen to hold this title. They had a son, Amenhotep I (Amenophis), who succeeded to the throne upon his father's death, and a daughter, Ahmose, who received the title God's Wife as well. Ahmose-Nofretari outlived her husband and became regent for her son, who was too young to rule. Ahmose-Nofretari was an influential and highly honored queen, as evidenced by depictions at Thebes of later pharaohs making offerings to her as a goddess. After her death she became the object of a religious cult, the center of which was at Deir el-Medina. Her name appears in at least fifty private tombs and on more than eighty monuments.

Ahmose-Nofretari
(Corbis / Roger Wood)

References

Grimal, Nicolas. *A History of Ancient Egypt.* Trans. Basil Blackwell Ltd. New York: Barnes & Noble Books, 1997. pp. 190, 195, 200–202, 283.

White, J.E. Manchip. *Ancient Egypt: Its Culture and History.* New York: Dover Publications, 1970. pp. 164–165.

Aissa Koli

Ruler of the Kanuri Empire of Bornu, West Africa (ca. 1562/1563–1570, or 1497–1504)

Kanem-Bornu was located in west Africa. Although some discrepancy exists about the dates and parentage of Aissa (also known as Aisa Kili Ngirmaramma), substantial evidence of her reign exists among local tradition. Arabic historians, who routinely ignored women sovereigns, failed to record her rule. Too, history records that her successor, Idris Aloma, imposed a Muslim bureacracy upon previously pagan subjects, all the more reason for Islamic sources to ignore her rule. By some accounts Aissa Koli was the daughter of Ali Gaji Zanani, who died in ca. 1545/1547 (or 1497, according to Panikker) after ruling only one year. By this account, when Ali Gaji Zanani died, he was succeeded by Dunama, a relative, who also died in 1497. Aissa

Koli then ruled alone for seven years, because it was believed that there was no male heir. However, she was unaware of the existence of a brother, whom his mother, a Bulala, had sent to the Bulala court because the interim ruler had threatened to kill all the former king's sons. The boy, Idris, was five years old at the time that Aissa Koli's rule began. When he reached the age of twelve, he wrote his mother and his sister the queen, informing them of his existence. Aissa Koli's term being up—the rulers of many of the African nations had a fixed term of seven years—she asked him to come home. By this account, he was crowned king in 1504. Aissa Koli continued in a position of influence and authority, advising her long-exiled brother.

Other sources say that she was the daughter of a relative of Ali, King Dunama, who succeeded Ali and reigned until ca. 1562/1563. This version says that Ali had left a young son of five, Idris, who had been spirited away to live with his mother's Bulala relatives in Kanem for fear that Dunama would have him killed. After Dunama's death, Aissa assumed the throne and ruled for seven years, as it was generally believed that there was no male heir. When Idris was twelve, he wrote to his mother and his sister (by some accounts) Aissa, informing them of his existence. When the queen's seven-year term was up, she invited him to come home. He was crowned king (*mai*) in ca. 1570 and went on to become the most famous king in the 1,000-year Sefawa dynasty of Kanem-Bornu. This version also maintains that Aissa continued in a position of influence and authority, as adviser to her brother on government procedures and the ways of his subjects, strengthening his position against interdynastic strife, until he grew to manhood.

References

Hunwick, John. "Songhay, Bornu and Hausaland in the 16th Century." In J.F.A. Ajayi and Michael Crowder, eds. *History of West Africa*. Vol. 1. New York: Columbia University Press, 1972. pp. 101–139.

Panikker, K. Madhu. *The Serpent and the Crescent: A History of the Negro Empires of West Africa*. Bombay: Asia Publishing House, 1963. p. 104.

Alaghai-bäki
Mongolian Queen of the Öngüt, Northern China (fl. 13th c.)

Alaghai-bäki was a daughter of Jenghiz Khan (Genghis Khan, r. 1206–1227), who rewarded the Turkish Öngüts who helped him overcome the Kins (Chins or Juchens) by giving her in marriage to Po-yao-ho, son of assassinated Öngüt chief Alaqush-tigin. Young Po-yao-ho had gone with Jenghiz Khan on his campaign against the Khwarizm to restore the Alaqush family to the leadership of the

Öngüt. Alaghai-bäki had no children of her own, but Po-yao-ho had three sons by a concubine. When he died, Alaghai-bäki ruled the Öngüt country with "a forceful hand." Described as "a woman of energy," her father's daughter, she treated her late husband's sons as her own, allowing each to marry into the clan.

References

Grousset, René. *The Empire of the Steppes.* Trans. Naomi Walford. New Brunswick, NJ: Rutgers University Press, 1970.

Alam al-Malika
Al-hurra, Ruled in Zubayd (ca. 1120–1130)

Zubayd (Zabīd) was a principality and city in western Yemen near San'a, with whom it was in a perpetual state of war. During the period from 1022 to 1158 Zubayd was ruled by a Muslim dynasty of Ethiopian Mamluks (slaves). The title *al-hurra* was bestowed on women in Yemen who were active in the political arena, but it did not denote queenship. Alam al-Malika al-hurra was a *jarya,* or singer slave of Zubayd's king, Mansur Ibn Najah (r. ca. 1111–1123). Her political astuteness, learning, and intelligence so impressed the king that he ultimately placed her in charge of the realm's management and "made no decision concerning it without consulting her." In 1123 King Mansur Ibn Najah was poisoned by his vizier, Mann Allah. After his death, Alam al-Malika al-hurra continued to govern, and it was written of her that "she discharged her task with distinction." However, she was denied the privilege of having the *khutba* proclaimed in her name. The *khutba,* the privilege reserved for the sovereign, was preached at Friday night prayer, affirming the sovereign's right to rule.

References

Mernissi, Fatima. *The Forgotten Queens of Islam.* Trans. Mary Jo Lakeland. Minneapolis: University of Minnesota Press, 1993. p. 140.

Alexandra
King of the Maccabees (Judaea) (76–67 B.C.)

Alexandra (Salome Alexandra or Alexandra Salome) was the wife of King Alexander Jannaeus of the Asmonean, or Hasmonean, dynasty, Syria, who ruled from 103 to 76 B.C., during one of the brief periods of Judaean independence. The couple had two sons, John Hyrcanus II and Aristobulus II. Before he died in 76 B.C., Alexander Jannaeus, realizing that strong religious support would be necessary for his successor, persuaded Alexandra Salome to assume the throne, thus restoring the Pharisees to a position of leadership. She became king, not queen, and her elder son was appointed high priest (as a woman, she could not become the high priest herself). She reversed the earlier policy of Hyrcanus I and elevated the Pharisees, who reinforced their temple regulations and resumed their position of power. Alexandra Salome's brother, Simon bar Shetah, held an important role in the new regime. She died in 67 B.C. and was succeeded by her son Hyrcanus II, who only three months later was driven from power, briefly, by her other son, Aristobulus II. On the advice of Antipater the Idumaean, Hyrcanus petitioned Aretas, king of the Nabataean Arabs, for help and eventually regained the throne; however, he was a puppet in the hands of various Roman factions.

References
Cooke, Jean, et al. *History's Timeline*. New York: Crescent Books, 1981. p. 33.
Langer, William L., ed. *World History*. Boston: Houghton Mifflin, 1948, 1980. p. 94.
Peters, F. E. *The Harvest of Hellenism*. New York: Barnes & Noble Books, 1996. pp. 294–295, 321–323.

Alexandra
Empress of Russia, Absolute Ruler in Her Husband's Absence (1915–1917)

Alexandra was born in 1872 in Darmstadt, the daughter of Alice, Queen Victoria's daughter, and Louis IV, duke of Hesse-Darmstadt. Darmstadt was located in present-day West Germany. Alexandra was often unbending and firm willed, with a strong and proud appreciation of her Teutonic blood. She married Nicholas II of Russia in 1894 and dominated their entire married life. She was not popular with the Russian people, who considered her a German interloper. As consolation, she immersed herself in religion; however, her interest in religion did not prevent her from exerting her influence to undo the 1905 reforms that limited the powers of the monarchy. The couple had four daughters before their son Alexis, a hemophiliac, was born. The boy's perilous health also put the future of the dynasty in peril. Alexandra turned for advice to Grigory Yefimovich Rasputin, a self-proclaimed holy man, upon whom she came to rely so heavily that her conduct became a public scandal. In August 1915, when Nicholas left for the front to assume command of Russian troops, Alexandra moved quickly to consolidate her own power. She dismissed valuable ministers and replaced them with puppets, choices of Rasputin. The government soon became paralyzed, and Alexandra was further alienated from an already suspicious and mistrusting public. Alexandra apparently believed that she was safely beyond justice, and even when Rasputin was murdered, she continued her despotic rule, paying no heed to public opinion. After the October Bolshevik Revolution, the entire family was imprisoned. On July 29, 1918, she was shot to death at Yekaterinburg, now Sverdlovsk, Russia. It might be concluded that she alone precipitated the collapse of the military government in March 1911, hastening the advent of the Bolshevik Revolution.

References

Thompson, John M. *Revolutionary Russia, 1917.* New York: John Scribner's Sons, 1981. pp. 14–23.

Alice
Princess, Regent of Antioch (1130 and 1135–1136)

Alexandra, Empress of Russia (Corbis-Bettmann)

Born ca. 1106, the second daughter of Jerusalem's King Baldwin II and Queen Morphia of Melitene, Alice married tall, fair-haired, handsome Prince Bohemond II of Antioch in 1126. They had a daughter, Constance, who was only two years old when her father died in 1130. Without waiting for her father King Baldwin II to appoint a regent, Alice at once assumed the regency for her daughter. But her ambition to rule, not as a regent but as a reigning sovereign, drove her to rash measures. When she heard that her father was on the way to Antioch to claim a regency, she sent an envoy to the atabeg Zengi, offering to pay him homage if he would guarantee her possession of the throne of Antioch. Baldwin intercepted the envoy and had him hanged. When Baldwin reached Antioch, he found the gates locked. After three days of negotiations, he entered the city, where Alice had barricaded herself in a tower, waiting for guarantees of her safety. When she and her father finally met, she knelt in terror and begged his forgiveness, which she received. Baldwin removed her from the regency, assumed it himself, and banished Alice to her dower lands of Lattakieh and Jabala. After Baldwin's death (1131), Alice reasserted her claims for the regency. She gathered a sizable following against her brother-in-law, King Fulk, who sailed from Jerusalem to claim the regency. Alice's revolt was put down (1132), but she remained safe at Lattakieh. In 1135, the Latin bishop of Mamistra, Radulph of Domfront, assumed the patriarchal throne without canonical election. Not wishing to be dominated by Jerusalem, he opened negotiations with Alice, who saw opportunity to regain power in Antioch. She appealed to her sister, Queen Melisende, Fulk's wife, who arranged Alice's return to Antioch. Although Fulk retained the title of regent, the governing power was actually shared by Alice and Radulph in what was characterized as an uneasy alliance. Radulph soon quarreled with his clergy, and Alice seized the opportunity to govern Antioch alone. She endeavored to strengthen her rather tenuous position by offering the hand of her nine-year-old daughter, the heir Princess Constance, to the Byzantine emperor's son Manuel. Radulph, fearing he would be replaced as patriarch by a Greek if such a union occurred, sent an urgent secret message to King Fulk advising him to find a suitable husband for Constance at once. Fulk, keeping both Alice and his wife Melisende uninformed, chose as Constance's consort Raymond of Poiters. Patriarch Radulph then requested audience with Alice to say that a handsome stranger had offered himself as a candidate for marriage to Alice. She was most receptive to the proposal, but while Alice waited for the arrival of her future husband, Constance was kidnapped and taken to the cathedral, where Radulph quickly performed the ceremony uniting the child and Raymond. Alice, seething at the betrayal and having no more claim to the rule of Antioch, retired again to Lattakieh. At the time, she was still under thirty years old.

References

Runciman, Steven. *History of the Crusades.* Vol. 2, *The Kingdom of Jerusalem.* Cambridge: Cambridge University Press, 1952, 1987. pp. 176–177, 183–184, 188–190, 198–200.

Aline Sitoe
Queen of the Diola Tribe, Casamance (ca. 1936–1943)

Casamance was located in modern-day Senegal, West Africa. Aline Sitoe (also known as Queen Sitoe) was born ca. 1920 in Kabrousse. Beginning in 1942, she turned her people against the French who ruled her country. She gained renown as far away as Mauritania, Mali, and Guinea-Bissau for her battle-cry, "The white man is not invincible." She instigated a boycott of French products, instead encouraging local artisans to produce more. She discouraged use of the French language and exhorted her people to develop their intellectual capacities and resurrect their own culture. She sought to strengthen community life by giving women a more vital role. She announced a return to the use of the Diola six-day-week calendar, which was based on the annual rainy season, harvest season, dry season, and pre-rainy season. When Diola warriors ambushed a truck and killed four men, three of them soldiers, the French advanced upon Kabrousse and held it under seige from January 13 to 29, 1943, when the queen surrendered to prevent the French from burning the town to the ground. She was arrested and condemned to ten years in exile in Timbuktu; however, she died on May 22, 1944, after a long bout with scurvy. She was buried in Timbuktu's Sidi el Wafi Cemetery, but in 1983 her remains were returned to Senegal, which had become independent from France nineteen years after her death. Legend claims that Queen Sitoe could change herself into a bird whenever she liked.

References

"Mystery Finally Solved: Rebellious Queen Sitoe Succumbs to Scurvy." *Houston Post.* 27 October 1983: W3.

Alix of Anjou
Ruler of Brittany (1203–1221), Regent (1221–1237)

Alix of Anjou was the daughter of Constance, daughter of Conan IV the Younger (r. 1156–deposed in 1166), and her second husband, Guy of Thouars. Alix inherited Brittany when her half-brother, Arthur I, died in 1203. In 1213 she married Peter I, Mauclerc, son of Robert II of Dreux. The couple had a son, John I the Red, who came to the rule when Peter died in 1221, with Alix as his regent. She died in 1250.

References

Morby, John. *Dynasties of the World.* Oxford: Oxford University Press, 1989. p. 83.

Alix of Vergy
Countess, Ruler of Burgundy (1248–?)

Alix of Vergy was the daughter of Count Otto II and his wife, Countess Beatrix, daughter of Count Otto I. Alix's brother, Otto III, became count in 1234, and she inherited Burgundy, located in present-day eastern France, upon his death in 1248. She was married to Hugh of Chalon, and their son, Otto IV, inherited Burgundy upon her death some time before 1290. Otto IV, in financial straits after protracted conflicts with the emperor, concluded two treaties (1291 and 1295) with King Philip IV of France wherein he ceded Burgundy to France.

References

Heer, Friedrich. *The Medieval World.* New York: Mentor/NAL, 1962. p. 318.

Amalswinthe
Queen, Regent of the Ostrogoths (Italy, Western Roman Empire) (526–534), then Co-ruler (534–535)

Amalswinthe (or Amalsuntha or Amalsontha) was born in 498, the daughter of King Theodoric the Great of the Ostrogoths and Audofleda, sister of King Clovis. Even by today's standards, Amalswinthe was an extremely well educated woman. She studied both Greek and Latin and became a lifelong patroness of literature and the arts. In 515 she married Theodoric's distant relative, Eutharic. They had a son, Athalric, and a daughter, Matasuntha. Eutharic died in 522, and Theodoric died four years later, after which time Amalswinthe served as regent for her ten-year-old son. She chose to continue the pro-Byzantine policies of her father, even though they were unpopular with the Ostrogoth nobility. Recognizing the danger her policies put her in, she took the precaution of arranging with Byzantine emperor Justinian that if she were deposed she would transfer herself and the entire Ostrogothic treasury to Constantinople. In 533 she successfully quelled a rebellion and put to death three of its instigators, Ostrogoth noblemen. Upon her son's death in 534, she shared the throne with her cousin Theodahad; however, he fell under the influence of the forces that opposed her, and he ordered her banished to an island in the lake of Bolsena (Tuscany, Italy). There, at the instigation of the empress Theodora, relatives of the three noblemen she had put to death strangled her in her bath in 535.

References
Gibbon, Edward. *The Decline and Fall of the Roman Empire.* Vol. 2. Chicago: Encyclopaedia Britannica, 1952. pp. 554–556.

Previté-Orton, C. W. *The Shorter Cambridge Medieval History.* Vol. 1, *The Later Roman Empire to the Twelfth Century.* Cambridge: Cambridge University Press, 1952, 1987. pp. 139–140, 190.

Amanishakhete
Queen, Ruler of Kush in Meroë (ca. 24–23 B.C.)

Queens were called Candace in Kush, which gave rise to the assumption by conquering Romans that Candace was Amanishakhete's name. The Merotic people adopted an African-style matriarchal regime and set up a dynasty of queens, known collectively as the Candaces. When the Romans under Petronius attacked the northern Kushian city of Napata, they were met by a "one-eyed lady of masculine status" who retreated to a neighboring fort, probably Meroë, and sent envoys to negotiate, hoping to dissuade the Romans from destroying the religious capital. Petronius brushed aside her pleas and destroyed the town and the great temple of Amun at Jebel Barlal. Two years later she returned to attack Petronius, but the Romans held their ground. The Romans then withdrew to Nubia, finding nothing more to interest them. After 27 B.C. the Ethiopian "Candace" maintained diplomatic relations with Augustus. Amanishakhete was succeeded by Queen Amantari and King Natakamani (Nelekamani), probably not only husband and wife but brother and sister as well, Amanishakhete's offspring. These two were able to carry on some measure of restoration of Napata.

References

Cooke, S. A., F. E. Adcock, and M. P. Charlesworth. Vol. 10. *The Cambridge Ancient History.* London; Cambridge University Press, 1971. pp. 42, 243, 778.

Fairservis, Walter A., Jr. *The Ancient Kingdoms of the Nile.* New York: Mentor/NAL, 1962. p. 193.

Grimal, Nicolas. *A History of Ancient Egypt.* Trans. Basil Blackwell Ltd. New York: Barnes & Noble Books, 1997. p. 387.

Josephy, Alvin M., Jr., ed. *The Horizon History of Africa.* New York: American Heritage Publishing, 1971. pp. 61–63.

Amina
Queen of Zaria (Zauzau) in Hausaland, Nigeria (15th or 16th c.)

One source postulates that Amina was the daughter of Turonku Batwa, who founded the city of Zaria, West Africa, in 1536, and therefore gives her rule as the end of the sixteenth century. Amina succeeded her mother as ruler, but she had no husband. Amina is credited in oral tradition with expanding the empire of Zaria to include Nupe and Kororofa (Kwararata), a Jukun kingdom. Her influence also extended over Kano and Katsina. She encouraged trade and built many of the famous Hausa earthworks. Under her remarkable leadership, Zaria became the most powerful state in Hausaland. Eventually her holdings stretched down to the sea. The Chronicles of Kano speak of her with great respect: "At this time Zaria under Queen Amina conquered all the towns as far as Kwarafara and Nupe. Every town paid tribute to her. The Sarikin Nupe sent forty eunuchs and ten thousand kolas to her. She was the first to have eunuchs and kolas in Hausaland. Her conquests extended over 34 years." The kola nut, which she introduced, is one of the great luxuries of Western Sudan; it is prized for its bitter taste, slightly aphrodisiac properties, and its ability to quench thirst. It was said that, although she never married, she took a new lover every night. After Amina's death, her sister Zaria succeeded to the throne, but Zaria, the kingdom, soon faded from history as a great west African power.

References

Adeleye, R. A. "Hausaland and Bornu, 1600–1800." In J.F.A. Ajayi and Michael Crowder, eds. *History of West Africa*. Vol. 1. New York: Columbia University Press, 1972. pp. 485–530.

Panikker, K. Madhu. *The Serpent and the Crescent: A History of the Negro Empires of West Africa*. Bombay: Asia Publishing House. 1963. pp. 113–114, 273.

Anches-en-Amen

See Ankhesenamun

Anga

See Maham Anga

Ankhesenamun

Egyptian Queen, Widow of Tutankhaten (ca. 1336–1327 B.C.)

Ankhesenamun, also known as Ankhesenaton or Anches-en-Amen, was formerly named Ankhesenpaaten. She married Tutankhaten ("living image of the aten"), who changed his name to Tutankhamun ("living image of Amun"); her name became Ankhesenamun. The couple had no living male heirs, although two fetuses found in the king's tomb might have been their two stillborn babies. After the king's death in 1336 B.C., Queen Ankhesenamun, hearing of the conquest of Amka, or Amki (adjacent to Lebanon) by the Hittites, wrote to Hittite King Suppiluliumas I (r. ca. 1375–1335 B.C.): "My husband has died, and not one son do I have. But of you it is said that you have many sons. If you will give me a son of yours, he could be my husband. For how may I take one of my slaves and make him a husband and honor him?" Under Egypt's laws of matrilinear succession, the new husband would be the pharaoh. The Hittite king was skeptical, commenting to the envoy he sent to investigate, "Perhaps they only wish to deride me." The queen sent an ambassador in return with the letter, "Why have you spoken these words: 'They wish only to deride me'? I have not written to any other country. To you alone have I written. It is said that you have many sons. Give me a son of yours; he shall be my husband and king over Egypt!" Suppiluliumas agreed to send a son, Prince Zennanza, but he was murdered before he reached Egypt. Queen Ankhesenamun then married Ay, the vizier of her dead husband (1327 B.C.). Ay was pharaoh of

Ankhesenamun (Foto Marburg/Art Resource, NY)

Egypt for four years. After the so-called marriage, she disappeared from the scene. In his tomb, Ay is depicted accompanied by his wife, Tiy II.

References

Ceram, C. W. *The Secret of the Hittites.* New York: Dorset Press, 1990. pp. 161–162.

Grimal, Nicolas. *A History of Ancient Egypt.* Trans. Basil Blackwell Ltd. New York: Barnes & Noble Books, 1997. pp. 204, 241–242.

Ankhnesneferibre
Queen of Egypt (584–525 B.C.)

Ankhnesneferibre was the granddaughter of Wahibre Necho II (r. 610–595 B.C.), who was succeeded by his son Neferibre Psammetichus II (r. 595–589 B.C.). Ankhnesneferibre ("Neferibre lives for her") was the daughter of Queen Takhut and King Neferibre Psammetichus. Before he died in 589, the king made sure that his daughter was adopted by the divine adoratarice Nitocris, whom she succeeded in 584. Ankhnesneferibre held the office until the conquest of Egypt by Persia in 525 B.C.

References
Grimal, Nicolas. *A History of Ancient Egypt.* Trans. Basil Blackwell Ltd. New York: Barnes & Noble Books, 1997. pp. 360–361.

Ankyeaa Nyame
Legendary Queen of Kumasi in West Africa (ca. 17th c.)

The so-called Kumasi Stool family are members of the Oyoko family of Asante. Ankyeaa Nyame is credited by oral tradition with being the founder of the tribe at Asumennya-Santemanso. Tradition says she simply appeared there, accompanied by an executioner, a court crier, and a stool (throne) carrier named Taasiri. She came with her own stool as queen. According to the account of her origins authorized by the *asantehene* (ruler) Osei Agyeman Prempe II (r. 1931–1970), she is said first to have appeared at a place located in Akyem Abuakwa called Toaa-ase, ruled by Chief Ntoni, "descended from the skies in a large Brass-pan suspended by a strong gold chain." After eating, she disappeared, later to arrive at Asumennya-Santemanso.

References
Barber, Karin, and P. F. de Moraes Farias. *Discourse and Its Disguises.* Birmingham, England: University of Birmingham Centre of West African Studies, 1989, p. 76.

Anna Anachoutlou
Queen of Trebizond (Trabzon, Trapezus) (1341 and 1341–1342)

The Empire of Trebizond was located in what is now northeastern Turkey. With the help of Georgian queen Thamar (r. 1184–1212), Trebizond was captured by David and Alexius Comnena, grandsons of Andronicus I, east Roman emperor. They established the Empire of Trebizond with Alexius I as its first ruler. Anna was one of three queens who ruled this empire, which lasted from 1204 until its capture by the Turks in 1461. She was the daughter of King Alexius II

(r. 1297–1330). She was brought to the throne twice in 1341, first following the deposition of Irene Palaeologina (r. 1340–1341). Anna Anachoutlou was briefly deposed in favor of Michael, son of former King John II (r. 1280–1284), but was restored that same year. She ruled until 1342, when Michael's son John III was brought to the throne.

References
Morby, John. *Dynasties of the World*. Oxford: Oxford University Press, 1989. p. 56.

Ostrogorsky, George. *History of the Byzantine State*. New Brunswick, NJ: Rutgers University Press, 1969. pp. 425–426.

Anna Dalassena
Acting Regent of Byzantine Empire (ca. 1081–1082)

Anna Dalassena was the formidable wife of John Comnenus, who was the brother of Isaac I (r. 1057–1059). With her help and the support of her son Isaac and the powerful Ducas family, her third son, Alexius, seized the Byzantine throne from Nicephorus III and founded the Comnenian dynasty as Emperor Alexius I (r. 1081–1118). She exercised great influence over Alexius and served as regent during his absence from Constantinople at the time of the war against invading Italian Normans headed by Robert Guiscard.

References
Ostrogorsky, George. *History of the Byzantine State*. New Brunswick, NJ: Rutgers University Press, 1969. p. 376.

Anna Leopoldovna
Regent of Russia (1740–1741)

Born in 1718, Anna Leopoldovna was a niece of Anne (Anna), empress of Russia. In 1739 Anna married Prince Anton Ulrich, nephew of Charles VI, Holy Roman emperor. They had a son, Ivan, born in 1740, the year Empress Anne died. Empress Anne had named the retarded two-month-old boy heir to the throne and made her lover Biren (Biron) his regent. The unpopular Biren was arrested a few weeks later by members of his own ruling German coalition, who then named Anna Leopoldovna regent. The Germans expected to play important roles in Anna's government; however, they were unpopular with the people and unable to maintain order even among themselves. In 1741, a palace favorite, Elizabeth I, Peter the Great's daughter, who also aspired to the throne, took advantage of the disorder in Anna's administration. She mounted a palace revolt, in which she donned a guard's uniform and marched with palace guards into the winter palace, personally woke Anna and her sleeping family, and had them imprisoned. In 1744 Elizabeth exiled them to Kholmogory. Anna died two years later in childbirth.

References

Asprey, Robert B. *Frederick the Great: The Magnificent Enigma.* New York: Ticknor and Fields, 1986. pp. 160, 230, 275.

Riasanovsky, Nicholas. *A History of Russia.* New York: Oxford University Press, 1963, 1993. p. 245.

Anna of Savoy
Regent of Byzantine Empire (1341–1347)

Anna (or Anne) of Savoy was the wife of Andronicus III, by whom she had a son, John V Palaeologus (1331). When Andronicus died in 1341, John V was only nine years old. A dispute broke out between Anna and John Cantacuzenus, the grand domestic, chief minister under Andronicus III, the late ruler's nearest friend, and the real power. John asserted his claim to the regency, but he left Constantinople to battle the Serbs in Thrace, and in his absence Anna had him declared a traitor and imprisoned his supporters. For a time Anna was formally recognized as senior sovereign in Constantinople. Her likeness appears on seals and coins of the period. Anna made vigorous attempts toward a reunion of the churches of Rome and Constantinople, even more decisive than the efforts of her late husband, but without lasting results. In 1341 John Cantacuzenus had himself declared emperor, but he held to the principle of legitimate succession, placing the names of Empress Anna and Emperor John V before those of himself and his wife Irene. At the beginning of the civil war that followed, Anna pawned the crown jewels in Venice for 30,000 ducats with which to defend her throne. The loan was never repaid. In 1345 John Cantacuzenus, giving Empress Anna the office of despot, asked the Ottoman Turks to come to his aid, even marrying his daughter Theodora to the sultan Orhan. By 1346 John was confident enough of victory to have himself crowned emperor in Andrianople. Although Anna's power was now limited to Constantinople and the immediate vicinity, the ambitious empress would not give in. She negotiated with the Turks for assistance. Instead of attacking John Cantacuzenus, they invaded and plundered Bulgaria, then on the way home did the same to outlying Constantinople. Despite last-minute appeals to the hesychasts (a sect of mystics), Anna was forced to surrender in 1347. John was crowned co-emperor with John V, and he ruled alone for ten years until John V was nineteen. To assure that Anna would wield no further influence over her son, John married his daughter Helena to John V.

References

Ostrogorsky, George. *History of the Byzantine State.* New Brunswick, NJ: Rutgers University Press, 1969. p. 510, 518, 520, 526, 535.

Anna Palaeologina
Despina, Regent of Epirus (1335–1340)

Anna Palaeologina was the wife of John Orsini, despot of Epirus from 1323 to 1335, and had a son, Nicephorus II. In 1335 Anna poisoned her husband and, with her son, took over the government. She immediately entered into negotiations with the Byzantine emperor, hoping that, once having recognized Byzantine suzerainty, she would be allowed to continue to rule unmolested. However, the emperor did not want anyone so closely tied to Epirian independence to rule Epirus, so Byzantine troops marched into Epirus and replaced Anna with an imperial governor. Anna and her son were compelled to move to Thessalonica. Much later, Nicephorous II attempted to win back his rule and undertook an extensive and fairly successful campaign in both Epirus and Thessaly, but he died in 1358 while fighting the Albanians.

References

Ostrogorsky, George. *History of the Byzantine State.* New Brunswick, NJ: Rutgers University Press, 1969. pp. 508, 534, 579, 581.

Anna Palaeologina-Cantacuzena
Despina, Regent of Epirus (1296–ca. 1313)

Anna Palaeologina-Cantacuzena was the daughter of Princess Eulogia (Irene), sister of Byzantine Emperor Michael VIII. Anna married Nicephorus I, despot of the Greek principality of Epirus from 1271 to 1296. They had two children: Thomas of Epirus and Thamar (Tamara), who married Philip of Tarento. Anna became regent for their son Thomas when Nicephorus died in 1296. With her close ties to the Byzantine Empire, the pro-Byzantine party of Epirus gained control. In 1306 anti-Byzantine forces under the leadership of Philip of Tarento joined forces with the Catholic Albanians, seized Dyrrachium, and were intent upon overthrowing Anna, but their campaign failed. Anna ruled until Thomas reached his majority, ca. 1313.

References

Ostrogorsky, George. *A History of the Byzantine State.* New Brunswick, NJ: Rutgers University Press, 1969. pp. 510, 518, 520, 526, 535.

Anne
Duchess, Ruler of Brittany (Bretagne) (1488–1514)

Anne was born in 1477, the daughter of Francois II (1458–1488). Anne inherited the duchy of Brittany upon her father's death, whereupon a French army invaded. Various countries sent aid, but the French forces prevailed. Anne was then forced to promise to marry only with the consent of the king. But she married Maximilian of Austria without such consent, touching off a new French invasion, after which the crown annulled her marriage. In 1491 she married Charles VII, king of France. When he died in 1498, King Louis XII obtained a divorce from his wife, Jeanne, and married Anne in order to keep this duchy for the crown. They had a daughter, Claude, who married King Francis I of France. Anne died in 1514, and thereafter Brittany became a part of France.

References
Egan, Edward W., Constance B. Hintz, and L. F. Wise, eds. *Kings, Rulers, and Statesmen.* New York: Sterling Publishing, 1976. p. 154.

Langer, William L., ed. *World History.* Boston: Houghton Mifflin, 1940, 1980. pp. 409–410.

Morby, John. *Dynasties of the World.* Oxford: Oxford University Press, 1989. p. 83.

Anne
Queen of England and Scotland (1702–1714)

Anne (b. 1665), the second daughter of King James II and Anne Hyde, did not impress her father as a particularly promising offspring. For one thing, she did not embrace his Catholicism. For another, her father and indeed her public considered her particularly dull and common, partially owing to the fact that she was sickly, plump, and plain—in later life, she was to bear a close resemblance to Queen Victoria, who would live a century later. From Mary Queen of Scots the Stuart line had inherited the blood affliction called porphyria, which plagued Anne all her life. During her childhood, at the insistence of her Protestant uncle, King Charles II, Anne lived away from court, estranged from her father, who himself has been described as arrogant, unattractive, humorless, and boorish. She developed an abiding friendship with Sarah Jennings Churchill, who wielded enormous influence over her for over twenty years and who convinced Anne to favor William III of Orange over James when William arrived on England's shores to claim the throne from Anne's Catholic father. William and Mary, Anne's sister, became constitutional monarchs in 1683, and Anne was placed in line for succession to the throne. That same year, at age eighteen, Anne married Prince George of Denmark, a handsome, fair-haired, blue-eyed prince who soon became as fat and phlegmatic and as fond of drink as she. She subsequently had seventeen pregnancies, most ending in miscarriage or infant death. Only one child survived to age eleven. During the six-year reign of her sister, with whom she quarreled bitterly—primarily over Anne's devotion to Sarah Churchill —Anne continued to live in

exile from court. However, following Mary's death in 1694, William welcomed Anne and her unpopular husband, and Sarah as well, at court. Shortly before his death, William embarked on the War of the Spanish Succession, which was his legacy to Anne. When Anne came to the throne at age thirty-seven (1702), she suffered from obesity, gout, and premature aging brought about by her blood disorder. Too ill to walk to her coronation, she made a heavy burden for the bearers of her sedan chair. Despite her obesity, or possibly because of it, her subjects perceived her as good natured and dubbed her Good Queen Anne. Her husband, Prince George, attempted to assist her in her royal duties, but he was unpopular with the English people. In 1704, partly as a result of her friendship with Sarah but also of John Churchill's illustrious victories in the continuing war, Anne named Sarah's husband the first duke of Marlborough. Eventually, however, Sarah became more queenly than Anne, even throwing a royal tantrum in Kensington Palace. Queen Anne dismissed Sarah and soon after, the duke as well. The death of Anne's beloved George in 1708 left her with few personal allies. But her political future was bright: When the war ended in 1713, England towered as the world's greatest power with many new far-flung aquisitions. England forged a legislative union with Scotland, forming the nucleus of the United Kingdom. In addition, Anne accepted the principle of a constitutional monarchy, a system that England maintains to this day. She was the last monarch to veto an act of Parliament or to preside over the majority of the cabinet meetings. Although she showed no interest in the literature, drama, and art that flourished during her reign—she felt taxed, in fact, by prolonged attempts at intellectual conversation—she established a receptive climate for the arts. Anne was also the last monarch to practice "touch healings" of her subjects for the lymphatic tubercular condition called scrofula. She died in 1714 leaving no heirs, a widowed and friendless old woman at age forty-nine, the last of the Stuart line.

References

Hodges, Margaret. *Lady Queen Anne.* New York: Farrar Straus & Giroux, 1969.

Hudson, M. E., and Mary Clark. *Crown of a Thousand Years.* New York: Crown Publishing, 1978. pp. 114–117.

Kenyon, J. P. *The Stuarts.* Glasgow: William Collins Sons, 1970. pp. 186–207.

Anne
Empress of Russia (1730–1740)

Anne (or Anna Ivanova) was born in 1693, the daughter of Ivan V, nominal tsar of Russia, a chronic invalid. She was the niece of Peter the Great. She married the Duke of Courland, but he died on their wedding trip (1710) to Courland. After the death of Peter II (at age fifteen, of smallpox), Anne was offered the throne by the privy council, which, conceiving of her as weak, expected her to act as a figurehead while it continued to govern. When she came to the throne, however, she tore up the conditions she had previously accepted, dismissed the council, and made herself absolute ruler. She brought from Courland a cadre of favorites and in general patronized not only Germans but other foreigners in preference to Russian nobility.

Criticized for her excesses in office, Anne was also responsible for beginning some social reform. In 1731 she repealed Peter the Great's law that only one son could inherit his father's estate. She gave away state lands to her gentry supporters, the peasants on the land becoming serfs. Also in 1731, she opened a cadet school in St. Petersburg where graduates could become officers without first serving in the lower ranks, a practice Peter the Great had opposed. In 1736 the law requiring gentry to serve the state for an unlimited amount of time was altered to specify a term of no more than twenty-five years. Furthermore, one son would be exempt from service to manage the estates.

Soon, however, the tedium of her office began to pall; she lost interest in governing, for which she was untrained. She left it in the hands of her ruthless lover, Ernst Johann Biren (or Biron), who brought in his German friends as advisers. They exploited the country while Anne held extravagant court in St. Petersburg. On the day before she died in 1740, she named her two-month-old nephew Ivan as her successor and Biren as regent. But within a month Biren was overthrown, and Ivan's mother, Anna Leopoldovna, became regent for one year. Then late in 1741, Ivan, his mother, and the entire cabinet were ousted in a coup led by Peter the Great's daughter Elizabeth, who ascended the throne.

References

Asprey, Robert B. *Frederick the Great: The Magnificent Enigma.* New York: Ticknor and Fields, 1986. pp. 119, 160.

Langer, William L., ed. *World History.* Boston: Houghton Mifflin, 1940, 1980. pp. 515–516.

Riasanovsky, Nicholas V. *A History of Russia.* New York: Oxford University Press, 1963, 1993. pp. 243, 245, 249, 250.

Anne-Marie-Louise d'Orléans
Mademoiselle de Montpensier, Ruler of Auvergne (1617)

Anne-Marie-Louise d'Orléans was the daughter of Marie de Bourbon Montpensier and Jean Baptist Gaston, duke of Orléans, who ruled from 1608 to 1617. She was the grandaughter of Henri de Bourbon, who ruled from 1602 to 1608. She was the last ruler of Auvergne, which became part of France.

Anne-Marie-Louise d'Orléans (Archive Photos)

References

Egan, Edward W., Constance B. Hintz, and L. F. Wise, eds. *Kings, Rulers, and Statesmen.* New York: Sterling Publishing, 1976. p. 151.

Anne of Austria
Queen Regent of France (1643–1651), Governor of Brittany (1647–1666)

Anne (Anne d'Autriche) was born in 1601 in Madrid, the daughter of Philip III of Spain. In 1615, at the age of fourteen, she became the

Anne of Austria (Erich Lessing / Art Resource, NY)

wife of Louis XIII of France. The royal couple had two sons, the future Louis XIV and Philippe, future duc d'Orleans, but they lived apart for twenty-three years as a result of the meddlings of Cardinal Richelieu. For political reasons the cardinal wished to alienate the king from his wife. In 1636 she was named governor of Paris. When the king died in 1643, Anne had his will, which deprived her of right of sole regency, annulled and became the queen regent for her son Louis XIV, who was only five years old. Although she was inexperienced, she immediately exercised shrewd judgment by choosing as her minister Cardinal Mazarin, a wise and diplomatic manager who helped her maintain the absolute power of the monarchy that Richelieu had established for Louis XIII. Anne served as regent for almost a decade, preserving a close relationship with the cardinal, her favorite—some have concluded that they were secretly married—and thus establishing on firm grounds her young son's throne. In 1647 she became governor of Brittany, the second female to govern a major province. She continued to exercise influence over her son's decisions and to govern Brittany until the time of her death in 1666.

References

Durant, Will and Ariel. *The Story of Civilization*. Vol. 8, *The Age of Louis XIV*. New York: Simon & Schuster, 1960. pp. 3–45.

Harding, Robert. *Anatomy of a Power Elite*. New Haven: Yale University Press, 1978. pp. 127, 221.

Sédillot, René. *An Outline of French History*. Trans. Gerard Hopkins. New York: Alfred A. Knopf, 1967. p. 209.

Anne of England
Regent of the Dutch Republic (1751–1766)

Anne of England (or Anne of Hanover) was the eldest daughter of King George II of Great Britain and Caroline of Ansbach. Anne was married to William IV of Orange-Nassau, who ruled the Dutch Republic from 1748 to 1751. When he died, their son, William V, was only five years old. Queen Anne acted as regent until William was eighteen.

References

Langer, William L., ed. *World History*. Boston: Houghton Mifflin, 1940, 1980. pp. 475–476.

Anne of France
De Facto Regent of France (1483–1491)

Anne of France was born in 1461, the daughter of King Louis XI of France. She was more intelligent and politically astute than her brother Charles (VIII), nine years her junior, or the man she married, Pierre de Bourbon, seigneur de Beaujeu. The couple had a daughter, Suzanne, who was named heir to her father's Bourbon lands. When King Louis died in 1483, Charles was singularly unfit to ascend to the throne. He was thirteen years old, with modest intellectual capacities and delicate health. Anne and her husband assumed the reins of power in an effort to surmount problems with many wealthy noblemen caused by her late father. To mollify these noblemen, she restored lands that had been confiscated under her father's rule, and she dismissed many of her father's court favorites who had been responsible, in the eyes of the noblemen, for their grievances. In 1483, by negotiations already begun before the death of Louis XI, Charles was betrothed to Margaret of Austria, duchess of Savoy. From this betrothal, he received Artois and the Franche-Comte; however, Anne had a more profitable union in mind: one that would bring the duchy of Brittany under France's dominion. In 1491 she persuaded Charles to repudiate his engagement to Margaret in favor of marriage to Anne of Brittany. After the marriage, Charles's wife and his friend, Etienne de Vesc, persuaded him to free himself from the influence of his sister. In addition to holding the reins of government for seven years, Anne had been the effective overseer of her husband's Bourbon lands during the whole of their marriage. When he died in 1503, she continued to administer her daughter Suzanne's lands, knowing from her own experiences the penchant of royalty for expanding their domains. Anne died in 1522.

References

Previté-Orton, C. W. *The Shorter Cambridge Medieval History*. Vol. 2, *The Twelfth Century to the Renaissance*. Cambridge: Cambridge University Press, 1952, 1987. p. 484.

Anula
Queen of Ceylon (Sri Lanka) (47–42 B.C.)

Anula was the wife of King Darubhatika Tissa, whose death in 47 B.C. threw the country into a period of great turmoil. For short periods during that year, three people—Siva, Vatuka, and Niliya—tried briefly to rule. Eventually Queen Anula was called upon to restore order. She ruled for five years and was succeeded by her son, King Kutakanna Tissa, in 42 B.C.

References
Codrington, H. W. *A Short History of Ceylon.* Cambridge: Cambridge University Press, 1947.

Egan, Edward W., Constance B. Hintz, and L. F. Wise, eds. *Kings, Rulers, and Statesmen.* New York: Sterling Publishing, 1976. p. 438.

Apumatec
Queen of North American Indian Tribe (1607)

Apumatec was encountered in Virginia by Captain Newport's expedition on its first exploration inland from Jamestown, which did not proceed beyond the present site of Richmond. She was described by Gabriel Archer: "She had much copper about her neck; a crownet of copper upon her head. She had long black haire, which hanged loose downe her back to her myddle; which only part was covered with a deare's skyn, and ells all naked. She had her woemen attending on her, adorned much like herselfe (save they wanted copper) . . . Our captain presented her with guyfts liberally; whereupon shee cheered somewhat her countenance. . . ."

References
Jones, Howard Mumford. *The Literature of Virginia in the Seventeenth Century.* Charlottesville: University of Virginia Press, 1968. pp. 19–20.

Aquino, María Corazon
President of Republic of the Philippines (1986–1992)

María Corazon (Cory) was born in 1933, the daughter of José Cojuangco Sr., the wealthiest man in Tarlac Province, and Demetria Sumulong Sojuangco. Corazon was educated at elite girls' schools in Manila, Philadelphia, and New York before attending the College of Mt. Saint Vincent in New York. She married Benigno S. Aquino Jr. in 1954 and became his political helpmate. They had five children: Elena, Aurora, Benigno S. III, Victoria, and Kristina. Her husband entered politics and rose to become the most popular opponent of President Ferdinand Marcos, who declared martial law in 1972 to prolong his presidency. Marcos jailed Benigno Aquino, whom he considered his greatest threat. When Aquino was released, the family sought refuge in the United States, where they lived in exile from 1980 to 1983. In August 1983, Benigno Aquino attempted to return to the Philippines but was assassinated in the Manila airport. This assassination was the rallying point that united the opposition and forced Corazon Aquino to choose a political career. She led the dis-

María Corazon Aquino (Courtesy: Embassy of the Philippines)

sidents calling for Marcos's resignation. In the meantime, she returned to school for postgraduate work in law, receiving an LL.D. degree from the University of the Philippines in 1986. In 1986 she ran for president on the Unido party ticket; abandoning the speeches that had been prepared for her, she spoke simply of her own victimization by Marcos. She was elected president and immediately attempted to forge unity, bring about order, and commence economic reform, all the while fending off attacks by political foes. She immediately appointed a constitution commission to replace the 1973 charter that had been passed by a show of hands shortly after former president Ferdinand E. Marcos declared martial law. In September 1986, she traveled to the United States seeking support for her government and for the country. Although President Reagan refused to give her an audience, she received assurance that the United States would retain its two military bases in the Philippines. Following her speech to the joint session of Congress, which Speaker Thomas P. O'Neill, Jr. labeled "the finest speech" he had heard in his congressional career, Congress approved $200 million additional aid to her country. Although she instituted an economic growth program, much of her presidency was marked by unrest among citizens who wanted quicker results. In 1988 her land redistribution law was criticized by the press as not going far enough. Her detractors charged her with downgrading human rights as a trade-off for military support. On one occasion her palace troops opened fire and killed twenty demonstrators. In 1989 she took on one of the most powerful groups in the Philippines, the big-industry loggers, citing environmental devastation caused by "the greed of commerce, the corruption of officials and the ignorance of men." She weathered numerous crises, including several coup attempts. Although untrained in politics, she was a member of the class of wealthy "oligarchs" who had long ruled the Philippines. She spoke English, French, Spanish, Japanese, and Tagalog, the native language. Eschewing Marcos's elaborate Malacanang Palace as too opulent in a country where wealth had too long been kept in the hands of a few, she lived in a more modest home/office nearby. She repeatedly denied Marcos permission to return to the Philippines in an effort to still opposition before it developed, buying time for her economic programs to work. In 1992, although her popularity was on the wane, her choice of president, Fidel Ramos, won the presidential election to succeed her. However, he won with only 23 percent of the vote in an election that was so close that the ballots had to be counted by hand.

References

Jones, Clayton. "Aquino Joins Bid to Protect Forests." *Christian Science Monitor.* 22 March 1989: 4.

Jones, Clayton. "Aquino Plans Cabinet Shifts." *Christian Science Monitor.* 10 November 1986: 11.

Komisar, Lucy. *Corazon Aquino: The Story of a Revolution.* New York: George Braziller, 1987.

Mydans, Seth. "Aquino Is Working on Some Laws to Rule By." *New York Times.* 1 June 1986: 3.

Sheehy, Gail. "The Passage of Corazon Aquino." *Parade Magazine.* 8 June 1986: 4–9.

"The Stalled Revolution." *World Press Review.* August 1988: 40.

Arsinde
Countess, Ruler of Carcassonne (934–957)

Arsinde was the daughter of Acfred II, count of Carcassonne, which was located in what is now southwestern France. Arsinde ruled during a time when Carcassonne went its own way. It was not until the reign of Philip III the Bold (1270–1285) that walls were built (1272) and royal power firmly established in southern France. Arsinde married Arnaud de Comminges. The couple had a son, Roger, who succeeded his mother, ruling as count Roger I in 957.

References

Egan, Edward W., Constance B. Hintz, and L. F. Wise, eds. *Kings, Rulers, and Statesmen.* New York: Sterling Publishing, 1976. p. 156.

Langer, William L., ed. *World History.* Boston: Houghton Mifflin, 1940, 1980. p. 247.

Arsinoë II

Queen first of Thrace, then of Macedonia, then of Egypt, Co-ruler of Egypt (277–270 B.C.).

Arsinoë was born ca. 316 B.C., the daughter of Berenice and Ptolemy I Soter of Egypt. In 300 B.C. she married Lysimachus, king of Thrace. Thrace was located in Asia Minor, bounded by the Aegean and Black Seas on the east and south and by the Danube River on the north. Arsinoë was leaving her homeland far behind when she married the king of Thrace. But as she was not his first wife, she had little prospect of furthering the futures of her offspring. Lysimachus already had an heir to the throne, his son Agathocles. In the same year that Ptolemy I died in Egypt (283 B.C.), his daughter orchestrated the demise of Agathocles; in an attempt to advance the rights of succession of her own three sons, Arsinoë accused Agathocles of treason, hoping to discredit him. An angry Lysimachus ordered his son Agathocles executed, and in the outbreak of violence that followed, which escalated into a war involving Agathocles's avenging allies in Selucia, Lysimachus was killed in battle (281 B.C.). Arsinoë escaped from Ephesus, taking her sons to safety in Cassandrea where her exiled half brother and new king of Macedonia, Ptolemy Ceraunus, cajoled her into marrying him, then murdered two of her sons. When Ptolemy Ceraunus died fighting the Gauls in 279 B.C., Arsinoë attempted to have her remaining son, Ptolemaeus, installed on the Macedonian throne, but she failed and was forced to flee to Egypt. There, in ca. 276 B.C., she married her brother, Ptolemy II, and became in every sense co-ruler. It was largely the result of her diplomatic skill that Egypt won the First Syrian War (ca. 274–271 B.C.), and following it, she was deified as Philadelphus (meaning "brother-loving") and displayed on the coinage of the realm. The new queen ruled the empire and managed its wars, meanwhile gathering around her such notable men of letters as the poet Callimachus. Ptolemy, also called Philadelphus, reigned among the chiefs and scholars of the court, while Arsinoë, a woman of great intelligence and mature experience, is thought to have played the dominant role in the formulation of royal policy as long as she lived. Several cities were named for her. Her interest in cultural pursuits led to the founding of a museum at Alexandria. She died in 270 B.C., but even before her death she was being worshipped as a goddess, an incentive that she herself may have initiated. The king erected a monument in her honor in Alexandria known as the Arsinoeum. This elevation to divinity of both king and his sister-queen might have ameliorated the deep Hellenistic taboos against incest. The precedent of marriage between siblings had already been set by Egyptian pharaohs. Thereafter, the practice of Hellenistic rulers to proclaim their own divinity became commonplace.

References
Bowder, Diana, ed. *Who Was Who in the Greek World*. Ithaca, NY: Cornell University Press, 1982. pp. 101–102.

Langer, William L, ed. *World History*. Boston: Houghton Mifflin Company, 1940, 1980. p. 96.

Peters, F. E. *The Harvest of Hellenism*. New York: Barnes & Noble Books, 1970.

Rawlinson, George. *Ancient History*. New York: Barnes & Noble, 1993. pp. 198, 200.

Artemisia I
Queen, Ruler of Halicarnassus and Cos (ca. 480 B.C.)

Halicarnassus was a Greek city-state in southwestern Anatolia, and Cos was an island off the coast. As a tribute-payer to Xerxes, king of Persia, Artemisia participated in his war of invasion against the Greeks in 480 B.C. She ably commanded five ships during the naval battle off the island of Salamis. Herodotus, a great admirer of her accomplishments, claimed that Xerxes, who was badly defeated, had sought Artemisia's advice. She advised him to retreat, which he did.

References
Bowder, Diana, ed. *Who Was Who in the Greek World*. Ithaca, NY: Cornell University Press, 1982. p. 106.

Hammond, N. G. L. *History of Greece*. Oxford: Clarendon Press, 1986. p. 239.

Herodotus. *The Histories*. Trans. Aubrey de Sèlincourt. New York: Penguin Books, 1954, 1988. pp. 8, 11, 14, 474, 545–546, 552–558.

Olmstead, A. T. *History of the Persian Empire*. Chicago: University of Chicago Press, 1948. pp. 253, 269, 433–434.

Artemisia II
Ruler of Caria (353/352–351/350 B.C.)

Caria was located in southwestern Anatolia. Artemisia was the daughter of King Hecatomnos of Caria and wife and sister of King Mausolus, who succeeded Hecatomnos. In her own right, she was a botanist and medical researcher. A plant genus, a sagebrush, is named for her. Artemisia and her husband were extremely devoted. When he died (353 or 352 B.C.), Artemisia succeeded him as sole ruler. During her approximately three-year reign, the Rhodians, believing that a woman's rule offered them excellent opportunity to rid themselves of Caria's dominion, charged the capital. Artemisia, apprised of their approach, ordered the citizens to pretend surrender. Even as the Rhodians landed and began plundering the marketplace, the hidden Carian fleet emerged from a man-made channel connected to a hidden harbor and seized the empty Rhodian ships. Soldiers hiding along the city walls shot down the plunderers. Then Artemisia wreathed the captured ships in laurel, signifying victory, and with her own forces aboard, sailed the Rhodian ships back to the island. Before her ruse was discovered, the Carians had entered the Rhodian harbor. The Rhodian leaders were executed, and Artemisia erected two monuments in Rhodes commemorating her conquest of the island. In the capital of Halicarnassus (modern-day Bodrum, Turkey), she had erected for her late husband a magnificent tomb for which all subsequent tombs that are splendid edifices are named. It was called the Mausoleum of Halicarnassus, one of the Seven Wonders of the World. Tradition holds that she never recovered from his death and died of grief (ca. 350 B.C.). A statue of Artemisia in Museo Archeologico Nazionale, Naples, shows her as a beautiful woman with a purposeful stride and an aura of strength.

References

Bowder, Diana, ed. *Who Was Who in the Greek World.* Ithaca, NY: Cornell University Press, 1982. pp. 299–300.

Durant, Will. *The Story of Civilization.* Vol. 2, *The Life of Greece.* New York: Simon & Schuster, 1939, 1966. pp. 586, 593.

Olmstead, A. T. *History of the Persian Empire.* Chicago: University of Chicago Press, 1948. pp. 426, 429, 432–435.

'Arwa Bint Ahmad al-Sulayhiyya
Shi'ite Malika (Queen) and Ruler of Yemen (1091–1138)

'Arwa was the wife of al-Mukarram Ahmad, ruler of Yemen from 1067 to 1084, who carried on his father's tradition of allowing his wife to share his power. Al-Mukarram came to power while his parents took a pilgrimage to Mecca. During the trip his father 'Ali al-Sulayhi was murdered by the Banu Najah family, and his mother Asma was taken prisoner by them. When Asma was released, she directed her son's rule until her death, along with 'Arwa. The unquestioned criterion of a head of state in the Muslim world was the right to have the *khutba* (sermon) pronounced in his name. The *khutba,* the privilege of the sovereign, was preached at Friday prayers, and it affirmed the sovereign's right to rule. Ordinarily it was not to be said in the name of a woman; however, 'Arwa had the right to have the *khutba* pronounced in her name. She bore the royal title, al-sayyida al-hurra, meaning, "the noble lady who is free and independent; the woman sovereign who bows to no superior authority." By late in his rule, the king saw the kingdom that his father had established threatened on the north by the Najabids and on the south by the Zuray'ids. Beset by illness, he transferred control of the principality to 'Arwa. The exact wording of her *khutba* was, "May Allah prolong the days of al-Hurra the perfect, the sovereign who carefully manages the affairs of the faithful." Although many Islamic scholars have swept under the table any mention of rule by women as if it were a shameful thing, Yemeni historians, both ancient and modern, point with pride to their women rulers. Of 'Arwa, contemporary historian 'Abdallah al-Thawr says she "held fast to her principles, loved her people, and was faithful to them." He notes that she left more monuments, buildings, roads, and mosques than the imams who governed San'a (the capital city) from 1591 to 1925. She ruled until her death in 1138.

References

Al-Dahbi. *Siyar 'alam al-nubala'*. Cairo: Dar al-Ma'arif, 1958. This reference contains a biography of 'Arwa.

al-Thawr, 'Abdallah Ahmad Muhammad. *Hadhihi hiyya al-Yaman*. Beirut: Dar al-'Awda, 1979. p. 331.

al-Zarkali, Khayr al-Din. *Al-a'lam, qamus ash'ar al-rijal wa al-nisa' min al-'arab wa al-musta'rabin wa al-mustashraqin*. Vol. 1. Beirut: Dar al-'Ilm li al-Malayin, 1983.

Asa
Queen of Norway (mid-9th c.)

Queen Asa is known to have lived in Viking Norway in the middle of the ninth century and to have died at about age twenty-five or thirty. In 1904 the bodies of two women were found in an elaborate burial ship in a grave in Oseberg, South Norway. The highly decorated vessel was the kind probably used by a king or chieftain, so one of the bodies was believed to be that of Queen Asa. With her was buried an older woman of about sixty or seventy, possibly a bondswoman who sacrificed herself so as to serve her mistress in the afterworld.

References

Donovan, Frank R. *The Vikings*. New York: American Heritage Publishing, 1964. p. 89.

Wilson, David. *The Vikings and Their Origins*. London: Thames and Hudson, 1970. pp. 57, 122.

Asma Bint Shihab al-Sulayhiyya
Shi'ite Malika (Queen) and Co-ruler of Yemen (1047–1067)

Asma Bint Shihab al-Sulayhiyya was married to 'Ali Ibn Muhammad al-Sulayhi, a Shi'ite imam who founded the Sulayhid dynasty and consolidated the principality of Yemen. He reigned from 1047 to 1067. 'Ali al-Sulayhi imposed his rule and his beliefs so easily upon Yemen because he was descended from the older culture as a member of the Yam clan of the Hamdan tribe from the realm of Sheba. Historians note that Asma "attended councils with her 'face uncovered'" and that "the *khutba* (a sermon affirming a sovereign's right to rule) was proclaimed from the pulpits of the mosques of Yemen in her husband's name and in her name." She bore the title of al-sayyida al-hurra, "the noble lady who is free and independent; the woman sovereign who bows to no superior authority." In 1066 'Ali decided to undertake a pilgrimage to Mecca. He and Asma took a splendid caravan of a thousand horsemen, a military force of five thousand Ethiopians, and all of the Yemeni princes whom he had conquered over the years, plus Asma's whole court entourage. 'Ali had designated their son al-Mukarram, married to 'Arwa, to govern in his stead during his absence. The caravan was attacked by the Ethiopian Banu Najah family in retribution for 'Ali's murder of their father. 'Ali was among the people killed, and Asma was taken prisoner. When she was finally freed and sent back to San'a, her son continued to take orders from his mother. She died in 1097.

References

al-Thawr, 'Abdallah Ahmad Muhammad. *Hadhihi hiyya al-Yaman.* Beirut: Dar al-'Awda, 1979. pp. 275, 281.

al-Zarkali, Khayr al-Din. *Al-a'lam, qamus ash'ar al-rijal wa al-nisa' min al-'arab wa al-musta'rabin wa al-mustashraqin.* Vol 1. Beirut: Dar al-'Ilm li al-Malayin, 1983. p. 299.

Athaliah
Ruler of Judah (ca. 844/845–837/839 B.C.)

Athaliah was the daughter of Queen Jezebel and King Ahab, seventh king of the northern kingdom of Israel, according to the Old Testament. She married Jeham (or Joram or Jehoram), king of Judah. Their son, Ahaziah, became the sixth king of Judah upon his father's death in 841. Athaliah served as queen mother in court, a position of honor, while her son went off to war. After a reign of only one year, Ahaziah was killed in battle by Jehu. Athaliah seized the throne and tried to put to death all her own grandsons, heirs to the throne, in

Athaliah (Archive Photos)

order to destroy the line of David and keep the throne for herself. One of the infants, Joash, was hidden away by followers loyal to Ahaziah. Athaliah reigned tyrannically for seven years. She eliminated the Omrites from Judah and eradicated the House of David. She also introduced the worship of Baal. When Joash was of age, he came out of hiding and in the revolution that followed, Athaliah was overthrown. She was executed ca. 839 or 837 B.C.

References

Langer, William L., ed. *World History.* Boston: Houghton Mifflin, 1980. p. 45.

Wilson, Robert Dick. *A Scientific Investigation of the Old Testament.* Rev. Edward J. Young. Chicago: Moody Press, 1959. p. 71.

Wright, Ernest. *Biblical Archaeology.* Philadelphia: Westminster Press, 1957. p. 162.

Awura Pokou

Queen of the Baule Tribe in West Africa (ca. 1730–1750)

Awura (or Aura) Pokou ruled over one branch of the Akans' great Ashanti kingdom, which moved into the southeast part of the Ivory Coast region early in the eighteenth century. Following a dispute over leadership, in which she refused to join the Ashanti confederacy in what is now Ghana, she led her group south to the banks of the Komoe River. When she questioned her priest about the hazardous crossing of the river, he informed her that if she offered a sacrifice, all would go well for her tribe's crossing. She offered her own son as a sacrifice, calling out, "Baouli—the child is dead." To this day, her descendants are called Baoules. Queen Pokou and her tribe crossed the river and cultivated the savanna that lay on the other side. This was the beginning of the Baule (Baoule) tribe, which populated the area between the Komoe and Bandama Rivers. Eventually her tribe assimilated many of the preexisting tribes of the area to became the largest, most powerful tribe on the Ivory Coast. Although the tribe lost much of its political power during the nineteenth century, it remains the largest tribe in the Ivory Coast today.

References

Kirtley, Michael and Aubine. "The Ivory Coast, African Success Story." *National Geographic.* July 1982: 95–125.

Āzarmēdukht
Sasanid Queen of Persia (631–632)

The younger daughter of King Khusrau II, who ruled Persia from 590 to 628, Āzarmēdukht succeeded her sister Bōrān on the throne. The reign of Āzarmēdukht was marred by pretenders and rival kings in various parts of the empire. She was succeeded by her nephew, Yazdgard III. Sasanid monarchs used the oriental title ahahanshah, or king of kings.

References

Morby, John E. *Dynasties of the World.* Oxford: Oxford University Press, 1989. p. 49.

B

Bāī
See Lakshmi Bāī; Tārā Bāī; Udham Bāī

Bailor-Caulker, Honoraria
Paramount Chief of the Shenge, Sierra Leone (fl. 20th c.)

Madame Honoraria Bailor-Caulker has been influential in Sierra Leone politics for several decades. Her family, the Caulkers, were slavers who ruled the coast of Yawri Bay in the vicinity of Freetown. Through slave trading, the Caulkers grew rich and powerful. While she was paramount chief, Madame Bailor-Caulker frequently mentioned this fact in public speeches, not only to assure some of her audiences that she had much for which to atone but also because she said that powerful chiefs prefer that their ancestry be rooted among the strong who ruled rather than the weak who were enslaved.

She was a flamboyant leader who dressed in voluminous silk gowns and wore a turban adorned with ornate jewelry. She was carried through the village in a palanquin, borne by relays of her subjects, and accompanied by a large entourage of singers, drummers, and dancers. At public meetings she promised her subjects who had elected her that she would soon bring water and electricity to the area. She presided over Shenge District Court, where she heard cases involving local grievances and dispensed judgments.

In 1977 she traveled to the United States to speak at an American Anthropological Association meeting on women in government and politics. In 1997, although no longer holding office, she was still an outspoken champion for the Shenge.

References
Reader, John. *Africa.* New York: Alfred A. Knopf, 1998, originally London: Hamish Hamilton, 1997. pp. 377–379.

Bakwa

See Turunku Bakwa

Balkis

Queen, Ruler of Axum (10th c. B.C.)

Conflicting legends abound concerning the queen of Sheba, whose legendary name was Balkis (Balqis, Bilqis; also Makeda). Arab historian Sir John Glubb believes the queen of Sheba was from Yemen, and although she is not mentioned by name in the Koran, sura 27, "The Ant," describes her meeting with King Solomon. The king, noticing that one of the birds, the hoopoe, was missing from review, vowed to punish it if it could not justify its absence. When the bird arrived (verse 22), he said, "I have found out a thing that thou apprehendest not, and I come to thee with sure tidings. (verse 23) Lo! I found a woman ruling over them [the people of Sheba, or Saba], and she hath been given (abundance) of all things, and hers is a mighty throne." The Yemenis honor all their queens by calling them *balqis al-sughra,* meaning "little queen of Sheba." According to the Muslim legend, the king's demons, fearing he might marry the queen of Sheba, told him that she had the hoof of an ass and hairy legs. The king had glass installed in the floor in front of his throne so that the queen, mistaking it for water, raised her skirts, revealing that she did not have hairy legs.

Fage mentions the existence in southwestern Arabia (in present-day Yemen) of a number of major kingdoms, among which Saba, or Sheba, was the most powerful for some period in pre-Islamic times. Between the sixth century B.C. and the first century A.D., Sabaean influences reached Ethiopia, which included among its traditions the story of the queen of Sheba. African legend says that in the tenth century B.C. an Ethiopian king on his deathbed named his daughter Makeda as his successor and that Makeda ruled as queen of Sheba. According to an Ethiopian manuscript now in the British Museum, when an Ethiopian merchant named Tamrin took building materials to Jerusalem for the construction of King Solomon's temple, as a show of gratitude, Solomon sent with the merchant valuable gifts for the queen. She was so impressed by the merchant's account of Solomon's wealthy court that she organized a large caravan laden with precious gifts and went to see for herself. A romance developed between them, resulting in the birth of a son, whom Makeda named David, who became Menelik I.

John Reader recounts a legend that Menelik went to the court of his father for a year and on his departure took the Ark of the

Covenant from the temple and brought it to Axum. (However, while Solomon was alive, Axum, or Aksum, did not exist.) Later, during the time of Queen Judith, Axum was destroyed, but monks carried the Ark to an island in Lake Zewai.

Balkis (Corbis-Bettmann)

By another account, Solomon recognized Menelik as his first-born son and decreed that only Menelik's male heirs would rule Ethiopia. Emperor Haile Selassie claimed direct lineage from Menelik.

Hirtle points out that if Makeda were a contemporary of Solomon's, she would have lived in the ninth century B.C., but the ruins of her purported palace at Axum have been dated from a few centuries A.D. to 500 B.C., "maybe further."

By yet another account mentioned by Vansina, the Kingdom of Rozwi, a Shona clan in Zimbabwe, was the true land ruled by the queen of Sheba.

References

de Villiers, Marq, and Sheila Hirtle. *Into Africa.* Toronto: Key Porter Books, 1997. pp. 23, 336–337, 346.

Fage, J. D. *A History of Africa.* New York: Alfred A. Knopf, 1978. pp. 54–55.

Glubb, Sir John. *A Short History of the Arab Peoples.* New York: Dorset Press, 1969. p. 24.

Jackson, John G. *Introduction to African Civilizations.* Secaucus, NJ: Citadel Press, 1970. pp. 268–269.

Mernissi, Fatima. *The Forgotten Queens of Islam.* Trans. Mary Jo Lakeland. Minneapolis: University of Minnesota Press, 1993. pp. 9, 43–44, 89, 118–119, 141–144.

Reader, John. *Africa*. NewYork: Alfred A. Knopf, 1998; originally published in London: Hamish Hamilton, 1997. pp. 220–222.

Vansina, Dr. Jan. "Inner Africa." In Alvin M. Josephy, Jr., ed. *The Horizon History of Africa*. NewYork: American Heritage Publishing, McGraw-Hill, 1971. p. 270.

Balthild
Regent of Neustria (657–664)

Neustria was located in the northeastern portion of present-day France. The daughter of Anglo-Saxon royalty, Balthild, being a Christian, was kidnapped by pagans as a child and made a slave. She escaped and eventually married King Clovis II (Chlodwig), ruler of Neustria and Burgundy (639–657). When he became deranged, she ruled in his stead. When he died in 664, Balthild became regent for Clothar III (Lothair), king of Neustria (657–673), king of all Franks (656–673), until he came of age in 664. Balthild, remembering her own tragic childhood, forbade the practice of selling Christians as slaves to pagans. She founded a monastery and made efforts to establish communication between Christian converts in Neustria and those across the English Channel.

References
Boulding, Elise. *The Underside of History, A View of Women through Time*. Boulder: Westview Press, 1976. p. 396.

Bandaranaike, Sirimavo Ratevatte Dias
Prime Minister of Sri Lanka (1960–1965 and 1970–1977)

Sirimavo Ratevatte Dias Bandaranaike was born in 1916 in Ratnapura, Balangoda, in southern Ceylon (now Sri Lanka). Although she received a Catholic education, she remained a Buddhist. In 1940 she married Solomon West Ridgeway Bandaranaike, an Oxford-educated attorney already committed to a life in politics, which Sirimavo loved as well. In 1956, as leader of the People's United Front, a coalition of four nationalist-socialist parties, he was appointed prime minister. Three years later he was assassinated by a Buddhist monk. Sirimavo became president of the Sri Lanka Freedom Party, which her husband had founded in 1952. In 1960, with no previous political experience, she became the world's first female prime minister, elected with the understanding that she would continue her husband's socialist policies. She followed a neutral policy with both communists and non-communists. She attempted to stabilize the economy by extending the government into various businesses, but worsening economic conditions and racial and religious clashes led to her party's ouster in 1965. Sirimavo did not retire from politics, however, and in 1970 her party again regained power. During her second term as prime minister she took more radical steps to bring the country's economic and ideological difficulties under control. Much of the turmoil of her administration had to do with ethnic problems that she failed to address adequately. These problems

Sirimavo Ratevatte Dias Bandaranaike (Courtesy: Embassy of Sri Lanka)

continued throughout the 1990s. The dominant population is Sinhalese. The minority Tamil group, Indian in origin, has agitated for years for a separate state. When Sirimavo nationalized key industries, a court determined that she had gone too far. It expelled her from parliament and stripped her of her civil rights (1977). The election of 1977 decimated her power base. The United National Party, under President Junius R. Jayewardene, was no more successful than she in solving the island's worsening problems.

Her daughter, Chandrika Kumaratunga, followed in her mother's footsteps, and in 1994 the People's Alliance that she headed narrowly defeated the ruling United National Party, making Chandrika the new prime minister. Sirimavo reentered the political arena to run for president in November 1994; however, she was defeated.

References

"A Family Affair?" *World Press Review.* October 1994: 24.

Seneviratne, Maureen. *Sirimavo Bandaranaike: The World's First Woman Prime Minister.* Sri Lanka: Colombo Press, 1975.

"Sri Lanka's Racial Riots Could Cost Us Dearly." *U. S. News & World Report.* 8 August 1983: 8.

Barbara, Agatha
President of Malta (1982–1987)

Agatha Barbara was born March 11, 1924, in Zabbar, Malta. Visually challenged, she nevertheless pursued careers in teaching and in politics as a member of the Malta Labour Party. In 1947, at the age of twenty-three, she was elected Malta's first woman member of parliament, representing the Second District. In 1955 she became the first and only woman to hold cabinet rank when she became minister of education, a post she held until 1958.

Although Malta gained independence from Great Britain in September 1964, at the citizens' request, during a transition period Queen Elizabeth II was named queen of Malta, and British forces were allowed to remain on the island for ten more years. In 1971 Agatha Barbara became minister of education and culture and held the post until 1974.

On December 13, 1974, Malta became a democratic republic within the British Commonwealth, and the office of president was established. Sir Anthony Mamo, formerly governor-general, became the first president. Agatha Barbara became minister of employment, labour, and welfare. In December 1976 Dr. Anton Buttigieg was elected president; he served until 1982.

Following a two-month period when Dr. Albert Hyzler served as acting president, Agatha Barbara became Malta's first woman president in 1982. She served until 1987, when the Nationalist Party defeated the Labour Party and gained control of the government, a position it continues to enjoy.

Agatha Barbara continued to maintain a keen interest in politics and also in sports; she had previously been named honorary president of St. Patrick's Football Club. Now retired, she resides in Zabbar, Malta.

References

Kay, Ernest, ed. *The World Who's Who of Women,* 3d ed. Cambridge: International Biographical Centre, 1976. p. 50.

Misokova, Cynthia. National Tourism Organisation, Malta. http://www.tourism.org.mt; cmiso@tourism.org.mt, March 1998.

Barrow, Ruth Nita
Governor-General of Barbados (1990–1995)

Barbados is the easternmost island of the West Indies. In 1966 it became an independent state in the Commonwealth of Nations. The British monarch, the nominal head of state, is represented by a governor-general, who presides over a privy council appointed by the governor-general on advice from the prime minister. Control of the government rests in the hands of the prime minister and other ministers answerable to parliament.

Ruth Nita Barrow was born in 1916. She was married to Errol Barrow, who was active in the Democratic Labor Party. In 1986 Errol

Barrow became prime minister, but he died a year later. Nita Barrow continued to take an active part in politics, and in 1990 she was appointed governor-general by Queen Elizabeth II. She held the post until her death in December 1995.

References

Funk & Wagnalls New Encyclopedia. Vol. 3. 1996. p. 273.

"History." Barbados Bureau on Information and Tourism, www. barbados.gov.

Bazao
See Turunku Bakwa

Bazao-Turunku
See Turunku Bakwa

Beatrice
Regent of Tuscany (1052–1076)

Tuscany was located in present-day northwestern Italy. Beatrice was married to Count Boniface of Canossa, marquess of Tuscany. They had three children, two of whom died early. Boniface was considered by Holy Roman emperor Henry III to be his most dangerous enemy in Italy. When Boniface was assassinated in 1052, the youngest child, Matilda, age six, became heiress to the house of Attoni, founded by her grandfather Atto Adalbert. Beatrice ruled Tuscany alone until 1054, when she married Godfrey the Bearded, duke of Upper Lorraine. Godfrey stood in no better stead with Henry III than Boniface. In 1055 Henry arrested Beatrice and Matilda and sent them to Germany while Godfrey went into hiding. In time, Godfrey had made peace with Henry, and in 1056 Beatrice and Matilda were released. Beatrice returned to Tuscany to rule over her daughter's lands. In 1069 Godfrey died. Matilda, who had meanwhile married Godfrey's son and settled in Lorraine, returned to Italy in 1070 to rule with her mother until Beatrice's death in 1076.

References

Langer, William L., ed. *World History.* Boston: Houghton Mifflin, 1980. p. 232.

Previté-Orton, C. W. *The Cambridge Shorter Medieval History.* Vol. 1, *The Later Roman Empire to the Twelfth Century.* Cambridge: Cambridge University Press, 1982. p.457.

Beatrice
Countess, Regent of Edessa (1150)

Edessa was a Crusader state in northern Syria. Beatrice was the wife of Joscelin II (r. 1131–1150). In April 1150 Count Joscelin was captured by the invading Muslims. Countess Beatrice sold what remained of the land to Byzantium in the summer of that year, thus ending the county's fifty-year history.

References
Carpenter, Clive. *The Guinness Book of Kings, Rulers & Statesmen.* Enfield, Middlesex: Guinness Superlatives 1978. p. 55.

Beatrice
Minority Ruler in Name Only of Portugal (1383–1384)

Beatrice was the daughter of Ferdinand I (the Handsome), ruler of Portugal (1367–1383), and Leonora Telles. Henry II, king of Castile, coerced Ferdinand to accept an arranged marriage between his infant daughter and John I of Castile so as to bring Portugal under the eventual dominance of Castile. When Ferdinand died in 1383, Leonora acted briefly as Beatrice's regent but was forced to acknowledge John I as king of Portugal as per the terms of the marriage agreement. In 1387, to strengthen a claim for the Castilian crown, John was married a second time to Phillipa of Lancaster, daughter of duke John of Gaunt. Thus from infancy onward Beatrice remained a helpless pawn in the drive for Castilian power.

References
Langer, William L., ed. *World History.* Boston: Houghton Mifflin, 1980. p. 306.

Beatrice, Countess
Ruler of Provence (1245–1267)

Beatrice was the daughter of Raymond Berengar V (r. 1209–1245). She inherited the rule of Provence upon his death in 1245. In 1246 she married Charles, count of Anjou, who in 1266 became Charles I, king of Naples and Sicily. However, he lost Sicily in 1282. Beatrice had a son, Charles II the Lame. She died in 1267, and her husband continued to rule until his death in 1285. Thereafter Charles II inherited the rule of Provence.

References
Morby, John E. *Dynasties of the World.* Oxford: Oxford University Press, 1989. p. 87.

Smith, Denis Mack. *A History of Sicily*. Vol. 1, *Medieval Sicily*. New York: Dorset Press, 1968. pp. 66f, 104.

Béatrix de Bourgogne
Baroness of Bourbon (1287–1310)

Béatrix de Bourgogne was the daughter of Agnes de Dampierre and Jean de Bourgogne. She married Robert de France, comte de Clermont, and succeeded as ruler of Bourbon when her mother died in 1287. Béatrix died in 1310.

References

Egan, Edward W., Constance B. Hintz, and L. F. Wise, eds. *Kings, Rulers, and Statesmen*. New York: Sterling Publishing 1976. p. 153.

Béatrix Wilhelmina Armgard
Queen of The Netherlands (1980–)

Béatrix was born in 1938 in Soestdijk, Baarn, the oldest of four daughters of Queen Juliana and Prince Bernhard. Because of the hardships of Nazi occupation of their country during World War II, the royal family was sensitive to public sentiment against unnecessary extravagances by the monarchy, even though the royal family continued to be much loved by the Dutch people. The daughters were reared in a much more democratic fashion than their counterparts in Great Britain. Béatrix attended Baarn grammar school and the State University of Leiden, where she earned a doctor of law degree (1961). In 1966 she made an unpopular marriage to Prince Claus von Amsberg, a German diplomat whose participation in the Hitler Youth Movement and the German Army during World War II did not make him a prime candidate in the eyes of the people. That he had been exonerated by an Allied court did not clear him in the opinion of the Dutch subjects. However, the union produced the first male heir to the House of Orange since the time of William III (d. 1890) when Willem-Alexander was born in 1967, and much of the public opposition to von Amsberg disappeared. Two other sons were born in 1968 and 1969. At the age of forty-two, when her youngest son had reached the age of eleven, Béatrix succeeded her mother upon Queen Juliana's abdication (1980), taking an oath as "king." Béatrix describes woman's role in Holland as much like her own: "She can do a lot but she can't decide. There's a traditional limit on all women." Described as having a "strong handshake" and as "stylish, magnetic with plumb-line posture," the queen does not engage in social controversy, understanding that her main function is to be a symbol of unity and of

continuity with the past. Her concern for the preservation of the historic led her to take great care in equipping the room of her seventeenth-century palace that she uses for her sculpture studio. The royal family, which engages in a certain amount of foreign diplomacy on an informal level, has enjoyed wide popularity throughout Europe. The Netherlands has now had a woman ruler for 100 years.

References

Langer, William L., ed. *World History.* Boston: Houghton Mifflin, 1980. p. 475.

McDowell, Bart. "The Dutch Touch." *National Geographic* 170. October 1986: 500–525.

Who's Who in the World, 1997. New Providence, RI: Marquis Who's Who/Reed Elsevier, 1996. p. 144.

Bendjou, Empress
Joint Ruler of Mali (ca. 1345)

Bendjou was a commoner and the second wife of Emperor Sulayman (Suleymon), who ruled Mali from ca. 1341 to 1360. Sulayman had divorced his first wife, Kossi, in order to marry Bendjou. However, either because of her commoner origins or because of Kossi's popularity, when Bendjou met the noble ladies in the audience chamber, none would pay homage to her by throwing earth on their heads. They only threw it on their hands, a sign of disrespect. Ibn Battuta, observing the customs of Mali in 1352, described this practice of groveling before the ruler: "If one of [the sultan's attendants] addresses the sultan and the latter replies, he uncovers the clothes from his back and sprinkles dust on his head and back, like one washing himself with water." When the ladies of the court refused to throw dirt on their heads to honor Bendjou, she complained to the sultan (emperor), whose anger was incited against his ex-wife. The incident, a reflection of a greater struggle for political power in Mali, escalated into a minor civil war that pitted Sulayman against the relatives of his ex-wife. Kossi and a prince launched an unsuccessful coup attempt, but Sulayman and his chiefs defeated the opposition that she spearheaded, and Bendjou assumed joint rule of Mali without further incident.

References

Dunn, Ross E. *The Adventures of Ibn Battuta.* Berkeley: The University of California Press, 1986. p.302.

Panikker, K. Madhu. *The Serpent and the Crescent: A History of the Negro Empires of West Africa.* Bombay: Asia Publishing House, 1963. p. 60.

Berenice
Co-ruler of Caesarea Paneas and Tiberias in Judaea (fl. ca. 52)

Berenice was born Julia Berenice in A.D. 28, the daughter of King Herod Agrippa I (10 B.C.–A.D. 44), who ruled Judaea from A.D. 37 to 44. She was the older sister of Drusilla, who was linked both to Aziz, Arab ruler of Emesa, and Feliz, the Roman procurator of Judaea. However, Berenice was much more active than her sister. She first reputedly married, or was sleeping with, Marcus, a nephew of Philo Judaeus of Alexandria, and lived in Alexandria, Egypt. After his premature death, she married her father's brother, Herod, who was given rule over Chalcis in Greece. To Herod, Berenice bore two sons, Berenicianus and Hyrcanus. Herod died in A.D. 48 while she was still in her twenties. In ca. 52, she shared the Chalcis throne and the business of the kingdom, in Batanala and Trachonites in southern Syria, with her brother, Agrippa II, who had succeeded as king of Judaea when their father died in A.D. 44. The couple was popularly believed to be cohabiting in Caesarea before and after Berenice's brief marriage to Polemon II, king of Olba in Cilicia (in present-day Turkey and Armenia). Her powers of persuasion were such that she convinced Polemon, a non-Jew, to be circumcised before she would consent to marry him. This marriage was also cut short by the husband's death.

From the historian Josephus's account of the Jewish revolt against Florus, Nero's chosen procurator of Judaea, Agrippa relied heavily upon Berenice. At one point, to dissuade the Jewish people from revolting against Rome, he placed Berenice conspicuously on the roof of the palace where she could be seen by the crowd while he pleaded for peace. At the end of his impassioned speech, both he and his sister burst out in tears, moving the crowd to accompany the couple to repair the temple that had been damaged in the uprising. Thus they were able to postpone a confrontation that would cost many Jewish lives.

When the Caesarean palace was burned down and Jerusalem sacked, Agrippa and Berenice became Flavian sympathizers. Commander-in-chief Titus (A.D. 41–81), a twenty-eight-year-old widower, fell under the charms of the forty-one-year-old widow and for thirteen years made her his mistress. But after Titus became emperor in A.D. 79, his intention to make her his empress—a Jewish princess thirteen years his senior—caused such an uproar among the court in Rome that he was compelled to banish her to Gaul, where she is thought to have lived until age seventy-two. Titus reigned barely two years before he died in A.D. 81.

References

Bowder, Diana, ed. *Who Was Who in the Roman World.* Ithaca, NY: Cornell University Press, 1980. p. 70.

Josephus. *The Jewish War.* Trans. G. A. Williamson. London: Penguin Books, 1959, 1970. pp. 143, 152–153, 155 156, 162, 166, 192–193.

Mommsen, Theodor. *The Provinces of the Roman Empire.* Trans. Wm. P. Dickson. Vol. 2. Chicago: Ares Publishers, 1974. pp. 201, 219.

Peters, F. E. *The Harvest of Hellenism.* New York: Barnes & Noble Books, 1996. p. 513n.

Berenice III
Queen of Egypt, Co-ruler (101–88 B.C.), then Sole Ruler (81–80 B.C.)

Berenice III (Cleopatra Berenice) was the daughter of Ptolemy Lathyrus (Ptolemy IX), who ruled from 117 to 81 B.C., and either Cleopatra IV or Cleopatra Selene, who first (prior to 101 B.C.) married Berenice to her uncle, Ptolemy Alexander (Ptolemy X). Although the reign of her father Lathyrus totaled thirty-six years, for the first ten years (117–107 B.C.) his mother Cleopatra ruled for him, and for the next eighteen years (107–89 B.C.) he was a fugitive, ruling only over Cyprus while his brother Alexander ruled Egypt with the dowager queen, Cleopatra III. When Cleopatra died in 101 B.C., Berenice became full queen and co-ruler. However, Alexander was suspected of having assassinated Cleopatra III and was driven from Egypt. He raised an army and attempted to return, but when it was learned that he had robbed the tomb of Alexander the Great to finance his army, he was once again driven out. Berenice accompanied him, but when he died, she returned. Meanwhile, Lathyrus had returned and had been restored as king. When Lathyrus died, he left only one legitimate heir, Berenice. She succeeded him on the throne and ruled for six months as sole monarch. The Roman dictator Lucius Cornelius Sulla arranged for Ptolemy Alexander X's son, her first cousin, to return to Egypt to marry her. It was his intent that they would rule jointly. However, Berenice had no intention of dividing her power and refused his proposition, so he simply had her assassinated (80 B.C.). The enraged populace, with whom Berenice had been very popular, killed Alexander, thus eliminating the last Ptolemaic ruler of Egypt.

References

Bowder, Diana, ed. *Who Was Who in the Greek World.* Ithaca, NY: Cornell University Press, 1982. pp. 405–406.

Egan, Edward W., Constance B. Hintz, and L. F. Wise, eds. *Kings, Rulers, and Statesmen.* New York: Sterling Publishing, 1976. p. 125.

Rawlinson, George. *Ancient History.* New York: Barnes & Noble, 1993. pp. 206–207.

Berenice IV
Ruler of Egypt (58–55 B.C.)

Berenice IV was the eldest daughter of Ptolemy XII Auletes (called "the flute player" because of his frivolous pursuits), Macedonian king of Egypt, and Cleopatra V Tryphaena. Berenice was the older sister of the famous Cleopatra VII. When Berenice's father went to Rome in 58 B.C. to seek military aid against an Alexandrian insurrection, he left the government in the hands of Berenice and her mother. However, the mother died shortly after, and Berenice was proclaimed queen of Egypt. She ruled alone for three years. In 56 B.C. the Alexandrians, anxious to replace the absent Ptolemy XII Auletes, found a suitable marriage candidate for Berenice in Archelaus, a Pontic prince. However, in 55 B.C. her father returned with Syrian reinforcements, regained control of the throne, and executed Berenice and her supporters.

References

Bowder, Diana, ed. *Who Was Who in the Greek World.* Ithaca, NY: Cornell University Press, 1982. p. 406.

Rawlinson, George. *Ancient History.* New York: Barnes & Noble, 1993. pp. 208–209.

West, John Anthony. *The Traveler's Key to Ancient Egypt.* New York: Alfred A. Knopf, 1985. pp. 428–429, 446.

Bergmann-Pohl, Sabine
President of the Parliament of the German Democratic Republic (1990)

Following World War II, Germany was divided into four zones by the Allies. In 1949 the zones administered by the Western Allies became the Federal Republic, or West Germany, a democratic republic, while the German Democratic Republic, or East Germany, was established under Soviet auspices as an independent communist state.

East Germany was led for more than a quarter of a century by Walter Ulbricht. Thereafter, no single leader dominated the government, although Erich Honecker functioned as head of state from 1976 to 1989, when he was forced to resign. After the communist government collapsed in 1989 and the reunification of Germany was anticipated, the Socialist Unity Party, a communist organization, held free elections for a new People's Chamber, which took office in March 1990. The charge to the chamber was to work out the economic and political merger of East Germany with West Germany.

Sabine Bergmann-Pohl, born in 1946, was elected to preside over this parliament. On August 23, 1990, the People's Chamber agreed to formal unification, and on October 3, 1990, East Germany became a part of the Federal Republic of Germany. Thus Sabine Bergmann-Pohl gained the distinction as the last head of state of East Germany.

References
"Germany." In Funk &*Wagnalls New Encyclopedia*. Vol. 11. 1986. pp. 355–364.

Bhutto, Benazir
Prime Minister of Pakistan (1988–1990, 1993–1996)

Benazir Bhutto was born in 1953, the eldest child of Zulfiqar Ali Bhutto, a Berkeley- and Oxford-trained Pakistani lawyer, and his number two wife, Nusrat, an Iranian. Ali Bhutto became a cabinet member at the age of thirty-two, when Benazir was five years old; thus she and her younger siblings were reared in proximity to power. When she was sixteen she entered Radcliffe, graduating cum laude with a B.A. degree. From there she went to Oxford, where she was elected president of the Oxford Union and received another B.A. cum laude. Her father became leader of the new truncated state of Pakistan in 1971. In 1979, in a U.S.-supported coup, Ali's rival, General Zia ul-Haq, sent tanks to surround the prime minister's house. Ali was dragged away before his family's eyes and sentenced to be hanged by a court rigged by Zia. Ali immediately became a national martyr, and his wife and daughter became symbols of resistance to Zia's military dictatorship. They were imprisoned and mistreated until their health failed. In 1983 Benazir received permission to be sent abroad for medical treatment. In 1984 Indira Gandhi personally intervened in behalf of Nusrat, believed to be suffering from cancer. The family was reunited in London, where Benazir began to organize her supporters. Zia lifted martial law in 1985, and Benazir returned the next year to a tumultuous welcome. She was promptly imprisoned and some of her supporters shot. But Zia's popularity was waning: His generals had grown wealthy from heroin money, and the whole country was weakened by heroin. She was released only a month later, when Zia realized that public sentiment was in her favor. In 1987 she consented to an arranged marriage with Asif Ali Zardari, of a wealthy landed family like her own. Ultimately the couple had two children, Bilawal and Bakhtawar. In 1988, Benazir was several months pregnant when the plane upon which Zia and

Benazir Bhutto
(Reuters/Corbis-Bettmann)

most of his high command were traveling exploded and crashed. Her People's Party won the election that followed despite discriminatory practices that prevented women and the poor from voting. Benazir was sworn in as prime minister of Pakistan. It was widely reported by Islamic news sources at the time that Bhutto was the first woman to lead an Islamic state; however, research has uncovered more than a dozen other women Islamic rulers, in Yemen, Egypt, Kirman, and the Maldive islands. Her mother, Nusrat, became a member of the parliament. Benazir faced enormous problems of a bankrupt economy, which included huge debts to the International Monetary Fund; a heroin mafia; 1.35 million heroin addicts; and thousands of Afghan refugees. In an interview with David Frost about her long political struggle, she said, "You can never survive on your fears. Only on your hopes." Meanwhile violence had erupted in the provinces of Sind and Baluchistan, forcing Bhutto to consider opposing central rule.

Bhutto ruled Pakistan from 1988 to 1990, but her government, the first democracy after a decade of military rule, was thrown out on corruption charges that were never substantiated. Under this government, her mother, Nusrat Bhutto, was a senior cabinet minister and her husband, Asif Ali Zardari, was a visible presence in government circles. However, after her downfall, Zardari, charged with taking kickbacks, spent more than two years in prison, although the charges were never proved. From 1990 to 1993 her Pakistan People's Party led the opposition, during which time she built a coalition of minor parties.

In October 1993, her party won a slim margin in the national elections, and the National Assembly named her prime minister for a second time. This time her husband was kept at a distance during the elections, and her aides reported that none of her family would be included in her new cabinet.

In 1994 she was able to facilitate the sale of Pakistan Telecom shares abroad, raising $1 billion, and the signing of deals with local industrialists by U.S. investors in the amount of $4 billion. However, although she had cut the budget deficit, privatized public utilities, and instituted an austerity drive, her success as judged by the International Monetary Fund did not translate to help for the common citizen. In September 1994, her long-time political opponent Nawaz Sharif, leader of the Pakistan Muslim League, called for a general strike. Another opponent to both factions, Zahid Sarfaraz, a member of a group of right-wing politicians and retired generals, called for the army to step in and save the country; yet another faction, led by Mir Zafarullah Jamali, to avert a military takeover, called for the military to back a vote of no-confidence against Bhutto.

During that same month Benazir attended the United Nations Population Conference in Cairo, where she spoke against abortion. Norwegian prime minister Gro Harlem Brundtland spoke in favor of abortion at the same conference.

In 1995 Owais Aslam Ali, with the Pakistan Press Foundation, reported that, after a decade of trends toward a freer press, Bhutto's government, as well as other political groups and terrorists, had turned against the media, particularly the newspapers in Karachi. Bhutto's officials complained that the papers sensationalized the violence that had gripped Karachi. In June the government of Karachi's Sind province banned six mass-circulation newspapers for sixty days. However, when a nationwide newspaper strike was threatened, the government rescinded the order. Journalists in other towns reported being harassed and physically assaulted by law enforcement officials and political groups. A prominent journalist in Lahore was arrested because his campaign against child labor was "against the national interest."

Bhutto's party was voted out in 1996, but she remains a formidable spokesperson for her country in the international arena.

References

Ali, Owais Aslam. "Regression in Pakistan" (from "IPI Report"). *World Press Review.* April 1996: 17–18.

Ali, Tariq. "Dynasty's Daughter." *Interview.* February 1989: 68–71.

Bhutto, Benazir. *Daughter of Destiny.* New York: Simon & Schuster, 1989. Or see Bhutto, Benazir. *Daughter of the East.* London: Hamish Hamilton, 1988.

Bokhari, Farhan. "Pakistan's Benazir Bhutto Gets a Second Chance." *Christian Science Monitor.* 20 October 1993: 2.

Brody, James. "In Step with David Frost." *Parade.* 18 February 1989: 18.

Mayer, Ann Elizabeth. " Benazir Bhutto and Islamic Law." *Christian Science Monitor.* 6 February 1989: 18.

"The 'Strongwomen' of South Asia." *World Press Review.* December 1994: 18–20.

Bianca
Queen, Vicar of Sicily (1410–1412)

Bianca was the wife of Martin I, king of Aragon from 1395 to 1410 and regent of Sicily. On the death of John I, who ruled Sicily from 1387 to 1395, Martin I left his only son, also named Martin, as king, or viceroy, of Sicily. The latter, then also called Martin I, died in 1409, willing the kingdom to his father, just as any other item of personal property. King Martin I of Aragon then became known also as Martin II, king of Sicily. He, too, died the following year, and as neither Martin had left an heir, the vacant throne of Sicily fell to Martin II's widow, Bianca. Count Cabrera of Modica, grand justiciar, defied Queen Bianca, hoping to secure the throne for himself. In addition, in each region, powerful feudal barons reasserted their rights and withheld revenues, so Queen Bianca had to resort to private borrowing to keep the kingdom running. Even the citizens of Messina, which supported her rule, took advantage of the situation by occupying the royal castles at Syracuse and Catania. A committee was appointed to select a candidate for king. Out of a list of six, the committee chose Ferdinand, king of Castile, who in 1412 proclaimed himself king of Sicily before the citizens of Sicily had even been consulted.

References
Langer, William L., ed. *World History.* Boston: Houghton Mifflin, 1980. p. 306.

Smith, Denis Mack. *A History of Sicily.* Vol. 1, *Medieval Sicily.* New York: Dorset Press, 1968. pp. 91–92.

Bianca Maria
Duchess, Regent of Milan (1466–1468)

Bianca Maria was the illegitimate and only child of Duke Filippo Maria Visconti of Milan and Maria of Savoy. In 1433 Bianca became betrothed to Francesco Sforza, whom she married in 1441. The couple had a son, Galeazzo Maril Sforza, born in 1444. Blanca thought she was the legal heir of Milan when her father died (1447), but instead he had named Alfonso of Aragon, king of Naples, as his successor.

*Bianca Maria
(Scala / Art Resource,
NY)*

Francesco battled Naples, Venice, Montferrat, and Savoy for the right to rule Milan in his wife's name. In 1450 he achieved that right and ruled until his death in 1466. Bianca ruled with her son for the first two years of his rule, but following his marriage in 1468 to Bona of Savoy, she retired and became a patron of the arts.

References

Langer, William L., ed. *World History.* Boston: Houghton Mifflin, 1980. p. 321.

Bilqis
See Balkis

Bjerregaard, Ritt
Premier of Denmark (1995)

Ritt Bjerregaard was born in Copenhagen in 1941. She entered politics as a member of the Danish parliament in 1971 and has held a seat ever since. A member of the Social Democratic Party, she was appointed minister of education in 1973. In the election of December 1973, because of dissension among the left-wing parties, the non-Socialist parties gained a majority. The Social Democratic government resigned, and Poul Hartling, of the Venstre (Liberal Democrat) Party, headed a minority government. An outspoken critic of French leadership and French policies, Bjerregaard was relieved of her position after criticizing French conservative Jacques Chirac, who was chosen in 1974 by French president Valéry Giscard d'Estaing as his prime minister, saying that she didn't think Chirac would grow in stature with his post. (Apparently the French minister proved too ambitious with his agenda favoring businessmen and was dismissed in 1976.) Hartling attempted to institute a firm savings program, which brought on increased unemployment and ultimately toppled his government in January 1975. The Social Democrats returned to power with Anker Jørgensen at the helm. During this period Ritt Bjerregaard was again appointed minister of education, a position she held until 1978. In 1979 she became minister of social affairs, remaining at that post until 1982. She was chairperson of the Parliamentary Group of the Social Democrat Party (1987–1992).

Years in politics did not alter her outspoken criticism of French policies of which she disapproved. When the French government began nuclear tests in the South Pacific, she publicly criticized them.

She took an active role in bringing Denmark into the European Economic Community, in 1990 becoming a member of the Parliamentary Assembly of the Countries of Europe. In 1992 she was elected vice president of that body. She also served as president of the Danish European Movement (1992–1994). She serves on the Trilateral Commission of the Center for European Policy Studies. In 1995 Ritt Bjerregaard, the first female premier of Denmark, was sent to Brussels as the European Union environment commissioner. She has written several books on politics and women's role in politics.

References

The Australian Magazine. April 1996: 22.

Who's Who in the World 1997. New Providence, NJ: Reed Elsevier, 1996. p. 149.

Blanca, Doña
Queen of Navarre (1425–1441)

In the Middle Ages, from 1134 to 1458, Navarre was an independent kingdom in present-day northern Spain. Blanca (Blanche) was the daughter of Charles III the Noble of the House of Evreux (r. Navarre 1387–1425). In ca. 1420 Blanca married Juan II of Portugal, king of Aragon. They had a son, Carlos de Viana, and two daughters, Leonor (Eleanor of Navarre) and Blanche of Aragon. In 1425 Blanca succeeded her father as queen of Navarre. She died in 1441, but the throne was not passed down to her heirs until after Juan's death thirty-eight years later. He was succeeded by her son Don Carlos (d. 1461) and then by her daughter Eleanor (Leonor). Juan's second marriage produced a son, Ferdinand, who married Isabella of Castile and who ultimately brought the southern part of the kingdom of Navarre under Aragonese control (1512).

References

Egan, Edward W., Constance B. Hintz, and L. F. Wise, eds. *Kings, Rulers, and Statesmen.* New York: Sterling Publishing, 1976. p. 430.

McKendrick, Melveena. *Ferdinand and Isabella.* New York: American Heritage Publishing, 1968. pp. 22–23.

Morby, John E. *Dynasties of the World.* Oxford: Oxford University Press, 1989. p. 114.

Blanche of Castile
Regent of France (1226–1236 and 1248–1252)

Blanche was born in 1188 in Palencia, Spain, to Alfonso VIII of Castile and Eleanor, daughter of Henry II of England. In 1199, when Blanche was only eleven years old, her marriage to the future Louis VIII of France was arranged by her grandmother, Eleanor of Aquitaine; in fact, the elderly Eleanor traveled from England to Spain to deliver Blanche to France herself, a gesture designed to emphasize the importance of the union for peace with both Spain and England. In 1214 Blanche and Louis had a son who would eventually become Louis IX. In 1216 when her uncle John of England died, Blanche tried to seize the English throne. Louis stormed England on her behalf but was defeated, and John's son was crowned Henry III. In 1223 Louis VIII succeeded to the throne of France, but he died three years later. Blanche became regent of France and guardian for their son, Louis IX, who was twelve years old. She proved to be a strong and able ruler. To quell rebellious nobles, Blanche rode into battle at the head of her own troops. When the nobles tried to abduct her son, she expelled them and replaced them with commoners. It was Blanche who was responsible for the Treaty of Paris, which ushered in an era of peace and prosperity. When her son reached twenty-one, Blanche was relieved of the regency, but she remained a large influence on his life and upon affairs of state. When Louis and his wife Margaret determined to embark on a crusade in 1248, Blanche, whose ability to rule had been proved during her son's minority, was once again made regent of France. There were foreign problems to solve: She had to persuade the English to keep the peace, and she had to maintain a delicate balance of relations with Holy Roman emperor Frederick. Louis was captured by the Turks in 1250, and most of his troops were shot. He was ransomed and sent home, but Blanche died in 1252 while her son was still out of the country.

References

Heer, Friedrich. *The Medieval World.* Trans. Janet Sondheimer. New York: Mentor/NAL, 1962. p. 319.

Runciman, Steven. *A History of the Crusades.* Vol. 3, *The Kingdom of Acre.* Cambridge: Cambridge University Press, 1987. pp. 256, 274, 279–280.

Bona of Savoy
Regent of Milan (1476–1479)

Bona was the wife of Galeazzo Maria Sforza, ruler of Milan from 1466 to 1476. They had a son, Gian Galeazzo. After her husband was assassinated in 1476, Bona served as regent, governing for her son. In 1478 she supported Florence against Naples after the Pazzi family conspiracy, an unsuccessful attempt to overthrow the Medici rulers of Florence. The Duchy of Milan was usurped in 1479 by Bona's brother-in-law, Ludovico il Moro.

References

Langer, William L., ed. *World History*. Boston: Houghton Mifflin, 1980. p. 322.

Bonaparte, Elisa

See Elisa Bonaparte

Bōrān

Sasanid Queen of Persia (630–631)

Bōrān was the daughter of King Khusrau II the Victorious, ruler of Persia from 590 to 628. During two chaotic years following his death, two of her brothers, Kavad II and Ardashir II, and a usurper, Shahrbaraz, each held the throne briefly. Bōrān was then placed on the throne, but the following year her sister, Āzarmēdukht, succeeded her.

References

Morby, John E. *Dynasties of the World*. Oxford: Oxford University Press, 1989. p. 49.

Boraqchin, Khatum

Regent of the Mongolian Khanate of Kipchak (1255–1257)

Khatum Boraqchin was the wife of Batu, who became khan of Kipchak in 1227. When he died in 1255, his son and heir Sartaq had gone to pay court to Grand Khan Mongka, his father's friend. But before Sartaq could return home and be crowned, he died. Mongka nominated a young prince, Ulaqchi, either Sartaq's younger brother or his son, to succeed to the throne of Kipchak, and he made the widow Boraqchin regent. She served until Ulaqchi died in 1257.

References

Grousset, René. *The Empire of the Steppes*. Trans. Naomi Walford. New Brunswick, NJ: Rutgers University Press, 1970. p. 397.

Boudicca
Queen of the Iceni (ca. 60)

Born ca. A.D. 26 of a royal family, Boudicca (or Boadicea) was married to King Prasutagus, who ruled the Iceni in what is now Norfolk, England, by special arrangement under Roman suzerainty. Boudicca was tall and comanding, with tawny hair and what was described as a "harsh voice." She had produced two daughters but no male heirs when King Prasutagus died. Under terms of his will, he left his estate to his daughters and to Nero, emperor of Rome, believing that he could count on the crown's protection of his family's holdings. However, the Romans immediately seized his kingdom, ousted his family, plundered his chief tribesmen, and installed Suetonius Paulinus as provisional governor. Boudicca was publicly flogged, and she watched her daughters, legendarily named Voada and Voadicia, being raped by the legionnaires. She immediately began organizing opposition, and while Paulinus was away, she initiated a determined revolt throughout East Anglia. During her brief reign of terror, her followers managed to sack Camulodunum (Colchester), Verulamium, Londinium (London), and various military installations and reportedly took the lives of 70,000 Romans and Roman sympathizers. She left the Roman Ninth Legion in shambles. However, her victory was short lived, for Paulinus retaliated with fresh troops and met the Britons somewhere near Fenny Stratford on Watling. After a bloody standoff, the exhausted Britons were cut down, and Roman rule was restored. Boudicca, unwilling to live under Roman rule and certain, at any rate, that she would be executed, took poison and died ca. A.D. 60.

References
Duff, Charles. *England and the English.* New York: G. P. Putnam's Sons, 1955. pp. 51, 52, 63, 232.

Langer, William L., ed. *World History.* Boston: Houghton Mifflin, 1980. pp. 120, 179.

Markdale, Jean. *Women of the Celts.* Trans. A. Mygind et al. Rochester, VT: Inner Traditions International, 1986. pp. 27, 32, 253.

Brigantia
Legendary Queen of the Brigantes (51)

Brigantia (or Brigit) is mentioned in inscriptions both in Britain and in Gaul. According to Cormac, she was the daughter of the Dagda (or lord of diverse talents, or good-at-everything god). She was the patron of poets and was called *banfile,* meaning "female poet." She is believed to be Christianized as St. Brigid.

References

Chadwick, Nora. *The Celts.* Harmondsworth, Middlesex: Penguin Books, 1976. p. 169.

Duff, Charles. *England and the English.* New York: G. P. Putnam's Sons, 1955. p. 42.

Brundtland, Gro Harlem
Prime Minister of Norway (1981 and 1986–1989, 1990–1996)

Gro Harlem Brundtland was born April 20, 1939, in Oslo, the daughter of Gundmund and Inga Brynolf Harlem. In 1960 she married Arne Olav Brundtland and had a daughter, Kaja, and three sons, Knut, Ivar, and Jorgen. She received her M.D. degree in 1963 from Oslo University, then attended Harvard University School of Public Health, where in 1965 she earned a master's degree in public health. She returned to Oslo and served for two years as medical officer for the National Directorate of Public Health before becoming the assistant medical director for the School of Health Services in Oslo in 1968.

Dr. Brundtland entered political life in 1974 when she was appointed minister of environment for the Norwegian government, a post she held until 1979. She was elected member of parliament in 1974 from the Norwegian Labour Party. She became leader of the party in 1981 and was first elected prime minister in February 1981. Her party held the majority until October of that year, and thereafter she became leader of the opposition until 1986, when she again became prime minister. She held the post until 1989. During that period she was chosen chairman of the World Commission of Environment from 1984 to 1987. In 1990 she again returned as prime minister, serving until 1996.

Three times Norway rejected joining the European Community before Brundtland launched a campaign to "persuade the voters that the nation will not develop into a competitive power if it remains outside the EEC and that the Scandinavian nations should form a bloc capable of defending their interests." Conservative factions observed that if Norway did join the EC, that organization would find "it has a bee under its shirt," because the prime minister was known as a forceful and opinionated politician.

In 1992 she surprised a Labour Party convention by announcing that, although she would continue as prime minister, she was withdrawing from the position of party leader. Prior to that time, the posts of prime minister and party leader of the Labour Party had traditionally been held by one person, but Dr. Brundtland wished to reduce the workload of holding both positions for so many years. The party elected Thorbjørn Jagland as new party leader, and the two had an excellent working relationship for the next four years.

At the United Nations Population Conference in Cairo held the first week of September 1994, Gro Harlem spoke in favor of abortion. At that same conference, Prime Minister Benazir Bhutto spoke against it, according to a television news report.

In October 1996, Dr. Brundtland announced her intention of resigning as head of the Norwegian Labour government in favor of Thorbjørn Jagland. She chose to do so at that time so that his position as prime minister would be well established before the party's convention in November 1996 and before the parliamentary elections the following year. "I have the intention to remain an active, working person also in the future, and I believe it is a privilege to leave as Head of Government," she said.

Dr. Brundtland was a strong proponent of a more active role for women in politics; women outnumbered men in her cabinet. She was quoted in the *China Daily* on the subject of women in politics and in the work force in general: "Men and women should have equal opportunity to fulfill their roles in society as well as at home. . . . Husbands will have to increase their domestic participation."

References
"Four's a Charm?" *World Press Review.* March 1993: 32.
International Who's Who 1987–1988. London: Europa Publishing, 1987. p. 200.
"The Office of the Prime Minister Press Release" Oslo, Norway. *Odin,* 23 October 1996.
Who's Who in the World 1997. New Providence, NJ: Marquis Who's Who/Reed Elsevier, 1996. p. 193.
"Women in Politics." *World Press Review.* March 1988. p. 53.

Brunhilde
Queen Regent for Austrasia and Burgundy (575–581 and 595–613)

Brunhilde (or Brunichildis) was born ca. 550, the daughter of the Visigothic king, Athanagild, and Goiswinth. She was the sister of Galswintha, who became the second wife of the Merovingian king Chilperic I, ruler of an area that is presently Belgium. Brunhilde married Chilperic's half-brother, Sigebert I, king of the eastern kingdom of Austrasia from 561 to 575. Between them, the two brothers and their two sister wives controlled the whole Frankish world. However, when Galswintha was murdered at the instigation of Chilperic to please his mistress Fredegund, Brunhilde vowed revenge, and thus began a feud that lasted and escalated for forty years amid plots and counterplots resulting in several murders. Sigebert was murdered by Fredegund's emissaries in 575, and Brunhilde's son Chilperic II was made king. During his minority, Brunhilde was made regent, and she soon married Merovech, Sigebert's nephew. In 581, Chilperic II was adopted by his uncle Chilperic I, and Brunhilde was free to devote herself to venting her revenge upon Fredegund. When Brunhilde's son died in 595, she was again made regent for her two grandsons: Theudoric II, king of Burgundy, and Theudebert II, king of Austrasia. She wielded tremendous power, and her only rival was Fredegund, who by that time was ruling Neustria for her young son, Clotaire II. On Fredegund's death in 598, Brunhilde seized Neustria as well, and so united under her dominion the entire Merovingian world. Her grandson Theudebert incurred her wrath in 612, and she persuaded his brother Theudoric to overthrow him. In 613, the Austrasian nobles who opposed her and favored Theudebert united under Clotaire II and were able to overthrow her government. Brunhilde was sentenced to death by being dragged behind a wild horse. Brunhilde probably inspired some of the ancient German heroic myths concerning a beautiful amazonian queen.

Brunhilde
(Corbis-Bettmann)

References

Gregory of Tours. *The History of the Franks.* Trans. Lewis Thorpe. Harmondsworth, Middlesex: Penguin Books, 1974. pp. 196, 221–222, 233, 247, 251, 254–256, 268, 272, 275, 279, 305, 370, 383, 401–402, 417, 426, 437, 453, 456–458, 480–481, 488–489, 491–492, 502–503, 505, 507, 514–515, 518, 524–526, 578.

Sullivan, Richard E. *Heirs of the Roman Empire.* Ithaca: Cornell University Press, 1960. pp. 39–40.

Busignani, Patricia
Co-captain-regent of San Marino (1993)

The Most Serene Republic of San Marino, the oldest independent republic in Europe, is completely surrounded by Italy, with which it has had a treaty of friendship since 1862. San Marino is governed by two heads of state, called co-captains regent, who are elected from the parliamentary body for a term of six months. A leader may not be re-elected sooner than three years later.

Patricia Busignani was first elected to a five-year term as a legislator in the Great and Good Council, and this group elected her, in April 1993, to the post of co-captain regent. In this position she presided over the ten-member Congress of State, the executive branch of the government. Her term expired October 1, 1993.

References
Delury, George, ed. *The World Almanac and Book of Facts.* New York: Newspaper Enterprise Association, 1994. pp. 273–274.

Cahina
See Kahina, Al-

Campbell, Kim
Prime Minister of Canada (1993)

Kim Campbell, who was born in 1947, was educated as a lawyer and became a professor before entering politics. In 1988 she was elected to parliament and moved swiftly through the ranks of Canada's ruling Progressive Conservative Party. She was soon appointed minister of Indian affairs and later minister of justice. In January 1993 she was appointed minister of defense. In June of that year she was elected Canada's first woman prime minister, after telling her supporters, "Whether I win or lose, our party is ready for a leader from either founding gender. . . . Our choice as a party is clear: We can respond to the winds of change or we can be swept away." She took over a country bitter over government cutbacks of social programs and an 11.4 percent unemployment rate.

One of her first tasks was to tackle the federal and provincial deficits by calling a special meeting with provincial premiers aimed at reaching a spending agreement before a scheduled summit with other world leaders. In July 1993 Campbell represented Canada at the three-day summit in Tokyo of the G-7, the Group of Seven of the world's leading industrial nations: Japan, Canada, Britain, Italy, France, Germany, and the United States. The group discussed terrorism, ethnic wars such as the one in Bosnia, and nuclear threats but could reach little consensus on how to deal with the violence in Bosnia. They did agree to supply aid to Boris Yeltsin's government in Russia. The summit allowed Campbell to stand out as the only woman among those world leaders.

Back home, Campbell worked to solidify the conservative base in Canada's western provinces before she faced elections. By law she

*Kim Campbell
(Reuters/Corbis-
Bettmann)*

had to call for elections no later than the end of November. Although an August 1993 Gallup poll showed Campbell's approval rating at 51 percent, the highest level for a prime minister in thirty years, her popularity was not enough to pull her Progressive Conservatives ahead of the Liberal Party, led by Jean Chrétien.

References
"Canada's Tories Name a
    Woman as New Premier."
    New York Times. 14 June
    1993: A1, A4.
Clayton, Mark. "Canada's
Campbell Turns to the Race Ahead." *Christian Science Monitor*. 15 June
    1993: 6.
————. "Kim Campbell Sets Out to Show She's No 'Kim Mulroney.'"
    Christian Science Monitor. 25 August 1993: 3.
Farnsworth, Clyde H. "How Women Moved Up in Canada." *New York
    Times*. 20 June 1993: E5.
Jones, Clayton. "Security Issues Crowd Agenda at Tokyo Summit."
    Christian Science Monitor. 9 July 1993: 1, 4.

Candace
*Traditional name for a dynasty of queens who ruled Meroë, Ethiopia, and
Kush. Also see Amanishakhete, whom Romans called Candace.*

Candace
Queen of Ethiopia and Meroë (42–52)

This particular Queen Candace is said to have learned of the new religion called Christianity from her treasurer, who had made a pilgrimage to Jerusalem and there had been baptized by Philip the Apostle. The episode is depicted in the book of Acts in the New Testament, where the treasurer is described as "a eunuch of great authority under Candace, queen of the Ethiopians, who had the charge of all her treasures, and had come to Jerusalem to worship."

References
de Villiers, Marq, and Sheila Hirtle. *Into Africa*. Toronto: Key Porter
    Books, 1997. p. 340.

Peters, F. E. *The Harvest of Hellenism.* New York: Barnes & Noble Books, 1996. p. 389.

Cartimandua
Queen, Ruler of Brigantia (41–60)

The Brigantes were a large northern British tribe during the time of the Roman invasion of Britain. Cartimandua's consort and sometimes adversary was Venutius, who had ambitions to rule on his own. In A.D. 43, when the Romans invaded Britain, in a Celtic practice known as *celsine,* she signed a treaty placing herself under Roman protection. Her decision was very unpopular with the Brigantes, who launched a series of revolts against her. In A.D. 48 she was forced to call on her Roman protectors to quell a rebellion. When Caratacus, Welsh leader of an unsuccessful anti-Roman rebellion, approached Queen Cartimandua seeking asylum and an alliance, the queen, in a display of loyalty designed to buy Roman favor, had him arrested and turned him over to the Romans in chains. Her husband called her a traitor and began rallying support for her overthrow. In A.D. 57 he attempted to seize control of the government, but the Romans again intervened on her behalf. The couple eventually reconciled and ruled jointly for a while. Then Queen Cartimandua ran off with Vellocatus, the royal armor bearer. Venutius and his troops gave chase, but again her Roman allies came to her rescue. Eventually in ca. A.D. 69, she abandoned the Brigantes altogether, and without her tie with the Romans, Vellocatus was powerless to prevent takeover. In 71, in a battle against the Roman general Venutius, Vellocatus and the Brigantes were defeated, and Rome annexed Brigantia.

References
Chadwick, Nora. *The Celts.* Harmondsworth, Middlesex: Penguin Books, 1976. p. 65.

Hubert, Henri. *The Greatness and Decline of the Celts.* New York: Arno Press, 1980. p. 159.

Markdale, Jean. *Women of the Celts.* Trans. A. Mygind et al. Rochester, VT: Inner Traditions International, 1986. p. 32.

Rutherford, Ward. *Celtic Mythology.* Wellingborough, Northamptonshire: The Aquarian Press, 1987. p. 31.

Catalinda d' Albret
Queen of Navarre (1483–1484), Co-ruler (1484–1516)

Catalinda d' Albret (or Catherine de Foix) was the grandaughter of Eleanor (Leonor, r. 1479) and Gaston IV of Foix. She succeeded her brother Fransesco Febo (Francis Febus, r. 1479–1483), who had married her mother, Eleanor (Leonore), grandaughter of John II of Aragon and Dona Blanca of Navarre. Catalinda married Jean d'Albret ca. 1502, and they had a son, Henry II, born in 1503. In 1512 King Ferdinand's troops succeeded in forcing southern Navarre to be annexed to Aragon and Castile, thus all but eliminating the throne of Navarre. She said to her husband at the time, "If we had been born you Catherine and I Don Jean, we would not have lost our kingdom." Catalinda died in 1516, and Henry became heir to the house of Albret claim. He gathered French forces and in 1521 invaded Navarre, intent on freeing it. He was defeated in his attempt; however, in 1530 Charles I of Spain, of his free will, ceded portions of Navarre back to Henry.

References

Carpenter, Clive. *The Guinness Book of Kings, Rulers & Statesmen.* Enfield, Middlesex: Guinness Superlatives 1978. p. 222.

Morby, John E. *Dynasties of the World.* Oxford: Oxford University Press, 1989. p. 115.

Caterina Sforza
Effective Ruler of Forli and Imola (1488–1500)

Caterina Sforza was born in 1462, the illegitimate daughter of Galeazza Maria Sforza, later duke of Milan, and his mistress. Reared by her grandmother, Cianca Vistonti-Sforza, Caterina received an excellent education. Her father was assassinated in 1476. In 1477 Caterina was married by proxy to Girolamo Riario of the Ordelaffi family, a nephew of Pope Sextus IV. When Venetian forces attempted to occupy her husband's lands in Forli, Caterina defended them in his absence (1483). When Sextus died, Caterina, seven months pregnant, held the fortress of Sant' Angelo until the new pope could arrive to take possession. During her husband's illness, she ruled Forli for him. In 1488 her husband was killed by the Orsi family, but she made the Orsi pay dearly, in public executions, mutilations, and dismemberings. While ruling on behalf of her son, she had to fight off neighbors, papal claims, and even the French. Her children were held hostage at one time, but she, being pregnant again, refused to yield the castle, explaining that she could always make more babies. Caterina took many lovers over the years. In 1489 her affair with Mario Ordelaffi so scandalized the pope that he used her conduct as an excuse to attempt to award her lands to his own son, whose conduct was no better. One of her lovers, Giacomo Feo, of whom her legitimate son was jealous, had been speared to death and mutilated by a cohort of her son's. She had the killer, his wife, and sons thrown down a well to drown (1495). Her second husband was Giovanni d'Medici (not the pope), son of

Pierofrancesco d'Medicis. In 1498 she had a son by Giovanni. The son, Giovanni Della Banda Nera (John of the Black Bands), became the greatest military leader of all the d'Medicis. In 1499, following the Treaty of Blois between France and Venice, the controversial and notorious Pope Alexander VI, citing a papal bull designating Caterina as a "daughter of iniquity," decided that was grounds for giving her lands to his son, Cesare

Caterina Sforza (Corbis-Bettmann)

Borgia. Caterina did not plan to give up without a fight; Borgia was acting captain general of the papal army and was aided by a large contingent of French troops, so she was aware that her chances of holding them off and surviving were slim. She wrote her uncle, "Should I perish, I want to perish like a man." Instead, she was captured in 1500 and repeatedly raped and sodomized for a year by Borgia's soldiers. She was released in 1501 and died in 1509.

References

Breisach, Ernest. *Caterina Sforza: A Renaissance Virago.* Chicago: University of Chicago Press, 1967.

Hare, Christopher. *The Most Illustrious Ladies of the Italian Renaissance.* Williamstown, MA: Corner House Publishers, 1972. pp. 36, 135, 229–256.

Catherine
Countess, Ruler of Vendôme (1374–1412)

Catherine was the daughter of Count Bouchard VI and Jeanne de Castile. When her father died in 1366, her mother and her brother, Count Bouchard VII, ruled Vendôme jointly until his death in 1374. Catherine married Jean de Bourbon and bore a son, Louis I de Bourbon. She succeeded her brother and ruled until her death in 1412. Her son, Louis I, succeeded her.

References

Egan, Edward W., Constance B. Hintz, and L. F. Wise, eds. *Kings, Rulers, and Statesmen.* New York: Sterling Publishing, 1876. p. 162.

Catherine I
Empress of Russia (1725–1727)

Catherine (or Ekaterina I Alekseyevna) was born Marta Skowronska, the daughter of Lithuanian peasants, in ca. 1683 in Marienburg, now Malbork, Poland. Orphaned when she was three years old, she was reared by a Lutheran minister who later made her his servant, an inauspicious beginning for a future empress. Her chief attribute was her beauty, and that alone, plus a misfortune of war, changed her fortunes. However, her more durable attributes were her intelligence, her diplomacy, and her ambition, and these would prove to be more valuable as she rose to prominence. During the Great Northern War, Russian troops swept through Marienburg, and Marta was taken prisoner by Marshal Boris Sheremetev, who made her his mistress. When he tired of her, she was handed over to a close adviser to Peter I, Prince Aleksandr Menshikov. Peter had put aside his wife, Eudoxia, banishing her to a nunnery, and it was not long before he took notice of Marta. She became his mistress in 1702 and the following year bore a son. The tsar set about making his heir more palatable to the court by having Marta received into the Orthodox Church and rechristened Catherine Alekseyevna. For the next nine years Catherine was Peter's companion, bearing many children, only two of whom, Elizabeth and Anna, survived past infancy. Peter, already having a legitimate heir in Alexis, his son by Eudoxia, and having no sons by Catherine, felt no need to marry her. In addition, his first wife still loomed in the background, having first taken vows and then rescinded them. However, in 1712, after some pressure from the outside, Peter and Catherine were married. In 1718 Alexis was implicated in a conspiracy against the crown, and Peter had him condemned to death, possibly by torturing. When Peter was well past fifty, he consented to allow Catherine to be crowned empress consort of Russia (1724). When he died nine months later without naming an heir, Menshikov and his other advisers, whose cases she had often supported before Peter, now supported her candidacy. She was declared sovereign of Russia "according to the desires of Peter the Great" by the senate and the Holy Synod, which had controlled the government during her husband's reign. She soon began to transfer control into a new governing body of her own design, the Supreme Privy Council, which effectively robbed the synod of its power. This council, formed to deal with "matters of exceptional significance," was comprised of six members, chiefly Menshikov, her former lover, and five others. During her reign, which lasted only two years and three months,

Menshikov remained the most influential member of the government. Shortly before her death, at the urging of her advisers, she named Peter's twelve-year-old grandson, Pyotr (Peter) Alekseyevich, as heir to the throne and sanctioned his marriage to Menshikov's daughter. She died in 1727 in St. Petersburg. Her daughter, Elizabeth, would later become empress, and Anna's son, Peter III, would later become tsar.

References

Dvornik, Francis. *The Slavs in European History and Civilization.* New Brunswick, NJ: Rutgers University Press, 1962. pp. 517, 533–534, 542.

Riasnovsky, Nicholas V. *A History of Russia.* Oxford: Oxford University Press, 1963, 1993. pp. 238–239, 243.

Catherine II the Great
Tsarina or Empress of Russia (1762–1796)

Catherine II (or Ekaterina II Alekseyevna) was born Princess Sophia Augusta Frederica in 1729 in Stettin, Anhalt-Zerbst, a small kingdom in Prussia. She was the daughter of Prince Karl Augustus and Joanna Elizabeth. Joanna was an indifferent mother; being vain and envious of the bond between father and daughter, she convinced Sophia that she was far homelier than she actually was. Smart, astute, self-disciplined, and energetic, Sophia concentrated on other interests than attracting suitors. Elizabeth I of Russia, looking for a suitable mate for her scrawny, pocked fifteen-year-old nephew/heir Peter (Prince Karl Peter Ulrich of Holstein-Gottorp), chose Sophia when she was only fourteen and not the beauty she was later to become. In the winter of 1743, Sophia, ambitious but ill prepared to become a tsaritsa (ruler's wife) by education or possessions (three shabby dresses in a half-filled trunk), traveled secretly with her mother to meet her future husband. At the Russian border, the party was met with a welcoming escort that paraded all the way to Moscow with much fanfare. In the beautiful Elizabeth, Sophia found the kindness that her own mother had never shown; the young girl idolized the empress and from the very first day tried to emulate her. Taking the name Catherine, she converted to Russian Orthodoxy and threw herself zealously into preparing for her role, studying and mastering Russian, a language her future husband (who was German) never bothered to learn.

The couple was married a year later, and Elizabeth personally escorted them to the marriage chamber and dressed the bride for bed. But the groom did not respond to the challenge, then or for years to

come; desultory and immature, he spent much of his time playing with toy soldiers. Catherine became a tall and slender beauty but was still an untouched maiden eight years later. Elizabeth, convinced that Peter was impotent, arranged for a clandestine lover for Catherine. However, once she had become pregnant and delivered a son, Catherine was again ignored. For years she could only see her child by appointment. At thirty, she took a lover, Gregory Orlov, a handsome war hero five years her junior, an officer in the imperial guard. Eventually she bore a child by him.

Upon Elizabeth's death, Peter, who refused to observe a period of mourning, began a disastrous reign of six months, during which he ended the war against his beloved Prussia and forced France and Austria to do likewise, restoring to Frederick the Great the lands he had lost. Still obsessed by his toy soldiers, he dressed his guards in Prussian-like uniforms. During Orthodox church services he would stick his tongue out at the priests. He then decided to have Catherine arrested and to divorce her so that he could marry his mistress, Elizabeth Woronotsov.

Catherine, near to term with Orlov's child, delivered in secret while a servant distracted Peter, who loved fires, by setting fire to his own cottage. Word spread of Peter's intentions, so Orlov spirited Catherine away to an army barracks, where she begged for protection. The soldiers rushed to kiss her hands, calling her savior. She was sworn in as empress on the spot. Peter was arrested and killed by a brother of Orlov.

Catherine II assembled more than 500 leaders and scholars, gave them each extracts from Montesquieu's *The Spirit of Laws,* and charged them with reform of the government. However, she later disbanded the commission and actually increased her own power. Her action was probably the direct cause of the 1917 revolution, although in later years of her reign she was to become more lenient. During her reign Russia became a world power. As a result of two wars with Turkey, Russia gained the Crimea and an outlet to the Black Sea. Its image as a barbaric state receded further as she established the Russian Academy and encouraged the arts, belatedly bringing the Renaissance to Russia. She became the protectoress of the philosopher Denis Diderot, chief editor of the *Encyclopedie*, the most important publishing enterprise of the century. She had Voltaire to visit in Russia; he had, in fact, advised her to take up arms and drive the Turks from Europe.

During the time of the Turkish wars, Catherine took a Crimean general, Gregory Potemkin, as lover. Well into old age, she took yet another lover, Platon Zubov, who was forty years younger than she. She ruled for thirty-four years. Her son, Paul I, who should have been Peter's successor, did not come to the throne until he was forty-four years old and ruled only five years. The other rightful heir, Ivan VI, who held the crown briefly as an infant before Elizabeth's rule, was imprisoned, never knowing his real identity. Catherine gave orders that if he became ill, he was not to be given medical treatment. He was eventually stabbed by a jailor during an escape attempt. She died in 1796 of a stroke at the age of sixty-seven. Among her papers was found her credo: "Be gentle, humane, accessible, compassionate and liberal-minded. Do not let your grandeur prevent you from being condescending with kindness toward the small and putting yourself in their place. . . . Behave so that the kind love you, the evil fear you, and all respect you."

References

Coughlan, Robert. *Elizabeth and Catherine.* New York: G. P. Putnam's Sons, 1974.

Durant, Will and Ariel. *The Story of Civilization.* Vol. 9, *The Age of Voltaire.* New York: Simon & Schuster, 1965. pp. 216, 360, 477–479, 510, 516, 575, 606, 644, 646, 665, 675, 679, 730, 733, 744, 774, 776, 779, 785.

Oldenbourg, Zoe. *Catherine the Great.* New York: Pantheon Books, 1965.

Catherine Cornaro
Regent Ruler of Jerusalem (on Cyprus) (1473–1489)

Catherine Cornaro was a Venetian noblewoman married to James II, bastard of the house of Lusignon, who ruled Cyprus from 1460 to

1473 and who had also become archbishop of Nicosia. When Jerusalem's ruling Lusignon family was driven from the mainland in 1291, it had retreated to Cyprus, but it still claimed to be rulers of the kingdom of Jerusalem. Catherine and James had a son, James III, who was too young to rule when his father died in 1473. Catherine and her son remained in Venice; from there she ruled for her son, who died only a year later. She continued to rule in the queen's name from Venice until 1489, when, partly by gift and partly by extortion, she deeded Cyprus to Venice and abdicated. Cyprus remained a Venetian possession until 1570.

References

Langer, William L., ed. *World History.* Boston: Houghton Mifflin, 1980. p. 279.

Catherine de Foix
See Catalinda d' Albret

Catherine de Médicis
Regent of France (1552, 1560–1563, and 1574)

Catherine de Médicis was born in 1519, the daughter of Lorenzo de' Medici, duke of Urbino, and Madelaine de la Tour d'Auvergne, a Bourbon princess. Catherine was the great-granddaughter of Lorenzo Il Magnifico, one of the greatest Italian leaders of all time. She was also the niece of Pope Clement VII. Her parents died when she was very young, and she was reared by nuns in Florence and Rome, who gave her an excellent education. In a prearranged marriage, she wed Henry, duke d'Orleans, in 1533, at the age of fourteen. Catherine had no children until she was twenty-four, and Henry took a mistress, Diane de Poitiers, who had a great influence on him and his affairs for the rest of his life. Catherine remained in the background from then until his death and only made her influence felt on the occasion of his absence when she received her first appointment as regent. In 1543, Catherine gave birth to a son who later became Francis II. She bore nine or ten children in all, seven of whom lived. Three of her sons became kings of France, and two of her daughters became queens of Spain. In 1547 Henry became King Henry II, ruler of France. In 1552 he went off to continue his father's war against the Holy Roman emperor Charles V, and Catherine was appointed

Catherine de Médicis (Erich Lessing / Art Resource, NY)

regent. In 1559 Henry was killed by the splinter of a broken lance while jousting. Francis II came to the throne but ruled less than two years. He was succeeded by his brother, Charles IX, a boy of ten, in 1560. Catherine, a devout Catholic, became regent of France, to the despair of the Huguenots, the Protestants. Her greatest challenge was the animosity between Catholics and Protestants, which her Edict of Toleration was aimed at alleviating. In 1561 Jean Nicot brought back from Portugal an American import, a new herb for the queen's use in treating wounds and ulcers. Called the "Queen's herb," it was later called tobacco. In 1562 the first of the Wars of Religion erupted in France. Catherine presided over three civil wars in a decade. Charles was declared of age when he reached thirteen, but he remained under her domination for the rest of his life. She tried playing off the parties of the Protestant Condés against the Catholic Guises, entering into a plot with the Guises to rid the country completely of the Huguenots. She is traditionally blamed for inducing Charles to order the Massacre of St. Bartholomew's Day in 1572 in which nearly all of the leading Huguenots in Paris were killed. All of Europe was scandalized by the bloodthirsty loss of life. Charles himself was guilt ridden over the ghastly massacre and died within two years, the victim of tuberculosis. In 1572 Catherine proposed her third and favorite son, Henry, for the throne of Poland, and in 1573 he was crowned. After Charles's death in 1574, Catherine again assumed the regency for three months until Henry could be induced to return and be crowned Henry III. Henry was easily persuaded; he abandoned Poland at once.

Catherine did not try to dominate her favorite son, who was considered a fop and a disgrace by the French people. She remained close and did his bidding, including making arduous diplomatic journeys on his behalf even in her later years. In 1589 he died as a result of a stab wound. Catherine died the same year at the age of seventy.

References
Sédillot, René. *An Outline of French History.* Trans. Gerard Hopkins. New York: Alfred A. Knopf, 1952, 1967. pp. 194, 199.
Williamson, Hugh R. *Catherine de' Medici.* New York: Viking Press, 1973.

Catherine of Aragon
Regent of England (1512–1514)

Catherine of Aragon was born in 1485, the second daughter of King Ferdinand II of Aragon and Queen Isabella of Castile. Catherine received an excellent education, particularly for a woman of her day, and was called a "miracle of learning." In 1501 she married Arthur, oldest son of King Henry VII of England, but he died a year later. In 1509 she became the first wife of Arthur's brother, Henry VIII. Unlike many royal couples of arranged marriages, the two appeared devoted on the many occasions when they entertained lavishly, and all might have gone well if Catherine had produced a male heir. During the next nine years she bore six children, but all died except Mary, who later became queen of England (1553–1558). Meanwhile, in 1512 Henry joined his father-in-law in a war against France, and Catherine served as regent in his absence. By 1527, since Catherine had produced no male heir, Henry appealed to Rome for an annulment on the grounds that she was his brother's widow. Catherine countered with an appeal arguing that her first marriage had never been consummated. The pope delayed for years on making a decision. In 1531 Henry separated from his wife and two years later—after his marriage to Anne Boleyn—he had his own archbishop of Canterbury annul his first marriage. Parliament then passed the Act of Supremacy making the king, not the pope, the head of the Church of England.

References
Hudson, M. E, and Mary Clark. *Crown of a Thousand Years.* New York: Crown Publishing, 1978. pp. 77, 78.
Mattingly, Garrett. *Catherine of Aragon.* Cambridge: Cambridge University Press, 1942.
McKendrick, Melveena. *Ferdinand and Isabella.* New York: American Heritage Publishing, 1968. pp. 99, 100, 134, 140.
Myers, A. R. *England in the Late Middle Ages.* Harmondsworth, Middlesex: Penguin Books, 1952. pp. 205, 237.

Catherine of Braganza
*Regent of Portugal
(1704–1705)*

Catherine of Braganza was the daughter of King John IV and Luisa Maria de Guzmán, who married Catherine in 1662 to King Charles II of Great Britain. In the next two decades Catherine was frequently pregnant. She had a number of miscarriages but produced no heir, although Charles had thirteen illegitimate offspring by a parade of mistresses. Catherine eventually returned to Portugal, ashamed of her own inadequacy and unable to tolerate his philandering. When he lay dying in 1685, he asked for his wife, but she sent a message asking that her absence be excused and "to beg his pardon if she had offended him all her life." He answered, "Alas, poor woman! She asks my pardon? I beg hers with all my heart; take her back that answer." Back in Portugal, Catherine made herself useful to the court: In 1704, while her brother was fighting in the War of Spanish Succession, she acted as regent on domestic matters.

References

Hudson, M. E., and Mary Clark. *Crown of a Thousand Years.* New York: Crown Publishing, 1978. p. 105.

Kenyon, J. P. *The Stuarts.* Glasgow: William Collins Sons, 1970. pp. 100–143.

Catherine of Valois
Titular Byzantine Empress (1313–1346, Sole Ruler after 1331)

Catherine of Valois was the daughter of Emperor Charles of Valois and Catherine of Courtenay. As a child, in 1313, she was given in marriage to Philip of Tarentum (or Tarento). They became co-rulers upon Charles's death in 1313. Catherine gave birth to three sons. Philip died in 1331, and Catherine ruled alone. In 1337, she also became ruler of the principality of Antioch. At her instigation, the governor of Dyrrachium stirred up a revolt in favor of the deposed

Despot Nicrophoros. Upon her death in 1346, her second son, Robert II, succeeded her.

References

Langer, William L., ed. *World History.* Boston: Houghton Mifflin, 1980. p. 282.

Ostrogorsky, George. *History of the Byzantine State.* New Brunswick, NJ: Rutgers University Press, 1969. pp. 497, 508, 510.

Ceccoli, Edda
Co-captain-regent of San Marino (1991–1992 and 1998)

The Most Serene Republic of San Marino, which lays claim to being the oldest independent republic in Europe, is completely surrounded by Italy, with which it has had a treaty of friendship since 1862. The republic is governed by co-captains-regent who are elected from the parliamentary body for a term of six months only and cannot be re-elected in less than three-year intervals.

Edda Ceccoli, elected to a five-year term in the Great and Good Council, the legislative branch of the government, was then elected by that body as co-captain-regent in October 1991. In this position, for a period of six months, she presided over the ten-member Congress of State, the executive branch of the government. She was re-elected for another five-year term to the Great and Good Council, and in April 1998, that body again named her co-captain-regent.

References

Delury, George, ed. *The World Almanac and Book of Facts.* New York: Newspaper Enterprise Association, 1992. pp. 573–574.

Famighetti, Robert. *The World Almanac and Book of Facts.* Mahwah, NJ: K-III Reference Corporation, 1998. p. 815.

Chamorro, Violeta Barrios de
President of Nicaragua (1990–1996)

Born Violeta Barrios in Rivas, Nicaragua, in 1929, she was the daughter of a wealthy cattle baron and his wife. She received her education in women's colleges in Texas and Virginia. At the age of twenty she married Pedro Juaquín Chamorro Cardenal, who became editor of the family newspaper *La Prensa* in 1952. The couple had four children: Pedro Juaquín, Claudia, Carlos Fernando, and Cristina. Chamorro Cardenal's crusades against Anastasio Somoza's regime resulted in the editor's imprisonment in 1956. After he was exiled to a remote village, he escaped to Puerto Rico, where Violeta and the children joined him and where the family lived for several years.

In 1978, while Violeta was in Miami, Chamorro Cardenal was assassinated. Violeta took over directorship of *La Prensa* that year and entered politics the following year, becoming one of five members of a revolutionary junta that brought Daniel Ortega Saavedra into power. Two of her children, Claudia and Carlos Fernando, took an active part in the revolution. But after nine months, Violeta Chamorro left the government, claim-

ing that what had promised to be a pluralistic democratic government had instead become a Marxist Communist government. Part of her husband's family broke away from *La Prensa* to form a pro-government newspaper, *El Nuevo Diario,* and Violeta Chamorro directed *La Prensa,* which became the focus of opposition to the Sandinista government. Two of her children, Pedro Juaquín and Cristina, followed her, while the other two remained in the Sandinista camp.

In 1990 a fourteen-party coalition chose Violeta Chamorro to be its candidate in a democratic election for president of Nicaragua. On February 15, 1990, she became the first woman to be elected president of a nation in the Western hemisphere.

After one year in office, her only solid accomplishment was bringing peace and a semblance of democracy to a country long ravaged by civil war and dictatorship. However, the economy, left in ruins by the Sandinistas, had continued to disintegrate.

By the summer of 1993, Chamorro had come under such intense political pressure both in Nicaragua and abroad that political observers wondered whether she would be able to finish the remaining three years of her term. Her government faced almost insurmountable problems as a result of a depressed economy, the accelerating guerrilla activity, and hostile political opposition from both extremes. Critics accused her of detachment, leaving government details to her controversial son-in-law and chief of staff, Antonio Lacayo. In public she continued to display a sense of humor and dignity, trademarks of

Nicaragua's first family, which has been compared to the Kennedy family in the United States.

In February 1995 Chamorro and the National Assembly began arguing over constitutional reforms. In June, she and the legislators finally agreed on a number of reforms she had requested, and the assembly approved her choices for Supreme Court judgeships.

In the months prior to the election in 1996, Chamorro and her supporters formed a new party, the National Project, one of whose goals was to overthrow the nepotism law that prohibited her son-in-law, Lacayo, from running for president in 1996. Former Sandinista vice president Sergio Ramírez, new leader of a breakaway party called the Renewed Sandinista Movement, agreed to back the removal of the law and allow Lacayo to run "in the interests of social peace."

Violeta Chamorro retired in 1996.

References

Constable, Pamela. "Nicaragua's Change Slow under Chamorro." *Houston Chronicle,* 28 April 1991: 23A.

Krauss, Clifford. "Bush's Uneasy Welcome for Violeta Chamorro." *New York Times,* 4 April 1991: 3E.

"Maneuvers at the Top." *World Press Review.* August 1995. p. 26.

Trotta, Dan. "Chamorro's Days Numbered in Nicaragua?" *Houston Chronicle,* 1 August 1993: 28A.

Who's Who in the World 1997. New Providence, RI: Marquis Who's Who/ Reed Elsevier, 1996. p. 238.

Charles, Mary Eugenia
Prime Minister of Dominica (1980–1995)

The granddaughter of former slaves, the daughter of John Baptiste and Josephine Delauney Charles was born in 1919 in Pointe Michel, Dominica. Dominica, an island in the Caribbean, was a British possession at that time. Her father, who lived to be 107 years old, was founder of the Penney Bank. Mary Eugenia received a B.A. degree from the University of Canada and studied law at the London School of Economics and Political Science. In 1949 she returned to Dominica, the first woman lawyer on the island. She became interested in politics in 1968 while fighting a sedition law that stifled dissent. She was appointed to the legislature in 1970 and to the house of assembly in 1975. There she became leader of the opposition. It was partly through the efforts of the Dominica Freedom Party, which she cofounded, that Dominica gained independence from Great Britain in 1978. In the election of 1980 her party gained the majority, and she became prime minister. Charles instituted immediate measures of economic reform. She set about corraling the tax evaders and putting an end to governmental corruption. In 1985 she won a second five-year term and was also made minister of foreign affairs, finance, economic affairs, and defense. Her primary concern was improving the quality of life for her people. "We should give the people not luxury but a little comfort—a job, the

Mary Eugenia Charles (UPI/ Corbis-Bettmann)

means to build a house, assistance for agricultural pursuits," she said in an interview. "We will never be rich, but I think we can be a self-reliant nation with a little thrift and a little development." To that end Charles sought to encourage tourism to some extent, but she was adamant about preserving the island's ecology and national identity. Dominica has no casinos, no night clubs, no duty-free shops, and Charles had no intention of encouraging them. "We want to bring in the kind of tourists who like what we already have here. We especially are encouraging naturalists. . . . We don't want hordes of tourists who expect to go to night clubs every night," she told an interviewer. She was described as a no-nonsense leader, a pragmatist. A strict constitutionalist, she was considered by her colleagues to be a brilliant lawyer and a savvy politician "with considerable charm." Of women's rights on her island, Charles said, "In Dominica, we really live women's lib. We don't have to expound it." It was Eugenia Charles who petitioned President Ronald Reagan's help against Cuban infiltration of Grenada, which led to the U.S. invasion of Grenada in 1983.

Charles, who has been called "the Iron Woman of the Caribbean," served two terms as prime minister, retiring in 1995.

References

International Who's Who 1987–1988. New Providence, RI: Reed Elsevier, 1997. p 256.

Moritz, Charles, ed. *Current Biography Yearbook, 1986.* New York: H. W. Wilson, 1986. pp. 88–91.

Okey, Roberta. "Trekking Nature's Terrarium." *Americas.* September/
   October 1987: 8–13.
Sanders, Charles L. "Interview." *Ebony.* January 1981: 16.
Walter, Greg. "Interview." *People.* November 1983: 20, 46.
Who's Who in the World 1997. New Providence, RI: Marquis Who's
   Who/ Reed Elsevier, 1996. p. 243.

Charlotte
Queen of Kingdom of Jerusalem (Cyprus) (1458–1464)

Charlotte was the elder daughter of John II, who ruled the remnants of the kingdom of Jerusalem, located on Cyprus, from 1432 to 1458. She married Louis of Savoy. When her father died in 1458 she ruled alone for two years and then shared the rule with her younger brother, James II. In 1464 she was deposed, when James came of age. James died in 1473, and his wife Catherine Cornaro ruled from Italy until her abdication in 1489, but Charlotte continued to exercise authority until her death in 1487.

References
Langer, William L., ed. *World History.* Boston: Houghton Mifflin, 1980.
   p. 279.

Charlotte
Grand Duchess, Ruler of Luxembourg (1919–1964)

Born Josephine-Charlotte in 1896, she was the daughter of Duke William IV. Her older sister was Maríe-Adelaïde, whom Charlotte succeeded in 1919. Marie-Adélaïde had been forced to abdicate during the German occupation of Luxembourg during World War I. In December 1918 the Chamber of Deputies (parliament) voted to continue the existence of the grand duchy of Luxembourg, and Charlotte became its ruler, thwarting a coalition of liberals and socialists that attempted to bring an end to the dynasty and unite Luxembourg with Belgium. Luxembourg then joined the League of Nations. Charlotte married Prince Felix of Bourbon, and in 1921 the future grand duke Jean was born. In 1922 Luxembourg concluded economic union with Belgium, but it was not until 1925 that French occupation troops were finally withdrawn from the land. In 1932, an agreement was made at the Ouchy Convention for the gradual reduction of economic barriers among Belgium, Luxembourg, and The Netherlands. Luxembourg enjoyed a period of relative prosperity under Charlotte until May 1940, when the Germans again invaded and occupied the country. Charlotte and her family fled to England and then to Canada, where they remained until U.S. troops liberated their country in September 1944. It was a more worldly Charlotte who returned to rule. In 1947 the grand duchy joined the Benelux union, and the following year it officially abandoned its long-held policy of "eternal neutrality." The country joined the North Atlantic Pact in 1949 and participated in the European Economic Community. On May 26, 1964, in one of Charlotte's last official duties, she joined with

Charlotte, Grand Duchess of Luxembourg (UPI/Corbis-Bettmann)

President Charles de Gaulle of France and President Heinrich Luebke of Germany in opening the Moselle Canal. In 1964 she abdicated in favor of her son, Grand Duke Jean, who presided over a duchy now firmly committed to cooperation with the rest of the European community.

References

Carpenter, Clive. *The Guinness Book of Kings, Rulers & Statesmen.* Enfield, Middlesex: Guinness Superlatives. p. 165.

Newcomer, James. *The Grand Duchy of Luxembourg.* Lanham, MD: University Press of America, 1984. p. 16.

Langer, William L., ed. *World History.* Boston: Houghton Mifflin, 1980. pp. 986, 1180, 1198.

Cheng-Chun
Empress, De Facto Co-ruler of China (48 B.C. to A.D. 13)

Cheng-Chun (also Wang Cheng-Chun) was a member of the Wang family, which had come to dominate the two-hundred-year-old Han Dynasty. She was married to Emperor Yuan Ti and came to the throne in 48 B.C. The couple had a son, Ch'eng Ti. When Yuan Ti died in 32 B.C., she was given the title of empress dowager, which carried much power and influence. She exercised her powers not only through her own office but also through those of her relatives. Ch'eng Ti reigned from 32 to 7 B.C., during which time the empress dowager appointed four of her relatives as his regents. She had eight brothers or half brothers, five of whom were appointed in succession to the equivalent of prime minister. She also bestowed titles of nobility upon a number of other relatives. She introduced changes in the state religious cults in an effort to secure blessings from various spiritual powers. Ch'eng Ti had several wives, and to please his favorite, he had his two sons by two other wives put to death. Therefore, he had no heir at the time of his own untimely death—probably murder—in 7 B.C. With her son's death, Cheng-Chun's influence waned, for Ai Ti, who succeeded him, was not of the Wang family. He tried to appease other families, primarily the Ting and Fu families, by assigning them court appointments against Cheng-Chun's judgment. The influence of the Wang family was thus diluted but was saved from further dilution by Ai Ti's death in 1 B.C. after only a five-year reign. Following Ai Ti's death, the empress summoned her nephew, Wang Mang, to the capital. A young boy, Ping Ti, had been chosen to become emperor, and the empress dowager chose Wang Mang to serve as regent. Wang Mang was an astute politician. When Ping died five years later—probably from poisoning—Wang Mang selected a one-year-old baby from more than fifty possible candidates, all legal heirs. In this way Wang Mang could be named acting emperor. Three years later he made himself emperor, declaring that Heaven had mandated that he establish a new dynasty, the Hsin Dynasty. Empress Cheng-Chun died in A.D. 13, distressed to see what she believed to be the end of the Han Dynasty, but confident that the Wang family name and influence would live on.

References

Langer, William L., ed. *World History.* Boston: Houghton Mifflin, 1940, 1980. p.146.

Latourette, Kenneth Scott. *The Chinese: Their History and Culture.* New York: Macmillan, 1934.

Morton, W. Scott. *China: Its History and Culture.* New York: McGraw-Hill, 1982. p. 57.

Reischauer, Edwin O., and John K. Fairbank. *East Asia: The Great Tradition.* Boston: Houghton Mifflin, 1960. p. 117.

Chindók Yówang
Queen of the Kingdom of Silla (647–654)

Silla, established in the third or fourth century, was originally located in South Korea. By the seventh century, it encompassed the entire Korean peninsula. Chindók, a cousin of Queen Sóndók (r. 632–647), came to the throne upon Sóndók's death to perpetuate the "hallowed-bone" lineage. This term refers to the institution that existed in Silla called "bone rank," or hereditary bloodlines, of which there were two. The "hallowed-bone" status was reserved for those in the royal house of Kim who possessed the qualifications to rule. The "true-bone" rank was held by members of the Kim royal house who lacked (originally) qualifications to rule.

Chindók continued her predecessor's alliance with China, whose influence was felt throughout the kingdom. During her reign, she adopted not only the literary culture of the T'ang Dynasty but its clothing fashions as well. She also began to use the Chinese calendar. Her state minister was Chukjvrang, a member of the organization of warriors called Hwarang. Considered uniquely competent, he continued as state minister under the three kings who followed her.

Chindók was the last of the "hallowed-bone" rulers and the last to preside over a divided Korean peninsula. Her successor, T'aejong, King Muyól Wang, of "true-bone" lineage, came to the throne after suppressing a rebellion of the head of the Council of Nobles and prevailing over his closest rival for kingship. During his reign, he consolidated the Korean peninsula under Silla's rule (668).

References

Lee, Ki-baik. *A New History of Korea.* Trans. Edward W. Wanger, with Edward J. Schulz. Cambridge: Harvard University Press, 1984. pp. 49–50, 74, 390.

Lee, Peter, trans. "Samguk Sagi," section 47, stanzas 437–438. In *Sourcebook of Korean Civilization VI.* New York: Columbia University Press, 1993. pp. 105–106.

Chinsóng Yówang
Queen of Silla (887–897)

Silla, first established in South Korea in the third or fourth century, had, by Queen Chinsóng's time, grown to encompass the entire Korean peninsula. Chinsóng was the daughter of Hón'gang Wang (r. 875–886) and the sister of Chónggang Wang, who succeeded his father but died after ruling only one year. Chinsóng presided over a Silla in decline. Her attempts to collect taxes were hampered by local warlords, who ignored her emissaries.

In addition, there was cautious growing unrest about the outdated entrenched class system. Confucianists made veiled criticisms of Silla's antiquated ranking system for royalty. One such protester, Wang Kó-in, was arrested and charged with having criticized the government by using language with hidden meaning. Another, Ch'oe Ch'i-wón, a renowned scholar, submitted a detailed proposal to the queen, suggesting changes aimed at dealing with problems besetting the realm. When his proposals were rejected out of hand, he went into self-imposed exile away from the capital.

Queen Chinsóng is remembered for having commissioned the monk Taegu and the high courtier Wihong to compile an anthology of *hyangga,* a poetic genre with themes having to do with religious practices in general and Buddhism in particular. The resulting collection, "Samdae mok" (Collection of Hyangga from the Three Periods of Silla History), has not survived.

One of the disgruntled warlords managed a successful rebellion against Chinsóng. She was succeeded by a cousin, Hyongong Wang (r. 897–912).

References

Lee, Ki-baik. *A New History of Korea.* Trans. Edward W. Wagner, with Edward J. Schulz. Cambridge: Harvard University Press, 1984. pp. 85–86, 94, 106, 391.

Christina
Queen of Sweden (1632–1654)

Christina was born in 1626 in Stockholm, the daughter of King Gustavus Adolphus and Maria Eleonora of Brandenburg. She succeeded her father when she was only six years old, although she was not crowned until 1644. Her chief regent was Axel Oxenstierna. Witty and bright, she was particularly well schooled: Descartes, for example, taught her philosophy. Under her reign education flourished, the first newspaper was established (1645), local rule was broadened, and industry was encouraged. Over the objection of Oxenstierna, she sought an end to the Thirty Years' War and was instrumental in concluding the Peace of Westphalia in 1648. She was easily persuaded to delegate her duties and give away crown lands. In 1654 she secretly became a convert to Roman Catholi-

Christina (Perry-Castaneda Library)

cism—forbidden in Sweden—and shocked her constituents by abdicating in favor of her cousin Charles X Gustavus. She moved to Paris and immersed herself in the literate and scientific communities and became a popular patroness of the arts. In such a stimulating atmosphere, she began taking a belated interest in affairs of state. She made vain attempts to obtain the crowns of both Naples and Poland, and when her cousin Charles X died in 1160, she vainly attempted to regain the Swedish throne. But the firmly entrenched state's ministers were set against her, primarily because of her Catholicism. She continued her associations with a brilliant entourage of friends and wrote a number of works, including her autobiography. She formed an intimate liason with Cardinal Decio Azzolino, even naming him her heir. She died in Rome in 1689 at the age of sixty-three. Azzolino died only two months later.

References

Derry, T. K. *A History of Scandinavia.* Minneapolis: University of Minnesota Press, 1979. pp. 120, 128–131.

Egan, Edward W., Constance B. Hintz, and L. F. Wise, eds. *Kings, Rulers, and Statesmen.* New York: Sterling Publishing, 1976. p. 449.

Masson, Georgina. *Queen Christina.* New York: Farrar, Straus & Giroux, 1969.

Trevor-Roper, Hugh. *The Golden Age of Europe.* New York: Bonanza/Crown, 1987. pp. 32, 126, 140, 144, 174.

Christine of France
Duchess, Regent of Savoy (1638–1648)

Christine was the daughter of Henry IV, king of France from 1589 to 1610, and his second wife, Marie de' Médicis. Christine married Victor Amadeus I of Savoy and bore three children: Francis Hyacinth; Henrietta, who married Ferdinand of Bavaria; and Charles Emmanuel II. Savoy was an independent state whose rulers also governed Piedmont. Victor Amadeus I ruled both states from 1630 to 1637. Following his death in 1637, their son Francis acceded to the throne, but civil war broke out. At the end of one year, Christine's younger son, Charles Emmanuel, came to the throne under her capable regency. Although the regency officially ended when he came of age in 1648, in reality Christine continued to dominate him until her death in 1663.

References

Langer, William L., ed. *World History.* Boston: Houghton Mifflin, 1980. pp. 426, 473, 494.

Tansu Çiller
(Courtesy: Turkish
Embassy)

Çiller, Tansu
Prime Minister of Turkey
(1993–1996)

Tansu Çiller was born in Istanbul, Turkey, in 1946. She studied economics at Roberts College (Bosphorus University in Istanbul) and the University of New Hampshire, received a Ph.D. from the University of Connecticut, and did postdoctoral work at Yale. She married Ozer Ucuran Çiller, and they had two children. She returned to Roberts College, where she headed the department of economics from 1976 to 1979. She entered politics in 1990 and in 1991 became the minister of state for economy. In that post, she proposed privatizing mismanaged state enterprises, restricting public spending, and lowering interest rates. Whenever her reforms were criticized, she blamed her opponents within Prime Minister Demirel's administration. Her strong free-market approach gained her the support of the business sector. She served as minister of economy until 1993. With only three years of political experience, in a surprising upset she defeated two long-serving cabinet members at the True Path Party convention in June 1993 and was appointed prime minister. As an English-speaking economist, a woman, and a devout secularist, she seemed the ideal person to counteract the Muslim fundamentalist movement and lead Turkey into the next century. However, in June 1996 the Welfare Party, an Islamic group, came into power in coalition with Çiller's party, forcing her resignation. In 1997 questions were raised as to the source of her wealth. Investigators examined her claim that she inherited more than $1 million in cash and gold from her mother, whom former neighbors described as a penniless pensioner, and also examined the 1992 purchase by her husband's company of $1.5 million in New Hampshire properties. Five coalitions attempted to govern in the next two years, but Çiller maintained strong rightist support, preventing their success.

References
Kinzer, Steven. "Once the Hope of Secular Turks, Ex-Leader Is Now Widely Reviled." *New York Times.* 6 April 1997: 2, 6.

Kohen, Sami. "Turkey's Reform-Minded Premier Faces Stiff
   Opposition." *Christian Science Monitor.* 17 June 1993: p. 7.
Who's Who in the World 1997. New Providence, RI: Marquis/Reed
   Elsevier, 1996. p. 267.

Cixi
Empress of China (1862–1873, 1875–1889, 1898–1908)

Cixi (or Tz'u-hsi) was born in Peking in 1835 and first came to court as a minor concubine to Emperor Xian Feng, who reigned from 1851 to 1862. In 1856 she bore his only son, Tong Zhi. When Xian Feng died in 1862, Cixi contrived, with the emperor's senior consort, Tz'u-an, to become Tong's co-regent. Cixi immediately assumed the dominant role, setting the groundwork for a remarkable career that brought China under her control for fifty years. Ruthless, politically astute, and power hungry, she continued, even after her son attained his maturity, to wield her power over affairs of state. The young emperor was completely dominated by her. He led a dissolute life, which she probably encouraged so as to have a freer rein herself. He died at the age of nineteen, the victim of his own excesses.

Cixi engineered the ascension of her four-year-old nephew, Guang Xu, by adopting him and naming him heir. The tradition of ancestor worship dictated that the next emperor should be of the next generation, which her nephew quite obviously was not, but this fact did not deter Cixi. The two empresses again served as regents until Tz'u-an's sudden death in 1881, possibly by poisoning.

Prince Gong, the principal court official, had instituted some crucial governmental reform measures that Cixi sabotaged whenever she could. In 1884 she dismissed him in favor of Li Hongzhang, who would cooperate with her more fully.

She was particularly fond of the theater. She often attended accompanied by one or both of her two favorite palace eunuchs, who, with her patronage, soon became wealthy and powerful in their own rights, to the disgust of Prince Gong, in particular.

In the late 1880s, urged on by her favorite eunuch and with the help of Li Hongzhang, Cixi appropriated funds from the navy to construct a magnificent summer palace northwest of Peking. There she retired, briefly, in 1889. The only new ship constructed during that time was a marble one, which was placed at the edge of an ornamental lake. Thus the Chinese navy was ill prepared when Japan struck Korea in 1894. China went to the aid of its ally but suffered a humiliating defeat. In 1895 Li Hongzhang was forced to sue for peace.

In 1898 the new young emperor Guang Xu was prevailed upon

Cixi (Archive Photos / Popperphoto)

to institute the far-reaching Hundred Days of Reform. Opposition to the reform rallied around Cixi, and in 1898 she came out of retirement as head of a military coup and had the emperor seized and six of the reformers put to death. She confined the emperor to his quarters for good and again assumed the regency. By 1900 the Boxer Rebellion had reached its peak, and when foreign troops invaded Peking, the court was forced to flee west to Xian. Before she left, out of pure spite, Cixi arranged for one of the emperor's favorites, the Pearl Concubine, to be drowned in a well. Cixi was forced to accept heavy peace terms before she was allowed to return to Peking two years later. Although the emperor Guang was not allowed to participate in the government, Cixi continued to rule, belatedly attempting to implement some of the preposed reforms in an attempt to salvage a crumbling dynasty. The day before she died in 1908, she issued an order for Guang's poisoning and from her deathbed named three-year-old Pu Yi as the new emperor, unable to relinquish the reins of power even at the end.

References

Morton, W. Scott. *China: Its History and Culture.* New York: McGraw-Hill, 1982. pp. 168–175.

Warner, Marina. *The Dragon Empress: Life and Times of Tz'u-hsi (1835–1908).* New York: Atheneum Press, 1986.

Claude
Duchess of Brittany (1514–1524)

Claude was born in 1499, the daughter of Louis XII and Anne, duchess of Brittany (r. 1488–1514), from whom she inherited the duchy. She became its last duchess. She married Francois III, who became Francois I, king of France. Upon her death in 1524, her husband annexed Brittany to France.

References

Carpenter, Clive. *The Guinness Book of Kings, Rulers & Statesmen.* Enfield, Middlesex: Guinness Superlatives, 1978. p. 90.

Claudine
Titular Sovereign of Monaco (1457–1465)

Claudine was born in 1451, the daughter of Catalan Grimaldi. In 1419 her grandfather John Grimaldi of the prominent Genoese family had succeeded in retaking Monaco from the French for the final time. The title of prince or princess of Monaco was not assumed by a Grimaldi until 1659. Claudine became sovereign at the age of six, when Catalan died. In 1465, at the age of fourteen, she married Lambert, who became seigneur. The couple's oldest son, John II, inherited his mother's claim in 1431. She died in 1514.

References

Carpenter, Clive. *The Guinness Book of Kings, Rulers & Statesmen.* Enfield, Middlesex: Guinness Superlatives, 1978. p. 173.

Cleopatra I
Co-ruler (193–181 B.C.), Regent of Egypt (181–173 or 176 B.C.)

Cleopatra was the daughter of Antiochus III, Seleucid king of the Hellenistic Syrian Empire, which had long been at war with Egypt. Her mother was Laodicé, a princess of Pontus. Cleopatra was given in marriage to Ptolemy V Epiphanes in 199 or 196 B.C., but the marriage was not celebrated until 193 B.C. Ptolemy V. Epiphanes ruled from 203–181 B.C. The marriage, a political move as a result of a peace treaty with Antiochus, also made Egypt a protectorate of Seleucia. Cleopatra ruled at Epiphanes's side. In ca. 189 B.C. the couple had a son, who was to become Ptolemy VI Philomater (also Philometor, "loving mother"), and later, a daughter, Cleopatra II. Philomater was still a child when his father was poisoned and died in 181 B.C. at the age of twenty-eight. Cleopatra I became regent and kept an iron grip on the government until her death in 173 B.C. She also taught her son well; Ptolemy VI is mentioned at the Egyptian ruin Kom Ombo as a kind, wise, and tolerant ruler. However, because of what was seen as his cowardice during the war with Antiochus (171–168 B.C.), the people of Alexandria demanded that he include his brother, Ptolemy VII, in his rule. Ptolemy VI's brother eventually expelled him.

References
Langer, William L., ed. *Encyclopedia of World History.* Boston: Houghton Mifflin, 1980. p. 97.
Peters, F. E. *The Harvest of Hellenism.* New York: Barnes & Noble Books, 1996. pp. 178–179, 256, 272fn, 381fn.
Rawlinson, George. *Ancient History.* New York: Barnes & Noble Books, 1993. p. 204, 205.

Cleopatra II
Co-ruler of Egypt (176–130 and again in 118–116 B.C.), Sole Ruler of Upper Egypt (130–118 B.C.)

Cleopatra II was the daughter of Ptolemy V Epiphanes. She married her brother, Ptolemy VI Philomater (or Philometor), who ruled Egypt from 180 to 145 B.C. She became co-ruler and bore him a daughter, Cleopatra III, and a son, Neos Philopater. During the war with Antiochus IV (171–168 B.C.), Philomater displayed such cowardice that thereafter the people of Alexandria insisted that the couple share the rule with their younger brother, Ptolemy VII Euergetes (Physcon). This arrangement lasted until 164, when Euergetes expelled Philomater. To settle the quarrel between the two brothers, the Roman senate restored Philomater, giving him and his wife Egypt to rule and giving Cyrene and Cyprus to Euergetes. In 145 B.C., while on a campaign in Syria, Philomater died. His son was to share the throne with Cleopatra, but Euergetes came back to Egypt, killed Neos Philopater, and married Cleopatra II. Thus the empire was united, but only briefly. Euergetes divorced his sister and married her daughter, Cleopatra III. In 130 B.C. Cleopatra II revolted against him and became queen of parts of Upper Egypt, which she ruled alone until 118 B.C., when she and her brother signed a peace and amnesty agreement. They both died in 116.

References
Peters, F. E. *The Harvest of Hellenism.* New York: Barnes & Noble Books, 1996. pp. 181, 182, 269fn.
Rawlinson, George. *Ancient History.* New York: Barnes & Noble Books, 1993. pp. 206–207.
West, John Anthony. *The Traveler's Key to Ancient Egypt.* New York: Alfred A. Knopf, 1985. p. 446.

Cleopatra III
Co-ruler of Egypt (116–101 B.C.)

Cleopatra III was the daughter of Cleopatra II and Ptolemy VI Philo-mater, who was also her mother's brother. She married her uncle, Ptolemy VII Euergetes II, and had two sons, Soter II Lathyrus and Alexander. When her father died in 116 B.C., he bequeathed the throne to her and her sons jointly. Soter II, being the elder, ruled with his mother from 116 to 110 B.C., as Ptolemy VIII. However, Cleopatra favored her younger son and doubtless encouraged him to expel his brother. Alexander, as Ptolemy IX, ruled briefly with his mother in 110 B.C., but Soter II gathered his forces and returned the next year to oust his brother. Two years later Alexander was again able to expel his brother and join Cleopatra in ruling Egypt until her death in 101 B.C.

References
Peters, F. E. *The Harvest of Hellenism.* New York: Barnes & Noble Books, 1996. pp. 181, 182.

Rawlinson, George. *Ancient History.* New York: Barnes & Noble Books, 1993. p. 207.

Cleopatra VI Tryphaena
Co-ruler of Egypt (58 B.C.)

Cleopatra VI was married to Ptolemy XI Auletes (the flute player), who ruled from 80 to 58 B.C. and from 55 to 51 B.C. Ptolemy had an illegitimate claim to the throne, so he faced much opposition to his rule. When he was driven into exile in 58 B.C., Cleopatra Tryphaena and his daughter Berenice took turns ruling. Cleopatra died shortly after he left, and Berenice was elected queen.

References
Langer, William L., ed. *Encyclopedia of World History.* Boston: Houghton Mifflin, 1980. p. 97.

Peters, F. E. *The Harvest of Hellenism.* New York: Barnes & Noble Books, 1996. pp. 380–381.

Cleopatra VII
Queen of Egypt (51–31 B.C.)

Cleopatra VII was born in 69 B.C., the daughter of Ptolemy XII Auletes. Although probably born in Egypt, she was not Egyptian, but Macedonian, Persian, and Greek. When she was fourteen, Mark Antony visited Alexandria and may have met her then for the first time. Her father had previously been forced to flee an incensed populace in Egypt

*Cleopatra VII
(Archive Photos /
Popperphoto)*

because of high taxes he had imposed, and he had only just been restored to the throne at the time of Mark Antony's visit. When her father died in 51 B.C., as the oldest surviving daughter she became joint ruler and bride of her younger brother Ptolemy XIII, the oldest surviving son. Their father's will made Rome the guardian of Egypt, for by that time the dynasty of the Ptolemys had become weak. Plutarch described the young queen as the epitome of beauty, and she obviously had great powers of persuasion. The chief ministers, Pothinus and Achillas, plotted to get rid of Cleopatra so that they could rule in her younger brother's name, and for two years they thwarted her attempts to rule and at last succeeded in expelling her to Syria. There she raised an army and set out for Egypt. Her forces met the opposition at Perlusium in 48 B.C., but before a battle could be waged, Julius Caesar arrived in Alexandria, and Cleopatra decided on a new tack. She concealed herself in a rolled-up rug and had herself delivered to Caesar's headquarters so that she could petition him to intervene in her behalf. The old general—he was fifty-six—was charmed by the young queen, and he quickly ordered that Cleopatra be restored to the throne. Pothinus, believing that he was too far away from Caesar to be challenged, instigated a rebellion against Caesar's forces that lasted three months and resulted in Pothinus's death. During the final battles, Ptolemy XIII drowned while trying to escape down the Nile on a barge. Caesar, who had originally traveled to Egypt to do battle with his former son-in-law Pompey, whom Pothinus had already killed, had no further reason to remain in Egypt except for his infatuation with the young queen, who even bore him a son. Caesar chose another of her younger brothers, Ptolemy XIII, then ten, to be her co-ruler.

Although there is not complete agreement on the activities of Cleopatra, at least one legend claims that she followed Caesar back to Rome, arriving in 46 B.C. with a large retinue that included her brother and her baby. She moved into Caesar's villa and entertained him frequently, by this account. He was assassinated in 44 B.C., and one version of the reason for that murder was that he asked the senate to pass a special law enabling him to divorce his wife so that he could marry Cleopatra, declare himself king, and make their son heir to the Roman Empire. He also placed a gold statue of her in the temple of Venus, an unpardonable sacrilege, since Cleopatra was a barbarian.

In the civil war that raged after his death, she fled to Egypt. She did not remain neutral in that struggle, however. She sent a fleet and four legions against Brutus and Cassius, Caesar's murderers, but her forces were intercepted and conscripted for Cassius. Again she raised a fleet, but it was turned back by a storm. The three victors of that war divided their spheres of influence: Octavian stayed in Rome, Lepidus took Spain and France, and Mark Antony took the east. One of Mark Antony's first acts, on arriving in Tarsus, was to summon Cleopatra to answer charges of conspiracy, since her troops had been used by Cassius. Cleopatra was prepared; she had not been idle in the meantime. Before her younger brother could reach the legal ruling age of fourteen, she had had him poisoned and had named her son, Caesarion, as her co-ruler. At twenty-eight, she had gained great confidence and theatrical timing. She took her time answering Mark Antony's summons and eventually arrived, just as he was holding audience, dressed as Venus aboard a gaudily festooned boat. The crowds turned from him and rushed to the bank of the Nile, where she waited, like a hostess, for him to come to her. Mark Antony did indeed come to her, and she gave him a queenly reception and proposed a great feast. By the time the revelry ended, Cleopatra had even managed to convince him to order the death of her one remaining sister, Arsinoe, so that no other threats remained to her sovereignty. The relationship between Antony and Cleopatra lasted for twelve years, although in its midst he returned to Rome and in 40 B.C., as a political move, married Octavian's sister, Octavia. He probably also married Cleopatra in 36 B.C. so as to legitimize the couple's three children.

Together the couple ruled Egypt and most of Asia Minor. Mark Antony designated Cleopatra as Queen of Kings and appointed her and Caesarion as joint rulers of Libya, Cyprus, and Coelesyria. They parceled out other lands to their children: Alexander, the older son, was made ruler of Armenia, Media, and Parthia; his twin sister Cleopatra was made ruler of Cyrene; and their brother Ptolemy Phoenicia was made ruler of Cilicia and Syria. Octavian then denounced Mark Antony in the senate and in 32 B.C. declared war on Cleopatra. The couple ignored the threat and spent the winter in feasting and revelry on the island of Samos. Octavian advanced across their lands, claiming them for Rome, until he met Antony's troops near Actium in Greece in 31 B.C. Although Antony had superior troops, Cleopatra persuaded him to fight a naval battle against Agrippa, Octavian's naval commander. During the battle, Cleopatra's boat sailed away, and Antony, thinking that she had fled, was so distraught that he left his command and sailed after her. His forces were defeated, so Cleopatra left for Alexandria to raise another fleet.

There she met Octavian. She offered to abdicate in favor of Caesarion, but Octavian was not interested. He offered her favorable treatment if she would kill Antony. After yet another losing battle, Cleopatra retreated to a mausoleum she had built for her own death and sent a messenger to tell Antony that she was dead. Distraught, he stabbed himself but did not die immediately. When he learned that Cleopatra was still alive, he had servants carry him to her mausoleum, where they raised him by ropes so that he could see her looking out the window. Plutarch said, "Those who were present say that there was never a more pitiable sight than the spectacle of Antony, covered with blood, struggling in his death agonies and stretching out his hands toward Cleopatra as he swung helplessly in the air." She pulled him up through the window, and Antony died in her arms. The year was 30 B.C.

When Antony died, Cleopatra, then thirty-nine, again tried to beguile Octavian, but she could see that he was not easily entranced by a middle-aged woman. Fearing poor treatment as a hostage in Rome, she attempted suicide, but Octavian removed all knives and weapons and threatened to harm her children when she went on a hunger strike. Legend maintains that loyal servants smuggled an asp into her mausoleum in a basket of figs. She held it to her breast until it killed her. To the Egyptians, the asp was the divine minister of the sun god. The symbolic meaning of an asp bite was that the sun god had rescued his daughter from humiliation and taken her to himself.

References

Ludwig, Emil. *Cleopatra.* New York: Viking Press, 1937.

Peters, F. E. *The Harvest of Hellenism.* New York: Barnes & Noble Books, 1996. pp. 183, 314fn, 381, 384–387, 402fn, 436.

Cleopatra of Cyrene
Ruler of Cyrene (c. 33–31 B.C.)

Cyrene, originally a Greek colony, was located off the coast of Libya. In 74 B.C. it was incorporated as a province of Rome. Cleopatra of Cyrene (Cleopatra Selene) was born in 40 B.C., the daughter of Mark Antony and Cleopatra VII and the twin sister of Alexander Helios, who ruled Armenia, Media, and Parthia. Another brother, Ptolemy Phoenicia, ruled Syria and Cilicia. Her parents gave Cleopatra Cyrene to rule ca. 33 B.C., but Octavian restored the lands to Roman rule after the battles of 31 B.C. His sister Octavia, who was a wife of Mark Antony's, arranged a marriage for the deposed Cleopatra with Juba of Mauretania, the king of Numidia, one of the most gifted rulers of his time.

References

Langer, William L., ed. *World History.* Boston; Houghton Mifflin, 1980. p. 97.

Peters, F. E. *The Harvest of Hellenism.* New York: Barnes & Noble Books, 1996. pp. 385, 510fn.

West, John Anthony. *The Traveler's Key to Ancient Egypt.* New York: Alfred A. Knopf, 1985. pp. 26, 420.

Cleopatra Thea
Ruler of the Seleucid Empire (125–120 B.C.)

Cleopatra Thea married Demetrius II Nicator, who ruled the Seleucid Empire and the kingdom of Pergamum in Mesopotamia from 145 to 139 B.C., when he was captured by Mithridates by treachery. Cleopatra Thea and Demetrius had two sons, Seleucus V and Antiochus VIII Epiphanes Philomater Callinicus Grypus. She also had at least one son by Antiochus VII Euergetes Eusebes Soter Sidates, who ruled while Demetrius was held prisoner. That son was Antiochus IX Philopater Cyzicenus. In 129 B.C. Demetrius II was released and sent back to Syria, to rule for four more years, but he was murdered by Alexander Zabinas, a pretender to the throne. Cleopatra and her son Seleucus V assumed the throne, but she soon had her son put to death. She ruled with her second son, Antiochus VIII Epiphanes, until her death in 120 B.C. Three years later, her youngest son, Antiochis IX, forced his brother to abdicate and ruled briefly. Later the two half brothers divided the realm.

References

Peters, F. E. *The Harvest of Hellenism.* New York: Barnes & Noble Books, 1996. pp. 271–272, 274.

Constance
Co-ruler of Antioch (1130–1163)

Constance was born in 1127, the daughter of Bohemund II, ruler of Antioch (1126–1130) and Alice of Jerusalem. When her father died, Constance was only two years old. Instead of waiting for King Baldwin, Alice's father, to appoint a regent, Alice assumed the regency for Constance at once. But rumors spread that Alice planned to immure Constance in a convent in order to rule not as regent but as reigning sovereign. When Baldwin arrived, he removed Alice from the regency and banished her to Lattakieh. He placed Constance under the guardianship of Joscelin. A year later Joscelin died, and Alice reasserted her claim to be her daughter's regent. Late in 1135 Alice, who had been allowed to return to Antioch and rule the city in her daughter's name but who did not have the regency, thought of a plan to enhance her own power. She offered the hand of the eight-year-old Constance to the Byzantine emperor's younger son, Manuel. Quickly the patriarch Radulph notified King Fulk that he must find a husband for Constance. In 1136 Fulk decided on handsome thirty-seven-year-old Raymond of Poiters, son of Duke William IX of Aquitaine. In a disguise, Raymond reached Antioch while Constance was kidnapped and brought to the church for a quick wedding and while Alice, deceived into believing Raymond was coming to ask for her hand, waited at the palace. Constance, once married, was then considered a legitimate ruler. The couple had at least three children: Bohemund III, Maria, and Philippa. Raymond died in 1149 when Constance was only twenty-two.

The throne was Constance's by right, but it was thought, since Muslims threatened and times were treacherous, that a man was needed at the head of government. Her son Bohemund III was only five. King Baldwin of Jerusalem, her nearest male relative, tried to find her a husband and offered her what he considered three suitable choices. Constance was not interested in any of them. Baldwin had no choice but to return to Jerusalem and leave Constance in charge of the government. Constance then sent word to Constantinople to ask the overlord, Emperor Manuel, to find her a suitable mate. Manuel chose his middle-aged brother-in-law John Roger, but Constance, whose first husband had been dashing and handsome, sent the older man packing. Her own choice was a young knight named Reynald of Chatillon. She married him in 1153, probably before she asked permission of King Baldwin. She did not ask Emperor Manuel's permission at all. The choice was not a popular one, since it was generally believed that she had married beneath her station. Reynald, ambitious but lacking in funds, embarked on an unpopular expedition against Cyprus while Constance stayed at home and bore at least one child, Agnes (who later married Bela III, king of Hungary). Reynald, after a humiliating groveling in the dirt at the feet of Emperor Manuel for his brash attack on Cyprus, never gained the prestige he longed for. In 1160 he made a raid into the Euphratean valley and was taken prisoner by Nur el-Din. Reynald was bound and sent on camel back to Aleppo, where he remained in jail for sixteen years, for neither King Baldwin nor Emperor Manuel was in any mood to ransom him.

Constance claimed the power to rule Antioch, which was hers, but public opinion leaned toward her son Bohemund, age fifteen. King Baldwin came back to Antioch, declared Bohemund III king, and appointed Patriarch Aimery as regent. Constance was immensely displeased, and the overlord, Emperor Manuel, was displeased that Baldwin had taken the decision into his own hands without consulting him. Constance appealed to Emperor Manuel to restore her and in addition proposed her daughter Maria as wife for the widowed emperor. Baldwin, fearing that a closer tie between Manuel and Antioch would diminish his own authority over Antioch, suggested Melisende of Tripoli as Manuel's wife instead. Miffed by Baldwin's affrontery in appointing Constance's son as ruler and acting amid rumors of Melisende's illegitimacy, Emperor Manuel chose Constance's daughter Maria as his wife and sent his emissaries to Antioch to establish Constance as ruler.

When Bohemund III reached eighteen, he wanted to take over the throne from his mother. Constance felt the throne should be hers until she died. She appealed to General Constantine Coloman for military aid to protect herself from being bodily removed from office by her son. The rumors of her actions provoked a riot in Antioch. She was exiled and died soon after, ca. 1163.

References

Egan, Edward W., Constance B. Hintz, and L. F. Wise, eds. *Kings, Rulers, and Statesmen.* New York: Sterling Publishing, 1976. p. 16.

Runciman, Steven A. *A History of the Crusades.* Vol. 2, *The Kingdom of Jerusalem.* Cambridge: Cambridge University Press, 1987. pp. 183–184, 198–200, 305–306, 330–333, 345–349, 352, 358–360.

Constance
Duchess of Brittany, Co-ruler (1171–1196)

Constance was the daughter of Conan IV (r. 1156–1171), from whom she inherited a weakened duchy of Brittany that Conan had allowed King Henry II of England to rule in part. Constance married King Henry's son Geoffroi II and ruled jointly with him. The couple had a son, Arthur I, born in 1187, who inherited the duchy upon her death in 1196.

References

Carpenter, Clive. *The Guinness Book of Kings, Rulers & Statesmen.* Enfield: Middlesex: Guinness Superlatives, 1978. p. 90.

Constance
Queen of Sicily (1189, 1194–1198) and Regent of Germany (1197–1198)

Constance was born in 1154, the daughter of King Roger II (of Apulia) and his third wife Beatrice of Rethel. In 1186 Constance became the future empress of the Holy Roman Empire by marrying the future Henry VI, the Lion, of the house of the Hohenstaufen (r. 1190–1197). When her nephew William II died in 1189, Constance, as legal heiress, claimed the throne of Sicily, but she was opposed by Count Roger and another of her nephews, Tancred of Lecce, son of her older brother Roger. The Sicilian people did not want Constance's husband, a German, for a ruler, and neither did the papacy. Tancred grabbed the crown briefly in 1190, and while his enemies cried, "Behold, an ape is crowned!" Henry sent troops to unseat him. Tancred took his aunt Constance captive, but the pope induced him to set her free. Tancred's death in 1194 cleared the way for Constance and Henry to assume the thrones of Sicily. Constance was installed as governor of the Regno (kingdom). That same year, their son Frederick II was born.

The people of Sicily hated the German Henry, who was a harsh ruler. Constance, and even Pope Celestine, may have been aware of a plot to assassinate him. When Henry discovered the plot, he took terrible vengeance, blinding all prisoners, even German ones. His death in 1197 of a fever was celebrated throughout the land. As regent ruler, Constance exercised particular political skill. She consolidated her power and secured the protection of Pope Innocent III in preserving her son's claim to the throne. She managed to have her son crowned king in April 1198 before he died in November of that same year.

References

Langer, William L., ed. *World History*. Boston: Houghton Mifflin, 1980. pp. 224–225.

Ostrogorsky, George. *History of the Byzantine State*. New Brunswick, NJ: Rutgers University Press, 1969. pp. 411–412.

Painter, Sidney. *The Rise of the Feudal Monarchies*. Ithaca, NY: Cornell University Press, 1951. p. 114.

Previté-Orton, C. W. *The Shorter Cambridge Medieval History*. Vol. 1, *The Later Roman Empire to the Twelfth Century*. Cambridge: Cambridge University Press, 1952, 1987. pp. 510, 605–615.

Runciman, Steven. *A History of the Crusades*. Vol. 2, *The Kingdom of Jerusalem and the Frankish East*. Cambridge: Cambridge University Press, 1952, 1987. p. 428.

Smith, Denis Mack. *A History of Sicily*. Vol. 1, *Medieval Sicily*. New York: Dorset Press, 1968. pp. 44–45, 47, 51, 55.

Constance
Queen of Sicily (1282–1302)

Constance was the daughter of King Manfred of Sicily, who ruled from 1258 to 1266, and his first wife Beatrix of Savoy and the grandaughter of Emperor Frederick II. Constance married Peter III, king of Aragon, who ruled from 1276 to 1285. Charles I of Anjou, son of Louis VIII of France, was out to create his own Mediterranean empire, and to that end he invaded Sicily, defeating King Manfred in 1266. The papacy awarded Charles the kingdom of Sicily. In 1282, Constance's husband, King Peter, launched a long-planned campaign to recapture the throne in Constance's name, disguising his trip as an African crusade. He landed at Callo in 1282, defeated Charles, placed himself and Constance upon the throne of Sicily, and refused to do homage to the pope. The pope naturally opposed their rule and endeavored to have them deposed, and even the local nobility was opposed to the Argonese takeover. The struggle to maintain their family's right to ascendancy continued even after Peter's death. Constance acted as regent for their eleven-year-old son James until he reached eighteen. The couple had four children: Alfonso III, who succeeded to the throne of Aragon; Isabella, who married Diniz, king of Portugal; James I, who succeeded to the throne of Sicily under his mother's regency and, as Jaime II, succeeded to the throne of Aragon in 1291; and Frederick III, who also ruled Sicily. James ruled for ten years, then exchanged Sicily for Corsica and Sardinia. He appointed his younger brother, then seventeen, as regent in 1291, when he took over Aragon from his brother. Four years later Frederick was elected king, and eventually the pope recognized him as such. Thus Constance's heirs were finally firmly established as rulers of Sicily.

References
Langer, William L., ed. *World History.* Boston: Houghton Mifflin, 1940, 1980. pp. 228, 306, 313.

Previté-Orton, C. W. *The Shorter Cambridge Medieval History.* Vol. 1, *The Later Roman Empire to the Twelfth Century.* Cambridge: Cambridge University Press, 1952, 1982. pp. 510, 557.

Crescentii
See Marozia Crescentii

Cresson, Edith
Prime Minister of France (1991–1992)

Born Edith Campion on January 27, 1934, in Boulogne-Billancourt, a suburb of Paris, she was raised with a British nurse, who taught her fluent English. Of her childhood, she later wrote, "One of the most obvious characteristics of the bourgeoisie is the boredom it produces." She attended a noted school of business, the School of Higher Commercial Studies, and earned a doctorate in demography. In 1959 she married a Peugeot executive, Jacques Cresson. At length her dissatisfaction with the bourgeois life led her to join the Socialist movement. Her enthusiasm and organizational abilities brought her to the attention of François Mitterrand during his 1965 failed presidential campaign. When he became head of the French Socialist Party in 1971, she remained his disciple. In 1975 the party asked her to run for parliament in a conservative district, and although she lost, her reputation as *la battante*—the fighter—was made. In 1977 she became mayor of Thuré, and in 1983 she became the only Socialist to defeat a sitting conservative mayor when she was elected mayor of Châtellerault.

After Mitterrand became president in 1981, Cresson became the first woman to serve as minister of agriculture, much to the disgust of French farmers, who referred to her as La Parisienne. However, in that post, she raised their income by 10 percent in 1982. In 1983 she was appointed minister of tourism and trade, and in 1984, minister of trade and industry. In 1988 she became minister of European affairs, but she resigned in October to enter the private sector; she joined Groupe Schneider, a French electrical manufacturer.

In less than three years the lure of politics had become too strong, and she returned to government service. She was chosen as France's first female prime minister in May 1991. Her appointment marked a milestone for French women, who did not obtain the right to vote until 1946.

Cresson said that she planned to turn France into an industrial power rivaling Germany. But when she announced the members of her cabinet, which included many holdovers from her predecessor, opposition leaders predicted that her coalition could not last. The headline in the newspaper *La Monde* read, "For How Long?"

In a magazine interview, Cresson said, "There are three places where women have always been excluded: the military, religion, and politics. I would say that today, it is still in politics where they have the least access." Her outspoken statements on several occasions soon caused problems. She was hampered by "perceived political ineptitude," creating diplomatic uproars for criticizing British masculinity, for one, and the Japanese social order, for another. In regional elections held in March 1992, amid rising unemployment figures and strikes by workers in areas that were traditionally her supporters, her party suffered a stunning defeat, receiving only 18.3 percent of the vote and losing a departmental council it had held since 1934. Cresson was forced to resign. President François Mitterrand replaced her with former finance minister Pierre Beregovoy.

Edith Cresson (AP Photo / Christian Lutz)

References
"A French First." *New York Times*. 19 May 1991: E7.

Greenhouse, Steven. "'The Fighter' of France." *New York Times*. 16 May 1991: A1, A31.

Greenhouse, Steven. "French Prime Minister Quits; Woman Named to Post." *New York Times*. 16 May 1991: A3.

"Seasonal Work." *New York Times*. 5 April 1992: 3A.

Cristina
See María Cristina I of Naples

da Lourdes-Pintasilgo, María
Prime Minister of Portugal (1979–1980)

María da Lourdes-Pintasilgo (or de Lurdes Pentassilgo) was born in 1930 and trained as an industrial engineer. From 1965 to 1974 she was agent for the Co-operative Chamber. An avid spokesperson for women's causes, she was the author of several books addressing the problem of the church's treatment of women, including: *The New Feminism, To Think the Church Anew,* and *Roads for Our Joint Effort.* She served as president of the interministerial commission dealing with the status of women in Portugal.

The revolution of April 25, 1974, toppled Portugal's dictatorship of Antonio de Oliveira Salazar (1932–1968) and his successors; in the aftermath the country was close to anarchy. From 1976 to 1983 sixteen provisional governments reigned over a Portugal in chaos. Romalho Eanes (b. 1935) was elected president in 1976 and reelected in 1980. María da Lourdes-Pintasilgo was pressed into service in a number of cabinet posts. She was minister of social affairs and state secretary for social security for the Second and Third Provisional Governments. In 1979–1980 she served as Portugal's first woman prime minister, of the Fifth Constitutional Government.

Eanes appointed her ambassador to UNESCO, where she was a member of the Executive Council and a part of the Portuguese delegation to the General Assembly. She was a member of the Graal, an international women's movement, and of the Women's Liaison Group between the Catholic Church and the Ecumenical Council of Churches.

In 1986 she ran for the office of president, winning the primary, but losing in the general election. In 1987 she was elected member of the European Parliament.

References
"Nuno Moura Portugal." www.uc.pt, April 1997.
Women's International Center Biography. World Wide Web, 1997.

Daura, Queen of
*Ruler of Daura State (ca. 9th c.), Founding Queen-grandmother of the
Hausa States of Northern Nigeria and Niger (10th c.)*

Daura is a town and emirate in present-day Kaduna State, northern
Nigeria, west Africa.

A queen (Magajiva, which means "the senior princess") was
founder of Daura, and she began a lineage of ruling queens that, according to de Villiers and Hirtle, lasted for several hundred years. According to Davidson, the last queen of Daura was the last of a line of
only nine queens in the area; however, it is possible that each of these
queens ruled for many decades. The queenly tradition survives to
some extent even today in Islamic Daura, for the senior princess in
the Daura emir's household holds the title of Magajiva.

According to Hausa lore, the last queen of Daura had offered half
her realm to the person who killed Sarki, the huge fetish snake living
in Daura's well. A son of the king of Baghdad, Bayajida (or
Anuyazidu), was traveling through the area with his wife, a princess
of Bornu to the east, and stopped for water at the well. He killed the
snake, cutting off its head, which he kept, and throwing the body onto
the ground. When the feat was reported to the queen, she called for
Bayajida to appear before him with proof of his deed. When he produced Sarki's head, she offered to give him half of her town. He answered, "Do not divide the town because I . . . will be amply rewarded if you will . . . take me as your consort." She married him and
he was given the title Makas-Sarki, "slayer of the snake."

She and Bayajida had a son named Bawogarior ("give back the
town"). Their six grandsons, plus a son of Bayajida's other wife, became the Seven Rulers of the Hausa Bakwai, the Seven True Hausa
Kingdoms (10th c.).

Women still draw water daily from Sarki's well in Daura.

References
Davidson, Basil. "The Niger to the Nile." In Alvin M. Josephy, Jr., ed.
   The Horizon History of Africa. New York: American Heritage Publishing,
   McGraw-Hill, 1971. 241–242.
de Villiers, Marq, and Sheila Hirtle. *Introduction to Africa.* Toronto: Key
   Porter Books, 1997. p. 287.
Layor, ChiChi. "The Land of the Long Horn." Hausa epics. Ebo State,
   Nigeria, Manuscript, 1996.

Dawlat Khatun
Ruler of Luristan (1316)

Luristan is located in southwestern Persia. Dawlat, who was married to 'Izz al-Din Muhammad, thirteenth sovereign of the Mongol Bani Khurshid dynasty, succeeded to the throne when he died in 1316. But she proved to be a poor administrator, "who was not successful in managing the affairs of state," and she abdicated after a short period of time in favor of her brother-in-law, 'Izz al-Din Hasan.

References
Mernissi, Fatima. *The Forgotten Queens of Islam.* Trans. Mary Jo Lakeland. Minneapolis: University of Minnesota Press, 1993. pp. 104–105.

Deborah
Judge, Ruler of Israel (ca. 1224–1184 B.C.)

Deborah lived in a time when Israel was ruled by judges (as was Sardinia 2,500 years later). The term carried a broader meaning than simply legal advisers. Judges were local and national leaders, chieftains, and battle commanders as well. Deborah was also a prophetess. She was the wife of Lapidoth, about whom nothing is known. She lived in the hill country of Ephraim, on the road between Ramah and Beth-el. She obviously possessed wisdom, because she became a counselor to passersby. She was also a keeper of the tabernacle lamps. Eventually she was elevated to judgeship, Israel's only woman judge. Although Athaliah is mentioned in the Bible as a ruler of Judah, Deborah is the only woman listed in the Bible who was raised to political power by the common consent of the people.

Her chief concern became dealing with marauders. For twenty years the king of neighboring Canaan, Jabin, had raided the camps of Israel using iron chariots, pillaging homes and vineyards, and raping and murdering women and children. (The Canaanites are believed to have been a Celtic tribe.) Jabin's army, under the command of Sisera, was said to possess 900 iron chariots, a formidable force for a people to face who still fought on foot, using arrows, slings, and swords. Deborah sent a message to neighboring Kedesh, where lived Barak, a man noted for his military skill. Deborah commanded Barak to raise an army and go to meet Sisera's forces near Mount Tabor, which rises 1,000 feet above the Plain of Jezreel. General Barak announced that unless Deborah accompanied him, he would not go. Deborah consented to accompany him, and they led the troops to the foot of Mount Tabor, near the Kishon River. They arrived in a cloudburst of hail, sleet, and rain that changed the Kishon into a raging torrent. Sisera's

Deborah (Corbis-Bettmann)

iron chariots became mired in the mud, making the charioteers easy marks for the foot soldiers. Sisera escaped and fled on foot. A woman named Jael, wife of Heber the Kenite, saw him and invited him to hide in her tent. Since the Kenites were at peace with the Canaanites, this tent seemed to offer safe refuge. After Sisera fell asleep, Jael drove a tent stake through his temple. When Barak arrived, searching for the retreating general, he found him dead. Without a commander, the Canaanites were defeated and retreated in disarray.

To celebrate the victory, Deborah and Barak sang a duet, the Ode of Deborah, one of the most ancient pieces of writing in the Old Testament and certainly the lengthiest: It runs through thirty-one verses in the fifth chapter of Judges. It was also one of the earliest military songs in history. Her story and song are recorded in the fourth and fifth chapters of the book of Judges in the Old Testament.

References

Alexander, David, and Patricia Alexander, eds. *Eerdman's Handbook to the Bible.* Berkhamsted, Herts, England: Lion Publishing, 1973. pp. 219–222.

Deen, Edith. *All the Women of the Bible.* New York: Harper and Brothers, 1955. pp. 69–74.

Josephus Flavius. *Life and Works.* Trans. William Whiston. Philadelphia: Winston Company, n.d. p. 150.

Packer, J. I. et al. *The Bible Almanac.* Nashville, TN: Thomas Nelson, 1980. pp. 44–52, 204, 427, 429.

Deidameia
Queen, Ruler of Epirus (ca. 235 B.C.)

Deidameia was the daughter of Alexandros II (r. 272–ca. 240 B.C.) and the sister of Pyrrhus II (r. 240–ca. 236 B.C.) and Ptolemaeus (r. ca. 236–ca. 235 B.C.). During a civil war, Ptolemaeus was killed, and Deidameia may be considered to have taken the throne briefly before she, too, was murdered. The Republican Party took over the government in 235 B.C.

> **References**
> Carpenter, Clive. *The Guinness Book of Kings, Rulers & Statesmen.* Enfield, Middlesex: Guinness Superlatives, 1978. p. 75.

Diane of Poitiers
Duchess, De Facto Co-ruler of France (1547–1559)

Diane, duchess of Valentinois, was born in 1499 and came to court as lady-in-waiting to Louise of Savoy and later to Queen Claude. Diana was married to Louis de Breze, comte de Maulevrier, who died in 1531. At that time she became the mistress of the future King Henry II, even though she was twenty years his senior. Henry II ruled France from 1547 to 1559. She so completely dominated him that he gave her many of the crown jewels and kept her prominently at court, while his wife, Catherine de Médicis, was obliged to remain in relative obscurity, being brought out only to serve as regent in his absence and after his death. Although Diane had absolute power over Henry's decisions, she did not usually concern herself with the larger affairs of state but focused her interests upon arts and letters, becoming a patron of both. However, it is doubtful that she refrained from expressing her preferences and dislikes of Henry's advisers or that she refused to express an opinion when Henry unburdened himself upon her. His complete enthrallment of and dependence upon an older woman suggests that she represented far more

Diane of Poitiers
(Archive Photos)

than a lover or companion; rather, she was the mother authority that he never outgrew. Despite the fact that she was so much older than he, she outlived him, because he died accidentally in 1559. She retired to the beautiful chateau built for her by Philibert Delorme at Anet in Eure-et-Loir, where she died in 1566.

References

Harvey, Sir Paul, and J. E. Heseltine. *The Oxford Companion to French Literature.* Oxford: Oxford University Press, 1959, 1993. p. 202.

Langer, William L., ed. *World History.* Boston: Houghton Mifflin, 1980. p. 411.

Didda
Queen, Regent of Kashmir (10th c.)

The *damaras,* or feudal landlords, having defeated the powerful Tantrins, had in turn become so powerful that they had been a threat to several rulers. When Queen Didda assumed the regency for her son, the landlords saw opportunity to refuse payment of tribute and to assert their independence. The era was rife with feudatories vying for power and Turks threatening the borders. In spite of much opposition, Queen Didda conducted affairs of state.

References

Thapar, Romila. *A History of India.* Vol. 1. London: Penguin Books, 1987. p. 226.

Dido
Queen of Phoenicians, Founder of Carthage (ca. 814 B.C.)

The oldest version of the founding of Carthage by Dido is from a history of Sicily by Timaeus in the early part of the third century B.C. The founding date is cited variously as 825 B.C. or 814 B.C. Dido is also called Elissa in Greek tradition and is associated with Tanit, tutelary goddess of Carthage. Dido, or Elissa, was said to be the daughter of Mutton, king of Tyre, and the sister of Pu'myaton (Pygmalion), who ruled the Sidonian state (r. 820–774 B.C.). She married Acerbas, who was killed by her brother. To escape her brother, during the seventh year of his reign she fled to northern Africa, near modern-day Tunis, where a local chief, Iarbus, sold her a piece of land upon which she founded a settlement that became Carthage. Carthage became the most important outpost of Phoenician civilization in the Western Hemisphere, with almost a million people within its walls. In the sixth century it was the wealthiest city in antiquity. To keep from having to marry Iarbus, Dido stabbed herself in the presence of a host of

witnesses atop her own funeral pyre, which she herself had caused to be constructed.

Dido (Corbis-Bettmann)

Virgil's version is that Dido met Aeneas when he landed in Africa and killed herself with his sword when he left her. She cursed him and his descendants, saying they would always be enemies of Carthage. Ovid tells the story of Dido's sister Anna, who came to Italy after Dido's death and many other misfortunes. There she was welcomed by Aeneas, but his wife Lavinia was jealous. Anna, warned of Lavinia's jealousy by Dido's ghost, left and disappeared in the Numicus River. Morford and Lenordon suggest the story may be genuine to a point.

References

Khader, Ben, Aïcha Ben Abed, and David Soren. *Carthage: A Mosaic of Ancient Tunis.* New York: The American Museum of Natural History and W. W. Norton, 1987. pp. 25–26, 100.

Morford, Mark P. O., and Robert J. Lenardon. *Classical Mythology.* New York: Longman, 1977. pp. 257, 261, 453, 455, 488.

Watts, A. E., tr. *The Metamorphoses of Ovid.* San Francisco: North Point Press, 1980. p. 319.

Dola
Queen of the Itsekiri Kingdom in Nigeria (ca. 1850)

Dola (Iye Idolorusan) was the half sister of Olu (king) Akengbuwa, who died in 1848. Following his death, a dispute broke out among several contenders for the throne. Dola finally set up an interregnum council of state, which she headed, in an attempt to hold the kingdom together. However, the Itsekiri divided into vying trade groups that Queen Dola was powerless to control. Her governor of the river, or minister of trade, became the most influential person in the kingdom. Queen Dola's influence quickly diminished, but no new *olu* was elected until 1936.

References
Ikime, Obaro. "The Changing Status of Chiefs among the Itsekiri." In Crowder, Michael, and Obaro Ikime, eds. *West African Chiefs.* New York: Africana Publishing, 1970. pp. 289–311.

Domitien, Élisabeth
Prime Minister of the Central African Republic (1975–1976)

The Central African Republic is a landlocked nation, bordered on the north by Chad, on the east by Sudan, on the south by Congo, and on the west by Cameroon. It is ruled by a head of state (president and, briefly, emperor) and a head of government (prime minister). The country gained independence from France in 1960 with David Dacko as president. Five years later, Dacko's cousin Jean-Bedel Bokassa seized power in a military coup. In 1972 the sole political party declared Bokassa president for life.

Thus he was still in power when, on January 1, 1975, Élisabeth Domitien began her term as prime minister, the first woman so designated on the continent. The choice of a woman head of government was particularly unusual in a dictatorship that was growing more repressive each year, but Bokassa had displayed a degree of sensitivity toward the plight of women. For example, in 1971, in commemoration of Mother's Day, he had released all women prisoners, at the same time ordering the execution of men accused of serious crimes against women. Élisabeth Domitien served until April 7, 1976.

References
Delury, George, ed. *The World Almanac and Book of Facts.* New York: Newspaper Enterprise Association, 1994. p. 523.

Lipschutz, Mark R., and R. Kent Rasmussen. *Dictionary of African Biography.* Berkeley: University of California Press, 1989. pp. 51, 261.

Drahomira
Queen, Regent of Bohemia (ca. 926–928 or 921–924/925)

Drahomira (or Dragomir) was born Drahomira von Stoder and married Duke Rastislav I (Vratislav), ruler of Bohemia from ca. 912 to 926. Rastislav's parents, Borivoj and Ludmila, were the first Czech rulers to adopt Christianity. The citizens of Bohemia were divided in their loyalty between their old pagan religions and the new Christianity. Drahomira and Rastislav had two sons, Wenceslas (b. 908) and Boleslav (the Cruel). Ludmila took it upon herself to educate Wenceslas, as heir to the throne, in the ways of Christianity, while Drahomira, a pagan, saw to Boleslav's upbringing.

When Rastislav died in ca. 926, Wenceslas was only fourteen. His Christian grandmother became his regent, to the consternation of anti-Christian factions throughout the land. Drahomira, an ambitious and conniving woman, is said to have been behind the plot whereby anti-Christian agents broke into Tetin Castle and strangled Ludmila. Drahomira then assumed the regency herself. Wenceslas remained a Christian and Boleslav a heathen. Civil strife between Christians and non-Christians characterized Drahomira's regime, and her intrigues at court were so flagrant that Wenceslas chose to assume the reins of government in ca. 930 when he was barely eighteen. Wencelas was a wise and beloved ruler who made the mistake of yielding to Henry the Fowler when the Germans threatened to invade, an action that further enraged the anti-Christian faction. In ca. 935 he was murdered by his brother at the door of the church. (Some sources give his death as 929 and Drahomira's regency as 921–924/925.) King Wenceslas became Bohemia's patron saint, which would have been the last thing that Queen Drahomira would have wanted. The Christmas carol, "Good King Wenceslas," refers to his deeds.

References
Cooke, Jean, et al. *History's Timeline.* New York: Crescent Books, 1981. pp. 47, 61.

Kinder, Hermann, and Werner Hilgemann. *Atlas of World History.* Trans. Ernest A. Menze. Vol. 1. Garden City, NY: Anchor/Doubleday, 1982. p. 169.

Langer, William L., ed. *World History.* Boston: Houghton Mifflin, 1980. p. 255.

Morby, John. *Dynasties of the World.* Oxford: Oxford University Press, 1989. p. 155.

Dreifuss, Ruth
President of Switzerland (1999)

Ruth Dreifuss was born into a Jewish family in January 1940 in St. Gallen in northeastern Switzerland. Her father, who worked in a textile importing company, volunteered with a group that helped Jewish refugees fleeing from the Holocaust. In 1945 he was caught helping falsify documents and lost his job, and the family moved to Geneva. Ruth Dreifuss received a degree in economics from Geneva University. She became a left-leaning union activist. In 1992 she was elected to the federal cabinet, becoming the second woman and first Jew to hold the post. She served as interior minister during the investigation of Swiss wartime actions, and she took tough stands for reform of the nation's health insurance and for addressing the nation's drug problem. In August 1998, Swiss banks agreed to a $1.25 billion settlement for money that Holocaust victims had deposited in Swiss banks. Dreifuss expressed relief that the banks had made a settlement, but she cautioned that the government's restitution work was not finished. In December 1998, she was elected by parliament to the one-year presidential post, which rotates among the seven-member Swiss cabinet. Her election was a symbol of success in a country where women were not allowed to vote on the national level until 1971.

References
Olson, Elizabeth. "A First for Swiss: A Woman as President." *New York Times International.* 27 December 1998: 7.

Durgavati
Rani, Queen of Gondwana (ca. 1545–1564)

Gondwana (also called Garha-Kalanga), outside of the southern boundary of the Indian Mughal Empire at the time, had been ruled by independent and tributary chiefs. Fed by the Mahandi River, Gondwana lay on the east-central side of India north of the Deccan. The Gonds were a group of Dravidian tribes, aboriginal (pre-Aryan) people of India. To this day the Raj Gonds still remain outside the Hindu caste system, neither acknowledging the superiority of Brahmins nor being bound by Hindu rules.

Queen Durgavati (or Durgawati) was a member of the Gond Chandels, the remnants of which are now in Bundelkhand in north-central India. She was the daughter of Kirāt Rai, chandella king of Mahoba and Kālinjar. She married Raja Dalpat Sa Garha Mandala of Gondwana, ca. 1545, but was soon left a widow to rule the kingdom in behalf of her infant son, Bir Narayan. With magnificent courage she maintained its sovereignty for the better part of two decades in the face of repeated threats of both Baj Bahādor of Mālwa and the Afghans of Bengal. Historians have termed her one of the most able and effective female leaders in Indian history. In 1564 the Moghul Akbar, intent upon enlarging his empire, sent General Āṣaf Khān with an army of 50,000 men to make an unprovoked invasion of Gondwana. Queen Durgavati and her son, now about eighteen, met the Moghul army with a seasoned force of their own at a bloody two-day pitched battle at Narhi. On the second day, her son was wounded and had to be escorted to safety by a large contingent of the rani's troops. Withdrawal of the escort so weakened her army that it was quickly overpowered. Durgavati, wounded by two arrows, stabbed herself to death to escape the disgrace of capture. Akbar then annexed her kingdom.

References

Bhattacharya, Sachchidananda. *A Dictionary of Indian History*. New York: George Braziller, 1967. pp. 321–322.

Gascoigne, Bamber. *The Great Moghuls*. New York: Dorset Press, 1971. p. 88.

Langer, William L., ed. *World History*. Boston: Houghton Mifflin, 1940, 1980. pp. 356–358, 569.

Dzeliwe Shongwe
Queen Regent of Swaziland (1982–1983)

Dzeliwe Shongwe was the senior wife of King Sobhuza II (or Mona) (1899–1982), who ruled for sixty years and died at the age of eighty-two. It had been arranged that Dzeliwe was to act as regent until Sobhuza's handpicked successor, Prince Mokhesetive (Mswati III, b. 1968), came of age. A fifteen-man National Council (Liquqo) and an "authorized person," Prince Sozisa Dlamini, were appointed to assist her. In 1983, Swaziland's first prime minister, Prince Mbandla (Makhosini) N. F. Dlamini, a great-grandson of Sobhuza I and the nephew of Sobhuza II, was ousted from his post by Dzeliwe and the Liquqo for his resistance to recognizing the authority of the Liquqo. Additionally, his reformist and modernist views clashed with the conservative and traditional Liquqo. He was forced to flee into Bophuthatswana while a more conservative candidate, Prince Bhakimpi Dlamini, was appointed prime minister.

However, the Liquqo kept asserting its authority and in August 1983 prepared a document for the queen regent to sign that would acknowledge the supreme authority of the Liquqo. When Dzeliwe refused to sign, she was physically removed as head of state and ordered out of the Royal Compound. She was suceeded by Queen Ntombi Thwala, mother of the king-designate.

References

Blaustein, Albert P., and Gisbert H. Flanz, eds. *Constitutions of the Countries of the World: A Series of Updated Texts, Constitutional Chronologies, and Annotated Bibliographies.* Dobbs Ferry, NY: Oceana Publications, 1991.

E

Ebuskun
Khatun, Regent of Turkestan (1242–1246)

She was the wife of Mütügen, eldest son of Jagatai. Jagatai was one of the four sons of Jenghiz-khan who shared in their father's empire, and Mütügen would then inherit the land of Jagatai when he died. However, Mütügen preceded his father in death; he was killed in 1221 at the siege of Bamian, leaving his wife, Ebuskun, and their son, Qara-Hulägu. So upon Jagatai's death in 1242, the throne went to his grandson, Qara-Hulägu, under the regency of his mother. Ebuskun served as regent for four years, when the new grand khan Güyük intervened and replaced Qara-Hulägo with a personal friend, Jagatai's younger brother, Prince Yissu-Mangu (Mongka).

References
Grousset, René. *The Empire of the Steppes: A History of Central Asia.* Trans. Naomi Walford. New Brunswick, NJ: Rutgers University Press, 1970. p. 329.

Eji
Co-ruler of Egypt (ca. 1351–1350 B.C.)

Eji (also Mutnedjmet or Metnedjenet) was the eldest sister of Queen Nefertiti, wife of King Akhenaton, whose rule Egyptologists place variously from ca. 1378–1352 B.C. to 1379–1362 B.C. Nefertiti either died or fell out of favor with her husband in about the twelfth year of his reign. Toward the end of his reign, he asked Sakere (or Smenkhkare), husband of their oldest daughter, Meritaton, to co-rule, probably because of an infirmity of Akhenaton's. When Sakere died, ca. 1361 or 1357, his child-brother Tutankhamen (Tut) ruled (ca. 1362–1352 B.C.). He was also married to a daughter of Akhenaton, Ankhesenpoaten. During Tutankhamen's rule, the actual power rested with his elderly regent, Ay, and with General Horemheb, the royal deputy. When King Tut died, ca. 1352 or 1351, the elderly Ay continued to hold power while the widow queen looked for a husband-successor. It is likely that Horemheb had a hand in the void that led to his own ascension, since the widow's husband-to-be was murdered, Ay died, and so, apparently, did Tut's widow. During this void, Queen Eji, as the sister of the late queen, was left as ruler for only a year or two. Horemheb married her to secure a claim to the throne, and Eji seemed to play little part in the government following the marriage. Although he was an elderly man, Horemheb ruled for over a quarter of a century, but he and Eji had no children. This rule marked the end of the Eighteenth Dynasty.

References

Egan, Edward W., Constance B. Hintz, and L. F. Wise, eds. *Kings, Rulers, and Statesmen.* New York: Sterling Publishing, 1976. p. 123.

Grimal, Nicolas. *Ancient Egypt.* Trans. Basil Blackwell Ltd. New York: Barnes & Noble Books, 1997. pp. 214, 226, 312, 317, 318.

Eleanor
Queen of Navarre (1441–1481)

Eleanor (or Leonor) was the younger daughter of King John of Aragon and Queen Doña Blanca (Bianca, or Blanche) of Navarre, who ruled Navarre until her death in 1441. Eleanor's older brother Charles de Viana succeeded his mother. He and his father had serious disagreements; when Charles died suddenly in 1441 it was assumed that he had been poisoned. The next heir after Charles was his sister Blanche, the queen whom King Henry the Impotent of Castile had divorced. King John had Blanche imprisoned, where she died suddenly, possibly poisoned by Eleanor's orders. King John had his younger daugher, Eleanor, enthroned in Blanche's stead. Eleanor was married to Gaston IV, count of Foix (r. 1436–1470). Through their daughter, Catalina, they established a dynasty that was to be short-lived, because in 1512 Ferdinand of Aragon conquered the Spanish portion of Navarre. The French portion of Navarre remained independent until 1610, when it was united with France. Eleanor's father continued to exercise dominion over her kingdom until his death in 1479. She died two years later, and her grandson, Francis Phoebus, who had become count of Foix on his father's death in 1470, became king of Navarre.

References

Chapman, Charles E. *A History of Spain.* New York: The Free Press/Macmillan, 1965. p. 134.

Egan, Edward W., Constance B. Hintz, and L. F. Wise, eds. *Kings, Rulers, and Statesmen.* New York: Sterling Publishing Company, 1976. pp. 157, 430.

Langer, William L., ed. *World History.* Boston: Houghton Mifflin, 1980. p. 307.

Morby, John E. *Dynasties of the World.* Oxford: Oxford University Press, 1989. p. 114.

Eleanor of Aquitaine

Duchess (of Aquitaine), Countess (of Poitiers), Queen (of both France and England), Regent of England (1189–1199)

To cite only the regency of this remarkable woman is to disregard the tremendous and far-reaching impact she had on the affairs of Europe during her lifetime. She was born ca. 1122, the daughter of William X, duke of Aquitaine and count of Poitiers. Upon her father's death in 1137, she inherited Aquitaine and Poitiers and married Louis VII the Young, who became king of France that year. She and Louis had two daughters: Marie, who married Henry of Champagne, and Alice, who married Thibault of Blois. Eleanor was considered far more intelligent than Louis.

In 1148 she and her retinue, dressed in battle garb, accompanied him on the Second Crusade. They went first to Antioch, where Eleanor's uncle Raymond of Tripoli sought Louis's help in recovering Montferrand from the Turks. Louis, however, was not quite ready to fight, or perhaps Raymond's proposal did not sound prestigious enough; at any rate, he said that he wanted to make a pilgrimage to Jerusalem before he began any military campaigns. Eleanor, the more sensible of the two, pleaded her uncle's cause; in fact, she and Raymond were in each other's company so much that tongues began to wag, and Louis, growing jealous, announced that he would set off for Jerusalem at once. Unwilling to be bullied, Eleanor announced that she would stay in Antioch and get a divorce, whereupon Louis dragged her by force from her uncle's palace. Historian William of Tyre assessed Eleanor as a "fatuous woman," but in the light of her long and illustrious career, his assessment would appear to be short sighted and biased. Kinder historians have described her as possessing good looks, charm, courage, passion, self-will, hot temper, sound sense, and a taste for poetry and romance. Louis lost all in the crusade: honor, the battle, even, for all practical purposes, his wife. He returned home in 1149, a temporarily chastened man. After a brief attempt at reconciliation, the couple separated and the marriage was annulled (1152)—no male heir had, after all, been produced.

Eleanor saw to it that her lands were returned to her and then promptly married Henry, duke of Normandy, who in 1154 became Henry I, king of England. During her marriage to the English king,

*Eleanor of Aquitaine
(Giraudon / Art
Resource, NY)*

she continued to administer her own lands, Aquitaine consisting of Guienne and Gascony. The couple had eight children: William; Henry; Richard I the Lionhearted ("ruled" 1189–1199); Geoffrey; John Lackland (r. 1199–1216); Matilda, who married Henry the Lion; Eleanor, who married King Alfonso VIII of Castile; and Joan, who married both King William II of Sicily and Count Raymond VI of Toulouse. In 1168 Queen Eleanor gave her favorite son, Richard, the duchy of Aquitaine and in 1172 made him duke of Poitiers.

In 1173 her sons revolted against their father, with not only Eleanor's blessing but also her military support. The sons were defeated in 1174, but it was Eleanor whom her husband sent to prison, for fifteen years. She was released upon her husband's death in 1189. Richard became king, but he left in a few months on the Third Crusade. Eleanor was given vice-regal powers, but she would much rather have sailed with her son. However, rules of the Third Crusade specifically barred the participation of women. After three years away from his throne, Richard was on the way home when he was captured by Duke Leopold of Austria and held for ransom of 150,000 marks, an astronomical sum to raise, even for Eleanor. She rounded up the money and traveled in person to escort her son home in 1194. He had been gone five years. The queen arranged for him to be crowned again, but a month following his coronation, he left again for Normandy, leaving the archbishop of Canterbury in charge, never going to England again. When he died in 1199, the great Richard the Lionhearted had actually served six months as king of England.

Eleanor, to solidify relations between England and France, quickly arranged a marriage between her grandaughter, Blanche of Castile, and the Dauphine of France; in fact, to ensure its success, in 1200, at almost eighty years of age, she traveled to Castile to fetch Blanche and deliver her personally to France. Then she returned to Aquitaine, which her son John had inherited from his brother, and defended it against her grandson Arthur of Brittany, who tried to claim it for France. She continued to be on hand to thwart Arthur during the campaign at Mirebeau in 1202, when at last John could take him prisoner. Triumphant but exhausted, she retired to the monastery at Fontevrault, Anjou, where she died in 1204.

References
Kibler, William W., ed. *Eleanor of Aquitaine: Patron and Politician.* Austin: The University of Texas Press, 1976.

Eleanor of Arborea
Ruler of Arborea (1383–1404)

Arborea, located in the center of Sardinia, was one of the four territorial divisions of that island, one of the largest in the western Mediterranean. Eleanor succeeded her father as queen, or "judge," of Arborea and is famous as a warrior queen. Her small realm had been invaded first by Pisans and then by Alfonso IV of Aragon, who drove out the Pisans. Eleanor fought valiantly in an effort to push the invaders out, but she did not succeed. She died in 1404 without securing her realm from invaders. However, another of her endeavors was more successful: It was through her efforts at codifying the laws, completing work begun by her father, that in 1421 her Carta de Logu was adopted by the Sard parliament, to be effective for the entire island. It remained in effect until the Treaty of Utrecht in 1713.

References
Delane, Mary. *Sardinia, The Undefeated Island.* London: Faber and Faber, 1968, pp. 149, 152, 185.

Elisa Bonaparte
Duchess of Tuscany, Princess of Piombino, and Ruler of the Principality of Lucca (1805/1809–1814)

Born Marie Anne (Elisa) Buonaparte (or Elisa Lucca) in 1777 on the island of Corsica, she was the oldest daughter and one of eight surviving children of Carlo Maria Buonaparte, a lawyer, and Maria Laelitia Ramolini (the family changed the spelling of their name to Bonaparte after 1796). Her father's family, of ancient Tuscan nobility, had emigrated to Corsica in the sixteenth century. She was the younger sister of Napoleon, who was born in 1782. She married Felix Bacciochi.

Napoleon was generous with his brothers and sisters; he first made Elisa the duchess of Tuscany. In 1805 he made her ruler of the principality of Lucca, in the Tuscany region of north-central Italy, and princess of Piombino. Elisa, like her famous brother, demonstrated

Elisa Bonaparte (Giraudon / Art Resource, NY)

remarkable administrative abilities. A woman of strong convictions, she occasionally found herself at odds with her family, even with Napoleon. At one point near the end of Napoleon's life he noted that all but Elisa had disappointed him. In 1815, following Napoleon's defeat, the Congress of Vienna assigned Lucca to the Spanish infanta Queen Maria Luisa of Etruria. Elisa withdrew to Bologna and later to Trieste, where she died in 1820, a year before her exiled brother.

References

Egan, Edward W., Constance B. Hintz, and L. F. Wise, eds. *Kings, Rulers, and Statesmen.* New York; Sterling Publishing, 1976. p. 277.

Morby, John. *Dynasties of the World.* Oxford: Oxford University Press, 1989. p. 108.

Putnam, John J. "Napoleon." *National Geographic* 161. February 1982: 142–189, particularly p. 168.

Elissa
See Dido

Elizabeth
Queen, Regent of Hungary and Croatia (1382–1385 and 1386)

Elizabeth was the daughter of Croatian Ban (supreme administrator of the realm, representing the king) Sjepan Kotromanic and the wife of Ljudevit I (r. 1342–1382), who also inherited the Polish throne when his uncle, King Kazimir, died. Elizabeth and Ljudevit had two daughters, Marija and Jadviga, both minors when Ljudevit died in 1386. Marija was betrothed as a child to Sigismund of Luxembourg, prince of Bohemia and son of Charles IV, emperor of the Holy Roman Empire and king of Bohemia. Jadviga inherited the Polish throne and later married Ladislav Jagielo, grand duke of Lithuania. Marija, at age twelve, inherited the Hungarian and Croatian thrones, with Elizabeth assuming the regency with the aid of Nikola Gorjanski, paladin of Hungary.

Croatian nobles resented the rule of the two queens, and Ivan Palizna, templar prior of Vrana, led a plot to invite Stjepan Tvrdko, king of Bosnia, to become king of Croatia. Gorjanski learned of the plot and brought both queens, with a strong army, from Hungary to Croatia to confront the rebels. The conspiracy collapsed, and the queens were welcomed royally in the capital, Zadar, where Marija presided over a session of the Croatian Sabor (parliament) before returning to Hungary. Soon, however, a new movement, spearheaded by the Horvat brothers, Ivaniz, ban of Macva, and Pavao, bishop of Zagreb, sought to install Marija's cousin, Prince Charles of Durazzo, on the throne. Charles accepted the invitation and traveled to Croatia to assume the throne. After a year, he went on to Hungary to oust Marija there as well. Marija abdicated, and Charles assumed that throne.

Elizabeth, Gorjanski, and Gorjanski's deputy, Forgacs, instigated a plot to assassinate Charles, and Marija was installed as queen of Hungary and Croatia for a second time (r. 1386–1395). Now Palizna, who had fled to Bosnia when his own plot failed, joined forces with the Horvat brothers and began another uprising. Gorjanski again set out for Croatia with an army and both queens, but this time the army was routed by the Horvats. Gorjanski and Forgacs were executed, and both queens were imprisoned in Palizna's palace, Novigrad on the Sea. On demand of Charles's widow, Elizabeth was put to death (1386). Marija was freed by her betrothed, Sigismund of Luxembourg, who had entered the breach and taken the Hungarian crown for himself in behalf of his wife.

References
Gazi, Stephen. *A History of Croatia.* New York: Barnes & Noble Books, 1993. pp. 58, 60–62.

Elizabeth
Queen, Ruler of Hungary (1439–1440)

Elizabeth was the daughter of Holy Roman emperor Sigismund, king of Hungary from 1387 to 1437, and his first wife, Barbara of Cilli. Elizabeth married Albert V, duke of Austria, who became King Albert II of Hungary upon her father's death. As Albert was also crowned king of Germany and Bohemia, Elizabeth became queen of those realms as well. The couple had a daughter, Elizabeth.

Albert II had the makings of a strong leader and immediately set about ending territorial feuds by appointing arbiters. He also divided Germany into governable administrative districts. However, he died after only two years (May 1439) while on an unsuccessful campaign against the Turks. Elizabeth was pregnant at the time. In 1440 she gave birth to their son, whom she named Ladeslov V Posthumus. In May 1440, to prevent Hungary from falling permanently under Polish rule, she compelled the primate to crown her baby king, exactly one year after her husband had died. She then made her cousin Frederick V of Styria (later Emperor Frederick II) the king's guardian. However, from 1440 to 1444 Hungary was nominally ruled by Vladislav VI of Poland.

Elizabeth was supported in her struggle to win her son's throne by some influential Croatian magnates and by the Serbian despot, George Brankovic, who had been granted large estates in Hungary. Elizabeth's forces met Vladislav's General Hunyadi in 1442 and were defeated. All might have been lost but for Vladislav's death in 1444, which cleared the way for Elizabeth's baby son to "rule." Her daughter, Elizabeth, married Casimir IV, king of Portugal, Vladislav's brother.

References
Dvornik, Francis. *The Slavs in European History and Civilization.* New Brunswick, NJ: Rutgers University Press, 1962. pp. 234, 349, 436.

Egan, Edward W., Constance B. Hintz, and L. F. Wise, eds. *Kings, Rulers, and Statesmen.* New York: Sterling Publishing, 1976. p. 229.

Langer, William L., ed. *World History.* Boston: Houghton Mifflin, 1980. pp. 337–339.

Elizabeth I
Queen of England (1558–1603)

Elizabeth I was born in 1533, the daughter of Henry VIII and his second wife, Anne Boleyn. Elizabeth's childhood and early adulthood were fraught with danger and disaster. Her mother was beheaded when Elizabeth was three years old. During the reign of her brother Edward VI, his protector, Edward Seymour, had his own brother Thomas tried for treason and executed, accused of plotting to marry Elizabeth and usurp the throne. Elizabeth, a nominal Protestant, was considered a constant threat to her Catholic sister, Mary, who ruled from 1553 to 1558. For a while during Mary's reign, Elizabeth was imprisoned in the Tower of London, suspected of having aided Sir Thomas Wyatt in a rebellion against the queen. These early experiences, whereby she was often saved by cautious circumspection, helped her perfect a technique that was to hold her in good stead throughout her reign: the technique of giving "answerless answers."

Elizabeth schooled herself particularly well; during her teens she could already speak six languages. In later years this facility with languages would place her at an advantage with foreign dignitaries, with whom she often conversed in their own languages. Elizabeth came to the throne in 1558, at the age of twenty-five, when Mary died. In later years of Elizabeth's forty-five-year reign, she would become known as the Virgin Queen and still later as Good Queen Bess. The greatest threat to her throne was posed by her cousin Mary Stuart, queen of Scots, a threat that Elizabeth ended by consenting to Mary's beheading once her involvement in an assassination plot by Anthony Babington was clearly proved.

In 1588 Elizabeth raised a fleet and force to defend against the Spanish Armada. She rode out to the mouth of the Thames to address her troops, saying in part, "I am come amongst you . . . not for my recreation and disport, but being resolved, in the midst and heat of the battle, to live or die amongst you all. . . ." Her presence and her speech so inspired the fleet that the Spanish Armada was routed and forced to retreat to the North Sea, where it was destroyed by storms. Elizabeth dabbled more frequently in foreign affairs after that, endeavoring to undermine, wherever possible, the Catholic influence.

She assisted The Netherlands in gaining independence from Spain, and she helped the Protestants gain a foothold in France.

The trait of hers that exasperated her ministers and foreign rulers alike, which they considered a terrible womanly weakness, was perhaps her greatest strength. That trait was what they considered to be indecisiveness. It was, instead, caution and circumspection. Elizabeth seemed to rule by instinct, knowing just when to withhold a decision, often until the need for decisive action had passed and a crisis had thus been averted. For years she used this trait to keep the nations of Europe guessing concerning her marriage plans. Half the monarchs of Europe curried her favor, hoping for a beneficial union. In her innate wisdom, she kept her plans to herself, neither rejecting nor accepting overtures. This technique was her special ploy to manipulate affairs of state. When it became apparent that she would not marry, would not produce an heir, she kept the world guessing, until she lay on her deathbed, about whom she would name as her successor.

At the end of her reign, England was poised to become a major world power and a colonial giant. During the latter years of her reign, literature flowered, as did, to a lesser degree, art and architecture. She personally attended the premier of the new playwright Shakespeare's *Twelfth Night*. Even today, Elizabeth is generally considered to be one of England's greatest monarchs. In 1603, when almost seventy years old, she named from her deathbed James VI of Scotland, the Protestant son of her cousin Mary, queen of Scots, as James I of England, first of the Stuart line.

References

Johnson, Paul. *Elizabeth I.* New York: Holt, Rinehart and Winston, 1974.

Luke, Mary M. *Gloriana: The Years of Elizabeth I.* New York: Coward McCann & Geoghegan, 1973.

Smith, Lacey Baldwin. *Elizabeth Tudor: Portrait of a Queen.* Boston: Little, Brown , 1975.

Elizabeth I
Tsarina of Russia (1741–1762)

Elizabeth I (or Elisaveta Petrovna) was born in 1709, the daughter of Peter the Great, who ruled Russia from 1682 to 1725, and Catherine I, who ruled from 1725 to 1727. When Elizabeth's mother was on her deathbed, she named her late husband's grandson, Peter II, to succeed her. Elizabeth was eighteen at the time, a beautiful, vivacious, and popular young woman at court. When Peter died in 1730, the throne was offered to Anna, a niece of Peter the Great. Anna ruled for ten years and on her deathbed named her grand-nephew Ivan as her successor and her niece Anna Leo-poldovna as regent. By this time Elizabeth was thirty-one, still very popular at court, particularly among the guards.

Elizabeth I, Tsarina of Russia (Corbis-Bettmann)

Anna Leopoldovna, be-lieving that Elizabeth's pop-ularity would make it more difficult for Anna to conduct her regency, had decided to banish Elizabeth to a con-vent, but the French ambas-sador and other anti-Ger-man factions in the court learned of the plan and ap-proached Elizabeth with the idea of staging a coup d'ètat. On a night late in 1741, Elizabeth dressed as a palace guard, stole into the palace with the other guards, and arrested the infant emperor, his regent-mother, and her advisers. Elizabeth was then proclaimed empress of Russia. She immediately reinstated the senate that had been created by her father but abolished by his successors. She then left control of most state affairs to her ministers while she turned her attention to westernizing her country.

Elizabeth established Russia's first university in Moscow and founded the Academy of Arts in St. Petersburg, now Leningrad. The privileged classes prospered in her reign while the lot of the serfs grew worse. The government's financial base deteriorated, although the country itself grew in stature as a European power. Russia fought a war with Sweden and gained a portion of Finland. Elizabeth joined with France and Austria in the Seven Years' War against Prussia's Fred-erick the Great, but by choosing her nephew Peter III as her succes-sor, she was paving the way for Peter to undo all the gains made against Prussia. She realized he was not a strong choice, so she chose his wife with extra care and groomed her for her future role. That young girl would become Catherine the Great. Elizabeth died in 1762.

References

Coughlan, Robert. *Elizabeth and Catherine.* New York: G. P. Putnam's Sons, 1974.

Riasanovsky, Nicholas V. *A History of Russia.* 5th ed. New York: Oxford University Press, 1993. pp. 242–243, 246–253 passim, 258f, 263.

Elizabeth II
Queen of Great Britain (1952–)

Elizabeth Alexandra Mary was born in 1926, the elder daughter of Prince Albert, duke of York (later to become King George VI, who ruled 1936–1952), and Lady Elizabeth, daughter of Claude Bowes-Lyon. With her younger sister, Margaret Rose, the future queen spent early childhood never expecting to be thrust into the limelight. When in 1936 her uncle Edward VIII abdicated and her father became king, Elizabeth suddenly found herself next in line for the throne. At age thirteen she first met her distant cousin, Lieutenant Philip Mountbatten, prince of Greece and prince of Denmark. Eight years later they were married. Their first son, Charles, was born the following year, 1948. Subsequently the couple had a daughter, Anne, and two more sons, Andrew and Edward.

Elizabeth acceded to the ostensibly symbolic position of queen in 1952. However, as queen, she has exercised more than ceremonial power, according to the London *Economist:* "Any prime minister who thinks that the weekly audition is a mere formality is in for a shock. The queen's experience tells. . . . She has seen every cabinet paper and important Foreign Office dispatch of the past 35 years and has held weekly meetings with eight consecutive prime ministers. She has met most foreign heads of state and has complained to the Foreign Office that its briefings are too simple. The queen is not only powerful but also popular. . . ." Both Winston Churchill and Harold Wilson were embarrassed to find that the queen was sometimes more up to date than her prime ministers. Wilson said when he retired, "I shall certainly advise my successor to do his homework before his audience."

The queen lives in 600-room Buckingham Palace in London, a dozen rooms of which are the royal apartment. Although the palace and its fifty-plus-acre grounds require a staff of 346 employees, the queen is thrifty. One authority, Robert Lacey, says the apartment is "visibly frayed at the edges." Yet the government allowance of the equivalent of $6.3 million for maintenance is usually inadequate, and the queen must make up the shortfall from her private funds. The queen is one of the wealthiest women in the world. She owns 52,000 acres of prime land. As alternate residences she has at her disposal Windsor Castle on the Thames near London and Holyroodhouse in Scotland. She also has estates at Sandringham in Norfolk and Balmoral in Scotland, both of which she maintains at her own expense. The British people regard the queen as a symbol of unity, stability, and tradition, and although the liberal British press occasionally criticizes the wealth of some of the royal family, the queen herself remained largely above criticism until the untimely death of her ex-daughter-in-law, Diana.

In 1994 Prince Charles had become increasingly unpopular when he announced that he never loved his estranged wife, Lady Diana Spencer. Liberal sources wrote that the best hope to save the monarchy was for Elizabeth to reign as long as Queen Victoria—for fifty-three years, until 2005. At that time, Charles and Diana's older son, William, would be twenty-one and could ascend the throne, bypassing his father entirely. In 1997 the divorced princess was killed in an automobile accident in Paris, occasioning an outpouring of grief of monumental proportions around the world. As England and the world mourned Diana's death, the queen remained in seclusion until public criticism compelled her to make an appearance to express the family's and the nation's grief.

References

Hudson, M. E., and Mary Clark. *Crown of a Thousand Years.* New York: Crown Publishing, 1978. pp. 148–150.

"Life in the Grand Style for Europe's Leaders." *U.S. News & World Report.* 21 June 1982.

"The Sleaze Factor." *World Press Review.* December 1994, p. 27.

"Throne Power." *World Press Review.* February 1988: 38.

Elizabeth of Görlitz
Co-ruler of Luxembourg (1412–1415), Ruled Alone (1415–1419 and 1425–1444)

Elizabeth of Görlitz (or Elizabeth of Luxembourg) was the second wife of Antoine of Burgundy, duke of Brabant, who in 1406 had been named successor to Limburg and Brabant by the childless Duchess Joanna, his great aunt. Elizabeth and Antoine had two sons: John IV, later duke of Brabant (1415–1427), and Philip, also later duke of Brabant (1427–1430).

During the reign of Holy Roman emperor Wenceslas IV (also king of Bohemia), the ruler spent so much time attending peace conferences in Prague trying to bring an end to the many internal conflicts that plagued his realm that the various princes of Germany began to demand some degree of separate rule for Germany. Anarchy reigned in much of the outlying areas of his realm. Wenceslas was eventually imprisoned as a heretic, and Antoine and Elizabeth, as heirs of the house of Limburg, saw opportunity to become pretenders to the duchy of Luxembourg. Wenceslas managed to get out of prison and restore himself briefly in ca. 1411, but when he returned to prison in 1412, Antoine and Elizabeth claimed the throne of Luxembourg. Wenceslas was executed in 1415, but Antoine died the same year.

Although Wenceslas's brother Sigismund became king of Germany, Elizabeth managed to hold onto Luxembourg. She ruled alone for five years while her son John IV became duke of Brabant. In 1419 Duke Johann of Bavaria assumed rule of the duchy until he died in 1425. Elizabeth then ruled alone again from 1425 until 1443 or 1444. In the meantime, her son John had died in 1427 and her younger son Philip became duke of Brabant until 1430, when he also died. Elizabeth, having outlived her heirs, continued as sole ruler of Luxembourg until ca. 1443, when she ceded it to Philip the Good, her husband's nephew. Luxembourg then joined the house of Burgundy.

References

Egan, Edward W., Constance B. Hintz, and L. F. Wise, eds. *Kings, Rulers, and Statesmen.* New York: Sterling Publishing, 1976. p. 297.

Langer, William L., ed. *World History.* Boston: Houghton Mifflin, 1980. pp. 406–407.

Elizabeth of Luxembourg
See Elizabeth of Görlitz

Elizabeth of Poland
Queen (of Hungary), Regent of Poland (1370–ca. 1377)

Elizabeth was the daughter of King Vladislav IV, king of Poland from 1305 to 1333. In 1320 she married Charles Robert of Anjou, king of Hungary (1310–1342). Their older son, Andrew, married Joanna I, queen of Naples. Their younger son was Louis I, king of Hungary (1342–1382) and king of Poland (1370–1382). Elizabeth's brother, Casimir III, succeeded their father as king of Poland in 1333 but died in 1370 leaving no male heir, so Elizabeth's son Louis I was named king of Poland. Louis had no interest in governing Poland and appointed his mother Elizabeth as regent. She ruled Poland until she died ca. 1377.

References

Dvornik, Francis. *The Slavs in European History and Civilization.* New Brunswick, NJ: Rutgers University Press, 1962. pp. 48, 82.

Egan, Edward W., Constance B. Hintz, and L. F. Wise, eds. *Kings, Rulers, and Statesmen.* New York: Sterling Publishing, 1976. pp. 338–339.

Emma

Queen, Regent of The Netherlands (1889–1898)

Emma (Archive Photos)

Born Emma of Waldeck Pyrmont, she became the second wife of King William III, ruler of The Netherlands from 1849 to 1890. In 1880 they had a daughter, Wilhelmina, who became second in the line of succession, the king's elder son by his first wife, Sophia, having died the previous year. In 1884 his other son, Alexander, died, making Wilhelmina heir apparent. During King William's final illness, Queen Emma served as regent. William died in 1890, and Emma continued as regent for ten-year-old Wilhelmina until she reached the age of eighteen. During Emma's rule, she was faced with putting down two serious revolts in the Dutch East Indies (1894 and 1896). The Liberal Party, in power at the time, passed a new electoral law in 1896 that more than doubled the number of citizens allowed to participate in the electoral process, but workers would not be satisfied with anything less than universal suffrage. The Liberal ministry continued to pass social legislation for the next five years. Queen Emma retired at the time of her daughter's majority.

References

Langer, William L. *World History.* Boston: Houghton Mifflin, 1980. pp. 475, 674.

Erato
Queen of the Ancient Kingdom of Armenia (?–A.D. 14)

Erato was the last ruler of the House of Artashes (Artaxias). In the first century B.C. Tigranes I, a descendant of the founder Artaxias, had deposed Artanes, the last king of Armenia Minor, and united the two Armenias under his rule. In 69 B.C. Tigranes I was defeated by Lucullus and stripped of his other possessions such as Syria but allowed to continue to rule over Armenia as a vassal of Rome. But after the first year, Tigranes paid tribute to no one, ruling for twenty-nine years and outlasting his overlord Antiochus by five years. Technically, Armenia remained at war with Rome, but in fact Armenia appeared to be a buffer state between the two greater warring factions of Rome and Parthia. However, when Tigranes's fourth-born son Artavsd-Artavasdes II came to the throne (55 B.C.), Armenia still managed to thrive as an independent state. Artavsd, although outwardly a Parthian ally since 53 B.C., appeared to submit when Mark Antony appeared on the scene. He guided Antony to his battle with Parthia, which Antony lost. Pretending friendship, Antony invited Artavsd and his family to his tent, where he seized them and took them off to Alexandria to be paraded as captives and to be turned over to Cleopatra. She tortured them unmercifully in an attempt to find the whereabouts of the Armenian crown jewels. But the entire family died in 33 B.C., with the exception of Artavsd's eldest son Artashes, who only two years later recaptured the Armenian throne and had all the Roman traders killed. Armenian disobedience continued despite Roman intimidation under Queen Erato, presumably Artashes's widow, who was herself twice dethroned by the Romans, the second time in A.D. 14.

References
Cahin, M. *The Kingdom of Armenia.* New York: Dorset Press, 1987, 1991, p. 245.

Ermengarde
Countess, Ruler of Carcassonne (1067–1070)

Carcassonne was located in the southwestern section of present-day France. Ermengarde was the daughter of Count Roger II, who ruled Carcassonne until his death in 1060. Her brother, Roger III, succeeded his father but died in 1067. Ermengarde married Raimond Bernard, vicomte d'Alby. She inherited the realm in 1067 from her brother and ruled until her death in 1070.

References.
Egan, Edward W., Constance B. Hintz, and L. F. Wise, eds. *Kings, Rulers, and Statesmen.* New York: Sterling Publishing, 1976. p. 156.

Ermengarde
Viscountess, Ruler of Narbonne (1143–1192)

Narbonne was located in the southeastern section of present-day France. Ermengarde was the daughter of Aimery II, who ruled from 1105 to 1134. When he died, he was succeeded by her brother, Alfonse Jourdain, count of Toulouse, who ruled from 1134 until he died in 1143. Ermengarde then presided over Narbonne for almost fifty years. She was the leader of the French royalist party in the south of France, which was in opposition to the English. She has been described as a nobly born Joan of Arc. She was married several times, but her husbands took no part in the government of Narbonne. Ermengarde fought numerous wars defending her domain and was a patron of troubadours and protector of the church. She gained renown as an arbiter and judge in complex cases of feudal law. She had no children, so when she died in 1192 she named as her heir her nephew, Pierre de Lara.

References
Egan, Edward W., Constance B. Hintz, and L. F. Wise, eds. *Kings, Rulers, and Statesmen.* New York: Sterling Publishing, 1976. p. 159.

Heer, Friedrich. *The Medieval World.* Trans. Janet Sondheimer. New York: Menton/NAL, 1962. p. 318.

Ermensinde
Countess, Ruler of Luxembourg (1196–1247)

Owing to the fact that her grandmother, Ermensinde I, a daughter of Conrad I (r. 1059–1086), had married Godfrey, count of Namur, Ermensinde II (or Ermensind) was of the house of Namur, originally a medieval county in present-day southeastern Belgium. Around the year 1100 the low-country territories began to expand and form principalities, weakening the hold of the German kings, so far away. With the decline of the power of German kings, emperors could do little to enforce their influence in the lowlands. Ermensinde inherited rule of the principality of Luxembourg in 1196 from her father, Count Henry IV the Blind, who ruled from 1136 to 1196. She married Walram III, duke of Limburg, and had a son, Count Henry V, born in 1217, who inherited the rule when Ermensinde died in 1247.

References
Egan, Edward W., Constance B. Hintz, and L. F. Wise, eds. *Kings, Rulers, and Statesmen.* New York: Sterling Publishing, 1976. p. 297.

Morby, John E. *Dynasties of the World.* Oxford: Oxford University Press, 1986. p. 92.

Esat
See Judith

Esato
See Judith

Eschiva of Ibelin, Lady
Queen of Beirut (1282–ca. 1291)

Eschiva of Ibelin was the younger daughter of John II of Beirut and Alice de la Roche of Athens. Her older sister, Isabella, became queen of the crusader state of Beirut following their father's death in 1264. Eschiva married Humphrey of Montfort, younger son of Philip of Montfort, lord of Toron and Tyre. The couple had a son, Roupen. When Isabella died in 1282, the fief of Beirut passed to Eschiva. When Humphrey's brother John of Montfort died ca. 1283, leaving no issue, Humphrey inherited Tyre. But he died ca. 1284, so Tyre then went to John's widow, Margaret. After a suitable interval, Eschiva was married (by King Hugh III of Cyprus and Jerusalem) to King Hugh's youngest son, Guy.

When the Mameluk sultan Qalawun was preparing to attack those of the Franks who were not protected by the truce of 1283, Eschiva hastened to ask him for a truce, which was granted in 1284. (Mameluks were former slaves from Russia and Central Asia who founded a dynasty in Egypt and Syria in 1250 that lasted almost 300 years. Mameluks made up an important part of Islamic armies from 833 forward.) The truce did not prevent Shujai, a later leader of the Mameluks, from driving out the crusaders and tearing down not only the walls of Beirut but also the castle of the Ibelins and turning the cathedral into a mosque in 1291.

References
Runciman, Steven. *A History of the Crusades.* Vol. 3. Cambridge: Cambridge University Press, 1952, 1987. pp. 329, 343, 393–395, 422.

Eudocia Macrembolitissa
Empress, Regent of the Byzantine Empire (1067), Co-ruler (1071)

Eudocia Macrembolitissa was born in 1021, the daughter of John Macrembolites. She was also the niece of the patriarch of Constantinople, Michael Cerularius. She married Emperor Constantine X Ducas. They had three sons, Michael VII, Andronicus, and Constantine, and two daughters, Zoe and Theodora Anna (also called Arete). When Constantine X died in 1067, according to the account of

Michael Psellus, one of Eudocia's advisers, she succeeded her husband as supreme ruler in accordance with his wishes. She assumed control of the administration in person, instructing her two sons (Andronicus had died earlier) in the nature of political affairs. Psellus said, "I do not know whether any other woman ever set such an example of wisdom or lived a life to hers up to this point." After a series of setbacks from the Turks who threatened along the frontier, Eudocia was convinced of the need for a strong military government. Psellus recalled praying aloud that she might enjoy power as long as she lived and Eudocia's calling the prayer a curse: "I hope it will not be my fate to enjoy power so long that I die an empress," she told him.

Despite the opposition of her advisers, Psellus and Caesar John, her brother-in-law, Eudocia married General Romanus IV Diogenes, who became ruler in 1068. He was an unpopular choice with the people. He fought the Turks with valor but was defeated in 1071 and taken prisoner. Again the throne was vacant. Some preferred that Michael succeed his stepfather, while others favored the complete restoration of Eudocia's rule to the exclusion of her sons. It was Psellus's suggestion that Eudocia and her son Michael assume joint and equal rule, which they did for a while. Meanwhile, Romanus concluded a treaty with the Turks that freed him if he paid an annual tribute to them. Romanus, intent on regaining the throne, wrote to Eudocia that he was free and wished to return. Eudocia, caught in an embarrassing situation, did not know what to do.

Michael did not want to lose his reign, so he decided to cut himself off from his mother and assume sole control. His advisers decreed that Eudocia should leave the city and live in a convent that she herself had founded. Michael refused to ratify such a decree. But with Romanus threatening, a constant stream of propaganda was directed against Eudocia. It was feared that she would allow Romanus to return and assume the throne. At length a second decree was issued stating that she must take the veil of a nun. In 1071 she was immured in a nunnery, and Michael was declared sole ruler. When Romanus returned, before he ever reached Constantinople, he was set upon by agents of Psellus, and his eyes were put out with hot irons. He died soon after, in 1072, as a result of his horrible injuries. Eudocia died in the nunnery in 1096, having been granted her wish not to die an empress.

References

Ostrogorsky, George. *History of the Byzantine State.* New Brunswick, NJ: Rutgers University Press, 1969. pp. 344–345.

Psellus, Michael. *Fourteen Byzantine Rulers.* Trans. E. R. A. Sewter. Harmondsworth, Middlesex: Penguin Books, 1982. pp. 339–360 passim.

Eudoxia

Augusta, De Facto Co-ruler of Eastern Roman Empire (400–404)

Eudoxia (or Eudocia) was the daughter of a mercenary general, the Frankish chief Bauto. In 395 she married Arcadus, emperor of the Byzantine Empire from 383 to 408. The marriage was engineered by a corrupt court eunuch, Eutropius, in an effort to weaken the status of a political rival. Eudoxia soon found that she was married to a weak and ineffectual ruler who let Eutropius dominate him. In time she decided to join Eutropius's opposition in order to bring about his ouster (399). Eudoxia and Arcadus had four children: Theodocius II, who, like his father, was weak; Pulcheria, who, like her mother, was strong; and two other daughters. Despite frequent pregnancies, Eudoxia exercised enormous influence over her husband's affairs. The period of her greatest influence dated from her designation as augusta in January 400. The patriarch of Constantinople, John Chrysotom, openly criticized her and her court and publicly reproached her and her court. She retaliated, after several bitter quarrels, by appealing to a rival archbishop for help in expelling John Chrysostom from his see (403) and permanently exiling him (404). She died shortly afterward of a miscarriage (A.D. 404).

References

Langer, William L., ed. *World History* Boston: Houghton Mifflin Company, 1940. p. 683.

Ostrogorsky, George. *History of the Byzantine State.* New Brunswick, NJ: Rutgers University Press, 1969. p. 54.

Previté-Orton, C. W. *The Shorter Cambridge Medieval History.* Vol. 1, *The Later Roman Empire to the Twelfth Century.* Cambridge: Cambridge University Press, 1952, 1982. pp. 77–83.

Eugénie-Marie
Countess (of Teba), Empress, Regent of France (1859, 1865, 1870)

María Eugénia Ignacia Augustina de Montijo de Guzmán (known as Eugénie-Marie) was born in a tent, to escape falling ceilings, during an earthquake in 1826. She was the daughter of a Spanish grandee, Don Cipriano de Guzmán y Palafox y Portocarrero, count of Teba, and Doña María Manuela. Her uncle Eugenio was the count of Montijo, and her father was his heir if Eugenio died childless.

In 1853 Eugénie-Marie married Louis Napoleon, who had been elected president of the French republic but who the year before had become Emperor Napoleon III when the monarchy was reestablished. The new red-haired empress was strikingly beautiful, brilliant, and charming, but pious, naive, and unschooled in affairs of state. Two events altered the degree of her involvement in political life: an assassination attempt against her husband in 1855 and the birth of their son Napoleon-Eugene-Louis in 1856, whom she hoped to see become the next emperor. Eugénie-Marie, a devout Catholic, became intent in fostering her faith. While her husband attempted to liberalize domestic policy, she worked for conservative causes, becoming the leader of the Clerical Party at the palace. Napoleon III concentrated much of his energies on war with Austria and on the Franco-Prussian War. In addition, he was afflicted with bouts of ill health throughout his reign.

On at least three occasions—1859, 1865, and 1870 and possibly more—Eugénie-Marie served as regent while her husband was out of the country. She was first appointed regent in 1859 during the war against Italy. In 1861 she was instrumental in the decision to create a Mexican Empire and to make Austrian archduke Maximilian its emperor. In 1862 Eugénie, believing that a united Italy was a threat to French security, suggested that Victor Emanuel's kingdom be broken up into four states of an Italian federation. But she was determined that Victor not take Rome, insisting that French troops stay there, for fear that the pope might excommunicate her and Napoleon if the French abandoned Rome. In 1869 she officially opened the Suez Canal with the Turkish khedive and Franz Joseph. In a time when entrance into medical school was denied women, she interceded in behalf of promising women applicants to gain them admittance. In 1870 she was appointed regent while Napoleon took supreme command of the army against the Prussians in the Franco-Prussian War. Napoleon's defeat and surrender following the Battle of Sedan (1870) left him a prisoner of war. Eugénie as regent refused to negotiate with the Prussians, who wanted her to cede them Alsace and Lorraine. She wrote a personal letter to King William of Prussia asking him not to annex those territories. In a courteous reply the king wrote that Prussia's security required their possession.

Napoleon's defeat made the likelihood of his reassuming his reign slim, so Eugénie-Marie sought exile in England. The deposed emperor died in 1873 following an operation for bladder stones, but Eugénie continued to play a part in politics, because her son was immediately proclaimed Napoleon IV by the Bonapartists. In 1879, hoping that her son would capture the imagination of the French people and return to claim the crown much as her husband had done, Eugénie encouraged him to mount an expedition to Africa to gain notoriety and military experience. But he was killed by Zulus, and Eugénie's aspirations died with him. She was not completely out of politics, however. Even though she was eighty-eight at the outbreak of World War I, she offered her yacht to the British Admiralty, which used it as a mine sweeper. She contacted the British War Office and offered to convert a wing of her forty-one-room mansion, Farnborough Hill, into a hospital. She continued to live in exile, becoming a well-loved celebrity wherever she went. She died at age ninety-four in 1920 while on a visit to Madrid.

References
Langer, William L., ed. *World History.* Boston: Houghton Mifflin, 1980. p. 683.
Ridley, Jasper. *Napoleon III and Eugenie.* New York: The Viking Press, 1980.
Weber, Eugen. *France.* Cambridge: The Belknap Press of Harvard University, 1986. pp. 95, 97, 181.

Euphrosine
Countess, Ruler of Vendôme (1085–1102)

Euphrosine was the sister of Bouchard III, who began his rule with the help of his guardian uncle, Giu de Nevers, and ruled from 1066 to 1085. She married Geoffroi Jourdain, sire de Previlly. When Count Bouchard III died in 1085, Euphrosine became countess and ruler. When she died in 1102, she was succeeded by Count Geoffroi Grisegonella.

References

Egan, Edward W., Constance B. Hintz, and L. F. Wise, eds. *Kings, Rulers and Statesmen.* New York: Sterling Publishing, 1976. p. 162.

Euphrosyne
Empress, De Facto Co-ruler of the Byzantine Empire (1195–1203)

Euphrosyne was the wife of Byzantine emperor Alexius III Angelus, who wanted to rule so badly that he blinded and deposed his own brother in 1195. Alexius, a weakling with a lust for power, adopted the name Comnenus after the great Comneni emperors, because he thought the name Angelus did not sound distinguished enough. The couple had three children: Irene, whose grandson became Michael VIII Palaeologus; Anna, whose husband became Theodore I Lascaris; and Eudocia, or Eudokia, whose second husband became Alexius IV. Alexius III busied himself with diplomatic affairs, at which he showed some aptitude, but home affairs were left to Euphrosyne. She proved to be extravagant and as corrupt as her brother-in-law Isaac had been.

References

Ostrogorsky, George. *History of the Byzantine State.* New Brunswick, NJ: Rutgers University Press, 1969. pp. 408, 410–416, 577.

Previté-Orton, C. W. *The Shorter Cambridge Medieval History,* Vol. 2, *The Twelfth Century to the Renaissance.* Cambridge: Cambridge University Press, 1952, 1982. p. 112.

Vasiliev, A. A. *History of the Byzantine Empire.* Madison: University of Wisconsin Press, 1952. pp. 440–445, 487.

F

Fatima
Sultana, Ruler of the Maldive Islands (1383–1388)

The Maldive Islands are located in the Indian Ocean, southwest of India's southern tip. When Islam was adopted in the twelfth century, the islands became a sultanate. For forty years, Muslim women ruled the Maldive Islands. Fatima's aunt, Sultana Rehendi Kabadi Kilege, called Khadija, had begun the dynasty, ruling from 1347 to 1379. The Muslim traveler Ibn Battuta spent a long period in Sultan Khadija's kingdom and even married four times while there, one of his wives being Sultana Khadija's stepmother. He described the kingdom in his work called the *Rihla* or *Rehla*.

Fatima was the daughter of Khadija's sister, Sultana Myriam, who had succeeded upon Khadija's death and reigned from 1379 to 1383. Upon her mother's death, Fatima ascended the throne and ruled until her death in 1388.

References
Dunn, Ross E. *The Adventures of Ibn Battuta.* Berkeley: University of California Press, 1986. pp. 230–235, 245.
Mernissi, Fatima. *The Forgotten Queens of Islam.* Trans. Mary Jo Lakeland. Minneapolis: University of Minnesota Press, 1993. p. 108.

Fatima
Queen of Zanzibar (ca. 1652–1696)

For over a century the small kingdoms on the south central coast of Africa were harassed by the Arabs and the Portuguese, each fighting for control. Several women ruled during that period, making their kingdoms easy targets, in the eyes of the Arabs. In 1652 Sultan ibn Seif of Oman drove the queen of Zanzibar off the island. For the next forty years, however, the Portuguese continued to maintain the upper hand and the queen was soon able to return to Zanzibar. In 1696 the Arabs lay seige to Fort Jesus at Kilindini in Mombasa, where many of the local citizens had taken refuge. The Portguese dispatched ships from Goa and Mozambique to intercept the Arabs, but the Omani slipped through. Queen Fatima had been attempting to send supplies to Fort Jesus, which was so understaffed that the women had to take turns as sentries. The Arabs captured Zanzibar and took the queen prisoner, deporting her to Muscat. After ten years, however, she was allowed to return, but her island remained under Arab control.

References

Clarke, Prof. John Henrik. "Time of Troubles." In Alvin M. Josephy, Jr., ed. *The Horizon History of Africa.* "Time of New York: American Heritage Publishing, McGraw-Hill, 1971. pp. 369–370.

Finnbogadóttir, Vigdis
President of Iceland (1980–1996)

In Iceland surnames are a combination of the father's first name and the suffix *dottir* (daughter) or *sson* (son). People are called by their first names, since surnames are usually lengthy and complex. A woman does not take her spouse's name when she marries but is known by her maiden name all her life. Vigdis was born in 1930 in Reykjavik to Finnbogi Ruter Thorvaldsson, a civil engineer and professor at the University of Iceland, and Sigridur Eriksdottir, a nurse, who was chairman of the Icelandic Nurses Association for thirty-six years. Vigdis was interested in the theater. She attended junior college in Reykjavik, then went abroad to study at the University of Grenoble and at the Sorbonne. She also attended the University of Copenhagen, where she studied theater history.

In 1953 she married but divorced after nine years; she returned to Iceland, where she taught French both in college and on television. At age forty-two she became the first single, divorced woman in her country to adopt a child: a daughter, Astridur. In 1972 she became director of the Reykjavik Theater Company, which flourished under her direction.

She became interested in politics in 1974 when she helped organize a petition campaign for the removal of the U.S. naval base at Keflavik. According to Washington columnist Betty Beale, Vigdis first ran for president in 1980 on a dare. Her opponents were three men. She was elected, the first popularly elected woman president in history, and she easily won reelections in 1984, 1988, and 1992. Although the post of president is largely ceremonial, with governing power vested in the prime minister, Vigdis did have some authority in the government. She signed all bills passed by the Althing, or parliament. If she vetoed a bill, it went before the people in a national referendum. In times of crisis—for example, the death of the prime minister—the president of Iceland would oversee the forming of a new government. As cultural ambassador for her country, Vigdis made state visits to other countries to educate the world to the fact that Iceland is not a place of snow and ice. On a five-city U.S. tour in 1987 called the "Scandinavia Today" celebra-

Vigdis Finnbogadóttir (Archive Photos)

tion, she took along Hilmar Jonsson, founder of Iceland's only gourmet magazine and known as the "gourmet ambassador," who prepared typical Icelandic foods to illustrate how far Icelanders have come from the days of eating large chunks of raw cod.

Although she encouraged the modernization of her country and was particularly interested in bettering the status of women, there are some areas of Icelandic life that are sacred, which she hoped progress would not alter. She was proud of the Norse heritage of her people, and she was unwilling to see Iceland become too worldly. The state-run television did not operate on Thursday night, for example, because that is traditionally family night. Until 1989, the manufacture and sale of beer were prohibited on the island. Vigdis described her position in an interview: "The role of the president is to be a symbol for the nation of unity and identity." In 1990 the Women's International Center presented President Finnbogadóttir with the International Leadership Living Legacy Award. When she stepped down from her post in 1996, she held the record as having the longest time in a democratically elected presidential office in the world.

References

Beale, Betty. "Word from Washington: Iceland's President Kicks off Scandinavian Culture Extravaganza." *Houston Chronicle.* 5 September 1982: 7:11.

"Exercising Patience." *World Press Review.* September 1990: 55.

Moritz, Charles, ed. *Current Biography Yearbook, 1987.* New York: H. W. Wilson, 1987. pp. 169–172.

Young, John Edward. "Iceland's 'Chef of State' Needs Plenty of Cod and Imagination." *Christian Science Monitor.* 8 July 1987: 25.

Fredegund
Queen, Regent of Neustria (584–597)

A study of the life of Fredegund (or Fredegond) should put to rest for all time the argument that if women ruled, peace would reign. She was at least the third wife of Merovian King Chilperic I, who ruled the western Frankish kingdom of Soissons from 561 to 584. Soissons was located in present-day western Belgium. The area has been called by several names. When the Frankish kingdom was divided among Chlotar I's four sons at the time of his death in 561, Chilperic's portion, the smallest part, was called Tournai, or the kingdom of Soissons. When Chilperic's half-brother died in 567, Chilperic received a large portion to the south, and later this entire area was designated as Neustria.

Chilperic was possibly the most barbaric king of the Franks. Gregory of Tours claimed that Chilperic had many wives, but the first of record were Audovera and Galswintha, sister of Queen Brunhilde. Fredegund, a former servant and Chilperic's mistress, induced him to repudiate Audoveda and to garrot Galswintha. This murder began a forty-year feud between Brunhilde and Fredegund. Fredegund and Chilperic married, and if the account of Gregory of Tours is accurate, she became one of the most bloodthirsty queens in history. She and Chilperic had many children, at least six known ones, most of whom died, and it was their deaths that motivated many of her bloodthirsty acts. Another motivation was the desire to rid the Frankish world of Brunhilde and her husband, Sigebert. Fredegund sent two emissaries to assassinate Sigebert, who was also planning an attack on Chilperic, his brother.

The entire Frankish world was infected with an epidemic of dysentery during Chilperic's reign. When her young son Samson became ill, Fredegund rejected him and wanted to have him put to death. She failed in her attempt, but he died anyway. When two more of her children were near death, she decided the disease was God's punishment because Chilperic had amassed so much wealth by taxing paupers. She ordered him to burn the tax demands. Chilperic sent messages to the people promising never to make such assessments again, but the children died anyway. She attempted to have two of her stepsons killed. She had her stepson Clovis's girl-friend and the girl's mother tortured before she had him stabbed for making "unforgivable remarks" about her. When she lost a fourth child to dysentery, she tortured and killed a number of Parisian housewives as alleged witches, charging that they had caused his death. She and Chilperic had Leudast, count of Tours, tortured to death for scurrilous behavior and perfidious talk. She had at least one daughter left, Rigunth, who in 584 was sent off to Toulouse with fifty carts of wealth, which Fredegund claimed was not from the country's treasury, as her dowry.

That same year, their baby Lothar was born, and shortly afterward, Chilperic was assassinated. Fredegund knew that she must preserve the child's life at all cost, as he was her last tie to power—although she did claim to be pregnant again at the time of Chilperic's death, just as a precaution. She took her wealth and took refuge in a cathedral, but she and the chief advisers of Chilperic's reign were removed to the manor of Rueil so that a new regime could be formed around the baby Lothar. But Fredegund was far from finished. She sent a cleric from her household to gain Queen Brunhilde's confidence and then assassinate her. When he failed, she murdered him. She then sent two priests to assassinate King Childebert II and his mother, Queen Brunhilde, but they were intercepted and executed. In 586, after she had had a bitter argument with Bishop Praetextatus, he was stabbed, apparently at her instigation. She came around to his room to watch him slowly die. She then poisoned a man who dared to berate her for murdering the bishop. She tried, but failed, to murder the bishop of Bayeux for investigating her part in the murder of Bishop Praetextatus.

Her daughter, Rigunth, back home after all her wealth was plundered, often insulted her mother, and they frequently exchanged slaps and punches. After a particularly vexing exchange, Fredegund tried to murder her daughter by closing the lid of a chest on her throat. She sent twelve assassins to murder King Childebert II, but they were all caught. She had three men decapitated with axes at a supper she gave for that specific purpose, because their constant family quarreling was causing a public nuisance. Other members of the victims' families wanted the queen arrested and executed, but she escaped and found refuge elsewhere. Later, in Paris, she sent word to King Guntram of Burgundy that was more a command than a request: "Will my lord the King please come to Paris? My son is his nephew. He should have the boy taken there and arrange for him to be baptised . . . and he should deign to treat him as his own son." The king took Fredegund, as regent, and Lothar (Clothar II) under his protection, but he had to be convinced by a large body of sworn depositions that the boy was Chilperic's legitimate son, since Fredegund had taken a few lovers in her time. King Guntram died in 592, and Brunhilde's son King Childebert II of Austrasia tried to take both Burgundy and Neustria, since he did not think that Fredegund and Lothar would be strong enough to resist an attack. This kind of attack and counterattack continued until Childebert's death three years later, and then the struggle was left to the two aging women, Fredegund and Brunhilde, who kept it up until Fredegund's death in Paris in 597.

References

Gregory of Tours. *The History of the Franks.* Trans. Lewis Thorpe.
    Harmondsworth, Middlesex: Penguin Books, 1974. pp. 222–587.
Previté-Orton, C. W. *The Shorter Cambridge Medieval History.* Vol. 1,
    The Later Roman Empire to the Twelfth Century. Cambridge: Cambridge
    University Press, 1952, 1982. pp. 156–157.

G

Galla Placidia
See Placidia, Galla

Gandhi, Indira
Prime Minister of India (1966–1977 and 1980–1984)

Born Priyadarshini Nehru in 1917, she was the only child of Jawaharlal Nehru, India's first prime minister, and his wife, Kamala. As leaders of the movement for India's independence, her parents were frequently imprisoned by the British during her childhood, but Nehru wrote his daughter many letters that inspired her to follow in his footsteps. As a girl of twelve, she organized the Monkey Brigade, an association of thousands of children who assisted the National Congress Party. Sporadically she attended boarding schools in India and Switzerland, then college in West Bengal and Oxford. At twenty-one she joined the National Congress Party and became actively involved in the revolution. Against her father's advice, she married a childhood friend, Feroze Gandhi, lawyer, economist, and member of parliament—and Parsi. The mixed marriage raised a public furor. The couple had two sons, Rajiv and Sanjay, in the ten years before they separated.

In 1947 India was free to choose its own leader, and Nehru was the obvious choice. Since his wife had died in 1936, Indira served as his first lady. In 1959 she was elected president of the Congress Party, the second-highest political position in India. In 1960 her husband died, but she never remarried. Her father died in 1964. His successor, Lal Badahur Shastri, brought her into his cabinet as minister of information and broadcasting. In 1966 Shastri died, and Indira Gandhi was elected prime minister, the first woman ever to lead a democracy, the world's largest democracy. In the 1967 election, her win was less than an absolute majority, and she had to accept a right wing deputy prime minister. In 1971 India annexed the kingdom of

Sikkim, exploded its first nuclear device, and put a satellite into orbit. Gandhi then called for another election and won handily, running on the slogan, "Abolish poverty." Her party won two-thirds of the seats in parliament. At that point she was probably the most popular leader in the world. U.S. secretary of state Henry Kissinger said of her at that time, "The lady is cold-blooded and tough," although Indians called her Mataji, "respected mother."

It was not possible for her both to abolish poverty and please the rich, to whom she owed her power. A voluntary sterilization program she had instituted was attacked by her right wing opponents as being a compulsory program. In 1975, amid riots and protests, she declared a state of emergency and severely limited personal freedoms with new laws and with prison terms for political opponents. In effect, she suspended the democratic process in which she professed to believe. Two years later, after she had restored democratic practices, she was voted out of office and replaced by the right wing Janata Party. She was charged with abuse of office by the new administration and even spent a week in jail. In December 1979 she was reelected by a large plurality with the help of her younger son, Sanjay, who was her heir-designate. When he died in a plane crash in 1960, there was speculation about the future of the Congress Party and Indira's rule, but her popular support remained strong for a long time. She began to groom her other son, Rajiv, to be her successor. In 1983 she told the World Energy Conference, "We are opposed to nuclear weapons and do not have any" but said that India was developing a nuclear program for peaceful purposes. Gandhi could not begin to solve India's economic, social, religious, linguistic, and cultural problems and contend with a devastating drought that affected 2.7 million Indians. She said in a 1982 interview, "Can democracy solve such vast problems, especially when we have this constant opposition in the way? People are hitting at our feet and still saying, 'You must go further, you must go faster.' But we believe in democracy; we were brought up with those ideals.

And in India we simply cannot have another way. . . . Only a democracy will allow our great diversity. . . . The only danger to democracy is if the people feel it is not solving their problems." Her chief detractors were the right wing and the two Communist parties. In 1984, after she had again placed restraints on personal freedoms and ordered a raid on a Sikh temple, she was assassinated. Her son, Rajiv Gandhi, became the new prime minister of India. In her autobiography, Indira Gandhi, the most powerful woman India has ever known, wrote simply, "To a woman, motherhood is the highest fulfilment."

References

Bhatin, Krishan. *A Biography of Prime Minister Gandhi.* New York: Praeger, 1974.

"Clouds over India Dim Gandhi's Global Star." *U.S. News & World Report.* 21 March 1983.

Gandhi, Indira. *My Truth.* New York: Grove Press, 1980.

"Gandhi on Atomic Power." *Houston Post.* 18 September 1983: A 3.

Szulc, Tad. "What Indira Gandhi Wants You To Know." *Parade* 25 July 1982: 6–8.

Tefft, Sheila. "Gandhi Murder Inquiry Released." *Christian Science Monitor.* 29 March 1989: 4.

Gemmei-tennō

Empress of Japan (708–714)

Originally named Abe, Gemmei-tennō was born in 662, the daughter of Emperor Tenchi, who ruled Japan from 662 to 673. Following his abdication in 673, two other rulers, his brother Temmu (673–686) and Tenchi's daughter and Temmu's consort Jitō (687–696), followed before Gemmei's son Mommu, Jitō's nephew, became emperor. He was fourteen years old when he ascended to the imperial throne. He ruled for eleven years. In the year following Mommu's death, Abe became Empress Gemmei-tennō at the age of forty-six. It was customary, no matter how early in the year a ruler's reign ended, to begin the succeeding ruler's reign no sooner than the following year.

She proved to be an exceptionally able ruler. It is due to her foresight that the early traditions of Japan have survived. At her instigation, the *Kojiki* (712) and the *Fudoki* (713) were written to preserve the ancient traditions. In keeping with the ancient belief that a dwelling place was polluted by death, it was customary upon the demise of a sovereign for the successor to move into a new palace. Emperor Tenchi had enacted an edict to regulate the capital in 646, but the edict was not carried out until 710, when Empress Gemmei moved the court from Asuka to Nara, or Heijo, as it was called then, in the province of Yamato in central Japan. She also ordered the coinage of the first copper money. She abdicated in 714 in favor of her daughter, Hitaka (Genshō-tennō), and died in 723 at the age of sixty-one.

References
Papinot, E. *Historical and Geological Dictionary of Japan.* Rutland, VT: Charles E. Tuttle, 1972. p. 115.

Reischauer, Edwin O. *East Asia: The Great Tradition.* Boston: Houghton Mifflin, 1960. p. 480.

Sansom, George. *A History of Japan to 1334.* Stanford: Stanford University Press, 1958. p. 82.

Genshō-tennō
Empress of Japan (715–723)

She was born Princess Hitaka in 679, the daughter of Empress Gemmei-tennō and the older sister of Emperor Mommu. She furthered the work of her mother by encouraging the arts, letters, science, and agriculture. The *Nihongi,* chronicles of Japan to the year 697, were completed and published during her reign (720). When her nephew Shōmu reached age twenty-five, she abdicated, at the age of forty-five, in favor of him. She died in 748 at the age of 69.

References
Papinot, E. *Historical and Geographical Dictionary of Japan.* Rutland, VT: Charles E. Tuttle, 1972. p. 117.

Gordon, Minita
Governor-General of Belize (1981–1993)

Belize, formerly the crown colony British Honduras, is located on the east coast of Central America. In 1973 the name was changed from British Honduras to Belize, and in 1981 the colony gained independence and became a member of the British Commonwealth of nations with Queen Elizabeth II as head of state. The governor-general of Belize, as in several other Commonwealth nations, is appointed by the British monarch and represents the monarch. The governor-general presides over national and international defense, foreign affairs, and the civil service but wields no real power for governing.

Minita Gordon was born in 1930. After receiving an excellent education, she served in several positions, including member of the national assembly. When Belize received its independence in 1981, Queen Elizabeth II appointed Minita Gordon its first governor-general. Because Guatemala refused to recognize Belize's independence, 1,500 British troops, under Gordon's command, remained on Belize soil to maintain peace. Gordon served for twelve years, retiring in 1993.

References

"Belize." *Funk & Wagnalls New Encyclopedia*. Vol. 3. 1986. p. 412.

Go-Sakuramachi-tennō
Empress of Japan (1763–1770)

Go-Sakuramachi-tennō was born Princess Toshi-ko in 1741, the daughter of Emperor Sakuramachi-tennō. After a reign of eleven years during which the shōgun Yoshemune had held actual power, the emperor had abdicated in favor of his eleven-year-old son Momosono. During the boy's reign, power rested with the shōgun Ieshige. When her brother died in 1763, Go-Sakuramachi-tennō, two years his junior, succeeded to the ceremonial position and permitted Ieshige to continue his government. She abdicated at the age of thirty in favor of her nephew Hidehito. She died in 1814 at the age of seventy-three.

References

Papinot, E. *Historical and Geographical Dictionary of Japan.* Rutland, VT: Charles E. Tuttle, 1972. pp. 127, 399, 535.

Grey, Lady Jane
Queen of England for Nine Days (1553)

Jane was born in 1537, the daughter of Henry Grey, marquess of Dorset, later duke of Suffolk, and Lady Frances Brandon, sister of Henry VIII. Jane was the great-grandaughter of Henry VII. She led a short and unhappy life. At the age of sixteen, at the instigation of the duke of Northumberland, she was married to his son, Lord Guildford Dudley, and went to live with Dudley's parents, whom she found disagreeable.

A few weeks later, the duke, an ambitious man who had plans to make his son the king, persuaded the dying King Edward VI to name Lady Jane as heir to the throne, bypassing the legal heirs, Edward's sister Mary Tudor, daughter of Henry VIII, and after her, Edward's other sister Elizabeth, then his cousin Mary of Scots. When Jane first learned of the scheme to name her queen, she fainted. Nevertheless, when Edward VI died in July 1553, she allowed herself to become a pawn in the political intrigues against Mary Tudor. Lady Jane and Guildford were escorted to the Tower of London, where she was proclaimed queen on July 10, 1553. But Mary had gained great popular support, and the

duke of Northumberland, realizing this, left town, leaving his son and daughter-in-law to their own devices. The mayor of London announced Mary as queen, and the duke of Suffolk, Jane's father, convinced her to step down. She left the tower in relief, saying that she never wanted to be queen in the first place.

Northumberland was executed, but Queen Mary "could not find it in her heart to put to death her unfortunate kinswoman, who had not even been an accomplice of Northumberland but merely an unresisting instrument in his hands." But in 1554, when Jane's father was involved in an insurrection led by Sir Thomas Wyatt, Queen Mary became convinced that her throne would be threatened so long as Jane lived. Jane, her father, and her husband were all executed in 1554.

References

Hudson, M. E., and Mary Clark. *Crown of a Thousand Years.* New York: Crown Publishing, 1978. pp. 82–85.

Plowden, Alison. *Lady Jane Grey and the House of Suffolk.* New York: Franklin Watts, 1986.

Gulama, Madame
Mende Chieftain in Sierra Leone, West Africa (1960s–1986)

For more than thirty years, Madame Gulama was a prominent and controversial leader in Sierra Leone affairs. Much of her power stemmed from arranging marriage between graduates of the Sande Bush (female initiation society, of which she herself was a graduate and then director) and men in strategic positions who could help her in her own ambitious plans. Graduates of the Sande Bush are always influential in their own right and thus a great asset to men in positions of leadership.

References

Boone, Sylvia Ardyn. *Radiance from the Waters.* New Haven: Yale University Press, 1986. pp. 86, 146.

Gwamile Mdluli
Queen, Chief Regent of Swaziland (1899–1921)

Gwamile Mdluli was the wife of King Mbandzeni (ca. 1857–1889), who reigned from 1874 until his death. Gold was discovered in 1882, bringing more and more Europeans into the area, so that, during the last five years of his reign, he signed almost 400 concessions granting the newly arrived Europeans sundry privileges. Shortly before his death in 1889, he signed one final concession granting Europeans control of Swaziland in return for £12,000 a year. Upon his death, his son Bhunu (b. 1873) succeeded as king at the age of sixteen. During his short life, Bhunu and his regents worked futilely to regain control of Swazi rights that his father had signed away. Bhunu died in 1899, leaving a newborn son Sobhuza II (or Mona) to inherit the throne.

Sobhuza's grandmother Gwamile served as chief regent, working to reverse the "sellout" of Swazi rights perpetrated by her husband. One of her first acts was to dissolve the concessionaires' committee.

In 1899 the Boer War began between Britain and the Transvaal and the Orange Free State. On October 1, 1899, the Transvaal government surrendered its powers over Swaziland to Queen Regent Gwamile. But by that time, the white man's encroachment into Swazi life could not be reversed. In 1903, after the war was over, Swaziland became a British protectorate. Gwamile continued as regent until her grandson was formally installed (1921). Swaziland would not gain full independence again until 1968.

References

Blaustein, Albert R., and Gisbert H. Flanz, eds. *Constitutions of the Countries of the World: A Series of Updated Texts, Constitutional Chronologies, and Annotated Bibliographies.* Dobbs Ferry, NY: Oceana Publications, 1991.

Lipschutz, Mark R., and R. Kent Rasmussen. *Dictionary of African Historical Biography.* Berkeley: The University of California Press, 1986. p. 220.

Gyda
Queen of English Jarldom (ca. 988–ca. 995)

Gyda was the daughter of a Viking king (by Snorre Sturlason's account, of Ireland) and the younger sister, or more likely half sister, of Anlaf Curaran (Olaf Kvaran, d. 992, or Amlaibh, who ruled Dublin 857–871), the king of Dublin in Ireland. During the era of numerous petty kingdoms, Gyda, described as "young and beautiful," first married a mighty jarl (chieftain) in England. (It might be noted that King Svein Forkbeard had a daughter, Gyda, who married the exiled son of Jarl Hakon of Norway, Eirik Hakonarson. Gyda, however, was the name of other early queens, among them Gyda, the wife of Edward the Confessor, and her mother, also named Gyda, or Githa, the mother of Harold, king of England.)

When Gyda's husband died, she ruled the land in her own right. A warrior and duelist named Alvini wooed her, but she said that she would choose her husband from among the men of her own country. The prospective husbands gathered dressed in their finery—all except Olav Trygvason, a Norwegian harrier who called himself Ali, later to become the great sea king. She chose Olav, but Alvini challenged him to a duel. Olav defeated Alvini, banished him from England, and married Gyda. They had a son who became Viking king Trygvi. For a while, Olav divided his time between England and Ireland, making raids. Later he returned to Norway to claim his heritage as Olav I, king of Norway (995). Presumably he left Queen Gyda behind. He had several wives, both before and after Gyda, but she is not mentioned again.

References
Jones, Gwyn. *A History of the Vikings.* Oxford: Oxford University Press, 1984. p. 137.
Sturlason, Snorre. *Heimskringla, or The Lives of Norse Kings.* Trans. A. H. Smith. Editorial notes by Erling Monsen. New York: Dover Publications, 1990. pp. 137–138, 471.

H

Hatshepsut
Queen of Egypt (Variously Given as 1479–1458, 1505–1484, 1503–1482, 1501–1480, or 1473–1458 B.C. in the Eighteenth Dynasty)

Hatshepsut (or Hatasu) was the daughter of King Thutmose I and Queen Ahmose I. She married her half brother, King Thutmose II. When their father died in ca. 1493 B.C., the couple ascended to the throne. Thutmose II died ca. 1479 B.C., before Hatshepsut could bear him a son, and a boy of six by a minor wife of his became Thutmose III. Hatshepsut assumed the regency, but very shortly usurped the throne and ordered herself crowned pharaoh, as selected by the god Amon-Re. She adopted the false beard signifying wisdom worn only by pharaohs. Occasionally she was depicted wearing masculine garb as well.

An extraordinary and able monarch, she forswore the military conquests of her forebears and concentrated instead on commercial enterprises. Her greatest economic triumph came in the ninth year of her reign (ca. 1471 B.C.), when she reestablished trade with the land of Punt, which was probably on the Somali coast along the Gulf of Aden, although scholars differ as to its exact location. Because the Nubians controlled the Nile route between Aswan and Khartoum and demanded toll to use it, another trade route had to be found. Hatshepsut's chancellor Nehsy led the trade expedition of five provision-laden ships that had to be carried across the desert from Thebes to the Red Sea to reach Punt. The chief of Punt, Parahu, and his wife, Atiya, met the expedition with gestures of great obeisance. In exchange for bread, beer, wine, meat, and fruit, the ships brought back "green" gold, ivory, ebony, herbs, myrrh, baboons, monkeys, hounds, and servants and their children. Many of the treasures collected in Punt were used to adorn the impressive edifices and monuments built during the queen's approximately twenty-year reign.

The military leaders chafed under her indifference and lack of

*Hatshepsut
(Corbis-Bettmann)*

military ambitions and rallied around Thutmose III, waiting for him to grow to manhood. Encouraged by them, Thutmose III became bent on acquiring a reputation as an empire-builder, and he rose to become head of the army, occupying himself with foreign wars while Hatshepsut occupied herself constructing monuments. Some of those monuments that survive are small chapels dedicated to the great architect of the day, Senmut, who rose to a position of eminence in her court. Their location within her temple suggests that Senmut must have been her lover. However, if he had the memorials placed there without her knowledge, as some suggest, she must have discovered them and hacked them from the walls of niches. Five years prior to the end of her reign, all record of Senmut's activities ceases.

In the last five years of her reign, Hatshepsut's power waned. Prince Thutmose III, doubtless irked by the usurpation of his aunt, either came to the throne in a coup d'état or acceded at the time of her death. Evidence of his vendetta against her memorials is irrefutable. Hatshepsut died in about 1458 B.C.

References

Fairservis, Walter A., Jr. *The Ancient Kingdoms of the Nile*. New York: Mentor/NAL, 1962. pp. 133–134, 141, 165.

Grimal, Nicolas. *A History of Ancient Egypt*. Trans. Basil Blackwell Ltd.

New York: Barnes & Noble Books, 1997. pp. 163, 174, 176, 200–217 passim, 246, 262, 264, 274, 295, 297, 300–302, 313.

Rawlinson, Nicolas. *Ancient History.* New York: Barnes & Noble Books, 1993. pp. 77, 163, 174, 176, 200–217, 246, 262–264, 274, 295, 297, 300–302, 313.

Reader, John. *Africa.* New York: Alfred A. Knopf, 1998; London: Hamish Hamilton, 1997. pp. 196–197.

Shinnie, Margaret. "Civilizations of the Nile." In Alvin M. Josephy, Jr., ed. *The Horizon History of Africa.* New York: American Heritage Publishing, McGraw-Hill, 1971.

West, John Anthony. *The Traveler's Key to Ancient Egypt.* New York: Alfred A. Knopf, 1985. pp. 342–343.

White, J. E. Manchip. *Ancient Egypt: Its Culture and History.* New York: Dover Publications, 1970. pp. 165–167.

Hazrat Mahal, Begum
Regent of Oudh (1856–1858)

Until 1856 the kingdom of Oudh in northern India, with its capital of Lucknow, had been ruled by a nominally independent king. But the exile of King Wajid Ali Shah and the annexation in 1856 of his kingdom by the British East India Company were two of the causes of the Sepoy War or Indian Mutiny of 1857. Begum Hazrat Mahal, a concubine of the harem, was the only one in the harem willing to commit herself to the rebellion. Raja Jai Lal visited her and made a bargain: He would present her young son, Birjis Qadr, to the army as the son and rightful heir of the deposed king if she, as new queen regent, would appoint Jai Lal as military leader. Hazrat agreed, although it was common gossip in Lucknow that the boy was really the son of her paramour, Mammu Khan. Birgis Qadr was accepted by the army and enthroned in 1857. Hazrat appointed her lover chief of the high court.

The new queen fought valiantly against the British and worked hard to retain the leadership of the revolt by fiery personal speeches to the troops, but during the final assault by the British in 1858, she could sense that she was losing control. People were leaving Lucknow in search of safety. She considered suing for a compromise peace, but the British were not willing. As the British advanced on Lucknow, the rebels escaped; Hazrat, her ailing son, and her court went northeast to Bithavli, where they attempted to regroup for a pitched defense. The British demanded surrender, but Hazrat and her party refused and tried to escape to Nepal. Among her party were the rani of Tulsipur, raja of Gonda, and Beni Madho, who was the rana of Shankerpur and one of Hazrat's most loyal followers. By that time Hazrat had come to realize that she and her son had been virtual prisoners of the sepoys (Indian soldiers in the British army); she berated them, saying they had made goats of her and her son, although the queen had never sought their support. The British tried to prevent the retreat of the rebels. Many were killed or captured. Hazrat and her party did escape capture, but it was presumed that they all died of exposure or disease soon after. Reporters at the time likened her to Penthesilea, queen of the Amazons, who in post-Homeric legends fought for Troy; hence, a strong commanding woman.

References

Pemble, John. *The Raj, the Indian Mutiny and the Kingdom of Oudh, 1801–1859*. Rutherford, NJ: Fairleigh Dickinson University Press, 1977. pp. 4, 210–211, 213, 222–223, 229, 234, 245–247.

Hedwig, Saint
Duchess of Silesia (ca. 1236, 1241–1243)

Hedwig was the daughter of Bertold III of Andrechs, marquis of Meran, count of Tirol, and prince (or duke) of Carinthis and Istria. Her mother was Agnes, daughter of the count of Rotletchs. At a very young age, Hedwig's parents placed her in a monastery. At the age of twelve, she became the wife of Henry I, duke of Silesia from 1201 to 1238. The couple had six children: Henry II the Pious, Conrad, Boleslas, Agnes, Sophia, and Gertrude. After the birth of their sixth child, at Hedwig's suggestion, the couple agreed not to cohabit, so as to remain pure, and never to meet except in public places. At her persuasion, and with her dower, Henry built the monastery of Cistercian nuns at Tretnitz, the construction of which took sixteen years.

In 1163 Silesia (now mostly in Poland) was divided into Upper and Lower Silesia, each ruled by a Piast prince. Henry and his son tried without success to reunite the territory, while Hedwig ruled Silesia. When her husband was taken prisoner by the duke of Kirne, her son Conrad raised an army to rescue him, but Hedwig, who had great faith in her own prayers, dissuaded him from attempting the rescue, saying that she was sure that in due time he would be released. In 1238 Henry I died, but Hedwig remained duchess of Silesia, although she concerned herself only with matters of the church. In 1241 Henry II was killed in the battle of Liegnitz, which pitted the Silesian Knights of the Teutonic Order against the Mongol army under the command of Baider, son of Jagatai. Hedwig died in 1243 and was canonized in 1266.

References

Butler, Alban. *The Lives of the Fathers, Martyrs and Other Principal Saints.*
Vol. 4. Chicago: The Catholic Press, 1961. pp. 1290–1295.

Löwenstein, Prince Hubertus Zu. *A Basic History of Germany.* Bonn: Inter
Nationes, 1964. p. 38.

Helen Glinski
See Yelena Glinskaya

Helena Lecapena
Co-ruler of Eastern Roman Empire (945–959)

Helena Lecapena was the daughter of the regent of the Roman Empire, Romanus Lecapenus. In 919 she married the young Emperor Constantine VII Porphyrogenitus, who wore the crown from 913 to 959 and who raised her father to the rank of caesar and the status of co-emperor of the Eastern Roman Empire. The father-in-law dominated Constantine and became one of the most important rulers in Byzantine history. But in 944, as he began to age noticeably, two of his sons, Helena's brothers, anxious that Constantine VII not gain control upon Romanus's death, staged a coup d'état and sent their father to a monastary. However, the coup did not have popular support. The brothers were executed, and Constantine VII was left in reluctant control of his throne.

Helena and Constantine had at least six children, one of whom was Romanus II, who became emperor of the Eastern Empire from 959 to 963, and another of whom was Theodora, who married John I Tzimisces, emperor of the Western Empire from 969 to 976. Constantine VII, a scholarly man who was more interested in intellectual pursuits, did not come into his full rights as sole ruler until he was nearly forty (945). By that time he had worn the crown for thirty-three years, most of his life. During the period of his sole rule, he was most apt to follow the lead of Helena, who had inherited her father's strong leadership abilities.

Of great historical importance was the visit of the Russian princess Olga, who came to Constantinople to cement Byzantine and Russian relations. As a measure of her esteem, Olga, a Christian, took at her baptism the name of the Byzantine empress Helena. This honor by the regent of the Kievan state and her stay with Helena and Constantine at the Imperial Palace at Constantinople ushered in a new era between the two nations and gave fresh impetus to the missionaries of the Byzantine church in Russia. In 959 Constantine VII died, and their son Romanus assumed the throne. He had married the beautiful and ambitious Theophano and was completely under her spell. To please Theophano, Helena had to retire from court, and her five daughters were forcibly removed to convents.

References

Ostrogorsky, George. *History of the Byzantine State.* New Brunswick, NJ: Rutgers University Press, 1969. pp. 262, 264, 279, 283–284.

Psellus, Michael. *Fourteen Byzantine Rulers.* Trans. E. R. A. Sewter. Harmondsworth, Middlesex: Penguin Books, 1982. pp. 63, 308.

Henriette de Cleves
Duchess, Ruler of Nevers (1564–1601)

Henriette was the daughter of Francois II, duke of Nevers from 1562 to 1563, and the sister of Jacques, duke of Nevers from 1563 to 1564. As was frequently the case with minor rulers, Henriette inherited the financial problems of several of the men in her family. By the time of her grandfather, Francois I, the concept of provincial governors had been well established (although actually the term *governor* had come into usage for royal provincial agents as early as 1330). Governors were originally appointed when there was no male heir. Four of the 142 major governors of the period from 1515 to 1560 were dukes of Nevers, the first being Henriette's grandfather, Francois I, who was appointed governor of Champagne. He dissipated much of his fortune in the discharge of his duties, particularly on military campaigns.

When Francois I died early in 1562, he left Henriette's father, Francois II, the new governor of Champagne, bankrupt. Francois II died in battle only ten months later, leaving the guardian of Henriette's young brother Jacques de Cleves the job of liquidating the debts. Henriette's dowry was lowered, and to protect her jewels from creditors, she hid them at the Paris townhouse of the president of the Parlement, Pierre de Seguier. Seguier's wife eventually filed a protest: "Since the day that the said lady left her family jewels (with us) . . . a merchant has not ceased to bother us. . . . We plead to be freed from the charge of keeping the jewels." Before the liquidation process had begun, Jacques also died, in 1564. Since there was no male heir in the Cleves line, the property could have been dispersed among others as was often the case. But in 1565 King Charles IX issued extraordinary permission for the family property and titles to pass to Henriette, and a marriage was arranged for her with the prospective heir of some large estates, Ludovico Gonzaga, or Louis de Gonzague. The two succeeded to the duchy and guided it for thirty-seven years.

The marriage did not solve Henriette's financial problems completely, for Gonzaga had debts of his own, and his inheritance was not as large as that of the Cleveses. In addition, Henriette had to provide dowries for her two sisters. Each received 700,000 livres worth of land and dowries totalling another 600,000 livres. Louis sold many properties, but much of the estate administration fell to Henriette. Louis was in the prime of his military career, serving as mobile army commander and courtier. He was wounded in 1568 and in 1573, and he was forced to borrow money to pay his men. Despite this, the Neverses were the chief creditors of the monarchy during this period.

Henriette had at least one daughter. In 1581 she had a son, Charles II (Charles de Gonzague or Gonzaga), who succeeded upon her death in 1601 but who actually had become co-governor of Champagne with his father in 1589 and who succeeded as duke when his father died in 1595.

References

Egan, Edward W., Constance B. Hintz, and L. F. Wise, eds. *Kings, Rulers, and Statesmen*. New York: Sterling Publishing, 1976. p. 159.

Harding, Robert R. *Anatomy of a Power Elite*. New Haven: Yale University Press, 1978. pp. 21, 143–149.

Hetepheres I
Queen Mother of the Fourth Dynasty, Egypt (ca. 2613–2494 B.C.)

Because of Egypt's law of matrilineal succession, Hetepheres I bore the title of daughter of God. She was the daughter of Huni and half sister of Meresankh, who was not of royal blood. Meresankh was the mother of Sneferu (Snofru), whom Hetepheres married and who ruled after Huni's death. Among the couple's children was Khufu (Cheops), who succeeded upon the death of his father. Hetepheres outlived her husband and was buried with great honors by her son.

References

Grimal, Nicolas. *The History of Ancient Egypt*. Trans. Basil Blackwell Ltd. New York: Barnes & Noble, 1997. pp. 67–68, 128.

Himiko
See Pimiku

Himnechildis
Queen, Guardian / Regent of Austrasia (662–675)

Himnechildis was the wife of Sigibert III, king of the eastern Frankish kingdom of Austrasia from 632 to 656. She had at least one child, a son, Dagobert II. When her husband died, Dagobert was shorn of his long royal hair and sent to an Irish monastery by Grimoald, father of the pretender Childebert. Sigibert's nephew Childeric II, age thirteen, was then proclaimed ruler of Austrasia under the joint guardianship of Queen Himnechildis and the mayor of the palace, Ebroin. When Childeric II was assassinated in 675, Himnechildis and the Austrasian mayor Vulfoald, with the help of Wilfrid, bishop of York, traced her son, Dagobert, who was twenty-six by that time, and restored him to his throne.

References
Previté-Orton, C. W. *The Shorter Cambridge Medieval History.* Vol. 1, *The Later Roman Empire to the Twelfth Century.* Cambridge: Cambridge University Press, 1952, 1982. p. 158.

Hind al-Hīrah
Queen, Regent of the Kingdom of Lakhm in Syrian Desert (554–?)

Hind al-Hīrah was a Christian princess of either Ghassan or Kindah who married Mundhir, al Mundhir III, whose mother was Mariyah or Mawiya. Al Mundhir III, the most illustrious ruler of the Lakhmids, ruled ca. 503 to 554. He raided Byzantine Syria and challenged the kingdom of Ghassan, possibly the homeland of Queen Hind. They had a son, Amr ibn-Hind, who inherited the throne in 554 when his father died and ruled until 569. Queen Hind, an independent and resourceful queen, served as regent for her son. Although she has been described as bloodthirsty, she founded a convent in the north Arabian capital that survived. She reared her son to appreciate the finer things of life; he became a patron of the poet Tarafah and other practitioners of the art of Mu'allaqat, or suspended odes.

References
Hitti, Philip K. *History of the Arabs.* New York: St. Martin's Press, 1968. p. 83.

Hinematioro
Paramount Chieftainess of the Ngati Porou (17th or 18th c.)

The Ngati Pirou is a Maori group of some forty tribes in New Zealand. The Maori are a Polynesian people that migrated to New Zealand in two waves, ca. the ninth and fourteenth centuries. The largest social division is the tribe, based on common ancestry. The subtribes are the principal landowners. Unlike other tribes, the Ngati Pirou have retained most of their ancestral lands and the *mana*—prestige and power—that comes with the land. Hinematioro was one of the rare women who attained lofty status, owing in part to the prestige of her ancestors. The Maori not only record their ancestors in the "treasured book" but also memorize these genealogies, and the most skilled orators relate them to guests. All that remains that attests to Hinematioro's ferocity and her status are ornately carved wooden openwork prows and figureheads outfitting her 100-foot-long war canoe.

References

Momatiuk, Yva, and John Eastcott. "Maoris: At Home in Two Worlds." *National Geographic* 166. October 1984. pp. 522–542.

Newton, Douglas. "The Maoris: Treasures of the Tradition." *National Geographic* 166. October 1984. pp. 542–553, particularly 546.

Hodierna of Jerusalem
Countess, Regent of Tripoli (1152–1164)

Hodierna was one of the four popular daughters of King Baldwin II of Jerusalem (ruled 1118–1131) and Queen Morphia. Her sisters were Melisende, who married King Fulk of Anjou and bore King Baldwin III; Alice, who married King Bohemond IIII of Antioch; and Joveta, who, because she had been captured by Turks as a child, was considered too tainted to make a suitable marriage and was sent off to become abbess of Bethany. Hodierna was married in 1133 to Count Raymond of Tripoli, a man of strong passions who was jealously devoted to her. In 1140 their son Raymond III was born. They also had a daughter of great beauty, Melisende. The marriage was not entirely happy; gossip was circulated concerning the legitimacy of Hodierna's daughter. Raymond, wildly jealous, attempted to keep his wife in a state of seclusion.

Early in 1152 their relationship was so bad that Hodierna's sister, Queen Melisende, felt it her duty to intervene. She persuaded her son, King Baldwin III, to accompany her to Tripoli to try to achieve a reconciliation between the two. Raymond and Hodierna agreed to call off their quarrel, but it was decided that Hodierna should take a long cooling-down holiday in Jerusalem. Queen Melisende and Hodierna set off southward for Jerusalem, accompanied for the first mile or so by Raymond. As he returned to the capital, he was attacked by a band of assassins as he entered the south gate and stabbed to death. King Baldwin III, who had remained behind at the castle playing dice, marshaled the garrison, which rushed out and killed every Muslim in sight but did not find the assassins. Baldwin sent messengers to bring back Queen Melisende and Hodierna and tell them the grim news. Hodierna then assumed the regency in the name of her twelve-year-old son Raymond III. Since the Turks were a constant threat, it was thought that a man was also needed as guardian of the government. Baldwin, as nearest male relative, obliged.

The Turks attacked Tortosa and were driven out, but with Hodierna's consent, Baldwin gave Tortosa to the Knights of the Temple and returned to Jerusalem. In 1164 King Amalric assumed the regency for Raymond III. Hodierna's daughter's questionable parentage cost her the opportunity to become the bride of Byzantine Emperor Manual.

References

Runciman, Steven. *A History of the Crusades.* Vol. 2, *The Kingdom of Jerusalem and the Frankish East.* Cambridge: Cambridge University Press, 1952, 1987. pp. 280, 332, 333, 335.

Hoho
South African Khoi Chieftainess (fl. 1750)

Although no written history existed at the time of Hoho's reign, evidence of the existence of this ruler of a Khoi, or Hottentot, clan is found in at least two old texts, one by Juju (1880), another by J. H. Soga (1930). Both describe the advance of the Xhosa people into Khoi territory. Some time after 1750 the Xhosa warriors led by Rharhabe (d. 1782), a son of Xhosa chief Phalo, crossed the Kei River and encountered three of Hoho's men. Tradition states that he incorporated them into his chiefdom as the isi'Thathu clan, *isithathu* meaning three. It is not known what her clan was called prior to that time. According to Soga, Hoho peacefully surrendered the Amatola Mountains to Rharhabe in exchange for tobacco, dagga, and dogs; however, Juju describes a battle against her that Rharhabe waged in order to bring about that surrender.

References

Juju. "Reminiscences of an Old Kaffir." *Cape Monthly Magazine,* 3d series, 3. 1880: 289–294.
Peires, J. B. *The House of Phalo.* Berkeley: The University of California Press, 1982. p. 23, 200.
Soga, John Henderson. *The South-Eastern Bantu.* Johannesburg: Witwatersrand University Press, 1930. p.130.

Homāy
Traditional Queen of Persia prior to 7th c. B.C.

Homāy (or Chehrzād or Sheherezade) appears in the first version of Persian traditional history, the Yashts, retold in the Persian epic *Shah-Nama* by Firdausi. She was the daughter of Ardashir (Bahman) and the sister of Sāsān, a lion hunter. She was "endowed with wisdom and perspicuous judgment" as well as beauty. According to custom (called pahlavi), her father married her, and she became pregnant. On his deathbed, Ardashir passed the crown to her and after her, to her unborn child, bypassing his son Sāsān. Dismayed at being shunned, Sāsān left Iran and married in Nishāpur. Homāy succeeded to the throne, establishing a new practice and a new order. She distributed money from her treasury to her troops and was said to surpass her father in judgment and equity. She gave birth to a boy, Dārāb, but kept his birth a secret so that she could continue to rule. She had an elaborate casket constructed and placed the baby in it, launching it in the Euphrates River, accompanied by two attendants who were to report back that the casket had traveled and arrived safely. A fuller (clothes washer) and his wife found the casket and raised the baby. When he was grown and joined the army, his commander wrote to Queen Homāy, informing her of his history. She summoned Dārāb to the capital and had him enthroned.

References

Firdausi. *Shah-Nama, The Epic of Kings.* Trans. Reuben Levy. Chicago: University of Chicago Press, 1967. pp. 219–228.

Hortense de Beauharnais
Queen, Regent of Holland (1810)

Hortense de Beauharnais was born in 1783, the daughter of Alexander, vicomte de Beauharnais, and Josephine Tascher de la Pagerie of Martinique. Reared in Paris, Hortense spent the years from age five to ten on Martinique when her parents separated. When her father died, Josephine married Napoleon I (1797), and that marriage was to change Hortense's future. Attractive, intelligent, and cultured, she later wrote in her memoirs, "My life has been so brilliant and so full of misfortune that the world has been forced to take notice of it." She was a gifted pianist and composer of popular songs, at least two of which were sung by French troops. In 1802 she married Louis Bonaparte, Napoleon's brother, and became, so to speak, sister-in-law to her stepfather Napoleon. She bore three sons: Charles Napoleon (b.1802, d.1807), Napoleon Louis (b. 1804), and Louis Napoleon,

later Napoleon III (b. 1808, possibly fathered by someone other than Louis).

Hortense became queen of Holland in 1806 when Napoleon gave her husband, Louis, the crown. In 1809 she took a lover, the comte de Flahault. In 1810 Louis abdicated in favor of his elder surviving son and appointed Hortense as regent of Holland. In 1811, nearly a year after her husband had gone into exile at Teplitz, she became pregnant. She went into hiding and gave birth to a son who was placed into the charge of his paternal grandmother, the novelist Madame de Souza.

After the surrender of Napoleon I, Hortense received 400,000 francs per year and the title of duchesse de Saint-Leu, although she lost the rank of queen. Her husband received a lower title, the comte de Saint-Leu, which annoyed him. When he returned in 1814 he sued for separation, demanding custody of their older son. The principle of paternal authority was enshrined in French law, and her lawyers told her it was pointless to contest, but she did. Although her lawyer made a brilliant impassioned appeal for the right of a mother against the archaic laws that considered only the rights of the father, the court ruled in favor of the father. Although Napoleon Louis did not comply immediately, he eventually went to live with his father. During the restoration and the Hundred Days, Napoleon I stayed in Hortense's home for four days. She once received protection of Alexander I, tsar of Russia, but after she had accepted the pension and title from King Louis XVIII and the friendship of the tsar, her support of Napoleon during the Hundred Days seemed traitorous. The tsar said of her, "She is the cause of all the troubles which have befallen France."

Napoleon Louis married his cousin Charlotte, daughter of King Joseph, and opened a paper factory, designing the machinery himself. He experimented with mechanical flight as well. Hortense and her younger son, Louis Napoleon, sought exile in England. Louis Napoleon joined the Bonapartists and, after an unsuccessful attempt or two, gained the election as president of France. Later, the republic reverted briefly to an empire, and Louis became Napoleon III. Hortense died of cancer in 1837 with her son at her side.

References

Ridley, Jasper. *Napoleon III and Eugenie*. New York: Viking Press, 1980. pp. 3–13.

Hsiao-shih
Queen, Regent of Khita (983–?)

Hsiao-shih was the wife of the Khitan khan Ye-lu Hsien, who died in 983. Their son, Ye-lu Lung-su, born in 971, acceded to the throne upon his father's death with Hsiao-shih as regent. The appearance of a minor ruler under the guardianship of a female regent generally sparked an attempt by neighboring foes to attempt to usurp the throne. In 986 the kingdom was attacked by the army of the second Chinese Sung emperor, T'ai-tsung, but Khitan general Ye-lu Hiou-ko defeated the Chinese, then threw the retreating troops into the Sha River to drown. In 989 the Chinese tried again to overcome the Khitans but were defeated near Paoting.

References

Grousset, René. *The Empire of the Steppes: A History of Central Asia*. Trans. Naomi Walford. New Brunswick, NJ: Rutgers University Press, 1970. pp. 131–132.

Hu
Queen, Ruler of the Toba in Central Asia (515–528)

Hu was the wife of King Toba K'iao, who ruled Toba from 499 to 515. Upon his death, his widow reigned for thirteen years. A descendant of the old Tabatch dynasty, she was a forceful leader and the last member of the Tabatch to display the ancient strength. Described as a woman of exceptional energy, even bloodthirsty on occasion, with a passion for power, nevertheless she was a devout Buddhist. She added to the adornment of the Lungmen sanctuaries and dispatched the Buddhist pilgrim Sung Yun on a mission to northwest India (518–521). He returned bringing Buddhist documents that she prized.

References

Grousset, René. *The Empire of the Steppes: A History of Central Asia*. Trans. Naomi Walford. New Brunswick, NJ: Rutgers University Press, 1970. pp. 64–65.

I

Ide d'Alsace
Countess of Boulogne (1173–1216)

Ide was the daughter of Countess Marie of Boulogne (countess from 1159–1173) and Matthieu d'Alsace. When her mother died in 1173, Ide became ruler of Boulogne. She married four times. When she died in 1216, she was succeeded by Mauhaut de Dammartin.

References
Egan, Edward W., Constance B. Hintz, and L. F. Wise, eds. *Kings, Rulers, and Statesmen*. New York: Sterling Publishing, 1976. p. 152.

'Inayat Shah Zakiyyat al-Din Shah
Sultana of Atjeh (1678–1688)

Atjeh, a small Muslim sultanate on the northern tip of Sumatra, was at one time a bustling trade center, dominating the world pepper market. 'Inayat was the third in a succession of four Muslim queens who ruled Atjeh for a total of forty years. She is listed in H. Djajadiningrat's article on "Atjeh" in the *Encyclopedia of Islam* as being the sixteenth sovereign of the dynasty. She came into power at the death of Sultana Nur al-'Alam Nakiyyat al-Din Shah in 1678 and ruled for ten years. She was succeeded by Kamalat Shah, possibly her daughter. The fact that the political enemies of these four sultanas had brought a *fatwa* from Mecca forbidding by law that a woman rule suggests that each woman wielded considerable power and was popular with her subjects.

References
Mernissi, Fatima. *The Forgotten Queens of Islam*. Trans. Mary Jo Lakeland. Minneapolis: University of Minnesota Press, 1993. pp. 30, 110.

Indzhova, Renata
Interim Prime Minister of Bulgaria (1994–1995)

Late in 1989, Premier Todor Zivkov, who had been head of state of Bulgaria since 1971 and had held power for thirty-five years, was ousted and also expelled from the Communist party. He was replaced as general secretary by Peter T. Mladenov, who went on to become president. Mladenov instituted some reforms, such as restoring civil rights of the Bulgarian Turks and instituting a multiparty system. In 1990, parliament voted to revoke the constitutionally guaranteed dominant position of the Communist party. In the nation's first democratic parliamentary elections since World War II, held in 1990, Mladenov's party lost, and he resigned shortly afterward. The opposition leader, Khelyu Khelev, was chosen to replace him.

A new constitution was put in place in 1991 that provided for the direct election of a president, and in the election held in 1992, Khelev again won the presidency. The post of prime minister, long held by longtime Communist leader Andrei Lukanov, was now chosen freely from among members of parliament. In 1994, as economic conditions and accompanying strikes worsened in Bulgaria, threatening to topple the government, Renata Indzhova, a member of parliament from her district, was elected as a coalition candidate to fill the post of prime minister until the next general election could be held and unpopular austerity measures could be instituted.

References

Famighetti, Robert, ed. *The World Almanac and Book of Facts.* Mahwah, NJ: K-III Reference Corporation, 1998. p. 747.

Irene
Empress, Co-ruler of Byzantine Empire (780–790 and 792–797), Emperor (797–802)

Irene was born ca. 752, the daughter of Athenian parents. In ca. 769 she married Leo IV, surnamed the Chazar (or Kahzar) for his barbarian mother. Leo ruled the Byzantine Empire from 775 to 780. They had a son, Constantine VI, in 770. The following year, the infant was crowned co-emperor to prevent Leo's stepbrother Nicephorus from claiming the throne. When Leo IV died prematurely in 780, Irene became co-emperor with her ten-year-old son. A person who venerated icons, with a lust for power, Irene could justify all her actions because she believed she was the chosen instrument of God. Her efforts were focused on gaining and keeping power, not on improving the welfare of the state.

Her first test came immediately, when Caesar Nicephorus, supported by the iconoclasts, attempted to overthrow her regime. She rapidly suppressed the rebellion and made it known that she was firmly in control. With cunning, diplomacy, and intrigue, she was instrumental in restoring the use of icons in the Eastern Roman Empire when the Seventh Ecumenical Council met in Nicea in 787. This action earned her the devotion of the Greek Church, and all her actions to follow could not deny her eventual sainthood. She forced a wife, Maria, on her son, Constantine VI, who, as he matured, grew resentful of his mother's power. A first attempt to wrest control from her was quelled, Constantine was flogged, and Irene

demanded to be recognized as senior ruler, with her name placed above Constantine's. Finally, in 790, the army, with whom she was unpopular, rejected the ambitious demands of Irene and proclaimed Constantine sole ruler. She abdicated and was banished from the court.

But Constantine VI proved disappointingly weak. In 792 he allowed his mother and her faithful lieutenant, the eunuch Stauracius, to return, and Irene was even allowed to resume the position of co-ruler. She incited her son to blind Alexius, the general who had led the attack against her on Constantine's behalf, and to mutilate his uncles who had plotted against her. In 795 she encouraged him in his lust for his mistress, Theodote, and persuaded him to divorce his wife, Maria. In marrying Theodote, he violated all ecclesiastical laws, outraging public opinion. With Constantine in such general disfavor, Irene was free to have him arrested, blinded, and deposed. In 797 she proclaimed herself sole reigning emperor, not empress. She was the first woman to control the empire as an independent ruler in her own right and not as a regent for a minor or an emperor unfit to rule.

The monks praised their benefactress, who bestowed large gifts upon them. She lowered taxes while raising endowments, making everyone happy, but ruining the finances of the Byzantine state. In 798 she opened diplomatic relations with Charlemagne. In 802 he was said to be contemplating marriage to Irene, but the plan never reached fruition.

In 802 a conspiracy led by the logothete-general Nicephorus seized the throne, and Irene was exiled to the island of Principio, then to Lesbos, where she died in 803. She is a saint of the Greek Orthodox Church.

References

Ostrogorsky, George. *History of the Byzantine State*. New Brunswick, NJ: Rutgers University Press, 1969. pp. 175–182, 186–188, 192–197, 220–225.

Previté-Orton, C. W. *The Shorter Cambridge Medieval History*. Vol. 1, *The Later Roman Empire to the Twelfth Century*. Cambridge: Cambridge University Press, 1952, 1982. p. 249.

Irene Godunova
Tsaritsa, Ruler of Russia (7–17 January 1598)

Irene Godunova (or Irina) was the widow of Fyodor I Ivanovich (Theodore, r. 1584–1598) and sister of Boris Godunov (r. 1598–1605). She took the throne for ten days after the death of her husband, then retired to a convent and became a nun. After a brief interregnum, her brother Boris was elected to succeed her. She died in 1603.

References

Carpenter, Clive. *The Guinness Book of Kings, Rulers & Statesmen*. Enfield, Middlesex: Guinness Superlatives, 1978. p. 245.

Riasnovsky, Nicolas V. *A History of Russia*. Oxford: Oxford University Press, 1993. p. 156.

Irene Palaeologina, Empress
Ruler of the Empire of Trebizond (1340–1341)

Trebizond, now Trabzon, located in northeastern Turkey on the Black Sea, was a Greek state founded after the fall of Constantinople by two grandsons of Byzantine emperor Andronicus I Comnenus. The first ruler was one of those two men, Alexius I (r. 1204–1222). The Commenian Dynasty remained in power in Trebizond, remote from the struggle for the restoration of Byzantium, for over 250 years, longer than any other Byzantine family. By the fourteenth century, Trebizond had been defeated by the Mongols and became their tributary vassal.

Irene was the wife of Basil (r. 1332–1340). After his death, Irene ruled for about a year and was deposed in favor of another woman, Anna Anachoutlou, daughter of King Alexius II (r. 1297–1330).

References

Morby, John E. *Dynasties of the World*. Oxford: Oxford University Press, 1989. p. 56.

Ostrogorsky, George. *History of the Byzantine State*. New Brunswick, N.J.: Rutgers University Press, 1969. pp. 426ff–439.

Isabel
Princess, Regent of Brazilian Empire (1871–1872 and 1876–1888)

Isabel was born in 1846, the daughter of Dom Pedro de Alantara, Pedro II, second and last emperor of the Brazilian Empire, who ruled from 1840 to 1889. King Pedro was a wise and able ruler, and his daughter was educated to become one as well. She married a Frenchman, Gaston d'Orleans, comte d'Eu. In 1871, 1876, and 1888, King Pedro, anxious to improve Brazil's relations with Europe, personally made extended visits to European heads of state. He also visited the U.S. president in 1876. During those protracted absences, Isabel acted as regent.

Although Pedro and Isabel as his regent did much to enhance education, remove corruption, abolish slavery, and enhance revenues, their popularity waned. In 1888 Isabel decreed complete emancipation without compensation to owners, and about 700,000 slaves were freed. The slave owners withdrew their support of the king. Support for a republic grew, as did disatisfaction with Isabel and her French husband. The army, which Pedro had barred from dabbling in politics, hatched a conspiracy and revolted in 1889. Pedro abdicated, and he and Isabel and their family sought exile in Europe. Isabel died in Europe in 1921.

References

Egan, Edward W., Constance B. Hintz, and L. F. Wise, eds. *Kings, Rulers, and Statesmen*. New York: Sterling Publishing, 1976. p. 61.

Langer, William L., ed. *World History*. Boston: Houghton Mifflin, 1980. p. 855.

Isabel
See Perón, Isabel

Isabella
Queen of Beirut (1264–1282)

Isabella was the daughter of John II of Beirut, who died in 1264, and the sister of Eschiva of Ibelin, queen of Cyprus. Isabella remained a figurehead all of her life. She was first married to the child king of Cyprus, Hugh II, who died in 1267 before the marriage could be consummated. She then married an Englishman, Hamo (Edmund) L'Etranger (the Foreigner), who soon died, leaving her under the protection of the sultan Baibars. King Hugh of Cyprus tried to carry her off and remarry her to the candidate of her choice, but the sultan Baibars, citing the pact that her late husband had made with him, demanded that she be sent back to Beirut, where a Mameluk guard "protected" her. She married twice more, to Nicholas L'Aleman and William Barlais. When she died in 1282, Beirut passed to her sister, Eschiva.

References
Runciman, Steven. *A History of the Crusades.* Vol. 3, *The Kingdom of Acre.* Cambridge: Cambridge University Press, 1952, 1987. pp. 329, 342.

Isabella
Countess, Ruler of Foix (1398–1412)

Isabella was the daughter of Gaston III Phebus, who ruled Foix from 1343 to 1391, and the sister of Matthieu de Castelbon, who succeeded his father upon his death in 1391 and ruled until 1398. She married Archambaud de Graille, and they had at least one son, Jean de Graille. She acceded upon her brother's death in 1398 and ruled until her own death in 1412. Her son Jean then became count of Foix.

References
Egan, Edward W., Constance B. Hintz, and L. F. Wise, eds. *Kings, Rulers, and Statesmen.* New York: Sterling Publishing, 1976. p. 157.

Isabella
See Zabel

Isabella I the Catholic
Queen of Castile and León, Queen of Spain (1474–1504)

Isabella I was born in 1451, the only daughter of Juan II, ruler of Castile from 1406 to 1454, and his second wife, Isabella of Portugal. Isabella I's half brother was Enrique IV (Henry IV), who ruled Castile and León when his father died, from 1454 to 1474. Because Isabella was Enrique's heir, he had plans for her marriage to which she violently objected, for she had larger ideas for a political match with the possibility of uniting Spain.

In a furtive ceremony in 1469, Isabella married her second cousin Ferdinand II, heir of the king of Aragon. This secret union would prove to be one of the most important events in Spanish history, for their heir would inherit both the kingdom of Aragon and the kingdom of Castile, thus forming Spain as we know it. And although theirs was not a love match, they grew to be the most devoted of couples, even insisting on being buried together at death. The couple had five children: John, Isabella, Juana, María, and Catherine. In 1474 Enrique died, and Isabella became queen of Castile and León. Enrique's daughter, Juana, contested the claim, and a civil war followed. When it ended in 1479, Isabella was the undisputed queen. That same year King Juan II of Aragon had died, and Ferdinand had become king of Aragon. The two countries were administered separately during the lifetimes of the couple.

Following a flagrant breach of the truce between the Moors in Granada and Castile, Isabella became determined to drive the Moors from her land. The battle lasted a decade (1482–1492). When she was well into her fourth pregnancy and prepared to join her husband in Cordoba, she was warned that it was foolish to travel so close to the Moorish capital, but she told her advisers, "Glory is not to be won without danger." Throughout the campaign, the king rode at the head of her army, and Isabella became quartermaster and financier. She also visited camps to encourage the soldiers and established field hospitals and front-line emergency tent-hospitals. The latter became known as Queen's Hospitals. The truce in 1492 made Spain an all-Christian nation again after 781 years.

In 1486 Christopher Columbus, seeking financial backing for his search for a shorter route to Asia, knew that he stood a better chance of impressing the intuitive and enthusiastic Isabella than her cautious husband. However, although Columbus's proposition excited her imagination, all her funds were being funneled into the war with Granada. It was not until 1492, when Santangel, Ferdinand's keeper of the privy purse, reminded Isabella that her goal had been to make her country preeminent in Europe, that she summoned Columbus to return to make a contract. During the next ten years she funded four voyages to the new world. Isabella is remembered for her support for Columbus, but she also was a great patron of literature, the arts, and the church. She died in 1504, shortly before Columbus returned from his fourth voyage.

References

Chapman, Charles E. *A History of Spain.* New York: The Free Press/Macmillan, 1965. pp. 111, 123–124, 133–134, 139, 154, 202–230, 292–294.

Langer, William L., ed. *World History.* Boston: Houghton Mifflin, 1980. pp. 304–305.

McKendrick, Melveena. *Ferdinand and Isabella.* New York: American Heritage Publishing, 1968.

Isabella II
Queen of Spain (1833–1868)

Isabella II was born in 1830, the elder daughter of King Ferdinand VII, who ruled Spain from 1814 to 1833, and his fourth wife, Maria Christina of Naples. Three months before he died, at the urging of his wife, Ferdinand set aside the Salic Law, or male succession law, to assure the succession of his infant daughter and deprive his brother, Don Carlos, of the throne. Isabella was proclaimed queen at age three with her mother as regent. Don Carlos's dispute of her claim culminated in the first Carlist War (1834–1839).

In 1840 General Baldomero Espartero, a Progressist, seized power, forced Maria Christina to leave the country, assumed the regency himself, and became a virtual dictator. In 1843 he was deposed by the military, and Isabella was declared of age to rule, although she was only thirteen. In 1846 she married her cousin, Francisco de Asiz de Borbon, the duke of Cádiz. She had four children: Isabella, María de la Paz, Eulalia, and Alfonso XII. In 1847 the second Carlist War and republican uprising weakened the liberal system that was in place. A new prime minister, O'Donnell, engaged the country in war against Morocco from 1859 to 1860. Isabella was separated from her husband, and it was rumored that she took lovers, including an actor, son of a cook, Carlos Marfori, whom she made minister of state.

Her reign continued to be plagued by political unrest and uprisings. In 1868 a revolution forced her to flee to France, and she was declared deposed. In 1870, however, she took the formal step of abdicating in favor of her son, Alfonso XII. After much shuffling of leadership in Spain, Alfonso declared for a constitutional monarchy when he came of age in 1874. Isabella died in Paris in 1904.

References

Chapman, Charles E. *A History of Spain.* New York: The Free Press/Macmillan, 1965. pp. 498–503, 506.

Langer, William L., ed. *World History.* Boston: Houghton Mifflin, 1980. pp. 694–697.

Ridley, Jasper. *Napoleon III and Eugénie.* New York: Viking Press, 1980. pp. 144, 154, 158, 162, 167–168, 205, 246, 323, 492, 539.

Isabella Clara Eugenia of Austria
Co-ruler of the Spanish Netherlands (1598–1621), Sole Governor (1621–1633)

Isabella Clara Eugenia was born in 1566, the daughter of King Philip II, who ruled Spain from 1556 to 1598, and his third wife, Elizabeth of Valois. Philip unsuccessfully proposed Isabella as successor to the English throne in 1587 after the execution of Mary Queen of Scots and to the throne of France in 1598 after the assassination of her uncle Henry III. She married Albert, archduke of Austria, and received as dowry the ten southern Spanish Netherlands provinces to rule (1598).

The rule of Isabella and Albert signaled a change in policy: Flemish Catholics were treated in a conciliatory manner rather than driven to hostility. Under their rule the southern Netherlands regained part of its earlier prosperity. The seven provinces of the northern Netherlands had a measure of autonomy, and Isabella and Albert attempted to reunite the provinces, first by diplomacy and later by force, but they failed. Albert died in 1621, and the Netherlands became a Spanish sovereignty, but Isabella remained and ruled as governor for her nephew the king (Philip IV) until her death in Brussels in 1633.

References

Geye, Pieter. *The Revolt of The Netherlands 1555–1609.* London: Ernest Benn, 1958. pp. 218, 223, 227, 232, 239–243.

Trevor-Roper, Hugh et al. *The Golden Age of Europe.* New York: Bonanza / Crown Publishers, 1987. pp. 53, 84–85, 89, 101.

Isabella d'Este (Erich Lessing / Art Resource, NY)

Isabella d'Este
Marquessa, Regent of Mantua (1495 and 1509)

Isabella received the kind of education usually reserved for a noble boy. At sixteen she married Francesco II Gonzaga, the marquis of Mantua. She administered his lands during his absence leading Venetian forces against Charles VIII in 1495. They had a son, Federico, born in 1500. In 1509, when her husband was taken prisoner by the Venetians, she ruled Mantua and held it against the threatening forces of the Venetians. Gonzaga was released by intervention of the pope. As a reward for Gonzaga's support of Emperor Maximilian I against Venice, their son was named duke of Mantua. Isabella, a great patron of the arts and letters, presided with her husband over a splendid and impressive court.

References

Mee, Charles L., Jr. *Daily Life in Renaissance Italy.* New York: American Heritage Publishing, 1975. pp. 70–72.

Isabella Farnesio of Parma
Queen and De Facto Co-ruler of Spain (1714–1746)

Isabella (or Isabel) Farnesio (or Elizabeth Farnese) was born in 1692 in Parma, Italy, the niece and stepdaughter of the duke of Parma. In 1714 she married Philip V of Spain after the death of his first wife, the popular Maria Louisa Gabriela of Savoy. Maria had been influenced by her maid of honor, Madame des Ursins, whom King Louis XIV had sent because she was familiar with the customs of Spain, being the widow of the Duke of Braciano, a Spanish grandee. After Maria's death, a young Italian abbot had suggested to Madame des Ursins that Isabella, being sweet and gentle of nature, would be a suitable wife for King Philip, and her pliable character would enable Madame des Ursins to retain her own power at court. After the marriage, Isabella, a handsome, ambitious woman, dismissed Madame des Ursins on their first meeting and took complete control of King Philip.

Her husband was so besotted by her that he sometimes struck her in a fit of jealous rage. However, Isabella was willing to overlook his capricious behavior in order to maintain her control over him. Early in 1715 she managed the elevation of the young Italian abbot, Alberoni, to head affairs of state. Eventually he would be made cardinal. Her chief ambitions were to break France's influence over the Spanish crown and to recover Italian possessions by exiling Austrians from Italy. Isabella and Philip had seven children: Charles, Francisco, Philip, Luis Antonio, Mariana, Teresa, and Antonia.

Since Philip had two sons by his first wife, Isabella had not much hope that her children would reign on the Spanish throne, so she spent much of her reign attempting to supplant Austrian power in Italy, securing Italian principalities for her children to govern. She was shrewd in her choice of ministers, selecting those who would carry out her foreign policy to the ends that Spain's imperialistic gains in Italy were significant. Isabella made improvements in the country's economy and enacted reforms in the military and administrative branches of the government. Her husband abdicated briefly in 1724 in favor of his oldest son, Luis, but returned when Luis died of smallpox that same year. Philip died in 1746 and was succeeded by Ferdinand VI, his son by his first wife. Isabella then retired from court. She died in 1766.

References
Chapman, Charles E. *A History of Spain.* New York: The Free Press/ Macmillan, 1965. pp. 374–375.
Langer, William L., ed. *World History.* Boston: Houghton Mifflin, 1980. pp. 487–489.

Isabella of Bavaria
Regent of France (1392–1422)

Isabella was born in 1371, the daughter of Stephen III, duke of Bavaria-Ingolstadt. In 1385 she married Charles VI, king of France, who ruled from 1380 to 1422. Her husband's first attack of insanity occurred in 1392. The following year the first of their six children was born. In the ensuing years she was frequently regent as Charles's seizures of insanity grew worse and more protracted. She chose Philip of Burgundy as an adviser, and later the king's brother Louis, duke of Orleans, became her constant adviser. When he was killed in 1407, she turned to John the Fearless, the new duke of Burgundy as of 1404. In 1415 Henry V of England invaded France and defeated the French at Agincourt, reconquering Normandy for the English.

In 1417 her son Charles, the dauphin, who would rule later as Charles VII (1422–1461), determined to gain control, had his mother imprisoned. She was rescued by John the Fearless, who assisted her in establishing a new seat of government, first at Chartres and then at Troyes. In 1419, as the English continued to advance, John the Fearless was assassinated. The following year King Charles VI, with Isabella's support, accepted the Treaty of Troyes, in which he repudiated the dauphin as illegitimate and adopted Henry V as heir. Henry V continued his steady conquest of France until his death in 1422. Isabella's husband died the same year. She faded from the political arena as the dauphin schemed to regain his rightful throne. She died in 1435 in Paris.

References
Langer, William L., ed. *World History.* Boston: Houghton Mifflin, 1980. pp. 299–301.

Runciman, Steven. *A History of the Crusades.* Vol. 3, *The Kingdom of Acre.* Cambridge: Cambridge University Press, 1952, 1987. p. 456.

Isabella of Cyprus
Regent of Jerusalem (1263)

Isabella of Cyprus was the eldest sister of King Henry of Cyprus. She married Henry of Antioch, youngest son of Bohemond IV. In 1253 the couple had a son, Hugh II of Cyprus. Isabella also reared her late sister's son, also named Hugh (of Brienne). Much information that remains about Isabella concerns her efforts to attain her rightful regency. When Queen Plaisance of Cyprus died in 1261, a new regent was required for Cyprus and Jerusalem, as Isabella's son, Hugh II, was only eight years old. Plaisance's late husband was Isabella's brother, and thus Isabella was the next in the line of succession as regent. The High Court of Cyprus refused Isabella as regent in favor of her young son, but the High Court of Jerusalem, in 1263, named her regent de facto, refusing to administer the oath of allegiance because King Conradin was not present. Isabella appointed her husband, Henry, as *bailli*. In the thirteenth century the *bailli* was much more powerful than the English bailiff. The *bailli* had authority to act for the monarch in collecting and dispensing funds, raising an army, defending the area, maintaining order, holding court, and overseeing minor officials.

Isabella died in 1264. Her son, who was by then eleven, became regent, although her nephew Hugh of Brienne put in a counterclaim. But as Isabella had been accepted as the last regent, the vote was unanimous that her son should succeed her.

References

Runciman, Steven. *A History of the Crusades.* Vol. 3, *The Kingdom of Acre.* Cambridge: Cambridge University Press, 1952, 1987. pp. 206, 288–289.

Isabelle
Princess, Co-ruler of Achaea (1289–1297, 1301–1307)

Achaea was a Frankish crusader principality in the area of Attica in Greece. Isabelle was the daughter of Guillaume II (r. 1246–1278). In 1276 Guillaume became a vassal of Carlo I, king of Sicily and Naples (r. 1278–1285), who passed the principality on to his son, Carlos II of Naples (r. 1285–1289). In 1289 Carlo II waived his rights, and Isabelle, with her first husband, Florent of Hainault, assumed the throne. When Florent died in 1297, Carlo II again took the throne until Isabelle's remarriage in 1301. She and her second husband, Philippe I of Savoy, ruled until 1307, when she was deposed in favor of Philippe II, son of Carlo II of Naples. Isabelle had a daughter, Mathilde, who assumed the throne in 1313.

References

Carpenter, Clive. *The Guinness Book of Kings, Rulers & Statesmen.* Enfield, Middlesex: Guinness Superlatives, 1978. p. 1.

Isabelle
Duchess, Co-ruler of Lorraine (1431–1453)

Isabelle was the daughter of Charles II the Bold (r. 1391–1431), who married her to the heir to Bar, René I (also Rinaldo, king of Naples) and thus consolidated the two parcels into a much-strengthened duchy of Lorraine, which she ruled with her husband after her father's death. She had two sons who ruled after her, Jean II (r. 1453–1470) and Nicolas (r. 1470–1473).

References

Carpenter, Clive. *The Guinness Book of Kings, Rulers & Statesmen.* Enfield, Middlesex: Guinness Superlatives, 1978. p. 92.

Isato
See Judith

J

Jacqueline
Countess, Ruler of Holland, Zeeland, and Hainault (1417–1433),
Duchess of Bavaria and Countess of Ostrevant (1433–1436)

The daughter of William IV of the house of Bavaria (r. Holland 1404–1417), Jacqueline (or Jacoba) assumed the throne upon his death. In 1415 she had married John of Touraine, dauphin of France, who died two years later. The German king Sigismund refused to recognize Jacqueline's right to rule, so in 1418 she married her cousin John IV, duke of Brabant. When John mortgaged Holland and Zeeland the following year, Jacqueline repudiated their marriage.

In 1421 she went to England and married Humphrey, duke of Gloucester. In 1424 the couple returned to Holland with an army to retake her lands; however, when the forces against them seemed overwhelming, Humphrey deserted and retreated to England the following year. Jacqueline was taken prisoner by Philip the Good, duke of Burgundy, who had his own designs on Holland, but she escaped and marshaled her English forces to combat Philip. In 1428 the pope intervened, declaring her English marriage null. She was forced to make peace with Philip and to promise not to marry without his consent.

In 1430 she secretly married Francis, lord of Zulen and St. Maartensdijk, with an eye to overthrowing Philip. But Francis was taken prisoner in 1432, and Jacqueline was forced to abdicate the following year. Thereafter Holland and Hainault were united with Burgundy. Jacqueline was made duchess of Bavaria and countess of Ostrevant in 1434. She died two years later.

References
Langer, William L. *World History.* Boston: Houghton Mifflin, 1980.
   p. 406.
Morby, John. *Dynasties of the World.* Oxford: Oxford University Press,
   1989. p. 91.

Jadwiga
"Maiden King" of Poland (1384–1399)

Jadwiga (or Hedwig) was born ca. 1373, the third daughter of Louis I of Anjou, king of Poland (1370–1382) and king of Hungary (1342–1382), and Elizabeth of Bosnia. Polish nobility had made a special agreement to accept any one of Louis's daughters as their next ruler. Louis did not have serious concerns about Poland, which he governed through his regent-mother, Elizabeth, until her death and thereafter through a council of regents. He was concerned, however, that the succession to the Hungarian throne should be secure. He had appointed Jadwiga as his successor and had betrothed her and formally celebrated her marriage at the age of five to William of Hapsburg, anticipating by such a union a closer relationship between Hungary and Austria.

After Louis died in 1382, the Hungarian nobles elected her sister Maria as "king of Hungary." Maria, who had been married to Sigismund, son of Emperor Charles IV, had been designated by Louis to inherit the throne of Poland after the oldest sister, Catherine, died in 1378. But Polish nobles, who did not want the Holy Roman emperor to have a hand in their future, urged Queen Elizabeth to name her younger daughter Jadwiga as successor to the Polish throne. However, they did not approve of Jadwiga's Austrian husband and decided that she should marry the new grand duke of Lithuania, Jagiello, who hoped that he would reclaim their territory lost to Hungary. During the interregnum following Louis's death (1382–1384), Poland suffered through civil wars and upheavals while Polish nobles vied to increase their own power and privileges.

In 1384 Jadwiga was formally elected and crowned "king" of Poland. William of Hapsburg, Jadwiga's former "husband," after trying in vain to defend his right by attempting to occupy Wawel castle in Cracow, returned to Vienna. Jadwiga had been genuinely fond of him, but she had to content herself with marrying the thirty-five-year-old Jagiello "for the good of her country" in 1386 at age twelve. Jagiello had converted to Catholicism and taken the name Wladyslaw II. He never intended merely to play the role of prince consort, but the young Jadwiga, being the hereditary claimant, had the right to rule on her own if she wished; therefore the ruling class of Poland did not wholeheartedly accept his attempts to rule. Frustrated in his ambitions, he was nevertheless able to unite his dukedom of Lithuania, three times the size of Poland, with Poland and to convert the country to Catholicism. Jadwiga remained somewhat intimidated by her older husband. She bore no children and died at the age of twenty-nine in 1399. Only then did Jagiello become ruler of Poland in his own right. He married again three times. His last wife, Sonia of Kiev, bore two sons who became kings of Poland.

References

Dvornik, Francis. *The Slavs in European History and Civilization*. New Brunswick, NJ: Rutgers University Press, 1962. pp. 83–84, 129–130, 169, 222, 224, 436.

Egan, Edward W., Constance B. Hintz, and L. F. Wise, eds. *Kings, Rulers, and Statesmen*. New York: Sterling Publishing, 1976. p. 361.

Langer, William L., ed. *World History*. Boston: Houghton Mifflin, 1980. pp. 337–340.

Jagan, Janet
Prime Minister (1997), President of Guyana (1997–)

Born Janet Rosenberg in 1921, she was the daughter of Jewish immigrants living in Chicago. She trained as a nurse at Northwestern University and met a young man training at Northwestern University Dental School, Cheddi Jagan (b. 1918 in Port Mourant, Jamaica, of East Indian parents). In 1943 they married and moved to Guyana, at that time a British colony called British Guiana on the northeastern shore of South America. The couple had two children and in time became citizens of Guyana. Fifty percent of Guyana's population is of East Indian extraction, and 31 percent is of black African extraction.

In the late 1940s she helped her husband found the People's Progressive Party, a predominantly East Indian (male) organization. While Cheddi Jagan became a member of the legislative council (1947–1953), Janet Jagan cofounded the Women's Political and Economic Development Organization in 1946 and founded its successor, the Women's Progressive Organization, in 1953. In that year, unlimited suffrage was granted to the citizens of Guyana by the British government. In 1955, after an ethnic split in the leadership of the Women's Progressive Organization, Indian members were encouraged to join the hitherto mostly male People's Progressive Party.

As her husband rose in positions of leadership, Janet Jagan served as a member of the legislative assembly. In 1961 Guyana achieved full self-government under the British umbrella, and the People's Progressive Party gained the majority in the legislative assembly. Cheddi Jagan became the first premier of Guyana, and Janet Jagan became health minister. But the austere economic measures that Premier Jagan introduced the following year resulted in riots that pitted African

and Indian factions against each other. British troops returned more than once to restore order.

In 1963 elections were held again, and when no one could secure a majority, Forbes Burnham of the People's National Congress was chosen to form a coalition government. On May 26, 1966, Guyana was declared an independent nation, and it became a member of the United Nations the same year. On February 23, 1970, Guyana became a republic, and Arthur Chung (b. 1918) of the People's National Congress became president.

In the elections of 1992, Cheddi Jagan's People's Progressive Party again gained a majority in the National Assembly, and he became president of Guyana, an office he held until his death in March 1997, of a heart attack. Jagan's deputy, Samuel A. Hinds, suceeded him pending elections the following December, and his widow, Janet Jagan, became prime minister, the first woman to hold that high post.

On September 1, 1997, she accepted her party's nomination to run for the presidency. On December 15, 1997, she won by an overall majority, and on December 19 she was sworn in as president of the Republic of Guyana, becoming the first woman to hold the highest office in the land. Samuel A. Hinds was elected prime minister, and Bharrat Jagdeo became vice president. As was expected, the opposition People's National Congress, which had been in power from 1970 to 1992, challenged the results, but her election was upheld.

The newly elected President Jagan expressed the desire that her son, Joey Jagan, who had been living in the Caribbean, return to Guyana and succeed at the helm of the People's Progressive Party. Thus she would be grooming him for future leadership of the republic. However, critics described the younger Jagan as a "loose cannon" who might destroy the fragile economic development of the country. During her first year in office she appointed a constitution reform commission and instituted a national development strategy, through which the country's chief industry announced layoffs that made the work of national development even more urgent. Her first year was marked by police brutality toward black women and by political unrest among

Guyana's black citizens, who called for a coalition government. President Jagan rejected their demands but decried police brutality.

References

Ishmael, Safraz W. "People's Progressive Party Civic Homepage." www.pppcivic.org. December, 1997. Prepared by Ishmael from University of Maryland School of Physics.

Persaud, Robert. "Editorial." *Starbroek News.* Lacytown, Georgetown, Guyana. April 22, 1999.

Seenarine, Moses. "Keeping the Natives at Bay: Janet Jagan in Guyana." Saxakali Publications, October 29, 1997 at http://saxakali.com.

Jane
See Grey, Lady Jane

Jane
See Joanna I

Jayaram, Jayalalitha
Chief of Tamil Nadu (1995–1996)

Jayalalitha Jayaram was born in India in 1947. In the 1960s she became an actress, starring in many Tamil-language films that established her reputation as a romantic heroine. She married M. G. Ramachandran, who was an even bigger star than she. Ramachandran was elected chief minister of Tamil Nadu State, located on the southeastern tip of the Indian peninsula and having a population of 55 million people. When he died while in office, Jayalalitha was elected by a landslide vote from poor villagers. She won the admiration of some villagers for projects such as improving irrigation, providing a local burial ground, and aiding orphans and the disabled. However, she was mocked for having eighty-five-foot plywood cutouts painted with her image erected at various intersections in Madras, the capital, as well as elsewhere throughout the land.

By mid 1995, local newspapers and magazines had printed lengthy exposés detailing governmental corruption said to have spread through every level as well as political ties to criminal gangs. She was accused of reinforcing her rule with hired thugs. In September of that year she staged a wedding of maharajah-like opulence for her "foster son," the nephew of her closest friend, Sasikala Natarajan. The bride was a granddaughter of Shivaji Gansean, considered the Madras studio's greatest star ever. The wedding drew more than

100,000 people, many of whom were bused in from faraway villages. Thousands of guests received invitations inscribed on silver salvers. At least 12,000 of the guests were served a wedding lunch by 3,500 cooks and waiters. A leading film designer was commissioned to construct a tableau of Tamil mythology running for miles between Jayalalitha's official residence and the wedding site. At least 20,000 special-duty policemen provided crowd control.

Minister Jayaram, stating, "My conscience is clear," filed more than 200 lawsuits against opponents and publicly accused Governor Channa Reddy, in his late seventies, of "misbehaving" toward her in their private meetings. In the elections of 1996 she was swept out of office.

References

Burns, John F. "For Indian Politician, an Opulent Wedding Means Political Bliss." *New York Times International.* 10 September 1995: 6.

Jeanne I
Countess, Ruler of Dreux (1345–1346)

Jeanne was the daughter of Count Robert, who ruled Dreux from 1309 to 1329. She succeeded her uncles, Jean II, who ruled from 1329, when his brother died, to 1331, and Pierre, who ruled from 1331, when Jean II died, to 1345. When she died a year later, her aunt, Jeanne II, succeeded her.

References

Egan, Edward W., Constance B. Hintz, and L. F. Wise, eds. *Kings, Rulers, and Statesmen.* New York: Sterling Publishing, 1976. p. 157.

Jeanne I, Countess of Champagne
See Juana I

Jeanne II
Countess, Ruler of Dreux (1346–1355)

Jeanne was the second daughter of Count Jean II, who ruled Dreux from 1282 to 1309, and the sister of Count Robert, who ruled from their father's death in 1309 to 1329. She married Louis, vicomte de Thouars, and bore a son, Simon. When her niece, Countess Jeanne I, died in 1346, Jeanne II succeeded to the reign. Her son Simon succeeded her in 1355.

References

Egan, Edward W., Constance B. Hintz, and L. F. Wise, eds. *Kings, Rulers, and Statesmen.* New York: Sterling Publishing, 1976. p. 157.

Jeanne d'Albret
Queen of Navarre
(1555–1572)

Jeanne (also Joan III or Juana III) was born ca. 1528, the daughter of Henry II, king of Navarre (1517–1555), and his second wife, Margaret of Angouleme. From 1521 until he died, Henry warred with France for the return of his Navarre territories lost by his parents in 1514. In 1548 Jeanne married Antoine de Bourbon, duke of Vendôme. They had a son, Henry, born in 1553, who had scant prospects of becoming King Henry IV of France because there were so many in the line of succession ahead of him.

In 1555, Jeanne became queen of Navarre when her father died. In a series of religious wars in France, Antoine, first a leader of the Protestant faction, eventually changed his mind and became a champion of the Catholics. Queen Jeanne, however, publicly announced her Calvinism on Christmas in 1560. In 1562 her estranged husband was killed fighting the Calvinists. In 1568 Queen Jeanne, who had remained neutral during the first two religious wars, entered the third war. When her brother-in-law Louis I, head of the army, was killed in Jarnac, she hurried to the scene and proclaimed her son Henry, age fifteen, the head of the army.

When the war ended in 1570, Jeanne and Catherine de Médicis began arrangements for a marriage between Henry and Catherine's daughter, Margaret of Valois. The marriage occurred two years later. Queen Jeanne traveled to Paris to prepare for the event but died of a respiratory infection two months before the ceremony took place. Henry became not only king of Navarre but also, in 1589, King Henry IV of France, and Navarre became a part of France.

References

Egan, Edward W., Constance B. Hintz, and L. F. Wise, eds. *Kings, Rulers, and Statesmen.* New York: Sterling Publishing, 1976. p. 162.

Harding, Robert R. *Anatomy of a Power Elite.* New Haven, CT: Yale University Press, 1978. pp. 39, 176, 188.

Langer, William L., ed. *World History.* Boston: Houghton Mifflin, 1980. pp. 410, 411.

Morby, John E. *Dynasties of the World.* Oxford: Oxford University Press, 1989. p. 115.

Trevor-Roper, Hugh. *The Golden Age of Europe.* New York: Bonanza/Crown, 1987. p. 162.

Tuchman, Barbara W. *A Distant Mirror, The Calamitous 14th Century.* New York: Ballantine Books, 1978. p. 595.

Jeanne de Castile
Co-ruler of Vendôme (1366–1374)

Jeanne was married to Count Jean VI, who ruled Vendôme from 1336 to 1366. They had two children, Catherine and Bouchard VII. When Jeanne's husband died in 1366, she served as co-ruler with her son, for whom she was guardian. Bouchard died in 1374, and her daughter assumed the reign.

References
Egan, Edward W., Constance B. Hintz, and L. F. Wise, eds. *Kings, Rulers, and Statesmen.* New York: Sterling Publishing, 1976. p. 162.

Jeanne de Chatillon
Countess, Ruler of Blois (1279–1292)

Jeanne de Chatillon was the daughter of Jean de Chatillon, count of Blois and Chartres, who ruled from 1241 to 1279. She married Pierre, count of Alençon. She succeeded to the rule of Blois on her father's death. She died in 1292, leaving no offspring, and was succeeded by her German cousin, Hugues de Chatillon.

References
Egan, Edward W., Constance B. Hintz, and L. F. Wise, eds. *Kings, Rulers, and Statesmen.* New York: Sterling Publishing, 1976. p. 152.

Jeanne de Nemours
Duchess, Regent of Savoy (1675–1684)

Savoy, located between France, Austria, and Italy (and now a part of Italy), had once been occupied by French forces. Although it had long since regained its sovereignty and had even expanded its holdings, it had constantly to play diplomatic dodgeball between the two powers, France and the Hapsburg empire. Jeanne de Nemours (or Marie de Savoie-Nemours) was the wife of Charles Emmanuel II, ruler of Savoy from 1638 to 1675. In 1666 they had a son, Victor Amadeus II, who succeeded as ruler when his father died in 1675. Jeanne acted as regent not only until he attained majority, but until 1684. Jeanne inherited a Francophile orientation of Savoy's policy, which she thought it wisest to continue. After Savoy had acquired Sicily and following the Treaty of Utrecht in 1713, Jeanne encouraged her son to engage in diplomatic maneuvering to trade his title of duke of Savoy by exchanging Sicily for Sardinia. He then became the king of Sardinia-Piedmont in 1720, but he abdicated in 1730. Jeanne did not live to see his abdication; she died in 1724.

References

Langer, William L., ed. *World History.* Boston: Houghton Mifflin, 1980. pp. 494–495.

Morby, John E. *Dynasties of the World.* Oxford: Oxford University Press, 1989. p. 110.

Jeanne de Penthièvre
Duchess, Ruler of Brittany (1341–1365)

Jeanne de Penthièvre was born in 1319, the daughter of Jean III (r. 1312–1341), whose death occasioned a dispute over the right of succession.

Her uncle, Jean IV de Montfort, the younger brother of Jean III, also claimed hereditary right, and for the first four years she fought for control of Brittany. In 1365 she was forced to cede her rights to her cousin, Jean V de Montfort (r. 1365–1399). Jeanne de Penthièvre died in 1384.

References

Carpenter, Clive. *The Guinness Book of Kings, Rulers & Statesmen.* Enfield: Middlesex: Guinness Superlatives, 1978. p. 90.

Jindan
Rani, Regent of the Sikh Kingdom of the Punjab (ca.1843–1846)

Jindan was the daughter of a chieftain of the Kanhayas and his wife, the domineering Sada Kaur. In 1795 Jindan became the first wife of Ranjit Singh, age fifteen, who had been chief of the Sukerchakias since he was twelve. For the first few years of their marriage, the rani's mother directed all of Ranjit's affairs. In 1801 he proclaimed himself maharajah of the Punjab. In 1838 the British viceroy persuaded him to assist in placing a British choice on the throne of Kabul in Afghanistan. Following the victory in Afghanistan, Ranjit fell ill and died (1843). He was succeeded by his youngest son, Dalip or Dulop Singh, with Ranjit's widow, Jindan, as regent.

In 1845 British encroachment on the Punjab made it necessary for the rani, the chief minister, and the commander in chief of the army to agree to attack the British. Their defeat in 1846 led to the

Treaty of Lahore, whereby they lost a number of territories, including Kashmir. Jindan was deposed as regent, and a council was appointed to govern. But a second Sikh revolt that erupted in 1848, which the new government was powerless to stop, was put down by the British. This time the British deposed the young king and sent him and Rani Jindan to England. He became a Christian and a landowner in Norfolk. A final bloody encounter in 1849 between the Sikhs and the British ended with British annexation of the Punjab.

References

Bhattacharya, Sachchidananda. *A Dictionary of Indian History.* New York: George Braziller, 1967. pp. 321–322.

Jinga
See Nzinga Mbandi

Jingō-kōgū
Empress, Regent of Japan (ca. 200–269)

Jingō-kōgū (or Kōgō) was born ca. 169, the daughter of Prince Okinaga no Sukune and Katsuraki no Taka-nuka-hime. She married Chūai-tennō (Tarashi-Naka-tsu-hiko), fourteenth emperor of Japan, who ruled from 192 to 200. The emperor had planned an expedition to conquer Korea but died in 200 before he could undertake it. The empress, although pregnant with their son at the time, conducted the expedition to Korea and brought the kings of Koryo, Pekche, and Silla (Kōrae, Hakusai, and Shinra) under her suzerainty. (Some descrepancy can be seen between Japanese and Korean dating of the expedition. According to Korean records, the expedition occurred in 346.) She returned to Japan in time to give birth to Homuda, the future emperor Ōjin. Two sons of one of her husband's concubines revolted, claiming succession by right of primogeniture. Jingō sent General Taki-shiuchi no Sukune to put them to death, thus ending all threat to her reign. She refused to ascend to the throne but ruled as regent for sixty-nine years. She died in 269 at the age of 100 and was honored with the name Kashi-dai-myōjin. (According to Korean histories, the empress died in 380.)

References

Aston, W. G., trans. *Nihongi: Chronicles of Japan from the Earliest Times to A.D. 697.* Rutland, VT: Charles E. Tuttle, 1972. pp. 224–253.

Papinot, E. *Historical and Geographical Dictionary of Japan.* Rutland, VT: Charles E. Tuttle, 1972. pp. 229–230.

Reischauer, Edwin O., and John K. Fairbank. *East Asia: The Great Tradition.* Boston: Houghton Mifflin, 1960. pp. 468–469.

Sansom, George A. *A History of Japan to 1334*. Stanford: Stanford
    University Press, 1958. pp. 16–17.

Jitō-tennō
Empress, Ruler of Japan (686–697)

Jitō-tennō was born in 625, named Hironu hime, or Uno no Sasara,
a daughter of the emperor Tenchi, who ruled Japan from 662 to 671,
and a sister of Kōbun-tennō, who ruled from 671 to 672. When their
father fell ill, he shaved his head and retired to Yoshino-zan. Kōbun-
tennō assumed the throne, but a civil war broke out. Tenchi's brother,
Ō-ama no Ōji, revolted and claimed the succession. Ō-ama defeated
the imperial troops, so Kōbun-tennō killed himself after a reign of
only eight months. Ō-ama ascended the throne and ruled for fourteen
years as Temmu-tennō. He married his niece, Jitō. When he died in
687, Jitō succeeded him, at the age of forty-two. During her reign she
made important administrative reforms, encouraged the development of agriculture, and had the first silver coin struck. Sensitive to
the religious plurality over which she reigned, she endeavored to remain impartial in her religious devotions and contributed to both
Buddhist and Shintō temples. After a reign of eleven years, she abdicated in favor of her nephew (and grandson) Mommu. Upon her retirement, she was the first to take the honorary title for past emperors, Dajō-tennō. She was also the first monarch to be cremated. She
died in 701.

References
Aston, W. G., trans. *Nihongi: Chronicles of Japan*. Rutland, VT: Charles E.
    Tuttle, 1972. pp. 382–423.
Papinot, E. *Historical and Geographical Dictionary of Japan*. Rutland, VT:
    Charles E. Tuttle, 1972. pp. 70, 232.
Sansom, George A. *A History of Japan to 1334*. Stanford: Stanford
    University Press, 1958. p. 65.

Joan
See Juana I

Joan I
Countess, Capetian Ruler of Artois (1329–1330)

Artois was located in northern France. Joan (or Jeanne) was the
daughter of Mahaut (r. 1302–1329) and Otto IV, count of Burgundy
(not to be confused with the duchy of Burgundy, of which Eudes IV,
Joan's future son-in-law, was duke at the time [r. 1315–1349]). Joan

married Philip V of France (r. 1316–1322) and had at least two daughters: Joan II (r. 1330–1346) and Margaret (r. 1361–1382). In 1329 Joan I succeeded her mother Mahaut but ruled only one year before she died. Her daughter Joan II succeeded her.

References

Morby, John E. *Dynasties of the World*. Oxford: Oxford University Press, 1980. p. 94.

Joan II
Countess, Capetian Ruler of Artois (1330–1347)

Artois was located in northern France. Joan II (or Jeanne) was the daughter of Joan I (r. 1329–1330) and Philip V (r. France 1316–1322). Joan II married Eudes IV, duke of Burgundy (r. 1315–1349) and inherited the rule of Artois at the death of her mother. Joan II and Eudes IV had a son, Philip, whose son Philip of Rouvres (r. 1347–1361) succeeded his grandmother. After 1349 Philip of Rouvres also ruled Burgundy.

References

Morby, John E. *Dynasties of the World*. Oxford: Oxford University Press, 1989. pp. 94–95.

Joanna I
Countess of Provence (1343–1382), Queen of Naples (1343–1381)

Joanna I (or Jane, Joan I, Giovanna I, or Giovanni I) was born in 1326, the daughter of Charles of Calabria and Maria of Valois and the grandaughter of Robert the Wise, king of Naples from 1309 to 1343. She succeeded Robert upon his death, becoming the first queen of Naples. Queen Joanna, intelligent and politically astute as well as beautiful, married her cousin, Andrew of Hungary, brother of Hungarian King Louis I (or Lewis), as a political ploy to reconcile Hungarian claims upon Naples. The influx of Hungarians brought by Andrew into Naples angered many, including Joanna, who feared that the Hungarians intended to take over Naples. Andrew was assassinated in 1845, if not by her instigation, at least with her consent.

In 1347 she married Louis of Taranto but was forced to take exile in Avignon when her former brother-in-law, King Louis I, invaded Naples to avenge his brother's death, accusing her of strangling him. During her five-year exile, she sold Avignon to Pope Innocent VI in return for a declaration by him of her innocence of the assassination. Her second husband died ten years after her return, and in 1862 she married King James of Majorca. He died in 1875, and the following year she married Otto of Brunswick, a military man.

At one time she named her niece's husband, Charles III of Durazzo, as her heir, but later she repudiated him and adopted Louis, duke of Anjou, brother of France's king Charles V. Durazzo appealed to Pope Urban VI, who in 1381 crowned him king of Naples in Rome. Durazzo then invaded Naples, imprisoned Joanna, and in 1382 had her murdered by suffocation.

References
Gibbon, Edward. *The Decline and Fall of the Roman Empire.* Vol. 2. Chicago: Encyclopaedia Britannica, 1952. pp. 509, 577.

Morby, John E. *Dynasties of the World.* Oxford: Oxford University Press, 1989. pp. 87, 102.

Tuchman, Barbara W. *A Distant Mirror, The Calamitous 14th Century.* New York: Ballantine Books, 1978. pp. 201, 330, 333, 334, 337, 399, 409.

Joanna II
Queen of Naples (1414–1435)

Joanna II (or Joan II, Giovanna II, or Giovanni II) was born in 1371, the daughter of Margaret of Durazzo and Charles III, who ruled Naples from 1382 to 1386 and Hungary from 1385 to 1386. She was the sister of Ladislas I, who succeeded as king of Naples after their father was murdered in 1386. She first married William of Austria, but after he died in 1406, her amorous escapades kept Italian diplomacy in an uproar. When her brother died in 1414, Joanna succeeded to the throne and appointed her current lover, Pandolfello Alopo, as grand chamberlain. The following year she married Jacques de Bourbon, comte de la Marche, who had her lover executed and then attempted to wrest the throne from her. But Italian barons, not wanting a French takeover, ousted him and sent him back to France.

Joanna used the succession unmercifully as a maneuvering device. She adopted, then renounced, Alfonso V of Aragon (the Magnanimous) as her heir; adopted, then disinherited, Louis III of Anjou as her heir; readopted, then redisinherited, Louis; and when Louis died, finally named his son René as her heir. She died in 1435, leaving Alfonso and René to fight it out. Alfonso was the victor and became the next king of Naples.

References

Carpenter, Clive. *The Guinness Book of Kings, Rulers & Statesmen.* Enfield, Middlesex: Guinness Superlatives, 1978. p. 147.

Langer, William L. *World History.* Boston; Houghton Mifflin, 1980. p. 314–315.

Joanna III
See Juana la Loca

Joanna of Austria
Regent of Portugal (1557–1562)

Joanna was the daughter of Charles V, Holy Roman emperor, and Isabella, daughter of King Manuel I of Portugal. Joanna married John of Portugal, second son of King John III (the Pious) of Portugal, who ruled Portugal from 1521 to 1557. In 1554, months before their son was born, John died. The boy, Sebastian I, succeeded to the throne three years later when his grandfather died. Joanna served as regent for five years. During her regency Portugal's overseas dominions frequently erupted in rebellions. In 1562 John III's brother, Cardinal Henry, was appointed to replace her for the remaining six years of the regency.

References

Langer, William L., ed. *World History.* Boston: Houghton Mifflin, 1980. pp. 418–419.

Jodit
See Judith

Johanna
Countess, Ruler of Flanders (1205–1244)

Johanna (or Joanna) was the daughter of Baldwin IX, emperor of Constantinople (1171–1195), and Maria of Champagne. Johanna became sole ruler from the House of Hainault of Flanders in 1205. In 1212 she married Ferdinand of Portugal, who served as co-regent until 1233, when he died. She then ruled alone during a difficult period of Belgian history, when the country was devastated by war. Upon her death in 1244, she was succeeded by her sister Margaret II. Flanders, a great center of economic activity and a much fought over territory, was ruled by women for sixty-five years.

References

Egan, Edward W., Constance B. Hintz, and L. F. Wise, eds. *Kings, Rulers, and Statesmen.* New York: Sterling Publishing, 1976. p. 52.

Heer, Friedrich. *The Medieval World.* Trans. Janet Sondheimer. New York: Mentor/NAL, 1962. p. 318.

Morby, John E. *Dynasties of the World.* Oxford: Oxford University Press, 1989. p. 90.

Johanna
Duchess, Ruler of Brabant (1355–1404/1406)

Johanna, of the House of Burgundy, was the daughter of John III, who ruled Brabant from 1312 to 1355, and she succeeded him at his death in 1355. She married Wenceslas, duke of Luxembourg. On a ceremonial visit to Brabant in 1356, she tendered upon her subjects a new constitution, called Joyeuse Entrée, which conferred broad liberties to her subjects. Johanna had no children. Owing to ill health, she abdicated in 1404, but no successor was named. On her deathbed she named as successor her great-nephew Antoine of Burgundy (r. 1406–1415), grandson of her sister, Margaret, and son of Philip the Bold. She died in 1406.

References

Langer, William L., ed. *World History.* Boston: Houghton Mifflin, 1980. p. 406–407.

Morby, John E. *Dynasties of the World.* Oxford: Oxford University Press, 1989. p. 94.

Jolanthe
Duchess, Co-ruler of Lorraine (1473–1480)

Jolanthe was a kinswoman of Jean II (r. 1453–1470) and Nicolas (r. 1470–1473). When Nicolas died, she inherited the duchy. She was married to René II, grandson of René I (co-ruled 1431–1453). René II ruled with her until her death in 1480, whereupon he became sole duke of Bar and Lorraine.

References

Carpenter, Clive. *The Guinness Book of Kings, Rulers & Statesmen.* Enfield, Middlesex: Guinness Superlatives, 1978. p. 92.

Juana I
Queen of Navarre
(1274–1305)

Juana I (or Joan I) was born in 1273, the daughter of Henry I (Enrique) the Fat (r. Navarre 1270–1274). She succeeded from the House of France to the rule of Navarre and Champagne upon his death when she was only an infant. From the mid-thirteenth century onward, the counts or countesses of Champagne were also kings or queens of Navarre.

In 1284, she was married to Philip IV the Fair of France (r. France 1285–1314), considered by his detractors as a cruel and greedy tyrant. During Philip's reign of France, the French feudal monarchy was at its apex. He forbade private feudal wars, decreeing as illegal the practice of nobles to ride about carrying arms. He effectively weakened the church's influence in politics. Queen Juana founded the College of Navarre. She died in 1305.

References

Heer, Friedrich. *The Medieval World.* Trans. Janet Sondheimer. New York: Mentor/NAL, 1962. p. 251.

Langer, William L., ed. *World History.* Boston: Houghton Mifflin, 1980. p. 298.

Morby, John E. *Dynasties of the World.* Oxford: Oxford University Press, 1989. pp. 70, 85, 114.

Painter, Sidney, *The Rise of the Feudal Monarchies.* Ithaca: Cornell University Press, 1951. pp. 37, 39–41.

Sédillot, René. *An Outline of French History.* Trans. Gerard Hopkins. New York: Alfred A. Knopf, 1967. pp. 115–116, 126–127, 152–153, 160.

Juana II
Queen of Navarre (1328–1349)

Juana II (or Joan II or Jeanne II) was born ca. 1311, the daughter of Margaret of Burgundy and King Louis X (r. France 1314–1316). Juana inherited the kingdom of Navarre at the death of her uncle, King Charles I (r. 1322–1328), who was also Charles IV, king of

France. She married Count Philip of Evreux (Philippe III). Under Juana, Navarre became an independent nation again. Philip died in 1343. Their son, Charles II the Bad (Carlos), inherited her throne when she died in 1349.

References
Morby, John E. *Dynasties of the World.* Oxford: Oxford University Press, 1989. p. 114.

Juana la Loca
Queen of Castile and León (1504–1506/1555), Queen of Aragon (1516–1555), Queen of Naples (1516–1555), Queen of Sicily (1516–1555)

Juana la Loca (the Mad) (or Giovanna III or Queen Jan) was born in 1479, the daughter of Isabella I of Castile and Ferdinand II of Aragon. She was married to Philip (the Handsome) of Burgundy and became archduccess of Burgundy. Philip became Philip I in 1504 when, upon Isabella's death, Juana inherited her mother's throne. Upon her father's death, she inherited the thrones of Aragon, Naples, and Sicily. Juana bore two sons: Charles, who first became Charles I, king of Spain, then Charles V, Holy Roman emperor; and Ferdinand, who succeeded his brother as Holy Roman emperor. She had four daughters: Eleanor, who married King Manuel I of Portugal; Isabella, who married King Christian II of Denmark; Maria, who married King Louis II of Hungary; and Catherine, who married King John III of Portugal. When Philip died in 1506, Juana lost her sanity completely. She toured the country with his coffin and finally retired three years later to Tordesillas, still accompanied by his embalmed corpse.

References
Chapman, Charles E. *A History of Spain.* New York: The Free Press/Macmillan, 1965. pp. 207–209, 235, 233.
Langer, William L., ed. *World History.* Boston: Houghton Mifflin, 1980. pp. 406, 415, 428.
McKendrick, Malveena. *Ferdinand and Isabella.* New York: American Heritage Publishing, 1968. pp. 99, 130–136, 140, 141, 144, 146–147.

Judith
Queen of the Falasha Agaw of Abyssinia (10th c.)

Historical records do not make it clear when the Agaw became the monarchs of old Abyssinia (now Ethiopia). However, it is fairly certain that the Zagwe Dynasty of the Agaw of Lasta held power in Abyssinia from 1137 to 1270. In the south of Ethiopia, between the fault of the lakes and the loop of the Blue Nile, lay the great Damot kingdom. The Damot are possibly identical to the Demdem people, who are known to have been near Lake Abaya, the homeland of the Galla people. A part of these turbulent populations, who to some degree converted to Judaism, launched frequent attacks against the Amhara-Tegre power, the Christian provinces of Ethiopia. The most serious of these attacks, led by a Falasha queen named Esato (Judith) in ca. 976, devastated the Christian empire as far as the mountains of Tigre.

Judith, or Esato ("the Monster") or Isato ("Fire") (also Jodit, Esat, or Yehudit), was the daughter of Gedeon, a member of the Falasha tribe, the black Jews of Ethiopia, who claim descent from Solomon. Judith launched her attack against the Christians of Axum when their king, Anbessa Wudim, was only ten years old. The Ethiopians saw Esato's invasion as a heavenly punishment for their having failed to be obedient to their Coptic patriarch, and they fled as her armies neared. Queen Judith did not stop until Axum was reduced to ruin, its churches destroyed and its holy relics looted. The one exception, according to legend, was the Ark of the Covenant, which monks had carried south to an island in Lakeewai.

Queen Judith ruled for the next forty years, wreaking havoc and killing many thousands of Christians. Only the rock churches of Tigrai survived her onslaught. Legend says she died while returning to her palace following a church-burning expedition, when God misdirected her to a place called Adi Nefas. There a whirlwind picked her up and dropped her from a great height to her death. Her burial place, marked only by a pile of stones, is at Ade Kaweh near Wukro.

Once the local Ethiopian Christians were delivered of Esato's terrible wrath, they tightened their bonds with the Egyptian church. While the Agaw held political control, the Amhara and Tegre culture entered what has been described as a "dark age" about which little is known. A large part of the Ethiopic civilization was lost or destroyed during that time.

References

de Villiers, Marq, and Sheila Hirtle. *Into Africa*. Toronto: Key Porter Books, 1997. p. 341.

Gamst, Frederick C. *The Quemant: A Pagan-Hebraic Peasantry of Ethiopia*. New York: Holt, Rinehart and Winston, 1969. pp. 13, 14, 124.

Judith
See Zauditu

Julia Avita Mammaea
Augusta, Regent of the Roman Empire (222–235)

Commonly referred to as Mammaea, she was the daughter of Julia Maesa and Julius Avitas and the sister of Julia Soaemias. Julia Mammaea married Gessius Marcianus, and in 208 they had a son, Severus Alexander, a personable and intelligent child. Julia Mammaea's mother persuaded her grandson, Emperor Elagabalus, to adopt Alexander as his heir. When Elagabalus was murdered, Alexander became emperor at age fourteen. His mother acted as regent with a senatorial advisory council

After the death of her mother in 226, Julia Mammaea emerged as the real power, totally dominating the young emperor. In 232 she even accompanied the army on the Persian campaign, the failure of which was then ascribed to her interference. While on campaign in 235, she and her son were slain at Mainz by mutinous Roman soldiers led by Maximus Julius Verus.

References
Gibbon, Edward. *The Decline and Fall of the Roman Empire*. Vol. 1. Chicago: Encyclopaedia Britannica Press, 1952. pp. 271–272.

Peters, F. E. *The Harvest of Hellenism*. New York: Barnes & Noble Books, 1996. pp. 559–560, 579.

Rawlinson, George. *Ancient History*. New York: Barnes & Noble Books, 1993. pp. 431–433.

Julia Berenice
See Berenice

Julia Domna
Empress, Regent of the Roman Empire (211–217 Intermittently)

Julia Domna was born in Emesa, Syria, the daughter of the prominent high priest Bassianus. Renowned for her intelligence and beauty, she was the elder sister of the famous and equally well endowed Julia Maesa. In 187 she married the governor of Gallia Lugdunansis, Lucius Septimius Severes, who became Roman emperor in 193. She had two children in Gaul: Caracella (born in 188) and Geta (born in 189). Devoutly religious, Julia introduced the Semitic goddess Tanit (as Caelestis Dea) into the Roman world. In 203 she began gathering about her in Rome a group of philisophers and other literary figures.

Julia's life was to change drastically in 207, when Severus mounted an expedition to Britain, taking her and their sons with him. He died in 211 while in Britain, and his sons became co-emperors and bitter antagonists. In 212 Caracella persuaded Julia to act as intermediary to bring the two together for a reconciliation. When Geta appeared, Caracella had his brother stabbed to death in his mother's arms. Caracella then ruled alone and was frequently gone on military campaigns, leaving Julia in charge of the administration of civil affairs. In 217 he was murdered by his praetorian prefect, Macrinus, who was then proclaimed emperor. On news of her son's death, Julia committed suicide (217), allegedly by starvation, either voluntarily or upon Macrinus's orders.

References

Bowder, Diana, ed. *Who Was Who in the Roman World*. Ithaca, NY: Cornell University Press, 1980. pp. 89–90, 226–227, 270–271, 491–494.

Gibbon, Edward. *The Decline and Fall of the Roman Empire*. Vol. 1. Chicago: Encyclopaedia Britannica Press, 1952. pp. 48, 52, 54–55, 58.

Peters, F. E. *The Harvest of Hellenism*. New York: Barnes & Noble Books, 1996. pp. 430, 547, 557, 558.

Julia Maesa
Augusta, De Facto Regent of the Roman Empire (217–226)

Julia Maesa was born in Emesa, Syria, the daughter of the high priest Bassianus and the younger sister of Empress Julia Domna. Julia Maesa married a Roman senator, Julius Avitus. They had two daughters: Julia Soaemias, mother of Emperor Elagabalus (r. 218–222), and Julia Mammaea, mother of Emperor Severus Alexander (r. 222–235). Elagabalus resembled his kinsman Caracella, so after Caracella had been murdered by Macrinus, Julia Maesa plotted the overthrow of Macrinus by having Syrian troops pass off Elagabalus as Caracellas's bastard son, proclaiming him emperor. Elagabalus succeeded to the throne, but his grandmother held the real power. She introduced the Syrian cult of Bael at Rome.

Elagabalus was bisexual and had a tendency toward transvestism. He took three different wives and had many casual sexual encounters with various other partners. His conduct so disgusted his soldiers that by 221 it was clear to Julia Maesa that he would soon be murdered. She persuaded him to adopt his cousin Alexander, age fourteen, as his son and caesar. Alexander was so popular that Elagabalus became jealous and tried to have him killed. The outraged soldiers murdered Elagabalus and his mother, Julia Soaemias, in 222. Julia Maesa continued to exercise her power until her death in ca. 226.

References

Bowder, Diana, ed. *Who Was Who in the Roman World*. Ithaca, NY: Cornell University Press, 1980. pp. 180–181, 271, 272.

Gibbon, Edward. *The Decline and Fall of the Roman Empire.* Vol. 1.
   Chicago: Encyclopaedia Britannica Press, 1952. pp. 58, 60–61.

Peters, F. E. *The Harvest of Hellenism.* New York: Barnes & Noble Books,
   1996. pp. 558, 559.

Rawlinson, George. *Ancient History.* New York: Barnes & Noble Books,
   1993. pp.431–433.

Juliana
Queen of The Netherlands (1948–1980)

Juliana Louise Emma Marie Wilhelmina was born in The Hague in 1909, the only child of Queen Wilhelmina and Prince Henry of Mecklenburg-Schwerin. As a teenage princess, she met her cousin Edward, Prince of Wales (the late duke of Windsor), and it was hoped in some circles that the two would be attracted to each other. Instead, the prince said, "Juliana, you have heavy legs," to which she retorted, "If the House of Windsor had been standing as long as the House of Orange, your legs wouldn't be so skinny." She studied at the University of Leiden from 1927 to 1930.

In 1937 Juliana married Prince Bernhard of Lippe-Biesterfeld. The couple had four daughters: Béatrix (1938), Irene (1939), Margaret (1943), and Marijke (1947). During World War II, Juliana and her children took refuge in Ottawa, Canada, returning to The Netherlands in 1945. In 1947 and 1948 she acted as regent during her mother's illness and became queen in September 1948, following her mother's abdication. Juliana was not crowned because in

Juliana (Archive Photos)

Holland the crown belongs to the people; instead the ceremony installing a new ruler is called inauguration.

In 1947 she freed from Dutch rule all the Netherlands East Indies except New Guinea, which later became the Republic of Indonesia. In the 1950s Juliana became interested in faith healing, and the news that she had put a faith healer on the payroll was met with public indignation. The marriage of her daughter Princess Irene to a Spanish Carlist and of Princess Béatrix to a German ex-Nazi aroused political controversy, as did the prince consort's acceptance of a large sum of money from Lockheed Aircraft Corporation in 1976. Juliana abdicated in 1980 in favor of her daughter Béatrix.

References
Clark, Sydney. *All the Best in Holland.* New York: Dodd Mead, 1960. p. 76.
Gunther, John. *Inside Europe Today.* New York: Harper & Bros., 1961. pp. 114–115.
Hoffman, William. *Queen Juliana: The Story of the Richest Woman in the World.* New York: Harcourt Brace Jovanovich, 1979.
Langer, William L., ed. *World History.* Boston: Houghton Mifflin, 1980. p. 475.
Uglow, Jennifer S., ed. *International Dictionary of Women's Biography.* New York: Continuum, 1982. p. 250.

Jumper, Betty Mae
Chief of Seminole Nation (1960s)

Betty Mae Jumper was born ca. 1927 in Florida and graduated from a reservation high school in Cherokee, North Carolina. She studied nursing in Oklahoma and went into field work with the U.S. Public Health Service. She then returned to Florida to the state Seminole Reservation, the Big Cypress Reservation, and has been active in the affairs of the tribe ever since.

In the Seminole Nation the clans are perpetuated through the women. Jumper was elected chief in the 1960s. An interviewer in 1969 described her as bright, jolly, and vivacious. As chief, her main concern was to raise the living standards of her tribe through education. She once cited the government-funded Head Start program as the most important boost for Seminole children's education. She said, "Many of the kids went into the first grade without knowing English. So they couldn't learn much, and they never did catch up. With Head Start they start out even." The program was dismantled by President Reagan. Of her people, Jumper said, "We don't want to be white people; we want to be Seminoles. We want the modern things, and we want to live nicely, but we want to do it among friends." Jumper mentioned the greatest trial of Indian youth who go away to college or military service is loneliness.

References

Capron, Lewis. "Florida's Emerging Seminoles." *National Geographic.* November 1969: 716–734.

Betty Mae Jumper (Courtesy: Seminole Nation)

Kaahumanu, Queen
Co-ruler of Hawaii (1823–1832)

Kaahumanu was the wife of Kamehameha I (r. 1795–1819), first ruler over the entire Hawaiian archipelago, whose greed almost ruined the islands. Under his rule, every sandalwood tree on the islands was chopped down and sold to Canton. Queen Kaahumanu had at least three children, one of whom, Liholiho, ascended the throne upon his father's death in 1819, just in time to play host to an influx from the West. He ruled as Kamehameha II (r. 1819–1823 or 1824).

In 1820, the first foreign whalers reached the islands. That same year, two Christian Congregationalist missionaries arrived from the United States. They made no inroads in converting the populace until the royal family agreed to be baptized. This conversion was eventually to have an impact on the sexual conduct of young Hawaiian girls upon whom, until that time, there had been no sexual taboos. The whalers had immediately taken advantage of the native girls, and as a result, venereal diseases swept the island.

In 1823 or 1824, Kamehameha II and his wife both died while in England on an official visit. His younger brother, Kauikeaouli, succeeded him and ruled, under his mother Queen Kaahumanu's supervision, as Kamehameha III (r. 1825–1854).

Queen Kaahumanu endeavored to raise the sexual moral standards of her subjects, an effort not appreciated by the foreign sailors. Her policy, called "stupid morality" by the whalers, was praised by U.S. president Andrew Jackson in 1829. After her death in 1832, the young king reverted to "lascivious ways," although otherwise he was considered a strong king. When he died in 1854, Queen Kaahumanu's daughter Kinau's son succeeded as Kamehameha IV (r. 1854–1863), followed by his brother Lut as Kamehameha V (r. 1863–1872).

References
Knappert, Jan. *Pacific Mythology.* London: Diamond Books, 1995. p. 109.

Morby, John E. *Dynasties of the World.* Oxford: Oxford University Press, 1989. p. 243.

Suggs, Robert C. *Island Civilizations of Polynesia.* New York: Mentor, 1960, p. 144.

Kahina, Al-

Priestess-queen of North African Berbers (ca. 695–703)

Prior to the capture of Byzantine-held Carthage by the Arabs and the establishment of the new Arab city of Tunis, the pastoral Berbers, the original inhabitants of northern Africa, had remained aloof from the struggle between Muslims and Christians, probably in the hope of benefiting from the aftermath. But around 695, the independent Berber tribes of the Aures mountains, part of the Atlas range in northern Africa, joined under the leadership of a queen of the Jerna tribe whom Gibbon called "Cahina," meaning "priestess."

Shortly after the capture of Carthage, Al-Kahina (or Cahina, Dhabba, or Dahiya al-Kahina) and her tribes swept down upon the Arabs with savage ferocity. In 703 the Berbers defeated the Arabs under Hassan ibn No'man near Mons Aurasius and drove the Saracens back to Egypt. After the victory, Al-Kahina assembled the Moorish chiefs and, according to Gibbon, suggested that because the gold and silver in their cities attracted the Arabs, they should burn the cities and bury the "vile metals" in their ruins. The fortifications from Tangier to Tripoli were burned. Even the fruit trees were cut down, leaving a desert. The populace was so devastated that the general of the Saracens was welcomed back. Al-Kahina was killed in the first battle against him. She died near a well that is still known as Bir al-Kahina. Thereafter the Berbers became allies of the Arabs. For her valiant effort, the priestess-queen earned the title of queen-mother of the Berbers. She is celebrated in Maghreb (Maghrib) epic literature.

References

Gibbon, Edward. *The Decline & Fall of the Roman Empire.* Vol. 3. Chicago: Encyclopaedia Britannica, 1952. p. 190.

Langer, William L., ed. *Encyclopedia of World History.* Boston: Houghton Mifflin, 1980. p. 202.

Marrouchi, Mustapha. "Breaking Up/Down/Out of the Boundaries: Tahar Ben Jelloun." *Research in African Literature* 21, no. 4 (1990): 79.

Oliver, Roland, and J. D. Fage. *A Short History of Africa.* Harmondsworth: Penguin Books, 1970. p. 71.

Kalyānavati
Queen of Sri Lanka (1202–1208)

Kalyānavati was a member of the non-Sinhalese faction of the Kaliṅga dynasty. She ruled during a chaotic period in Ceylonese history that followed the reign of Parākramabāhu I, who for the first time had united the island under one rule (1153–1186). Following his death, the country was ruled by a succession of relatives of his Kaliṅgan wife, none of whom ruled for very long. Queen Kalyānavati was the fifth ruler to take the throne in sixteen years. She succeeded King Sahassamalla, who had ruled for only two years. Following her six-year reign, she was succeeded by another relative, King Dharmasoka, who ruled for only one year.

References
Egan, Edward W., Constance B. Hintz, and L. F. Wise, eds. *Kings, Rulers, and Statesmen.* New York: Sterling Publishing, 1976. p. 441.

Kamalat Shah, Zaynt al-Din
Sultana of Atjeh in Indonesia (1688–1699)

Atjeh, a small Muslim sultanate on the northern tip of Sumatra, was once a busy trade center, dominating the world pepper market. Kamalat was the fourth in a succession of Muslim sultanas who ruled Atjeh for a total of forty years. She succeeded Sultana ʻInayat Shah Zakiyyat al-Din Shah, possibly her mother, who ruled from 1678 to 1688. In his article on "Atjeh" in the *Encyclopedia of Islam,* H. Djajadiningrat lists Kamalat Shah as the seventeenth sovereign of the dynasty. She ruled from 1688 to 1699. Despite decrees from Mecca and opposition from the caliphs, the sultanas were apparently popular enough to override the *fatwa* forbidding a woman to rule.

References
Mernissi, Fatima. *The Forgotten Queens of Islam.* Trans. Mary Jo Lakeland. Minneapolis: University of Minnesota Press, 1993. pp. 30, 86, 110.

Kanal-Ikal, Lady
Maya "King" of Palenque (583–604)

Kanal-Ikal was the daughter of King Chan-Bahlum I (b. 524, r. 572–583). She did not come to the throne as a consort or a regent but inherited the crown from her father. Surviving records do not name her husband, but her son was Ac-Kan, who ascended to the throne on January 4, 605, after her death on November 7, 604. Another son, Pacal I, had a daughter, Lady Kanal-Ikal's granddaughter,

named Zac-Kuk, who later also inherited the throne. The fact that Lady Kanal-Ikal appears prominently in her great-grandson Pacal the Great's records makes it likely that she commissioned the inscriptions and temple constructions during her reign.

References

Schele, Linda, and David Freidel. *A Forest of Kings: The Untold Story of the Ancient Maya.* New York: Quill/ William Morrow, 1990. pp. 219–221, 223, 224, 467.

Kassi
Empress of Mali (1341–?)

Kassi was the principal wife and paternal cousin of Emperor Suleyman, who ruled Mali from 1341 to 1360. According to Mali custom, the emperor and his principal wife ruled jointly. Kassi was extremely popular with the royal court, many members of which were her relatives. She was not, however, as popular with her husband as was a commoner named Bendjou. Eventually the emperor divorced Kassi in order to marry Bendjou. Kassi rallied support of the noble ladies of the court, who refused to pay homage to the new empress. Instead, Kassi was still regarded as empress by the noble ladies, who would do obeisance by throwing earth on their heads and who showed their disdain for Bendjou by throwing earth on their hands. This insubordination angered both Bendjou and the emperor, and Kassi was forced to seek sanctuary in the mosque. From this vantage, she incited the nobles, particularly her cousins, to revolt. The struggle that followed was actually a reflection of the larger division into two ideological factions vying for ascendancy. One party in the empire supported Suleyman while the other supported the sons of the former ruler, Mansa Maghan I, Suleyman's nephew. The latter faction also supported Kassi. Suleyman and his military chiefs eventually defeated Kassi and her cousins. This he did by discrediting her with her party by proving that she was intriguing with her cousin, Djathal, who had previously been expelled for treason. Suleyman was succeeded by Kassi's son, Kassa, who ruled only nine months before his cousin Mari Diata seized power.

References

Panikker, K. Madhu. *The Serpent and the Crescent: A History of the Negro Empires of West Africa.* Bombay: Asia Publishing House, 1963. p. 60.

Kazimiera-Daniute Prunskiene
See Prunskiene, Kazimiera-Daniute

Khadija
Sultana of the Maldives (1347–1379)

Khadija was one of three daughters of Sultan Salah al-Din Salih Al-bendjaly. When her father died, her brother Shihab-ud-din became king at a very young age. The vizier, 'Abdallah, son of Muhammad al-Hazrami, married the young king's mother and overpowered him and had him put to death. Meanwhile, Khadija had married Jamal-ud-din, who managed to take over the reins of power for his wife. As vizier, he issued orders in Sultana Khadija's name. The orders were written on palm leaves with a bent piece of iron, because paper was not used except for writing the Koran and books of learning. She ruled for thirty-three years, during which time Ibn Battuta traveled to the Maldives. He wrote: "One of the wonders of these islands is that its ruler [*sultana*] is a woman named Khadija. . . ." She died in 1379 and was succeeded by her sister Myriam.

References

Ibn Battuta. *Travels of Ibn Battuta A.D. 1325–1354.* Trans. H. A. R. Gibb from the French translation of C. Defremery and B. B. Sanguinetti. Vol. 2. Cambridge: Cambridge University Press, 1962.

Khentkaues
Co-ruler of Egypt (ca. 2494–2472 B.C.)

Khentkaues (also Khentkawes or Khamerernebti II) was the daughter of Khafre, also called Cephren (r. ca. 2520–2494 B.C.). Her mother was most likely the king's sister, Khamerernebti I, his first wife. Khentkaues was the sister and wife of Mycernius (also called Menhaure or Menkure), fifth ruler of the Fourth Dynasty (r. ca. 2494–2472 B.C.). Mycernius began construction on the third and smallest pyramid of Giza. Although the king was supreme, sculpture that survives indicates that Khentaues shared the rule. In the Fourth Dynasty kingship reached the peak of centralized authority.

According to Herodotus, Mycernius only had one child, a daughter, who died. The king had a hollow wooden cow made, plated with gold, to hold her. The cow was still standing during Herodotus's time

(ca. 490–425 B.C.). In an adjoining chamber from the one housing the cow were some statues representing, by one account, concubines of Mycernius. By a second account, the daughter hanged herself because her father had violated her, so her mother cut off the hands of the servants who allowed the king access to her daughter. The statues in the adjoining chamber, with missing hands, represent the servants.

References

Grimal, Nicolas. *A History of Ancient Egypt.* Trans. Basil Blackwell Ltd. New York: Barnes & Noble Books, 1997. pp. 68, 72, 74–75, 115–116, 128.

West, John Anthony. *The Traveler's Key to Ancient Egypt.* New York: Alfred A. Knopf, 1985. p. 110, 134.

Kinigi, Sylvie
Prime Minister of Burundi (1993)

Burundi, located in central east Africa, is bounded on the east and south by Tanzania, on the north by Rwanda, and on the west by Zaire and Lake Tanganyika. During the entire time that it has been a political entity since the fifteenth century, first as a kingdom, now as a republic, a power struggle between the Hutu and the Tutsi tribes has characterized its government. In 1981 a new constitution confirmed Burundi's status as a one-party state. At that time, the Tutsi faction held power over the majority Hutu peasants. In 1987 the president was ousted in a military coups headed by Major Pierre Buyoya, and this was followed within the year by ethnic violence that left 5,000 dead.

Sylvie Kinigi, the well-educated daughter of a prominent Bujumbura family and the first woman to serve her country's government, had been a chairperson in women's organizations concerned with health and education before entering the national political arena. She was nominated from a field of clashing factions within her party as a compromise candidate for prime minister. At approximately the same time, neighboring Rwanda also elected a woman prime minister, and the two looked forward to amicable relations. But Kinigi's election was greeted with surprise and hostility even from within her own party. In placing herself in public service, she was aware of the danger accompanying victory. She served only a matter of months before political upheaval forced her out, but she was more fortunate than her Rwandan counterpart, Agathe Uwilingiuamana, who was assassinated.

References
"Women on the Run." *World Press Review.* February 1996: 38–39.

Kirum
Queen, Mayor of Khaya-Sumu's City in Ilansura (ca. 1790–1745 B.C.)

Kirum was one of many daughters of King Zimri-Lim, who ruled Mari in the mid-1700s B.C. The king arranged her marriage to Khaya-Sumu, who ruled Ilansura, and also appointed her mayor of Khaya-Sumu's city. A high-spirited woman, she not only administered the city, writing her father for advice, but also dispensed political advice to her father. Her independence and her seeking her father's political opinion about Khaya-Sumu's realm displeased her husband. He also married her sister or half-sister, Shimatum, creating a bitter rivalry. Kirum eventually asked her father for permission to return home. She quoted her husband as saying, "You exercise the mayorship here. (But) since I will (surely) kill you, let him come . . . and take you back." Apparently her father did not reply, for she wrote again, threatening, "If my lord does not bring me back, I will head toward Mari (and) jump (fall) from the roof." This time the king instructed his wife, Queen Shibtu, to bring Kirum home.

References
Lerner, Gerda. *The Creation of Patriarchy.* New York: Oxford University Press, 1986. pp. 70–74.

Kōgyoku-tennō
Empress, Twice Ruler of Japan (642–645 and, as Saimei-tennō, 655–ca. 662)

Kōgyoku-tennō was born in 594, the daughter of Prince Chinu no Ōji and Princess Kibi and the granddaughter of Shōtoku-taishi, a Japanese regent from 593 to 621. Her birth name was Ame-toyo-takara-ikashihitarashi hime, or Hitarashi-hime, or Tarashi for short. She first married Emperor Yōmei-tennō, who ruled from 586 to 587, and bore the Imperial prince Aya. After her first husband died in 587, she then married her uncle, Emperor Jōmei-tennō, who ruled from 629 until his death in 641. She bore two more sons and a daughter. At the age of forty-eight she succeeded her husband in 642, having been chosen by the Soga clan, which planned to wrest the ultimate control.

During her first reign, she was influenced by two powerful Soga ministers, Iruku and Emishi, who, at the instigation of her younger brother, Kōtoku, were assassinated in her presence in ca. 644. The next morning she abdicated in his favor. When he died ten years later, she reascended the throne at the age of sixty-two. (In early Japanese history, the outgoing ruler is considered to have ruled the entire year, and the incoming ruler's reign officially begins the following year.) This time she did not allow herself to be influenced by her ministers. She built a palace at Yamato, the first to be covered with tiles. The feast of the dead was first celebrated during her second reign. She sent a force to Ezo to subdue the Ebisu. In 660 China attacked the two Korean kingdoms of Koma and Kudara, which asked for Japan's help. The empress prepared to lead an army bound for Korea personally but died unexpectedly on the way, at the palace at Asakura, at the age of sixty-eight. For her second term as empress, she received the posthumous name of Saimei-tennō.

References

Aston, W. G., trans. *Nihongi: Chronicles of Japan,* vol. 2. Rutland, VT: Charles E. Tuttle, 1972. pp. 171, 248–273.

Papinot, E. *Historical and Geographical Dictionary of Japan.* Rutland, VT: Charles E. Tuttle, 1972. pp. 296, 527–528.

Sansom, George. *A History of Japan to 1334.* Stanford: Stanford University Press, 1958. p. 54.

Kōken-tennō
Empress, Twice Ruler of Japan (749–758 and, as Shōtoku-tennō, 764–770)

Kōken-tennō was born Abe-naishinnō in 716, the daughter of Shō-mu-tennō, who ruled Japan from 724 to 748. In 749 he shaved his head and abdicated in favor of his unmarried daughter, Kōken, then age thirty-three. An ardent Buddhist like her father, she assembled some 5,000 bonzes (priests) in the Tō-daiji temple, the Eastern Great Monastery, to read the sacred books. She exacted severe penalties for the killing of any living things. More interested in religion than government, she was eventually persuaded by an adviser, Nakamaro, to abdicate in favor of a kinsman, Junnin, whom Nakamaro then dominated completely.

Kōken shaved her head and took the name of Takano-tennō. She allowed herself to be dominated by the bonze (Buddhist priest), Dōkyō, who may also have been her lover. Dōkyō was a bitter rival of Nakamaro. In 764 the latter raised an army and marched against Dōkyō but was killed in the fighting. Dōkyō persuaded Kōken, now age forty-eight, to return to the throne, while Junnin-tennō was banished to the island of Awaji, where he died a year later.

The empress bestowed favors and titles upon Dōkyō, but he aspired for more: He wanted to be emperor, and in 768 he tried to persuade the empress to abdicate in his favor. However, the throne had been held by the same lineage for fourteen centuries, and before the empress could bring herself to step down in favor of a usurper, she consulted an oracle. The oracle brought an answer from the god Hachiman to the effect that a subject should never become emperor. She kept the throne but died the following year. Because of her second term, she received the posthumous name of Shōtoku-tennō. Her amorous abandon with the ambitious Dōkyō prompted Japanese nobles to vow that no more women would rule. Since her time, only two women have ruled.

References

Papinot, E. *Historical and Geographical Dictionary of Japan.* Rutland, VT: Charles E. Tuttle, 1972. pp. 237, 299–301.

Reischauer, Edwin O., and John K. Fairbank. *East Asia: The Great Tradition.* Boston: Houghton Mifflin, 1960. p. 484.

Sansom, George. *A History of Japan to 1334.* Stanford: Stanford University Press, 1958. p. 89.

Kossamak
Queen, Joint Ruler of Cambodia (1955–1960)

She was born Kossamak Nearirath, the daughter of King Sisowath, who ruled from 1904 to 1927, and the sister of King Monivong, who ruled Cambodia from 1927 to 1941. She married Prince Norodom Suramarit, and they had a son, Sihanouk, born in 1922. When Monivong died in 1941, Sihanouk was placed on the throne by the French governor general of Indochina, Admiral Jean Decoux. In 1952 Sihanouk dissolved the cabinet, declared martial law and went into voluntary exile to dramatize Cambodian demands for complete independence from France. In 1954 the Geneva Conference confirmed complete independence. A referendum the following year approved King Sihanouk's rule, but he abdicated in favor of his father and became prime minister. According to Egan, Hintz, and Wise, Queen Kossamak ruled jointly with her husband until his death in 1960,

Kossamak (Archive Photos)

when her son, Sihanouk, re-assumed the position of head of state.

References

Abercrombie, Thomas J. "Cambodia: Indochina's 'Neutral Corner.'" *National Geographic* 126. October 1964: 514–551.

Egan, Edward W., Constance B. Hintz, and L. F. Wise, eds. *Kings, Rulers, and Statesmen.* New York: Sterling Publishing, 1976. p. 69.

Ku-Baba

Queen, Founder of the Dynasty of Kish in Sumeria (ca. 2350 B.C.)

According to the king list, Queen Ku-Baba, founder of the Third Dynasty, appears to have reigned a hundred years, for she is the only ruler listed for the period. According to earliest Sumerian records, Ku-Baba, formerly a tavern keeper, holds the distinction of being the only woman listed in the king list as reigning in her own right. She led Kish's war for independence from Uruk. Later she was deified—not an uncommon occurrence at the time—and worshipped in northern Mesopotamia as the goddess Kubaba.

References

Carpenter, Clive. *The Guiness Book of Kings, Rulers & Statesmen.* Enfield, Middlesex: Guinness Superlatives, 1978. p. 15.

Edwards, I. E. S. et al., eds. *Cambridge Ancient History.* 3d ed. Vol. 1, pt. 2. Cambridge: Cambridge University Press, 1970–1971. p. 115.

Oppenheim, A. Leo. *Ancient Mesopotamia.* Chicago: The University of Chicago Press, 1977. p. 151.

Roux, Georges. *Ancient Iraq.* Harmondsworth, Middlesex: Penguin, 1980. p. 459.

Kumaratunga, Chandrika

Prime Minister of Sri Lanka (1994–1995), President (1995–1996)

Born in 1945, Chandrika Kumaratunga was the daughter of Solomon Bandaranaike, prime minister from 1956 to 1959, and Sirimavo Bandaranaiko, who succeeded her husband as the island nation's first woman prime minister in 1959. Chandrika had a brother, Anura, and a sister, Sunethra. When Chandrika was thirteen, her father was assassinated before her eyes by a fanatical Buddhist monk. Solomon's widow was elected to succeed him, becoming the first woman to be elected prime minister anywhere in the world and instituting some economically devastating socialist experiments.

Chandrika was educated in Paris, studying political science and embracing the radical socialism of Mao Zedong and North Korea. She married Vijaya Kumaratunga, Sri Lanka's most popular movie star, and the couple had two children. But Vijaya, who was one of the country's most radical left-wing politicians as well, was shot by Sinhalese fascists, again before Chandrika's eyes. Following the assassination, she and her family fled abroad for three years. Meanwhile, her younger brother, Anura, had been his mother's first choice as heir to the political dynasty, but he declined. Chandrika was her mother's next choice, but Chandrika had cast off her socialist leanings and embraced the free market policies that had resulted in improved economic conditions. She announced that she sought "capitalism with a human face."

In 1993 she became the first woman to head a provincial government in Sri Lanka. In the spring of 1994, she defeated the long-governing United National Party in its home territory, the south. In elections of August 1994, she headed a nine-party parliamentary alliance that was able to put an end to the seventeen-year reign of the United National Party to become the new prime minister.

In 1995 she was elected president on the promise of striking a "peace deal" with the separatist Liberation Tigers of Tamil Eelam, led by Vellupillai Prabhakaran. Prior to her election, the country had been involved in a civil war between the government and the separatist forces of Prabhakaran, who has been labeled "one of the century's most vicious and treacherous leaders" by Lindsay Murdoch of the *Sydney Morning Herald*. In January 1995, she persuaded both sides to agree to a 100-day cease-fire; however, when the cease-fire expired, guerrilla activity resumed.

By then the country had been gripped for twelve years by civil war in which more than 50,000 people had been killed. Kumaratunga then offered to grant broad new autonomy to the Tamil minority in hopes that the Tamil Tigers would lay down their arms. However, although her message received a good reception among the Tamil population, the Tigers rejected her peace offer that would have caused the guerrillas to lose their iron grip on the region. Her party lost the election in 1996 and she resigned.

References
"A Family Affair?" *World Press Review*. October 1994, p. 24.
"Peace at Hand?" *World Press Review*. November 1995, p. 26.
"Return of the Tigers." *World Press Review*. August 1995, pp. 28–29.
"The 'Strongwomen' of South Asia." *World Press Review*. December 1994, pp. 18–20.

Kutlugh Khatun
Queen of Kirman, Persia (1257–1282)

Since there were many women on the political scene of that era with the name of Turkan Khatun, in order to avoid confusion this queen will be referred to as Kutlugh Khaten. She was also known as Turkan Khatun or Kutlugh Turkhan. She was the daughter of Barak Hajib, ruler of Kirman as Kutlugh Khan and, later, Kutlugh Sultan. She was married to her father's cousin, Qutb al-Din. After her father's death in 1234, her brother, Rukn al-Din, acceded to the throne. His reign was followed by that of his cousin, Qutb al-Din, Kutlugh's husband, in 1252. When Qutb al-Din died in 1257, their son, Hajjaj, was underage, so the officials at Kirman requested the Mongol court to allow Qutb al-Din's widow to reign, which she did for twenty-six years.

She sent her son, Hajjaj, to fight in Mongolian ruler Hulägu's army and married her daughter, Padishah Khatun, to Hulägu's son, Abaka Khan. This union was most unusual in that Padishah was Muslim and Abaka was Bhuddist. In addition, in order to save her daughter from an obligatory marriage, Kutlugh Turkhan had reared her daughter as a boy. Officially Hulägu confirmed Kutlugh Turkhan's title seven years later, in 1264. Her title was 'Ismat al-dunya wa al-din, and she had the right to have the *khutba* proclaimed in her name in all the mosques.

Her reign was marked by prosperity, and her power and popularity were at their peak when one of her stepsons, Suyurghatamish, appeared to contest her reign. To appease him, she had his name added to hers in the *khutba,* but she complained to her daughter, Padishah, who used her influence to obtain a *yarligh* forbidding Suyurghatamish from interfering in the affairs of Kirman.

Toward the end of Kutlugh Khatun's life, her son-in-law, Abaka, died. He was replaced by his brother, who converted to Islam and took the name of Ahmad Teguder. Ahmad had Kutlugh Khatun removed and installed her stepson Suyurghatamish on the throne of Kirman. Although she traveled to the Mongol court at Tabriz to plead her case, Ahmad refused to rescind his order. She died a year later without having regained her throne or having witnessed the unanticipated reign of her daughter, Padishah Khatun.

References

Grousset, René. *The Empire of the Steppes.* Trans. Naomi Walford. New Brunswick, NJ: Rutgers University Press, 1970. p. 237.

Mernissi, Fatima. *The Forgotten Queens of Islam.* Trans. Mary Jo Lakeland. Minneapolis: University of Minnesota Press, 1993. pp. 29, 100–101.

L

Lakshmi Bāī
Rani, Regent Ruler of Jhānsi (1853 and 1857–1858)

Jhānsi is located in Uttar Pradesh state in northern India. Lakshmi Bāī, originally named Manukarnika, was born ca. 1833 in Benares, the daughter of Moropant Tambe, a Brahmin official. She married Ganyadhar Rao, rajah of Jhānsi, and on her wedding day took the name of Lakshmi, the wife of the god Vishnu. The couple had one son, who died at the age of three months. When Ganyadhar Rao became seriously ill in 1853, to assure the continuation of his line, the couple adopted five-year-old Damodar Rao, a descendant of Rao's grandfather. Majarajah Ramachandra Rao died the same year, and by his will Lakshmi assumed the rule of Jhānsi for their adopted son.

At this point, the British saw the opportunity to annex Jhānsi and declared that Damodar was not a legal heir. For over a year Lakshmi battled in the courts, but ultimately she was deposed by the British East India Company. In 1857, however, when the Indian Mutiny escalated into a Jhānsian uprising against the British, Lakshmi was hastily recalled by the same people who had deposed her and was requested to restore order: "We suggest that you take your kingdom and hold it, along with the adjoining territory, until the British authority is established. We shall be eternally grateful if you will also protect our lives." Lakshmi resumed the reins of government with her father as minister. Later in 1857 the British moved to recapture Jhānsi, and Lakshmi's forces, with Lakshmi at their head dressed in male attire, resisted.

The rebel leader Ramchandra Panduranga, who called himself Tantia Topi, rode to assist her, but the British defeated their combined forces. Lakshmi and her father escaped and were welcomed by Topi at Kalpi. They all proceeded to Gwalior and recaptured it from the British, but in 1858, the British again took Gwalior, and Lakshmi's father was captured and hanged. The rani, who was still leading her troops, died a soldier's death on the battlefield.

References

Bhattacharya, Sachchinananda. *A Dictionary of Indian History.* New York: George Braziller, 1967. p. 538.

Premble, John. *The Raj, the Indian Mutiny, and the Kingdom of Oudh 1801–1859.* Rutherford, NJ: Fairleigh Dickinson University Press, 1977. p. 192.

Spear, Percival. *A History of India.* Vol. 2. London: Penguin Books, 1987. p. 142.

Laodicé
Queen of Cappadocia (ca. 131/130 B.C.–ca. 126 B.C.)

Cappadocia was a small kingdom in eastern Anatolia. Laodicé (or Nysa) was the wife of Ariarathes V, king of Cappadocia (r. ca. 163–ca. 131/130 B.C.) The couple had six sons. When Ariathes was killed in battle, Laodicé poisoned five of her sons before they were old enough to assume the throne so as to be able to rule herself. One son, the youngest, was saved. After Laodicé was removed by an outraged public and assassinated, he ascended the throne as Ariarathes VI.

References

Carpenter, Clive. *The Guinness Book of Kings, Rulers & Statesmen.* Enfield, Middlesex: Guinness Superlatives, 1978. p. 40.

Rawlinson, George. *Ancient History.* New York: Barnes & Noble Books, 1993. p. 247.

Leonora Telles
Queen, Regent of Portugal (1383–1384)

Kings usually married for political gain and seldom for love. The marriage of Leonora Telles (or Leonor Teles de Meneses) to King Ferdinand I the Handsome, who ruled Portugal from 1367 to 1383, followed the love-smitten Ferdinand's repudiation of a previous betrothal to a Castilian princess and precipitated a war between Portugal and Castile. Leonora and Ferdinand had a daughter, Beatrice, who was later married to John I of Castile. When Ferdinand died in 1383, Queen Leonora became regent for her daughter for the Portugese throne. This arrangement led to strong opposition among the people, who detested both the regent and her Galician lover-adviser, João Fernandes Andeiro, count of Ourém. An illegitimate brother of Pedro I, John of Aviz, led a successful revolt and murdered Andeiro. Queen Leonora fled the country and appealed to the king of Castile for help. The Castilian army marched upon Lisbon in May 1384, but an outbreak of plague forced it to retreat four months later. John I was proclaimed king in 1385, becoming the first ruler of the Avis dynasty. Leonora was imprisoned in a convent at Tordesillas. She died in 1386.

References

Langer, William L., ed. *World History.* Boston: Houghton Mifflin, 1980. pp. 306–307, 309.

Liang
Empress, Regent in China (144–150)

Following the reign of Emperor Ho-Ti (r. 88–105), there were civil wars and anarchy in China, as many local warlords managed to establish their independence. Liang was the first of six powerful empresses from three great families who, with court eunuchs, managed to keep the court's wealth and power in their hands by seeing to it that infants and young children were appointed to the throne. Of the twelve emperors of the Eastern Han Dynasty, eight were between the ages of three months and fifteen years. In 132, Empress Liang secured influence for her father, and the Liang family captured control of the court. Empress Liang's father held power for twelve years until he died in 144. Beginning in 144, three young emperors were appointed for whom Empress Liang served as regent. One was her brother, Liang Chi. She died in 150, to be replaced by another young empress. In 159 Emperor Huan Ti put Liang Chi to death and wiped out the last of the Liangs.

References

Langer, William L., ed. *World History.* Boston: Houghton Mifflin, 1940, 1980. pp. 148–149.

Morton, W. Scott. *China: Its History and Culture.* New York: McGraw-Hill, 1980. p. 63.

Reischauer, Edwin O., and John K. Fairbank. *East Asia: The Great Tradition.* Boston: Houghton Mifflin, 1960. pp. 125–126.

Lilavati
Queen, Ruler of the Sinhala Kingdom, Ceylon (1197–1200, 1209–1210, 1211–1212)

During a period of political instability in Sri Lanka, Queen Lilavati was called to the throne on three separate occasions. Frequent incursions from south India kept the island in turmoil. In addition, political factions would frequently break away to form a separate feudal state.

Lilavati, a Kaliṅgan, married Parakramabahu I (r. ca. 1153– 1186). Following his death, her brother Nissankamalla reigned for approximately ten years. Briefly the island fell into the hands of Codaganga before Queen Lilavati came to the throne on her own in 1197. She ruled for three years and was deposed. Her first reign was followed by the two-year reign of King Sahassamalla, the six-year reign of Queen Kalyanavati, and the one-year reigns each of King Dharmasoka and King Anikanga. In 1209 Queen Lilavati was restored for one year and again deposed; in 1210 she was replaced by King Lokesvara, but she was reinstated for another brief reign the following year. In 1212 she was again deposed in favor of King Parakráma Pandu.

This frequent unseating of the monarch is an indication of the general anarchy that existed, which allowed a ruthless south Indian fortune-seeker named Magha to invade in 1215, seize power, and rule dictatorially for over two decades.

References

Carpenter, Clive. *The Guinness Book of Kings, Rulers & Statesmen.* Enfield, Middlesex: Guinness Superlatives, 1978. p. 228.

Liliuokalani
Queen, Ruler of Hawaii (1891–1895)

The future queen was born Lydia Paki Kamekeha Liliuokalani in 1838. Her mother was Keohokalole, an adviser to King Kamehameha III, who ruled from 1825 to 1854. Before his death in 1824, the king adopted his nephew, who ruled as Kamehameha IV from 1855 to 1862. When Kamehameha IV's only son died, the king withdrew from public office, grief stricken. He was replaced by Lunalilo, who had the support of the ex-king and his wife, Queen Emma. Lunalilo died in 1874 without appointing a successor. The contest that followed pitted the partisans of Dowager Queen Emma against the supporters of the lineage of Keohokalole, Lydia's mother. The latter faction was victorious.

Lydia's brother, David Kalakaua, reigned from 1874 to 1891. In 1877 her younger brother, Prince Regent W. P. Leleiohoku, died, and Lydia was named heir presumptive. She succeeded to the throne at the age of fifty-three upon the king's death (1891). Shortly after her succession, her husband, John Owen Dominis, whom she had married in 1862, died. U.S. colonists led by Sanford Dole, who controlled most of Hawaii's economy, revolted when the queen attempted to restore some of the monarchy's power dissipated during her brother's reign. Dole's faction asked for her abdication in 1893, and she had to appeal to U.S. president Grover Cleveland for reinstatement. Dole defied the president's orders and set up a republic of

his own. The royalists revolted, but Dole's forces
squelched the revolt and
jailed the queen's supporters. She abdicated in 1895
in order to win pardons for
them.

In 1898, the year the
islands were formally transferred to the United States,
she composed "Aloha Oe,"
which quickly became the
farewell song for her country. She died in 1917.

References

James, Edward T., ed.
*Notable American
Women 1607–1950.*
Vol. 2. Cambridge:
Belknap Press of Har-
vard University Press,
1971. pp. 403–404.
Langer, William L., ed.
World History. Boston: Houghton Mifflin, 1940, 1980. p. 938.

*Liliuokalani
(Hawaiian Historical
Society)*

Louise de Savoy
Duchess, Regent of France (1515–1516 and 1525–1526)

Louise de Savoy was born in 1476, the daughter of Philip II, duke of
Savoy, and Marguerite de Bourbon. She married Charles de Valois-
Orleans, count (later duke) of Angoulême, and had two children:
Margaret, who became queen of Navarre, and Francis, who married
Claude, daughter of King Louis XII, and became King Francis I in
1515. A strong and ambitious woman with great diplomatic skills,
Louise, who was never a queen, was appointed regent during both
her son's expeditions to Italy. When Holy Roman emperor Charles V
captured Francis I and held him prisoner, Louise kept the country
running, negotiated Francis's release, and was able to convince England's King Henry VIII to sign a treaty of alliance with France,
Venice, and Pope Clement VII against Charles V. When the wars between Francis and Charles threatened to bankrupt both, they were
forced, in 1529, to negotiate. Again Louise was called upon, this time
to negotiate the peace with Charles's aunt, Margaret of Austria. The

Louise de Savoy (Corbis-Bettmann)

two arranged the Treaty of Cambrai, called the "Ladies' Peace." Louise died in 1531.

References

Langer, William L., ed. *World History.* Boston; Houghton Mifflin, 1980. pp. 410, 422, 429.

Louise Hippolyte
Princess, Titular Ruler of Monaco (1731)

Louise Hippolyte was born in 1697, the daughter of Prince Antoine I of the house of Grimaldi. She married James, duke of Estouteville, who then became Prince James I. She bore a son, Honore III. Her father died in 1731. Princess Louise, heir to the throne, died the same year, and the prince consort ruled for two years. He abdicated in 1733 in favor of their son and died in 1751.

References

Egan, Edward W., Constance B. Hintz, and L. F. Wise, eds. *Kings, Rulers, and Statesmen.* New York: Sterling Publishing, 1976. p. 316.

Morby, John E. *Dynasties of the World.* Oxford; Oxford University Press, 1989. p. 89.

Lourdes-Pintasilgo
See da Lourdes-Pintasilgo, María

Lucia of Antioch
Princess of Antioch and Countess, Titular Ruler of Tripoli (1288–1289)

This Tripoli is located in Lebanon, not to be confused with Tripoli, Libya. During the time of the latter Crusades, Tripoli became part of the kingdom of Acre.

Lucia (Lucy) was the daughter of Bohemond III (Tripoli) and VI (Antioch), prince of Antioch and count of Tripoli (r. 1252–1275), during whose reign Antioch was captured by the Mamluks. She was the younger sister of Bohemond IV (Tripoli) and VII (Antioch), titular prince of Antioch and count of Tripoli (1275–1287). She married Narjot of Toucy, the former grand admiral under Charles of Anjou, and went to live in Apula. Her brother died childless in 1287, naming Lucia as his heir. Her mother, Dowager Princess Sibylla of Armenia, fought bitterly to obtain the rule; meanwhile, a commune was established that was to be the real sovereign authority. But with help and maneuvering, Lucia was able to garner acceptance by opposing factions of Tripoli and was given supreme authority by the nobles and the commune. Foes had traveled to Cairo to ask Sultan Qalawun to intervene against Lucia's reign. In 1289, the sultan brought a huge army and launched a general assault on Tripoli. Countess Lucia was able to escape to Cyprus, but the majority of the men were massacred and the women and children captured as slaves. Tripoli officially fell to the Muslims on April 26, 1289.

References

Runciman, Steven. *A History of the Crusades.* Vol. 3, *The Kingdom of Acre.* Cambridge: Cambridge University Press, 1952, 1987. pp. 343, 403–407.

Lucienne
Princess, Regent of Antioch (ca. 1252–1258)

Born Lucienne of Segui, she was a great-niece of Pope Innocent III and a cousin of Pope Gregory IX. When Prince Bohemond V of Antioch and Tripoli divorced Alice of Cyprus by reason of consanguinity and began looking for a second wife, he asked Pope Gregory to choose the woman. Gregory chose his kinswoman Lucienne. This choice pleased Bohemond, for he could thus claim fortuitous ties with the papacy; however, the number of her Roman relatives and friends that flocked to visit Tripoli at her invitation irritated both Bohemond and the local barons. The couple took little interest in Antioch but held court at Tripoli.

Lucienne had two children: Plaisance, who married King Henry of Cyprus, and Bohemond VI, who was fifteen years old when his father died in 1252. Lucienne assumed the regency for her son. She was described as a feckless woman who never left Tripoli and who left the governing of Antioch to her Roman relatives. In ca. 1258, members of the Embriaco family gained control of Tripoli. Lucienne was removed from the regency but managed to keep many of her Roman relatives in high places. The irate local barons, who had long resented interference by foreigners, marched upon Tripoli and actually wounded Bohemond in an effort to rid the city of Lucienne's relatives. Later Bohemond arranged for the murder of Bertrand, head of the younger branch of the Embriaco, and the rebels withdrew. This murder precipitated a long blood feud between the houses of Antioch and Embriaco.

References

Runciman, Steven. *A History of the Crusades.* Vol. 3, *The Kingdom of Acre.* Cambridge: Cambridge University Press, 1952, 1987. pp. 207, 230–231, 233, 278, 288, 343.

Ludmila
Regent of Bohemia (ca. 921)

Ludmila was born ca. 820 in what is now the Czech Republic. She married Prince Borivoj, ruler of Bohemia. They converted to Christianity, becoming the first Czech sovereigns to do so. They built Bohemia's first Christian church, near Prague. Their son, Ratislav, married Drahomira, a pagan. Ludmila's grandsons from this union were Wenceslas and Boleslav. Ludmila reared Wenceslas as a Christian, while her daughter-in-law reared Boleslav as a pagan. When Ratislav died in 920, the anti-Christian faction attempted to seize control of the government, but Ludmila urged Wenceslas, age about thirteen, to take over the reins of government in the name of Christianity. Ludmila acted as regent when Wenceslas became ruler of Bohemia in ca. 921. However, at Drahomira's instigation, agents stole into Tetin Castle and strangled Ludmila in 921. She became a martyr and a saint, as did Wenceslas some eight years later. The carol "Good King Wenceslas" sings his virtues.

References

Cooke, Jean et al. *History's Timeline.* New York: Crescent Books, 1981. pp. 46, 61.

Kinder, Hermann, and Werner Hilgemann. *Atlas of World History.* Trans. Ernest A. Menze. Vol. 1. Garden City, NY: Anchor/Doubleday, 1982. p. 169.

Langer, William L., ed. *World History.* Boston: Houghton Mifflin, 1980. p. 255.

Lü Hou
Empress, Regent of China (188–179 B.C. or 195–180 B.C.)

Lü Hou was married to a former peasant named Gao Zu (or Kao Tsu), whom she had goaded into power and who ruled as first emperor of the Han dynasty from 206 or 202 to 195 B.C. Over the centuries, it became the custom that when the child of an emperor was made heir apparent, the mother was then recognized as empress. On accession of her son, she, as dowager empress, often became the real ruler. This tradition began with Lü. Having ambitions of her own, she saw to it that her son, Hui Ti, was formally named heir apparent. After her husband's death, the child Hui Ti ascended, and Lü was able to ignore the more important members of the imperial clan who were located in various kingdoms and marquisates some distance from the seat of government. She dominated the palace by replacing her husband's relatives with members of her own family in all positions of power.

When her son died, Empress Lü designated another young child to succeed him. When the new young emperor began to question her authority, she simply had him imprisoned and then seized absolute power and designated a third child as emperor. Her efforts to usurp the throne for her family posed a serious threat to the central government, which the late emperor's kinsmen eventually recognized. His loyal ministers put her to death in 180 B.C., massacred the whole Lü clan, and placed Wen Ti, Gao Zu's son by another wife, on the throne. Lü Hou has been compared with a later Chinese strongwoman, Madame Mao.

References

Bloodworth, Dennis, and Ching Ping Bloodworth. *The Chinese Machiavelli: 3,000 Years of Chinese Statecraft.* New York: Dell, 1976. pp. 143, 148.

Morton, W. Scott. *China: Its History and Culture.* New York: McGraw-Hill, 1980. p. 50.

Reischauer, Edwin O., and John K. Fairbank. *East Asia: The Great Tradition.* Boston: Houghton Mifflin, 1960. pp. 94, 117.

Luisa
Regent of Etruria (1803–1807), Duchess of Lucca (1815–1824)

Etruria was a kingdom that only existed from 1801 to 1807 by terms of the Treaty of Luneville between Austria and Napoleon. Located in Tuscany in present-day Italy, Etruria was created especially for the house of Bourbon-Parma by Napoleon Buonaparte. Luisa was born in 1782, the daughter of Charles IV, who ruled Spain from 1788 to 1808, and Maria Luisa of Parma. Luisa married Louis, ruler of Etruria from 1801 to his death in 1803. They had two children, Luisa and Charles, king of Etruria (1803–1807), for whom she served as regent. After the fall of Napoleon, Luisa was awarded the duchy of Lucca (1815), which she ruled until her death in 1824.

References

Langer, William L., ed. *World History.* Boston: Houghton Mifflin, 1980. p. 700.

Luisa María de Guzmán
Regent of Portugal (1656–1662)

Luisa María de Guzmán was the wife of John IV of the house of Braganza, king of Portugal from 1640 to 1656. They had three children: Catherine, who married Charles II of England; Alfonso IV, who ruled as king of Portugal from 1656 to 1667; and Pedro II, who ruled as regent from 1667 to 1683 and as king from 1683 to 1706. When John IV died in 1656, Alfonso, age thirteen, ascended to the throne with Luisa María serving as regent during his minority. Alfonso proved to be both frivolous and vicious. Some also characterized him as feeble-minded. His outrageous conduct prompted his brother, Pedro, considered to be wise and just, to imprison Alfonso and set himself up as regent in 1667. When Alfonso died in 1683, Pedro II could legally ascend to the throne.

References

Langer, William L., ed. *World History.* Boston: Houghton Mifflin, 1980. pp. 490, 491.

Luise-Marie
Duchess, Regent of Parma and Piacenza (1854–1859)

Luise-Marie (or Louise of Bourbon-Berry) was born in 1819, the daughter of Ferdinand, the last duke of Berry, and Caroline of the Two Sicilies. Luise-Marie married Duke Charles III, ruler of Parma from 1849 to 1854. Within five years they had four children: Margarita, Robert, Alicia, and Enrico. When Duke Charles was assassinated in 1854, their son Robert, age six, became duke of Parma. Luise-Marie served as regent until 1859, when she transferred her powers to a provisional government. Robert, age ten, was deposed. Parma was incorporated in Piedmont-Sardinia in 1860 and into Italy in 1861. Luise-Marie died in 1864; Robert died in 1907.

References

Egan, Edward W., Constance B. Hintz, and L. F. Wise, eds. *Kings, Rulers, and Statesmen.* New York: Sterling Publishing, 1976. p. 270.

Morby, John E. *Dynasties of the World.* Oxford: Oxford University Press, 1989. p. 109.

M

Maham Anga
De Facto Regent of Mughal Empire (1560–1562)

Maham Anga was Akbar's chief nurse prior to his enthronement at age thirteen as emperor (Kalanaur, 1556). Her own son, Adham Khān, as Akbar's foster brother, was regarded as almost one of the family. Maham Anga, shrewd and ambitious and very much in charge of the household and the harem, sought to advance her own authority and that of her son. In 1560 the two tricked Akbar into coming to India without his chief minister and guardian Bairam, and they were able to convince Akbar that now that he was seventeen, he did not need Bairam. Akbar dismissed his minister and sent him on a pilgrimage to Mecca. Months later Bairam was murdered by an Afghan, and much of his former power passed to Maham Anga.

Her son was sent to invade Malwa, but his conduct following his victory was reprehensible. He kept the treasure and the harem for himself and had the other captives butchered while he and his fellow officer sat jesting. Akbar, enraged when he heard of the outrage, set off for Malwa at such speed that Maham Anga had no chance to send a warning to her son. Adham Khān, chastened but not dismissed, handed over the booty to Akbar and was forgiven, but he secretly kept back two young girls for himself. When Akbar heard rumors of this last treachery, Maham Anga had the girls murdered before they could testify against her son.

Her power began to wane in 1561, however, when Akbar appointed Atkah Khānn, a man outside her sphere of influence, as his new chief minister. Five months later (1562), her son attempted to assassinate the new minister and was thrown off the parapet—twice—as execution. Akbar himself informed Maham Anga of her son's death, and she died shortly afterward. The emperor, age nineteen, was then able to rule without interference.

References

Gascoigne, Bamber. *The Great Moghuls.* New York: Dorset Press, 1971.
pp. 79–81.

Spear, Percival. *History of India.* Vol. 2. London: Penguin Books. 1987.
pp. 29–30.

Mahaut
Countess, Capetian Ruler of Artois (1302–1329)

Mahaut was the daughter of Robert II, the Noble (r. 1250–1302), from whom she inherited the county of Artois. She married Otto IV, count of Burgundy. At the time, there were two Burgundys: a county and a duchy. The couple had a daughter, Johanna (Joan I), who succeeded Mahaut upon her death. Mahaut's granddaughter, Johanna II, married the duke of Burgundy, thus reuniting the two Burgundys for a short period.

References

Morby, John E. *Dynasties of the World.* Oxford: Oxford University Press, 1989. p. 94.

Mahaut I
Dame, Ruler of Bourbon (1215–1242)

Mahaut I was the heir of Archambaud V, ruler of Bourbon from 1116 to 1171. She first married Gautier de Vienne, who ruled Bourbon upon Archambaud's death in 1171 until his own death in 1215. Mahaut then ruled in her own right from 1215 to 1242. She married Gui II de Dampierre and had two daughters, Mahaut II de Dampierre and Agnes. She was succeeded by Archambaud VII in 1242.

References

Egan, Edward W., Constance B. Hintz, and L. F. Wise, eds. *Kings, Rulers, and Statesmen.* New York: Sterling Publishing, 1976. p. 153.

Mahaut II de Dampierre
Countess, Ruler of Bourbon (1249–1262), Ruler of Nevers (1257–1266)

Mahaut II de Dampierre was the daughter of Gui II de Dampierre and Dame Mahaut I, who ruled Bourbon from 1215 to 1242. Mahaut II succeeded Baron Archambaud VII, who ruled from 1242 to 1249. She married Eudes de Bourgogne, and they had a daughter, Yolande de Bourgogne. Mahaut II was the granddaughter of Countess Mahaut de Courtenay, who ruled Nevers for over a half-century, from 1182 to 1257, and whom she succeeded as ruler of Nevers upon her grandmother's death in 1257. In 1262 she was succeeded by her sister

Agnes as ruler of Bourbon, but she ruled Nevers until her death in 1266. She was succeeded in Nevers by her daughter Yolande.

References

Egan, Edward W., Constance B. Hintz, and L. F. Wise, eds. *Kings, Rulers, and Statesmen*. New York: Sterling Publishing, 1976. p. 153.

Kemp-Welch, Alice. *Six Medieval Women*. London: Macmillan, 1913. pp. 93, 102.

Mahaut de Boulogne
Countess, Ruler of Boulogne (1125–1150)

Mahaut (or Matilda) de Boulogne's father was Eustache III, who ruled Boulogne from 1095 to 1125. He retired to a Cluniac monastary in 1125, leaving Boulogne to his daughter to rule. She married Etienne de Blois, who in 1135 became King Stephen of England (1135–1154) by usurpation from his cousin, also named Matilda (and called Empress Maud). Mahaut, who was also sometimes called Empress Maud by the British, was much more popular with the English people than Empress Maud, the other Matilda, who, to further confuse matters, was also Mahaut's cousin on the other side of the family. Thus Mahaut and Etienne were both cousins to England's Empress Maud, but not to each other. Mahaut and Etienne had five children, three of whom succeeded her sequentially as rulers of Boulogne: Eustache IV, Guillaume, and Marie. Eustache IV succeeded her upon her death in 1150.

References

Egan, Edward W., Constance B. Hintz, and L. F. Wise, eds. *Kings, Rulers, and Statesmen*. New York: Sterling Publishing, 1976. p. 152.

Mahaut de Courtenay
Countess, Ruler of Nevers (1192–1257)

Mahaut de Courtenay was the daughter of Pierre de Courtenay and Countess Agnes de Nevers, who ruled from 1181 to 1182 and whom she succeeded in 1192. In 1199 Mahaut married Count Herve de Donzy. After he died, she took a second husband, Guy de Forez, in 1226. Upon her death in 1257 her grandaughter, Mahaut II de Bourbon, succeeded her. In 1259 Guy de Forez sold all his French property to Cardinal Mazarin.

References

Egan, Edward W., Constance B. Hintz, and L. F. Wise, eds. *Kings, Rulers, and Statesmen*. New York: Sterling Publishing, 1976. p. 159.

Mahaut de Dammartin
Countess, Ruler of Boulogne (1216–1269)

Mahaut de Dammartin succeeded upon the death of Countess Ide d'Alsace, who ruled Boulogne from 1173 to 1216. Mahaut married Philippe Hurepel, the son of Philip Augustus. She died in 1260.

References
Egan, Edward W., Constance B. Hintz, and L. F. Wise, eds. *Kings, Rulers, and Statesmen.* New York: Sterling Publishing, 1976. p. 152.

Makeda
See Balkis

Mamochisane
Queen of the Kololo in Zambia (1851)

The Kololo are a Sotho people who, under Chief Sebitwane, fled in ca. 1839 from the advancing Mfecane, crossing the Zambizi and occupying western Zambia. There they conquered the Lozi (Barotse) kingdom, but during the fighting the Lozi captured Sebitwane's daughter, Mamochisane (Ma-Muchisane) (ca. 1840). They released her to her father unharmed, and the Lozi's kind treatment of her apparently influenced King Sebitwane to deal leniently with the Lozi. He divided the conquered territory, known as Bulozi or Barotseland, into four provinces and appointed Mamochisane as governor of a central province. Apparently she was an able leader, for on his deathbed in 1851, the king nominated her to succeed him. Mamochisane ruled briefly, but soon abdicated in favor of her brother, Sekeletu, ostensibly so as to marry and have a family.

References
Lipschutz, Mark R., and R. Kent Rasmussen. *Dictionary of African Historical Biography.* Berkeley: University of California Press, 1978, 1986.

Mandughai
Khatun, Regent of Mongolia (1470–ca. 1492)

Mandughai was the very young widow of Grand Khan Mandaghol, Jenghiz-khan's twenty-seventh successor, who died in 1467 of war wounds. His great-nephew and heir, Bolkho, succeeded him but was assassinated in 1470 before he could be proclaimed khan. The mother of Bolkho's five-year-old son Dayan had deserted the child, so Mandughai took him under her protection, proclaimed him khan, and became his regent. She assumed command of the Mongol troops and defeated their enemy, the Oirat. In 1481 she married Dayan, who was then sixteen. In 1491–1492 she again led the army to fend off the Oirat. History gives Mandughai credit for abolishing Oirat supremacy and restoring that of the eastern Mongols. She, and after her Dayan, infused new life into the Jenghiz-khanate's fading authority.

References

Grousset, René. *The Empire of the Steppes.* Trans. Naomi Walford. New Brunswick, NJ: Rutgers University Press, 1970. p. 509.

Mankiller, Wilma T.
Chief of Cherokee Nation (1985–1995)

Wilma Pearl T. Mankiller was born in 1944, the daughter of Charlie and Irene Mankiller. Her father was full-blood Cherokee; her mother was Dutch-Irish. Wilma and ten brothers and sisters grew up in a four-room frame house with no plumbing located on the family allotment in Mankiller Flats in Adair County in eastern Oklahoma. In 1956, when she was eleven years old, the family was moved to San Fransisco by the Bureau of Indian Affairs. This move was part of a government program to force the assimilation of Native Americans. The family lived in a tenement in Hunter's Point, then a high crime primarily poor black neighborhood. After high school, at age seventeen she married a wealthy Ecuadorian and toured Europe with him. They had two daughters, in 1963 and 1965. Wilma studied sociology at San Francisco State University, where she became interested in bettering the plight of Native Americans. The nation's attention was focused on the problems of Native Americans when a group, including some of Mankiller's relatives, occupied Alcatraz Island for nineteen months (1969–1970). A number of celebrities went to Alcatraz to show their support, but Mankiller remained on the mainland working for Native American causes.

In 1971 her father died and was returned to Oklahoma to be buried. When her activist work to help the Pit River Indians recover their lands and her other civil rights struggles led to her divorce three years later, she felt compelled to return to her roots. She moved with her daughters back to Oklahoma and completed her degree in 1975 at Flaming Rainbow University. It was not until that year that the U.S. government granted the Cherokees self-determination. In 1977 she began working for the then 65,000 known members of the Cherokee tribe as an economic coordinator and commuted to the University of Arkansas to work toward a master's degree in community planning.

Wilma T. Mankiller (UPI/Corbis-Bettmann)

An auto accident enroute to classes in 1979 resulted in seventeen surgeries in one year. The following year she contracted myasthenia gravis and had surgery on her thymus gland. Despite her difficulties, in 1983 she was elected deputy chief of the Cherokee Nation, which had grown to 108,000 registered members.

In 1985 she moved from the second spot to become the first female chief when Chief Ross Swimmer became head of the Bureau of Indian Affairs. Many U.S. tribes trace their ancestry matrilineally, and Chief Mankiller looked upon her ascension as a return to the historical role women held in tribal affairs. Historically, a woman selected the chief; the head of the women's council had a great deal of power, Mankiller has explained. In 1987 she ran for a full four-year term and was elected on her own merits. In 1991, despite a recent kidney transplant—donated by her brother, Donald Mankiller—she ran again and was reelected by a majority of 82 percent. She was the tribe's first principal chief in recorded history.

She lives with her second husband, Charlie Soap, a full-blood Cherokee, and his son Winterhawk in Tahlequah, Oklahoma, capital of the Cherokee Nation, located eighty miles east of Tulsa. Of her duties, she said, "It is sort of like running a small country and sort of like running a middle-sized corporation." Mankiller has attributed her resilience to her Cherokee blood. She noted that most Cherokees were marched from their southeastern U.S. homeland by soldiers in the 1838 Trail of Tears. Although 4,000 died along the way, those who survived quickly established themselves as a literate nation. They opened the first school west of the Mississippi and established several newspapers in the Cherokee language. Mankiller said in an interview, "We are fighters and survivors. We were not shy about war, but we also fought a lot of battles in court. We were devastated, uprooted and driven like cattle to this land, but we made the best of it."

Mankiller worked throughout her time in office overseeing tremendous growth in tribal membership and encouraging new business ventures for the Cherokee Nation. She was inducted into the National Women's Hall of Fame and received the Humanitarian Award from the Ford Foundation. Following her decision not to run for another term, she was honored by President Clinton for her many years of public service in a special ceremony at the White House.

References

Flood, Mary. "First Female Cherokee Chief Ready for Job." *Houston Post.* 7 April 1984: A 1, A 26.

Mankiller, Wilma, with Michael Wallis. *Mankiller.* New York: St. Martin's Press. 1994.

Sowers, Leslie. "Wilma Mankiller: The First Woman Chief of the Cherokee Nation Is as Comfortable in the White House as She Is at a Stomp Dance." *Texas.* 20 January 1991: 10–11.

Whittemore, Hank. "She Leads a Nation." *Parade Magazine.* 18 August 1991: 4–5.

"Who's News." *USA Weekend.* 2–4 March 1990: 2.

Zakin, Susan. "Woman Chief Blazing an Indian Trail." *Mother Jones.* September 1986: 8, 10.

Mansarico
Mani Warrior Queen in West Africa (mid-16th c.)

The Mani (Mane) were a Mandinko (Mande-speaking) people arising from the Mali Empire. Queen Mansarico, who had perhaps been exiled by the Mansa (king) of Mali, left that country and led her followers south, then west, eventually establishing, by the mid-1540s, a base of operations in the vicinity of Cape Mount in Liberia. From there, she dispatched her armies into the borderland of present-day Sierra Leone, subjugating the local populace and establishing subkingdoms, which were forced to pay tribute to her. This pattern of waves of invasions eventually had the result of developing the Mende as the largest ethnic group in Sierra Leone.

Mansarico and other Mani women were equipped for leadership because they apparently possessed not only such essential skills as knowledge of herbal medicine and agriculture and such serendipitous skills as knowledge of the fine arts but also expertise in statecraft. The basis for this knowledge and expertise appears to have been education obtained through a hierarchical initiation society. Thus Mani women were always powerful, often regents or rulers in their own right.

References

Boone, Sylvia Ardyn. *Radiance from the Waters.* New Haven: Yale University Press, 1986, pp. 4, 25, 246.

Mantantisi
Queen-regent of the baTlokwa in South Africa (ca.1817–ca.1824)

Mantantisi (Mmanthatisi, Mma Ntatisi, Matatisi) was born ca. 1780, a member of the Sia, a branch of the Sotho-speaking people of present-day Orange Free State. She married Mokotjo, chief of the Tlokwa branch, and in ca. 1804 had a son, Sekonyela. When her husband died (ca. 1817), she sent her son to live with her people while she remained to rule the Tlokwa.

In ca. 1820 a Nguni army under Mpangazitha invaded from the east coast, driving the Tlokwa westward. Mantantisi then led her people in a series of raids against neighboring armies that lasted several years and became known as the Difaqane. Soon her reputation as a predator was widespread. A corruption of her name, "Mantatee," became the term for the various predatory bands that ravaged the region of the Orange and Vaal Rivers.

She is described, in epic literature about the exploits of the Zulu emperor Shaka the Great (r. 1816–1828), as a fierce woman who personally led her army, raiding and terrorizing the Maluti nations of the Sothos. She not only fought Shaka's chief enemy, Matiwane, but also conquered the army of Shaka's ally, the great king of the Bathos and founder of the Sotho nation, Moshoeshoe (Mshweshwe). She subdued the fierce nation of the Fukengs as well and defeated the army of the Kwena nation. Only the Hlubis of Mpangazitha were able to withstand her army's onslaught. After her defeat, Shaka, pleased to hear people "rain curses against Queen Mantantisi," is reported to have said, "I always marvel at how men could be terrorized by a woman. . . ." Shaka's commander-in chief, Mdlaka, reporting her various brave exploits to his emperor, said that the entire southern region of Khahlamba mountains "curses her very name and ancestry." Shaka commented, "How strange is all this courage in a woman!" He termed her a "homeless vagabond."

Eventually she settled in northern Lesotho, where, in ca. 1824, her son joined her and assumed the kingship. She continued to play a central role in Tlokwa affairs until the mid-1830s; after ca. 1836 no more is known.

References
Kunene, Mazisi. *Emperor Shaka the Great.* Trans. Mazisi Kunene. London: Heinemann Educational Books, 1979. pp. 112, 253–254.
Lipschutz, Mark R., and R. Kent Rasmussen. *Dictionary of African Historical Biography.* Berkeley: University of California Press, 1986. pp. 148–149.

Margaret
Duchess of Carinthia, Countess of Tirol (1335–1362)

Born Margaretha Maultasch in 1318, she was the daughter of the duke of Carinthia and count of Tirol. In 1330 she was married to John Henry of Luxembourg, age nine. When her father died in 1335, she inherited Tirol but was forced to cede Carinthia, which had been given to her family by Rudolph I in 1286, back to Germany. Margaret's marriage was still childless after eleven years. She acted in collusion with the Tirolese to expel John Henry, whose brother Charles (later Emperor Charles IV) had stepped in to rule.

In 1342 Holy Roman emperor Louis IV the Bavarian annulled Margaret's previous marriage and married her to his son Louis, margrave of Brandenburg. This marriage displeased not only the pope and the Luxembourgians but the Tirolese as well, who did not want to be ruled by the Germans. An uprising against Margaret and her new husband had to be suppressed, and there was serious doubt that she would be able to maintain control. But after Louis IV was deposed in 1346, the successor Charles IV favored the status quo for Tirol's rulers, who would remain in control as long as there was an heir. If Margaret produced no heir, she would cede Tirol to the Hapsburgs.

Margaret bore one son, Meinhard, and the lineage of Tirol seemed secure. However, her husband died in 1361, and after she had passed child-bearing years, her only son died in 1363. Holy Roman emperor Rudolph IV persuaded her to cede Tirol to him, and she retired to Vienna, where she died in 1369 at age fifty-one.

References

Dvornik, Francis. *The Slavs in European History and Civilization.* New Brunswick, NJ: Rutgers University Press, 1962. pp. 44, 52, 53, 54.

Margaret
Queen of Denmark and Norway (1375–1412), Regent of Sweden (1389–1412)

Margaret (or Margrete or Margarethe) was born in Denmark in 1353, the daughter of King Valdemar IV Atterdag, ruler of Denmark from 1340 to 1375, and Helvig, sister of the duke of Schleswig. When Margaret was six years old, she was married to King Haakon VI, ruler of Norway from 1343 to 1380. She spent her youth in the court in Norway. In 1370 she bore a son, Olaf V, and began to take an active interest in government soon afterward. After her father's death in 1375, she succeeded in getting her five-year-old son elected to the Danish throne with herself as regent. After her husband's death in

1380, she also ruled Norway for her son. When Olaf died in 1387, Margaret adopted her six-year-old nephew, Erik of Pomerania, as heir to the throne.

She was asked by Swedish nobles to assist in an uprising against Swedish king Albert. The nobles proclaimed her queen of Sweden in 1388 and granted her a large domain consisting of lands belonging to former chancellor Bo Jonsson Grip. Her forces captured Albert in 1389 and held him prisoner for six years until peace was concluded. In 1397 she united the three Scandinavian countries in the Union of Kalmar, which lasted unchanged until 1523. Despite her heir's coronation in 1397, Margaret remained the sole ruler for the rest of her life. She strengthened her influence over the church and kept the ambitious German princes at bay, primarily through diplomacy. However, she was obliged to use force against Holstein in 1412, and during the conflict, she died suddenly.

References
Dahmus, Joseph. *Seven Medieval Queens.* Garden City, NY: Doubleday, 1972. pp. 233–275.
Egan, Edward W., Constance B. Hintz, and L. F. Wise, eds. *Kings, Rulers, and Statesmen.* New York: Sterling Publishing, 1976. pp. 112–113, 447.
Langer, William L., ed. *World History.* Boston: Houghton Mifflin, 1980. pp. 334–336.
Morby, John E. *Dynasties of the World.* Oxford: Oxford University Press, 1989. p. 149.

Margaret II
Countess, Ruler of Flanders (1244–1278), Ruler of Hainault (1244–1280)

Margaret II (or Black Meg) was born ca. 1200, the daughter of Maria of Champagne and Baldwin IX, count of Flanders and Hainault, who in 1204 was crowned Baldwin I, first Latin emperor of Constantinople. Margaret was the sister of Johanna, who ruled Belgium from 1206 to 1244. Margaret was first married to Buchard of Avenes, who had been pledged to serve the church. His marriage led to his excommunication and his imprisonment by his sister-in-law, Countess Johanna. Although she had borne him a son, Margaret was persuaded to seek a divorce or an annulment. She later married William of Dampierre and bore another son, Guy.

When her sister died in 1244, Margaret acceded to the throne. In 1278 she abdicated, naming as her successor her younger son, Guy. However, her first son resorted to force in protesting her decision. The civil war that followed was resolved by a compromise by which each son would rule a portion of the land. However, in the end Margaret outlived them both. She died in 1280.

References

Egan, Edward W., Constance B. Hintz, and L. F. Wise, eds. *Kings, Rulers, and Statesmen.* New York: Sterling Publishing, 1976. p. 52.

Morby, John E. *Dynasties of the World.* Oxford: Oxford University Press, 1989. p. 90.

Margaret III
Countess, Ruler of Belgium (1384–1405)

Margaret III (or Margaret of Flanders or Margaret of Mâle) was born in 1350, the daughter of Margaret of Brabant (r. Artois 1362–1382) and Louis II de Mâle (of Nevers), count of Flanders. In 1369 she married Philip le Hardi, duke of Burgundy (1384–1404). She was heiress to the county of Burgundy, Artois, Nevers, and Rethel, making her a countess in her own right and a duchess by marriage. The couple had four children: John, duke of Burgundy; Philip, count of Nevers; Margaret; and Antoine, duke of Brabant. Belgium had been under the duchy of Burgundy's rule from 1334 to 1377, so Louis II de Mâle actually ruled Flanders from 1377 to 1384. Margaret ruled from her father's death in 1384 until her own death in 1405. At that time Flanders became unified with the duchy of Burgundy.

References

Egan, Edward W., Constance B. Hintz, and L. F. Wise, eds. *Kings, Rulers, and Statesmen.* New York: Sterling Publishing, 1976. pp. 52, 160.

Langer, William L., ed. *World History.* Boston: Houghton Mifflin, 1980. pp. 299, 300, 406–407.

Morby, John E. *Dynasties of the World.* Oxford: Oxford University Press, 1989. p. 90.

Margaret of Anjou
Queen, Lancastrian Leader (1455–1485), Acting Regent of England (1460–1461)

Margaret of Anjou was born in 1430, the daughter of René I of Anjou, titular king of Naples (1435–1442), and Isabella, duchess of Lorraine from 1431 to 1453. In a 1445 marriage arranged as part of a two-year truce in the Hundred Years' War, she became the wife of King Henry VI, who ruled England from 1422 to 1461. The couple had one son, Edward, born in 1453. Margaret was not popular with her English subjects. Her husband suffered bouts of insanity and was never declared fit to rule. Richard, duke of York, served as lord protector.

Margaret of Anjou (Perry-Castaneda Library)

In 1455 a civil war (the War of the Roses) broke out between the houses of Lancaster and York. Richard of York asserted his hereditary claim to the throne, and the lords decided that he should be next in the line of succession, excluding Margaret's son, Edward. Richard actually gained control of the government until Margaret ousted him in 1456. At that time the qualities with which Shakespeare described her became evident: "stern, obdurant, flinty, rough, remorseless" (*Henry VI,* part III, act 1, scene 4). She was more than capable of acting in the interests of the king: Both her mother and her grandmother had ruled their lands. In 1459 the second round of hostilities erupted. During the Battle of Northampton in 1460, Henry VI was taken prisoner, and Margaret refused to accept the terms for his release, which would exclude her son as Henry's heir. Instead, she raised an army in the north and defeated Richard of York, who died on the field in Wakefield, Yorkshire.

But southern England had not forgotten the Hundred Years' War with France and had not forgotten that Margaret was French. Londoners rallied around York's son, also named Edward, defeated Margaret's army, and proclaimed Edward of York king in 1461. Margaret and her son fled to Scotland with Henry VI. In 1464 a fresh Lancastrian uprising brought them back to England. In 1465 Henry VI was again captured and imprisoned in the Tower of London. In 1470 Margaret, then in France, entered into collusion with Richard, duke of Warwick, in a plot to restore Henry VI to the throne. However, Warwick was killed in battle on the day that she returned to England in 1471. Margaret and her son headed the forces at Tewksbury that attempted to hold off Edward of York, but they were defeated for the final time. Margaret's son was killed, and she was taken prisoner. Henry VI was murdered in prison. In 1475 King Louis XI of France ransomed Margaret. She returned to France, where she died in poverty in 1482.

References

Dahmus, Joseph. *Seven Medieval Queens.* Garden City, NY: Doubleday, 1972. pp. 276–327.

Myers, A. R. *England in the Late Middle Ages.* Harmondsworth, Middlesex: Penguin Books, 1976. pp. 126–130, 193.

Margaret of Antioch-Lusignan
Regent of Tyre (1283–1291)

Called "the loveliest girl of her generation," Margaret of Antioch-Lusignan was the daughter of Henry of Antioch and Isabella of Cyprus and the sister of King Hugh III, ruler of Cyprus and Jerusalem. She married John of Montfort, lord of Tyre, who died ca. 1283. When Sultan Qalawun was preparing to attack those Franks not protected by the truce of 1283, Lady Margaret asked him for a truce, which was granted. She renewed the truce in 1290 after Qalawun invaded Tripoli. Early in 1291 she handed Tyre over to her nephew Amalric, brother of King Henry II of Cyprus.

References

Runciman, Steven. *A History of the Crusades.* Vol. 3, *The Kingdom of Acre and the Later Crusades.* Cambridge: Cambridge University Press, 1952, 1987. pp. 329, 394–395, 408, 421.

Margaret of Austria
Duchess of Savoy, Regent of The Netherlands (1507–1515 and 1519–1530)

Margaret of Austria (Marguerite d'Autriche) was born in 1480, the daughter of the future emperor Maximilian I (r. 1486–1519) and Mary, duchess of Burgundy (r. 1477–1482). Margaret was the sister of Philip the Handsome. In 1483 she was betrothed to the future Charles VI, who later repudiated her. She then married the infante John of Spain, who died shortly after the marriage (1497). In 1501, she married Philbert II, duke of Savoy, who died in 1504. In his memory, she built the beautiful church of Brou near Lyons.

In 1507 her father appointed her successor to her late brother, Philip, as regent of The Netherlands for her nephew Charles. In 1508 she also represented another young nephew, Ferdinand of Aragon (Holy Roman emperor Ferdinand I) and her father in negotiating a settlement of the French claims in the Burgundian Netherlands. Her nephew Charles was declared of age in 1515, but he reappointed her in 1519 while he was occupied in securing the Hapsburg throne. He ruled as Charles V from 1519 to 1556. In 1529 Margaret negotiated the Treaty of Cambrai, "The Ladies' Peace," with Louise of Savoy, settling claims of France upon Italy, Flanders, and Artois and claims of Germany upon Burgundy. Margaret continued to rule The Netherlands until she died in 1530.

References

Harvey, Sir Paul, and J. E. Heseltine, comps. *The Oxford Companion to French Literature*. Oxford: Oxford University Press, 1959. p. 452.

Langer, William L., ed. *World History.* Boston: Houghton Mifflin, 1980. pp. 422, 429.

Margaret of Austria
Duchess of Parma, Governor General of The Netherlands (1559–1567)

Margaret of Austria was born in 1522, the illegitimate daughter of Holy Roman emperor Charles V (Charles I of Spain), who ruled Spain from 1516 to 1556 and the empire from 1510 to 1556, and Johanna van der Gheenst. In 1536 Margaret married Alesssandro de' Medici, duke of Florence, but she was widowed in less than a year. In 1538 she married Ottavio Farnese, who became duke of Parma in 1547. They had a son, Alessandro Farnese.

Her half brother, King Philip II of Spain, appointed her governor general of The Netherlands in 1559. Under her regency the provinces prospered, despite heavy taxation. She presided over the three governing councils, Privy, State, and Finances, which were to see to it that the Protestants (Calvinists) were suppressed and that King

Margaret of Austria, Duchess of Parma (Erich Lessing / Art Resource, NY)

Philip's demands for funds were met. She was saddled with carrying out a highly unpopular program without military backing, for her subjects had no desire to pay for a foreigner's military campaigns. The northern part of her territory (Holland) had embraced Calvinism while the southern part (Belgium) was still Catholic. Both segments opposed Spanish rule, the Spanish garrison, the introduction of the Spanish inquisition, and the penal edicts against heretics. She rejected a petition submitted to her by 300 nobles objecting to religious persecution. An adviser referred to the signers as "beggars," and soon all those opposed to Spanish rule took as their appellation, "Beggars."

In 1566 Calvinist riots led Margaret, who still had no troops from King Philip, to call in German mercenary troops. In 1567 she dealt with religious uprisings by mass executions. Philip II eventually sent in the duke of Alva with 10,000 troops to replace Margaret and to repress the uprisings. In 1580 she returned to The Netherlands as head of the civil administration under her son, Alessandro. She returned to Italy in 1583, where she died in 1586.

References

Clough, Shepard B. et al. *European History in a World Perspective.* Vol. 2, *Early Modern Times.* Lexington, MA: D. C. Heath, 1975. pp. 638, 713–715.

Geye, Pieter. *The Revolt of the Netherlands, 1555–1609.* London: Ernest Benn, 1958. pp. 70, 75, 78, 79, 87–92, 98, 100, 101, 154.

Langer, William L., ed. *World History.* Boston: Houghton Mifflin, 1980. pp. 407–408.

Masselman, George. *The Cradle of Colonialism.* New Haven: Yale University Press, 1963. p. 27.

Trevor-Roper, Hugh. *The Golden Age of Europe.* New York: Bonanza/Crown, 1987. pp. 66, 80, 82.

Margaret of Brabant
Countess, Burgundian Ruler of Artois (1361–1382)

Margaret of Brabant was the daughter of Joan I (Jeanne, r. 1329–1330) and Philip V (r. France 1316–1322). Margaret married Louis of Nevers (Louis II of Crecy), count of Flanders (r. 1322–1346). They had a son, Louis III of Mâle (r. Flanders 1346–1384), and a daughter, Margaret II (r. Flanders 1384–1405). Margaret succeeded her mother as ruler of Artois in 1362. Upon her death, Artois was united with Flanders under first her son's and then her daughter's rule.

References

Morby, John E. *Dynasties of the World.* Oxford: Oxford University Press, 1989. p. 94.

Margaret of Navarre
Queen, Regent of Sicily (1166–1168)

Margaret of Navarre was the wife of William I, ruler of Norman Sicily from 1154 to 1166. It was claimed that she took as her lover the chief minister, Maio of Bari. In 1153 she had a son, William II, who succeeded his father at the age of thirteen. Margaret, as regent, first ruled through her favorite, Peter, a Saracen eunuch, a former slave who had been freed by her husband. But barons who had earlier been exiled by William I saw the chance to regain their estates under the regency of a woman, and they began to return and rebuild their castles. Peter decided to escape to Morocco to avoid the inevitable conflict building between the barons and Queen Margaret.

In 1167 she appointed her cousin Stephen of Le Perche chief minister and Peter of Blois as her son's tutor. But Stephen's harsh manner made him unpopular. When rumor spread that he was siphoning money to France, a riot quickly spread at Messina. Stephen fled to Jerusalem, and Peter went back to France. Into the void stepped an Englishman, Walter Offamillo, who seized power and used the Palermo mob to help him become archbishop. He remained the center of power for twenty years. In effect, Margaret's influence was at an end. Even after William II came of age in 1172, he did not openly cross the archbishop. Offamillo effectively ended Margaret's attempt to rule.

References

Smith, Denis Mack. *A History of Sicily.* Vol. 1, *Medieval Sicily.* New York: Dorset Press, 1968. pp. 38–40.

Margaret of Norway
Child Queen of Scotland (1286–1290)

Margaret of Norway (or the maid of Norway) was born ca. 1282, the daughter of King Eric II Magnusson, who ruled Norway from 1280 to 1299, and Margaret, daughter of King Alexander III of Scotland (1249–1286). Margaret, the mother of Margaret of Norway, died in 1283, and none of King Alexander's children survived him. When he died in 1286, Scottish nobles declared his grandaughter, Margaret, age four, queen. In 1290 her great-uncle, England's King Edward I, arranged for her marriage to his son, the future King Edward II. On the voyage to England, Margaret fell ill and died at the age of eight.

References

Langer, William L., ed. *World History.* Boston: Houghton Mifflin, 1980. pp. 214, 217, 218.

Mackie, J. D. *A History of Scotland.* Harmondsworth, Middlesex: Penguin Books, 1984. pp. 35, 45, 61–63, 135.

Runciman, Steven. *A History of the Crusades.* Vol. 3, *The Kingdom of Acre.* Cambridge: Cambridge University Press, 1952, 1987. pp. 401–402.

Margaret Tudor
Queen, Regent of Scotland
(1513–1514)

Margaret Tudor
(Archive Photos)

Margaret Tudor was born in 1489, the elder daughter of King Henry VII, who ruled England from 1485 to 1509, and Elizabeth, daughter of King Edward IV, who ruled from 1461 to 1483. In 1503 Margaret married James IV, king of Scotland from 1488 to 1513, and bore a son who became James V when his father died in 1513. Margaret ruled as regent for her son.

In 1514 she married Archibald Douglas, earl of Angus. Since he was a partisan of England, the Scottish parliament removed her from the regency. In 1527 she divorced Douglas and married Henry Stewart, whom her son made Lord Methven when he came to the throne the following year. Margaret and her third husband were James's most trusted advisers for the first six years of his majority, but James became angry at his mother for sharing state secrets with her brother, King Henry VIII of England. She retired to Methven Castle where she died in 1541.

References
Langer, William L., ed. *World History.* Boston: Houghton Mifflin, 1980. p. 396.
Myers, A. R. *England in the Late Middle Ages.* Vol. 4. Harmondsworth, Middlesex: Penguin Books, 1952. p. 205.

Margareta
Countess, Ruler of Flanders (1191–1194)

Margareta (or Margaret of Alsace or Margaret I) was the daughter of Gertrude, whose father Robert I ruled from 1071 to 1093, and Thierry I (or Dirk I) of Lorraine. She was the sister of Thierry of Alsace, who ruled Flanders from 1128 to 1157/1168, and the aunt of Count Philip, who ruled from 1157/1168 to 1191. (Philip was co-regent with his father, Thierry, from 1157 to 1168.) In 1171 Margareta married Baldwin V, count of Hainault, who then became Baldwin VIII, count of Flanders. In 1172 they had a son, Baldwin IX, who would become count of Flanders and Hainault in 1244 and, in 1278, emperor of Constantinople. When her nephew Philip died in 1191, Margareta succeeded him, but she died in 1194. Her son succeeded her that year.

References

Egan, Edward W., Constance B. Hintz, and L. F. Wise, eds. *Kings, Rulers, and Statesmen.* New York: Sterling Publishing, 1976. p. 52.

Morby, John E. *Dynasties of the World.* Oxford: Oxford University Press, 1989. pp. 90, 93.

Margaretha
Guardian for Otto II the Lame, Count of Gelderland and Zutphen
(1229–1234)

Margaretha was the daughter of Duke Henry I of Brabant. In 1206 she married Gerhard III of Gelre (Gelderland), count of Gelderland and Zutphen. It was a marriage designed to unite two antagonistic dynasties. In ca. 1220 they had a son, Otto II, called Otto the Lame (not to be confused with Otto the Lame of Lüneburg, r. 1434–1446). When Gerhard III died in 1229, Otto succeeded his father, with Margaretha serving as guardian until he came of age in 1234.

References

Britannica Micropaedia. Vol. 7. Chicago: The University of Chicago Press/Encyclopaedia Britannica, 1983. p. 626.

Margrethe II
Queen of Denmark (1972–)

Margrethe II (Margaret) was born in 1940, the daughter of Frederick IX, king of Denmark from 1947 to 1972, and Ingrid, who was the daughter of Crown Prince Gustaf VI Adolf (or Adolphus) of Sweden (r. 1950–1973). In 1953 King Frederick signed a new constitution that permitted female succession to the throne for the first time in over 500 years. In 1967 Margrethe married Henri de Laborde de Monpezat, a French diplomat, who was then referred to as Prince Consort Henrik. The couple has two sons: Frederick, born in 1968, and Joachim, born in 1969. She acceded to the throne when her father died in 1972, the first queen to rule Denmark since 1412. She became, at age thirty-one, the youngest queen regnant in the world, in the world's oldest existing monarchy. She is popularly called the Queen of Democracy. A talented artist, she is best known for her illustrations of *The Lord of the Rings.* With her husband, she wrote *All Men Are Mortal.* Denmark has a constitutional monarchy, with the queen as head of state and a prime minister as head of government. The queen's duties are largely ceremonial, but her opinions carry great weight with the voters. It was due to her influence that voters ratified the Maastricht Treaty, the basic document of the European Union, in 1993 after rejecting it in 1992. She has indicated no plans to abdicate in favor of her son.

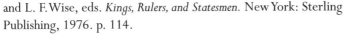

Margrethe II
(Archive Photos)

References

Egan, Edward W., Constance B. Hintz, and L. F. Wise, eds. *Kings, Rulers, and Statesmen.* New York: Sterling Publishing, 1976. p. 114.

International Who's Who 1987–1988. London: Europa Publications, 1987. p. 963.

Morby, John E. *Dynasties of the World.* Oxford: Oxford University Press, 1989. pp. 150, 152.

Moritz, Charles, ed. *Current Biography Yearbook 1972.* New Haven: H. W. Wilson, 1972. pp. 306–308.

Marguerite
Countess, Ruler of Blois (1218–1230)

Marguerite was the eldest daughter of Isabella, daughter of King Louis IX of France, and Thibault V (Theobald), king of Navarre, who also ruled Blois until his death in 1218. Marguerite acceded to the throne when her father died. She married three times. Her third husband, Gauthier d'Avesnes, ruled with her. She died in 1230 and was succeeded by Marie de Chatillon.

References

Egan, Edward W., Constance B. Hintz, and L. F. Wise, eds. *Kings, Rulers, and Statesmen.* New York: Sterling Publishing, 1976. p. 152.

Marguerite II
See Margaret II

Marguerite de Thouars
Joint Ruler of Dreux (1365–1377)

Marguerite de Thouars was the daughter of Simon of Dreux and the sister of Peronelle. She and Peronelle were parceners (joint heirs) of Dreux when their father died in 1365. In 1377 or 1378 they sold it to King Charles VI of France, who conferred it on the house of Albret.

References
Egan, Edward W., Constance B. Hintz, and L. F. Wise, eds. *Kings, Rulers, and Statesmen.* New York: Sterling Publishing, 1976. p. 157.

Maria
Queen of Sicily (1377–1402)

Maria was the daughter of Frederick IV, ruler of Sicily from 1355 to 1377, except that until 1372 Sicily was claimed by Naples. She acceded to the throne in name only when he died in 1377. In 1390 she was abducted from Catania Castle and taken to Barcelona to marry her cousin, Martin the Younger, prince of Aragon, son of King Pedro IV. In 1392 her husband was crowned Martin I, king of Sicily. Martin and his relatives then set about to bring Sicily under Aragonese control. Maria had one son, who died in 1402; she died the same year, having served her purpose, as far as the Aragonese were concerned. Martin ruled for seven more years and was succeeded by his father.

References
Egan, Edward W., Constance B. Hintz, and L. F. Wise, eds. *Kings, Rulers, and Statesmen.* New York: Sterling Publishing, 1976. p. 274.

Smith, Denis Mack. *History of Sicily.* Vol. 1 *Medieval Sicily.* New York: Dorset Press, 1968. p. 87.

María I of Braganza
Queen of Portugal (1777–1816)

Born María Victoria in 1734, she was the daughter of King Joseph I Emanuel, ruler of Portugal from 1750 to 1777, and María Ana Victoria of Spain. María Victoria's father suffered from insanity from 1774 on, and her mother became regent. When he died in 1777, María succeeded him as María I. She married her uncle, Pedro III, and ruled jointly with him until his death in 1786, and from then on she ruled alone. She consented to the trial of the dictator Pombal, who had usurped her father's power and authority, but she pardoned him because of his old age and sent him into exile. Her reign was characterized by peace and prosperity. She and Pedro had one son, John VI. In 1792 Queen María suffered a mental breakdown, and her son took over the government. In 1799 John assumed the title of prince regent. In 1807 Napoleon invaded Portugal and the family was forced to flee to Brazil. María remained in Brazil even after Napoleon's defeat. She died there in 1816.

María I of Braganza
(Corbis-Bettmann)

References

Chapman, Charles E. *A History of Spain.* New York: The Free Press/Macmillan, 1965. p. 392.

Egan, Edward W., Constance B. Hintz, and L. F. Wise, eds. *Kings, Rulers, and Statesmen.* New York: Sterling Publishing, 1976. p. 378.

Langer, William L., ed. *World History.* Boston: Houghton Mifflin, 1980. pp. 491, 492.

Maria II da Gloria
Queen of Portugal (1826–1828 and 1834–1853)

Maria da Gloria was born in 1819 in Brazil, the daughter of King Pedro IV, ruler of Brazil from 1826 to 1831, and Leopoldina of Austria. Pedro inherited the Portuguese throne from his father, John VI, who ruled as a constitutional monarch. Pedro drew up a charter providing for a parliamentary government similar to Britain's for Portugal, but he refused to leave Brazil to implement it. After a few months he abdicated and ceded the throne to his seven-year-old daughter Maria da Gloria, with her uncle Miguel as regent.

She was betrothed to her uncle but did not marry him. In 1828, Miguel led a coup d'état and proclaimed himself king. Maria da Gloria fled to England and contacted her father, asking him to come to her aid. In 1831 Pedro abdicated the Brazilian throne and traveled to England to lead the fight for the restoration of Maria to the Portuguese throne. With the help of England and France, the Miguelists were defeated. Maria was restored in 1833 and assumed power in 1834.

She was first married to Auguste Beauharnais, who soon died. In 1836 she married Duke Ferdinand of Saxe-Coburg. They had five children: Pedro V, who ruled from 1853 to 1861; Fernando; Luis I, who

*Maria II da Gloria
(Archive Photos)*

ruled from 1861 to 1889; John, and Leopoldina. Maria da Gloria's reign was a troubled one, primarily because of her choice of chief ministers. She appointed the ambitious duque de Saldanha, who dominated politics during much of her reign and who brought Portugal to the brink of civil war at one point. She died in childbirth in 1853.

References

Egan, Edward W., Constance B. Hintz, and L. F. Wise, eds. *Kings, Rulers, and Statesmen.* New York: Sterling Publishing, 1976. p. 379.

Langer, William L., ed. *World History.* Boston: Houghton Mifflin, 1980. pp. 491, 698, 699.

Morby, John E. *Dynasties of the World.* Oxford: Oxford University Press, 1989. p. 120.

Ridley, Jasper. *Napoleon III and Eugenie.* New York: Viking Press, 1980. p. 85.

Maria Adélaïde
Grand Duchess of the Grand Duchy of Luxembourg (1912–1969)

Maria Adélaïde was born in 1894, the eldest daughter of Grand Duke William IV, who reigned from 1905 to 1912. She succeeded him at the age of eighteen upon his death in 1912. Maria Adélaïde was not a popular ruler because of her reactionary policies. In August 1914 Luxembourg was invaded by the German Fifth Army under the command of Crown Prince Wilhelm, and the country was occupied for the remainder of World War I. Early in 1919, when German occupation had ended, Maria Adélaïde was forced by popular opinion to abdicate in favor of her younger sister, Charlotte, whose cooperative economic and political policies more accurately reflected the times. Maria Adélaïde died in 1924 at the age of thirty.

References

Egan, Edward W., Constance B. Hintz, and L. F. Wise, eds. *Kings, Rulers, and Statesmen.* New York: Sterling Publishing, 1976. p. 298.

Morby, John E. *Dynasties of the World.* Oxford: Oxford University Press, 1989. p. 97.

María Ana Victoria of Spain
Queen, Regent of Portugal (1774–1777)

Born María Ana Victoria (or Mariana) in 1718, she was the daughter of Isabella of Parma and King Philip V, who ruled Spain (1700–1724 and 1724- 1746). She was the sister of Philip VI (r. 1746–1759) and Charles III (r. 1759–1788). In 1721 / 1722, at the age of two or three, she was contracted in marriage to Louis XV, age eleven. She was delivered to Paris, but in 1725 the Marquise de Prie, mistress of the Duc de Bourbon (Louis's minister), hoping to maintain influence at court, conspired to have the marriage annulled so that Louis could marry Marie Leszczyńzska, daughter of the deposed king of Poland. María Victoria was sent back to Spain in disgrace, causing strained relations between Spain and France. María Victoria then married Joseph I, who later became ruler of Portugal (1750–1777). Joseph showed no interest in affairs of state. His entire reign was dominated by Sebastião José Carvalho e Mello, who became marquis of Pombal in 1770. A ruthless dictator, Pombal nevertheless reformed finances and the army, broke the power of the nobility and the church, and encouraged industry and trade. María Victoria and Joseph had a daughter, María I, born in 1734. In 1774 Joseph was declared insane, and María Victoria was appointed regent. She began gradually to erode the power of Pombal. In 1777 her husband died, having never regained his health, and the reign was passed to María I.

References

Chapman, Charles E. *A History of Spain.* New York: The Free Press/Macmillan, 1965. pp. 378, 392.

Durant, Will and Ariel. *The Story of Civilization.* Vol. 9, *The Age of Voltaire.* New York: Simon & Schuster, 1965. pp. 32, 273.

Langer, William L., ed. *World History.* Boston: Houghton Mifflin, 1980. pp. 491–492.

Maria Anna of Austria
Queen, Regent of Spain (1665–1676)

Maria Anna of Austria (María Ana) was born in 1634, the daughter of Ferdinand III, king of Hungary (1625–1657), king of Bohemia (1637–1657), Holy Roman emperor (1637–1657), and his first wife, María Anna of Spain. In a lavish and extravagant ceremony, Archduchess Maria Anna of Austria became the second wife of Philip IV, who was king of Spain from 1621 to 1665. She had two children: Margareta Teresa, born in 1651, who married Emperor Leopold I; and Charles V, born in 1661, who succeeded to the throne at the age of four upon his father's death (1665). Maria Anna served as regent for over ten years,

but her leadership was hampered by her dependence upon her Jesuit advisers and her preference for foreigners. In addition, she was preoccupied in combating French king Louis XIV's attack on Spanish possessions in The Netherlands. Court nobles led by John Joseph of Austria gained the upper hand in the government and eventually forced Maria Anna to resign. She died in 1696.

References

Chapman, Charles E. *A History of Spain.* New York: The Free Press/ Macmillan, 1965. pp. 269, 284.

Langer, William L., ed. *World History.* Boston: Houghton Mifflin, 1980. pp. 417, 486.

Maria Carolina
Queen, De Facto Ruler of Naples and Sicily (1777–1798 and 1799–1806)

Maria Carolina was born in 1752, the daughter of Maria Theresa, empress of Austria from 1740 to 1780, and Holy Roman emperor Francis I. Maria Carolina, the sister of Marie Antoinette, in 1768 married King Ferdinand IV, king of Naples (1759–1808), and later, as Ferdinand I, king of the Two Sicilys (1816–1825). Ferdinand allowed Maria Carolina to assume much of the authority to rule that had hitherto been held by the regent Tanucci. Affairs of state were conducted chiefly by her. The birth of a male heir, Francis I, in 1777, gave her the authority, according to her marriage contract, to sit on the council of state. She soon brought about the complete downfall of Tanucci and allied herself, perhaps romantically as well as politically, with an English adventurer, Lord Acton, of obvious British persuasion.

When her sister, Marie Antoinette was executed, Maria Carolina engaged Naples in the Austro-British campaign against the French Revolution. In 1798 the French seized Naples and renamed it the Parthenopean Republic. Maria Carolina, Ferdinand, and their children were forced to flee for their lives. A year later, after the overthrow of the new republic, the royal family returned to Naples and ordered the execution of the republic's partisans. In 1805 she requested the aid of Russian and British fleets in yet another conflict with France. Again in 1806, Naples was overrun by the French, and the royal family fled to Sicily.

She had long since acquired a hatred of Sicilians. She once wrote, "The priests are completely corrupted, the people savage, the nobility of questionable loyalty." Once she even suggested that the British buy Sicily from her for £6 million. When the Sicilians adopted a new constitution, she could see what it took others years to see: that it was a baronial document that discriminated against the common people and that parliament was a farce designed to divert people's attention from what the nobles were doing. After she quarreled with the British ambassador, he persuaded Ferdinand to exile her from Sicily.

She returned to Austria alone in 1811, where she died three years later. In addition to her son, she was survived by five daughters: Maria Teresa, who married Emperor Francis I of Austria; Louisa Amelia, who married Ferdinand III of Tuscany; Maria Amelia, who married Louis Philippe, king of France; Cristina, who married Felix of Sardinia; and Maria Antonia, who married Ferdinand VII, king of Spain.

References

Langer, William L., ed. *World History*. Boston: Houghton Mifflin, 1980. pp. 496, 497, 702.

Smith, Denis Mack. *History of Sicily*. Vol. 2, *Modern Sicily: After 1713*. New York: Dorset Press, 1968. pp. 325, 335–338, 341, 348.

Maria Christina
Duchess, Governor General of Austrian Netherlands (1780–1789)

Maria Christina (or Christina) was born in 1742, one of sixteen children of Maria Theresa, empress of Hungary and Bohemia (1740–1780) and Holy Roman emperor Francis I, who ruled from 1745 to 1765. She married Albert, duke of Saxe-Teschen. Maria Christina governed the Austrian Netherlands, which is present-day Belgium, during the reign of her brother, Holy Roman emperor Joseph II, whose edicts abolishing many religious bodies were so unpopular that Maria Christina was hesitant to implement them. In retaliation to the edicts, the estates of Hainault and Brabant refused to pay taxes in 1788, and in 1789 revolution erupted. The Austrians were forced to retreat to Luxembourg. Maria Christina died in 1798.

References

Egan, Edward W., Constance B. Hintz, and L. F. Wise, eds. *Kings, Rulers, and Statesmen*. New York: Sterling Publishing, 1976. p. 52.

Maria Christina of Austria
Queen, Regent of Spain (1885–1902)

Maria Christina of Austria was born in 1858 in an area of Austria that is now in the Czech Republic. In 1879 she became the second wife of King Alfonso XII, ruler of Spain from 1874 to 1885. They had three

Maria Christina of Austria (Erich Lessing / Art Resource, NY)

children: María de la Mercedes, Maria Teresa, and Alfonso XIII, who was born after his father died. When Alfonso XII died in 1885, María de la Mercedes technically became hereditary queen until her brother was born in 1886. The ex-queen, Isabella II, attempted to intervene, but her meddling only strengthened Maria Christina's position. Maria Christina served as regent for both children until Alfonso XIII was declared of age to govern in 1902.

Even then, Alfonso at first allowed his mother to continue to rule. During her regency, she alternated power between the liberals, led by Praxedes Mateo Sagasta, and the conservatives, led by Antonio Canovas del Castillo. The Spanish-American War of 1898 left Spain weakened and the Spanish Empire decimated, with the loss of Cuba, Puerto Rico, Guam, and the Philippines. Maria Christina resigned her regency in 1902. She died in 1929 in Madrid.

References

Chapman, Charles E. *A History of Spain*. New York: The Free Press/Macmillan, 1965. p. 506.

Langer, William L., ed. *World History*. Boston: Houghton Mifflin, 1980. pp. 695, 696–697.

María Cristina I of Naples
Queen, Regent of Spain (1833–1840)

María Cristina (or Cristina) was born in Naples in 1806 and became the fourth wife of King Ferdinand VII, who ruled Spain from 1814 to 1833. They had two daughters: Isabella II and Luisa Fernanda. In 1833, two months before her husband's death, María Cristina influenced him to set aside the Salic Law, thus allowing their daughter, María Isabel (Isabella II), to succeed him and depriving his brother, Don Carlos, of the throne. On the death of Ferdinand, María Cristina became regent with absolute power. Realizing she needed the support of the liberals, she liberalized the constitution and sanctioned certain anticlerical measures. In 1833 she made a secret morganatic marriage to Fernando Muñoz that, when discovered, made her highly unpopular.

In 1834 Don Carlos, determined to win the throne for himself, instigated the First Carlist War, aimed at María Cristina and the liberals. The Carlists were defeated in 1837, but the war was not officially concluded until 1839. Don Carlos left the country for France. In the meantime, María Cristina was pressured into appointing a Progressist minister and accepting a new compromise constitution (1837). In 1840 General Baldomero Esparto, Progressist leader, revolted, forcing María Cristina to resign her regency and leave the country, making way for Esparto to assume the regency. She later made an attempt to return and participate in the government, but failed, and she retired in exile to France in 1854, where she died in 1878.

References
Chapman, Charles E. *A History of Spain*. New York: The Free Press/Macmillan, 1965. pp. 497–500.

Langer, William L., ed. *World History*. Boston: Houghton Mifflin, 1980. pp. 694–696.

Ridley, Jasper. *Napoleon III and Eugenie*. New York: Viking Press, 1980. pp. 142, 144, 152, 157.

María de la Mercedes
Queen Infanta of Spain (1885–1886)

María de la Mercedes (or Mercedes) was born in 1880, the elder daughter of King Alfonso XII, who ruled Spain from 1875 to 1885, and Maria Christina of Austria. When María de la Mercedes's father died in 1885, there was no male heir, so she succeeded him, at age five. However, several months later her mother gave birth to a boy, Alfonso XIII, who became the new king at birth. María de la Mercedes was married to Carlo, conti de Caserta di Bourbon, but she had no children. She died in 1904.

References
Langer, William L., ed. *World History*. Boston: Houghton Mifflin, 1980. p. 695.

María Estela Martínez de Perón
See Perón, Isabel

Maria of Anjou
"King" of Hungary, Queen of Croatia (1382–1385 and 1386–1395)

Maria (or Mary or Marija) of Anjou was born in 1370, the daughter of Elizabeth of Bosnia and Polish king Ljudevit, or Louis the Great, king of Hungary (1342–1382) and king of Poland (1370–1382), and the older sister of Jadwiga (Jadviga), who inherited the Polish throne. While Maria was still a child, she was betrothed to Sigismund of Luxemburg. They were married in 1378, when she was eight and he was ten.

Sigismund was prince of Bohemia and son of Holy Roman emperor and king of Bohemia Charles IV. Sigismund was later to become king of Hungary from 1387, king of Germany from 1411, king of the Lombards from 1431, and Holy Roman emperor from 1433. The couple had no children. When Maria's father died in 1382, the Hungarian nobility, which had previously agreed to accept Jadwiga as "king of Hungary," elected instead Maria, age twelve, who also inherited the throne of Croatia, with her mother assuming the regency.

Croatian nobility, however, objected to the rule of the two queens. A conspiracy headed by Ivan Palizna planned to detach Croatia and invite Stjepan Tvrdko, king of Bosnia, to rule. When Nikola Gorjanski, the queen's adviser, learned of the conspiracy, he brought both queens, backed by a strong army, from Hungary to Croatia. The plot failed, and Palizna fled to Bosnia, while the queens received a royal welcome. Before her return to Hungary, Maria presided over a session of the parliament, the Sabor.

Soon, however, her position was challenged again. A new plot to unseat the queen was organized by the Horvat brothers: Pavao, bishop of Zagreb, and Ivanis, *ban* of Macva. They invited Maria's cousin, Prince Charles II of Durazzo and Naples, whose father, Steven V, had ruled Hungary (1270–1272), to assume the Croatian throne. Charles gladly traveled from Naples to accept the reins of government. After a year in Croatia, he moved on to Hungary, determined to unseat Maria there, as well, which he did (1385). However, Queen Elizabeth and her advisers devised their own plan to overthrow him, and Charles was assassinated. Maria returned to the throne for a second time in 1386.

Following Charles's assassination, the Horvat brothers joined forces with Palizna, who returned from Bosnia, and determined to take control of the Croatian government. Again Gorjanski and the two queens set out for Croatia with an army. This time, however, the army was defeated. Both queens were captured and taken to Palizna's castle, Novigrad on the Sea. Charles's widow insisted that Elizabeth be executed.

When Maria's husband, Sigismund of Luxemburg, learned that she was being held prisoner, he left for Hungary to assume the crown for himself. In 1387 he was crowned king consort. The Hungarians received him warmly, and he assembled a strong army and requested help from the Venetian navy so as to invade Croatia and free Maria. With the Venetians blockading Novigrad's sea approach, the army laid siege by land. Eventually Palizna surrendered Maria in exchange for his own safe return to Bosnia. The Horvats also took refuge in Bosnia while Maria and Sigismund returned to Hungary to face mounting threats by the Turks for the rest of their reign. She died in 1395 at the age of twenty-five.

References

Dvornik, Francis. *The Slavs in European History and Civilization.* New Brunswick, NJ: Rutgers University Press, 1962. pp. 60–62, 83, 436.

Langer, William L., ed. *World History.* Boston: Houghton Mifflin, 1980 pp. 339, 342.

Maria of Austria
Dowager Queen of Hungary, Governor of The Netherlands (1530–1555)

Maria of Austria was the daughter of Queen Juana of Spain and Philip of Hapsburg. Maria was the sister of Holy Roman emperor Charles V and of Ferdinand, king of Bohemia. She married Louis II, who was king of Hungary from 1516 to 1526. Following his death in 1526 and the death in 1530 of Margaret, duchess of Savoy and governor of The Netherlands, Dowager Queen Maria was appointed governor of The Netherlands by her brother, Emperor Charles. She ruled until her death in 1555.

References

Geye, Pieter. *The Revolt of The Netherlands.* London: Ernest Benn, 1958. p. 38.

Maria Theresa (Perry-Castaneda Library)

Maria Theresa

Empress of Hapsburg Empire, Queen of Bohemia and Hungary, Archduchess of Austria, Ruler of Luxembourg, and So On (1740–1780)

Maria Theresa was born in 1717, the older daughter of Charles VI, king of Bohemia and Hungary from 1711 to 1740, and Elizabeth Christina of Brunswick. When her father died in 1740, Maria Theresa succeeded him in the midst of the War of Austrian Succession. That same year she married Francis Stephen of the house of Lorraine, grand duke of Tuscany from 1737 to 1765, later Francis I, emperor of the Hapsburg Empire (1745–1765). Two of their children, Joseph II and Leopold II, were emperors, and one was Marie Antoinette.

At the time of Maria Theresa's accession the monarchy was exhausted, the people discontented, and the army weak. Only seven weeks after her father's death, Frederick III the Great of Prussia marched in and took over the Austrian province of Silesia, precipitating the Silesian Wars of 1740–1742 and 1744. She lost Silesia to Frederick and never forgave the loss. The Seven Years' War that ensued (1756–1763) was a world war, fought not only in Europe but also in North America and India, with Britain and Prussia fighting France, Austria, and Russia.

Maria Theresa managed to bear sixteen children in 20 years while she first established her right to rule, then negotiated an imperial crown for her husband, and meanwhile introduced economic reforms and strengthened the central government and the army. She improved the economic climate of The Netherlands and enjoyed wide popularity there. She died at the age of sixty-three in 1780.

References

Crankshaw, Edward. *Maria Theresa.* New York: Viking Press, 1969, 1971.

Roider, Karl A., Jr., ed. *Maria Theresa.* Englewood Cliffs, NJ: Prentice Hall, 1973.

Marie
Countess, Ruler of Boulogne (1159–1173)

Marie was the daughter of Countess Mahaut de Boulogne (who was Queen Matilda of England), ruler of Boulogne from 1125 to 1150, and King Stephen I, who ruled England from 1135 to 1154. She was the sister of Count Eustache IV, who succeeded their mother upon her death and ruled from 1150 to 1153, and of Guillaume II, who ruled from the time of his brother's death in 1153 until 1159. When Guillaume died in 1159, Marie succeeded him. She was married to Matthieu d'Alcase. They had a daughter, Ide, who succeeded her mother upon Marie's death in 1173.

References
Egan, Edward W., Constance B. Hintz, and L. F. Wise, eds. *Kings, Rulers, and Statesmen.* New York: Sterling Publishing, 1976. p. 152.

Marie
Regent of Jerusalem (1205–1212)

Marie (also Maria La Marquise or Maria of Montferrat) was born ca. 1192, the oldest daughter of Princess Isabella, heiress of the kingdom of Jerusalem, and her second husband, Conrad of Montferrat, who was murdered shortly after Marie was born. In 1198 Isabella and her fourth husband, Amalric II, were crowned king and queen of Jerusalem. In the kingdom of Jerusalem, hereditary right to rule dictated that Maria would inherit the throne, but the High Court preserved its claim to elect a ruler.

Isabella died in ca. 1205, as did Amalric. Maria, at age thirteen, acceded to the throne, and John of Ibelin, lord of Beirut, was appointed regent for three years. In 1208, at age seventeen, she was married to a penniless knight from Champagne, John of Brienne, who was already sixty years old. In 1212 they had a daughter, Yolanda (also called Yolande or Isabella II). That same year Marie died. Her husband continued to rule for their daughter.

References
Runciman, Steven. *A History of the Crusades.* Vol. 3, *The Kingdom of Acre and the Later Crusades.* Cambridge: Cambridge University Press, 1952, 1987. pp. 32, 66, 84, 94–95, 104, 132–134, 320.

Marie
Countess, Ruler of Brabant (1260)

Marie (or Mary of Brabant) was the second wife of Holy Roman emperor Otto IV, whom she married ca. 1213. Otto was deposed in

1215 and died in 1218. Marie did not remarry and had no children. When Countess Mahaut de Dammartin died in 1260, the fief of Boulogne passed to Marie. Eventually it passed to Robert VI, comte d'Auvergne.

References

Egan, Edward W., Constance B. Hintz, and L. F. Wise, eds. *Kings, Rulers, and Statesmen.* New York: Sterling Publishing, 1976. p. 152.

Langer, William L., ed. *World History.* Boston: Houghton Mifflin, 1980. p. 224.

Marie de Bourbon
Princess, Ruler of Achaea (1364–1370)

Marie de Bourbon was the widow of Robert II (r. 1333–1364). His brother, Philippe II, disputed her right to rule and eventually won out (r. 1364–1373).

References

Carpenter, Clive. *The Guinness Book of Kings, Rulers & Statesmen.* Enfield, Middlesex: Guinness Superlatives, 1978. p. 1.

Marie de Bourbon Montpensier
Duchess, Ruler of Auvergne (1608–1627)

Marie de Bourbon Montpensier was born in 1605, the daughter of Henri, duke of Montpensier, who ruled Auvergne from 1602 to 1608, and Henriette de Joyeuse. At age three, Marie succeeded her father upon his death. She married Jean Baptist Gaston, duke of Orléans. In 1627 they had a daughter, Anne-Marie-Louise, who inherited her mother's rule when Marie died the same year.

References

Egan, Edward W., Constance B. Hintz, and L. F. Wise, eds. *Kings, Rulers, and Statesmen.* New York: Sterling Publishing, 1976. p. 151.

Marie de Chatillon
Countess, Ruler of Blois (1230–1241)

Marie de Chatillon inherited Blois when Countess Marguerite of Navarre died in 1230. Marie was married to Hugues de Chatillon, count of Saint-Pol. They had a son, Jean de Chatillon, who became count of Blois and Chartres when his mother died in 1241.

References

Egan, Edward W., Constance B. Hintz, and L. F. Wise, eds. *Kings, Rulers, and Statesmen.* New York: Sterling Publishing, 1976. p. 152.

Marie de Médicis

Regent of France
(1610–1617), De Facto Ruler
until 1631, Governor of
Normandy (1612–1619)

*Marie de Médicis
(Scala/Art Resource,
NY)*

Marie de Médicis was born in 1573 in Florence, Italy, the daughter of Francesco de Medici, grand duke of Tuscany, and Joanna of Austria. In 1600 Marie married King Henry IV (r. France 1589–1610). In 1601 she gave birth to the future Louis XIII and subsequently had five more children. When Henry was assassinated in 1610, Marie was named regent for her son Louis XIII. She chose as her chief minister a Florentine friend, Concino Concini, whom she named marquis d'Ancre. In 1612 she became governor of Normandy as well, a post she held until 1619. She was the first woman governor of a major province. She later traded this post for the government of Anjou.

Even after Louis came of age in 1614, she continued to rule France. In 1619 Concini was assassinated, and Marie was banished to Blois, but she escaped and, with the help of the future cardinal-duke of Richelieu, she set up court at Angers. After the death of the king's favorite, the duke of Luynes, in 1621, Marie and Richelieu gained control of affairs. She obtained a cardinal's hat for Richelieu and saw to it that Louis appointed him chief minister. When Richelieu rejected alliance with Spain and opted to side with the Huguenots, Marie demanded that he be dismissed. Eventually, instead, Louis banished his mother again (1631). She went to the Spanish Netherlands, then to Cologne, where she died in 1642, penniless.

References

Durant, Will and Ariel. *The Story of Civilization*. Vol. 9, *The Age of Voltaire*. New York: Simon & Schuster, 1965. pp. 26, 313.

Harding, Robert R. *Anatomy of a Power Elite*. New Haven, CT: Yale University Press, 1978. pp. 127, 129, 175, 226.

Hare, Christopher. *The Most Illustrious Ladies of the Italian Renaissance*. Williamstown, MA: Corner House, 1972. p. 211.

Trevor-Roper, Hugh. *The Golden Age of Europe*. New York: Bonanza/Crown, 1987. pp. 153, 158, 166, 172, 173.

Marie-Louise
(Scala/Art Resource,
NY)

Marie d'Savoy-Nemours

See Jeanne de Nemours

Marie-Louise

Regent of France (1812),
Duchess of Parma
(1815–1847)

Marie-Louise was born in Vienna in 1791, the eldest of twelve children of Holy Roman emperor Francis II (r. 1792–1806), ruler of Austria as Francis I (1804–1835), and his second wife, Maria Theresa of Naples-Sicily. When Napoleon, eager for a royal heir, decided to divorce his beloved Josephine, the Austrian foreign minister, Count (later Prince) Klemens von Metternich, suggested nineteen-year-old Marie-Louise as Napoleon's second wife. They married in 1810, and in 1811 their son, Napoleon II, was born. In 1812, during Napoleon's Russian campaign, Marie-Louise served as regent.

The marriage marked a turning point for Napoleon. According to historian Owen Connelly in Putnam, "Marie-Louise made him so happy that he lost his compulsion to work." Whether she was equally happy is questionable. Napoleon still corresponded with Josephine, and there were rumors that he was the father of the children of Marie-Louise's sister-in-law, Archduchess Sophie. After his first abdication in 1814, Marie-Louise's father whisked her and her son back to Austria.

The Congress of Vienna gave Marie-Louise the Italian duchies of Parma, Piacenza, and Guastalla, with sovereign power to rule in her own right, reverting to the house of Bourbon at her death. She refused to accompany Napoleon to Elba, and after he threatened to abduct her, they became completely estranged. By the time he died in 1821, she had already given birth to two children by Adam Adalbert,

Graf von Neipperg. They married shortly after Napoleon's death. She established a moderate rule in Parma and maintained the previously enacted French reforms. Neipperg died only two years after their marriage, and in 1824 she took a third husband, Charles-René, comte de Bombelles. In 1832 her son Napoleon II died in Vienna of tuberculosis. Marie-Louise died in Parma in 1847.

References

Langer, William L., ed. *World History.* Boston: Houghton Mifflin, 1980. pp. 644, 650.

Putnam, John J. "Napoleon." *National Geographic* 161. February 1982: 165–170.

Sédillot, René. *An Outline of French History.* Trans. Gerard Hopkins. New York: Alfred A. Knopf, 1967. pp. 290, 306.

Marija
See Maria of Anjou

Marozia Crescentii
Ruler of Rome (928–932)

Marozia Crescentii was the daughter of Roman senator Theophylact Crescentii and his wife, Theodora. The patrician Crescentii family was of the landed aristocracy that controlled Rome during the nadir of the papacy. At the time of Marozia, the papacy was a local and secular institution. Italy was without effective native rule. Marozia was the mistress of Pope Sergius III and mother of his son John, later Pope John XI. She married Alberic I of Spoleto, margrave of Camerino, who, with her father, restored Sergius III to the papacy. Alberic and Marozia had a son, Alberic II. After Alberic I died in 928, Marozia overthrew and imprisoned Pope John X, raised her illegitimate son to the papacy, and took control of Rome until her son Alberic II assumed power in 932. Following the death of her first husband, she married, successively, Marquess Guido, Guy of Tuscany, and, after he died, his half-brother, Hugh of Provence, king of Italy from 926 to 932. In 932 her son, Alberic II, rose up against her and drove out King Hugh.

References

Langer, William L., ed. *World History.* Boston: Houghton Mifflin, 1980. p. 230.

Previté-Orton, C. W. *The Shorter Cambridge History of the Crusades.* Vol. 1, *The Later Roman Empire to the Twelfth Century.* Cambridge: Cambridge University Press, 1952, 1982. pp. 359, 437.

Martha
Queen Mother, De Facto Ruler of Russia (1613–1619)

Martha was the wife of Philaret Romanov, who had been placed in captivity in Poland while she had been forced into a convent by Boris Godunov. She was the mother of Michael Romanov, elected tsar of Russia in 1613. Young Michael had no education preparing him to rule, so he left the direction of affairs of state to the ambitious Martha, who left the convent, and to other relatives. In 1619 Philaret was freed to return to Moscow, where he was elevated to patriarch. He assumed the reins of government and ruled "brutally" in the name of his son, eliminating other relatives and even Martha.

References

Dvornik, Francis. *The Slavs in European History and Civilization.* New Brunswick, NJ: Rutgers University Press, 1962. p. 490.

Mary
Queen, Regent of Georgia (1027–ca. 1036)

Mary was the daughter of Sennacherib-John of Vaspurahan and the wife of George I (Giorgi), Bagratid king of Georgia from 1014 to 1027. They had a son, Bagrat, born in 1018. During George's reign, he determined to restore the lands of David of Tao to Georgia, and when he occupied Tao in 1015–1016, he broke the peace with Byzantium. Eventually, in 1021, King Basil II and his Armenian Bagratid allies swept through Georgia and devastated the land, slaughtering women and children as well. When he invaded again in 1022, King George submitted to the emperor, relinquished all claim to Tao, and gave up his three-year-old son Bagrat as a hostage. Both Georgia and Armenia were left under the Byzantine thumb.

George died in 1027, and Bagrat IV succeeded his father as a minor of eight. Queen Mary served as regent during a troubled time in Georgia's history but was able to secure for her son a kingdom that was the major indigenous power in Caucasia. In 1031, after the Katholikos (or takeover of the Byzantine empire) of Iberia (a country adjacent to Armenia), Queen Mary and the minister Melchisedech journeyed to Constantinople on a diplomatic mission on behalf of her son. Peace was concluded, and young Bagrat received the dignity of Curopalate, which had been denied his father. Bagrat was able to use his power as Curopalate to remove recalcitrant princes holding hereditary possessions, reducing those who opposed him to a lowly status, and to elevate loyal followers into the upper nobility. Mary also made arrangements at the time of her journey to Constantinople for her son to marry the Emperor's niece, Helena. Bagrat IV reigned for forty-five years.

References

Allen, W.E.D. *A History of the Georgian People from the Beginning Down to the Russian Conquest in the Nineteenth Century.* New York: Barnes & Noble Books, 1971. pp. 87–90.

Hussey, J. M., ed. *The Cambridge Medieval History.* Vol. 4, pt. 1. Cambridge: Cambridge University Press, 1966. p. 621.

Suny, Ronald Grigor. *The Making of the Georgian Nation.* Bloomington: Indiana University Press, in association with Hoover Institutions Press, Stanford University, 1988. pp. 33–34.

Mary
Duchess, Ruler of Burgundy and Luxembourg (1477–1482)

Mary, Duchess of Burgundy and Luxembourg (Corbis-Bettmann)

Mary was born in 1457, the daughter of Charles the Bold (r. 1467–1477) and Margaret of York. In 1474, Louis XI (the Spider) formed the Union of Constance, a coalition of foes of Burgundy, and opened war on Charles the Bold. Charles was killed in battle in 1477. Louis attempted to unite Burgundy with the crown, but Flanders stood firmly by Mary. The Union of Constance was a formidable foe for a widow alone; she soon married Archduke Maximilian of Austria (r. Hapsburg Empire 1493–1519). The couple had two children: Philip (the Handsome), who married Joanna of Castile and was regent of Spain, and Margaret, who first married John of Spain and then Philip of Savoy. Mary died in 1482. Their son Philip became duke of Burgundy.

References

Langer, William L., ed. *World History.* Boston: Houghton Mifflin, 1980. pp. 303, 324, 327, 406, 427.

Mary I
*Queen of England
(1553–1558)*

Mary I (or Bloody Mary or Mary the Catholic) was born in 1516, the daughter of Henry VIII, king of England (r. 1509–1547), and Catherine of Aragon. Henry divorced Catherine in 1533, claiming marriage to his brother's widow was incestuous and thus Mary was a bastard. His next wife, Anne Boleyn, forced Mary to serve as lady-in-waiting for her own daughter, Elizabeth. Mary was also coerced into admitting the illegality of her mother's marriage to her father.

After Anne Boleyn was beheaded, Mary's lot became easier; she was made godmother to Edward, son of Henry's third wife, Jane Seymour. One by one she watched Henry's wives come and go, secretly practicing her Catholicism, waiting for a marriage partner to materialize. Her bastard status limited her marital opportunities, even though, in 1544, she was named in succession to the throne after Edward. When Edward died in 1553, one threat to her succession, Lady Jany Grey, had to be deposed after a nine-day "reign," and then Mary became, at age thirty-seven, the first queen to rule all of England in her own right.

She set about restoring the ties to the Catholic Church severed during her father's reign. To that end, she determined to marry Philip of Spain, son of Holy Roman emperor Charles V. The people of Tudor England distrusted Spaniards, and his Catholicism was of grave concern to nobles who had profited when Henry VIII confiscated Catholic lands. Sir Thomas Wyatt led a Protestant insurrection that Mary countered with an impassioned plea to her citizenry. Wyatt was executed, and Mary married Philip in 1554. Soon after, the papal legate absolved England from the sin of its twenty-year break with Rome. The church restored heresy laws (1555), and some 280 heretics were burned. "Bloody Mary" was blamed for the slaughter.

Philip returned to Spain when his father died (1555) and came to England only once more during their marriage. That was in 1556, to persuade her to take arms against France to assist Spain's interests.

In 1558 Calais, an English possession for more than two centuries, was taken by the duke of Guise. This loss was one from which she never recovered. Ten months later she was dead.

References

Hudson, M. E., and Mary Clark. *Crown of a Thousand Years.* New York: Crown Publishers, 1978. pp. 78, 82–89.

Langer, William L., ed. *World History.* Boston: Houghton Mifflin, 1980. pp. 395–396, 398–399, 417.

Trevor-Roper, Hugh. *The Golden Age of Europe.* New York: Bonanza/Crown, 1987. pp. 26, 40, 190.

Mary II
Queen of England (1689–1694)

Mary II was born in 1662, the daughter of James II, ruler of England from 1685 to 1688, and Anne Hyde. Although both parents were Catholic converts, Mary was reared as a Protestant. In 1677, at age fifteen, she was married to her cousin, William of Orange, stadholder of Holland, and went to Holland to live. Her initial disappointment on meeting William, who was twelve years older than she and four inches shorter, eventually disappeared. However, she never reconciled to William's long-standing love affair with her lady-in-waiting, Elizabeth Villiers. Despite Mary's obvious dislike of Elizabeth, William insisted that she be retained in the queen's retinue.

In 1688 English bishops wrote to William, a champion of Protestant causes, inviting him to invade England. It was an invitation that William and Mary welcomed. William's invasion met with scant resistance, for the country wanted a Protestant ruler. King James fled to France, and after a half-hearted attempt to regain his throne, retired to France permanently. Mary quickly made it known that she had no intention of reigning alone: She was the prince's wife, she said, and never meant to be "other than in subjection to him." They were crowned joint sovereigns in 1689. However, during her six years as queen of England, she reigned alone for much of the time, since William was abroad attending to matters of state in Holland or was conducting his military campaigns against France or Ireland. Mary enjoyed great popularity and ruled with vigor, sensitivity, and dynamism during William's absences, but when he was in England, she quickly retired. Her chaplain wrote that if her husband retained the throne of England, "it would be done by her skill and talents for governing."

Her estrangement from her father and from her adopted homeland, Holland, troubled her, but more vexing were her constant quarrels with her sister Anne, whose friends, Sarah and John Churchill, actively disliked William. She, in turn, mistrusted them and thought that Anne was entirely too much in their thrall. Mary died prematurely of smallpox at the age of thirty-two (1694).

References

Hudson, M. E., and Mary Clark. *Crown of a Thousand Years.* New York: Crown Publishers, 1978. pp. 112–114.

Langer, William L., ed. *World History.* Boston: Houghton Mifflin, 1980. pp. 463, 465–467, 553.

Mary Bosomworth
"Princess," Ruler of Ossabaw, Sapelo, and St. Catherines Islands (1747–?)

A Creek Indian, Mary Bosomworth was the daughter of "an Indian woman of no note," according to one Georgia account. She served General James Oglethorpe, the founder of Georgia, as an interpreter to the Creek Indians. As her third husband she took the Reverend Thomas Bosomworth, Oglethorpe's chaplain. Together they persuaded the Creeks that Mary was their princess in the maternal line. The Creeks accepted her and honored her request to give her three islands to command off the Georgia coast: Ossabaw, Sapelo, and St. Catherines. The British attempted to recover the islands, but Mary raised an army of Creeks and marched into Savannah, threatening a massacre. The British backed down, but eventually ransomed Ossabaw and Sapelo for large sums. Mary kept the island of St. Catherines.

References

Cerutis, James. "Sea Islands: The South's Surprising Coast." *National Geographic* 139. March 1971: 373–374.

Mary of Antioch
Empress, Regent of Byzantine Empire (1180–1183)

Mary (or Maria) of Antioch was the daughter of Constance of Antioch and Raymond of Poitiers and the sister of King Bohemond III. In 1160, in an undeclared contest between Mary and Melisende, daughter of Raymond II of Tripoli, she was chosen by Byzantine emperor Manuel I (1143–1180) as his second wife. The couple had a son, Alexius II, who acceded to the throne at the age of eleven with his mother as regent.

Empress Mary was the first Latin to be ruler of the empire, and as such, she was resented by the people. Italian opportunistic merchants had all but gained a monopoly on trade in Constantinople. To confound her problem with her subjects, Mary took as her adviser and, as rumors had it, possibly her lover, her husband's nephew, the protosebastus Alexius Comnenus, uncle of Maria of Jerusalem. He, too, was unpopular. The porphyrogennete Maria and her husband, Ranier of Montferrat, plotted to kill her uncle Alexius II, but their plot went awry.

In 1182 Empress Mary's cousin-in-law, Andronicus Comnenus, invaded Constantinople; it was the opportunity the people had needed to fall upon all the hated Latins in their midst. The citizens slaughtered the haughty Italian merchants who had controlled the city's trade. Andronicus then eliminated his rivals one by one, beginning with the porphyrogennete and her husband, whom he murdered. Young Alexius II was forced to sign a warrant condemning his mother Mary to be strangled to death (1182). The boy himself was murdered two months later.

References
Ostrogorsky, George. *History of the Byzantine State*. New Brunswick, NJ: Rutgers University Press, 1969. pp. 394, 396.
Previté-Orton, C. W. *The Shorter Cambridge Medieval History*. Vol. 1, *The Later Roman Empire to the Twelfth Century*. Cambridge: Cambridge University Press, 1982. p. 536.
Runciman, Steven. *A History of the Crusades*. Vol. 2, *The Kingdom of Jerusalem*. Cambridge: Cambridge University Press, 1952, 1987. pp. 359–360, 427–428.

Mary of Guise
Queen, Regent of Scotland (1554–1560)

Mary of Guise (or Mary of Lorraine) was born in 1515, the eldest daughter of Claude of Lorraine, founding duc de Guise who ruled from 1528 to 1550, and Antoinette de Bourbon-Vendôme. In 1533 Mary married Louis d'Orléans, duc de Longueville. They had one son, François, born in 1534. In 1537 her husband died. The following year she married King James V, ruler of Scotland from 1513 to 1542. Their daughter, Mary Stuart, was born a few days before James died in 1542. English King Henry VIII tried in vain to gain control of the kingdom at that time, but he failed.

In 1554 James, earl of Arran, was deposed from the regency for twelve-year-old Mary Stuart in favor of Queen Mary. In the beginning of her regency, Mary, a Catholic, actually cultivated Protestants and ruled with such religious tolerance that the Protestants even supported her 1558 decision to marry her daughter to the future king of France, Francis II. However, heavy-handed French influence soon induced her to change her tolerant attitude toward Protestants and to attempt to suppress the growth of Protestantism in Scotland. Her actions sparked a civil war in which the Protestants were aided by England and the Catholics by France. Queen Mary was driven from office but returned, only to be on the verge of defeat again. Her health failed, and from her deathbed she called a conference of nobles from both sides and pleaded for reason and for a compromise. She died in 1560 before she could see her request honored.

References

Mackie, J. D. *A History of Scotland.* Harmondsworth, Middlesex: Penguin Books, 1984. pp. 133, 136–139, 149.

Mary of Lorraine
See Mary of Guise

Mary Stuart
Queen of Scots (1542–1567)

Born in 1542, she was the only child of King James V, ruler of Scotland from 1513 to 1542, and Mary of Guise. Mary Stuart was born the year her father died. To keep Henry VIII from gaining control of the fatherless child, Mary's mother sent her to France when she was five years old, where she was reared in the household of King Henry II and Catherine de Médicis. In 1558, at age sixteen, she was married to their eldest son, fourteen-year-old Francis II, later ruler of France from 1559 to 1560. That same year, Elizabeth Tudor, a Protestant, acceded to the throne of England, and Mary Stuart, a Catholic, was next in the line of succession. Two years later her husband died, and she soon returned to Scotland.

*Mary Stuart
(Gustavo Tomsich /
Corbis-Bettmann)*

For the first years of her majority rule, she refrained from interfering in religious affairs, even choosing Protestant advisers. Then she made the fatal mistake of falling in love with her cousin, Lord Darnley, who was unpopular with all factions. Despite all protests, she married him in 1565. Through plots and counterplots, including the murder of her secretary Rizzio before her eyes, Darnley tried to ensure the succession for his heirs. Mary bore a son, James VI, in 1566, but by now she was convinced that Darnley had meant to kill her.

One account says that Mary developed an adulturous relationship with the earl of Bothwell before he murdered Darnley in 1567 and that Mary was aware of Bothwell's plot. Whatever her foreknowledge of events was, afterward Bothwell abducted her, ravished her, and subsequently married her. But the marriage set Scottish nobles up in arms; they exiled Bothwell, imprisoned Mary on the island of Loch Leven, and forced her to abdicate in favor of her son. The following year she fled to England, but Elizabeth held her in prison for eighteen years. Then, in 1586, suspecting Mary of being involved in a plot to assassinate her, Elizabeth consented to have Mary put to death.

References

Mackie, J. D. *A History of Scotland.* Harmondsworth, Middlesex: Penguin Books, 1984. pp. 134, 136–139, 153–175, 202, 308.

Orfield, Olivia. *Death Trap.* Elgin, IL: Performance Publishing, 1979.

Mathilde
Countess, Ruler of Nevers (992–1028)

Mathilde was the daughter of Otto Guillaume, count of Burgundy and Nevers from 987 to 992. She married Seigneur of Maers, Moncearx, and Auxerre. They had a son, Renaud, who succeeded his mother as Count Renaud I of Auxerre and Nevers, on her death in 1028.

References

Egan, Edward W., Constance B. Hintz, and L. F. Wise, eds. *Kings, Rulers, and Statesmen.* New York: Sterling Publishing, 1976. p. 159.

Matilda
Abbess, Regent of Germany (996)

Matilda was the daughter of Otto the Great, Holy Roman emperor from 962 to 972, and Adelaide of Burgundy. Matilda was a sister of Otto II, emperor from 973 to 983. From 954 to 968 she was abbess of Quedlinburg. When her fifteen-year-old nephew, Otto III, went to Italy to receive his imperial crown in 996, he installed his very able aunt Matilda, described as "a woman of great wisdom and strength," as his regent.

References

Löwenstein, Prince Hubertus Zu. *A Basic History of Germany.* Bonn: Inter Nationes, 1964. p. 30.

Matilda

*Uncrowned Queen of England (1141), Regent of England (Intermittently
from 1154), Duchess of Normandy*

Matilda (or Empress Maud) was born in 1102, the only daughter of
King Henry I, ruler of England from 1100 to 1135, and Edith (also
called Matilda) of Scotland. Matilda was the grandaughter of
William the Conqueror. Fierce, proud, and cynical, she developed
an early, consuming interest in politics. In 1114, at the age of
twelve, she was married to Holy Roman emperor Henry V, who lost
her estates in his second campaign for expansion. The couple had no
children. In 1120 her brother William, heir to the English throne,
died, and in 1125 her husband died. Her father then recalled her to
England, naming her his heir and arranging her marriage to fourteen-year-old Godfrey Plantagenet, count of Anjou. She was
twenty-nine years old. In 1133 the couple had a son, Henry II, des-
tined to rule England from 1154 to 1189. She had two more sons,
Geoffrey and William.

When King Henry I died in 1135, her cousin Stephen of Blois,
son of Henry's sister Adela, usurped the throne in a sudden coup

d'état. It took Matilda four years to gather her supporters in France, but in 1139, she invaded England to claim her throne from the usurper. It was two years before her forces could capture Stephen and send him in chains to Bristol Castle. She was proclaimed *Domina Anglorum*, "lady of the English," and queen in April 1141, although she was not crowned at the time. But by November, her demands for money and her quarrels with the church had soured many of her supporters, who had second thoughts about crowning her. Hostility toward her mounted to such an extent that at one time she was forced to masquerade as a corpse to escape Stephen's supporters.

Eventually Stephen was set free, and Matilda was again obliged to elude her would-be captors, this time by wearing white so as to blend with the snow around Oxford Castle. Finally, after many battles and much intrigue, Matilda could see that she was beaten, and in 1148 she retired to Normandy. Her son Henry II acceded to the throne in 1154, and she ably performed her duties as regent for him during the first few years of his reign, for although he ruled for 34 years, he spent an aggregate of only 14 years in England. She died in 1167, having composed the words to appear on her tombstone: "Here lies Henry's daughter, wife and mother; great by birth, greater by marriage, greatest by motherhood."

References

Hudson, M. E., and Mary Clark. *Crown of a Thousand Years.* New York: Crown Publishers, 1978. pp. 26–27.

Stenton, Doris Mary. *English Society in the Early Middle Ages.* Harmondsworth, Middlesex: Penguin Books, 1965. pp. 35–36, 225.

Matilda
Princess, Ruler of Achaea (1313–1318)

Matilda (or Mathilde) was the daughter of Isabelle, ruler of Achaea from 1301 to 1307, when she was deposed by Philippe II (r. 1307–1313). When Philippe died, Matilda assumed the throne. Following her death in 1318, Robert, king of Naples, succeeded her.

References

Carpenter, Clive. *The Guinness Book of Kings, Rulers & Statesmen.* Enfield, Middlesex: Guinness Superlatives, 1978. p. 1.

Matilda of Flanders
Duchess, Regent of Normandy (ca. 1066–?)

Matilda of Flanders was the daughter of Count Baldwin (Beaudoin) V of Flanders and the wife of William I (later, the Conqueror), duke of Normandy. William based his claim for the throne of England on the fact that Matilda was a descendant of Alfred the Great. Her father was a descendant of Baldwin II, who married Alfred's daughter Aelfthryth. While William was conquering England (1066), Matilda ruled Normandy. The couple had four children: Robert Curthose, later duke of Normandy; William II Rufus (the Red), ruler of England (1087–1100); Adela, wife of Stephen II of Blois, ruler of England (1135–1154); and Henry I, ruler of England (1100–1135). Matilda died in 1083.

References
Duff, Charles. *England and the English*. New York: G. P. Putnam's Sons, 1955. p. 83.

Heer, Friedrich. *The Medieval World*. Trans. Janet Sondheimer. New York: Mentor/NAL, 1962. p. 318.

Previté-Orton, C. W. *The Shorter Cambridge Medieval History*. Vol. 1, *The Later Roman Empire to the Twelfth Century*. Cambridge: Cambridge University Press, 1982. pp. 382, 608.

Matilda of Tuscany
Duchess, Co-ruler of Central Italy (1071–1076), Sole Ruler (1076–1089)

Matilda of Tuscany was born in 1046, the daughter of Boniface of Canossa, marquis of Tuscany, and his wife, Beatrice. Matilda's father's assassination in 1052 and the deaths of her older brother and sister left her the sole heir of an enormous fortune, including the holdings amassed by her grandfather, Otto Adalbert, founder of the House of Attoni. In 1054 Beatrice married Godfrey the Bearded of Upper Lorraine, Emperor Henry III's most dangerous foe in Germany. In 1055 Henry arrested Beatrice and Matilda, age nine, sending them to Germany, while Godfrey fled. Later Henry and Godfrey became reconciled and released Beatrice and Matilda. Godfrey died in 1069, and Matilda married his son, Godfrey the Hunchback, and settled in Lorraine. In 1071 she lost her only child, so she returned to Italy, where she reigned with her mother until Beatrice's death in 1076.

Matilda then became sole ruler of a large, wealthy, and powerful domain. She remained all her life a powerful ally of the papacy. It was at her castle of Canossa that Emperor Henry IV stood barefoot in the snow for three days in order to receive absolution from the pope.

There were few aspects of Italian or papal life about which her wishes did not have to be considered. In 1089 Pope Urban II arranged a marriage between Matilda and Welf V, duke of Bavaria and Carinthia. She was forty-three and he only seventeen.

*Matilda of Tuscany
(Corbis-Bettmann)*

Henry IV, intent on enlarging his holdings, invaded northern Italy, but Matilda, with her vast resources, was able to hold out against him in the hills. After he had seized the crown of Italy, Matilda and Pope Urban convinced Henry IV's son Conrad to revolt against Henry (1093). Her death in 1115 created a furor, for in 1086 and 1102 she had donated her nonfeudal lands to the papacy, whereas her will named Henry IV's son and successor Henry V as the recipient. The resolution of the dilemma this caused was reached only after years of strife.

References
Duff, Nora. *Matilda of Tuscany.* London: Cambridge Press, 1909.
Langer, William L., ed. *World History.* Boston: Houghton Mifflin, 1980. pp. 221–223, 232–236, 314.
Painter, Sidney. *The Rise of the Feudal Monarchies.* Westport, CT: Greenwood Press, 1982. pp. 103–104.
Previté-Orton, C. W. *The Shorter Cambridge Medieval History.* Vol. 1, *The Later Roman Empire to the Twelfth Century.* Cambridge: Cambridge University Press, 1982. pp. 457, 485, 491, 494, 496, 497.

Maud, Empress
See Matilda (Uncrowned Queen of England)

Mavia
Queen of the Saracens (ca. 370–380)

Mavia (or Mawia) was married to the king of the Saracens, a Bedouin tribe living in the area around the Sinai Peninsula. When her husband died, Mavia succeeded him. She organized raids against Rome's eastern frontier into Phoenicia and Palestine. Riding at the head of her army, she defeated a Roman army and made peace only on the condition that a certain hermit named Moses be forcibly consecrated as bishop of her tribe. Her daughter was married to the Roman commander-in-chief, Victor, a Samaritan from across the Danube. In 378 Mavia sent her Arab cavalry to aid the Romans in defending Constantinople; its shockingly bloodthirsty mode of fighting intimidated even the Goths. She is probably the person described elsewhere as Mawia, queen of Syria, possibly a Ghassanid. Ghassar was an Arabian kingdom bounded on the northeast by the Euphrates River and extending into the Sinai Peninsula.

References
Bowder, Diana, ed. *Who Was Who in the Roman World*. Ithaca, NY: Cornell University Press, 1980. pp. 335, 575.

Mawa
Leader of Zulu Political Refugees (ca. 1842–1848)

Mawa was born ca. 1770, the youngest sister of regent Mnkabayi and of Senzangakhona, who became the father of three Zulu kings. During the reigns of two of her nephews, Shaka (r. ca. 1815–1828) and Dingane (r. 1828–1840), she served as royal liaison in a British military town. In 1840 another nephew ousted Dingane and, in ca. 1842, had his brother Gqugqa assassinated. Mawa, who apparently had supported Gqugqa's bid for the throne, fled with several thousand followers to Natal. There she gathered additional supporters and eventually negotiated a treaty with the new British administration to settle permanently in Natal. She died in 1848.

References
Bryant, A. T. *Olden Times in Zululand and Natal*. London: Longman Green, 1929.

Mawia
See Mavia

McAleese, Mary
President of Ireland (1997–)

Mary McAleese was born in 1951 in Belfast, Northern Ireland, the first of nine children in a Catholic family. Her father owned a pub in the Falls area of Belfast, but the family lost both business and home during sectarian violence in the 1970s. At that time the family moved to Rostrevo in County Down.

She studied law at Queen's University in Belfast, receiving LL.B. (1973), M.A., M.I.L., and F.R.S.A. degrees. After studying to be a barrister, in 1974 she began practice in Belfast, primarily criminal and family law. In 1975, at age twenty-four, she moved to Dublin to accept the post as Reid Professor of Criminal Law, Criminology, and Penology at Trinity College.

In 1976 she married Martin McAleese, a former athlete who trained as an accountant in Dublin. In 1980 he went back to Trinity College to study dentistry. The couple had three children: Emma (1982) and twins Sara Mai and Justin (1985). In 1987, when Martin set up practice in County Armagh, the family moved to Rostrevor, County Down. In 1987 Mary McAleese was appointed director of the Institute of Professional Legal Studies, a department of Queen's University. In 1994 she was made pro vice-chancellor of Queen's. She was the first female to hold one of the three pro vice-chancellor positions.

In 1997 Ireland's popular president Mary Robinson announced that she would not seek reelection but would accept a post as the United Nations commissioner on human rights. Among the candidates to replace her were Mary McAleese, a professed devout Roman Catholic and nationalist, and Mary Banotti, a member of the European Parliament and political party Fianna Fail. Despite a smear campaign suggesting pro–Sinn Fein leanings, with a surprising show of voter strength Mary McAleese was elected the eighth president of Ireland, the first native of Northern Ireland ever to win an election in the Irish Republic.

Following her sweeping win, McAleese declared the dawn of "the true age of the Irish" and said she hoped her victory would help banish guerrilla strife from Ireland. Promising that hers would be a bridge-building presidency, to help end the sectarian conflict between Catholics and Protestants, she said, "I hope we may find our way back to a spirit of mutual generosity." One of her first gestures of religious healing, which she described as an attempt to improve Catholic-Protestant relations, was to receive communion at a Protestant service in Dublin. A Northern Ireland Catholic priest and an archbishop declared that she had violated church law, and the papal nuncio in Dublin was reported to have informed the Vatican.

The Irish president does not exercise executive power. She has only a limited political role. She appoints all seven judges to the supreme court, signs and promulgates bills passed by parliament, and on the advice of the prime minister she summons and dissolves parliament, although in some circumstances she may refuse a dissolution. Her post is largely ceremonial. McAleese has described her most important function as building bridges between people.

References

Casey, Patricia. "President Defies Media Stereotypes." *Irish Times* "Opinion." 16 December 1997: 1.

Clarity, James F. "In Ireland, Gesture of Religious Healing Inflames the Faithful." *New York Times.* 21 December 1997: 10Y.

Graham, William. "McAleese Triumphs over Rivals to Take Presidency." *Irish News.* 16 October 1997: 1.

Honore, Carl. "Battle Lines Begin to Fade across Northern Ireland." *Houston Chronicle.* 16 November 1997: 25A.

"Presidential Election Home Page" Worldwide Web, December 1997.

Mehr-n-Nesā
See Nūr Jahān

Mei
Queen of Cambodia (1835–1847)

Mei, the daughter of King Ang Chan (r. 1797–1835), came to the throne upon her father's death. At the time Cambodia was a vassal of Vietnam, so Mei exercised very little power during her twelve-year reign. In 1847 she was deposed in favor of Ang Duang, son of former king Ang Eng. She died in 1875.

References

Morby, John E. *Dynasties of the World.* Oxford: Oxford University Press, 1989. p. 231.

Meir, Golda
Premier of Israel
(1969–1974)

Golda Meir was born Goldie Mabovitch in 1898 in Kiev, Russia, to Moshe Mabovitz and his wife. To escape persecution, the family migrated in 1906 to Milwaukee, Wisconsin, where Golda's father became a railroad worker and her mother a grocery clerk. Golda attended Milwaukee Teachers Training College. She joined the Poale Zion, a faction of the Labor Zionists Party. In 1917 she married Morris Myerson, a sign painter she had met while visiting her sister in Denver. In 1921 she persuaded her husband to emigrate to Palestine and live in a kibbutz. In 1924, after their first child was born, they moved to Jerusalem, where Morris worked as a bookeeper and Golda took in laundry. They had another child, born in Jerusalem.

By 1929 Golda had immersed herself in the Zionist movement, quickly becoming a leader. During World War II she emerged as a forceful spokesperson to the British in behalf of Zionism. Her husband hated his life in Israel, but Golda was possessed by her mission. In 1945 they were divorced; he died in Tel Aviv in 1951. Golda was a signer of Israel's Proclamation of Independence, and in 1948, during the war for independence, Golda traveled to the United States to raise $50 million for the cause. In 1949 she was elected to the legislature, where she served for twenty-five years; prime minister David Ben-Gurion called her "the only man in the cabinet." In 1956, at Ben-Gurion's suggestion, she Hebraized her name to Golda Meir.

In 1969 she became Israel's fourth prime minister. Meir faced both the hostility of Israel's neighbors, necessitating a huge defense budget in a struggling economy, and mass disunity, not only within her own Labor party but in the country as a whole, which was a mixture of occidental and oriental Jews. In 1974, after the outbreak of the fourth Arab-Israeli War late the year before, she was forced to resign, although she continued to work in politics. Her private life and her political career had been ones of constant struggle, but her ability to see humor in the bitterest of moments helped her to keep her perspective. She once said, "Can you imagine Moses dragging us forty years through the desert to bring us to the one place in the Middle East where there is no oil?" When she died in 1978 at the age of eighty, it was discovered that she had had leukemia for twelve years.

References

Avallone, Michael. *A Woman Called Golda*. New York: Leisure Books, 1982.

Meir, Golda. *My Life*. New York: G. P. Putnam's Sons, 1975.

Melisende
Queen of Jerusalem (1131–1152)

Melisende (or Melissande) was the eldest of four daughters of Queen Morphia (the daughter of Gabriel of Melitene) and King Baldwin II, ruler of Jerusalem from 1118 to 1131. Before Melisende's marriage, her chief companion was Hugh of Le Puiset, lord of Jaffy, a tall, handsome man who had lived in the court as a boy. In 1129 her parents married her to Fulk V, who was short, wiry, red-faced, and middle-aged; she never cared for him.

After she and Fulk ascended to the throne following her father's death in 1131, she continued her intimate friendship with Hugh, now married to an older woman, Emma, widow of Eustace I of Sidon. Fulk grew jealous, and soon the court was divided between Count Hugh and the king. Emma's son, to protect his mother's honor, challenged Hugh to a duel. Hugh did not appear for the duel, a sign of his cowardice and his guilt. Sometime soon afterward, supporters of either Fulk or Emma, the aggrieved parties, stabbed Hugh, but he did not die. Because Fulk was suspected of being behind the plot to kill Hugh, when the would-be assassin was caught, Fulk arranged for a public execution. The assassin had his limbs cut off one by one, but while his head remained, he was to continue to repeat his confession. Melisende was still so angry over the incident that for many months afterward Hugh's enemies and even Fulk himself feared for their lives.

Melisende had several children by Fulk, but only two survived: Baldwin III, born in 1130, who ruled from 1143 to 1162; and Amalric I, born in 1136, who ruled from 1162 to 1174. In 1143 Fulk died, thrown from a horse while on a family picnic. Melisende appointed her older son, Baldwin, as her colleague and assumed the government herself. When Baldwin reached the age of twenty-two, he wanted to rule alone, but Melisende, conscious of her own hereditary right, declined to hand over the power to him completely. She made arrangement for his coronation with the stipulation that she would be crowned again by his side so that her joint authority would be specifically honored. However, Baldwin secretly changed the date of the coronation and was crowned without her. The act created dissention between supporters of each side, but Melisende, striken at her own son's perfidy, yielded to him and retired from politics. She died in 1161.

References
Runciman, Steven. *A History of the Crusades.* Vol. 2, *The Kingdom of Jerusalem.* Cambridge: Cambridge University Press, 1952, 1987. pp. 177–178, 185–187, 191–193, 231–236, 247, 279–283, 311, 333–337, 360–161.

Mentewab
Empress/Regent of Ethiopia (1730–1769)

Mentewab (or Mantuab) was born Walata Giorgis or Berhan Mogasa and claimed descent in part from Portuguese settlers who had come to Ethiopia during the reign of Galawdewos (ca. 1522–1559). In the 1720s she became the wife of Emperor Baqaffa (Bakaffa), who ruled Ethiopia from 1721 to 1730. During his reign she watched over the reestablishment of Christianity in the southern provinces, a duty she was to continue for the rest of her life.

When Baqaffa died in 1730, she served as regent during the minority of her son Iyasu II. When Iyasu came of age, he showed little interest in government, so she continued to wield power, promoting various relatives into positions of influence and angering much of the nobility. With Mentewab, Iyasu had the splendid Abbey of Kusquan built. To free himself of his mother's rule, he married the daughter of one of the Gallas chiefs and introduced Gallas warriors into the capital. When Iyasu died in 1755, Mentewab helped to bring her infant grandson, Ioyas, to the throne and again served as regent. During the reign of Ioyas, who ruled from 1755 to 1769, a rival faction arose headed by Mikael Sehul. Sehul had Ioyas assassinated in 1769, removed Mentewab, and put Tekle-Haimanot II on the throne. She retired to Gojjam and later met a Scottish explorer, who wrote about her life.

References
Budge, E. A. *A History of Ethiopia.* London: Methuen, 1928. pp. 221–222.
Egan, Edward W., Constance B. Hintz, and L. F. Wise, eds. *Kings, Rulers, and Statesmen.* New York: Sterling Publishing, 1976, p. 130.
Lipschutz, Mark R., and R. Kent Rasmussen. *Dictionary of African Historical Biography.* Berkeley: University of California Press, 1989. p. 145.

Meryit-Net
*Queen, Ruler of Egypt
(ca. 300 B.C.)*

According to the ancient historian Manetho, cited in Emery, it was during the reign of Neteren that it was decided that women might occupy the throne; however, there is evidence that has convinced some historians to suppose that Meryit-Nct ("beloved of Neith") (or Merneith) was the successor of Zir (Djer) and possibly the third sovereign of the First Dynasty. She was likely Djer's daughter, the wife and apparent co-ruler of his successor Wadjit and the mother of Den, the fourth king of the dynasty.

Since among the royal ladies of the dynasty, Meryet-Nit is the only one to have great monuments both at Abydos and Sakkara adjacent to those of kings, it could be surmised that she herself was a reigning monarch. Her Abydos monument is one of the largest and best built of all.

References

Emery, W. B. *Archaic Egypt.* New York: Viking Penguin, 1987. pp. 32, 65, 66, 68, 69, 94, 126.

Grimal, Nicolas. *A History of Ancient Egypt.* Trans. Basil Blackwell Ltd. New York: Barnes & Noble Books, 1997. pp. 50, 52.

Mfalma Fatima
Ruler of Pate in East Africa (early 18th c.)

Pate is an island off the coast of Kenya, part of the Lamu archipelago. Pate is also the name of the town on the island. From 1652 forward, Pate became the center of resistance to Portuguese rule and maintained its preeminence in the Lamu islands for more than a century and a half. During that time the rulers of Pate frequently called on the Imān of Oman for assistance in combating the Portuguese.

In 1696, in answer to an appeal from Pate, the Imān of Oman attacked Mombasa with a fleet of over 3,000 men. In 1698 Sayf ibn Sultān brought about a Portuguese surrender, ousting the Europeans from Fort Jesus, the great Mombasan castle.

However, soon the Omani developed imperial ambitions and attempted to dominate the Swahili seacoast and monopolize ocean-borne commerce. In 1727 Pate, anxious to preserve its independence, switched allegiance and joined with the Portuguese to oust the Omani.

It was during this period that Mfalma Fatima ruled Pate. Two of her letters, written in Swahili, are among a collection of fourteen, dating between 1711 and 1729, preserved in the Historical Archives of Goa. Portuguese translation describes her only as "a female ruler of Pate."

References

Biersteker, Ann, and Mark Plane. "Swahili Manuscripts and the Study of Swahili Literature." *Research in African Literature* 20, no. 3 (Fall 1989): 449–472 (specifically 468).

Davidson, Basil. *African History.* New York: Collier/Macmillan Publishing, 1991. p. 196.

Mtoro bin Mwinyi Babari. *The Customs of the Swahili People. The Desturi za Waswahili.* Ed. and trans. J. W. T. Allen. Berkeley: University of California Press, 1981. pp. 305, 307.

Min

Queen, Twenty-fifth Regent Ruler of Yi Dynasty in Chosŏn (Korea)
(1873–1882 and 1882–1895)

The Yi Dynasty, with twenty-six monarchs, ruled Korea until the Japanese annexation in 1910. During the first ten years (1864–1874) of the reign of King Kojong, usually known as Yi T'ae Wang, power was in the hands of his father, Taewŏn-gun, who was first driven out in 1873 by Confucian officials whom he had antagonized and by the powerful Min family. Although Taewŏn-gun had arranged for Kojong's marriage to a member of the Yohung Min clan, this wife, Queen Min (or Bin) used the occasion of a public denunciation of Taewŏn-gun to end his regency.

Power then passed to Min, who at first opposed all efforts at modernizing or westernizing Korea. But after an expedition to Japan by Korean fact-finders resulted in the adoption of a policy of enlightenment that would establish ties with Japan and Western powers, which the Confucian literati opposed, Taewŏn-gun's popularity began to rise again. He made plans to return to power, and in 1881 he determined to put his eldest son Yi Chae-son, born of a secondary wife, on Kojong's throne. He also planned to eliminate the advocates of enlightenment. The plot was uncovered, however, and although

Taewŏn-gun was not prosecuted, Yi Chae-son and more than thirty of his followers were put to death.

Taewŏn-gun was now pitted against Queen Min as the country reacted violently to the expansion of Japanese influence in Korea. In 1882 a mutiny by old-line soldiers resulted in an attack on the Japanese legation, and the building was burned to the ground. The soldiers next invaded the palace, and Queen Min escaped assassination by hiding. To quell the violence, King Kojong had no choice but to recall Taewŏn-gun to power. His return was a vote for a policy of exclusion, but now both Japan and China vied for power over Korean affairs. When Taewŏn-gun paid a courtesy call to Chinese headquarters, he was kidnapped (1882) and taken to Tientsin in China. A coup in 1884 resulted in the progressives pressing for his return, not because they favored his policies but because they needed his help in overcoming the entrenched influence of Queen Min's family. Eventually, Kojong and the Min oligarchs could only maintain power by enlisting foreign support.

Min was characterized as "the one vital ruling spark in the effete Korean court." She was assassinated in 1895 in a plot engineered with the connivance of the Japanese resident, Viscount Miura, because she was suspected of being the mastermind behind the anti-Japanese attitude of the Korean government.

References

Bergamini, David. *Japan's Imperial Conspiracy*. New York: William Morrow, 1972. pp. 282–283.

Langer, William L., ed. *World History*. Boston: Houghton Mifflin, 1940, 1980. pp. 916–917, 922.

Lee, Ki-baik. *A New History of Korea*. Trans. Edward W. Wagner with Edward J. Schulz. Cambridge: Harvard University Press, 1984. pp. 268, 273–274, 278, 281, 294, 295, 300, 316.

Mnkabayi
Regent Ruler of the Zulus (ca. 1780s)

Described as the most important political figure in Zululand, Mnkabayi (Mkabayi, Mkhabayi) was born a Zulu princess ca. 1760. She was the older sister of the future Zulu chief Senzangakhona, for whom she served as regent after their father died. She remained single in order to retain her political independence and her influence over her brother. Shortly before he ascended to the throne, Senzangakhona disgraced himself by impregnating his lover, Nandi, before their wedding, but he married her anyway, and she bore a son, Shaka (ca. 1787). The Zulu chief married others and had other sons, who would eventually succeed him. His harsh treatment of Nandi and Shaka, however, caused them to leave. Mnkabayi remained friendly with Nandi, and following Senzangakhona's death in ca. 1815, Mnkabayi encouraged Shaka to return and seize power from his half-brother Sigujana, which he did. In 1827 Nandi died, and Mnkabayi is believed to have blamed Shaka for her death. She encouraged two other nephews, Dingane and Mhlangana, to assassinate him. Later she persuaded Dingane to eliminate Mhlangana as well.

Mnkabayi was last reported alive in 1835. At the time she was said to be extremely old.

References

Kunene, Mazisi. *Emperor Shaka the Great*. Trans. Mazisi Kunene. London: Heinemann Educational Books, 1979.

Lipschutz, Mark R., and R. Kent Rasmussen. *Dictionary of African Historical Biography*. Berkeley: University of California Press, 1986.

Mo-ki-lien, Khatun of
Regent of Mongolia (734–741)

Although the name of this Turkish queen did not survive, we know that she was married to Turkish khan Mo-ki-lien, who ruled in Mongolia starting in 716 and who was poisoned by his minister in 724. The couple had a son, Yi-jan, who succeeded his father and for whom the khatun served as regent. When Yi-jan died, Mo-ki-lien's younger brother, Tängri khagan, took the throne, also as a minor, and Mo-ki-lien's widow continued to serve as regent and adviser until Tängri khagan's death in 741.

References

Grousset, René. *The Empire of the Steppes*. Trans. Naomi Walford. New Brunswich, NJ: Rutgers University Press, 1970. p. 69.

Mother of the King of Kongo
Queen, Ruler of Mpemba Kazi (ca. 12th c.?)

Long before the Kongo coalesced into a kingdom in the fourteenth century, there is a tradition as to its beginnings. Although this queen carried the title "Mother of the King of Kongo," she may or may not have been the queen-mother of Mbene, founder of the Kongo kings, but she was doubtless the strongest person and the one whom Mbene (Motinobene or Mutinu Mbene) most trusted.

With ambitions to expand his area of influence, Mbene married the daughter of ManiKabungo and set about founding a dynasty. He conquered all the indigenous chiefs in the area except Mbata, with

whom he made an alliance. In the future all Kongo kings were to marry daughters of the ManiMbata.

Mbene established his first capital at Mpemba Kazi. As he sought to enlarge his territory, it became his custom to conquer one area, then leave a local ruler in charge and move on. When he moved farther south to M'banza Congo, he left the queen to rule at the old capital, giving her the title "Mother of the King of Kongo."

References

de Villiers, Marq, and Sheila Hirtle. *Into Africa.* Toronto: Key Porter Books, 1997. p. 159.

Mout
Queen of the Sudan
(fl. 730 B.C.)

Mout is mentioned in accounts of the life of Egyptian commander Taharqa (Khunefertemre Taharqa, the Biblical Tirhakah, r. 689–664 B.C.), who led the Egyptian forces into Asia against the Assyrian Sennachirib. Queen Mout was married to King Piankhi of Sudan (ca. 751–716 B.C.), who laid the foundation for his brother Shabaka to found the Twenty-fifth Egyptian Dynasty by invading and subduing the various rebel forces in Lower Egypt. Taharqa was the youngest son of Mout and Piankhi. After Piankhi's death, Shabaka became pharaoh of Egypt. After Shabaka died in 701 B.C., his nephew

Shabataka became pharaoh. In 689 B.C., Taharqa had Shabataka assassinated and ascended the throne, proclaiming himself the son of Mout, queen of the Sudan, and erecting a temple in her honor.

References

Diop, Cheikh Anta. *The African Origin of Civilization.* Trans. Mercer Cook. Chicago: Lawrence Hill Books, Chicago Review Press, 1974.

Mujaji I, II, III, IV
"Rain Queen" of the Lovedu in South Africa (19th–20th Centuries)

The Lovedu (Lobedu) are a Bantu-speaking people of the northern Transvaal. Mujaji is the dynastic title of the female rulers. According to legend, King Mugodo's father, to deceive people, had treated his son with disrespect in public but privately had taught him the secrets of the tribe's rain charms. When Mugodo came to the throne, his people refused to respect him because of his own father's apparent disrespect, and his reign ended in confusion, ushering in the reign of queens. Mugodo went to one daughter with a plan to save the kingdom by fathering a child by her, but she refused his proposal, which she considered a sin. He then went to his next daughter, Mujaji, who agreed to give birth to an heir to the throne, with Mugodo as the father. She gained ascendancy while Mugodo was still on the throne, but she remained in seclusion, and the people began to believe in her great wisdom and immortality. They called her "white-faced," "radiant as the sun," and "one who gives water to wash the face." Word of her powers spread south to the Zulus and north to the Sothos, both of which sent emissaries bearing gifts to the great queen.

Mujaji II's reign was less successful. When Zulus invaded her land, she attempted to conjure a drought to destroy them. White Europeans came next, encroaching on her territory, desecrating the tribe's holy places. She went into seclusion and induced a half-sister to present herself as "she who must be obeyed." Her ploy did not keep the Europeans at bay, and in 1894, despondent, she took poison and died.

The Europeans had discovered Mujaji II's deception and, to punish the Lovedu, refused to recognize the next queen, Mujaji III, until the bogus "she who must be obeyed" had died. Still, it was only Mujaji who inherited the secret medicines and objects for making rain and for denying it to their enemies, and so her people recognized her as their divinely ordained ruler, although they did not rebel against their overlords. The Lovedu, a peaceful people, practice the ideals of cooperativeness and reciprocity.

Mujaji IV, the current queen, is called "transformer of clouds" and functions more as a rainmaker than a monarch. With the assistance of her rain doctor, who uses medicine to help remove the forces that occasionally block the queen's powers, she guarantees the cycle of the seasons, bringing rain throughout the year. Her health is of utmost importance to the tribe. During times of great drought, people bring gifts and long dances are performed. Mujaji's ability to control the rain depends on cooperation from her ancestors, whose skins she uses in her rain pots.

References

Krige, E. J., and J. D. Krige. *The Realm of a Rain-Queen.* London: Oxford University Press, 1943.

Parrinder, Geoffrey. *African Mythology.* New York: Peter Bedrick Books, 1982. pp. 120–121.

Munjŏng, Queen Dowager
Regent of Chosŏn Dynasty in Korea (1545–?)

Munjŏng was the strong-willed wife of King Chungjong (r. 1506–1544), who was succeeded by his eldest son, Imjong, by a different wife. Imjong was favored by the Neo-Confucian literati. However, in a purge by a rival, more traditional political faction known as the Meritorius Elite, the new king was killed, and Queen Munjŏng's eleven-year-old son Myŏngjong (r. 1545–1567) was brought to the throne with the queen dowager as regent. Her intention was to reestablish the country's traditional social and religious practices.

During her regency the famous monk Pou was given important responsibilities in encouraging and revitalizing Buddhism, which had been declining as Confucianism had become more influential. The temple Pongun-sa was made the main temple of the Son (Zen) School of Buddhism and of the Textual School. In 1552 the "monk examination" was reinstituted. But with Munjŏng's death, Buddhism again went into decline and became a faith practiced primarily by women.

References

Lee, Ki-baik. *A New History of Korea.* Trans. Edward W. Wagner with Edward J. Schulz. Cambridge: Harvard University Press, 1984. pp. 199–200, 206, 394.

Myōjō-tennō
Empress of Japan (1629–1643)

Myōjō-tennō (or Myōshō or Meishō) was born in 1623, the daughter of Emperor Go-Mi-no-o, who ruled Japan from 1612 to 1629, and his consort Tōfuku-mon-in (Tokugawa Kazu-ko), who was the sister of Shōgun Iemitsu. Myōjō's father abdicated when she reached the age of six, and she succeeded him. During her reign, the power was primarily in the hands of her uncle, Shōgun Iemetsu. She abdicated in 1643 in favor of her brother, Go-Kōomyō, and lived in retirement for fifty-three years. She died in 1696.

References

Papinot, E. *Historical and Geographical Dictionary of Japan.* Rutland, VT: Charles E. Tuttle, 1972. pp. 124, 417.

Myōshō

See Myōjō-tennō

Myriam

Sultana of the Maldive Islands (1379–1383)

The Maldive Islands are located in the Indian Ocean, southwest of the southern tip of India. Myriam was the middle daughter of Sultan Salah al-Din Salih Albendjaly, ruler of the Maldives. When the father died, Myriam's young brother Shihab-ud-din became king. But their mother married the vizier 'Abdallah, who overpowered the young king and took over the reins of government. Later 'Abdallah married Myriam's older sister, Khadija, after her first husband died. Khadija then reigned for thirty-three years and died in 1379. Myriam succeeded her sister to the throne, where she remained until 1383. Her husband occupied the post as vizier. The couple had a daughter, Fatima, who succeeded her mother in 1383.

References

Mernissi, Fatima. *The Forgotten Queens of Islam.* Trans. Mary Jo Lakeland. Minneapolis: University of Minnesota Press, 1993.

Nandi
Queen Mother of the Zulus (ca. 1815–1827)

Nandi was born ca. 1760, a member of the Langeni tribe in South Africa. In ca. 1787 she had an illicit affair with Zulu chief Senzangakhona and became pregnant. Although pregnancy out of wedlock was considered a tribal disgrace, the king nevertheless married her, and she bore a son, Shaka. The Zulu people treated Nandi and Shaka badly and forced her out of the capital, so she took her son and returned to her people, who treated her no better. She then took Shaka to the Mthethwa people, where he grew to manhood and served in the army of Chief Dingiswayo, rising to a high position.

When Zulu chief Senzangakhona died in ca. 1815, Shaka returned to claim his throne. Nandi, as queen mother, wreaked retribution on those who had previously mistreated her. Shaka, the empire builder, was frequently absent during military maneuvers. He never married, so Nandi exercised full authority during his absence. She remained the king's most important influence until her death in 1927. When she died, Shaka and the entire nation went into protracted mourning: "a fearful mourning exploded throughout the land." The king called in his counselors and told them: "There have been two rulers in Zululand: One gentle, who excelled in her kindness and generosity. . . . Such duality has never been known in all history."

References
Clarke, Prof. John Henrik. "Time of Troubles." In Alvin M. Josephy, Jr., ed. *The Horizon History of Africa.* New York: American Heritage Publishing, McGraw-Hill, 1971. pp. 374–375.
Kunene, Mazisi. *Emperor Shaka the Great.* London: Heinemann, 1979. pp. 2ff.–422.
Lipshutz, Mark. R., and R. Kent Rasmussen. *Dictionary of African Biography.* Berkeley: University of California Press, 1986. p. 169.

Naqi'a
Regent of Assyria (ca. 689 B.C.)

Confusion exists over the identity of the builder queen whom Herodotus called Nitocris. Because of the building activity associated with Naqi'a, she has mistakenly been identified as the Nitocris of whom Herodotus wrote. However, that "queen" was probably either Addagoppe, who was never a queen at all, or Sammuramat. Naqi'a was the wife of Sennacherib, who ruled Assyria from 705 to 681 B.C., when, according to the biblical account (II Kings 19: 37), he was murdered in Babylon by two of his sons. One of these sons, called Adrammelech in the Bible, has now been identified as Arad-Mulissi. Naqi'a's name indicates that she was probably either Jewish or Armaean.

In ca. 700 B.C. Sennacherib and Naqi'a transformed the capital city of Nineveh into a city of unparalleled splendor, building for themselves an eighty-room palace to overlook it. To water the botanical gardens and orchards surrounding the palace, the king constructed major irrigation works. In 689 B.C., after having defended the city of Babylon several times, Sennacherib sacked it. Naqi'a may have served as regent during his absences on military campaign, for in the old Assyrian capital Ashur, among the steles devoted to kings, one of three devoted to women was for a "lady of Sennacherib." Presumably this refers to his queen, although the title is now lost.

One of her sons—not one of the patricides—was a younger son, Esarhaddon, who had been picked by his father to succeed him. Esarhaddon ruled ca. 680 to 669/670 B.C. Sennacherib was murdered while Esarhaddon was far away on the field of battle, possibly so that one of his brothers could claim the throne. Esarhaddon had to rush home to fight to win his crown. Presumably with Naqi'a's help, Esarhaddon rebuilt the city of Babylon, which his father had destroyed, and placed it under the rule of his son, Shamash-shum-ukin. In 670 B.C. Esarhaddon was killed while on campaign to Egypt, and his other son, Ashurbanipa, ascended (669 B.C.).

References

Fairservis, Walter A., Jr. *The Ancient Kingdoms of the Nile.* New York: Mentor/NAL, 1962. pp. 182–187.

Saggs, H.W.F. *The Might That Was Assyria.* London: Sidgwick and Jackson, 1984. p. 79, 98–99.

White, J. E. Manchip. *Ancient Egypt: Its Culture and History.* New York: Dover Publications, 1970. pp. 188, 192.

Naryshkina, Natalya Kirillovna
Queen-mother, De Facto Ruler of Russia (1689–1694)

A member of the influential Naryshkin family, Natalya Kirillovna (Nathalie) was educated by a guardian, Artamon Sergeyevich Matveyev, in Western ways. She had a powerful brother, the boyar, Leo Naryshkin. She became the second wife of Tsar Alexis and had a son, Peter (Peter I the Great). Tsar Alexis died in 1676 when Peter was only four years old. The tsar was succeeded by Peter's half brother, Fyodor III, although his mother's relatives, the Miloslavskys, held ultimate power. After Fyodor died in 1682 without leaving an heir, Peter was first named tsar over his feeble-minded half brother Ivan, but after a revolt by the Miloslavsky faction, the two brothers were proclaimed co-tsars, with Peter's twenty-five-year-old half sister Sofya as regent.

Sofya went to great lengths to keep Peter and Natalya at a distance from power; in fact, they lived in some fear for Peter's safety in the village of Preobrazhenskoye. There, Peter received a much more liberal education than he would have received in the confines of the palace. In 1689, in an attempt to show the world that Peter was old enough to govern, Queen Natalya arranged a political marriage for her seventeen-year-old son with Yevdokiya Fyodorovna Lopukhina (Eudoxia). However, Peter had no interest in his wife and later banished her to a convent. When an attempted coup by Sofya's adherents was uncovered, Peter and the Naryshkins removed Sofya as regent and sent her to a Moscow convent. When the coup failed, Peter was at last acknowledged.

Ivan V was still nominally a joint ruler, and Peter, at seventeen, showed no inclination to take personal charge of the government. The direction of the state fell into the hands of Natalya, her brother Leo, and Patriarch Joachim. After Joachim's death in 1690, Patriarch Hadrian also assumed some power. During that time, with Natalya assuming a role as acting regent, Muscovite isolationism and suspicion of anything foreign again flourished. But when Natalya died in 1694, Peter I, at age twenty-two, finally assumed the reins of government.

References
Riasnovsky, Nicholas V. *A History of Russia.* Oxford: Oxford University Press, 1863, 1993. pp. 213–216.

Nefrusobek
Last Queen of the Theban Twelfth Dynasty, Egypt (ca. 1790/1787–1785/1783 B.C.)

Nefrusobek (also Sebekkare, Sebeknefru, Skemiophris, or Sobekne-feru ["the beauty of Sobek"]) was the daughter of Amenemhet (Ammenemes) III who ruled from ca. 1844/1842 to 1797 B.C., and the half-sister of Amenemhet (Ammenemes or Aman-m-he) IV, who succeeded his father at an elderly age after his father's forty-five-year reign. When her brother died approximately a decade after ascending to the throne, the absence of a male heir made Nefrusobek the next in line of succession.

She ruled as king and full pharaoh but did not attempt to depict herself as a man, as did Queen Hatshepsut (Eighteenth Dynasty). In Nefrusobek's titulature, she was described, for the first time in Egyptian history, as a woman-pharaoh. Her father had enabled a long period of peace and prosperity for Egypt. Although White termed her "insignificant," she did maintain the peaceful and prosperous rule set by her predecessors, until she was ready to choose a successor. The kingship was inherited through the daughter of the monarch. In order to preserve the royal succession within the same family, the custom was adopted of having the oldest son of the king marry his oldest sister, which Amenemhet had done. Since he died childless, Nefrusobek was privileged to select the next king by marrying him.

She was expected to marry a member of the Theban nobility and elevate him to the throne, but she had other ideas. Instead, she married a commoner from Lower Egypt. Her choice so enraged the citizenry that civil war broke out, since the northerners believed that they were far superior to the southerners. However, the sides were too evenly matched, and no one could gain a decisive victory. While this senseless war raged on, a tribe of nomads from Asia, the Hyskos ("shepherd kings") invaded and took over. Nefrusobek died ca. 1783 B.C., and the Twelfth Dynasty ended.

References
Grimal, Nicolas. *A History of Ancient Egypt.* Trans. Basil Blackwell Ltd. New York: Barnes & Noble Books, 1997. pp. 118, 171, 179, 182, 391.

Jackson, John G. *Introduction to African Civilization.* Secaucus, NJ: Citadel Press, 1970. pp. 107–108.

Rawlinson, George. *Ancient History.* New York: Barnes & Noble Books, 1993. p. 60.

White, J. E. *Ancient Egypt: Its Culture and History.* New York: Dover Publishing, 1970. p. 158.

Nicole
Duchess, Ruler of Lorraine (1624–1625)

Nicole (or Nicola) was the daughter of Henry II, duke of Lorraine, who ruled from 1608 to 1624. She became duchess of Lorraine upon her father's death in 1624. That same year she married her cousin Charles (later Charles IV, r. 1625–1634), son of her father's brother Francis II of Vaudémont. Francis, in a neat bit of finagling, arranged the marriage in order to wrest the duchy out of her control. The following year Francis abolished female succession so that he himself could be proclaimed duke. He then abdicated in favor of his son Charles IV (sometimes called Charles III). Nicole died in 1657.

References
Britannica Micropaedia. Vol. 2. Chicago: Encyclopaedia Britannica Press, 1983. p. 758.

Egan, Edward W., Constance B. Hintz, and L. F. Wise, eds. *Kings, Rulers, and Statesmen.* New York: Sterling Publishing, 1976. p. 128.

Morby, John E. *Dynasties of the World.* Oxford: Oxford University Press, 1989. p. 158.

Nitocris
Queen of Egypt (ca. 2475 B.C.)

Although no archaeological evidence has survived of the reign of Nitocris, the Turin Canon lists her as the last ruler of the Sixth Dynasty and the wife of Merenre II, whom she succeeded. She was the first known queen to exercise political power over Egypt. She is associated with the legendary courtesan Phodopis, mythical builder of the third pyramid of Giza. Herodotus (b. ca. 484 B.C.), who traveled in Egypt after 454 B.C. and received much of his information from word of mouth, tells of an Egyptian queen, Nitocris. To avenge the murder of her brother-king, whom she succeeded, she built a huge underground chamber. As an inaugural ceremony she held a banquet and invited all those responsible for her brother's death. When the banquet was in full swing, she opened a large concealed conduit and allowed her guests to drown in river water. To escape her punishment, she threw herself into a roomful of ashes. No other source supports Herodotus's account.

References
Grimal, Nicolas. *A History of Ancient Egypt.* Trans. Basil Blackwell Ltd. New York: Barnes & Noble Books, 1997. p. 89.

Herodotus. *The Histories.* Trans. Aubrey de Sélincourt. New York: Penguin Books, 1954. p. 166.

Nitocris
See Addagoppe of Harran

Ntombe Twala
Queen Regent of Swaziland (1983–1986); iNlovukazi,
or Ndlovukazi (Queen Mother) (1986–)

Swaziland is a landlocked independent kingdom bounded on three sides by South Africa and on the east by Mozambique. Ntombe Twala (or Thwala) was the mother of king designate, Prince Mokhesetive (b. 1968) and a junior wife of King Sobhuza II. When the king died in 1982, his senior wife, Queen Dzeliwe, was to act as regent for the king's hand-picked successor, Mokhesetive. However, in August 1983, Dzeliwe was removed by the Liqoqo, or national council, for refusing to sign a paper acknowledging the council as the supreme authority. She was replaced as regent by Crown Prince Mokhesetive's mother, Ntombe, who signed a decree in September 1983 that apparently gave the Liqoqo (or Libandla) the supreme authority to act. Constitutional matters continued to be vested in the king.

That same month, the crown prince returned from England, where he had been in school, to preside over his first official function. In a traditional ceremony at Lobamba, he was formally introduced to the chiefs and the Swazi people. In April 1986 he was crowned King Mswati III, at age eighteen, the youngest monarch to rule Swaziland. His first order of government was to restore support for the crown that had been eroded by power-hungry members of the council. He dissolved the Liqoqo and dismissed the prime minister.

In Swaziland power is shared between the king (Ngwenyama, signifying "hardness" as typified by thunder) and the queen mother (iNdlovukazi, signifying "she elephant" as typified by the softness of water). The national council (Liqoqo, or Libandla), the traditional side of government, is appointed by the king and headed by the king and queen mother. Her main duty is to uphold the traditional and cultural elements of Swazi society; however, she may make diplomatic foreign policy decisions and national executive decisions. She is present at all policymaking meetings and is the first addressed by the king in all his public speeches. The governing power is vested in the king, who appoints a prime minister. A People's Parliament was re-established in 1988. It is an open forum that offers the public an opportunity to express their views on policies of the Swazi nation.

Each year, in August or September, the young maidens of Swazi congregate from every part of the kingdom to honor the queen

mother with the Umhlanga, or Reed Dance, a celebration that takes
more than a week to prepare.

References

Blaustein, Albert P., and Gisbert H. Flanz, eds. *Constitutions of the
Countries of the World: A Series of Updated Texts, Constitutional Chronologies
and Annotated Bibliographies.* Dobbs Ferry, NY: Oceana Publications,
1991.

Hussey, Hazel. "Ceremonies," "Choosing the King of Swaziland," and
"Umhlanga Reed Dance." Mbabane: *Swaziland Jumbo Tourist Guide,*
1997.

Ntsusa
Chief of the South African amaRharhabe / Ngqika (1782)

Ntsusa was the daughter of Xhosa chief Rharhabe, who, along with
his "great son" (eldest and heir) Mlawu, died in battle against the
Thembu tribe in 1782. Mlawu's son Ngqika was only four years old
at the time. The age of Ntimbo, Mlawu's other son, is not known.
One tradition reported by Stephen Kay says Ntsusa was appointed
chief by King Khawuta, while two factions squabbled over which of
Mlawu's sons should be chief. Most of the former chief's councilors
supported Ntimbo, while Rharhabe's son Ndlambe and his party
backed Ngqika. Ndlambe secured the king's support and thereafter
ruled as regent for his nephew, even continuing to exercise real
power after he installed Ngqika as chief. It is Ndlambe who is credited as the architect of Rharhabe greatness. Eventually, however,
Ngqika rebelled and tried to wrest control from his uncle, enlisting
support from the Boer colonists. War broke out between the two factions that continued for years. Meanwhile, a clan with many chiefs
had developed under Ngqika's aunt Ntsusa, whom Ngqika's son Tyhali
accused in the theft of some Boer military horses, calling Ntsusa's
clan "the terror of the country." As a result, a Boer commando group
was sent out against the Ntsusa, the clan named for Ntsusa. Ntsusa
died in 1826.

References

Kay, Stephen. *Travels and Researches in Caffraria.* London: John Mason,
1833. p. 152.

Peires, J. B. *The House of Phalo.* Berkeley: The University of California
Press, 1982. pp. 49, 81, 212.

Nur al-'Alam Nakiyyat al-Din Shah
Sultana of Atjeh in Indonesia (1675–1678)

Atjeh was a small Muslim sultanate on the northern tip of Sumatra, which was a center of trade, dominating the world supply of pepper. Nur al-'Alam is listed by H. Djajadiningrat in his article on "Atjeh" in the *Encyclopedia of Islam* as the fifteenth sovereign of the dynasty. She succeeded another woman, probably her mother, Sultana Tadj al-'Alam Safiyyat al-Din Shah, who had reigned from 1641 to 1675. Nur al-'Alam ruled for only three years. She was also followed by another woman, probably a sister or daughter, 'Inayat Shah Zakiyyat al-Din Shah. The fact that their political enemies had brought from Mecca a *fatwa* forbidding by law that a woman rule further suggests that the women wielded considerable power.

References

Jones, Russell, trans. *Hikayat Sultan Ibrahim Ibn Adham*. Lanham, MD: University Press of America, 1985.

Mernissi, Fatima. *The Forgotten Queens of Islam*. Trans. Mary Jo Lakeland. Minneapolis: University of Minnesota Press, 1993. pp. 30, 110.

Nūr Jahān
Empress, De Facto Ruler of India (1611–1627 Intermittently)

Originally called Mehrunissa, Nūr Jahān (also Mehr-n-Nesā or Mihn-un-Nisa) was born in 1577, the daughter of a Persian, Sher Alkun (or I'timād-ud-Dawlah), who was in the service of the moghul Jahāngīr, who ruled from 1605 to 1627. Mehrunissa married a Persian, Sher Afkun, whom Jahāngīr posted to Bengal. She had a daughter, Lādilī Begam, who married Prince Shahiryār, a son of Jahāngīr.

Sher Afkun died in 1607, possibly at Jahāngīr's instigation. The widow Mehrunissa was brought to court as lady-in-waiting to Salima, a widow of the previous moghul, Akbar. Janāngīr married Mehrunissa four years later and gave her the name Nūr Mahal, "light of the palace." Her brother, Āsaf Khān, was given a high-ranking position second only to that of her father, who was promoted to chief minister. Mehrunissa soon made herself indispensable to the dependent, alcoholic king, who gave her a new name, Nūr Jahān, "light of the world." Her mother discovered attar of roses and was rewarded with a pearl necklace. The family had clearly taken over the palace. Jahān Jahān, her brother, and her father dominated the politics of the realm, with Nūr Jahān making the decisions and the others carrying them out. British ambassador Sir Thomas Roe wrote home to the future King Charles I that Nūr Jahān "governs him and wynds him up at her pleasure."

Jahāngīr fell ill in 1620, and from then on his poor health, compounded by alcohol, opium, and asthma, made it imperative for Nūr Jahān to exercise control. Her father died, and her brother was occupied elsewhere during the final five years of Jahāngīr's life, and Nūr Jahān ruled alone, from inside the harem. There is no evidence that she ever broke purdah. She even hunted tigers from a closed howdah on top of an elephant with only the barrel of her musket exposed between the curtains. In 1626 she even rode into battle in an elephant litter, dispensing her orders through her eunuch. She also carried on a business, specializing in indigo and cloth trades. After her daughter married Shahiryār, Nūr Jahān began actively to work against Shāh Jahān, Jahāngīr's appointed heir to the throne. After her husband died in 1628, Shāh Jahān was able to sieze control, and Nūr Jahān quickly accepted retirement and a pension of 200,000 rupees a year. She died in 1646.

References

Gascoigne, Bamber. *The Great Moghuls.* New York: Dorset Press, 1971. pp. 136–137, 141, 154, 158–160, 165–172, 178–179, 181.

Nyakaima
Queen, Founder of the Bunyoro, or Babito, Dynasty (ca. 16th c.)

The Babito dynasty was located in the Great Rift area of east central Africa between the Great Lakes. Nyakaima was a member of the Luo group of Nilotic-speaking tribes of southern Sudan. A member of the MuChwezi tribe from east central Africa migrated to her area and married her. The couple established a clan that became the ruling Bunyoro dynasty known as Babito. Eventually the kingdom absorbed the BaChwezi people and inherited their kingdom. The Babito dynasty endured for some ten generations.

Even today, priestesses who claim descendance from Nyakaima still attend a shrine honoring her located at the base of a 400-year-old, 130-foot tall "witch tree." The tree is located on the top of Mubende at the center of the Great Lakes region. There, the priestesses make offerings and sacrifice white chickens.

References

de Villiers, Marq, and Sheila Hirtle. *Into Africa.* Toronto: Key Porter Books, 1997. p. 351.

Nyamazana
Queen of the Ngoni in East Africa (1835–1890s)

The Ngoni people, more than a million strong, consist of a dozen sub-groups of Bantu-speaking people scattered throughout eastern Africa, each forming an independent state with its own ruler. Nyamazana was reputedly the niece of Zwangendaba, who led a migration from Zululand ca. 1819, and in Zimbabwe became leader of a branch of the Ngoni. In 1835 he led his Ngoni across the Zambezi River, but his niece remained behind with her followers. One story alleges that Zwangendaba barred her from coming farther with him, possibly for reasons having to do with logistics.

For approximately the next two years, Nyamazana led her Ngoni tribesmen through Shona territory, pillaging native settlements until, in ca. 1839, the warriors of King Mzilikazi (ca. 1795–1868), founding king of the Ndebele state, arrived in Zimbabwe. Nyamazana surrendered to them, married the king, and allowed her followers to be integrated into the Ndebele state. She is said to have outlived the king by more than three decades, dying in the early 1900s.

References

Lipschutz, Mark R., and R. Kent Rasmussen. *Dictionary of African Historical Biography.* Berkeley: University of California Press, 1986.

Rasmussen, R. Kent. *Mzilikazi of the Ndelebe.* London: Heinemann Educational Books, 1977.

Nysa
See Laodicé

Nzinga Mbandi
Queen (Ngola) of the Mbundu in the Kingdoms of Ndongo (1624–1626) and Matamba (ca. 1630–1663) in Northwest Angola

Nzinga Mbandi (also Singa, Jinga [Jingha], Zhinga, Nzinga Pande, Ann Zingha, Njinga Oande, and Dona Ana de Sousa) was born ca. 1580, the daughter and sister of kings. One of her predecessors was Nzinga Mhemba, baptized in 1491 by the Portuguese as Alfonso, who came to the throne in 1507 and ruled as an "ardent and enlightened Christian" until he died in 1543. In 1618 the Portuguese finally conquered the Ndongo kingdom in Angola. (The name Angola comes from *ngola,* meaning ruler.) Nzinga's early attempts to become the ruler of her tribe failed, and her brother was made ngola in the early 1620s. In ca. 1622 he sent her to Luanda to negotiate with the imperious Gover-

nor de Sousa. The governor sat upon a throne while Nzinga was expected to stand before him. She ordered a slave to kneel so that she could sit. According to one account, when the interview was at an end, she ordered the slave slaughtered before the horrified governor's eyes to show him that she never had to sit in the same chair twice.

Nzinga first attempted to use the Portuguese to secure her leadership, even allowing herself to be baptized and to take the name Dona Ana de Sousa, being named after the Portuguese governor. Her sister Mukumbu had become Lady Barbara, and her sister Kifunji had become Lady Grace. Nzinga's brother died in 1624 as did his son, both possibly at Nzinga's instigation, and Nzinga became the undisputed queen. Two years later the Portuguese drove her out and installed a more cooperative ruler. In retaliation for the Portuguese attempt at a coup, Nzinga made an alliance with the neighboring kingdom of Kasanji, closing the slave routes to the Portuguese. She then went east into the interior and recruited a powerful army. In the early 1630s she conquered the kingdom of Matamba and made herself queen. From there she continued to harass the Ndongo kingdom and to control the interior slave trade, so that the Portuguese were still required to negotiate with her. She dressed as a male chief and was accompanied by an entourage of concubines, who were young men dressed as women. She was the first monarch to initiate a policy of aggressive military expansion, hence the term *jingoism* (a distortion of the name Jinga).

She could be diplomatic if it suited her purposes, or she could put on a great show of barbarism, which seemed to work more effectively to gain respect from the European intruders. Once, she had put on such a show of savagery across the river from the horrified Dutch, in the form of a gory ceremonial dance, that she could be certain of not being hindered by them. In 1626 the Portuguese decided to drive Nzinga out and set up a puppet ruler. Lady Grace was taken prisoner, but from captivity she supplied Nzinga with intelligence for years concerning Portuguese affairs. Nzinga's people remained loyal to her and refused to obey the puppet chief.

In the 1640s she formed an alliance with the Dutch, who had forced the Portuguese out of Luanda in 1641. In 1648 the Portuguese recaptured Luanda and began waging war on the inland kingdoms, including Matamba. In 1643, 1647, and 1648 she attacked the Portuguese and drove them back each time. On one of these raids the Portuguese drowned their prisoner Lady Grace as they retreated, and on another Lady Barbara was captured. In 1648 the Portuguese reconquered Luanda and were thus free to reconsolidate their hold on their African possessions.

In 1656/1659 they finally negotiated a treaty with Queen Nzinga in which she would engage in slave trade with the Portuguese and assist them in their military campaigns. She signed this treaty in 1659 at over the age of seventy-five, having dealt with incursions by the white man all of her life. She also agreed to accept missionaries in Matamba, once again embracing Christianity herself. One term of the official peace with the Portuguese was the release of Lady Barbara in exchange for 130 slaves. Nzinga, a Roman Catholic, continued to rule well into her eighties until her death, collaborating with the Portuguese in slave trade. She never married but was said to keep as many as thirty slaves as sexual partners, supposedly killing them off when she had finished with them.

Upon her death in 1663, she was given a Christian burial.

References

Birmingham, David. *Trade and Conflict in Angola: The Mbundu and Their Neighbors Under the Influence of the Portuguese.* Oxford: Oxford University Press, 1966. pp. 6, 226, 236–246, 268, 270.

Clarke, John Henrik. "Time of Troubles." In Alvin M. Josephy, Jr., ed. *The Horizon History of Africa.* New York: American Heritage Publishing, McGraw-Hill, 1971. pp. 320, 365–357, 405.

de Villiers, Marq, and Sheila Hirtle. *Into Africa.* Toronto: Key Porter Books, 1997. pp. 13, 15, 154, 168–169.

Fage, J. D. *A History of Africa.* New York: Alfred A. Knopf, 1978. pp. 303–304, 316.

Gray, Richard, ed. *The Cambridge History of Africa.* Vol. 4. London: Cambridge University Press, 1975. p. 8.

Lipschutz, Mark R., and R. Kent Rasmussen. *Dictionary of African Historical Biography.* Berkeley: University of California Press, 1986. pp. 181–182.

Oghul Qamish
Empress, Regent of Karakorum (1248–1251)

Karakorum, capital of the Mongol empire, was located on the Orhon Gol river in the Arhangay province of the present-day Mongolian People's Republic. Oghul Qamish was the wife of Güyük, great khan of the Mongols, who ruled from 1246 to 1248. She was believed to be of Markit birth. She had three young sons, Qucha, Naqu, and Qughu, for whom she acted as regent when their father died in 1248.

Jenghiz-khan had given each of his four sons a khanate over which to rule. The four khans then elected a supreme or great khan who was head of the entire empire. Since her husband had been great khan, Oghul was not only regent of the land of the house of Ogödäi but regent for the empire as well. In 1250, in the patrimonial lands of the house of Ogödäi, she received three envoys of Louis IX of France, who arrived by way of Persia. As an example of her avarice, she accepted their presents from King Louis as tribute and demanded that the king of France make more explicit submission to her.

It would later be claimed by her rival that during Oghul's regency she was given to the practice of sorcery. Oghul Qamish wanted the throne of the great khan to pass to a member of the house of Ogödäi: either to Güyük's nephew Shiramon, whom the former khan, his grandfather Ogödäi, had groomed for succession, or better still, to her own son Qucha. However, although Qucha was the eldest of her sons, he was too young. The head of the Jenghiz-khanite family, Batu, wanted to set the Ogödäi line aside and was persuaded to nominate as supreme khan a member of the Tolui family, Mongka, at an assembly not attended by representatives of the house of Ogödäi and their supporters from the house of Jagatai. The Ogödäis obviously refused to ratify such a nomination, and Mongka was elected by default.

The relegation of the house of Ogödäi was a violation of legitimacy, and Shiramon and his cousins did not intend to let the election stand. They plotted to surprise Mongka and his supporters during the drunken feast following the inauguration ceremony, overpower them, and depose Mongka. The plot miscarried and a civil war erupted, the houses of Ogödäi and Jagatai on one side and the houses of Jochi and Tolui on the other. After a year of bloodshed, Mongka triumphed over all his rivals. He had the sons of Oghul Qamish exiled and saved his venom for their mother. She was stripped of her clothes for questioning, convicted of sorcery, sewn up in a sack, and drowned (May July 1252).

References

Grousset, René. *The Empire of the Steppes: A History of Central Asia.* Trans. Naomi Walford. New Brunswick, NJ: Rutgers University Press, 1970. pp. 272–274, 330, 349, 596.

Runciman, Steven. *A History of the Crusades.* Vol. 3, *The Kingdom of Acre.* Cambridge: Cambridge University Press, 1952, 1987. pp. 260, 293–294.

Olga (Corbis-Bettmann)

Olga
Queen, Regent of Greece (1920)

Olga was the wife of King Alexander I, ruler of Greece from 1917 to 1920. On October 25, 1920, King Alexander died from blood poisoning, having been bitten by a pet monkey. Queen Olga became regent until December, when former King Constantine I, Alexander's father who had previously abdicated, resumed the throne.

References

Langer, William L., ed. *World History.* Boston: Houghton Mifflin, 1980. p. 1024.

Olga, Saint
Princess, Regent of Kiev (945–964)

Olga was born ca. 890 in Russia and became the wife of Grand Prince Igor I and the mother of a son, Svyatoslav. In 945 Igor was assassinated for exorting huge sums from his subjects to pay for his campaigns against the Byzantines. Olga became regent of the grand principality of Kiev until her son reached his majority. She hunted down Igor's murderers and ordered them scalded to death. In ca. 955 to 957 she became an Orthodox Christian and shortly afterward ushered in a new era in Byzantine-Kievian relations by visiting Constantinople. There she was baptized, or rebaptized, taking as her Christian name Helena, in honor of the Byzantine empress. It was through her efforts and those of her grandson Vladimir that Christianity was brought to Russia. However, during her lifetime she did not see her conversion affect the pagan faith of her subjects; in fact, during the first part of Vladimir's reign there was even a strong pagan revival. She died in 969 and was canonized by the Orthodox Church; her feast day is July 11.

References

Langer, William L., ed. *World History*. Boston: Houghton Mifflin, 1948, 1980. pp. 195, 259, 260.

Ostrogorsky, George. *History of the Byzantine State*. New Brunswick, NJ: Rutgers University Press, 1969. pp. 283, 292.

Previté-Orton, C. W. *The Shorter Cambridge Medieval History*. Vol. 1, *The Later Roman Empire to the Twelfth Century*. Cambridge: Cambridge University Press, 1952, 1982. p. 265.

Riasanovsky, Nicholas V. *A History of Russia*. Oxford: Oxford University Press, 1963, 1993. pp. 31, 34, 53.

Olympias
Queen, Regent of Macedonia (317 B.C.)

Olympias (or Olumpias, Myrtale, Polyxena, or Stratonice) was born ca. 375 B.C., the daughter of King Neoptolemus of Epirus. A follower of Orpheus and Dionysus, she met King Philip II of Macedon at the Sanctuary of the Gods on the island of Samothrace and in 357 B.C. became his principal wife. At that time she had apparently been called Myrtale and was perhaps renamed Olympias beginning the following year after Philip's victory in the Olympic Games. That same year, their son, Alexander III (the Great) was born in Pella, in Macedonia.

Two decades later, in 337 B.C., when Philip married Cleopatra Eurydice, Olympias and Alexander fled to Epirus. Alexander later moved on to Illyria and eventually reconciled with his father. After Philip was assassinated in 336 B.C., possibly by his wife or his twenty-year-old son, Olympias returned to Macedonia. With her son now in power, she forced Cleopatra Eurydice to commit suicide.

While Alexander was absent on military expeditions to Asia, Olympias quarrelled repeatedly over governing policy with the

Macedonian viceroy, Antipater, but Alexander invariably supported Antipater against his mother. Eventually, she returned to Epirus (c. 331 B.C.). Alexander died in 323 B.C., and Antipater died four years later, having appointed Polyperchon as his successor over the European part of the empire. This threatened the power of Antipater's son Cassander.

Antipater had brought Alexander's Bactrian wife, Roxane, and their son Alexander IV (ca. 323–c. 311 B.C.) to Macedonia. After Antipater's death, Roxane fled with the infant king to Epirus, to take refuge with Queen Olympias.

After Antipater's death, Polycheron invited Olympias to return to Macedonia to serve as regent for her grandson, Alexander IV, but at first she refused. Finally, in 317 B.C., when Cassander put Philip II's mentally handicapped son Phillip III Arrhidaeus on the throne, Olympias returned with Polyperchon and invaded Macedonia in the name of her grandson. In this endeavor she was supported by Macedonian soldiers. She killed Philip III and many others and forced his wife, Adea, to commit suicide. But in 316 B.C. Cassander blockaded Olympias at Pynda. He imprisoned Roxane and Alexander IV and condemned Olympias to death, but his soldiers preferred to desert to her rather than carry out her execution.

Her death eventually came at the hands of relatives of her former victims, whom she had slain at the time of the invasion. Alexander IV was murdered in ca. 310–309 B.C.

References

Bowder, Diana, ed. *Who Was Who in the Greek World*. Ithaca, NY: Cornell University Press, 1982. pp. 324–325.

Carney, E. D. "Olympias, Adea Eurydice, and the End of the Argead Dynasty." In Ian Worthington, ed. *Ventures into Greek History*. Oxford: Clarendon Press, 1994. pp. 357–380.

Peters, F. E. *The Harvest of Hellenism*. New York: Barnes & Noble Books, 1996. pp. 48, 53, 72, 76–77, 79.

Orghana

Princess, Regent of the Mongolian Khanate of Jagatai (1252–1261)

Orghana was first the wife of Qara-Hulägu, a grandson of Jenghiz-khan's son Jagatai and the ruler of the Turkestan khanate from 1242 to 1246. She had two sons, Buri and Mobarak Sha. In 1246 the new great khan Güyük replaced Qara-Hulägu with Jagatai's younger brother, Yissu-Mangu. In 1252, with the election of a new great khan, Mongka, Yissu-Mangu was deposed and Qara-Hulägu was reinstated and ordered to execute Yissu-Mangu. However, Qara-Hulägu died on the way to reclaim his throne, and it was up to Princess Orghana as regent to have Yissu-Mangu executed. Her husband's former minister Habash 'Amid took care of the matter without waiting for the executioner.

Orghana took over control of the khanate and held it for nine years. She was described as beautiful, wise, and discerning. Upon the great khan Mongka's death, one of his sons, Hulägu, became khan of Persia, while the other two, Kublai and Ariq-bögä, vied to become the supreme khan. Kublai outwitted his brother and became grand khan, but Ariq-bögä planned to dethrone him. To keep his other brother from sending reinforcements from Persia to Kublai, he decided to take over the khanate of Jagatai, sending Prince Alghu to remove Orghana from power and become regent himself.

Alghu had ambitions of his own: to make the Jagatai khanate independent. He seized Ariq-bögä's tax collectors and executed them, keeping the wealth for himself. In the war that followed, Ariq-bögä suffered severe losses. After two years, he tried to make peace with Alghun. At the time, he had with him Princess Orghana, who had come to protest her removal from the khanate. He sent her and Mas'ud Yalavach to Alghun's camp in Samarkaland with peace proposals. But on her arrival, Alghu married her and made Mas'ud his finance minister. With the money Mas'ud raised, Alghun and Orghana raised another large army. In 1264, Ariq-bögä was forced to surrender to Kublai. Alghun died in 1255 or 1266, and Orghana placed on the throne her son by her first marriage, Mobarek-shah, who became the first Jagataite to be converted to Islam.

References

Grousset, René. *The Empire of the Steppes.* tr. Naomi Walford. New Brunswick, NJ: Rutgers University Press, 1970. pp. 274–275, 286, 329–332.

Runciman, Steven. *A History of the Crusades.* Vol. 3, *The Kingdom of Acre.* Cambridge: Cambridge University Press, 1952, 1987. p. 309, and Appendix III.

P

Padishah Khatun
Queen of Kirman, Persia (1291–1295)

Padishah Khatun was the daughter of Kutlugh Turkhan, or Turkan Khatun, queen of Kirman from 1257 to 1282. At that time, the Mongols subjected the princesses of their "colonies" to obligatory marriages. To escape this fate, Padishah was reared as a boy among the boys. Nevertheless, eventually Padishah, a beautiful and gifted poet, was married to Abaka Khan, son of the great Mongolian Khan Hulägu. Ultimately Abaka inherited the Ilkhan court of his father, but when Abaka died in 1282, his successor-brother converted to Islam and took the name of Ahmad Teguder. He was dethroned two years later by Abaka's son Arghun, a strong Buddhist.

Meanwhile, Ahmad Teguder had removed Padishah's mother from the throne of Kirman and replaced her with her stepson Suyurghatamish. Eventually, Padisha charmed the fifth ruler of the Ilkhan dynasty, Gaykhatu, who was one of the sons of her former husband. When he succeeded to power in 1291, Padishah asked that as proof of his love, he give her the throne of the Persian province of Kirman, which he did. As soon as she came to power as head of state, she had her stepbrother Suyurghatamish arrested and thrown in prison. After an escape attempt, she ordered him strangled; she then took the title of Safwat al-dunya wa al-din ("purity of the earthly world and of the faith") and became the sixth sovereign of the Kutlugh-Khanid dynasty. Some of the gold and silver coins she had minted in her name still exist.

She ruled until the death of her husband in 1295. At that time his successor, Baydu, on advice of the leader of Suyurghatamish's clan, his widow Khurdudjin, a descendant of Hulägu, had Padishah put to death.

References

Mernissi, Fatima. *The Forgotten Queens of Islam.* Trans. Mary Jo Lakeland. Minneapolis: University of Minnesota Press, 1993. pp. 21, 99, 100, 101–102.

Pandit, Vijaya Lakshmi

*President of United Nations
General Assembly (1953)*

Vijaya Lakshmi Pandit was born Swarup Kumari Nehru in 1900, the daughter of Sarup Rani Nehru and Motilal Nehru, a Kashmiri Brahmin, prominent lawyer and one of Mahatma Gandhi's lieutenants. Vijaya was the sister of Jawaharlal Nehru, who became the first prime minister of independent India; and the aunt of Indira Gandhi, first woman prime minister of India. Vijaya was privately educated in India and abroad and, along with the rest of her family, worked for Indian independence. In 1921 she married Ranjit S. Pandit, a co-worker. In connection with her efforts for India's independence, the British imprisoned her for one year (1931). Her husband died in 1944, three years before India achieved independence from Britain.

Madame Pandit embarked on a distinguished political career, heading the Indian delegation to the United Nations from 1946 to 1948 and again from 1952 to 1953. She served as ambassador to Moscow from 1947 to 1949 and afterwards to the United States and Mexico until 1951. In 1953 she became the first woman to serve as president of the United Nations General Assembly. From 1954 to 1961 she served as ambassador in England and Ireland. During that time, she wrote *The Evolution of India* (1953). She became the governor of the state of Maharashtra in 1962, and two years later she accepted the seat in India's parliament formerly held by her brother Jawaharlal Nehru. In 1978 she became the Indian representative to the Human Rights Committee of the United Nations. In 1977 she left the Congress Party to join the Congress for Democracy. In 1977 she wrote her memoirs, *The Scope of Happiness.* She was placed on the Board of the Mountbatten Memorial Trust in 1980.

References

International Who's Who, 1987–1988. London: Europa Publishing, 1987. pp. xvi, 1130.

Mehta, Ved. *The New India*. Harmondsworth, Middlesex: Penguin Books, 1978. pp. 154–155.

Pāndyan Queen
Ruler in South India (2d. c. B.C.)

The Pāndya was a Tamil dynasty in the extreme south of India first mentioned by Greek authors in the fourth century B.C. Megasthenes mentioned that the Pāndyan kingdom was ruled by a daughter of Herakles. If poetry and heroic ballads that survive are any indication, the Cheras, the Cholas, and the Pāndyas were in constant conflict with one another. The Pāndyan queen is credited by Megasthenes with having an army of 4,000 cavalry, 13,000 infantry, and 500 elephants with which to fight her wars.

References
Thapar, Romila. *A History of India*. Vol. 1. London: Penguin Books, 1987. p. 103.

Pao-Ssŭ
Queen, Possible Co-ruler of Chou, or Zhou (ca. 1st or 2d Millennium B.C.)

The Chou, Chow, or Zhou Dynasty in China lasted from 1122 to 221 B.C. Although the Chinese tradition contains a Chou genealogy, no dates can definitely be assigned to the reigns. Legend surrounding Pao-Ssŭ's infancy claims that attempts were made to destroy her but proved fruitless. Such legends abounded about larger-than-life heroes such as King Cyrus the Great, Queen Semiramis, Moses, and King Gilgamish. This would suggest that Queen Pao-Ssŭ was a heroic, well-revered queen.

References
Waley, Arthur, trans. *The Book of Songs*. New York: Grove Press, 1960. p. 239.

Parysatis
Queen, Regent of Persia (424–404 B.C.)

Parysatis was the daughter of Xerxes I, who ruled Persia from 486 to 466 B.C. He was murdered by his chamberlain, Aspamitres, and the captain of his guard, Artabanus, the latter choosing Xerxes's youngest son and Parasatis's brother, Artaxerxes I, to succeed him. Artaxerxes I reigned for nearly forty years, dying in 425 B.C. His son, Parysatis's nephew, Xerxes II, succeeded him but was assassinated after only forty-five days by his half brother, Secydianus (or Sogdianus), who was in turn murdered after only six and a half months by Ochus, another brother. Ochus, who became known as Darius Nothus, was married to his aunt, Parysatis. Under her tutelage, he reigned for nineteen years (424–404 B.C.) The couple had at least two sons. When Darius Northus died, Parysatis attempted to put her younger son, Cyrus, on the throne—possibly so that she could control his affairs—but the older son, Arsaces (Artaxerxes II), was named to succeed his father. Parysatis urged Cyrus to take up arms against his brother in an attempt to overthrow him, which Cyrus did. But Cyrus was killed in battle at Cunaxa, thus ending Parysatis's influence.

References

Peters, F. E. *The Harvest of Hellenism.* New York: Barnes & Noble Books, 1996. p. 29.

Rawlinson, George. *Ancient History.* New York: Barnes & Noble Books, 1993. pp. 88–90.

Pascal-Trouillot, Ertha
Provisional President of Haiti (1990–1991)

Born Ertha Pascal in 1943 or 1944, she was a member of the wealthy mulatto professional elite that dominated Haitian politics prior to the rule of Francois Duvalier. She married Ernst Trouillot, a prominent lawyer who presided over the Port-au-Prince Bar Association until his death in 1989. The couple had one daughter.

Ertha Pascal-Trouillot earned her own law degree in 1971 and soon gained respect as a legal scholar. She authored several books on law; the first and best known, *The Judicial Status of Haitian Women in Social Legislation,* was written only two years after her graduation. She worked to reform Haiti's outmoded laws affecting the rights of women. Although Haiti's constitutions have provided for women's suffrage since 1950, until the 1970s women were considered "minors" and were not permitted to conduct business or have a bank account without the signature of their husbands. In 1984 Ertha Pascal-Trouillot was named Appeals Court judge, and in 1986, after the fall from power of Jean-Claude Duvalier, Minister of Justice Francois Latortue appointed her to a ten-year term as Supreme Court justice. Although other women had served as judges in Haiti, Ertha Pascal-Trouillot was the first woman to sit on the Supreme Court.

On March 10, 1990, Haitian ruler Lt. Gen. Prosper Avril resigned during a popular uprising against his military regime, turning over power to acting army chief of staff Maj. Gen. Herard Abraham, who promised to transfer power to a civilian leader within seventy-two hours. According to the constitution, Chief Justice Gilbert Austin was next in line; however, the opposition coalition Unity Assembly rejected his claim on the grounds that he was a puppet of the military. Austin extracted a pledge from the other eleven justices not to accept the nomination over him, and three other justices refused to accept the nomination. On the evening of March 11 the nominating committee visited Ertha Pascal-Trouillot, the court's

newest justice, to offer her the nomination. After a brief consultation with her sister and brother-in-law, she decided, in the interest of unity, to forgo her commitment to Justice Austin. She would take a leave of absence from the bench so as to preside over the provisional government for several months in order to oversee, with an advisory council of nineteen members, the democratic election of a Haitian president. Because roving assassination squads threatened her life, she was taken into hiding until her inauguration the following day.

In her inauguration speech, delivered in both French and Creole, she said, "I have accepted this heavy task in the name of the Haitian woman, who for the first time in the history of our country, has been called upon to go beyond her traditional daily sacrifices made with courage and true patriotism. . . . In the short time I have, I will work to clean the face of Haiti." In Haiti's first free election, Catholic priest Jean Bertrand Aristide was chosen to succeed her (January 1991). However, before due process could be enacted, on January 7, 1991, the capital was attacked by a military coup led by the former defense minister, Col. Christofe Dardompre, who declared himself ruler. Ertha Pascal-Trouillot announced that she was resigning immediately and returning to her post on the Supreme Court. She disappeared, and word reached the capital that she was being held hostage. The coup failed, Pascal-Trouillot was released, and Dardompre, who headed the National Palace Guard under ousted military ruler Prosper Avril, was arrested in April 1991. Earlier that month, Ertha Pascal-Trouillot had been arrested and questioned about the January coup. She was actually held at gunpoint by Roger Lafontant, a former interior minister during Duvalier's dictatorship. The government and courts were under military control for three years. It was not until 1994, when Aristide was restored to office with help from the United Nations, that the Supreme Court was able to resume. Following her term as justice, she retired.

References

French, Howard W. "Haiti's Class Divisions Deepen, Threatening Efforts to Return Aristide to Presidency." *New York Times.* 3 November 1991: 9.

————. "New Leader of Haitians Offers U. S. a Wary Hand." *New York Times.* 23 December 1990: 2.

"Haiti Coup Suspect Held." *Houston Chronicle.* 21 April 1991: 23A.

Norton, Michael. "Pascal-Trouillot Blazes a Trail for Women." *Houston Chronicle.* 13 March 1990: 8A.

Treaster, Joseph B. "Civilian Sworn in as Haiti's President." *New York Times.* 14 March 1990: A3.

Pauline

Princess and Duchess, Ruler of Guastalla (1806)

Guastalla, located in northern Italy, was probably founded by the Lombards in the seventh century. In 1406 it was designated a county, and from 1539 on it was ruled by the Gonzagas of Mantua. In 1621 it became a duchy, and in 1746 it passed to Austria and to the Spanish Bourbons.

Napoleon I, wanting to found a dynasty bearing his name, realized that someday one of the plots against his life might succeed. He knew that the individual is mortal but family endures. He sought to protect his place in history by bestowing kingdoms upon his brothers and sisters. In 1806 he revived the tiny six-square-mile duchy of Guastalla as an "independent principality," appointing his second surviving sister, Pauline Bonaparte, as its ruler. This feckless lady, whose likeness Canova had carved in stone, was known for her beauty, vanity, lusts, and extravagance. Although she found it amusing to have been made a sovereign, she could not bother to leave the luxuries of Paris in order to rule. She took office on March 30, 1806, and abdicated on May 24 of the same year. She was the principality's only ruler.

References

Carpenter, Clive. *The Guinness Book of Kings, Rulers & Statesmen.* Enfield, Middlesex: Guinness Superlatives, 1978. p. 145.

Sédillot, René. *An Outline of French History.* Trans. Gerard Hopkins. New York: Alfred A. Knopf, 1967. p. 306.

Pedini-Angelini, Maria Lea
Co-captain-regent of San Marino (1981)

San Marino, located on the Adriatic side of central Italy, and surrounded on all sides by Italy, is the world's oldest independent republic. It has a unique system of government, which calls for two captains-regent, elected by the Great and General Council, a parliament of sixty members elected for five-year terms. These captains-regent serve as heads of state, to preside over the executive branch, called the Congress of State, which is composed of ten members chosen by the council. The captains-regent serve only a six-month term and may not be reelected until after a three-year period has passed.

From 1945 to 1957, the country was ruled by a coalition of communists and socialists. In 1957 the Christian Democratic Party, aided by communist dissidents, took control. In 1978 a coalition led by communists again came to power, and it was during this period that Maria Lea Pedini-Angelini served as co-captain regent.

References
Britannica Macropaedia. Vol. 16. 1983. pp. 223–224.
Funk &Wagnalls New Encyclopedia. Vol. 23. 1986. p. 123.

Pemba, Queen of
Ruler of Pemba (?–ca. 1679)

Pemba is an island off the coast of east Africa near the port of Tanga, Tanzania. During the seventeenth century queens ruled on several of the islands in the area. In ca. 1679 a queen was ruling, but an antagonistic faction from a distant branch drove her into exile. In 1687 she went to the Portuguese colony of Goa, seeking refuge. There she ended all chance of regaining her throne by becoming a Christian. Nevertheless, the queen continued to speak for her people on Pemba. In an act of gratitude for the refuge she had received, she willed her kingdom to the Portuguese upon her death, but they were never able to claim this inheritance. In 1694, with conditions on Pemba still in a state of upheaval, Portugal discontinued its attempts to subject its populace. The queen died about 1694.

References
Clarke, John Henrik. "Time of Troubles." In Alvin M. Josephy, Jr., ed.
The Horizon History of Africa. New York: American Heritage Publishing, McGraw-Hill, 1971. pp. 369–370.

Perón, Isabel
President of Argentina
(1974–1976)

Isabel (Isabelita) Perón was born María Estela Martínez in 1931, one of five children of a small town bank manager in northwest Argentina. The family moved to Buenos Aires in 1933, and her father died four years later. Her mother worked to keep the family together, but María Estela quit school after the sixth grade to pursue a career in music and ballet. She studied ballet and piano and became a qualified piano teacher. When she was twenty she joined a professional ballet company, changing her name to Isabel, her saint's name.

One story claims that in mid-tour of her dance company in 1956, she was stranded in Panama City and met the exiled Juan Perón, president of Argentina from 1946 to 1955. She became his personal secretary and traveling companion and settled with him in Madrid. In 1961, at the age of thirty, she became the sixty-five-year-old Perón's wife. Since she was not in exile, she was free to return to her homeland, so in 1964 she began to travel around Argentina, speaking on behalf of Peronista candidates.

In 1973 Perón was recalled to Argentina and elected president, with his wife Isabel as vice president. Isabel had the handicap of following Perón's popular second wife, Eva (Evita). Later in 1973, Perón, who was seventy-eight and in poor health, fell ill, and he delegated full power to Isabel. In 1974 he died, and she acceded to the presidency, becoming the first woman chief of state to serve in her own right in South America. Although the liberal unions had always been the bastions of Peronist support, the right-wing military had supported Perón as well. These two factions had warred for years. To combat the terrorism that had interrupted the government from time to time for years, Isabel suspended constitutional rights and imposed de facto martial law. Inflation was running at 200 percent per year, so she imposed austere fiscal measures which precipitated a union strike that crippled the nation. Eventually she had to give in to union demands for large wage hikes just to get the country moving again. In 1976, while she suffered a gall bladder attack, her regime was overthrown by a military junta. She went into self-exile in Spain in 1981 but returned in 1983 for the inauguration at the request of the new constitutional president, Raul Alfonsín.

References

Egan, Edward W., Constance B. Hintz, and L. F. Wise, eds. *Kings, Rulers, and Statesmen.* New York: Sterling Publishing, 1976. p. 18.

"Intelligence Report." *Parade.* 27 February 1983: 2.

"Isabel Perón Pardoned." *Houston Post.* 10 September 1983: 4A.

"Isabel Perón's Return Confirmed." *Houston Post.* 27 August 1982: 3A.

Perry, Ruth
President of Liberia (1996–1997)

Liberia, located on the west coast of Africa, was founded in 1822 by U.S. black freedmen. Modeling its government after that of the United States, it became a republic in 1847.

Ruth Perry was born in 1939, received a good education, and married. She was first elected to the legislature early in 1980. During the military rule of Samuel Doe, Ruth Perry served as a senator. In 1990, Doe was executed by one of the warring factions vying for control of the government.

After six years of turbulence, during which more than 150,000 Liberians were killed and over half the 2.6 million population was forced to flee to surrounding countries, west African heads of state met in Abuja, Nigeria, on August 17, 1996, to choose a ruler of Liberia. This leader was to replace university professor Wilton Sankswulo as president until elections could be held the following year. Ruth Perry was named chairman of the Council of State, a six-member collective presidency. She told the assemblage that had elected her that she had the "touch of velvet" but could be "as hard as steel." When peace was finally restored, Perry, who had remained in Liberia throughout the bloody civil war, later credited help not only from outsiders (the Economic Community of West African States) but also from a constituency composed in part of victimized groups such as women.

Elections, originally slated for May 30, 1997, were postponed at the request of eleven of Liberia's sixteen political parties on the grounds that more time was needed to ensure stable conditions for free and fair elections. One of the leading candidates was another woman, Harvard-educated Ellen Johnson-Sirleaf, who resigned as head of the United Nations Development Programme's Regional Bureau for Africa to run for the post. She campaigned as being the obvious choice to continue Ruth Perry's policies of finding nonviolent modes for resolving differences. However, when elections were finally held in August 1997, Charles Taylor was elected.

Three months later, Ruth Perry opened a three-day United Nations interagency workshop in Addis Ababa, Ethiopia. The purpose of the meeting, composed of some sixty African women involved in government or in nongovernmental social organizations, was to identify the women's role in "peace-building and nonviolent means of conflict resolution."

References

Hagos, Ghion. "African Women Seek Role in Peace Building." Panafrican News Agency. *Africa News Online*. 24 November 1997.

Oyo, Remi. "Liberia Parties Want Elections Postponed." *Electronic Mail & Guardian*. 15 May 1997. IPS/Misonet.

Reuter Information Service. "Africa's First Woman Head of State Pledges to Work for Peace." *Nando Times*. 18 August 1996. p. 1.

Petronilla
Queen of Aragon (1137–1164)

Petronilla was born ca. 1136, the daughter of King Ramiro II, ruler of Aragon from 1134 to 1137. Ramiro was a monk, the brother of King Alfonso I, ruler from 1102 to 1134, who named Ramiro to succeed him on his death. The pope freed Ramiro from his vows so that Ramiro could emerge from retirement only long enough to marry and produce an heir. Ramiro betrothed Petronilla to Ramón Berenguer IV, count of Barcelona, then soon abdicated and returned to his monastery, leaving Queen Petronilla under the guardianship of Ramón, who was only six at the time.

Thirteen years later, in 1150, Petronilla married Berenguer, now king of Catalonia. She was never allowed to exercise authority during Berenguer's life. She had a son, Ramón Berenguer, who changed his name to the more Aragonese-sounding Alfonso II. By inheritance, Alfonso acceded to the throne of Catalonia in 1162 when his father died. Queen Petronilla abdicated the throne of Aragon in 1164, in favor of Alfonso. He was the first to rule in his own right over Aragon and Catalonia, which came to be known as the kingdom of Aragon.

References

Chapman, Charles E. *A History of Spain*. New York: The Free Press/
  Macmillan, 1965. pp. 78–79.
Langer, William L., ed. *World History*. Boston: Houghton Mifflin, 1980.
  pp. 250, 252.

Pheretima
Queen of Cyrene, or Cyrenaica (ca. 518)

Pheretima was the wife of Battus the Lame, fifth ruler of Cyrene, located in northern Libya. Battus was a Libyan word meaning "king." The couple had a son, Arcesilaus. The misfortunes that had befallen the realm prior to Battus's reign (the murder of his father and mother and Battus's lameness) had prompted the people to send to Delphi to ask the oracle for advice about changing their luck. The priestess advised them to employ Demonax of Mantinea in Arcadia to make some changes in the kingdom. Once employed, Demonax segregated the people into three groups and gave them many of the privileges previously enjoyed only by the rulers.

After Battus died, his son, Arcesilaus, acceded to the throne with the idea of rescinding Demonax's changes. His demands for a restoration of his ancestral rights led to civil war in which he was defeated. He fled to Samos, while Queen Pheretima went to Salamis in Cyprus. There she asked the ruler Euelthon for an army with which to recapture the throne. Instead of honoring her request, he sent her a golden spindle and distaff with wool on it, saying that he sent her a present that, unlike an army, he thought suitable for her sex. Meanwhile, Arcesilaus was able to raise an army in Samos, and he went back to Cyrene and recovered his throne.

Fearing a warning of the oracle, he was afraid to remain in Cyrene, so he went to Barca, leaving Queen Pheretima to represent him, running the government in Cyrene. But her son was assassinated in Barca, and when the queen learned of his death, she fled to Egypt for asylum. Intent on avenging her son's death, she convinced Aryandes to send troops from Egypt to Barca to assist her in laying seige to the town. They called on the citizens to surrender those responsible for Arcesilaus's death, but the people refused, claiming that everyone was equally responsible. The siege then continued for nine months. The Persians, meantime, were interested in mining operations in Barca and were eventually allowed by the Barcans to enter. The Persians then delivered to Queen Pheretima the men responsible for her son's murder. She had them impaled on stakes around the city wall.

The wives of the murderers fared no better. She cut off their breasts and stuck them up on stakes, too. She gave the rest of the people, other than those of the house of Bothus, to the Persians, who pillaged their homes and reduced them to slavery.

Cyrene and Euesperides were incorporated in a Persian satrapy in ca. 518. According to Herodotus, no sooner had Pheretima returned to Egypt than she died a horrible death, "her body seething with worms while she was still alive."

References

Hammond, N.G.L. *A History of Greece to 322 B.C.* Oxford: Clarendon Press, 1986. p. 178.

Herodotus. *The Histories.* Trans. Aubrey de Sélincourt. New York: Penguin Books, 1954, 1988. pp. 326–328, 337–339.

Pimiku
Queen, First Known Ruler of Japan (ca. 190–247)

In Chinese and Korean histories, Pimiku is called Pimiho, a corruption of Hime-ko. Pimiku (or Himiko, Pimisho, Pimiko, Yametsu-hime, or Yamato-hime-mikoto) was reputed to be the daughter of Suinin, who entrusted her with the sacred mirror, symbol of the sun goddess. In archaic Japanese, Pimiko meant "sun daughter." She was said to have built the Great Shrine of Ise, the most important Shinto shrine in Japan. She remained unmarried and, according to the *Wei chih,* ancient Chinese records considered more accurate than Japanese records, she ruled in Yamatai, which may have been Yamato. Other research indicates her realm was in western Japan. She seems also to have been a priestess. The *Wei* records say that she bewitched her subjects with magic and sorcery. A list survives of the names of the lands over which she presided. In 234 she had a daughter, Iyo-hime. After she conquered the savage tribes in southern Tsukushi, Chinese emperor Ming-ti awarded her with a golden seal inscribed with the title of "king" of the country of Wo (238). At her death in 247, over 100 of her servants buried themselves alive around her tomb.

References

Reischauer, Edwin O., and John K. Fairbank. *East Asia: The Great Tradition.* Boston: Houghton Mifflin, 1960. p. 463.

Sansom, George. *A History of Japan to 1334.* Vol. 1. Stanford: Stanford University Press, 1958. pp. 22, 45.

Placidia, Galla
Augusta, Regent of the Western Roman Empire (425–433)

Galla (or Aelia) Placidia was born in 390, the daughter of Emperor Theodosius I, ruler from 379 to 395, and his second wife Galla, daughter of Valentinian I. Galla Placidia was the half sister of Flavius Honorius, who ruled from 393 to 423. In 410 the Goths, under the command of Alaric, sacked Rome and took Galla Placidia prisoner. In 414 she married Alaric's successor, Athaulf, in Narbonne. Athaulf was assassinated the following year.

In 416 Galla Placidia was restored to the Romans, and the next year she unwillingly submitted to a political union, marriage to her half-brother's generalissimo, Constantius. They had a son, Valentinian, born in 419, and at least one daughter, Honoria. In 421 Constantius was declared augustus and co-emperor, but he died. Flavius Honorius died in 423 and, after a brief usurpation by Johannes during which Galla Placidia fled with her son to Constantinople, was succeeded in 425 by Galla Placidia's son, Valentinian, age six. Galla, as regent, was actively supported by Bonifatius (Boniface), who bore the title master of the soldiers of the eastern army. At first her influence was dominant in affairs of state, but when she tried to replace her own master of soldiers, Aëtius, with Boniface, Aëtius enlisted the help of the Huns, and by 433 his authority was unchallenged. Galla Placidia then turned her attention to adorning the city of Ravenna with a number of churches. She died in Rome in 450.

References
Bowder, Diana, ed. *Who Was Who in the Roman World.* Ithaca, NY: Cornell University Press, 1980. pp. 4–5, 46, 146, 413–414, 556–557.
Langer, William L., ed. *World History.* Boston: Houghton Mifflin, 1980. pp. 134, 158–159.
Previté-Orton, C. W. *The Shorter Cambridge Medieval History.* Vol. 1, *The Later Roman Empire to the Twelfth Century.* Cambridge: Cambridge University Press, 1952, 1982. pp. 78, 86–88.

Plaisance of Antioch
Queen, Regent of Cyprus and Jerusalem (1253–1261)

Plaisance of Antioch was the daughter of Bohemond V, prince of Antioch from 1233 to 1252, and his second wife, Lucienne of Segni. Plaisance's brother was Bohemond VI, prince of Antioch from 1252 to 1287. In 1251 she became the third wife of King Henry I, ruler of Jerusalem and Cyprus, and a year later bore him a son, Hugh II. King Henry died in January 1253. As their son was only a few months old, Queen Plaisance claimed the regency of Cyprus and the titular regency of Jerusalem. The High Courts of Cyprus confirmed her position there immediately, but the Jerusalem barons required her attendance in person before they would recognize her. She was formally recognized as regent of Jerusalem upon her visit to Acre in 1258. An efficient ruler of high integrity, she was deeply mourned when she died in 1261, leaving her son Hugh II an orphan at age eight.

References

Runciman, Steven. *A History of the Crusades*. Vol. 3, *The Kingdom of Acre*. Cambridge: Cambridge University Press, 1952, 1987. pp. 278, 281, 284–286, 288–289.

Plavsic, Biljana
President of the Bosnian Serb Republic (1996–1997)

Biljana Plavsic was born in 1930 into a wealthy merchant family from Visoko. Her father, a biologist, was director of natural sciences at Sarajevo's museum. She also became a biologist, studying botany and plant viruses in Zagreb and in New York in the early 1970s as a Fulbright scholar. She was married briefly to a prominent Sarajevo lawyer, then divorced and became dean of natural sciences at Sarajevo University. When she failed to get the post as biology chair at the Academy for Arts and Sciences in 1990, she became active in the newly formed Serbian Democratic Party and rose rapidly to a position of prominence.

Plavsic became an ardent supporter of Radovan Karadzic and the Serb cause: ethnic partition and a pure Serb state. When Karadzic was elected president of the self-proclaimed Republika Srpska, she became vice president. She was elected president when Karadzic, charged with masterminding "ethnic cleansing" genocide against the Muslims, was deposed under the terms of the Dayton peace accords. He was forced into hiding in Pale, where he planned to continue to direct the republic from behind the scenes, setting up his own police force, government, and state media.

Following her inauguration, Plavsic unexpectedly turned against the ideological irredentist Karadzic, renouncing his involvement in Serbian war crimes. The country, financially crippled by blockage of aid for noncompliance with the Dayton peace agreement of November 1995, was torn between loyalty to Karadzic and Plavsic, who had the cautious support of NATO and the United States. Still fiercely nationalistic, she favored a return to the monarchy. "With a parliamentary monarchy, each four years you can change the prime minister, but there is always stability in the state," she said in a September 1997 interview. "Now there is one stable roof over the Serb people, our church. Why not have the other roof, a monarchy?"

Biljana Plavsic (AP Photo / Radivoje Pavicic)

Foreign assistance, however, was not enough to overcome the hard-liners in parliament. In August 1997, NATO-led forces of British and Czech peacekeepers took over a police station in Banja Luka when it was learned that a large quantity of arms were stored there in preparation for a coup attempt against Plavsic's government. Later in the month a similar police station seizure in Brcko was carried out in the presence of an angry mob sympathetic to former president Karadzic. Subsequently, Plavsic, a pragmatic nationalist, was ousted from the ruling Serbian Democratic Party, calling into question her political survival as well as the fate of the Bosnian Serb Republic. Labeled a "name-only head of state" after her attempt to dissolve the parliament was ignored, Plavsic retired after the November 1997 election.

References
"Cracking Down on Bosnia's War Criminals." *World Press Review.* September 1997: 5.
"Difficult Choices." *World Press Review.* November 1997: 19.
Erlanger, Steven. "NATO Faces a Crossroads in Bosnia." *New York Times.* 31 August 1997: 6.
Hedges, Chris. "Bosnian Vote Could Backfire on West." *New York Times.* 23 November 1997: 4.
———. "Officials See Risk in New NATO Push for Bosnia Peace." *New York Times.* 24 August 1997: 1, 4.
Rüb, Matthias. "Threats to Bosnia's Peace." *World Press Review.* October 1997: 4.

Rubin, Elizabeth. "The Enemy of Our Enemy." *New York Times Magazine.* 14 September 1997: 58–61.

"U.S. Warns Bosnian Serbs to Honor Accords." *New York Times.* 31 August 1997: 6.

Plectrudis
Queen, Regent of Austrasia and Neustria (714–716)

Plectrudis was the wife of Pepin II of Herstol, mayor of Austrasia and Neustria from 687 to 714. (The title of mayor did not have the same connotation there as it has in the United States today.) The couple had at least one son, Grimoald, who died in 714, the same year his father died. All of Pepin's sons had predeceased him except one illegitimate son, Charles the Bold (Martel). Following the Frankish custom, Pepin's will divided the kingdoms among his grandsons as mayors under the regency of Queen Plectrudis. She did not rule long before civil war broke out among various rival factions. Between 716 and 719 Pepin's illegitimate son, Charles, overcame the Neustrians in three battles and took control of the kingdoms.

References
Previté-Orton, C. W. *The Shorter Cambridge Medieval History.* Cambridge: Cambridge University Press, 1952, 1982. p. 159.

Pokou, Aura
See Awura Pokou

Pomare IV
Queen, Ruler on Tonga (ca. 19th c.)

According to Knappert, Pomare is the name of a series of queens on the island of Tonga. One, Queen Pomare IV, is "credited" with inadvertently inviting Western diseases to her island by lifting the ban on marriages with non-Polynesians.

References
Knappert, Jan. *Pacific Mythology.* London: Diamond Books, 1995. p. 232.

Pomare V
Queen, Ruler on Tahiti (fl. 1835–1836)

Pomare is a family name that appears throughout the South Pacific. It was the name of several kings of Tahiti, but it was also the name of at least one queen. Queen Pomare V is remembered for having expelled two French Roman Catholic missionary priests from the Protestant island in ca. 1835 or 1836. As a result of this action, France demanded reparations from the Tahitians. In 1842 the Tahitians asked for a protectorate, which was granted in 1843. Eventually, Tahiti became a colony (1880).

References

Langer, William L., ed. *World History*. Boston: Houghton Mifflin, 1980. p. 925.

Prabhāvatī Gupta
Regent of the Kingdom of the Vākātakas (ca. 390–410)

Prabhāvatī Gupta was the daughter of Chandra Gupta II, who ruled northern India from 380 to 415. To strengthen his southern boundaries, Emperor Chandra married his daughter to King Rudrasena II, ruler of the Vākātakas (ca. 385–390). The Vākātaka kingdom was based on what remained of the earlier Sātavāhana kingdom and was located in the central Deccan region of India. When Rudrasena died ca. 390 after a reign of only five years, his sons were infants. His widow Prabhāvatī served as regent from ca. 390 to 410. During her unusually lengthy regency, her Gupta culture and her ties to the northern Indian kingdom enabled her to make a significant impact on Vākātakas culture.

References

Thaper, Romila. *A History of India*. Vol. 1. London: Penguin Books, 1987. pp. 139–140.

Prunskiene, Kazimiera-Daniute
Prime Minister of Lithuania (1990–1991)

Kazimiera-Daniute Prunskiene (Courtesy: Lithuanian-European Institute)

Born in 1943, Prunskiene was a member of the Lithuanian Parliament and the leader of her party when Lithuania declared its independence from the former Soviet Union. She was elected prime minister in 1990 and served for only one year.

References

World Almanac. Mahwah, NJ: K-III Reference Company, 1998.

Pu-abi
Queen, Co-ruler of Ur (ca. 2500 B.C.)

The Sumerian Dynasty of Ur was located on the Euphrates River. There are several surviving indications of the importance of Pu-abi (or Puabi, formerly Shubad). Her name is one of only two with the title *nim* (meaning "queen") inscribed on a cylinder-seal of lapis lazuli in the Royal Cemetery of Ur. She was the wife of an unknown king. Her body, along with several other bodies of presumed attendants, was found in a stone chamber. The queen's body was on a bier. She wore a headdress of gold, lapis lazuli, and carnelian, and she held a gold cup in her hand. Her burial place showed signs of human sacrifice, an indication that more than kingship was being honored. This would indicate that she was considered a god as well or at least that she represented a god on earth and thus was entitled to take her court with her into the next life. Apparently at this early period, the royal/divine quality meriting human sacrifice could be possessed by a woman as well as a man.

References
Glubok, Shirley, ed. *Discovering the Royal Tombs at Ur.* London: Macmillan, 1969. pp. 48–49.

Roux, Georges. *Ancient Iraq.* Harmondsworth, Middlesex: Penguin Books, 1980. pp. 132–133.

Puduhepa
Queen, Co-ruler of the Hittites (ca. 1275–ca. 1250 B.C.), Co-regent (ca. 1250–? B.C.)

Puduhepa (or Pudu-Kheba) was the daughter of a priest and grew up in Kizzuwatna (or Kizzuwadnian), a town on the coast of what is now Turkey. She was educated in history and literature and became a priestess until she married the man who would become King Hattusilis III (r. ca. 1275–ca. 1250 B.C.). He was the younger brother of King Muwatallis (r. ca. 1306–1282 B.C.), who had appointed Hattusilis as viceroy over his northern provinces as a reward for Hattusilis's victories over the Kashas. When Muwatallis died, his son, Urhi-Teshup (r. ca. 1283–1275 B.C.), succeeded him, but the new king soon began to belittle his uncle, Hattusilis. In ca. 1275 B.C. Hattusilis usurped the throne from his weak nephew. Later, in justifying his actions, he wrote that he was following the will of the goddess Ishtar.

Together, the king and queen reconstructed and reoccupied the old capital at Hattusa (present-day Boğazköy, Turkey). The two shared the rule for twenty-four years. A strong and influential woman,

Puduhepa had her own seal, with which she signed the king's international correspondence.

The couple had several children; a surviving self-critical, self-justifying autobiography from her husband says, "God granted us the love of husband and wife, and we had sons and daughters." This document is the first such in recorded history. One of their daughters, Naptera, was given in marriage as chief wife to Pharaoh Ramses II, as part of an "everlasting peace" between the Hittites and the Egyptians. This peace treaty (c. 1269 B.C.), written in both languages, the oldest written document of its kind, heralded a peace that lasted for some seventy years. Their son, Tudhaliyas IV (or Tudkhaliash, r. ca. 1250–1220 B.C.) succeeded Hattusilis upon his death, and because he was a weak ruler, Puduhepa became co-regent with him.

References

Ceram, C. W. *The Secret of the Hittites.* New York: Alfred A. Knopf, 1955.

Lehman, Johannes. *The Hittites.* Chicago: The University of Chicago Press, 1975.

Pulcheria
Augusta, Regent of the Eastern Empire (414–453)

Pulcheria was born in Constantinople in 399, the daughter of Eastern Roman emperor Flavius Arcadius, ruler from 383 to 408, and his wife Eudoxia. Pulcheria was the older sister of Theodosius II, born in 401, who ruled from 408 to 450. When her father died in 408, Pulcheria was appointed augusta and made regent for her brother, although she was only two years his senior. She took her responsibilities very seriously and assumed a personal hand in Theodosius's education. A devout Christian, she maintained her court with great piety and chastity. In 421 she arranged the marriage of her brother to Athenais (Eudocia), who eventually became her rival in court. In 443 friction between the two had mounted to such an extent that Eudocia voluntarily withdrew to Jerusalem. The eunuch chamberlain Chrysaphius gradually worked his way into the emperor's favor and eventually gained dominance over him for a while, but Pulcheria had recovered the initiative before Theodosius's death in 450. She selected a retired soldier, Marcian, as her brother's successor and married him to preserve the dynasty. She died in 453.

References

Bowder, Diana, ed. *Who Was Who in the Roman World.* Ithaca, NY: Cornell University Press, 1980. p. 452.

Purea

*Queen of the Landward Teva of Tahiti, Self-proclaimed Queen of
All of Otaheite, or Tahiti (mid-18th c.)*

Purea (or Oberea) and her mate Amo were the leaders of the Landward Teva tribe. She had a son, Teri-i-reree (b. ca. 1758/1759). On
June 26, 1767, Captain Samuel Wallis, captain of the English ship *Dolphin,* being ill in bed, sent his second lieutenant, Tobias Furneaux, to
take possession of Tahiti for the British. Two weeks after the ship's arrival and the rituals of possession, the English had seen a procession
of canoes bearing colorful pennants passing in review. Ten days later a
member of the crew came upon a "palace," where he was entertained
by the "queen," who was fed by her "ladies in waiting." In their reports
the men of the *Dolphin* invariably used quotation marks when describing the queen or her court, for to their way of thinking, the only
"authentic" courts were European. In July the queen made her first
visit aboard the ship. The captain treated her royally, but behind her
back the Englishmen laughed at her awkward use of Western cutlery
and at the tatoos on her rear.

There began a series of social exchanges designed by the English
to present to their own government the idea that they had established
diplomatic relations with the Tahitians. In reality the English sailors
found the Tahitian women's lack of sexual inhibition the most promising coin of social exchange. When Samuel Wallis sailed the *Dolphin*
for home, it is recorded that Queen Purea evinced "extravagant sorrow" at its leaving. However, the Englishmen left behind a legacy of
venereal diseases.

The Admiralty contracted with Dr. John Hawkesworth, a geog-
rapher of sorts, to record in a book the voyages of the various English explorers of the South Pacific. In this account there appears an
engraving entitled "A representation of the surrender of the island
of Otaheite to Captain Wallis by the supposed Queen Oberea." This
depicted a purely fictitious event. In 1767–1768 Purea and her mate
Amo (Suggs omits mention of the mate) built Mahaiatea, a sacred
place that was intended to be the ritual center of the island, for their
son, Teri-i-reree, in hopes of establishing him as the ruler over all of
Tahiti. One account says that when Purea imposed certain prohibi-
tions of food and behavior on the people, her sister and her sister-
in-law paid her formal visits, challenging the imposed fast. Ordinarily, formal visits among equals demanded hospitality, thus having the
effect of lifting Purea's ban. But, intent upon upholding the fast,
Purea refused to acknowledge their equality, and according to one

account, this rift precipitated a battle.

Another account of the cause of the uprising says that after Teri-i-reree's investiture and the ceremonial procession of symbols around the island began, Purea and Amo demanded submission of the subjects as the ceremony passed. But the Seaward Teva tribe refused to submit to a new authority, and they evinced their outrage with violence.

Whatever the cause, when Captain James Cook with young Joseph Banks sailed for Tahiti in 1768, they found that Purea and

Purea (NorthWind Picture Archives)

Amo had failed in their attempt to establish Teri-i-reree as the supreme ruler of all of Tahiti. The Seaward Teva had massacred many of the people of Papara, destroyed Mahaitea, and would ultimately defeat Purea.

The queen was said to be enamored of young Banks; one account tells of Banks's loss of his waistcoat and pistol while he slept on "Oberea's" canoe. At one point she directed a ritual at the gate of Fort Venus, which Cook observed, of the public copulation of a young man and a girl of ten or twelve. Letters exist in London, one dated 1775, from "Oberea, Queen of Otaheite to Joseph Banks, Esq." as well as one of Banks's replies, written after Cook had returned from his first voyage. Supposedly she also wrote a letter to Wallis. No record of her exists after the time of these documents.

References

Dening, Greg. *Performances.* Chicago: The University of Chicago Press, 1996. pp. 147, 151, 153–156, 161–167.

Suggs, Robert C. *The Island Civilizations of Polynesia.* New York: Mentor, 1960. pp. 133, 144.

Pu-su-wan
See Ye-lü Shih

R

Radiyya, Sultana
Sultana, Muslim Queen of Delhi, Northern India (1236–1240),
Called "Pillar of Women, Queen of the Times"

Radiyya (or Raẓiyya [or Razia] Iltutmi<u>sh</u>, or Altamsh, or Malika Iltutmish) was the Turkish daughter of <u>Sh</u>amsudīn Iltutmi<u>sh</u>, a former
slave who rose to be the third and greatest sultan of the Muslim Slave
Dynasty in Delhi. Her mother was the daughter of Qutb-ud-Din Aybak, the second sultan of Delhi. Sultan <u>Sh</u>amsudīn, originally a Turkish slave, a Mamluk, as general of the army had helped found the Muslim state of India in 1229.

Mamluks were Turks from the Asian steppes who were captured
as white slaves by slave merchants who sold them to the sultans. They
received a military education and then joined the military caste of the
palaces. After a period of apprenticeship, the Mamluks were named
to important posts in the military hierarchy, thus becoming part of
the military elite. Iltutmi<u>sh</u>'s bravery so impressed the sultan, Qutb
al-Dīn Aybak, that he married the young Turk to his daughter. At Aybak's death in 1211, Iltutmi<u>sh</u> took power and declared himself independent of the Ghaznah masters. He reigned for twenty-six years
and, realizing that his two sons by other wives were both feeble
minded, designated his daughter, Radiyya, as his successor.

When he died in 1236, she became the first Muslim woman to
rule northern India, but not without opposition. One of the sons,
Rukn al-Dīn, rebelled and killed his half brother, hoping to intimidate
Radiyya into stepping down. Radiyya, adopting a custom instituted by
her father, donned a garment dyed to indicate that she was a victim.
When her brother emerged from the palace to attend Friday prayers
at the mosque, she mounted the balcony and addressed the army, saying, "My brother killed his brother and he now wants to kill me." She
reminded the people of her father's many good deeds. The crowd became incensed, captured Rukn al-Dīn, and put him to death. The

army declared that Radiyya, a spinster, was queen. Thirteenth-century historian Amīr Khusrau said in Hardy's *Historians of Medieval India*, "Since there were no worthy sons, worthy opinion turned to Raẓiyya."

One of her first acts was to unveil. She "cut her hair and dressed like a man and in this fashion mounted the throne," according to an account by Badriye Uçok Un in Mernissi. According to Ibn Battuta's account, "She ruled as an absolute monarch for four years. She mounted horse like men armed with bow and quiver, and she would not cover her face." (Ibn Battuta, *The Rehla*).

Radiyya came to the throne at a difficult time in her country's history. During her reign, the two dominant sects of Islam, the Sunnis (the orthodox sect traditionally favored by the sultanate) and the Shias (a more radical splinter group), were pitted against each other. The Shias, joining some other schismatics, revolted against the sultanate but were roundly put down by Radiyya's forces. After that time, the Shias ceased to be a serious challenge to Sunnis during the history of the sultanate. Radiyya's subjects turned on her, however, when she began a rapid promotion of Jamāl al-Dīn Yaqat, an Abyssinian Ethiopian slave, who soon became master of the horse. It was suspected that she had embarked on a torrid love affair with him. Once, according to Ibn Battuta's account, when she was mounting her horse, "He slid his arms under her armpits in order to hoist her up on to her mount." Word spread rapidly that she had violated ethical behavior by allowing herself to be touched by her slave.

Although she was courageous and intelligent, after three and a half years on the throne she was nevertheless toppled in a palace coup. An army, raised by the governor, Ikhtiyar al-Din Altuniyya, agreed to depose her and have her marry. Radiyya left Delhi with her own army to combat Altuniyya. She lost the battle and was taken prisoner, but her charms proved too much for Altuniyya. He freed her, married her, and took her, wearing men's clothing over her own, and their armies back to Delhi to recapture her throne. But they were defeated, and Radiyya fled.

She wandered into a peasant's cottage and begged for food. The peasant, spying her jeweled gown under her disguise, killed her, drove away her horse, and buried her in his field. The peasant took some of her finery into the market to sell, but the *shihna* (magistrate) became suspicious and forced him into confessing his crime. Her body was disinterred, washed, shrouded, and given a proper burial. According to Ibn Battuta, "A dome was built over her grave which is now visited, and people obtain blessings from it."

Historian Yaḥyā ibn Aḥmad then wrote of the tragic event, "Every head that the celestial globe raises up/It will likewise throw a noose around the neck of that very same."

The historian Sirāj (S̲h̲ams al-dīn Sirāj) said in Eliot and Dowson, "Sultana Raẓiyya was a great monarch. She was wise, just and generous, a benefactor to her kingdom, a dispenser of justice, the protector of her subjects and the leader of her armies. She was endowed with all the qualities befitting a king, but she was not born of the right sex, so, in the estimation of men, all these virtues were worthless."

She was succeeded by a grandchild of her father's.

References

Ali, Tariq. "Dynasty's Daughter." *Interview*. February 1989. p. 124.

Eliot, H. M., and J. Dowson. *A History of India as Told by Its Own Historians*. Vol. 1. Cambridge: Cambridge University Press, 1931. pp. 185, 332.

Hardy, Peter. *Historians of Medieval India*. Westport, CT: Greenwood Press, 1982. pp. 65, 91.

Ibn Battuta. *The Rehla of Ibn Battuta. India, Maldive Islands and Ceylon*. Trans. Mahdi Husain. Baroda, India: Oriental Institute, 1976. pp. 34–35.

———. *Travels of Ibn Battuta AD 1325–1354*. Trans. H. A. R. Gibb from the French translation of C. Defremery and B. B. Sanguinetti. Vol. 1. Cambridge: Cambridge University Press, 1958.

Mernissi, Fatima. *The Forgotten Queens of Islam*. Trans. Mary Jo Lakeland. Minneapolis: University of Minnesota Press, 1993. pp. 89–90, 93–97.

Thapar, Romila. *A History of India*. Vol. 1. London: Penguin Books, 1987. pp. 269, 301.

Ranavalona I
Queen, Titular Ruler of the Kingdom of Madagascar (1828–1861)

The kingdom of Madagascar, which united most of the island, lasted from 1810 to 1896, when Madagascar became a French colony. Of its six rulers, four were women. The kingdom was founded by King Radama I (r. 1809–1828), who, in exchange for assistance from the British governor of nearby Mauritius, agreed to cooperate in ending slave trade thoughout his territory. He also allowed into his country European tradesmen and members of the London Missionary Society. He married his cousin, Ranavalona I, a member of the Merina, or Andriana, Dynasty and the grandniece of Andrianjafy (r. 1760–1783). The couple had a son, Radama II.

When Radama I died prematurely in 1828, Ranavalona succeeded him and ruled for thirty-three years. Because she did not share his romance with the Europeans, she moved quickly to reverse her late husband's liberal Europeanization policies. Over a number of years she expelled the Europeans, and eventually she had so purged the kingdom of outsiders that the British and French joined forces to unseat her. They were defeated at Tamatave in 1845. She ruled unmolested until her death in 1861. Her son Radama II (r. 1861–1863), who succeeded her, married her niece Rasoherina, a daughter of her sister.

References

Egan, Edward W., Constance B. Hintz, and L. F. Wise, eds. *Kings, Rulers, and Statesmen.* New York: Sterling Publishing, 1976. p. 302.

Morby, John E. *Dynasties of the World.* Oxford: Oxford University Press, 1989. p. 237.

Ranavalona II
Queen of Madagascar (1868–1883)

Madagascar, an island located off the southeastern shore of Africa, is populated by a mixture of African and Indonesian people. Ranavalona II was a member of the Merina, or Andriana, Dynasty and the niece of Queen Ranavalona I (r. 1828–1861), her mother being the queen's sister. The first Ranavalona's son Radama II had succeeded upon his mother's death in 1861, but he was assassinated two years later at the instigation of the Merina oligarchy, tribes of a "higher" pure Indonesian caste. His former army chief, Rainilaiarivony, asserted himself into the position of prime minister, marrying the king's widow, Rasoherina (r. 1863–1868), who was another niece of Ranavalona I. When Rasoherina died five years later, Ranavalona II succeeded her, and Rainilaiarivony married her as well.

The following year (1869), Christianity was adopted as the official religion of Madagascar, and the traditional Malagasy religion was suppressed. The kingdom soon took on many of the European characteristics once adopted by the queen's uncle and so long fought by her aunt. Ranavalona II's fifteen-year reign was the last peaceful reign of the dynasty. When she died in 1883, leaving no heir, a distant cousin, Ranavalona III, was found to succeed her.

References

Egan, Edward W., Constance B. Hintz, and L. F. Wise, eds. *Kings, Rulers, and Statesmen.* New York: Sterling Publishing, 1976. p. 302.

Morby, John E. *Dynasties of the World.* Oxford: Oxford University Press, 1989. p. 237.

Ranavalona III
Queen of Madagascar (1883–1896)

Ranavalona III was born in 1861, presumably a distant cousin of King Radama II (r. 1861–1863), Queen Rasoaherina (r. 1863–1868), and Queen Ranavalona II (r. 1868–1883). The last ruler of the Merina, or Andriana, Dynasty, she succeeded Queen Ranavalona II upon her death in 1883. In 1883, Ranavalona III married the prime minister, Rainilaiarivony, who had been married to the two preceding queens and who was implicated in the death of Radama II. In 1895 French troops forced her husband into exile. She was forced to sign a treaty allowing Madagascar to become a French protectorate. She was not officially deposed but remained as a figurehead until, in 1916 or 1917, she died. Thereafter, Madagascar was united with the French empire.

References
Egan, Edward W., Constance B. Hintz, and L. F. Wise, eds. *Kings, Rulers, and Statesmen.* New York: Sterling Publishing, 1976. p. 302.
Morby, John E. *Dynasties of the World.* Oxford: Oxford University Press, 1989. p. 237.

Ranocchini, Glorianna
Co-captain-regent of San Marino (1984, 1989–1990)

San Marino, a land-locked country completely surrounded by Italy, is the oldest independent country in the world. The republic is led by heads of state called co-captains-regent, who are elected for six-month terms and reelectable only after three years. The co-captains-regent preside over the ten-member Congress of State, the executive branch of the government. These members and the captains-regent are all elected from among the parliamentary body, called the Great and General Council, members of which are elected for terms of five years.

Glorianna Ranocchini, who had been elected to a seat on the Great and General Council, first became co-captain-regent in 1984, while a coalition led by Communists controlled the council. In 1986 a new Christian Democrat–Communist coalition was formed. Glorianna Rancchini, returned to the council in the general elections of 1988, was again named to the post of captain-regent in 1989, serving until April 1990.

References
"San Marino." *Britannica Macropaedia.* Vol. 16. 1990. pp. 223–224.
"San Marino." *Funk & Wagnalls New Encyclopedia.* Vol. 23. 1986. p. 123.

Rasoherina
Queen of Madagascar (1863–1868)

A member of the Merina, or Andriana Dynasty, she was related to King Andrianjafy (r. 1760–1783) and to Queen Ranavalona I (r. 1828–1861), who was her mother's sister. Rasoherina married her cousin, Radama II, Queen Ranavalona I's son, who ascended to the throne in 1861 but was assassinated only two years later. Rasoherina ruled for five years. Radama II's former army chief, who was implicated in his murder, married Rasoherina, possibly against her will, and rose to become prime minister. On her death she was replaced by another of Ranavalona's nieces, Ranavalona II.

References
Egan, Edward W., Constance B. Hintz, and L. F. Wise, eds. *Kings, Rulers, and Statesmen.* New York: Sterling Publishing, 1976. p. 302.
Morby, John E. *Dynasties of the World.* Oxford: Oxford University Press, 1989. p. 237.

Robinson, Mary
President of Ireland (1990–1997)

Born Mary Bourke in Ballina, County Mayo, in 1944, she was educated in a convent school in Dublin. Her parents, Aubrey Bourke and Tessa O'Donnell, were doctors who subscribed to the *Irish Times,* considered a Protestant newspaper, which was banned at her school. Mary Bourke campaigned successfully for the ban to be lifted. She studied law, did postgraduate work at Harvard Law School, and at twenty-five became Trinity College's youngest law professor. Although her family was staunchly Catholic, she married a Protestant solicitor, Nicholas Robinson, and they had three children.

As a civil liberties lawyer, she entered politics and became a senator at age twenty-five. As a former member of the Irish Labor Party, she campaigned for the underdogs in Irish society. She also campaigned for the decriminalization of homosexuality, for equal rights for women, and against the prohibition of information on abortion. On her run for the presidency, she asked for and received a mandate to extend the hand of friendship to Northern Ireland's two communities. She was sworn in as the first woman president of Ireland on December 3, 1990. Of voters who elected her to what was then a largely symbolic but representative position, she said, "Instead of rocking the table, they rocked the system."

Prior to Robinson's tenure in office, successive presidents did little but sign documents and appear at state occasions. But Robinson changed the image of the Irish presidency into one of vitality and action and became one of the most admired leaders in the world.

In May 1995, President Robinson described the 150th anniversary of the great potato famine of 1845–1847 as a time to break the silence about this national disgrace and to decipher the puzzles and mysteries surrouding it. Was the famine a national disaster, was the landlord system at fault, or was the British laissez-faire colonial system in effect an act of genocide? Whatever the causes, the famine changed the country's character forever. It marked the end of the Celtic church, the Irish language, and the landlord class. It brought on the massive exodus to North America, so that today there are more Irish in the United States than in Ireland. The famine has been considered so shameful that even Irish literature has shunned it. However, Robinson hoped the commemoration would be cathartic, such that the Irish people would then look back to the golden age of the seventh and eighth centuries with renewed pride in Ireland's accomplishments.

*Mary Robinson
(Courtesy: Consulate
General of Ireland)*

She became a key figure in helping consolidate the peace process between the two Irelands. She was the first Irish president to open dialogue with the British royal family, paying a visit to Buckingham Palace for tea with the queen and hosting a visit of the queen's children in Ireland.

Robinson did not confine her interest to civil rights at home. She took several fact-finding trips to parts of Africa suffering from famine and the ravages of war. In 1996 her name was being mentioned as a possible successor to Boutros-Ghali as UN secretary-general. Her popularity among diverse factions had grown during her first term, which was a seven-year one. The recipient of numerous honorary degrees and international humanitarian awards, she was said to be admired by Queen Elizabeth. She instilled great loyalty among her staff at Phoenix Park. Loyalist women from Belfast sang her praises, as did Lord Jenkins, co-founder of Britain's Social Democratic Party, who praised her for her "wisdom and humanity."

Acknowledged as a "fervent internationalist," Robinson was quoted in the London *Observer* (21 April 1996) as believing that order, national or international, would be attained one step at a time. "We need to build lots of bridges," she said.

At the end of her term, she announced "with great reluctance" her decision not to run for reelection, although her success was assured, as no candidate opposed her. Upon leaving her post, she joined the United Nations as commissioner of human rights.

References

Connolly, Anne. "Ghosts of the Famine." *South China Morning Post,* Hong Kong, 11 November 1995. Reprinted in *World Press Review.* February 1996: 39–40.

"Here's to You, Mrs. Robinson." *World Press Review.* July 1996: 49.

Makem, Peter. "President Robinson Departs," in "Letter from Ireland." *Irish Edition.* www.us-irish.com. 24 November 1997.

"Outpouring of Warmth for Retiring Irish President." www.us-irish.com. 24 November 1997.

Russudan
Queen, Ruler of Georgia (1223–1234), Co-ruler (1234–1245/1247)

Russudan (or Rusudani or Rusudan) was the daughter of Queen Thamar (Tamara) the Great, who ruled Georgia from 1186 to 1212, and Thamar's cousin and consort, David Soslan, who ruled jointly from 1193 to 1207. Russudan's brother, King George III (Giorgi III Lasha, or the Brilliant, or the Resplendent), co-ruler from 1205 to 1212, then sole ruler until 1223, had many mistresses and even fathered an illegitimate child, but he had no legitimate heir to succeed him other than his sister. In 1221 the Georgian troops had been cut to ribbons at Khunani by Mongol generals of Jenghiz-khan, Jebe and Sübötäi. Russudan, having something of the same disposition as her brother and little of her mother's Christian piety, described in fact as "an unmarried but not a virgin queen," acceded to the throne when her brother died, and was proclaimed King of Karthalinia. Karthalinia, or Kartlia, was a section in present-day Georgia.

In 1225 Jelal ad-Din Mängüberti (Jalal on-Din or Jelal ad-Din), heir to the Khwarizmian empire who had been driven into exile by Jenghiz-khan, invaded Georgia. Queen Russudan sent an army to meet him, but her troops had not regained their strength since their trouncing by Jenghiz-khan: They were defeated at Garnhi on her southern frontier. The invaders, after ravaging southern Georgia, moved on into Russia. Queen Russudan wrote to the pope: "A savage people of Tartars [a play on words for the Tatars, *tartar* meaning *hell*], hellish of aspect, as voracious as wolves in their hunger for spoils and brave as lions, have invaded my country. . . . The brave knighthood of Georgia has hunted them out of the country, killing 25,000 of the invaders."

Learning that nearby Persia had been weakened by Mongol attack, she took advantage of the recent disaster and attacked Persia. But in 1225 Jelal ad-Din swooped down again and attacked the capital of Tiflis. Queen Russudan fled to Kutais while Jelal ad-Din occupied and sacked the capital, destroying all the Christian churches. In 1228 she attempted to regain control of the provinces along the Kur River that Jelal ad-Din held, but she was driven back. In 1231 the Mongol army reappeared to challenge Jelal ad-Din under the leadership of General Chormaqan. Jelal ad-Din, who had been defeated by Mongols before, retreated hastily, to die in Kurdestan in 1231. That year, with the Mongols fighting the Turks, Queen Russudan reoccupied her capital of Tiflis, but five years later Chormaqan invaded Georgia, and she was forced to take refuge once again in Kutais.

Around 1241 Chormaqan was stricken with the inability to speak and was replaced by Baiji. Queen Russudan soon became an irritant to him because of her stubborn refusal to give in to the Mongols. Eventually, however, in 1243 she herself became a vassal of the Mongols with the understanding that the whole kingdom of Georgia would be given to her son David Narin to rule under Mongol suzerainty. However, David Narin was in actuality only given Imeretia, while David Lasha, an heir of Russudan's brother, was given Kartlia.

References

Buchan, John, ed. *The Baltic and Caucasian States.* Boston: Houghton Mifflin, 1923. pp. 173–174.

Grousset, René. *The Empire of the Steppes.* Trans. Naomi Walford. New Brunswick, NJ: Rutgers University Press, 1970. pp. 260, 263, 272, 350.

Hussey, J. M., ed. *The Cambridge Medieval History.* Vol. 4, pt. 1. Cambridge: Cambridge University Press, 1966. p. 783.

Runciman, Steven. *A History of the Crusades.* Vol. 3, *The Kingdom of Acre.* Cambridge: Cambridge University Press, 1952, 1987. pp. 249–250.

Storm Across Georgia. London: Cassel, 1981. p. 40.

Suny, Ronald Grigor. *The Making of the Georgian Nation.* Bloomington: Indiana University Press, in association with Hoover Institution Press, Stanford University, 1988. pp. 40–41.

Rweej
Queen of the Lunda (before 1600)

The Lunda live in the savanna belts of central Africa, specifically the grasslands of Congo-Angola-Zambia. Queen Rweej was from a distinguished family of leaders. Rweej herself was the local Lunda queen when, toward 1600, a handsome Luba (another related people) hunter named Kibinda Ilunga took a band of followers west to the river Kasai. There he met the queen, charmed her, and married her. Thereafter Rweej let Kibinda Ilunga rule. This angered her twin brothers, who left the kingdom for the interior of Angola to establish chiefdoms of their own. Her brother Kinguri was the founding hero of the Imbangala in Angola. Another brother migrated south with a band of followers and formed the Lwena people, who today occupy the territory along the headwaters of the Zambezi. Queen Rweej and Kibinda Ilunga had a son, Luseeng, who, along with his son, Naweej, built a mighty empire called Lundaland, of which Naweej was the first Mwata Yamvo, or "lord of the viper."

References

Davidson, Basil. *African History.* New York: Collier Books, 1991. pp. 160–161.

Fage, J. D. *A History of Africa.* New York: Alfred A. Knopf, 1978. pp. 137–138.

Vansina, Dr. Jan. "Inner Africa." In Alvin M. Josephy, Jr., ed. *The Horizon History of Africa.* New York: American Heritage Publishing, McGraw-Hill, 1971. p. 267.

S

Sada Kaur
Rani, De Facto Co-ruler of Śukerchakīās, Pakistan (1795–ca. 1801)

Sada Kaur was the widow of a chieftain of the Kanhayas, whose daughter Jindan married fifteen-year-old Ranjit Singh, chief since he was twelve of the Śukerchakīās, a Sikh group. For many years Sada Kaur directed his affairs. Eventually Ranjit Singh proclaimed himself maharaja of the Punjab, a state that he single-handedly created.

References
Spear, Percival. *A History of India.* Vol. 2. London: Penguin Books, 1987. pp. 76, 104, 107, 117, 132, 135.

Saimei-tennō
See Kōgyoku-tennō

Salome Alexandra
See Alexandra

Salote Tupou III
Queen, Ruler of Tonga (1918–1965)

Salote Tupou was born in 1900, the daughter of King Tupou II, ruler of Tonga from 1893 to 1918, member of a dynasty that had ruled from at least the tenth century. During her father's reign, Tonga became a British protectorate because of financial difficulties. Salote came to the throne at the age of eighteen, following her father's death. A commanding figure at six feet two inches tall—size and stateliness have characterized the ruling family for generations—the queen guided the islands with wisdom and grace for forty-seven years, endearing herself to the people of Britain as well as to her own. To encourage Tonga's traditional crafts, she organized a women's cooperative that maintains at least one handicraft shop in a local hotel.

Salote Tupou III (Corbis / Hulton-Deutsch Collection)

In 1917 she married Sione (John) Fe'iloakitau Kaho (Prince Viliami Tungi). Their son, Taufa (or Tung, born in 1918), succeeded upon his mother's death (1965) as King Tafua'ahou Tupou IV. The queen who ruled so long and well did not live to see Tonga regain complete independence in 1970.

References

Candee, Marjorie Dent, ed. *Current Biography 1952.* New York: H. W. Wilson, 1954. pp. 552–554.

Egan, Edward W., Constance B. Hintz, and L. F. Wise, eds. *Kings, Rulers, and Statesmen.* New York: Sterling Publishing, 1976. p. 465.

Grosvenor, Melville Belle. "South Seas' Tonga Hails a King." *National Geographic* 133. March 1968: 322–344.

International Who's Who, 1987–1988. London: Europa Publishing, 1987. p. xvi.

Marden, Luis. "The Friendly Faces of Tonga." *National Geographic* 133. March 1968: 345–367.

Samsia
Queen, Ruler of Southern Arabia (ca. 732 B.C.)

In 734 B.C. King Ahaz of Judah asked the help of his suzerain Tiglath-Pileser III, who had taken over the New Assyrian Empire (745–727 B.C.), in defending against a coalition of the forces of Rezen of Damascus and Pekah (Pakaha) of Israel. Tiglath-Pileser obliged by first demolishing Israel's forces and then, in 732 B.C., marching against Damascus. He turned Damascus and outlying parts of Israel into provinces. In the central part of Israel he devastated the stately gardens outside Jerusalem, then swept through the capital and killed King Pekah, replacing him with Hoshea. Two queens of the Arabs sent tribute to Tiglath-Pileser. Records mention that a Queen Samsia, queen of southern Arabia at the time, was forced to pay tribute to Tiglath-Pileser in return for use of the harbor of Gaza, over which he had gained control. Another ruler called Zabibê, designated as "queen of the Arabs," also brought him tribute.

References

Biblical records: I Chronicles 5:26; II Kings 15 and 16 (in biblical accounts, Tiglath-Pileser is called Pul or Pulu).

Oppenheim, A. Leo. *Ancient Mesopotamia.* Chicago: University of Chicago Press, 1977. p. 169.

Packer, J. I. et al. *The Bible Almanac.* Nashville, TN: Thomas Nelson, 1980. pp. 134, 316, 500, 675.

Roux, Georges. *Ancient Iraq.* Harmondsworth, Middlesex: Penguin Books, 1980. p. 285.

Sancha, Queen
Titular Ruler of León (1037–1038)

Sancha was the daughter of Alfonso V (r. 999–1028) and Urraca I and the sister of Vermudo III (r. 1028–1037), who died without leaving an heir. Sancha's mother was the sister of Sancho el Mayor, king of Navarre (r. 1000–1035), who, during his lifetime, managed to bring all of Christian Spain under his influence.

Following the death of Alfonso V in 1028, García Sanchez, count of Castile, negotiated a marriage with the young Sancha that would have bolstered his position in relation to both León and Navarre. But before the marriage could be celebrated, he was assassinated in the city of León (1029). King Sancho of Navarre, because he was married to García Sanchez's sister, immediately claimed Castile in his wife's name and installed his son Ferdinand I (Fernando) as count. He then arranged a marriage between his son and his niece, Sancha. In 1034 the Navarrese king seized control of the city of León, forcing Vermudo to flee to Galicia. But King Sancho died the next year, and Vermudo immediately repossessed León. Thus Sancha was once again in line to inherit the throne upon Vermudo's death in 1037.

Her husband, Fernando, then ruled from 1038 until his death in 1065. The couple had three sons who ruled: García, the youngest, who ruled Galicia (1065–1071) until his brother Sancho took it from him; Sancho II the Strong, who ruled Castile (1065–1072) and was killed while wresting León from his other brother; and Alfonso VI, who ruled León (1065–1109), having reclaimed it after his brother Sancho's assassination. Alfonso's daughter, Urraca, managed to do what her grandmother could not: She ruled León in her own right (1109–1126).

References

Reilly, Bernard F. *The Kingdom of León-Castilla under Queen Urraca.* Princeton: Princeton University Press, 1982. pp. 6–9.

Sarraounia
Sorceress-queen of the Azna Kingdom (fl. 1899)

The Azna occupied the Dallol Mawri, a broad valley in the Hausa country of the present-day Dogondoutchi district of Niger in northwest Africa. As has happened with so many heroes of history, myths have grown about Sarraounia's childhood. She had a Spartan upbringing with adoptive parents. At the age of eighteen she already knew how to lead men into battle, and as a tribal sorceress, she held her warriors and her enemies alike in thrall. When the Fulani of Sokoto attempted to convert her and her people to Islam, she and her warriors fought bravely to drive them back. She had also successfully resisted invasion by the Tuaregs from the north before the white man appeared.

In January 1899, French troops—primarily black mercenaries—commanded by captains Voulet and Chanoine left Segou in Mali, crossed the territories of the Zarma and of the Gourma, and entered the dense vegetation of the Dallol Mawri. On April 17, 1899, they laid siege with cannon fire to the village of Lugu, which Queen Sarraounia and her fierce warriors defended valiantly, determined not to let the invaders drive her out: "We won't move a single inch from here . . . even if we must die to the last person!" But the superior French arms proved too powerful for the natives. Forced to retreat, she took her warriors into the forest, confiding to her adoptive father, "They are many and well-armed. . . . They burn everything along their route. . . ." After her initial defeat, she reorganized and vowed to resist "in spite of hunger. If there is no grain, we will eat vines and roots, but we will resist. . . ." She continued to harass her enemies, so intimidating the mercenaries that many of them abandoned the French. While the French captains, watching her rituals from afar, at first dismissed them as "drunkeness" and "incoherent ramblings of a superstitious woman," the mercenaries came to believe her to be the Nkomo woman, the femme fatale, the Dogoua, or demon-woman. Their abandonment greatly weakened the French forces. However, the Fulani, who, having failed to convert her to Islam, looked upon Sarraounia as a "rebellious, unclean, faithless woman" and her city as "accursed," opted to join forces with the French ultimately to bring about French subjugation of the entire area.

References
Mamani, Abdoulaye. *Sarraounia, ou "le drame d'une reine magicienne."* Paris: L'Harmattan, 1980.

Sati Beg
Il-Khanid Sultana of Persia (1338–1339)

The daughter of Mongol sultan Öljeitü of the Chingizid Dynasty (r. 1304–1316) and the sister of Abū Saʾīd (r. 1316–1335), Sati Beg (or Sati Bek) was one of four to come to the throne in the three years following her brother's death. Her first husband was Amir Tchoban, grandson of one of Hulägu's generals and commander-in-chief of the armed forces. After he died, she married Sultan Arpa (r. 1335–1336). When he died, two more men accended to the throne briefly before Sati Beg became head of state in her own right. During her reign the *khutba* was proclaimed in her name in the temple, signifying her right to rule. She had coins struck that read, "The just sultana Sati Bek Khan, may Allah perpetuate her reign." She was deposed after only nine months, and she took one of her two successors, Sulaymān Amin Yusuf Shah (r. 1339–1343), as her third husband. Following his rule, the Il-Khanid state broke into petty kingdoms. The title īl-khān denoted nominal subordination to the great Mongolian khan.

References

Mernissi, Fatima. *The Forgotten Queens of Islam.* Minneapolis: University of Minnesota Press, 1993. p. 105.

Morby, John E. *Dynasties of the World.* Oxford: Oxford University Press, 1989. p. 200.

Sauvé, Jeanne Mathilde
Governor-General of Canada (1984–1990)

She was born Jeanne Mathilde Benoit in 1992 in Prud'homme, Saskatchewan. In 1925 her family moved to Ottawa, where she was educated, graduating from the University of Ottawa. In 1942 she became president of Jeunesse Étudiante Catholique in Montreal, where she remained for five years. She married Maurice Sauvé, an economist, and the couple lived in Europe for four years. On their return to Canada as union organizers, she worked as a television commentator on CBC.

In 1972 she was elected as a Liberal to the House of Commons, and shortly afterward Prime Minister Pierre Elliott Trudeau named her successively minister of science and technology, environment, and communications. In 1980 she became the first woman to be Speaker of the House. In 1984, she assumed the post as Canada's first woman governor-general, replacing Edward R. Schreyer.

The governor-general is the nominal head of the government, appointed by the reigning monarch as the representative of the British crown. Following the prime minister's advice, the governor-general appoints the cabinet. It submits its decisions to the governor-general, who in turn, in most cases, is constitutionally bound to approve them. In theory, the governor-general is the head of the national government; the actual head is the prime minister, who is appointed to that post by the governor-general on the recommendation of the House of Commons.

Jeanne Sauvé retired in 1990 and died in 1993.

References

Filon, John, ed. *The World Almanac and Book of Facts.* New York: Newspaper Enterprise Association, 1994. pp. 522–523.

Funk & Wagnalls New Encyclopedia. Vol. 23. 1986. p. 175.

Saw
Chief Queen, Virtual Ruler of Pagan (1255–1287)

Ma (Lady, or literally "Sister") Saw (or Mi Cō Ū or Phwā Cō was born (c. 1229) in a Burmese village, the beautiful, talented daughter of peasants. At about the age of sixteen she became a "deputy queen" of a Pagan king who in a fictionalized account is called Usana (r. ca. 1211–1254/1255). Pagan was a walled dynastic fortress and the capital of Burma during a period when the region was comprised of five other major dynastic cities or kingdoms and two smaller kingdoms, all of which were dominated by Pagan and paid tribute to it. During his reign, Saw showed herself to be wise and diplomatic and so impressed the powerful chief minister that, when the king died, the minister made her chief queen of the king's successor, his bastard son Narathihapade (or Narasihapati, r. 1255–1287). This young man was chosen over the legitimate heir by the chief minister, who wished to maintain his own position. The young king was ignorant and unschooled in matters of the court. Both he and the chief minister came to rely upon Queen Saw's counsel, and she became the most influential figure in the kingdom of Pagan. Beginning in 1271 Kublai Khan sent missions to Pagan demanding tribute be paid. When their demands were rejected, the Mongols invaded. The king and his family fled the capital to a small town in the south. But he was lured to Prome and taken captive by his younger son, Sīhasū, Prome's governor, who offered him a choice of dying by poison or by the sword. The queen advised him that it would be nobler to die by poison than by "thy blood gushing red at point of sword." Following his death, she retired with her retinue to her village.

References

Aung-Thwin, Michael A. *Myth and History in the Historiography of Early*

Burma. Singapore: Institute of Southeast Asia Studies, 1998. pp. 56, 59, 177–178 fn., 186 fn.

Collis, Maurice. *She Was a Queen.* New York: New Directions Books, 1991.

Seaxburh
Queen of the Kingdom of Wessex (West Saxons) (672–674)

Seaxburh was the daughter of Pybba and the sister of Penda of Mercia. She married Cenwalh (Cenwealh), who ruled from 642–672. When Cenwalh repudiated his wife, her brother Penda drove Cenwalh from his throne. After Cenwalh died, Seaxburh ruled for two years. She was followed by Aescwine, a descendant of King Cynric (r. 534–560).

References
Aycock, Leslie. *Arthur's Britain.* Harmondsworth, Middlesex: Penguin Books, 1971. p. 343.

Morby, John E. *Dynasties of the World.* Oxford: Oxford University Press, 1989. p. 66.

Sebekkare
See Nefrusobek

Sebeknefru
See Nefrusobek

Shagshag
Queen, Administrator in Lagash (Early 3d Millennium B.C.)

Shagshag was the wife of King Urukagina. Her duties included but were not confined to administration of the temple of the goddess Bau, whose area extended over approximately one square mile and which employed 1,000–1,200 people. Shagshag also managed the temple devoted to the children of Bau. As administrator of these two temples, she exercised legal and economic authority over them and in addition functioned as chief priestess.

References
Batto, Bernard Frank. *Studies on Women at Mari.* Baltimore: Johns Hopkins University Press, 1974. p. 8.

Shajar Al Durr
Queen, Regent of Egypt (1250, Officially for 80 Days)

Shajar Al Durr (Shajarat al-Durr, Spray or Tree of Pearls) was Turkish, or possibly Armenian, and was the devoted slave-wife of Sultan Al Salih Ayyub, Ayyubid sultan of Egypt from 1240 to 1249. After she bore him a son, he gave her her freedom. During a campaign against the French Crusaders under King Louis in Africa, the sultan died in his tent in Mansoora in 1249. With the Crusaders on the way, Shajar Al Durr kept his death a secret. Daily she assured the officers that the sultan was much better, and she issued orders under the sultan's forged signature. Faced with a major battle against a well-armed force, this extraordinary woman commanded the army and at the same time ruled the land, all under cover, concealing a rotting corpse. The Crusaders were beaten by dysentery and starvation when the Muslims cut off their supply route.

Early the next year, the sultan's oldest son, Turan Shah, arrived in Cairo from Syria to be proclaimed sultan. But in May 1250, the Mamluks murdered him and hailed Spray of Pearls, to whom they were devoted, as queen of Egypt. She assumed sovereign power and ruled for eighty days, striking her own coins and having herself mentioned in Friday prayers as sultan of Egypt. Syria refused to recognize the accession of Spray of Pearls: The Abbasid Khalif wrote, quoting the Prophet, "Unhappy is the nation which is governed by a woman," adding with sarcasm, "If you have no men, I will send you one." As a result, Spray of Pearls was deposed in favor of a Mamluk general of the late sultan, Aybak, her commander-in-chief.

Shajar Al Durr, who was endowed with both intelligence and beauty, immediately set out to marry Aybak. Some sources say she married him before he became sultan, and then her Egyptian emirs nominated him as sultan. Whatever the scenario, it was through Shajar Al Durr that Aybak, who divorced his former wife, Umm 'Ali, to marry Shajar Al Durr, became the first Mamluk sultan (r. 1250–1257). In order not to be confined once more to a harem, Shajar Al Durr saw to it that the *khutba* (Friday prayer) was said in both her husband's and her name in every mosque in Cairo and that every official document bore both their signatures.

However, it was not a happy marriage. In 1257, when she learned that her husband intended to marry the daughter of the atabeg of Mosul, Badr al-Din Lu'lu, Shajar Al Durr was both humiliated and enraged. With her husband's servants, she devised an elaborate plan to murder Aybak. On April 12, 1257, when Aybak entered the *hammam,* or Turkish bath, at Citadel del Cairo, his servants surrounded and killed him.

The sultan's assassination threw the troops in an uproar. Some remained loyal to Shajar Al Durr, but a few days later Aybak's supporters retaliated. She was brought to the Burj al-Ahmar (Red Fort) and "battered to death with wooden shoes by the slave women of Aybak's first wife. . . ." They threw her half-nude body off the battlements of the citadel of Cairo overhanging a cliff. Her body lay in a ditch for several days before it was buried in the courtyard of a school that she founded. It is known today as Jami' Shajarat al-Durr, the mosque of Shajar Al Durr.

References

Chahin, M. *The Kingdom of Armenia*. New York: Dorset Press, 1987, 1991. p. 286.

Glubb, Sir John. *A Short History of the Arab Peoples*. New York: Dorset Press, 1969. pp. 202–205, 210.

Hitti, Philip K. *History of the Arabs*. New York: St. Martin's Press, 1968. p. 672.

Mernissi, Fatima. *The Forgotten Queens of Islam*. Minneapolis: University of Minnesota Press, 1993. pp. 14, 28–29, 86, 89, 90–93, 97–99, 110.

Shammu-ramat
Queen, Regent of New Assyrian Empire (ca. 811–806/809 B.C.)

Shammu-ramat (Shamiran, Sammuramat, or Semiramis) was born in Babylonia and married King Shamshi-Adad V, ruler of Assyria (823–811 B.C.). Following her husband's death, Shammu-ramat, as capable, energetic regent, ruled for three or five years before passing the reins of government to her son, Adad-nirari III. Proof that she clearly held the real power survives in dedications made in her own name, placed before that of her son. A memorial stele to her was found at Assur along with those of kings and other high officials, a singular honor for a woman then. The historical evidence stops there, but Greek historian Diodorus Siculus (ca. 1st century B.C.) credited her with rebuilding Babylon, a task historians attribute in part to a priestess, Addagoppe. Armenian legend attributes to "Queen Semiramis" much of the surviving construction of the kingdom of Urartu, which also belonged to Assyria at the time; however, there is no historical evidence to suggest that Shammu-ramat ever intervened in governing Urartu.

References

Chahin, M. *The Kingdom of Armenia*. New York: Dorset Press, 1987. pp. 67–71.

Herodotus. *The Histories.* Trans. Aubrey de Sélincourt. New York: Penguin Books, 1954, 1988. p. 115.

Langer, William L., ed. *World History.* Boston: Houghton Mifflin, 1940, 1980. p. 33.

Oates, Joan. *Babylon.* London: Thames and Hudson, 1979. p. 111.

Omstead, A. T. *History of the Persian Empire.* Chicago: University of Chicago Press, 1948. pp. 118, 163, 321–322, 380.

Oppenheim, A. Leo. *Ancient Mesopotamia.* Chicago: University of Chicago Press, 1977. p. 104.

Roux, Georges. *Ancient Iraq.* Harmondsworth, Middlesex: Penguin Books, 1980. p. 279.

Sheba

See Balkis

Shibtu

Queen, Frequent Regent of Mari (ca. 1790–1745 B.C.)

Shibtu was the wife of King Zimri-Lim, who ruled Mari in the mid-1700s B.C., and she acted as his deputy during his frequent absences. She had a variety of duties. The governor of Terqa, a neighboring city, addressing her as "his mistress," reported to the queen on business matters, and carried out her directives. Governors and vassal kings paid homage to her. She offered sacrifices, supervised oracles, and executed the king's orders.

References

Batto, Bernard Frank. *Studies on Women at Mari.* Baltimore: Johns Hopkins University Press, 1974. pp. 16, 20.

Shipley, Jenny

Prime Minister of New Zealand (1997–)

Jenny Shipley was born in 1952 in Gore, New Zealand, in the southern reaches of the South Island. She was the second daughter in a family that ultimately was to consist of four daughters. She grew up in Wellington, on the southern tip of the North Island, and Blenheim, on the northern part of the South Island. She graduated from Christchurch Teachers College in 1971 and taught in the primary grades for a number of years. She married Burton Shipley, who was to become a business development manager for a New Zealand bank. The two had a farming partnership for a number of years. After the birth of her children, Anna (b. 1977) and Ben (b. 1978), she became involved in politics at the local level.

In 1987 she entered national politics as a member of the New Zealand National Party and was elected as a legislator. In 1990 she was appointed minister of social welfare and minister of women's affairs, a position she held until 1996. In 1993 she was also appointed minister of health, and in 1996 she accepted an appointment to the portfolios of state services, transportation, state owned enterprises, accident rehabilitation compensation insurance, and Ra-

Jenny Shipley (AP Photo/Koji Sasahara)

dio New Zealand. In September 1997 she again became minister of women's affairs, at which time she relinquished the portfolio of state services. As leader of the National Party, she formed a coalition government with Winston Peters, leader of the New Zealand First Party. In November 1997 she was chosen prime minister–elect, and she was sworn in on December 8 as New Zealand's first woman prime minister.

During an interview following her inauguration, Shipley said, "I hope I've won this task on my merit. If it means that other young women in New Zealand will aspire to be the best that they can be, I'll feel very pleased." She described New Zealand as "a small but cheeky nation which seems to . . . do most things rather better than our size would suggest."

Speaking to the Auckland Regional Chamber of Commerce, she summed up the philosophy of her governmental style: "I am proud of the Government's determination to be realistic about the balance between what we would like and what we can afford." During 1998 Shipley traveled thoughout southeast Asia working to restore growth in the Asian Pacific Economic Community economies and to formulate an agreement opening markets in the World Trade Organization. In September 1999 she became the chairperson of APEC.

References

Peterson, Kara J. "Ungentle Coup." *World Press Review.* February 1998: 20.

Shipley, Jenny. Speech to the Auckland Regional Chamber of

Commerce, 16 December 1997. New Zealand Executive
Government News Release Archive.

Shipley, Jenny. Singapore Speech. New Zealand Executive Government
News Release, 20 November 1998.

Shipley, Jenny, and Simon Robinson. "A Small but Cheeky Nation." *Time.*
15 December 1997: 50.

Shōtoku-tennō

See Kōken-tennō

Shu-lü Shih

Khatum, Regent of Turkish Mongolia (926–?)

Shu-lü shih is not the empress's name. It simply means "of the Shu-lü clan"; unfortunately, although all the other names in this account are known, the empress's name was not preserved. She was the wife of A-pao-ki, chief of the Ye-lü clan of Khitan in the tenth century. The couple had two sons, T'u-yu and Tö-kuang. When her husband died in 926, the dowager empress rigged a popularity contest between her sons so that her favorite second son, Tö-kuang, would win. She then governed "with" him for the first few years, although she in fact held sole power and had indefatigable staying power. Each time a minister displeased her, she dispatched him to "take news of her to her late husband." Guards at her husband's tomb would then speed him on his way to join the departed. One sage Chinese minister, Chao Ssu-wen, upon being named the next victim, respectfully demurred with true oriental courtesy, deferring such a high honor to the widow, who was far more deserving than he. The khatum (empress) acknowledged that this was so, but much as she would like to go, her presence was essential to the horde. But just to be a sport about it, she lopped off one hand and sent it along to be buried in the tomb.

References

Grousset, René. *Empire of the Steppes: A History of Central Asia.* Trans.
Naomi Walford. New Brunswick, NJ: Rutgers University Press, 1970.
pp. 128–129.

Sibylla

Queen of Jerusalem (1186–1190)

Sibylla (or Sibyl or Sybil) was born in 1160, the daughter of King Amalric I, ruler from 1162 to 1174, and his first wife, Agnes of Courtenay. Sibylla was the sister of Baldwin IV, who acceded upon his father's death in 1174 and ruled until 1183. When Baldwin IV was nine years old, his instructor realized he was a leper and might not live to reign. So special care was given to Sibylla's education and choice of a mate, since he might be called upon to act as regent or, if need be, even as king. She first married William of Montferrat, count of Jaffa (1176). They had a son, Baldwin V, born posthumously, his father having died of malaria two months before.

In 1180 she took as her lover Guy of Lusignan, of whom her brother the king disapproved on the grounds that he was a weak and foolish boy. When the king discovered this relationship, he wanted to put Guy to death, but at the request of the Templars, he reluctantly allowed Sibylla to marry him. The marriage produced two daughters. Guy was to prove the king's estimation of him was correct. Baldwin IV, from his sickbed, first appointed Guy regent, then rescinded the order, banished him, and proclaimed Sibylla's son Baldwin V as his heir. Baldwin IV died in 1185, but the child died only one year later.

Of the two contenders for the throne, Sibylla and Isabella (by Amalric's second wife, Maria Comnena), the public favored Sibylla, even though her husband was generally despised. Backers of Sibylla, through subterfuge, managed to trick the other side and to proclaim Sibylla queen. At the coronation, only she was crowned, because of Guy's unpopularity. She was then asked to crown whatever man she thought worthy to serve; she of course crowned her husband. As an indirect result of Guy's foibles, Jerusalem was soon embroiled in a disastrous war with Sultan Saladin. Saladin took Guy prisoner and asked for Ascalon in exchange for his release, but the people, ashamed of Guy's selfishness on numerous occasions, refused to give up Ascalon for the ransom. After Ascalon fell anyway, Queen Sibylla wrote Saladin, asking that he release her husband (1188), and he complied with her request. In 1190 the queen and her two young daughters all died of a disease that swept through the countryside.

References

Runciman, Steven. *A History of the Crusades.* Vol. 2, *The Kingdom of Jerusalem and the Frankish East;* Vol. 3, *The Kingdom of Acre.* Cambridge: Cambridge University Press, 1952, 1987. pp. 362, 392–393, 404, 407, 423–449; 19–21, 30.

Sibylle
Princess, Ruler of Tripoli (October 1287)

Sibylle was the widow of Count Bohemond III and VI (r. 1252–1275) and the mother of Bohemond IV and VII (r. 1275–1287). When her son died, she ruled briefly in the month of October 1287. In

November of that year a republic was established, called the Commune of Tripoli, that lasted for one year.

References

Carpenter, Clive. *The Guinnes Book of Kings, Rulers & Statesmen*. Enfield, Middlesex: Guinness Superlatives, 1978. p. 55.

Sinqobile Bahle Mabhena

Chief of the Ndebele Tribe in Zimbabwe (1996–)

The name Sinqobile Bahle Mabhena means "we have conquered." She was born in 1974, the oldest of four daughters of the clan chief, Howard Mabhena. She had no brothers and no male cousins to inherit the chiefdom. She attended college at the University of Zimbabwe and became a teacher. When her father died, Mabhena, age twenty-three, was elected chief of the Ndebele according to her father's wishes. Her election was met by hostility by other chiefs, among them Khayisa Ndiweni, who claimed that even talking about "this girl" caused his blood pressure to go up. Despite threats that were made to harm her and to use black magic against her, Mabhena expressed determination to continue in office, voicing puzzlement as to why "men and other chiefs" were opposed to her election. She promised to do her best for her people. Her college friends supported her, dubbing her the "iron lady of Matabeleland."

Mabhena began by working to establish more secondary schools and more job-creating projects like pig and poultry cooperatives. Her primary responsibilities are to preside over hearings to settle family disputes and property matters for her tribe of over 100,000, minor suits that would otherwise clog Zimbabwe's court system. Her rulings in civil and criminal cases can be appealed in court.

References

Shelby, Barry. "Iron Lady of Matabele." *World Press Review*. March 1997. p. 23.

Sirikit

Queen, Regent of Thailand (1956)

Sirikit was born Princess Mom Rajawong Sirikit Kitiyakara in 1932, the daughter of a titled Thai diplomat, H. H. Prince Nakkhatra Mongkol Kitiyakara, and Krommuen Chandaburi Suranat. Sirikit was soon noted for her striking beauty. In April 1950 she married Bhumibol Adulyadej, who assumed office as ruler June 9, 1946, but was crowned one month after the wedding as King Rama IX, ruler of Thailand. In 1956 she was named regent of Thailand while the king,

who is considered holy by his people, performed his meditations and the duties of a Buddhist monk. At that time she took an oath before the National Assembly: "We will reign with righteousness for the benefits and happiness of the Siamese people." Although the constitutional monarchy wields little real political power, the monarch is head of state and commander of the armed forces and a stabilizing and unifying force.

Queen Sirikit's special project was promoting the export of handwoven Thai silk. The queen traveled to remote provinces to promote various cottage industries and to encourage rural people to practice their traditional crafts. She then obtained markets for these crafts. In some cases, where knowledge of the crafts had been lost, Queen Sirikit sent instructors to reteach the natives. To achieve those ends she established the Foundation for the Promotion of Supplementary Occupations and Related Techniques, which not only provides a chain of shops selling native crafts but also gives rural women the training and provides materials to set up artisans' cooperatives. She used her organizational skills for the Thai Red Cross, for aid to refugees, orphans, wounded soldiers and flood victims. Of Thai women, she said, "They never had the feeling of being inferior to their menfolk."

The royal couple had four children: Princess Ubol Ratana, an M.I.T. graduate who renounced her title and married an American, Peter Ladd Jensen; Crown Prince Ma Ha Vajiralongkorn, who, with his two wives and six children, calls himself the family "black sheep"; Princess Maha Chakri Sindhorn, who is president of the Foundation for Development set up by her father to improve the quality of life in Bangkok; and Princess Chulabhorn, a scientist with a doctorate in organic chemistry, married to a Thai commoner. The crown prince seemed little interested in civilian pursuits, and there was speculation that he might remove himself from succession. In 1979 the popular and brilliant Princess Sindhorn was accorded a special dynastic title by the National Assembly: Ma Ha Chakri (in effect, making her "crown princess"), and in the early 1980s the parliament revised royal law to permit a woman monarch for the first time in Thai history.

In 1985 Queen Sirikit abruptly withdrew from public life; in a much later television interview Princess Chulabhorn made the only explanation ever to come from the royal family about the queen's retirement. The princess described her mother as an insomniac who was exhausted and who had been "ordered to rest."

References
Crossette, Barbara. "King Bhumibol's Reign." *New York Times Magazine.* 21 May 1989: 30–36.

Gray, Denis, and Bart McDowell. "Thailand's Working Royalty." *National Geographic* 162. October 1982: 486–499.

International Who's Who, 1987–1988. London: Europa Publishing, 1987. p. xvi.

Sirimavo
See Bandaranaike, Sirimavo Ratevatte Dias

Sitoe, Aline
See Aline Sitoe

Sitre-meryetamun Tawosret
See Twosret

Sitt al-Mulk
Fatamid Queen of Cairo, Regent (1020–1024)

Sitt al-Mulk ("lady of power") was born ca. 970, the daughter of the caliph, al-'Aziz (r. 975–996). Her mother was a Christian. By all accounts, Sitt al-Mulk was one of the most beautiful Fatimid princesses. She was sixteen years older than her brother, al-Hakim, who was to be the next caliph. When her father died in a freak accident at the age of forty-two, al-Hakim, who had constantly tormented his sister, became caliph.

Al-Hakim's reign was characterized by oppression. He continued to harass his sister, whom he accused of having lovers. He ordered all dogs killed. He forbade laughing, weeping, and singing in the kingdom. Walking along the banks of the Nile, taking a pleasure boat ride, or even opening one's doors or windows onto a pleasant view were all forbidden. He put a ban on many food items and on the sale of wine. Grapes and raisins were dumped into the Nile. He forbade women to go into the streets, ordered shoemakers to cease making shoes for women, and closed women's bathhouses. Women were prisoners in their own homes for seven years and seven months. When women objected to this treatment, he simply had them put to death. He next focused his attention on the Jews and Christians, destroying their places of worship and subjecting them to public humiliation and persecution. Then another fanatic, Hamza Ibn ʿAli, convinced al-Hakim that he was actually God, and the caliph compelled the Muslims to worship him. The majority of the populace was enraged.

Eventually al-Hakim disappeared, and for four months during his "absence" Sitt al-Mulk simply assumed power, an unheard-of occurrence. Eventually the caliph's body was found, and she moved quickly to have his young son named caliph with herself as regent, although usually the caliph was required to be an adult. She immediately organized her regency and began to put the country's economy in order.

Now historians reveal that Sitt al-Mulk conspired with a general, Ibn Daws, to have her brother killed, promising to share power with him after the caliph was dead. After she gained the regency, it was necessary to remove Daws as well. She had some guards point him out as the murderer and he was killed on the spot.

Although she ruled for four years, she did not ask that the *khutba* (ritual Friday prayers affirming the ruler's right to rule) be said in her name. The *khutba* was preached in the name of her nephew, al-Dhahir. It was said that she showed "exceptional ability, especially in legal matters" and that she "made herself loved by the people."

References
Mernissi, Fatima. *The Forgotten Queens of Islam*. Trans. Mary Jo Lakeland. Minneapolis: University of Minnesota Press, 1993. pp. 159–178.

Sivali
Queen, Ruler of Ceylon (Sri Lanka) (35)

For a brief period following the death of King Chulabhaya (r. 34–35), Queen Sivali, who was probably his wife, reigned. However, before the year was out, she was succeeded by King Ilanaga, probably a usurper (r. 35–44).

References
Egan, Edward W., Constance B. Hintz, and L. F. Wise, eds. *Kings, Rulers, and Statesmen*. New York: Sterling Publishing, 1976. p. 438.

Gray, Denis, and Bart McDowell. "Thailand's Working Royalty." *National Geographic* 162. October 1982: p. 23.

Skemiophris

See Nefrusobek

Sobekneferu

See Nefrusobek

Sofya Alekseyevna

Regent of Russia (1682–1689)

Sofya Alekseyevna (or Sophia) was born in 1657, the eldest daughter of Tsar Alexis, who ruled Russia from 1645 to 1676, and his first wife, Mariya Miloslavskaya. Sofya was the sister of Fyodor III (Theodore), who acceded to the throne upon his father's death and ruled for six years. When Fyodor died in 1682, Peter (the Great), Sofya's half-brother by Alexis's second wife, Natalya Naryshkina, was proclaimed tsar. Sofya, indignant that the rights of her younger brother, Ivan, sickly and feeble-minded though he was, had been ignored, incited the already discontented palace guard to riot, terrorizing and actually murdering members of Peter's clan.

Sofya effected a compromise co-tsarship between Peter I and Ivan V, for which she assumed the regency. With the advice of her favorite (by some accounts lover), Prince Vasily (Basil) V. Golitsyn, who was enlightened and cosmopolitan, Sofya immediately moved to strengthen her position by arming the frontier and by removing from positions of authority those whom she did not trust. They included Peter, whom she exiled from the Kremlin. Well educated by Russian standards of the day, she invited skilled craftsmen from Europe to settle in Russia. These western Europeans profoundly influenced Peter, who later introduced elements of their style and culture into his reign.

With Golitsyn's help, Russia and Poland signed a treaty of "eternal peace" that confirmed Russia's ownership of Kiev and territory east of the Dnieper River. Sofya took Golitsyn's advice and engaged in two costly and disastrous military campaigns against the Tatars in exchange for this peace treaty. Her military failures, as compared with Peter's consuming interest in military skills, led to her unpopularity among the disgruntled military, which had supported her originally but which had since suffered loss of face in defeat. By 1689 Sofya had shown signs of her intention to get rid of Peter and to reign as tsaritsa. Theodore Shaklovity, whom she had appointed to command the Streltsy (musketeers), apparently attempted to incite his troops to stage a coup that would place Sofya on the throne. The plot was revealed to Peter, who fled in the middle of the night to the Holy Trinity–St. Sergius Monastery. In the days following, the patriarch, much of the populace, and even several regiments of the streltsy rallied behind Peter. The matter was resolved without open military action while Peter remained sequestered.

Following several riots by her supporters, in which Sofya, faced with certain defeat, took no active part, she was tried and sentenced to take the veil. Although Peter, at age seventeen, became the effective ruler, with Ivan retaining his position as co-tsar, the government actually fell into the hands of Peter's mother, Nathalie, and her associates. Shaklovity and two of his aides were executed. Golitsyn and several others were exiled. Sofya died in a monastery in 1704.

*Sofya Alekseyevna
(Corbis-Bettmann)*

References

Dvornik, Francis. *The Slavs in European History and Civilization.* New Brunswick, NJ: Rutgers University Press, 1962. pp. 491–492, 510, 526.

Grey, Ian. *Peter the Great: Emperor of All Russia.* Harmondsworth, Middlesex: Penguin Books, 1960. pp. 4–30.

Langer, William L., ed. *World History.* Boston: Houghton Mifflin, 1940, 1980. pp. 514–515.

Riasanovsky, Nicholas V. *A History of Russia.* Oxford: Oxford University Press, 1963, 1993. pp. 214–216, 220–221.

Sóndók Yówang
Queen of Silla (632–647)

The kingdom of Silla was originally located in South Korea, having its beginnings in the third or fourth century. By the end of the seventh century, it encompassed the entire peninsula. Sóndók (Sunduk) Yowang was the daughter of King Chinp'yóng Wang (r. 579–632), who had no sons and bequeathed the throne to his daughter.

The story is told that when she was seven years old, her father received as a gift a box of peony seeds accompanied by a painting of what the flowers would look like. Sóndók examined the picture and commented that, while the bloom was pretty, it was unfortunate that it had no odor. She deduced this from the fact that the painting showed no butterflies or bees around the blossom. This astute observation proved her intelligence and her competence for assuming the throne.

Sóndók became sole ruler of Silla in 632. As she grew older, she was revered for her facility of anticipating events. She formed an alliance with China, sending scholars there to study and to bring back knowledge to Silla. Són (Zen) Buddhism is said first to have come to Korea during her reign. She presided over the building of Buddhist temples: the nine-tiered pagoda of Hwanguyongsa was built during her reign, and the temples at Punhwangsa and Yóngmyosa were completed during her reign. She also presided over the building of the first observatory in the Far East. Called the Tower of the Moon and Stars, it still stands today in the old Sillan capital, Kyongju.

Sóndók's reign was characterized by rebellions and agressions in the kingdom of Paekche, her neighbor to the west, and Koguryo, to the north. Nevertheless, she ruled successfully for fourteen years, choosing a strong and capable general, Kim Yusin, to lead her military forces. She was succeeded by another woman, her cousin Chindók. Sóndók's tomb is located in Silla.

References

Lee, Ki-baik. *A New History of Korea.* Trans. Edward W. Wagner with Edward J. Schulz. Cambridge: Harvard University Press, 1984. pp. 74, 106, 390.

Soong Ch'ing-ling, Madame
Acting Head of State, The People's Republic of China (1976–1978)

Madame Soong (or Sung) Ch'ing-ling was born ca. 1892 in Shanghai, the elder sister of prominent industrialist, financier, and Chinese government official T. V. Soong, and of Soong Mei-ling, also known as Madame Chiang Kai-shek. In 1914 Soong Ch'ing-ling married revolutionary leader Sun Yat-sen, who was twenty-six years her senior. After his death in 1925, she became an active leader in the left wing of the Nationalist Party, which her husband had founded, while her brother-in-law, Chiang Kai-shek, became the leader of the right wing. In 1949 Chiang Kai-shek established the People's Republic of China, or Nationalist China, and moved to Taiwan, while Soong Ch'ing-ling remained on the mainland, where she became an important official in the new government. In 1951 she was awarded the Stalin Peace Prize for her efforts on welfare and peace initiatives. As chairperson of the Standing Committee of the National People's Congress, she was acting head of state from July 6, 1976, to March 4, 1978. In 1981, a few months before her death, she was made a member of the Communist Party.

References

Carpenter, Clive. *The Guinness Book of Kings, Rulers & Statesmen.* Enfield, Middlesex: Guinness Superlatives, 1978. p. 49.

Spray of Pearls
See Shajar Al Durr

Suchocka, Hanna
Prime Minister of Poland (1992–1993)

Hanna Suchocka was born on April 3, 1946, in the western Polish village of Pleszew, about sixty miles from the city of Poznan. Her family, considered leading citizens of the community, owned a pharmacy and lived in a large apartment above it. Although church attendance was not condoned in Communist-dominated Poland, her family weekly attended the Roman Catholic Church across the street from their home. When she enrolled in the University of Adam Mickiewicz in Poznan, she wanted to study literature, languages, or fine arts, but her parents wanted her to study pharmacy. As a compromise, she studied constitutional law, graduating in 1968. She was offered a one-year appointment as a junior faculty member contingent upon her joining the Communist Party. She refused, because she wanted to have the freedom to attend church.

To save her legal career, she joined the Democratic Party, which was tolerated by the Communists but was neither Marxist nor atheist. After entering politics as a member of the Democratic Party, she was elected to the Communist parliament in 1980, where she quickly gained a reputation as a compromiser.

In December 1981, martial law was imposed, and thousands of Solidarity leaders were sent to prison. Suchocka left the Democratic Party soon afterward, and when her term was up in 1984, she retired from parliament. However, when the new postcommunist government was installed, she returned to politics and was again elected to parliament in 1989. She was in London in 1992 when a party member phoned to inform her that she was wanted to serve as prime minister. At first she refused, but within weeks it became apparent that she was the only politician trusted by both moderates and the new

fundamentalist Catholic parties. When she took office in July 1992 amid a severe economic recession, her primary task was to be steering the once-communist country into a system of free market economy. She began to institute austere measures to bring the country toward prosperity. Under her coalition government, the fourth government in as many years, Poland began to experience the first political stability since the demise of communism in 1989. She persuaded the Sejm (parliament) to accept a "mini-constitution" and to adopt an austere budget that would enable the country to obtain foreign aid. After much negotiation and compromise, she was able to procure passage of a mass privatization plan for state-owned industry. Her personal popularity was strong among all segments of Polish society, but her coalition government was less well liked. In the election in the fall of 1993 her coalition had dissolved, and her party, the Democratic Union, was defeated.

References

Engelberg, Stephen. "Her Year of Living Dangerously." *New York Times Magazine.* 12 September 1993: 41,52,55.

Kiefer, Francine S. "Poland's Prime Minister Looks Ahead to Reform." *Christian Science Monitor.* 5 May 1993: 8.

Sugandha
Queen, Regent of Kashmir (?–914)

During the tenth century, two opposing military factions vied for ascendancy in Kashmir: the Ekangas and the Tantrins, a wild, ungovernable, and unpredictable clan. Queen Sugandha allied herself with the Ekangas in order to maintain her control of Kashmir as a whole. In a 914 clash between the two factions, Queen Sugandha's forces were defeated, leaving the Tantrins in complete control. Queen Sugandha was deposed, and none of the succeeding rulers was able to assert his authority over the Tantrins.

References
Thapar, Romila. *A History of India*. Vol. 1. London: Penguin Books, 1987. pp. 225–226.

Suiko-tennō
Empress, Ruler of Japan (592–628)

Suiko-tennō was born Toyo-mike-kashikiya-hime in 554, the third daughter of Emperor Kimmei-tennō, who reigned from 548 to 571. Her mother was the daughter of Sōga Iname. The Soga was a Samurai family of great distinction. Suiko's half brother, Bidatsu, acceded to the throne when their father died (571) and reigned until 585. In 576 she married Bidatsu and bore seven sons. Bidatsu died in 585 and was succeeded by his brother, Yōmei, who died in 587, and his brother, Sushun, who was murdered in 592 by Sōga Umako, the head of the Sōga family. Sōga Umako then placed his own niece, Suiko, on the throne.

Although Chinese ancient history records earlier reigning women in Japan, and although Japanese history records the earlier rule of Jingō-kōgō as regent for her son Ōjin, Suiko is the first reigning empress listed in Japanese recorded history. During her reign the total supremacy of the monarch was established. She encouraged the efforts of her nephew, Shōtoku-taishi, to implant Buddhism in Japan. Through her nephew, the empress invited craftsmen from Korea and China to come to Japan. The *Nihongi Chronicles* record not only the first embassy to be sent to China (607) but also much intercourse between Japan and the mainland, resulting in the adoption of the Chinese bureaucratic system and even the Chinese calendar. Suiko died in 628 at the age of seventy-five.

References
Aston, W. G., trans. *Nihongi: Chronicles of Japan*. Vol. 2. Rutland, VT: Charles E. Tuttle, 1979. pp. 120–156.

Papinot, E. *Historical and Geographical Dictionary of Japan*. Rutland, VT: Charles E. Tuttle, 1972. p. 605.

Reischauer, Edwin O., and John K. Fairbank. *East Asia: The Great Tradition*. Boston: Houghton Mifflin, 1960. p. 475.

Sansom, George. *A History of Japan to 1334*. Vol. 1. Stanford: Stanford University Press, 1958. p. 50.

Sung
Empress, Regent of China (ca. 1021–?)

Since this empress's given name is not recorded, she will be referred to as an empress of the Sung dynasty, or Empress Sung. She was the wife of Sung Chen Tsung (Tseng Tsung), third emperor of the Sung Dynasty, who ruled from 998 to 1022. When her husband became insane, she assumed power. Following his death in 1022, his teen-aged son by a minor concubine of humble rank acceded to the throne with Empress Sung as regent. The dowager empress was frequently at odds with the young emperor, and his young wife sided with her against him as well. After Empress Sung died, the emperor divorced his wife for favoring the dowager empress, causing a scandal in the court, which practiced strict Confucian morality.

References
Grousset, René. *The Empire of the Steppes.* Trans. Naomi Walford. New Brunswick, NJ: Rutgers University Press, 1970. p. 132.

Sung
Empress, Regent of China (1274–1276)

Since the name of this empress is not recorded, she will be referred to by the name of her dynasty, Empress Sung. She was the wife of Sung emperor Tu-Tsung, ruler of China from 1265 to 1274. Following the death of her husband in 1274, she became regent for his son, Kung-Ti, age two, with minister Chia Ssu-tao in charge. The Mongolian general Bayan, under Kublai Khan, invaded the Sung capital city of Hangchow in 1276. The empress regent handed over the empire to Kublai Khan, whereupon Bayan sent the young emperor, now age four, to Kublai, who treated him kindly. How the Empress Sung was treated is not recorded.

References
Grousset, René. *The Empire of the Steppes.* Trans. Naomi Walford. New Brunswick, NJ: Rutgers University Press, 1970. p. 287.

Langer, William L., ed. *World History.* Boston: Houghton Mifflin, 1940, 1980. p. 369.

Susanne de Bourbon
Duchess, Ruler of Bourbonnais (1503–1521)

Susanne (or Suzanne) de Bourbon was born in 1491, the daughter of Pierre II, sire of Beaujeu and duke of Bourbon from 1488 to 1505, and Anne of France. Susanne's only brother, Charles, died young. When her father died (ca. 1503), Susanne inherited the duchy of Bourbonnais. In 1505 she married Charles III, count of Montpensier, and had three sons, who all died young. She and Charles, who was the great-grandson of John I, duke of Bourbon (r. 1410–1434), administered the duchy until her death in 1521. Charles continued to rule,

but a charge of treason against him led to the confiscation of Bourbonnais by the French crown upon his death in 1527.

References

Egan, Edward W., Constance B. Hintz, and L. F. Wise, eds. *Kings, Rulers, and Statesmen*. New York: Sterling Publishing, 1976. p. 153.

Morby, John E. *Dynasties of the World*. Oxford: Oxford University Press, 1989. p. 82.

T

Tadj al-'Alam Safiyyat al-Din Shah
Sultana of Atjeh in Indonesia (1641–1675)

Atjeh was a Muslim sultanate on the northern tip of Sumatra. It was a center of trade and at one time dominated the world supply of pepper. Religious scholars noted throughout southeast Asia were located there. As early as 1514 several small states along the coast were brought under the control of an Atjehnese sultan. The country continued to expand and reached the peak of its power and influence during the reign of Sultan Iskandar Moeda (1607–1636), and it is believed that Sultana Tadj came to the throne as the surviving heir after the death of Moeda's successor. There is mention in an early manuscript of an Atjehnese queen in ca. 1640 making a gift of a four-tusked elephant to Gujerat. She is listed, along with the dates of her reign, as the fourteenth sovereign of the dynasty by H. Djajadiningrat in his article on "Atjeh" in the *Encyclopedia of Islam*. The length of her reign, and the fact that she was succeeded by another woman, Sultana Nur al-'Alam Nakiyyat al-Din Shah, probably her daughter, would suggest that she was a popular ruler. The fact that her political enemies had brought from Mecca a *fatwa* forbidding by law that a woman rule further suggests that she wielded considerable power.

References
Jones, Russell. *Hikayat Sultan Ibrahim Ibn Adham*. Berkeley: University of California Center for South and Southeast Asia Studies, 1985.

Mernissi, Fatima. *The Forgotten Queens of Islam*. Trans. Mary Jo Lakeland. Minneapolis: University of Minnesota Press, 1993.

Taitu
Empress, De Facto Ruler of Ethiopia (1906–1913)

Taitu (or Taytu Betul) was born ca. 1844. She married several times and had several affairs. In 1883 she became the fourth wife of King Sahle Mariam of Shoa and helped him rise to become Emperor Mene-

lik II, ruling all of Ethiopia from 1889 to 1913. It was Taitu who persuaded her husband to construct a home near a warm springs and to
grant parcels of land surrounding it to families of the nobility. From
this beginning, the new capital city of Ethiopia was founded in 1887.
Empress Taitu named it Addis Ababa, meaning "new flower." In 1902
Taitu personally led a successful military campaign to quell a revolt in
Tigre.

In 1906 Menelik suffered the first of a series of strokes that over
the years would debilitate him completely. Empress Taitu, who had always been a strong woman with great influence, then exercised her
ruling power. She attempted to have her stepdaughter, Zauditu,
named as her husband's successor, but he named his grandson, Lij
Iyasu V, to succeed him. Even after 1908, when Ras Tesemma was
named regent for Iyasu, Empress Taitu's authority remained supreme.
Ras Tessama died in 1911, and Lij Iyasu was proclaimed emperor;
however, he proved to be inept at governing. Empress Taitu's influence waned after her bedridden husband died in 1913. She retired
from court but returned in 1916 after Iyasu's government was toppled. Again she supported Zauditu's candidacy, and this time Zauditu
was crowned empress. However, Taitu was unable to gain the position
of regent. Tafari Makonnen (Haile Selassie) was named instead. Again
she returned to her mountain home, where she died in 1918.

References
Langer, William L., ed. *World History*. Boston: Houghton Mifflin, 1940,
    1980. p. 872.
Lipschutz, Mark R., and R. Kent Rasmussen. *Dictionary of African
    Historical Biography*. Berkeley: University of California Press, 1989.
    p. 230.

Takano-tennō
See *Kōken-tennō*

Tamara
*Queen, Co-ruler (1178–1184), then "King" of Karthalinia (Georgia)
(1184–1212)*

Tamara (or Thamar) was born ca. 1156, the daughter of King George
III (Giorgi), who ruled Georgia from 1165 to 1184. Georgia included
the ancient countries of Colchis and Iberia in the Caucasus. In 1178,
six years before his death, King George had Tamara, "the bright light
of his eyes," crowned as co-ruler. He gave her the official name
"mountain of god." The most celebrated monarch of the era, she has

been described as being "remarkable for her moderation, humanity, and personal culture."

She became sole ruler when the king died in 1184, but she was put under the guardianship of her aunt, Rusudani, her father's sister. In 1187 Tamara married George Bogolyuaski of Kiev, but the marriage was still childless after two years. She exiled him and in ca. 1193 married again, a cousin, David Sosland, who was of the house of Bagrationi, as was she. She made him co-ruler from ca. 1193 until 1207. In 1194 they had a son, George, and in 1195, a daughter, Rusudani. A devout Christian, Queen Tamara requested of Sultan Saladin that he sell her the Holy Cross for 200,000 dinars, but he refused. In 1191 her still disgruntled cast-off first husband, with the help of the Seljuk sultan of Erzerum, attempted to depose her but failed. In 1200, with the aid of Turkish troops, he tried again. She fought off repeated attacks by Rukn ad-Din; by then she had built an invincible military power.

In 1205 she made her son, George, co-ruler. She helped her nephews, Alexius and David Comnenus, grandsons of the Emperor Andronicus, to occupy Trebiz and establish a domain along the Black Sea shores of Asia Minor. David Comnenus was killed in 1206, but Alexius lived to become emperor and to found a dynasty that lasted 250 years. In 1207 her husband, David Soslan, died. Her son George IV succeeded her when she died in 1212. For her work in furthering the cause of Christianity, she was canonized by the Georgian Church.

References
Buchan, John, ed. *The Baltic and Caucasian States.* Boston: Houghton Mifflin, 1923. p. 173.

Hussey, J. M., ed. *The Cambridge Medieval History.* Vol. 4, pt. 1. Cambridge: Cambridge University Press, 1966. p. 783.

Runciman, Steven. *A History of the Crusades.* Vol. 3, *The Kingdom of Acre.* Cambridge: Cambridge University Press, 1952, 1987. pp. 3, 74, 101, 126, 163, 247.

Suny, Ronald Grigor. *The Making of the Georgian Nation.* Bloomington: Indiana University Press, 1988. pp. 37–41, 49, 87, 283, 290.

Ta-pu-yen
Queen, Regent of Kara-Khitai Empire (1142–1150)

The Kara-Khitai Empire, located in eastern Turkestan, was founded by the gur-khan Ye-lü Ta-shih, who ruled ca. 1130 to 1142. This pagan Mongol line in Muslim Turkic territory was looked upon so contemptuously by Arabian/Persian historians that they did not record the names of the rulers; as a result, they are known only by the Chinese transcriptions of their names. After the death of Ye-lü Ta-shih in 1142, his widow, Ta-pu-yen, became regent of the empire for their son, Ye-lü Yi-li, who reached his majority in 1150. Their daughter, Pu-su-wan (Ye-lü Shih), also ruled following her brother's death in 1163.

References
Grousset, René. *The Empire of the Steppes: A History of Central Asia.* Trans. Naomi Walford. New Brunswick, NJ: Rutgers University Press, 1970. pp. 165–166.

Tārā Bāī
Empress, Ruler of the Marāthā State of the Deccan (1700–1707)

Tārā Bāī was the wife of Raja Ram (r. 1687–1700), who succeeded to the throne when Mughals hacked to death his brother Sambhaji (or Shambhuji, r. 1680–1687). Raja Ram had escaped the advancing Mughal forces of the fanatical Muslim Aurangzeb and had gone to Jinji, a fort southwest of Madras, at the foot of which a Mughal army was camped off and on for seven years. When Aurangzeb demanded that Mughals finally attack, the Mughal commander arranged for his friend Raja Ram to escape before the fort fell. Raja Ram took up the fight against the Mughals who had long persecuted and threatened to overrun his Hindu kingdom. When Raja Ram was killed, his widow, Tārā Bāī, took up leadership, not only of the kingdom but also of the military movement against the invaders. When Aurangzeb died of old age (1707), the Mughal threat ended. Sambhaji's son, Shahu, who with his clever and talented mother, Yesubai, had been held prisoner by the Mughals, escaped and returned to claim the crown. Tārā Bāī challenged Shahu's succession, and for years he was engaged in internal struggles, leaving the government in the hands of his ministers.

References
Carpenter, Clive. *The Guinness Book of Kings, Rulers & Statesmen.* Enfield, Middlesex: Guinness Superlatives, 1978. pp. 130–131.
Gascoigne, Bamber. *The Great Moghuls.* New York: Dorset Press, 1971. p. 236.

Tausert
See Twosret

Tejada, Lidia Gueiler
President of Bolivia (1979–1980)

During a tumultuous period in Bolivia's history, the elections of July 1979 pitted three candidates representing three equally strong factions: military, political, and union. The election produced no majority, and an interim president, Walter Guevara Arze, was chosen by the parliament to serve until elections could be held in 1980. However, he was seen as being too biased against the military, and on November 1, 1979, Arze was deposed by Colonel Alberto Nalusch Busch, who held power for slightly over two weeks, until November 16. During that time a noncontroversial, compromise candidate, Lidia Gueiler Tejada, was chosen by leaders representing the union, political, and military interests. Tejada, born in 1926, had been active in politics and had held a number of committee positions, but she had the reputation of being open minded. She became Bolivia's first woman president, chosen to serve a one-year term. She was ousted in a military coup in 1980 before her term expired.

References
"Bolivia, History." *Britannica Macropaedia.* Vol. 3. 1983. p. 13.

Telles, Leonora
See Leonora Telles

Teng
Empress, Regent of China (105–121)

During the Later or Eastern Han Dynasty, following the death of Emperor Ho Ti, ruler from 88 to 105, Teng ruled as dowager queen regent for her infant son until her own death in 121. At the time of her death, most of her prominent relatives, as befitted their noble status, chose suicide.

References
Langer, William L., ed. *World History.* Boston: Houghton Mifflin, 1948, 1980. p. 146.

Teresa of Castile
Countess, Regent of Portugal (1112–1128)

Teresa of Castile (or Teresa of Portugal) was the illegitimate daughter of King Alfonso VI, ruler of Castile from 1072 to 1109, and Jimena Muñoz. Teresa was the half sister of Urraca (r. León-Castile 1109–1126). Teresa married Henry of Burgundy (or of Lorraine), to whom, possibly as early as 1093/1095, Alfonso VI granted land called the county of Portugal. In 1109 they had a son, Alfonso Henriques (Enríquez), who at age three succeeded as count of Portugal upon Henry's death (1112). Soon after Teresa assumed the post as regent, she became embroiled in a struggle with Galicia and Castile. After the death of Queen Urraca in 1126, there followed ten years of wars between Portugal and Castile, as first Teresa and later her son attempted to gain independence from Castile. Portuguese defenses were easily overcome, and Teresa, being the daughter, half sister, and aunt of Castilian kings, agreed to accept Castilian domination of Portugal. Her son, at age nineteen, took command of the army, defeated the Castilians, and drove his mother into exile (1128). In 1139 Portugal at last became a kingdom, and Alfonso was proclaimed king. He continued to rule until 1185.

References
Chapman, Charles E. *A History of Spain*. New York: The Free Press/Macmillan, 1965. pp. 74–75.
Langer, William L., ed. *World History*. Boston: Houghton Mifflin, 1980. pp. 253–254.
Reilly, Bernard F. *The Kingdom of León-Castilla Under Queen Urraca*. Princeton, NJ: Princeton University Press, 1982. pp. 28, 129.

Teuta
Queen of Illyria (ca. 231–227 B.C.)

Historians have dubbed Queen Teuta the Catherine the Great of Illyria. In Roman times, during and after the First Punic War, Illyria occupied a strip east of the Adriatic Sea making up the northwestern part of the Balkan peninsula, which had been inhabited by an Indo-European people called the Illyrians since about the tenth century B.C. At the height of its dominance in the region, Illyria extended from the Danube River to the Gulf of Ambracia on the Adriatic, to the Sar mountains. The Illyrian tribes, influenced by their equally barbarous Thracian neighbors, were adept at mounted warfare using the iron weapons from Inner Asia. Illyria consisted of many small backward kingdoms, the best known being located in present-day Albania with its capital at Scodra (Shkodër). In its prime, it was ruled by King Agron, whose wife was the celebrated Queen Teuta. Agron, with Demetrius II of Macedonia, defeated the Aetolians in ca. 231 B.C. But Agron died, leaving a young son, for whom his widow Teuta became regent.

Queen Teuta took an aggressive stance against her neighbors. With part of her navy, she attacked Sicily and the Greek colonies on the coast, while at the same time her pirates harassed Roman commerce. Her activities so disrupted the republic's rising commercial development that the Roman senate declared war on her in 229 B.C. Rome sent a huge army and fleet of 200 vessels under the command of Sentumalus and Alvinus to suppress her piracy. After two years of protracted warfare, Queen Teuta sued for peace (227 B.C.). Thereafter she was forced to pay tributes to Rome. The Hellenes, whom Teuta's pirates had also harassed, were so grateful that they admitted the Romans to the Isthmian Games and the Eleusinian Mysteries.

The rude tribes of Illyria were far from destroyed, however; in the difficult mountains and valleys of the interior, Teuta's successor Scerdilaidas had gathered his forces and was aided by Philip V of Macedonia. In 219 B.C. the Romans sent a second naval expedition that, after a protracted war, conquered the whole Balkan Peninsula. The last Illyrian king, Genthius, surrendered in 168 (or 165) B.C.

References
Çomo, Andi. "Albanian History: The Illyrians." www:albanian.com, 1998.

Kinder, Hermann, and Werner Hilgemann. *The Anchor Atlas of World History*. Trans. Ernest A. Menze. Vol. 1. Garden City: Anchor/ Doubleday, 1974. p. 81.

Langer, William L. *An Encyclopedia of World History*. Boston: Houghton Mifflin Company, 1980. p. 99.

Thatcher, Margaret
Prime Minister of Great Britain (1979–1990)

Margaret Thatcher was born Hilda Roberts in 1925, the daughter of Alfred Roberts, one-time mayor of Grantham, Lincolnshire. She attended Somerville College, Oxford, where she received a B.A. degree in chemistry and M.A. in law, specializing in taxation. She worked as a research chemist from 1947 to 1951. In 1951 she married Denis Thatcher; the couple had twins, a son and a daughter. She was called to the bar in 1953 and elected to Parliament six years later. After holding a number of political offices, in 1970 she became leader of the opposition, and four years later succeeded Edward Heath as leader of the Tories.

In May 1979 the conservatives won the election, and Mrs. Thatcher, who belongs to the right wing of the conservative party, became the first woman in history to serve as Britain's prime minister. She became Britain's longest continuously serving prime minister in 160 years and the longest serving leader in Western Europe. When Margaret Thatcher came into office, former deputy prime minister Lord William Whittlaw said, "England had reached an economic and social equivalent of Dunkirk." A breakdown in public services, labor unrest, and industrial decline plagued the country. By and large, Margaret Thatcher's ultraconservative economic moves reached far into the future. Once asked what she had changed in Britain, she answered, "everything." Preaching free market, private enterprise, the

value of hard work, self-discipline, and thrift, she made respectable in Britain the spirit of capitalism, which elsewhere in the world had become synonymous with greed and exploitation.

In 1982 Argentine forces invaded and captured Britain's Falkland Islands, and Thatcher, rejecting a UN peace proposal, retaliated with a large naval arsenal that the Argentines could not withstand. They surrendered 72 days after hostilities began. The undeclared war that claimed almost 1,000 lives and cost at least two billion dollars secured Thatcher's reelection.

However, for all her positive economic impact, a Gallup survey taken on the eve of her tenth year in office concluded that after Edward Heath, she was the least popular of English leaders. The survey found public perception that under Thatcher's rule there was more poverty, selfishness, greed, and crime in Britain. Her attempt at censorship of criticism of her administration was widely condemned, both at home and abroad. Too, the alleged business activities of her son, Mark, tainted the waning years of her administration. As early as 1984 she sent him to the United States when reports surfaced that he had made a career of questionable, perhaps illegal dealings. He was reported to have made his first fortune of some $18 million by parlaying his mother's position into becoming middleman in a controversial $30 billion deal to sell British arms to Saudi Arabia. Although Margaret Thatcher would later maintain that the arms deal was proper, private reports held that she was "heartbroken."

On November 22, 1990, urged by Conservative advisers, Margaret Thatcher resigned, throwing her support to John Major, who was elected her successor. However, the press's uncovering of her son's activities during and immediately after her term continued to throw a shadow across her record. The younger Thatcher had risen to director of Emergency Networks, which allegedly deducted $3 million in taxes from its employees' paychecks but failed to pass the money on to the government. Also pending were lawsuits alleging that the company pocketed medical insurance premiums as well. He next became involved with Ameristar Fuels Corporation, which filed for bankruptcy and was sold in 1995, with four senior financial managers of the company being charged with serious malpractice. In 1996 the younger Thatcher faced trial for tax evasion.

References

Baum, Julian. "Sizing up a Decade of British Radicalism." *Christian Science Monitor.* 4 May 1989: 1–2.

Junor, Penny. *Margaret Thatcher:Wife, Mother, Politician.* London: Sidgwick & London, 1983.

"Sinking Son." *World Press Review.* June 1995: 43.

"The Sleaze Factor." *World Press Review.* December 1994: 27.

Thecla
Co-regent of Byzantine Empire (ca. 842)

Thecla was the daughter of Emperor Theophilus, ruler of the Eastern Roman Empire from 829 to 842, and Empress Theodora. Thecla was the sister of Michael III, who acceded to the throne as a child of three upon their father's death; of Constantine, who died ca. 830; and of four sisters: Mary, Anna, Anastasia, and Pulcheria. When Michael came to the throne, their mother, Theodora, served as regent. Apparently Thecla, the oldest surviving sister, was entitled to share in the regency of her mother, since she was portrayed on the coins together with Michael and Theodora and was named with them on official government documents of the period. But there is no indication that Thecla took any actual part in the conduct of government.

When Theodora was forced to surrender control of the government in 856, her daughters were shut up in a nunnery. If Thecla was among them, she apparently did not remain long, because she soon surfaced as the mistress of Byzantine emperor Basil I, who ruled from 867 to 886. Basil, in a fruit-basket-turnover of wives, took as his second wife Eudoxia Ingerina, Thecla's brother Michael's former mistress. Michael made Basil co-emperor in 866, but in 867 Basil repaid the compliment by having the drunken emperor murdered in his bed chamber.

References

Ostrogorsky, George. *History of the Byzantine State.* New Brunswick, NJ: Rutgers University Press, 1969. pp. 219, 232.

Previté-Orton, C. W. *The Shorter Cambridge Medieval History.* Vol. 1, *The Later Roman Empire to the Twelfth Century.* Cambridge: Cambridge University Press, 1952, 1982. pp. 249, 252–253.

Theodolinda
Queen, Ruler of Lombards Briefly (590), Regent of Lombards (616–622)

The daughter of Duke Garibold of Bavaria, in ca. 590 Theodolinda (or Theodelinda) married King Authari, Lombard king from 584 to 590. When Authari died shortly after their marriage, the nobles of Lombard allowed Theodolinda to choose a new husband who would then also be king. She selected a Thuringian, Agilulf, duke of Turin. In 602 the couple had a son, Adaloald, who acceded to the throne when his father died in 616 and for whom Theodolinda was regent during his minority. A devout Catholic, she used her influence to help Catholicism triumph over Arianism in northern Italy. Theodolinda and Agilulf also had a daughter, Gundeberga, who married the Arian Rothari (Rother of legend), duke of Brescia, who ruled the Arians from 636 to 652 and who allowed the Catholic heirarchy to be reestablished in his kingdom. In 622 Theodolinda's son came of age, but shortly afterward, in 624, he went berserk, went on a killing rampage, and murdered twelve Lombard nobles. He was deposed and later poisoned (ca. 626). At that time,

Theodolinda, who had devoted her life to religion and good works, retired in sorrow and died two years later.

References

Gibbon, Edward. *The Decline and Fall of the Roman Empire.* Vol. 1; vol. 2. Chicago: Encyclopaedia Britannica Press, 1952. pp. 607; 107, 630.

Langer, William L., ed. *World History.* Boston: Houghton Mifflin, 1980. p. 165.

Previté-Orton, C. W. *The Shorter Cambridge Medieval History.* Vol. 1, *The Later Roman Empire to the Twelfth Century.* Cambridge: Cambridge University Press, 1982. p. 220.

Theodora
Empress, De Facto Co-ruler of Macedonian Dynasty, Byzantium (527–548)

A woman of humble origins, a former actress, in 525 Theodora married Justinian, also born of peasant stock, who ruled Byzantium from 527 to 565. It is generally conceded by today's historians that the historian Procopius, who in 551, 553, and 554 wrote books on the ruler and his wife, unduly maligned them both. In fact, Theodora's unswerving will, superior intelligence, and acute political acumen lead many modern-day historians to the conclusion that it was she, rather than Justinian, who ruled Byzantium.

In 527 Justinian was made co-emperor with his uncle, the emperor Justin, and was given the rank of august. At the same time, Theodora, who exercised considerable power and influence over him even at that time, was crowned augusta. While Justinian's entire reign was troubled by wars in both the east and the west and by frequent attacks from the north by barbarians, Theodora's spheres of influence, although not wholly confined to the domestic issues, concerned themselves with every facet of administrative, legislative, and ecclesiastical matters. Her name is mentioned in nearly every law passed during the period. She was one of the first rulers to champion women's rights, passing strict laws prohibiting white slavery and altering divorce laws to make them more favorable to women. In 531 she arranged the dismissal of the praetorian prefect, John of Cappadocia, whose collection of revenues and general attention to the financing of Justinian's military campaigns she thought inadequate.

In 532 two factions (the Greens and the Blues) united against Justinian and proclaimed the late emperor Anastasius's nephew, Hypatius, emperor. Justinian, believing all was lost, prepared for flight. But the indominable courage of Theodora prevented a coup. She persuaded Justinian to stand his ground, and those troops loyal to the emperor were able to quell the revolt. In the field of foreign affairs, she corresponded with and received diplomats and in general conducted any foreign policy that did not pertain to fighting battles.

Her championship of the cause of Monophysitism, the Christian teaching emphasizing the divine nature of Christ, counterbalanced the orthodox view set forth by the Council of Chalcedon in 451, that human and divine natures coexist in the Christ. She died of cancer in 548, leaving her bereft husband, toward the end of his life, to grapple with the theological mysteries and questions she had posed. Following her death, although her husband ruled almost two more decades, no notable legislation was passed.

References

Browning, Robert. *Justinian and Theodora*. New York: Praeger Publishers, 1971.

Ostrogorsky, George. *History of the Byzantine State*. New Brunswick, NJ: Rutgers University Press, 1969. pp. 25, 69, 73.

Previté-Orton, C. W. *The Shorter Cambridge Medieval History*. Vol. 1, *The Later Roman Empire to the Twelfth Century*. Cambridge: Cambridge University Press, 1952, 1982. pp. 78, 185–188.

Theodora
Empress, Regent of Eastern Roman Empire (842–856)

Theodora was the wife of Emperor Theophilus, who ruled the Byzantine Empire from 829 to 842. The couple had seven children: Maria, Thecla, Anna, Anastasia, Pulcheria, Constantine, and Michael II (later called the drunkard), who at the age of three acceded to the throne upon his father's death (842) with his mother as regent. Her ministers and her brother, Bardas, advised her to restore orthodoxy, which had been recanted by her late husband. She did so with a vengance: She reinstated icons (as pictures, not statues) and gave the Paulicians the choice of conversion or death. Paulicians who survived the ensuing bloodbath that her edict caused in Constantinople made a mass exodus to Thrace. Her government was then forced to undertake a new campaign against the Slavic tribes in southern Greece. After a long bitter struggle, the Slavs were subdued and forced to pay tribute and to recognize Byzantine supremacy. In 856 Theodora's brother, Bardas, acting in secret agreement with her son, Michael, murdered her adviser, Theoctistus, and had the senate proclaim Michael an independent ruler. Theodora was obliged to retire, and her daughters were shut up in a nunnery. Ten years later, after she attempted an attack against her brother, she too was sent away to a nunnery.

References

Durant, Will. *The Story of Civilization.* Vol. 4, *The Age of Faith.* New York: Simon & Schuster, 1950. p. 427.

Ostrogorsky, George. *History of the Byzantine State.* New Brunswick, NJ: Rutgers University Press, 1969. pp. 215, 219–223, 225, 250, 575.

Previté-Orton, C. W. *The Shorter Cambridge Medieval History.* Vol. 1, *The Later Roman Empire to the Twelfth Century.* Cambridge: Cambridge University Press, 1952, 1982. pp. 249, 252–253.

Sullivan, Richard E. *Heirs of the Roman Empire.* Ithaca, NY: Cornell University Press, 1960. pp. 103, 125.

Theodora
Empress, Ruler of Byzantine Empire (1042 and 1055–1056)

Born ca. 981, Theodora (or Augusta Theodora) was the youngest daughter of Constantine VIII, ruler of Byzantium from 963 to 1028, and his wife, Helena of Alypius. Psellus described her as "tall, curt and glib of tongue, cheerful and smiling" and as having "a placid disposition and in one way . . . a dull one" and as "self-controlled in money matters." Her eldest sister, Eudocia, pock-faced from an early age, entered a nunnery. Her second sister, Zoë, was singled out by their dying father to be married to Romanus II, who, with Zoë, inherited the reign upon the emperor's death (1028). During their reign, Theodora was exiled to a convent in Petrion. She never married, but by some quirk of disposition, she seemed not to hold a serious grudge against her sister for her treatment.

Zoë, always the adventurous one of the two, took a lover, Michael IV, and together they conspired to murder Romanus, whereupon Zoë married Michael and made him emperor. Although Michael IV treated Zoë poorly once he was installed, he nevertheless convinced her to adopt his nephew, Michael V, as her heir and his successor. Michael IV died, and Michael V came to the throne. But he made the mistake of exiling Zoë, arousing the populace against him. Michael quickly brought Zoë back, but the people were not appeased. They brought Theodora out of exile and proclaimed her empress (1042). She ruled alone briefly, then allowed her sister to join her and even gave her the more prominent role.

Zoë could not be satisfied; she seized power again by marrying a third time (Constantine IX, 1042–1055). Zoë died during this reign (1050), and when Constantine died (1055), Theodora was again summoned to take control. This time she superintended all affairs of state herself. She appointed all officials, dispensed justice from the throne, issued decrees, gave orders. According to Psellus, during her reign the empire prospered and its glory increased. She died in 1056 at the age of seventy-six, having named as her successor Michael VI, an aged man of the court suggested by her advisers when she was on her deathbed.

References

Ostrogorsky, George. *History of the Byzantine State*. New Brunswick, NJ: Rutgers University Press, 1969. pp. 321, 326, 337–338, 576.

Previté-Orton, C. W. *The Shorter Cambridge Medieval History*. Vol. 1, *The Later Roman Empire to the Twelfth Century*. Cambridge: Cambridge University Press, 1952, 1982. pp. 273–274, 277.

Psellus, Michael. *Fourteen Byzantine Rulers*. Trans. E. R. A. Sewter. Harmondsworth, Middlesex: Penguin Books, 1982. pp. 143–162, 261–271.

Theodora
Queen, Ruler of the Empire of Trebizond (Trabzon) (1284–1285)

Trebizond, both empire and city, also called Trabzond or, in ancient times, Trapezus, was located on the southeast coast of the Black Sea in northeastern Turkey. The empire was founded in 1204, after the fall of Constantinople, by the Grand Comneni, Alexius and David, two grandsons of Emperor Andronicus I (ruled the Byzantine empire 1183–1185). After the fall of their grandfather, the boys were taken to the Georgian court of their relatives where, in 1204, their aunt, Queen Thamar (r. 1184–1212), helped them to capture Trebizond and found an empire. Alexius I (r. 1204–1222) was the first ruler and the patriarch of the Trebezondian Comnenian Dynasty; David was killed in 1206 in battle.

Theodora was the youngest daughter of Manuel I (r. 1238–1263), a son of Alexius I. She was the sister of George (r. 1266–1280) and John II (r. 1280–1284), both of whom were deposed. After one year on the throne, Theodora was also deposed, and her brother John was restored (r. 1285–1287).

References

Morby, John E. *Dynasties of the World*. Oxford: Oxford University Press, 1989. p. 56.

Ostrogorsky, George. *History of the Byzantine Empire*. New Brunswick, NJ: Rutgers University Press, 1969. pp. 401, 426.

Runciman, Steven A. *A History of the Crusades,* Vol. 3. Cambridge: Cambridge University Press, 1987. pp. 126, 359, 398, 451.

Theophano
Empress, Regent of Byzantine Empire (963)

Born the daughter of a publican, Anastaso, Theophano was an extraordinarily beautiful woman who attracted the attention of the future Byzantine emperor Romanus II, who married her ca. 956. When Romanus became emperor in 959, she took the name of Theophano. A historian describes her as "entirely immoral and immeasurably ambitious." The couple had two sons, Basil II and Constantine VIII. Upon Romanus's death in 963, Theophano assumed the regency for the small boys. Being a shrewd student of political affairs, she knew her regency could not last long, so she came to an understanding with the elderly Nicephories Phocas, offering herself in marriage to him. The supreme military command was entrusted to the brilliant General John Tzimisces, with whom Theophano conducted a heated affair. She cooperated with conspirators of Tzimisces who murdered her elderly husband in his bed chamber in 969, expecting that she and John would then be married. But Patriarch Polyeuctus, in the sort of slap-on-the-wrist justice that was so often meted out to the powerful, demanded that before John could become emperor, he should do penance for his part in the murder, and that he should expel Theophano from the palace. She died in 991.

References

Ostrogorsky, George. *History of the Byzantine State.* New Brunswick, NJ: Rutgers University Press, 1969. pp. 284, 285, 293.

Previté-Orton, C. W. *The Shorter Cambridge Medieval History.* Vol. 1, *The Later Roman Empire to the Twelfth Century.* Cambridge: Cambridge University Press, 1952, 1982. pp. 258–259.

Theophano
Regent of Germany (984–991)

Although historians have called Theophano one of the greatest women in world history, they do not agree on her history. She was either the daughter of the Eastern Roman emperor Romanus II, ruler from 959 to 963, and his wife, Theophano, or the niece or grandniece of Emperor John Tzimisces, ruler from 969 to 976, who had a licentious affair with Romanus's wife, Theophano. In ca. 972, the younger Theophano married Otto II, who ruled the German Empire from 973 to 983. In 980 they had a son, Otto III, who succeeded his father at age three upon Otto II's death of a fever. Immediately revolts flared up among the Slavs on one side and the Danes and Franks on another, all intent upon wresting power from the throne. It was the genius of

Theophano, Regent of Germany (Corbis-Bettmann)

Theophano that saved the empire. In her castle at Quedlinburg she maintained a brilliant court attended by scholars of great note. She presided over a magnificent diet at Nijmwegen, attended by numerous princes. Her forceful and intelligent presence quelled the dissent, which did not surface again until after her death in 991. She was succeeded in the regency by her mother-in-law, Adelaide.

References

Gibbon, Edward. *The Decline and Fall of the Roman Empire.* Vol. 2. Chicago: Encylopaedia Britannica Press, 1952. 320.

Langer, William L., ed. *World History.* Boston: Houghton Mifflin, 1980. pp. 176, 195, 230–231.

Löwenstein, Prince Hubertus Zu. *A Basic History of Germany.* Bonn: Inter Nationes, 1964. pp. 21–24.

Ostrogorsky, George. *History of the Byzantine State.* New Brunswick, NJ: Rutgers University Press, 1969, pp. 296, 314.

Tindu

Mongol Queen of Iraq (1411–1419)

Tindu belonged to the Jallarid dynasty, a branch of the Ilkhan dynasty that ruled Iraq from 1336 to 1411. She was the beautiful daughter of the great Mongol king Awis. During a trip to Egypt with her uncle, she caught the fancy of Mamluk king al-Zahir Barquq, who asked for her hand in marriage. Her father was more than happy to oblige, in exchange for Egyptian military aid against the invasions by Tamerlane's armies. But Tindu was not happy in Cairo, and because Barquq loved her very much, he allowed her to return to her homeland of Iraq. Eventually she married her cousin Shah Walad, ruler of Baghdad, and after his death in 1411, she acceded to the throne. She ruled until her death in 1419, at which time her son claimed the throne.

References

Mernissi, Fatima. *The Forgotten Queens of Islam.* Trans. Mary Jo Lakeland. Minneapolis: The University of Minnesota Press, 1993, pp. 72, 105–106.

Tiy

Queen, De Facto Regent-ruler of Egypt (ca. 1370 B.C.)

Tiy was a commoner, possibly of Asiatic blood and possibly from a military family. Her father was Yuya of Akhmin, an officer in the Chariotry and master of the stud farms and possibly also the father of the queen-mother, Mutemwia. Tiy's mother's name was Tuya. Tiy's parents were eventually able to promote one of their sons, the divine father Ay, to succeed to the throne following Tutankhamun.

Tiy married Amenophis (or Amenhotep) III, ruler of Egypt from

Tiy (Corbis/Gianni Dagli Orti)

ca. 1405 to 1370 B.C., during the second year of his reign. The king, having departed from the "God's Wife" concept of marrying the royal heiress (usually one's sister) who would become the chief queen, bestowed upon his commoner wife the august title of "great royal wife." Variously described as "formidable," "a woman of long-suffering character," possessing "compelling physical appeal," she maintained her influence over him despite his many other feminine distractions. The king enjoyed sailing with Tiy on the artificial lake outside the palace, while Tiy enjoyed unusual power within the palace. In the ceremonies held renewing kingly power, Queen Tiy participated as well.

She bore the king six children. The first died without reigning. The second was Akhenaton (Amenophis IV), who ruled from ca. 1370 to 1352 B.C. Of her four daughters, two (Satamun and Isis) were given the title of queen. Tiy stood alongside her husband as the personification of Maat and was therefore afforded certain royal privileges such as participation in the various festivals. She played an important part in formulating foreign policy.

The king's last years were spent in illness, and it is possible that during those years Tiy's son was already elevated to ruler or co-ruler. In the early years of her son's reign, she acted as regent. Her father had elevated her brother, Inen, to the important post of second prophet of Amon (Amun). Given the amount of evidence remaining of Tiy's influence and participation, it is safe to assume that during the waning years of her husband's life, this influence and participation increased, especially on behalf of her son. She died in the eighth year of her son's reign. As an indication of her exalted position, she was allowed to have herself represented in the form of a sphinx, and a temple was dedicated to her at the Nubian site of Sedeinga.

References

Grimal, Nicolas. *A History of Ancient Egypt*. Trans. Basil Blackwell Ltd. New York: Barnes & Noble Books, 1997. pp. 214, 221–222, 226–227, 234, 237, 271.

West, John Anthony. *The Traveler's Key to Ancient Egypt*. New York: Alfred A. Knopf, 1985. pp. 226, 235, 338, 378.

White, J. S. *Ancient Egypt: Its Culture and History*. New York: Dover Publishing, 1970. pp. 169, 172, 173.

Tizard, Dame Catherine

Governor-General of New Zealand (1990–1996)

Catherine Tizard was born Catherine Anne Maclean on April 4, 1931, the daughter of Neil and Helen Montgomery Maclean. She received her education from Manamata College, in the north central part of the North Island, and at the University of Auckland. In 1951 she married Robert James Tizard. The couple had four children; they divorced in 1983. In the interim, she was a tutor in zoology at the University of Auckland (1967–1984), served on the Auckland City Council (1971–1983), and was a member of the Auckland Regional Authority (1980–1983). In 1984 she was elected mayor of the City of Auckland, a post she held until December 1990, when she was named Queen Elizabeth II's representative, governor-general of New Zealand. Tizard continued in this position until September 1996, when she was appointed chairperson of the Historic Trust. She lives in Auckland, New Zealand.

References

Who's Who in the World. 14th ed. New Providence, RI: Marquis/Reed Elsevier, 1997. p. 1461.

New Zealand Executive Government News Release Archive, September 10, 1996.

Tomyris
Queen of the Massagetae (ca. 529/530 B.C.)

The Massagetae was a large, warlike, half-nomadic Sakan tribe whose land lay eastward beyond the Araxes River in Eastern Persia. Tomyris was the widow of a Sakan chief and was both queen and leader of the army. She had at least one son, Spargapises.

Cyrus the Great, not content with his latest conquest of Assyria, turned his attention to adding the country of the Massagetae to his ever expanding Persian Empire. According to Herodotus, Cyrus, camped across the river from the Massagetae, first sent word to Queen Tomyris pretending to want her hand in marriage, but Tomyris, not so easily duped, refused. She sent him word, "King of the Medes, I advise you to abandon this enterprise. . . . Rule your own people, and try to bear the sight of me ruling mine. But of course, you will refuse my advice, as the last thing you wish for is to live in peace." She then offered him an alternative: allow her army to withdraw a three-days' march from the river, and then the two rulers could meet. Cyrus was at first inclined to accept this proposal until advised by Croesus against any compromise.

Croesus suggested tricking the Massagetae by preparing a feast as a trap, luring the Massagetae to descend upon it, and, once they had sated themselves and had drunk themselves into a stupor, having his troops come out of hiding and massacre them. Croesus pointed out, "It would surely be an intolerable disgrace for Cyrus son of Cambyses

to give ground before a woman." Cyrus took his advice, and the plot went off as planned, except for one small hitch: One of those captured in the plot was the queen's son, Spargapises. When the queen learned of this, she sent word that her son be released, or she would give Cyrus more blood than he could drink. Actually, Cyrus could not return Spargapises even if he had wanted to because the boy had committed suicide in captivity. The Massagetae attacked and massacred the Persians, including Cyrus. By Herodotus's account, the queen, learning that her son had committed suicide, filled a skin with blood and stuffed Cyrus's head in it, fulfilling her promise to give him more blood than he could drink. According to other accounts, Cyrus was only mortally wounded at the time and didn't die until three days later.

References

Herodotus. *The Histories.* Trans. Aubrey de Sélincourt. New York: Penguin Books, 1954, 1988. pp. 123–127.

Olmstead, A. T. *History of the Persian Empire.* Chicago: University of Chicago Press, 1948. p. 66.

Töregene
Khatun, Regent of Outer Mongolia (1241–1246)

A Naiman princess, Töregene (also Turakina, Töragina, or Törägänä) has been described as energetic but avaricious. She was the wife of Ögodei (or Ogötäi or Ogödöi), a son of Jenghiz-khan and ruler of the Mongolian Empire from 1229 to 1241. Jenghiz-khan had divided his realm among his four sons, making each a khan over the chieftains in his own realm; however, the khans then elected one great khan to rule over all.

In 1229 Ögodei was elected great khan by the plenary Kuriltai. Prior to his death of a drinking bout in 1241, he had had a quarrel with his eldest son, Güyük, and had sent him disgraced into exile. Ögodei had named as his successor his grandson, Shirämon, whose father, Kuchu, had been killed fighting the Chinese. But Töregene, determined that Güyük should have the throne, took over the regency. She summoned a Kuriltay (gathering of the official ruling body), which recognized her authority until a new great khan should be appointed. For five years she ruled while trying to convince the clan chieftains and princes of the blood to appoint Güyük. During her reign, she chose as her adviser, not a Christian like herself, but a Muslim, Abd ar-Rahman. Gossipers accused Abd ar-Rahman of aiding in Ögodei's untimely demise. Töregene eventually convinced the Kuriltai of Güyük's suitability, and she handed over the throne to him in 1246.

References

Grousset, René. *The Empire of the Steppes.* Trans. Naomi Walford. New Brunswick, NJ: Rutgers University Press, 1970. pp. 268–269.

Reischauer, Edwin O., and John K. Fairbank. *East Asia: The Great Tradition.* Boston: Houghton Mifflin, 1960. pp. 267, 270, 273.

Runciman, Steven. *A History of the Crusades.* Vol. 3, *The Kingdom of Acre.* Cambridge: Cambridge University Press, 1952, 1987. pp. 249, 251–252, 293.

Tou Hsien
Empress, Regent of China (88–97)

During the Later or Eastern Han Dynasty, dowager empresses and their eunuchs gained the power by choosing infants as successors to the throne. Tou Hsien, who came from a great land-owning family that dated back to the second century B.C., became all powerful at court by this ploy. Empress Tou altered the succession and, with her family, ruled as dowager empress from A.D. 88 to her death in 97.

References

Langer, William L., ed. *World History.* Boston: Houghton Mifflin, 1940, 1980. p. 146.

Morton, W. Scott. *China: Its History and Culture.* New York: McGraw-Hill, 1982. p. 63.

Reischauer, Edwin O., and John K. Fairbank. *East Asia: The Great Tradition.* Boston: Houghton Mifflin, 1960, pp. 125–126.

Tribhuvana
Queen, Majapahit Ruler of Java (1328–1350)

Tribhuvana succeeded her father, Jayanagara, who was slain by his physician, Tancha. Her minister, Gajah Mada, instigator of the assassination plot, became the empire's most powerful figure. In 1350 she abdicated in favor of her son, Hayam Wuruk, the Majapahit empire's most famous king.

References
"Gajah Maja." *Britannica Macropaedia*. Vol. 7. Chicago: Encyclopaedia Britannica, 1983. pp. 825–826.

Trieu Au
Vietnamese Hill-people "Ruler" (ca. 248)

Although not a queen, Trieu Au was a leader at a time when Vietnam was not unified but was instead a territory occupied by the Chinese. Born in 222, she was orphaned and taken by her brother and his wife, who treated her cruelly, more like a slave than a sister. Trieu Au killed her sister-in-law, perhaps a Chinese, and escaped to the hills. A commanding and charismatic speaker, she took it upon herself to enumerate the indignities that her people had endured at the hands of the Chinese. She set up her administration in the hills and raised 1,000 troops, with which she launched a revolt against the hated Chinese. Wearing golden armor, she rode at the front of her troops on the back of an elephant. She was defeated in only six months and, in honorable fashion, rather than surrender, committed suicide by throwing herself into a river. She is remembered today in Vietnam by a temple built in her honor and by her defiant declaration, "I want to rail against the wind and the tide, kill the whale in the sea, sweep the whole country to save the people from slavery, and I refuse to be abused."

References
Karnow, Stanley. *Vietnam: A History.* New York: Viking Press, 1983. p. 100.

Trung Nhi and Trung Trac
Co-queens of Vietnam (39–42)

Between 111 B.C. and A.D. 221, Vietnam was in the hands of the Han Dynasty overlords of China. For more than a century the Vietnamese made no serious challenge to the Han rule. Then, in ca. A.D. 39, a Chinese commander murdered a dissident Vietnamese nobleman and raped his widow, Trung Trac. She and her sister, Trung Nhi, organized the surrounding tribal lords and mustered an army that included at least one other outstanding woman, Phung Thi Chinh, who was pregnant at the time. The sisters attacked Chinese strongholds and either cleared out or massacred the enemy Chinese. Phung Thi Chinh reportedly gave birth to a baby but strapped it on her back and got back into the fray. The Vietnamese carved out an independent kingdom, purged of Chinese, which stretched from Hue into southern China. The Trung sisters were proclaimed co-queens of this new kingdom. They ruled until A.D. 42, when the Han emperor sent a large force to recapture the kingdom. Unable to meet such mighty opposition, the Trung sisters took the honorable route of committing suicide: they drowned themselves in a river. The Vietnamese still venerate the sisters at temples in Hanoi and Saigon. Madame Ngo Dinh Nhu, the sister-in-law of South Vietnam's president Ngo Dinh Diem, erected statues in their honor in Saigon in 1962.

References

Karnow, Stanley. *Vietnam: A History.* New York: Viking Press, 1983. p. 100.

Tuckabatchee, Queen of
Legendary Queen of Tuckabatchee Creek (late 18th c.)

According to Janice Woods Windle, family lore maintains that the queen of Tuckabatchee was a "full-breasted woman" whose relationship to the Woods family is legendary. She was said to have been the mother of Cherokee Hawkins Lawshe and the grandmother of Texas pioneer Georgia Lawshe Woods.

References

Windle, Janice Woods. *True Women.* New York: G. P. Putnam's Sons, 1993. pp. 169–170, 174–175.

Turunku Bakwa
Queen, Founder and Ruler of Zaria (1536–?)

Turunku Bakwa (or Bazao) was the mother of Amina and Zaria, both of whom ruled Zaria after her. Turunku Bakwa was an immigrant, a Fulani who moved into Macina, the eastern Niger region. Some argue that she might have come from the south because she had acquired guns from traders on the coast. She belonged to a matriarchal clan. In 1536 she founded the city of Zaria in north central Nigeria, naming it for her younger daughter.

References

Panikker, K. Madhu. *The Serpent and the Crescent: A History of the Negro Empires of West Africa.* Bombay: Asia Publishing House, 1963. pp. 112–113.

Twosret
King, Last Ruler of Nineteenth Dynasty, Egypt (ca. 1202–1200 B.C.).

Twosret (or Tausert or Twosre) was probably the daughter of Merneptah, who ruled ca. 1236 to 1223 B.C. She was the wife and probably also the sister of Sethos II (Seti II), ruler from ca. 1216 to 1210 B.C. Sethos married three queens, the first of whom, Takhat II, apparently did not provide him with an heir. Twosret was his second wife; she bore a son named Sethos Merneptah, but he died young. The third queen provided the heir, Ramesses Siptah. Apparently Sethos II died or was murdered in 1210 B.C. A Syrian officer, Bay, who had become powerful as chancellor of Egypt, brought Siptah to the throne. Because Siptah was too young, Twosret, his stepmother and matrilineal link to the throne, acted as regent and married him. Both Bay and Twosret acquired evil reputations. When Siptah died in 1202 B.C. (by one dating 1196 B.C.), possibly at her hand, Twosret herself ruled as "king," appropriating her husband's regnal years and restoring her first husband's name over his. Supposedly Bay seduced her and had free access to the treasury. The throne was probably usurped by Selnakht in 1200 B.C.

References

Grimal, Nicolas. *A History of Ancient Egypt.* Trans. Basil Blackwell Ltd. New York: Barnes & Noble Books, 1997. pp. 204, 270–271.
West, John Anthony. *The Traveler's Key to Ancient Egypt.* New York: Alfred A. Knopf, 1985. pp. 142, 162.

Tz'u-hsi
See Cixi

Tz'u-an
Queen, Regent of China (1862–1873 and 1875–1881)

Tz'u-an was at one time the senior consort of the Hsien-feng emperor, who reigned from 1851 to 1862, until another consort, Tz'u-hsi (Cixi), bore a son and heir, T'ung-chih. When the emperor died in 1862, the five-year-old boy became emperor with a council of eight elders acting as regents. Through clever plotting with Prince Kung, brother of the late king, the two dowager empresses managed to get the regency transferred to them. They then named Kung as the prince councilor. The women gradually brought about some westernization of the government and put an end to much of the government corruption. The regency ended when T'ung-chih reached his majority in 1973; however, he died only two years later. Tz'u-hsi violated succession laws, which called for an emperor of the next generation, by adopting her three-year-old nephew as heir. Again the two empresses served as regents until Tz'u-an's sudden death in 1881, possibly from poisoning.

References

Morton, W. Scott. *China: Its History and Culture.* New York: McGraw-Hill, 1982. pp. 168–175.

Udham Bāī
Queen, De Facto Co-ruler of Mughal India (1748–1754)

Udham Bāī was the daughter of Farrukh-Siyar, who in the twilight years of the Mughal empire married Muḥammad Shāh (Rawshan Akhtar), ruler from 1719 to 1748, the fourth in a row of weak rulers. Under his leadership, the empire lost the province of Kābul to Persia's Nādir Shāh and the province of Katehr to another soldier of fortune, Ruhēla, and several other provinces became practically independent. Udham Bāī's son, Aḥmad Shāh Badāhur, born in 1725, was no stronger. He had already reached his majority when he crowned himself king upon his father's death (1748), but his mother knew that he was cut from the same cloth as his four predecessors. If India was to continue under the Mughals, someone besides the good natured, lackadaisical Aḥmad Shāh would have to take the reins.

It was not difficult for Udham Bāī to dominate her son completely. She did not attempt to encourage responsibility in her son, and in the end the weaknesses that she encouraged sealed her fate as well as his. She had as her cohort the emperor's eunuch vicar and superintendent of the harem, Javid Khān. Despite their meddling, Aḥmad Shāh, who was easily intimidated, gave the Punjab and Multan to Nādir Shāh's lieutenant, Abdālī. Then, at a demonstration by the Marāthās in Sikandrābād, Aḥmad Shāh, who invariably chose flight to fight, abandoned the women of his family, including Udham Bāī, to captivity by the Marāthās. He was blinded and deposed in 1754 by a force consisting of Doab Afghans and Marāthās. He lived in confinement until his death in 1775.

References
Burn, Sir R., ed. *Cambridge History of India.* Vol. 4, *The Moghal Period.* Cambridge: Cambridge University Press, 1937. p. 462.
Gascoigne, Bamber. *The Great Moghuls.* New York: Dorset Press, 1971. pp. 245, 250.

Glubb, Sir John. *A Short History of the Arab Peoples.* New York: Dorset Press, 1969. pp. 235–236, 244.

Uicab, María
"Queen" of Tulum (1871)

María Uicab was a Mayan woman living on the Yucutan Peninsula who was known as the patron saint of Tulum and was given the title of queen. In 1871 the sacred Mayan ruins of the city of Tulum became an Indian shrine where a "talking cross" was set up. The city of Tulum and especially the "talking cross" were placed in the care of Queen María.

References
Las ruinas de Tulum. Ciudad de Mexico: Instituto Nacional de Antropologia e Historia, 1969. p. 14.

Ulrica Eleanora
Queen of Sweden (1718–1720)

Ulrica Eleanora was born in 1688, the daughter of King Charles XI, ruler of Sweden from 1660 to 1697, and Ulrica Eleanora of Denmark. The brother of the younger Ulrica Eleanora, Charles XII, succeeded their father on the throne. She was betrothed to Frederick of Hesse-Cassel, a Calvinist, but refused to marry him until her brother assured her the marriage would not jeopardize her accession to the throne in that Catholic country. The couple married in 1715 but remained childless.

In 1718, while on a military expedition to Norway, Charles XII was shot and killed, and Ulrica Eleanora acceded to the throne. Charles Frederick, son of her late older sister Hedvig Sofia, challenged her right to rule. However, the Riksdag accepted her reign on the condition that a new constitution be drawn up. This new document provided for a joint rule by the monarchy and the council when the Riksdag was not in session. When the Riksdag was sitting, principal decisions would be made by a secret committee made up of nobles, clergy, and burghers. Peasants were to have a voice in matters concerning taxes. This new constitution ushered in Sweden's so-called Age of Freedom. Ulrica Eleanora, being completely devoted to her husband, bowed to his ambitions in 1720 by abdicating in his favor. She died in 1741.

References
Derry, T. K. *A History of Scandinavia.* Minneapolis: University of Minnesota Press, 1979. pp. 159, 163, 166, 178.

Langer, William L., ed. *World History.* Boston: Houghton Mifflin, 1980. pp. 441, 508.

Urraca, Doña
Queen, Ruler of León and Castile United (1109–1126)

Doña Urraca was born ca. 1081, the daughter of Constance and Alfonso VI, king of León from 1065 and king of Castile from 1072. Urraca first married Raymond of Burgundy, a French knight who had come to participate in the Wars of Reconquista. She and Raymond had two sons before he died sometime prior to 1109. Her father spent most of his time fighting the Muslims. In his last battle with the Almoravids in 1108, his only son and Urraca's brother, Sancho, was killed.

Alfonso immediately began making arrangements for his widowed daughter, who would now inherit the throne, to marry someone on whom he could count to continue to fight the Muslims. When her father died the next year, Urraca, still a widow, inherited both thrones, León and Castile. She bowed to her father's wishes and married King Alfonso I (the Battler) of Aragon, whom she detested. Evidence shows that she ruled her own kingdom and had no intention of giving up her authority to him. Their constant scrapping kept the government in a turmoil and even curtailed the progress of the Cross in Spain during the First Crusade. Eventually she sent him back to Aragon via annulment. Neither her lover, the Count of Lara, nor her confidant, Archbishop Bernardo of Toledo, held sway over her decisions. Before her death in 1126, to assure that the throne did not fall into the hands of the greedy Aragonese, she had her son, Alfonso VII, crowned with her.

References
Langer, William L., ed. *World History.* Boston: Houghton Mifflin 1980. p. 250.

Reilly, Bernard F. *The Kingdom of León-Castilla under Queen Urraca 1109–1126.* Princeton: Princeton University Press, 1982.

Runciman, Steven. *A History of the Crusades.* Vol. 2, *The Kingdom of Jerusalem.* Cambridge: Cambridge University Press, 1952. pp. 249–250.

Uwilingiyimana, Agathe
Prime Minister of Rwanda (1993–1994)

Rwanda, located in east-central Africa, has long been the scene of conflict between the Hutu agricultural peasants and the Tutsi, a pastoral group that arrived in the fifteenth century and gained dominance over the Hutu. Throughout Africa the number of women in politics has been small, with only the most outstanding women managing to reach the upper tiers of power. Agathe Uwilingiyimana was such a woman, having been born of educated and influential Kigali parents and having received an outstanding education herself. Uwilingiyimama entered politics because she was interested in health and education reform as well as in the general betterment of the status of women. In 1993 she became the first woman ever nominated to head her party and the first to serve as chief executive of Rwanda. She worked hand-in-glove with neighboring Burundi's prime minister, Sylvie Kinigi, and together they planned extensive social reforms. However, Uwilingiyimana's leadership was not welcomed even by a substantial faction within her own party. In April 1994 she was assassinated, thus effectively ending any meaningful reform in Rwanda.

References

Humarau, Beatrice. "Women on the Run." *World Press Review*. February 1996: 38–39.

V

Vaekehu
Queen, Ruler of the Taiohae Tribe (1891)

Remnants of the Taiohae tribe live in the Marquesas Islands, two volcanic clusters of islands forty miles northeast of Tahiti. The main harbor and port on the northern island of Nuku Hiva is a town, also the administrative seat of the Marquesas, called Haka Pehi, or Taiolae, from the Polynesian tribe of Queen Vaekehu. The French annexed the whole group of islands in 1842. The French mission, backed by a military force, wiped out native culture by gradually weeding out recalcitrant chiefs, requiring that natives wear European-style clothing, and banning native songs and dances, musical instruments, and tatoos. By 1890, the time of Queen Vaekehu, the native culture was well broken, and she ruled at the French behest. The introduction by the French of venereal diseases, tuberculosis, smallpox, and leprosy all but obliterated the tribe. Some improvement in their numbers has been made in this century, although their culture is lost forever. Queen Vaekehu's reign was documented in 1891 by F. W. Christian, who collected her genealogy for a paper entitled "Notes on the Marquesas," published in the *Journal of the Polynesian Society,* (vol. 4, 1895, p. 194).

References
Suggs, Robert C. *The Island Civilizations of Polynesia.* New York: Mentor Books, NAL, 1960. pp. 53–54.

Victoria
Queen of Great Britain and Ireland (1837–1901)

She was born Alexandrina Victoria, in 1819, the daughter of Edward, Duke of Kent, and Princess Victore of Saxe-Coborg. Victoria's father died eight months later, and she was reared by her overbearing and pretentious mother, who would have been her regent but for the fact that King William IV of Hanover, Victoria's uncle and ruler since

Victoria
(Corbis-Bettmann)

1830, managed to live until shortly after Victoria's eighteenth birthday. Although Victoria inherited the crown of England, the crown of Hanover was barred to her by Salic law and went instead to her uncle Ernest, duke of Cumberland.

For the first two and one-half years of her reign as queen of England she remained unmarried, vacillating about becoming betrothed to her cousin, Prince Albert of Saxe-Coburg-Gotha. She eventually married him, and thus began one of the happiest royal marriages on record. The couple had nine children, who married into all the royal houses of Europe: Victoria married German emperor Frederick III; English king Edward VII married Alexandra of Denmark; Alice married Louis of Hesse-Darmstadt; Alfred married Marie of Russia; Helena married Christian of Schleswig-Holstein; Louis married the Duke of Argyll; Arthur married Louise of Prussia; Leopold married Helena of Woldech; and Beatrice married Prince Henry of Battenburg. Not the most supportive of mothers, Victoria often openly criticized her oldest son, Edward, in terms that would have crushed a lesser boy or man.

Albert died of typhoid in 1861, and Victoria mourned for him for the next forty years. Her long association with Benjamin Disraeli, the Conservative prime minister, and her grating relationship with his rival, William Ewart Gladstone, the Liberal leader, dominated her political concerns for many years. In a brilliant bit of public relations strategy in 1876, Disraeli secured for her the title of "empress of India," and she became the symbol of the national mood and enthusiasm for expansion and empire building. By the very length of her tenure during a time of unprecedented growth, she outlived her detractors and gained the devotion of the nation. She celebrated both a Golden Jubilee in 1887 and a Diamond Jubilee in 1897. By the time of her death in 1901, she had restored, as Britain's longest-reigning monarch, both dignity and respect to the crown and affection for its wearer. She was succeeded by her eldest son, Edward VII.

References

Fulford, Roger. *Hanover to Windsor.* Glasgow: Fontana/Collins, 1981. pp. 38–113.

Hudson, M. E., and Mary Clark. *Crown of a Thousand Years.* New York: Crown Publishing, 1978. pp. 132–135.

Longford, Elizabeth. *Queen Victoria: Born to Succeed.* New York: Harper & Row, 1914.

Ridley, Jasper. *Napoleon III and Eugenie.* New York: Viking Press, 1980. pp. 579–588, 603–617, 622–623.

Vigdis

See Finnbogadóttir, Vigdis

Vittoria

Duchess, Ruler of Urbino (1623)

Urbino was a dukedom in central Italy, famous for its majolica, a tin-glazed earthenware. Vittoria was the heir of Duke Federigo Ubaldo (1621–1623), of the family of Della Rovere. She married Ferdinando II de'Medici, who in 1627 became grand duke of Tuscany and who was a brilliant inventor of scientific instruments and a patron of the sciences. Vittoria acceded to the throne of Urbino upon the untimely death of Duke Ubaldo in 1623. At her death in 1631, Urbino was incorporated by reversion into the Papal States by Pope Urban VIII. In 1680 Urbino became part of the kingdom of Italy.

References

Egan, Edward W., Constance B. Hintz, and L. F. Wise, eds. *Kings, Rulers, and Statesmen.* New York: Sterling Publishing, 1976. p. 277.

Langer, William L., ed. *World History.* Boston: Houghton Mifflin, 1980. p. 425.

Wac-Chanil-Ahau, Lady

Maya Queen, Regent of Naranjo (682–ca. 699)

Lady Wac-Chanil-Ahau ("Six Celestial Lord," also Lady 6 Sky) was the daughter of Flint-Sky-God K, king of the Maya of Dos Pilas (r. 645–?). Following the Caracol-Tikal-Naranjo wars in which both Naranjo and Tikal fared badly at the hands of Caracol, Flint-Sky-God K set up the new kingdom called Dos Pilas near Lake Petexbatún and the Pasión River in the southern lowlands of the Yucatán. To solidify his position, he sent women, possibly sisters or daughters, to marry rulers of El Charro and El Pato. In 682, he sent Lady Wac-Chanil-Ahau, with an elaborate wedding caravan, to Naranjo to marry a nobleman and establish a new royal family.

On her arrival in Naranjo, she performed a three-day blood-letting sacrificial ritual (August 30–September 1, 682). She did not marry a king, and her husband was not important enough to be

Lady Wac-Chanil-Ahau (Library of Congress)

depicted on a stela. Their son, Smoking-Squirrel, was born on January 1, 68, and acceded to the throne at the age of five. Only twenty days after his accession, Naranjo warriors attacked the neighboring kingdom of Ucanal, taking prisoner one important lord named Kinichil-Cab. A stela depicting this capture shows Lady Wac-Chanil-Ahau standing on the captive's body (June 20, 693). Although Kinichil-Cab survived, on April 19, 699, Lady Wac-Chanil-Ahau conducted a public ritual in which she is again depicted standing on his body. This is the last date of which there is any record of her activities.

She lived many years into Smoking-Squirrel's reign, and every time he erected a monument commemorating his accession, he erected another dedicated to his mother. These monuments depict her engaging in the same rituals of state as her son. She was never given the designation "king" but appears to have ruled, first as viceroy or regent for her father from 682 to 693 and then as regent for her son for a number of years.

References

Schele, Linda, and David Freidel. *A Forest of Kings: The Untold Story of the Ancient Maya.* New York: Quill/William Morrow, 1990, pp. 168, 183–186, 221, 459, 460, 461, 478.

Waizero
See Zauditu

Wajed, Hasina
Prime Minister of Bangladesh (1997–)

Hasina Wajed (or Wazed) was born in 1946, the daughter of Mujibur Rahman, founder of Bangladesh in 1971 and its first prime minister. He, along with more than a dozen members of his family, was gunned down in his home in 1975 by renegade army officers. Hasina escaped and later became leader of the Awami League, the main opposition party to Prime Minister Khaleda Zia.

A "family feud" between the two leaders began with Mujibur Rahman's assassination, which was linked to followers of Khaleda Zia's husband, a former president who was in turn assassinated in Chittagong in 1981. In 1995–1996 Hasina Wajed launched a series of crippling strikes against the Khaleda Zia government, eventually bringing it down in the next parliamentary election. The Awami League won the election, making its leader prime minister.

During Hasina Wajed's first year in office, Bangladesh's economy grew as foreign investment dollars poured in. But she failed to bring about much needed governmental and social reforms, and there was ample evidence that the bitter feud continued. During 1998 at least thirty-one opposition party politicians were murdered, leading former prime minister Zia to call for the same paralyzing strikes that had caused her own government to fall.

References

"The 'Strongwomen' of South Asia"; see Arshad Mahmud, "Zia's Faltering Rule," reprinted from *The Guardian* (London) in *World Press Review.* December 1994. pp. 18–20.

"War of the Ladies." *World Press Review.* September 1998. p. 21.

Wang
See Cheng-Chun

Werleigh, Claudette
Prime Minister of Haiti (1994–1995)

In 1991 Haitian president Jean-Bertrand Aristide was arrested in a military coup and expelled from the country. Over the next two years thousands of Haitian refugees attempted to enter the United States to escape the military dictatorship. In 1993 the United Nations imposed a worldwide embargo of arms, oil, and financial aid upon Haiti. In 1994 the United Nations Security Council authorized an invasion of Haiti to unseat the usurpers, but at the last minute the military agreed to step down and allow the duly elected president to return. After thousands of U.S. troops arrived to assure his safety, Aristide returned to resume his office October 15, 1994.

Claudette Werleigh, a member of a distinguished family of jurists in Port au Prince and a minister of the Ministry of Foreign Affairs, was chosen to serve as prime minister. A United Nations peacekeeping force took over responsibility of Haiti on March 31, 1995. In the elections held at the close of the year, René Préval was voted Aristide's successor, and Rosny Smarth was chosen as the new prime minister. Préval took office on February 7, 1996.

References

Famighetti, Robert, ed. dir. *The World Almanac and Book of Facts.* Mahwah, NJ: KIII Reference Corporation, 1998. p. 772.

Who's Who in the World 1996. New Providence, RI: Marquis/Reed Elsevier, 1995. p. 1432.

Wilhelmina
(Corbis-Bettmann)

Wilhelmina
Queen, Ruler of The Netherlands (1890–1949)

Wilhelmina was born in 1880, the daughter of King William, ruler of the Netherlands from 1849 to 1890, and his second wife, Emma of Waldeck-Pyrmont. When Wilhelmina's father died (1890), she became queen of The Netherlands at the age of ten, under the regency of Queen Emma. Wilhelmina was inaugurated (not crowned, because the crown belongs to the Dutch people) in 1898. The liberal ministry passed much social legislation during the first two years of her majority, including bills calling for improved housing, compulsory education for children, and accident insurance. In 1901 she married Duke Henry of Mecklenburg-Schwerin. The couple had a daughter, Juliana, born in 1909.

Wilhelmina kept her country neutral during World War I, and after the German defeat, Kaiser Wilhelm sought and received refuge in The Netherlands. In 1920, the Dutch refused the Allied demand for his surrender. He lived in retirement, first at Amerongen, then at Doorn, where he died in 1941. Ironically, the Dutch kindness to the ex-ruler of Germany did not prevent the Nazis under Adolph Hitler from overrunning The Netherlands in May 1940.

May was to become a pivotal month for the queen for the rest of the decade. She escaped with her family and the government to London the day before The Netherlands formally surrendered, May 14, 1940. Throughout the war, Queen Wilhelmina sent messages from England of hope for her people over Radio Orange. She returned May 3, 1945, after the Nazi surrender, to find that her country had suffered extensive damage. Imminent large-scale famine was averted only by aid from the Allies. On May 17, 1948, the countries of The Netherlands, Belgium, Luxembourg, France, and Britain signed a fifty-year mutual assistance pact in Brussels. Four months later, owing to ill health, Wilhelmina abdicated in favor of her daughter, Juliana.

Wilhelmina lived in retirement at her palace, Het Loo, until her death in 1962 at the age of eighty-two.

References
Langer, William L., ed. *World History*. Boston: Houghton Mifflin, 1980. pp. 674, 986, 1136, 1172, 1179.

Shirer, William L. *The Rise and Fall of the Third Reich*. New York: Simon & Schuster, 1960. pp. 561, 640, 652, 721–723, 729.

Wu Hou
Empress, De Facto Ruler of China (660–684), Regent of China (684–690), "Emperor," Ruler in Her Own Right (690–705)

Wu Hou (or Wu Chao or Wu Tso Tien) was born in 625 and at the age of thirteen came as a junior concubine to the court of T'ang emperor Tai-tsung, ruler from 627 to 649. When he died, she was chosen by his heir and possibly already her lover, Kao-tsung (649–684), first as his favored concubine and then, in 655, as his empress. On her way to ultimate power, she is said to have poisoned one of her own sons, her sister, and her niece; forced another son to hang himself; had four grandchildren whipped to death; ordered the execution of two step-sons and sixteen of their male heirs; killed four daughters-in-law and thirty-six government officials and generals; and ordered another 3,000 families to be slaughtered. By 660 she had eliminated all her opponents.

The emperor was often too ill to attend to affairs of state for months at a time and relied entirely on Wu Hou. For the last twenty-three years of his life, empress Wu Hou ran the country with consummate ability and efficiency. Military spending was reduced, the country experienced peace and prosperity, and commerce and agriculture thrived. When Kao-tsung died in 683, she became regent for their son, Chung Tsung. But she had disagreements with the new emperor's wife almost immediately, so she deposed her son after only one month and installed her second son, Jui Tsung, over whom she had more control.

In 690 she simply usurped the throne for herself, naming herself "emperor" and ruling with great wisdom in her own name for fifteen years. Described as self-confident and assertive, she took great pains to encourage independent thinking and bold behavior in her children. So long as she remained strong, no one dared attempt to usurp her power, but when she reached the age of eighty, her opponents grew more courageous. She was deposed in a palace coup in 705 and died in retirement ten months later.

References

Bloodworth, Dennis. *The Chinese Looking Glass.* New York: Farrar, Straus and Giroux, 1967. pp. 90–92.

Bloodworth, Dennis, and Ching Ping Bloodworth. *The Chinese Machiavelli: 3000 Years of Chinese Statecraft.* New York: Dell Publishing, 1976. pp. 214–215, 218, 258–259.

Grousset, René. *The Empire of the Steppes: A History of Central Asia.* Trans. Naomi Walford. New Brunswick, NJ: Rutgers University Press, 1970. pp. 107–108.

Hook, Brian, ed. *The Cambridge Encyclopedia of China.* Cambridge: Cambridge University Press, 1982. pp. 189–190, 191.

Morton, W. Scott. *China, Its History and Culture.* New York: McGraw-Hill, 1980, 1982. pp. 87, 89.

Reischauer, Edwin O., and John K. Fairbank. *East Asia: The Great Tradition.* Boston: Houghton Mifflin, 1960. pp. 157, 170, 190.

Y

Yaa Akyaa

*Asantehemaa, Queen Mother of the West African Asante (Ashanti) Empire
(ca. 1883–1896)*

Yaa Akyaa was born ca. 1837 of the royal matriclan Oyoko. She was
selected from among the women of the royal Oyoko dynasty to succeed Queen Afua Kobi as asantehemaa. Asantehemaa, meaning "queen
mother," does not carry the same connotation as it does in Europe.
Each district or group had its own chief and queen mother, but there
was one grand chief and one grand queen mother, who might not be
the mother of anyone, who ruled over all. It was the asantehemaa, in
many ways the most vital person in the tribe, who nominated the
chief and who made many of the diplomatic decisions. The asantehemaa was completely in charge during the long periods, stretching
sometimes into years, when no one occupied the Golden Stool.

Yaa Akyaa was married to the akyebiakyerehene Kwasi Gyam-
bibi. The akyebiakyerehene was a secretary or adviser to the chief and
the council. The couple had thirteen children, several of whom in
their turn were to be nominated to sit upon the Golden Stool. Even
prior to her election as asantehemaa, as queen mother of her own
tribe or district, she wielded considerable power.

In 1883 two factions were vying for supremacy and the right to
name the next asantehene, or chief of the chiefs. The duty of the asantehene was to act as judge. He decided cases of extreme seriousness
that could not be solved within the individual districts. The mamponhene, or leader of the Mampone district, sent word that he was coming to intercede in the dispute. Yaa Akyaa sent several messages instructing him to withdraw and to remove his guns from Kumase
because the two factions were going to fight. The mamponhene did as
he was told. The battle took place, and the Kumasi people headed by Yaa
Akyaa were victorious (1883). Her son Kwaka Dua II was placed on the
Golden Stool, and another son, Agyemon Badu, became heir apparent.

Following the premature death of Kwaka Dua II of smallpox only a few months later, and apparently the death of the heir as well and the subsequent death of his predecessor and rival, the kingdom was plunged into confusion. As the Asante attempted to recover from the devastation caused by the outbreak of this strange disease, a lawless people, the Adansis, took advantage of the confusion to rob and plunder travelers enroute to and from the coast. When the Asante retaliated, the Adansis sent false reports to the British blaming the Asante for the attacks on travelers and requesting aid to defeat the Asante. For a while, until they bothered to investigate the matter, the British intervened on behalf of the marauders. Meanwhile, Yaa Akyaa called a third son, Agyeman Prempe, to the stool, but a contender from another district had emerged, contesting Prempe's right since he was not the so-named heir apparent. Yaa Akyaa, in despair at the indecision, saw that there was imminent danger of the collapse of the empire and sent an urgent message to the chiefs requesting that they meet together and elect a king.

Still reeling from the unwarranted attacks by the British troops, the chiefs consented to come only if the British government would agree to support the man chosen. She then dispatched an emissary to the local British government requesting that a representative be present at the election so as to observe who was the duly elected ruler. The British took no notice of the message for two years, and it was yet another two years beyond that before the British deigned to comply. This unconscionable delay culminated in the appearance, in 1888, of the long-awaited British representative.

Yaa Akyaa, by this time age fifty, short, white-haired, characterized as proud, tenacious, energetic, cunning, and intelligent, in a dramatic bit of political maneuvering demanded that the chief sponsor of the rival candidate return the 3,200 ounces of gold that a deposed chief had "deposited" in Saawua. In fact, he had sewn it into a mattress. She was thus able to prevail over the Council of Kumase, and Agyeman Prempe was duly elected.

In 1890 she sent envoys to the British about the refugee problem: Many Asante had been lured to the British colony on the coast with promises of riches as servants and laborers, and they had acquired undesirable habits from the white men. She requested that the British instruct all Asante citizens residing in the colony to return to Asante in order to "make Asante as it was in the olden days." In exchange, the Asante would affirm its policy of "peace, trade and open roads."

In 1894 she led the more traditional councilors among the west African peoples in insisting that the British desist from interfering with their system of domestic slavery, which was integral to the Asante social structure and national plantation economy. The British colonial governor, Maxwell, believed that the arrest and detention of the asantehene would precipitate the collapse of the Asante government, and to that end, in 1890, the British government surrounded the town of Kumase and, in a surprise coup, took Yaa Akyaa, her son, and others in charge under British "protection." Two days later they were formally arrested. Her son, who was wrongly accused of killing people but knew that he would be proven innocent, allowed himself to be taken away without struggle, providing that the queen mother would go with him. She agreed to go. The two told the British and their people that there was no need to fight; they did not want their nation destroyed. The Asante people, instructed to be proud and not to react, nevertheless all cried. As one Asante wrote, "Kumase was a sea of tears." Prempe told his people that he and Yaa Akyaa would return, so, in the words of another reporter, "We went to our villages quietly and waited." They would wait for a very long time, for in 1896 the two leaders, never tried but only held in captivity, were deported to Sierra Leone, and in 1900 they were exiled to the remote Seychelles Islands.

Ironically, Prempe's and Yaa Akyaa's submission failed to save the sovereignty of the Asante kindom. Prempe was not allowed to return (as a "private citizen") until 1924; apparently Yaa Akyaa had died on Seychelles in the interim. On the surface, the British succeeded in "neutralizing" the Asante nation, but so long as the British remained in the villages the chant never ceased: "This nation is not yours, / It belongs to Nana Yaa, / This nation is not yours! / It belongs to Yaa Akyaa. / This nation is not your nation! / It belongs to Nana Prempe. / Nana Prempe is away, and you are occupying his office."

References

Balmer, W. T. *A History of the Akan People*. New York: Atlantis Press, 1925. pp. 168–185.

Lewin, Thomas J. *Asante Before the British*. Lawrence: Regents Press of Kansas, 1978. pp. 69–206.

Yaa Asantewaa

Edwesohemaa, Queen Mother of the Edweso Tribe of the Asante and Symbolic Leader of the Asante War for Independence (1900–1901)

Yaa Asantewaa was born ca. 1850 and had been elected queen mother, or edwesohemaa, of the Edweso tribe. Following the arrest by the British of her son, Edwesohene (chief of the Edweso) Kwasi Afrane, the queen mother and two others ran the local administration. The Edweso was one tribe of the Asante empire. The British reported that under the new leaders, "Edweso appears to be flourishing."

Following the British arrest in 1896 of Asantehene Agyeman Prempe and Asantehemaa Yaa Akyaa, the people hid the Golden Stool, symbol of Asante political sovereignty. The British levied stiff taxes to help recoup the cost of their campaigns against the Asante and to meet costs of building a fort to house British troops and to build the resident's office and home. In addition, the Europeans had taken over the state-owned "secret" gold mines, which had provided the capital for operating the Asante government.

By 1897, thirteen Basel and six Wesleyan missionary schools had been established. But soon the missionaries were interfering in local political and domestic affairs, intruding upon the private lives of the citizens. These conditions and more led to widespread Asante unrest, which the British sought to quell one way or another. The British governor then made the shocking demand that the Asante surrender the Golden Stool, and he sent a military attache, Capt. C. H. Armitage, to force the people to tell him where the stool was hidden.

Armitage went to Edweso and confronted Yaa Asantewaa, but the edwesohemaa told him that she did not have the Golden Stool. The captain went from village to village demanding the stool. At the village of Bare, Armitage lost patience. By one citizen's account, when the people of Bare learned that Armitage was on the way, they left the village, leaving only the children on the streets. The children told the captain their fathers were gone hunting and that they knew nothing about the Golden Stool. The captain ordered the children beaten, and the elderly came out of hiding to defend the children. The citizens were bound hand and foot and beaten.

This brutality sparked the beginning of the Yaa Asantewaa War for Independence, so named because the outraged queen mother of the Edweso, described as feisty and gallant, inspired and directed it. But the Asante were no match for the British, who not only killed the citizens but plundered and pillaged their farms and plantations and confiscated their lands so that the Asante were left completely dependent upon their victors for survival. The queen mother and her close companions were deported as political prisoners, along with the exiled Asantehene Agyeman and the queen mother of Asante, Yaa Akyaa, to the Seychelles Islands.

References

Lewin, Thomas J. *Asante Before the British*. Lawrence: Regents Press of Kansas, 1978. pp. 221–222.

Yehudit

See Judith

Yelena Glinskaya

Grand Princess, Regent of Russia (1533–1538)

Yelena Glinskaya (or Helen Glinski, Glinskij, or Glinskaia) was born ca. 1506 of a noble Tatar family, the niece of Prince Michael Glinski (Glinskij). Michael Glinski was a converted Orthodox Lithuanian magnate who, during a dispute between Alexander I and Sigismund I, contenders for the Polish-Lithuanian throne, had switched sides, deserted, and emigrated to Russia. In ca. 1529 Yelena became the second wife of Grand Prince Vasily III (Basil III), ruler of Russia from 1505 to 1533, whose marriage to his first wife, Solomonia, had been childless. Yelena bore Vasily two sons. Their firstborn son, born in 1530, became Ivan IV (later called the Terrible), ruler of Russia at the age of three when Vasily died. Grand Princess Yelena ruled in Ivan's name, disregarding the boyar duma and relying instead on her uncle, Prince Michael, until his death. Then she turned for counsel to her young lover, Ivan Ovchina-Telepnev-Oblensky, sparking unfounded rumors that Ivan was his son.

Her late husband, Basil III, had engaged in territorial disputes with Poland-Lithuania without receiving asked-for assistance of the Hapsburgs. The Russians had made substantial gain in that ten-year conflict, acquiring the key city of Smolensk in 1514. In 1533 Yelena sent emissaries both to Ferdinand I, king of both Hungary and Bohemia, and his brother, Holy Roman emperor Charles V, hoping to bolster friendship with the Hapsburgs in case of another conflict with Poland-Lithuania. The dispute did flare again over the ownership of Smolensk: In 1534–1536 another war resulted in no gain for the Poles. Russia was able to keep possession of Smolensk. Meanwhile, the boyars families of Sujskij and Belskij fought among themselves for the privilege of then overpowering Yelena's regency and assuming it themselves. In 1538 Yelena died suddenly, possibly of poisoning, allegedly at the provocation of the boyars. Ivan IV imprisoned Yelena's adviser Oblensky and his sister, although he did not formally accuse them of implementing the murder plot.

References

Dvornik, Francis. *The Slavs in European History and Civilization.* New Brunswick, NJ: Rutgers University Press, 1962. pp. 273, 343, 378, 439, 442.

Langer, William L., ed. *World History.* Boston: Houghton Mifflin, 1980. pp. 442, 444, 446.

Riasanovsky, Nicholas V. *A History of Russia.* Oxford: Oxford University Press, 1963, 1993. p. 143.

Ye-lü Shih
Regent of Kara-Khitai (1163–1178)

The Kara-Khitai empire was located in eastern Turkestan. Ye-lü Shih was born Pu-su-wan (Chinese transcription), a member of a pagan Mongol line ruling in Muslim Turkic territory. She was the daughter of Ye-lü Ta-shih, who ruled ca. 1130 to 1142, and his wife, Ta-pu-yen. Upon the death of the king in 1142, the aggressive Queen Ta-pu-yen served as regent until their son, Ye-lü Yi-lie, reached majority. When he died in 1163, Pu-su-wan assumed the regency on behalf of her nephew, Ye-lü Che-lu-ku, son of her late brother. (Although as ruler she was called Ye-lü Shih, for the sake of clarity she will continue to be referred to here by her birth name.)

During her reign, Pu-su-wan's army entered Khurasan to plunder Balkh (1165). In 1172 she took sides in the dispute of a neighbor, the Khwarizmian empire. Two sons of the late shah vied for the throne. The loser, Takash, sought refuge in her country. She charged her husband with the task of leading an army into Kwarizmia to reinstate Takash and drive out his brother, Sultan-shah. Once this was accomplished, Pu-su-wan demanded payment of tribute under extremely exacting conditions. When Takash rebelled, she reversed her policy and attempted to reinstate Sultan-shah. Although the Kara-Khitai were unable to accomplish this, they lent him an army with which he conquered another land, Khurasan (1181). When Ye-lü Che-lu-ku reached his majority in 1178, Pu-su-wan retired.

References
Grousset, René. *The Empire of the Steppes: A History of Central Asia.* Trans. Naomi Walford. New Brunswick, NJ: Rutgers University Press, 1970. pp. 165–167.

Yoko, Madame
Ruler of the Kpa Mende Confederacy in Sierra Leone
(1878 / 1885–1905 / 1906)

Yoko was born ca. 1849 and married three times. She divorced her first husband and was widowed by her second. A charming and personable woman, she then became the head wife of a powerful chief in western Mendeland, taking an active diplomatic role in his government. In 1878, when the chief was near death, he named her as his successor.

Madame Yoko immediately set out to form alliances with her neighbors, building one of the largest political confederacies in Sierra Leone's hinterland. She allied herself with the British, whose influence was expanding into the country's interior. The British stationed a police unit at her capital to help her keep peace and even deported a rival chief after she complained about him.

She started her own Sande Bush (female initiation society to train women leaders), which became so renowned in Mendeland that mothers vied to get their daughters accepted. She selected only the most promising young women for her Bush and, according to Sierra Leone historian M. C. F. Easmon, to enter her Bush was like being "presented at court." When the young women graduated, she married them off to "leading men who would help her own advancement."

In 1898 war broke out against the British, who two years earlier had declared a protectorate and imposed a property tax on its subjects. Yoko remained loyal to the British during this uprising, and as a reward, she was allowed to expand the territory under her jurisdiction and to exercise more control over the Kpa chiefs. She took liberties with her expanded power, engaging in acts of aggression to bring other tribes into her realm of influence. Her territory became so large and unwieldy that at her death the Kpa Mende Confederacy had to be divided into fifteen separate chiefdoms. According to some accounts, fearing old age, she took her own life in 1906.

References

Easmon, M.C.F. "Madame Yoko, Ruler of the Mende Confederacy." *Sierra Leone Studies*. December 1958: 166–167.

Hoffer, C. P. "Madam Yoko: Ruler of the Kpa Mende Confederacy." In M. Rosaldo and L. Lamphere, eds. *Women, Culture and Society*. Stanford: Stanford University Press, 1974.

Lipschutz, Mark R., and R. Kent Rasmussen. *Dictionary of African Historical Biography*. Berkeley: University of California Press, 1989. p. 253.

Yolanda
Titular Queen of Jerusalem (1212–1228)

Yolanda (or Isabella II or Yolanta) was born in 1212, the daughter of hereditary Queen Maria La Marquise, regent from 1205 to 1212, and King John of Brienne, ruler from 1210 to 1225. Queen Maria died the year Yolanda was born, and Yolanda (actually usually called Isabella, but here referred to as Yolanda to lessen confusion with other Isabellas) inherited the throne. Her father, who then had no legal right to govern except as regent, married (1114) Princess Stephanie of Armenia. Stephanie proved to be a malelovent stepmother. She died in 1219, reportedly as a result of a severe beating at the hands of her husband for having tried to poison Yolanda.

In 1225 the young queen was sent off to Italy to become the second wife of Holy Roman emperor Frederick II. On her way to Italy, she stopped in Cyprus to see her aunt, Queen Alice, for the last time. Both queens and their courts were in tears as Yolanda said goodbye to her "sweet land of Syria" that she would never see again. Frederick was thirty-one, and she was fourteen. Although he was handsome and intelligent, he was also said to be cruel, sly, selfish, and given to erotic conduct of the basest sort. He sent his new wife to a harem that he kept at Palermo, where she was obliged to live in seclusion. In 1228, at the age of sixteen, she gave birth to a son, Conrad, and having given the emperor his heir, she died six days later, never having ruled the kingdom that had been rightfully hers all of her short life.

References

Löwenstein, Prince Hubertus Zu. *A Basic History of Germany.* Bonn: Inter Nationes, 1964. p. 38.

Runciman, Steven A. *A History of the Crusades.* Vol. 3, *The Kingdom of Acre.* Cambridge: Cambridge University Press, 1987. pp. 134, 173–177, 179–182, 221.

Yolande
Empress, Regent of Latin Empire (1217–1219)

Yolande was the wife of Peter of Courtenay, emperor in name only of Constantinople from 1216 to 1217. She was the sister of both Baldwin I (formerly Count Baldwin IX of Flanders and Hainault), Latin emperor from 1204 to 1205, and Henry I, Latin emperor from 1205 to 1216. Yolande and Peter had three children: Marie, who married Theodore Lascaris; Robert, who ruled from 1219 to 1228; and Baldwin II, who ruled from 1228 to 1261. Her husband, Peter, was in Europe when his brother-in-law Henry died, and Peter set out for Rome, where the pope crowned him emperor. He was then on his way from Durazzo to Thessalonica when he was captured by Theodore Dukas of Epirus (1217). Peter died in captivity in 1218, never having ruled a single day. Yolande, who was the legal heir, became regent for her feeble son Robert. She died prematurely in 1219.

References

Langer, William L., ed. *World History.* Boston: Houghton Mifflin, 1980. pp. 281–282.

Ostrogorsky, George. *History of the Byzantine State.* New Brunswick, NJ: Rutgers University Press, 1969. pp. 430, 433.

Yolande de Bourgogne
Countess, Ruler of Nevers (1266–1296)

Yolande de Bourgogne was the daughter of Countess Mahaut II de Bourbon (ruled Nevers 1257–1266) and Eudes de Bourgogne. Yolande inherited the rule of Nevers when her mother died in 1266. She first married Jean Tristan de France, count of Valois, and after his death, she married Robert de Dampierre. She was succeeded in 1296 by Louis I of Flanders.

References
Egan, Edward W., Constance B. Hintz, and L. F. Wise, eds. *Kings, Rulers, and Statesmen.* New York: Sterling Publishing, 1976. p. 160.

Yüan Yu
Regent of Sung Dynasty, China (1085–1093)

Yüan Yu was the mother of Sung Shen Tsung, ruler from 1067 to 1085. He had appointed as chief councilor Wang an-Shih, who carried out a program of radical "socialist" reform of the government. He cut the budget by 40 percent, raised the salaries of officials to make honesty possible, gave aid to farmers, and made large assessments for public services. When Emperor Shen Tsung died in 1085, the grand dowager empress, ruling under the reign title of Yüan Yu, was regent for her grandson, Che Tsung, ruler from 1085 to 1100. Empress Yüan Yu, who was opposed to the reforms of Wang an-Shih, recalled the conservative ministers and rescinded the whole reform program. She died in 1093 and was succeeded by her grandson, Che Tsung.

References
Langer, William L., ed. *World History.* Boston: Houghton Mifflin, 1980. pp. 365–366.

Reischauer, Edwin O., and John K. Fairbank. *East Asia: The Great Tradition.* Boston: Houghton Mifflin, 1960. pp. 206–208.

Ywahoo, Dhyani
Cherokee Nation Clan Chief (fl. 1969–)

Dhyani Ywahoo is the chief of the Green Mountain (Vermont) Ani Yunwiwa, laying claim as holder of the Ywahoo lineage, said to be 2,860 years old. Her teachings were passed to her by her grandfather, Eonah Fisher (Bear Fishing), who received them from his father-in-law, Eli Ywahoo; and from her grandmother, Nellie Ywahoo. In 1969 the elders of the Etowah Band and the Ywahoo bloodline conferred and concluded that their teachings should be shared with the world.

Venerable Dhyani Ywahoo founded and directs the Sunray Meditation Society, near Bristol, Vermont.

In addition to leading her clan of the Cherokees, Dhyani Ywahoo is a champion of Native American cultures and the author of *Voices of Our Ancestors*. She has taken as part of her mission educating the world about the gifts to humanity from Native Americans. She informed a reporter that there are 128 foods now consumed worldwide that were cultivated by Native Americans for thousands of years. In addition, much of Western pharmacopoeia can be traced to Native American herbal knowledge. The Native Americans have led the world in their concern for living in harmony with nature and with protecting their environment.

When the countries of the Western Hemisphere celebrated the 500th anniversary of the arrival of Christopher Colombus in the New World, Dhyani Ywahoo traveled to Spain, where she met with Queen Sofia and others. She was invited to participate in the opening of Madrid's Casa de Americas, Europe's only institute devoted to Native American studies.

References

"Thanksgiving 1991: Food for Thought." *Parade.* 24 November 1991: 11.
"Ven Dhyani Ywahoo." www.sunray.org, 1998.

Z

Zabel
Queen, Ruler of Lesser (Little) Armenia (Cicilia) (1219–1269)

Little Armenia was located in modern-day Turkey. Zabel (or Isabella) was born in 1215, the younger daughter of Leo II (or Leon) the Great, ruler of Armenia from 1198 to 1219, and his second wife, Princess Sibylla of Cyprus and Jerusalem. Leo had no sons, and his older daughter, Stephanie, was the wife of John of Brienne, king of Jerusalem. On his deathbed (1219), Leo II named Zabel his successor under the regency of Baron Constantine of Lambron. Since King Leo had earlier promised the succession to his niece, Alice Roupen, married to Raymond of Antioch, John of Brienne decided to put in a claim on behalf of his Armenian wife Stephanie and their infant son as well. But his wife died, reputedly because of a battering he inflicted, and soon afterward the baby also died.

On Leo's death, the Hethumid baron Constantine was elected Zabel's protector and regent. He imprisoned Leo's grandnephew, Alice Roupen, and Raymond of Antioch's son, Raymond-Roupen (or Ruben-Raymond), who had declared himself king. Raymond-Roupen soon died in prison, leaving Zabel's claim unchallenged. With the consent of Armenian nobles, Zabel was married as a child to Philip, fourth son of Bohemond IV of Antioch, who did not comply with the marriage agreement: He refused, although already excommunicated by the Catholic Church, to embrace the separated Armenian Church as his father Bohemond IV had promised he would do. In addition, he spent as much time in Antioch as possible.

Philip stole the crown jewels of Armenia and sent them to his father. In 1224, as he set out again from Armenia for Antioch, he was arrested at Sis by Constantine, who demanded the return of the jewels as ransom. But Bohemond preferred to allow his son to die in prison rather than relinquish the jewels. Philip was poisoned at Sis a few months later. Zabel, broken hearted, fled to Seleucia, and the Hospitallers, or Templars, who previously had openly favored the heretical Armenian, to avoid the shame of surrendering Zabel in person, handed the whole town over to the regent Constantine. In 1226 Constantine arranged to have his own son, Hethoum I (Hayton) of Lambron, marry Zabel, although for many years she refused to live with him. Finally she relented, and in 1226 the two were crowned together. Bohemond IV, still seething over the murder of his son Philip at the hands of Constantine, tried vainly to persuade the pope to arrange a divorce between Zabel and Hethoum so as to deprive Hethoum of the right to rule. The couple had at least five children: Leo III, who became king of Armenia on his mother's death in 1269; Thoros; Sibylla, who married Prince Bohemond VI of Antioch; Euphemia, who married John of Sidon; and Maria, who married Guy of Ibelin. In 1254–1255 Hethoum, an ally of the Mongols, journeyed to Karakorum and back by way of Samarkaland and Persia. His travels were chronicled by Kirakos Gandzaketse in an account that provides some of the best source material on early Mongolian life and culture. As Hethoum the Great, he ruled from 1226 until 1269.

References

Chahin, M. *The Kingdom of Armenia*. New York: Dorset Press, 1987, 1991, pp. 275, 282–283.

Egan, Edward W., Constance B. Hintz, and L. F. Wise, eds. *Kings, Rulers, and Statesmen*. New York: Sterling Publishing, 1976. p. 21.

Grousset, René. *The Empire of the Steppes: A History of Central Asia*. Trans. Naomi Walford. New Brunswick, NJ: Rutgers University Press, 1970. pp. 281–282, 360–363.

Runciman, Steven A. *A History of the Crusades*. Vol. 3, *The Kingdom of Acre*. Cambridge: Cambridge University Press, 1987. pp. 164, 172–173, 230.

Zabibi

Queen, Ruler of an Arabian State (ca. 738 B.C.)

In ancient Mesopotamia the term *queen* was applied only to goddesses and to those queens of Arabia who served as rulers. If a king were ruling, both his spouse and his mother were also politically important. In 738 B.C. Azriyau, king of Sam'al (Ya'diya or Yaudi) of northern Syria, formed a coalition of principalities to obstruct the advance of King Tiglath-Pileser III of the New Assyrian Empire (r. 744–727 B.C.). The coalition was defeated, and Tiglath-Pileser exacted tribute from rulers of all the important states of Syria-Palestine, including Menahem, king of Israel, and Rezin (Rasunu), king of Damascus. Queen Zabibi (or Zabibê), referred to in ancient documents as "queen of the Arabs," was among those rulers, including another queen of the Arabs, required to send him tribute.

References

Laessøe, Jørgen. *People of Ancient Assyria*. Trans. F. S. Leigh-Browne. London: Routledge and Kegan Paul, 1963. p. 113.

Langer, William L., ed. *World History*. Boston: Houghton Mifflin, 1980. p. 33.

Olmstead, A. T. *History of the Persian Empire*. Chicago: University of Chicago Press, 1948. p. 22.

Oppenheim, A. Leo. *Ancient Mesopotamia*. Chicago: University of Chicago Press, 1977. pp. 104, 169.

Roux, Georges. *Ancient Iraq*. Harmondsworth, Middlesex: Penguin Books, 1964, 1980. p. 285.

Zac-Kuk, Lady

"King" of the Mayas of Palenque (October 22, 612–615),
Co-ruler (615 –640)

Palenque was a city-state in Mexico. Lady Zac-Kuk was the daughter of Pacal I (d. March 9, 612), the younger brother of a king, Ac-Kan (d. August 11, 612). She was the granddaughter of woman ruler Lady Kanal-Ikal (r. 583–604). Zac-Kuk was married to Kan-Bahlum-Mo', but she did not come to the throne as a consort, for her husband was never king. Nor was she regent for a king. She inherited the throne, presumably as her uncle's next-of-kin. She is depicted in Mayan art as having crossed eyes and tattoos over her whole body. She took the throne in 612 and ruled through "three pregnancies" until her son Hanab Pacal (b. 603) reached the age of twelve. At that time she handed her royal headdress over to him, as depicted in an ancient tablet carving in the Oval Palace. Even then Zac-Kuk continued as co-ruler, not just until Pacal became a man, but for many years beyond that time.

In the Temple of Inscriptions are two great vaulted chambers containing three panels carved with glyphs recounting the history of Pacal's ancestors.

Lady Zac-Kuk (Perry-Castaneda Library)

Pacal started the pyramid and after his death in 683, his son Chan-Bahlum (crowned January 10, 690) finished it. On these panels, Zac-Kuk is designated as being analogous to the mother of the gods, thus inferring Pacal's own godlike status. In his case, the mother was the parent critical to his claim to the throne.

Apparently, Zac-Kuk kept a tight hold on power until she died (640), because no major works were commissioned by her son, Pacal, until after that time. In 647, at the age of forty-three, he dedicated the first of his construction projects, Temple Olvidado. It had been seven years since her death and four years since his father's death.

References

Schele, Linda, and David Freidel. *A Forest of Kings. The Untold Story of the Ancient Maya*. New York: Quill, William Morrow, 1990, pp. 221–225, 227–228, 266, 467, 468, 478.

Zainab al-Nafzawiyya
Berber Queen of Morocco Who Shared Power with Her Husband
(1061 or 1071–1106)

Zainab al-Nafzawiyya was married to Yusuf Ibn Tashfeen (or Tashfin), prince of the Murabits, the famed founder of the Tashufinid Dynasty and Almoravid empire in Spain and north Africa, as well as the city of Marrakesh. Yusuf was independent ruler in Marrakesh until 1073, when he assumed the title of *amīr al-muslimīn*. Although it was common knowledge that Zainab shared the power with her husband, she did not have the right to have the *khutba* (a sermon preached in the mosques that gives the sovereign the right to rule) said in her name. Zainab's power was not the only indication of the liberal nature of Yusuf's dynasty. A theologian from another Berber sect, Muhammad Ibn Toumert, was returning to the Maghrib from Baghdad when he saw their daughter riding through Marrakesh among a party of girls, all with their faces unveiled. Outraged, he beat their mules so violently that the young ladies fell off. Zainab's power came to an end in 1106 when the king died and their son 'Ali assumed the throne.

References

Glubb, Sir John. *A Short History of the Arab Peoples*. New York: Dorset Press, 1969, p. 192.

Mernissi, Fatima. *The Forgotten Queens of Islam*. Trans. Mary Jo Lakeland. Minneapolis: University of Minnesota Press, 1993. pp. 14, 205.

Morby, John E. *Dynasties of the World*. Oxford: Oxford University Press, 1989. p. 181.

Zauditu
Empress, Titular Ruler of Ethiopia (1916–1930)

Zauditu (also Zawditu, Zewditu, Waizero, or Judith) was born in 1916, the daughter of Emperor Menelik II, ruler of Ethiopia from 1889 to 1913. Her stepmother was Empress Taitu. In 1902 Zauditu married Ras Gugsa (Gugsa Wolie). Because Menelik had no sons and was reluctant to name a woman to succeed him, he had named his grandson, Lij Iyasu, as his heir, but the heir apparent refused to ready himself for the position. He refused all schooling after the age of fifteen. When Menelik died in 1913, despite Taitu's objections in favor of her stepdaughter, Iyasu V became emperor. Three years later, he announced his conversion to Islam (1916). As he had not yet been officially crowned, the Ethiopian Church and the local chiefs removed him and, with Taitu as her champion, named Menelik's daughter Zauditu as empress, with Ras Tafari Makonnen (later to be known as Haile Selassie) as her regent and heir. Her appointment was contingent upon her divorcing her husband.

Gradually, Zauditu became concerned about Ras Tafari's usurping more and more power. Her reign was marked by turmoil between the conservative pro-church group, led by war minister Hapta Giorgis, and the liberal, pro-Western group, led by Ras Tafari. In 1923 Ethiopia joined the League of Nations, which later authorized an Ethiopian protest against Britain's plan for division. In 1924 slavery was abolished in Ethiopia. Eventually the country regained access to the sea that had been lost along both the Red Sea coast and the Gulf of Aden. After the death of his old rival Giorgis in 1928, Ras Tafari, not daring to usurp the throne from the empress, nevertheless staged a palace coup and had Zauditu name him "king." Two years later, Zaudita's estranged husband, Ras Gugsa, who had been made governor-general of the northern provinces, organized a revolt. Ras Gugsa was killed and the revolt was squelched by Ras Tafari's forces with great effort.

On the day that she heard the news of Ras Gugsa's death, Empress Zauditu died (1930), and Ras Tafari was immediately crowned emperor with the title of Haile Selassi I. Twenty-five years later he enacted a law barring females from becoming monarchs in Ethiopia.

References
Langer, William L. *World History.* Boston: Houghton Mifflin, 1980. pp. 872, 1078–1079.

Lipschutz, Mark R., and R. Kent Rasmussen. *Dictionary of African Historical Biography.* Berkeley: University of California Press, 1989. p. 255.

Zenobia
*Queen, Ruler of Palmyra, Syria
(266–272)*

She was born Bat Zabbai, or
Septima Zenobia. Arabians
knew her as Az-Zabbā. A
beautiful and wise woman
with aggressive energy, she
became the second wife of
King Odaenathus, ruler of
Palmyra for Rome ca. 260
to 266. She bore three sons:
Wahballat or Vaballath,
Herennianus, and Timolaus.
She reputedly instigated the
murder of her husband and
his heir by his first wife and then became regent for her own son, ruling extremely effectively. At the time of her reign a certain Paul of
Samosata was bishop of Antioch in Syria, when Antioch was subject to
Palmyra. Paul held the belief that Jesus was not God incarnated as man
but rather a human who became divine. His beliefs were thought by
many to be heretical, and in 268 the church denounced his doctrine
and attempted to depose him. But Zenobia's patronage mitigated
harsh judgment against him and prevented his removal.

Not content to remain under Roman cliency, Zenobia decided
to extend her power. In 269–270, she moved into Egypt and then
occupied most of Asia Minor. In 271 she had her son proclaimed augustus. Roman emperor Aurelian, who had not taken her seriously
up until her move into Egypt, marshalled his considerable forces
and marched against her. He recovered Egypt and Asia Minor, then
besieged Palmyra itself. After its surrender, Zenobia and a son fled
to a waiting boat in an attempt to gain sanction among her Sasanian
allies on the other side of the Euphrates. But she was apprehended.
She and her two younger sons were taken back to Rome and paraded in golden chains in Aurelian's triumphal processsion (272 or
274). Wahballat's fate is unknown; Zenobia was granted a pension.
It was not until after her defeat that Paul's sentence of deposition
could be carried out. Conjecture exists as to the direction the
Christian church might have taken had Zenobia prevailed against
the Romans and Paul of Samosata had continued to promulgate his
doctrine.

Zenobia later married a Roman senator and lived into old age in Italy.

References
Bowder, Diana, ed. *Who Was Who in the Roman World.* Ithaca, NY: Cornell University Press, 1980. pp. 586–587.

Fusfield, Bob. *Zenobia, Queen of Palmyra.* Pacific Palisades, CA: Morningbird Press, 1997.

Mommsen, Theodor. *Provinces of the Roman Empire,* vol. II. Trans. William P. Dickson. Chicago: Ares Publishers, 1974. pp. 106–110, 249.

Peters, F. E. *The Harvest of Hellenism.* New York: Barnes & Nobles Books, 1996. pp. 598–601.

Zia, Begum Khaleda
Prime Minister of Bangladesh (1991–1996)

Born in 1945 to a middle-class family with no connections to politics, Khaleda Zia was married at the age of fifteen, just after she finished school. The marriage to an army captain, Ziaur Rahman (Zia ur-Rahman), had been arranged by her parents. She and her husband had two sons. Ziaur rose to become a major general. During a military coup in 1975, he emerged as the country's "strong man," although a civilian, Abusadat Mohammad Sayem, remained as titular head of state for almost two years. In May 1977 General Zia held a national referendum that resulted in a 99 percent vote in his favor.

During his five-year rule, his wife, Khaleda Zia, showed no interest in affairs of state. But in 1981, following her husband's assassination in Chittagong, the Bangladesh Nationalist Party that he had founded drafted her to lead it. It was generally believed that she accepted the challenge in order to avenge her husband's murder, which she believed was masterminded by Zia's successor, General Hussein Muhammad Ershad. She waged a tireless nine-year war against Ershad's corrupt regime, vowing not to take part in any elections under him. Finally, in 1990, he was brought to justice for some of his excesses and was sentenced to twenty years in prison. Khaleda Zia was praised as an "uncompromising" leader. Her party was swept into power in the 1991 general election.

Unlike her counterpart in Pakistan, Benazir Bhutto, Prime Minister Zia took immediate steps to address the literacy problem in her country, where the average Bangladeshi received about two years of schooling, and only a third of the students were girls. She began agressively promoting education and vocational training, especially of girls, and expanding small, no-collateral loans to women-owned businesses. However, by late 1994, much of her popularity had eroded.

Begum Khaleda Zia (Reuters / Corbis-Bettmann)

The critical view was that, by concentrating all her efforts on staying in power, she had become increasingly isolated from the people. She was accused of pandering to fundamentalist causes when she refused to come to the defense of feminist writer Taslima Nasrin, who had made fervent demands for women's rights and an end to purdah and other institutions of sexual repression. The Bangladesh government charged the writer with defaming Islam, forcing her into hiding in Sweden. Zia's most vocal opponent was leader of the Awami League, Hasina Wajed, born in 1946, daughter of Bangladesh's founder and first prime minister, Mujibur Rahman.

By 1996 it appeared that Bangladesh's five-year experiment in democracy was failing. In late March of 1996 Zia gave in to public demands for new elections to be held and petitioned the president to form a caretaker government. However, although Zia's party retained control by default, only 15 percent of registered voters participated in the May elections, which were marred by widespread protests and violence that left sixteen people dead and several hundred injured.

References
Baker, Deborah. "Exiled Feminist Writer Tells Her Own Story." *New York Times.* 28 August 1994: 4 E.

Crossette, Barbara. "A Woman Leader for a Land That Defies Islamic Stereotypes." *New York Times.* 17 October 1993: 3.

"Shaky Democracy." *World Press Review.* May 1996: 24.

"The 'Strongwomen' of South Asia." *World Press Review.* December 1994: 18–20.

Zoë
Empress of Byzantine Empire (1028–1050)

Zoë was born in 980, the middle daughter of King Constantine VIII, ruler of Byzantium from 963 to 1028, and his wife, Helena of Alypius. Psellus described Zoë as "very regal in her ways, a woman of great beauty, most imposing in her manner, and commanding respect." As her pock-faced older sister Eudocia had entered a nunnery, Zoë was named by her dying father to be married to Romanus III. The two inherited the reign when Constantine died in 1028, and Zoë exiled her other sister to a nunnery, probably at Romanus's suggestion. Romanus immediately lost interest in Zoë, even keeping her short of money. She took a lover, a peasant's son, handsome Michael IV, and together they conspired to murder Romanus in his bath.

Zoë claimed the right to rule after Romanus's death, not for herself but for her adored Michael, whom she married and made emperor. Although Michael treated her badly, confining her to the women's quarters, he nevertheless convinced her to adopt his nephew, Michael V, as his successor. When Michael IV died in 1042, Michael V became ruler, but to avoid the possibility of a usurpation of his power, he made the mistake of exiling the aging Zoë to the island of Prinkipo. Indignation at the treatment of the rightful empress swept through the land, and mobs quickly assembled to protest her exile. Michael quickly brought Zoë back and made a great show of his regard for her, but it was of no avail: The mob tracked him down in a local church and gouged his eyes out after he had been forced to watch as the same treatment was given to his minister.

Meanwhile, the youngest sister, Theodora, had been brought back by another faction, which had proclaimed her queen, while across town another crowd had pledged loyalty to Zoë. Eventually Zoë made the first move of reconciliation, welcoming her sister back with an embrace. The sisters ruled jointly for a while, although Theodora bowed to her older sister's seniority and, if Psellus was correct, did not show the slightest rancor about having spent the best years of her life in a nunnery. Then in 1042, the sixty-four-year-old Zoë, ever warm blooded and impulsive, seized power again by marrying a forty-two-year-old senator, Constantine Monomachus, who ruled with her as Constantine IX. More tolerant with the passing of years, aware that her own charms had faded, Zoë ignored her husband's open affair with Sclerina, a niece of his second wife. He gave his mistress the title of Sebaste, and she took her place beside Zoë and Theodora at all court ceremonies. Zoë died in 1050, and when her husband died three years later, her sister Theodora at last ruled alone.

References

Ostrogorsky, George. *History of the Byzantine State*. New Brunswick, NJ: Rutgers University Press, 1969. pp. 321, 323, 326–327.

Psellus, Michael. *Fourteen Byzantine Rulers*. Trans. E. R. A. Sewter. Harmondsworth, Middlesex: Penguin Books, 1982. pp. 55–59, 63–65, 75–81, 87–240 passim, 250.

Zungu, Dr. Sibongile
Chief of the South African Madlebe Tribe (1993)

Sibongile Zungu was born in Durban and educated as a medical doctor. She married the Madlebe chief, who died in an automobile accident in 1993. After his death, she was chosen to succeed him, officiating over the rural South African tribe of 70,000. Of her election, she said, "People are waiting to see if I fall flat on my face. I'm going to make sure that doesn't happen."

Natal Province, where she is located, has been noted for its violent acts of bloodshed. Dr. Zungu vowed not to "get involved in politics" but gave the opinion that violence was "nature's way of changing this country—her way of cleansing away all the man-made suffering."

She was replaced by a kinsman, John Zungu, who was assassinated in 1997.

References
"Hail to The Chief" *World Press Review.* March 1993: 50.

Bibliography

Abercrombie, Thomas J. "Cambodia: Indochina's 'Neutral Corner'. *National Geographic* 126. October 1964: 514–551.

Adeleye, R. A. "Hausaland and Bornu, 1600–1800." In J.F.A. Ajayi and Michael Crowder, eds., *History of West Africa.* Vol. 1. New York: Columbia University Press, 1972.

"Africa's First Woman Head of State Pledges to Work for Peace." Reuter Information Service, *Nando Times,* 18 August 1996: 1.

Al-Dahbi. *Siyar 'alam al-nubala'.* Cairo: Dar al-Ma'arif, 1958.

Alexander, David, and Patricia Alexander, eds. *Eerdman's Handbook to the Bible.* Berkhamsted, Herts, England: Lion Publishing, 1973.

Ali, Owais Aslam. "Regression in Pakistan," from "IPI Report." *World Press Review.* April 1996: 17–18.

Ali, Tariq. "Dynasty's Daughter." *Interview.* February 1989: 68–71, 124.

Allen, W.E.D. *A History of the Georgian People from the Beginning Down to the Russian Conquest in the Nineteenth Century.* New York: Barnes & Noble Books, 1971.

al-Thawr, 'Abdallah Ahmad Muhammad. *Hadhihi hiyya al-Yaman.* Beirut: Dar al-'Awda, 1979.

al-Zarkali, Khayr al-Din. *Al-'alam, qamus ash'ar al-rijal wa al-nisa' min al-'arab wa al-musta'rabin wa al-mustashraqin,* vol. 1 of 8 vols. Beirut: Dar al-'Ilm li al-Malayin, 1983.

Asprey, Robert B. *Frederick the Great: The Magnificent Enigma.* New York: Ticknor and Fields, 1986.

Aston, W. G., trans. *Nihongi: Chronicles of Japan from the Earliest Times to A.D. 697.* Rutland, VT: Charles E. Tuttle, 1972.

Aung-Thwin, Michael A. *Myth and History in the Historiography of Early Burma.* Singapore: Institute of Southeast Asia Studies, 1998.

Australian Magazine. April 1996: 22.

Avallone, Michael. *A Woman Called Golda.* New York: Leisure Books, 1982.

Aycock, Leslie. *Arthur's Britain.* Harmondsworth, Middlesex: Penguin Books, 1971.

Baker, Deborah. "Exiled Feminist Writer Tells Her Own Story." *New York Times.* 28 August 1994: 4 E.

Balmer, W. T. *A History of the Akan Peoples.* New York: Atlantis Press, 1925.

Barber, Karin, and P. F. de Moraes Farias. *Discourse and Its Disguises*. Birmingham, England: University of Birmingham Centre of West African Studies, 1989.

Batto, Bernard Frank. *Studies on Women at Mari*. Baltimore: Johns Hopkins University Press, 1974.

Baum, Julian. "Sizing up a Decade of British Radicalism." *Christian Science Monitor*. 4 May 1989: 1–2.

Beale, Betty. "Word from Washington: Iceland's President Kicks off Scandinavian Culture Extravaganza." *Houston Chronicle*. 5 September 1982: section 7, p.11.

Bergami, David. *Japan's Imperial Conspiracy*. New York: William Morrow, 1972.

Bhatin, Krishan. *A Biography of Prime Minister Gandhi*. New York: Praeger, 1974.

Bhattacharya, Sachchidananda. *A Dictionary of Indian History*. New York: George Braziller, 1967.

Bhutto, Benazir. *Daughter of Destiny*. New York: Simon & Schuster, 1989.

———. *Daughter of the East*. London: Hamish Hamilton, 1988.

Biersteker, Ann, and Mark Plane. "Swahili Manuscripts and the Study of Swahili Literature." *Research in African Literature* 20, no. 3 (Fall 1989): 449–472; specifically 468.

Birmingham, David. *Trade and Conflict in Angola: The Mbundu and Their Neighbors Under the Influence of the Portuguese*. Oxford: Oxford University Press, 1966.

Blaustein, Albert P., and Gisbert H. Flanz, eds. *Constitutions of the Countries of the World: A Series of Updated Texts, Constitutional Chronologies and Annotated Bibliographies*. Dobbs Ferry, NY: Oceana Publications, 1991.

Bloodworth, Dennis. *The Chinese Looking Glass*. New York: Farrar, Straus and Giroux, 1967.

Bloodworth, Dennis, and Ching Ping Bloodworth. *The Chinese Machiavelli: 3,000 Years of Chinese Statecraft*. New York: Dell Publishing, 1976.

Bokhari, Farhan. "Pakistan's Benazir Bhutto Gets a Second Chance." *Christian Science Monitor*. 20 October 1993: 2.

Boone, Sylvia Ardyn. *Radiance from the Waters*. New Haven: Yale University Press, 1986.

Boulding, Elise. *The Underside of History: A View of Women through Time*. Boulder: Westview Press, 1976.

Bowder, Diana, ed. *Who Was Who in the Greek World*. Ithaca, NY: Cornell University Press, 1982.

———. *Who Was Who in the Roman World*. Ithaca, NY: Cornell University Press, 1980.

Breisach, Ernest. *Caterina Sforza: A Renaissance Virago*. Chicago: University of Chicago Press, 1967.

Britannica Micropaedia. Vol. 2. 1983.

———. Vol. 3. s.v. "Bolivia, History." 1983.

———. Vol. 7. s.v. "Gajah Maja." 1983.

————. Vol. 16. s.v. "San Marino." 1983.

Brody, James. "In Step with David Frost." *Parade.* 18 February 1989: 18.

Browning, Robert. *Justinian and Theodora.* New York: Praeger, 1971.

Bryant, A. T. *Olden Times in Zululand and Natal.* London: Longman Green, 1929.

Buchan, John, ed. *The Baltic and Caucasian States.* Boston: Houghton Mifflin, 1923.

Budge, E. A. *A History of Ethiopia.* London: Methuen, 1928.

Burn, Sir R., ed. *Cambridge History of India.* Vol. 4, *The Moghal Period.* Cambridge: Cambridge University Press, 1937.

Burns, John F. "For Indian Politician, an Opulent Wedding Means Political Bliss." *New York Times International.* 10 September 1995: 6.

Butler, Alban. *The Lives of the Fathers, Martyrs, and Other Principal Saints.* Vol. 4. Chicago: The Catholic Press, 1961.

Cahin, M. *The Kingdom of Armenia.* New York: Dorset Press, 1987, 1991.

Cambridge Ancient History. 3d. ed. Vol. 1. Cambridge: Cambridge University Press, 1970–1971.

"Canada's Tories Name a Woman as New Premier." *New York Times.* 14 June 1993: A1, A4.

Candee, Marjorie Dent, ed. *Current Biography 1953.* New York: H. W. Wilson, 1954.

Capron, Lewis. "Florida's Emerging Seminoles." *National Geographic.* November 1969: 716–734.

Carney, E. D. "Olympias, Adea Eurydice, and the End of the Argead Dynasty." In Ian Worthington, ed. *Ventures into Greek History.* Oxford: Clarendon Press, 1994.

Carpenter, Clive. *The Guinness Book of Kings, Rulers & Statesmen.* Enfield, Middlesex: Guinness Superlatives, 1978.

Casey, Patricia. "President Defies Media Stereotypes." *Irish Times* "Opinion." 16 December 1997: 1.

Ceram, C. W. *The Secret of the Hittites.* New York: Alfred A. Knopf, 1955. Reprint Dorset Press, 1990.

Cerutis, James. "Sea Islands: The South's Surprising Coast." *National Geographic* 139. March 1971: 373–374.

Chadwick, Nora. *The Celts.* Harmondsworth, Middlesex: Penguin Books, 1976.

Chapman, Charles E. *A History of Spain.* New York: The Free Press/Macmillan, 1965.

Clarity, James F. "In Ireland, Gesture of Religious Healing Inflames the Faithful." *New York Times.* 21 December 1997: 10Y.

Clark, Sydney. *All the Best in Holland.* New York: Dodd Mead, 1960.

Clarke, John Henrik. "Time of Troubles." In Alvin M. Josephy, Jr., ed., *The Horizon History of Africa.* New York: American Heritage Publishing, McGraw-Hill, 1971.

Clayton, Mark. "Canada's Campbell Turns to the Race Ahead." *Christian Science Monitor.* 15 June 1993: 6.

———. "Kim Campbell Sets Out to Show She's No 'Kim Mulroney.'" *Christian Science Monitor.* 25 August 1993: 3.

"Clouds over India Dim Gandhi's Global Star." *U.S. News &World Report.* 21 March 1983.

Clough, Shepard B., David L. Hicks, David J. Brandenburg, and Peter Gray. *European History in aWorld Perspective.* Vol 2, *Early Modern Times.* Lexington, MA: D. C. Heath, 1975.

Codrington, H. W. *A Short History of Ceylon.* Cambridge: Cambridge University Press, 1947.

Collis, Maurice. *SheWas a Queen.* New York: New Directions Books, 1991.

Çomo, Andi. "Albanian History: The Illyrians." www.albanian.com, 1998.

Connolly, Anne. "Ghosts of the Famine." *South China Morning Post,* Hong Kong, 11 November 1995. Reprinted in *World Press Review,* February 1996: 39–40.

Constable, Pamela. "Nicaragua's Change Slow under Chamorro." *Houston Chronicle.* 28 April 1991: 23A.

Cooke, Jean, Ann Kramer, and Theodore Rowland-Entwistle. *History's Timeline.* New York: Crescent Books, 1981.

Cooke, S. A., F. E. Adcock, and M. P. Charlesworth. *The Cambridge Ancient History.* Vol. 10. London: Cambridge University Press, 1971.

Coughlan, Robert. *Elizabeth and Catherine.* New York: G. P. Putnam's Sons, 1974.

"Cracking Down on Bosnia's War Criminals." *World Press Review.* September 1997: 5.

Crankshaw, Edward. *Maria Theresa.* New York: Viking Press, 1969, 1971.

Crossette, Barbara. "King Bhumibol's Reign." *New York Times Magazine.* 21 May 1989: 30–36.

———. "A Woman Leader for a LandThat Defies Islamic Stereotypes." *NewYork Times.* 17 October 1993: 3.

Dahmus, Joseph. *Seven Medieval Queens.* Garden City, NY: Doubleday, 1972.

Davidson, Basil. *African History.* New York: Collier/Macmillan Publishing, 1991.

———. "The Niger to the Nile." In Alvin M. Josephy, Jr., ed., *The Horizon History of Africa.* New York: American Heritage Publishing, McGraw-Hill, 1971.

Deen, Edith. *All theWomen of the Bible.* New York: Harper and Brothers, 1955.

Delane, Mary. *Sardinia, The Undefeated Island.* London: Faber & Faber, 1968.

Delury, George, ed. *TheWorld Almanac and Book of Facts.* NewYork: Newspaper Enterprise Association, 1994.

———. *The World Almanac and Book of Facts.* New York: Newspaper Enterprise Association, 1992.

Dening, Greg. *Performances*. Chicago: The University of Chicago Press, 1996.

Derry, T. K. *A History of Scandinavia*. Minneapolis: University of Minnesota Press, 1979.

de Villiers, Marq, and Sheila Hirtle. *Into Africa*. Toronto: Key Porter Books, 1997.

"Difficult Choices." *World Press Review*. November 1997: 19.

Diop, Cheikh Anta. *The African Origin of Civilization*. Trans. Mercer Cook. Chicago: Lawrence Hill Books, Chicago Review Press, 1974.

Donovan, Frank R. *The Vikings*. New York: American Heritage Publishing, 1964.

Duff, Charles. *England and the English*. New York: G. P. Putnam's Sons, 1955.

Duff, Nora. *Matilda of Tuscany*. London: Cambridge Press, 1909.

Dunn, Ross E. *The Adventures of Ibn Battuta*. Berkeley: The University of California Press, 1986.

Durant, Will. *The Story of Civilization*. Vol. 2, *The Life of Greece*. New York: Simon & Schuster, 1939, 1966.

———. *The Story of Civilization*. Vol. 4, *The Age of Faith*. New York: Simon & Schuster, 1950.

Durant, Will and Ariel. *The Story of Civilization*. Vol. 8, *The Age of Louis XIV*. New York: Simon & Schuster, 1960.

Durant, Will and Ariel. *The Story of Civilization*. Vol. 9, *The Age of Voltaire*. New York: Simon & Schuster, 1965.

Dvornik, Francis. *The Slavs in European History and Civilization*. New Brunswick, NJ: Rutgers University Press, 1962.

Easmon, M. C. F. "Madame Yoko, Ruler of the Mende Confederacy." *Sierra Leone Studies*. December 1958: 166–167.

Edwards, I. E. S. et al., eds. *Cambridge Ancient History*. 3d ed. Vol. 1, pt. 2. Cambridge: Cambridge University Press, 1970–1971.

Egan, Edward W., Constance B. Hintz, and L. F. Wise, eds. *Kings, Rulers, and Statesmen*. New York: Sterling Publishing, 1976.

Eliot, H. M., and J. Dowson. *A History of India as Told by Its Own Historians*. Vol. 2. Cambridge: Cambridge University Press, 1931.

Emery, W. B. *Archaic Egypt*. New York: Viking Penguin, 1987.

Engelberg, Stephen. "Her Year of Living Dangerously." *New York Times Magazine*. September 12, 1993: 41, 52, 55.

Erlanger, Steven. "NATO Faces a Crossroads in Bosnia." *New York Times*. 31 August 1997: 6.

"Exercising Patience." *World Press Review*. September 1990: 55.

Fage, J. D. *A History of Africa*. New York: Alfred A. Knopf, 1978.

Fairservis, Walter A., Jr. *The Ancient Kingdoms of the Nile*. New York: Mentor/NAL, 1962.

Famighetti, Robert. *The World Almanac and Book of Facts*. Mahwah, NJ: K-III Reference Corporation, 1998.

"A Family Affair?" *World Press Review*. October 1994: 24.

Farnsworth, Clyde H. "How Women Moved Up in Canada." *New York Times*. 20 June 1993: E5.

Filon, John, ed. *The World Almanac and Book of Facts*. New York: Newspaper Enterprise Association, 1994.

Firdausi. *Shah-Nama, The Epic of Kings*. Trans. Reuben Levy. Chicago: University of Chicago Press, 1967.

Flood, Mary. "First Female Cherokee Chief Ready for Job." *Houston Post*. 7 April 1984: A 1, A 26.

"Four's a Charm?" *World Press Review*. March 1993: 32.

"A French First." *New York Times*. 19 May 1991: E7.

French, Howard W. "Haiti's Class Divisions Deepen, Threatening Efforts to Return Aristide to Presidency." *New York Times*. 3 November 1991: 9.

————. "New Leader of Haitians Offers U. S. a Wary Hand." *New York Times*. 23 December 1990: 2.

Fulford, Roger. *Hanover to Windsor*. Glasgow: Fontana/Collins, 1981.

Funk & Wagnalls New Encyclopedia. Vol. 3. s.v. "Belize." 1996.

————. Vol. 11. s.v. "Germany." 1996.

————. Vol. 23. s.v. "San Marino." 1996.

Fusfield, Bob. *Zenobia, Queen of Palmyra*. Pacific Palisades, CA: Morningbird Press, 1997.

Gamst, Frederick C. *The Quemant: A Pagan-Hebraic Peasantry of Ethiopia*. New York: Holt, Rinehart and Winston, 1969.

"Gandhi on Atomic Power." *Houston Post*. 18 September 1983: A 3.

Gandhi, Indira. *My Truth*. New York: Grove Press, 1980.

Gascoigne, Bamber. *The Great Moghuls*. New York: Dorset Press, 1971.

Gazi, Stephen. *A History of Croatia*. New York: Barnes & Noble Books, 1993.

Geye, Pieter. *The Revolt of The Netherlands 1555–1609*. London: Ernest Benn, 1958.

Gibbon, Edward. *The Decline and Fall of the Roman Empire,* multiple volumes. Chicago: Encyclopaedia Britannica, 1952.

Glubb, Sir John. *A Short History of the Arab Peoples*. New York: Dorset Press, 1969.

Glubok, Shirley, ed. *Discovering the Royal Tombs at Ur*. London: Macmillan, 1969.

Graham, William. "McAleese Triumphs over Rivals to Take Presidency." *Irish News*. 16 October 1997: 1.

Gray, Denis, and Bart McDowell. "Thailand's Working Royalty." *National Geographic* 162. October 1982: 486–499.

Gray, Richard, ed. *The Cambridge History of Africa.* London: Cambridge University Press, 1975.

Greenhouse, Steven. "'The Fighter' of France." *New York Times.* 16 May 1991: A1, A31.

———. "French Prime Minister Quits; Woman Named to Post." *New York Times.* 16 May 1991: A3.

Gregory of Tours. *The History of the Franks.* Trans. Lewis Thorpe. Harmondsworth, Middlesex: Penguin Books, 1974.

Grey, Ian. *Peter the Great: Emperor of All Russia.* Harmondsworth, Middlesex: Penguin Books, 1960.

Grimal, Nicolas. *A History of Ancient Egypt.* Trans. Basil Blackwell Ltd. New York: Barnes & Noble Books, 1997.

Grosvenor, Melville Belle. "South Seas' Tonga Hails a King." *National Geographic* 133. March 1968: 322–344.

Grousset, René. *The Empire of the Steppes: A History of Central Asia.* Trans. Naomi Walford. New Brunswick: Rutgers University Press, 1970.

Grun, Bernard. *The Timetables of History.* New York: Simon & Schuster, 1979.

Gunther, John. *Inside Europe Today.* New York: Harper & Bros., 1961.

Hagos, Ghion. "African Women Seek Role in Peace Building." Panafrican News Agency. *Africa News Online.* 24 November 1997.

"Hail To the Chief." *World Press Review.* March 1993: 50.

"Haiti Coup Suspect Held." *Houston Chronicle.* 21 April 1991: 23A.

Hammond, N. G. L. *A History of Greece to 322 B.C.* Oxford: Clarendon Press, 1986.

Harding, Robert R. *Anatomy of a Power Elite.* New Haven: Yale University Press, 1978.

Hardy, Peter. *Historians of Medieval India.* Westport, CT: Greenwood Press, 1982.

Hare, Christopher. *The Most Illustrious Ladies of the Italian Renaissance.* Williamstown, MA: Corner House Publishers, 1972.

Harvey, Sir Paul, and J. E. Heseltine. *The Oxford Companion to French Literature.* Oxford: Oxford University Press, 1959, 1993.

Hedges, Chris. "Bosnian Vote Could Backfire on West." *New York Times.* 23 November 1997: 4.

———. "Officials See Risk in New NATO Push for Bosnia Peace." *New York Times.* 24 August 1997: 1, 4.

Heer, Friedrich. *The Medieval World.* Trans. Janet Sondheimer. New York: Mentor/NAL, 1962.

"Here's to You, Mrs. Robinson." *World Press Review.* July 1996: 49.

Herodotus. *The Histories*. Trans. Aubrey de Sélincourt. New York: Penguin Books, 1954, 1988.

Hitti, Philip K. *History of the Arabs*. New York: St. Martin's Press, 1968.

Hodges, Margaret. *Lady Queen Anne*. New York: Farrar Straus & Giroux, 1969.

Hoffer, C. P. "Madam Yoko: Ruler of the Kpa Mende Confederacy." In M. Rosaldo and L. Lamphere, eds., *Women, Culture and Society*. Stanford: Stanford University Press, 1974.

Hoffman, William. *Queen Juliana: The Story of the Richest Woman in the World*. New York: Harcourt Brace Jovanovich, 1979.

Honore, Carl. "Battle Lines Begin to Fade across Northern Ireland." *Houston Chronicle*. 16 November 1997: 25A.

Hook, Brian, ed. *The Cambridge Encyclopedia of China*. Cambridge: Cambridge University Press, 1982.

Hubert, Henri. *The Greatness and Decline of the Celts*. New York: Arno Press, 1980.

Hudson, M. E., and Mary Clark. *Crown of a Thousand Years*. Harmondsworth, Middlesex: Penguin Books, 1952.

Humarau, Beatrice. "Women on the Run." *World Press Review*. February 1996: 38–39.

Hunwick, John. 1972. "Songhay, Bornu and Hausaland in the 16th Century." In J.F.A. Ajayi and Michael Crowder, eds., *History of West Africa*, vol. 1. New York: Columbia University Press.

Hussey, J. M., ed. *The Cambridge Medieval History*. Vol. 4, pt. 1. Cambridge: Cambridge University Press, 1966.

Ibn Battuta. *The Rehla of Ibn Battuta. India, Maldive Islands and Ceylon*. Trans. Mahdi Husain. Baroda, India: Oriental Institute, 1976.

————. *Travels of Ibn Battuta AD 1325–1354*. Trans. H. A. R. Gibb from the French translation of C. Defremery and B. B. Sanguinetti. Cambridge: Cambridge University Press, vol. 1., 1958; vol. 2, 1962.

Ikime, Obaro. "The Changing Status of Chiefs among the Itsekiri." In Michael Crowder and Obaro Ikime, eds., *West African Chiefs*. New York: Africana Publishing, 1970.

"Intelligence Report." *Parade*. 27 February 1983: 2.

International Who's Who 1987–1988. London: Europa Publications, 1987–1988.

"Isabel Perón Pardoned." *Houston Post*. 10 September 1983: 4A.

"Isabel Perón's Return Confirmed." *Houston Post*. 27 August 1982: 3A.

Jackson, John G. *Introduction to African Civilizations*. Secaucus, NJ: Citadel Press, 1970.

James, Edward T., ed. *Notable American Women 1607–1950*. Vol. 2. Cambridge: Belknap Press of Harvard University Press, 1971.

Johnson, Paul. *Elizabeth I*. New York: Holt, Rinehart and Winston, 1974.

Jones, Clayton. "Aquino Joins Bid to Protect Forests." *Christian Science Monitor*. 22 March 1989: 4.

————. "Aquino Plans Cabinet Shifts." *Christian Science Monitor.* 10 November 1986: 11.

————. "Security Issues Crowd Agenda at Tokyo Summit." *Christian Science Monitor.* 9 July 1993: 1, 4.

Jones, Gwyn. *A History of the Vikings.* Oxford: Oxford University Press, 1984.

Jones, Howard Mumford. *The Literature of Virginia in the Seventeenth Century.* Charlottesville: University of Virginia Press, 1968.

Jones, Russell, trans. *Hikayat Sultan Ibrahim Ibn Adham.* Lanham, MD: University Press of America, 1985.

Josephus. *The Jewish War.* Trans. G. A. Williamson. London: Penguin Books, 1959, 1970.

Josephus Flavius. *Life and Works.* Trans. William Whiston. Philadelphia: Winston Company, n.d.

Josephy, Alvin M., Jr., ed. *The Horizon History of Africa.* New York: American Heritage Publishing, McGraw-Hill, 1971.

Juju. "Reminiscences of an Old Kaffir." *Cape Monthly Magazine,* 3d series, 3. 1880: 289–294.

Junor, Penny. *Margaret Thatcher: Wife, Mother, Politician.* London: Sidgwick & London, 1983.

Karnow, Stanley. *Vietnam: A History.* New York: Viking Press, 1983.

Kay, Ernest, ed. *The World Who's Who of Women.* 3d ed. Cambridge: International Biographical Centre, 1976.

Kay, Stephen. *Travels and Researches in Caffraria.* London: John Mason, 1833.

Kemp-Welch, Alice. *Six Medieval Women.* London: Macmillan, 1913.

Kenyatta, Jomo. *Facing Mt. Kenya.* New York: Vintage/Random House, 1965.

Kenyon, J. P. *The Stuarts.* Glasgow: William Collins Sons, 1970.

Khader, Ben, Aïcha Ben Abed, and David Soren. *Carthage: A Mosaic of Ancient Tunis.* New York: The American Museum of Natural History and W. W. Norton, 1987.

Kibler, William W., ed. *Eleanor of Aquitaine: Patron and Politician.* Austin: The University of Texas Press, 1976.

Kiefer, Francine S. "Poland's Prime Minister Looks Ahead to Reform." *Christian Science Monitor.* 7 May 1993: 8.

Kinder, Hermann, and Werner Hilgemann. *The Anchor Atlas of World History.* Trans. Ernest A. Menze. Vol. 1. Garden City, NY: Anchor/Doubleday, 1982.

Kinzer, Steven. "Once the Hope of Secular Turks, Ex-Leader is Now Widely Reviled." *New York Times.* 6 April 1997: 2, 6.

Kirtley, Michael and Aubine. "The Ivory Coast, African Success Story." *National Geographic.* July 1982: 95–125.

Knappert, Jan. *Pacific Mythology.* London: Diamond Books, 1995.

Komisar, Lucy. *Corazon Aquino: The Story of a Revolution*. New York: George Braziller, 1987.

Krauss, Clifford. "Bush's Uneasy Welcome for Violeta Chamorro." *New York Times*. 4 April 1991: 3E.

Krige, E. J., and J. D. Krige. *The Realm of a Rain-Queen*. London: Oxford University Press, 1943.

Kunene, Mazisi. *Emperor Shaka the Great*. Trans. Mazisi Kunene. London: Heinemann Educational Books, 1979.

Laessøe, Jørgen. *People of Ancient Assyria*. Trans. F. S. Leigh-Browne. London: Routledge and Kegan Paul, 1963.

Langer, William L., ed. *World History*. Boston: Houghton Mifflin, 1980.

Las ruinas de Tulum. Ciudad de Mexico: Instituto Nacional de Antropologia e Historia, 1969.

Latourette, Kenneth Scott. *The Chinese: Their History and Culture*. New York: Macmillan, 1934.

Layor, ChiChi. "The Land of the Long Horn." Hausa epics. Ebo State, Nigeria. Manuscript, 1996.

Lee, Ki-baik. *A New History of Korea*. Trans. Edward W. Wagner with Edward J. Schulz. Cambridge: Harvard University Press, 1984.

Lee, Peter, trans. "Samguk Sagi." In *Sourcebook of Korean Civilization 6*. New York: Columbia University Press, 1993.

Lehman, Johannes. *The Hittites*. Chicago: The University of Chicago Press, 1975.

Lerner, Gerda. *The Creation of Patriarchy*. New York: Oxford University Press, 1986.

Lewin, Thomas J. *Asante before the British*. Lawrence: Regents Press of Kansas, 1978.

"Life in the Grand Style for Europe's Leaders." *U.S. News & World Report*. 21 June 1982.

Lipschutz, Mark R., and R. Kent Rasmussen. *Dictionary of African Historical Biography*. Berkeley: University of California Press, 1989.

Longford, Elizabeth. *The Queen: The Life of Elizabeth II*. New York: Alfred A. Knopf, 1983.

————. *Queen Victoria: Born to Succeed*. New York: Harper & Row, 1964.

Löwenstein, Prince Hubertus Zu. *A Basic History of Germany*. Bonn: Inter Nationes, 1964.

Ludowyk, E. F. C. *The Modern History of Ceylon*. New York: Frederick A. Prager, 1966.

Ludwig, Emil. *Cleopatra*. New York: Viking Press, 1937.

Luke, Mary M. *Gloriana: The Years of Elizabeth I*. New York: Coward, McCann & Geoghegan, 1973.

Mackie, J. D. *A History of Scotland*. Harmondsworth, Middlesex: Penguin Books, 1984.

Mamani, Abdoulaye. *Sarraounia, ou "le drame d'une reine magicienne."* Paris: L'Harmattan, 1980.

"Maneuvers at the Top." *World Press Review.* August 1995: 26.

Mankiller, Wilma, with Michael Wallis. *Mankiller.* New York: St. Martin's Press, 1994.

Marden, Luis. "The Friendly Faces of Tonga." *National Geographic* 133. March 1968: 345–367.

Markdale, Jean. *Women of the Celts.* Trans. A. Mygind, C. Hauch, and P. Henry. Rochester, VT: Inner Traditions International, 1986.

Marquis Who's Who in the World. 14th. ed. New Providence, NJ: Reed Elsevier, 1996.

Marrouchi, Mustapha. "Breaking Up/Down/Out of the Boundaries: Tahar Ben Jelloun." *Research in African Literature* 21, no. 4 (1990): 79.

Masselman, George. *The Cradle of Colonialism.* New Haven: Yale University Press, 1963.

Massie, Robert K. *Nicholas and Alexandra.* New York: Atheneum Press, 1974.

Masson, Georgina. *Queen Christina.* New York: Farrar, Straus & Giroux, 1969.

Mattingly, Garrett. *Catherine of Aragon.* Cambridge: Cambridge University Press, 1942.

Mayer, Ann Elizabeth. "Benazir Bhutto and Islamic Law." *Christian Science Monitor.* 6 February 1989: 18.

McDowell, Bart. "The Dutch Touch." *National Geographic* 170. October 1986: 500–525.

McKendrick, Malveena. *Ferdinand and Isabella.* New York: American Heritage Publishing, 1968.

Mee, Charles L., Jr. *Daily Life in Renaissance Italy.* New York: American Heritage Publishing, 1975.

Mehta, Ved. *The New India.* Harmondsworth, Middlesex: Penguin Books, 1978.

Meir, Golda. *My Life.* New York: G. P. Putnam's Sons, 1975.

Mernissi, Fatima. *The Forgotten Queens of Islam.* Trans. Mary Jo Lakeland. Minneapolis: University of Minnesota Press, 1993.

Momatiuk, Yva, and John Eastcott. "Maoris: At Home in Two Worlds." *National Geographic* 166. October 1984: 522–542.

Mommsen, Theodor. *Provinces of the Roman Empire.* Trans. William P. Dickson. Chicago: Ares Publishers, 1974.

Morby, John E. *Dynasties of the World.* Oxford: Oxford University Press, 1989.

Morford, Mark P.O., and Robert J. Lenardon. *Classical Mythology.* New York: Longman, 1977.

Moritz, Charles, ed. *Current Biography Yearbook 1972.* New Haven, CT: H. W. Wilson, 1972.

———. *Current Biography Yearbook, 1986.* New York: H. W. Wilson, 1986.

———. *Current Biography Yearbook, 1987.* New York: H. W. Wilson, 1987.

Morton, W. Scott. *China: Its History and Culture.* New York: McGraw-Hill, 1980, 1982.

Mtoro bin Mwinyi Babari. *The Customs of the Swahili People. The Desturi za Waswahili.* Ed and trans. J. W. T. Allen. Berkeley: University of California Press, 1981.

Murphy, E. Jefferson. *Understanding Africa.* New York: Thomas Y. Crowell, 1969.

Mydans, Seth. "Aquino Is Working on Some Laws to Rule By." *New York Times.* 1 June 1986: 3.

Myers, A. R. *England in the Late Middle Ages.* Harmondsworth, Middlesex: Penguin Books, 1976.

"Mystery Finally Solved: Rebellious Queen Sitoe Succumbs to Scurvy." *Houston Post.* 27 October 1983: W3.

Newcomer, James. *The Grand Duchy of Luxembourg.* Lanham, MD: University Press of America, 1984.

Newton, Douglas. "The Maoris: Treasures of the Tradition." *National Geographic* 166. October 1984: 542–553, particularly 546.

Norton, Michael. "Pascal-Trouillot Blazes a Trail for Women." *Houston Chronicle.* 13 March 1990: 8A.

"Nuno Moura Portugal." www.uc.pt, April 1997.

Nyakatura, J. W. *Anatomy of an African Kingdom,* ed. Godfrey Uzoigwe, trans. Teopista Maganwa. Garden City: Anchor/Doubleday, 1973.

Oates, Joan. *Babylon.* London: Thames and Hudson, 1979.

Okey, Roberta. "Trekking Nature's Terrarium." *Americas.* September/October 1987: 8–13.

Oldenbourg, Zoe. *Catherine the Great.* New York: Pantheon Books, 1965.

Oliver, Roland, and J. D. Fage. *A Short History of Africa.* Harmondsworth, Middlesex: Penguin Books, 1970.

Olmstead, A. T. *History of the Persian Empire.* Chicago: University of Chicago Press, 1948.

Olson, Elizabeth. "A First for Swiss: A Woman as President." *New York Times International.* 27 December 1998: 7.

Oppenheim, A. Leo. *Ancient Mesopotamia.* Chicago: University of Chicago Press, 1977.

Orfield, Olivia. *Death Trap.* Elgin, IL: Performance Publishing, 1979.

Ostrogorsky, George. *History of the Byzantine State.* New Brunswick, NJ: Rutgers University Press, 1969.

"Outpouring of Warmth for Retiring Irish President." www.us-irish.com. 24 November 1997.

Oyo, Remi. "Liberia Parties Want Elections Postponed." *Electronic Mail & Guardian* 15 May 1997. IPS/Misonet.

Packer, James I., Merril C. Tenney, and William White, Jr. *The Bible Almanac.* Nashville, TN: Thomas Nelson, 1980.

Painter, Sidney. *The Rise of the Feudal Monarchies.* Ithaca: Cornell University Press, 1951; reprint Greenwood Press, 1982.

Panikker, K. Madhu. *The Serpent and the Crescent: A History of the Negro Empires of West Africa.* Bombay: Asia Publishing House, 1963.

Papinot, E. *Historical and Geographical Dictionary of Japan.* Rutland, VT: Charles E. Tuttle, 1972.

Parrinder, Geoffrey. *African Mythology.* New York: Peter Bedrick Books, 1982.

"Peace at Hand?" *World Press Review.* November 1995.

Peires, J. B. *The House of Phalo.* Berkeley: The University of California Press, 1982.

Pemble, John. *The Raj, the Indian Mutiny, and the Kingdom of Oudh, 1801–1859.* Rutherford, NJ: Fairleigh Dickinson University Press, 1977.

Peters, F. E. *The Harvest of Hellenism.* New York: Barnes & Noble Books, 1996.

Peterson, Kara J. "Ungentle Coup." *World Press Review.* February 1998: 20.

Plowden, Alison. *Lady Jane Grey and the House of Suffolk.* New York: Franklin Watts, 1986.

Plutarch. *Makers of Rome.* Trans. Ian Scott-Kilvert. Harmondsworth, Middlesex: Penguin Books, 1980.

Previté-Orton, C. W. *The Shorter Cambridge Medieval History.* Vol. 1, *The Later Roman Empire to the Twelfth Century.* Vol. 2, *The Twelfth Century to the Renaissance.* Cambridge: Cambridge University Press, 1952, 1982.

Psellus, Michael. *Fourteen Byzantine Rulers.* Trans. E. R. A. Sewter. Harmondsworth, Middlesex: Penguin Books, 1982.

Putnam, John J. "Napoleon." *National Geographic.* 161. February 1982: 165–170.

Rasmussen, R. Kent. *Mzilikazi of the Ndelebe.* London: Heinemann Educational Books, 1977.

Rawlinson, George. *Ancient History.* New York: Barnes & Noble Books, 1993.

Reader, John. *Africa.* New York: Alfred A. Knopf, 1998, originally London: Hamish Hamilton, 1997.

Reilly, Bernard F. *The Kingdom of León-Castilla under Queen Urraca, 1109–1126.* Princeton: Princeton University Press, 1982.

Reischauer, Edwin O., and John K. Fairbank. *East Asia: The Great Tradition.* Boston: Houghton Mifflin, 1960.

"Return of the Tigers." *World Press Review.* August 1995: 28–29.

Riasanovsky, Nicholas V. *A History of Russia.* Oxford: Oxford University Press, 1963, 1993.

Ridley, Jasper. *Napoleon III and Eugenie.* New York: Viking Press, 1980.

Roider, Karl A., Jr., ed. *Maria Theresa.* Englewood Cliffs, NJ: Prentice Hall, 1973.

Roux, Georges. *Ancient Iraq.* Harmondsworth, Middlesex: Penguin Books, 1964, 1980.

Rüb, Matthias. "Threats to Bosnia's Peace." *World Press Review.* October 1997: 4.

Rubin, Elizabeth. "The Enemy of Our Enemy." *New York Times Magazine.* 14 September 1997: 58–61.

Runciman, Steven A. *A History of the Crusades* 3 vols. Cambridge: Cambridge University Press, 1987.

Rutherford, Ward. *Celtic Mythology.* Wellingborough, Northamptonshire: The Aquarian Press, 1987.

Saggs, H.W.F. *The Might That Was Assyria.* London: Sidgwick and Jackson, 1984.

Sanders, Charles L. "Interview." *Ebony.* January 1981: 16.

Sansom, George A. *A History of Japan to 1334.* Stanford: Stanford University Press, 1958.

————. *A History of Japan, 1334–1615.* Stanford: Stanford University Press, 1961.

Schele, Linda, and David Freidel. *A Forest of Kings: The Untold Story of the Ancient Maya.* New York: Quill/William Morrow, 1990.

"Seasonal Work." *New York Times.* 5 April 1992: 3A.

Sédillot, René. *An Outline of French History.* Trans. Gerard Hopkins. New York: Alfred A. Knopf, 1967.

Seenarine, Moses. "Keeping the Natives at Bay: Janet Jagan in Guyana." Saxakali Publications. 29 October 1997.

Seneviratne, Maureen. *Sirimavo Bandaranaike: The World's First Woman Prime Minister.* Colombo, Sri Lanka: Colombo Press, 1975.

"Shaky Democracy." *World Press Review.* May 1996: 24.

Sheehy, Gail. "The Passage of Corazon Aquino." *Parade Magazine.* 8 June 1986: 4–9.

Shelby, Barry. "Iron Lady of Matabele." *World Press Review.* March 1997: 23.

Shinnie, Margaret. "Civilizations of the Nile." In Alvin M. Josephy, Jr., ed., *The Horizon History of Africa.* New York: American Heritage Publishing, McGraw-Hill, 1971.

Shipley, Jenny, and Simon Robinson. "A Small but Cheeky Nation." *Time.* 15 December 1997: 50.

Shirer, William L. *The Rise and Fall of the Third Reich.* New York: Simon & Schuster, 1960.

"Sinking Son." *World Press Review.* June 1995: 43.

"The Sleaze Factor." *World Press Review.* December 1994: 27.

Smith, Denis Mack. *A History of Sicily.* Vol. 1, *Medieval Sicily.* Vol. 2, *Modern Sicily.* New York: Dorset Press, 1968.

Smith, Lacey Baldwin. *Elizabeth Tudor: Portrait of a Queen.* Boston: Little, Brown, 1975.

Smith, Vincent A. *The Oxford History of India.* London: Oxford University Press, 1958.

Soga, John Henderson. *The South-Eastern Bantu.* Johannesburg: Witwatersrand University Press, 1930.

Sowers, Leslie. "Wilma Mankiller: The First Woman Chief of the Cherokee Nation Is as

Comfortable in the White House as She Is at a Stomp Dance." *Texas*. 20 January 1991: 10–11.

Spear, Percival. *A History of India*. Vol. 2. London: Penguin Books, 1987.

"Sri Lanka's Racial Riots Could Cost Us Dearly." *U. S. News &World Report*. 8 August 1983: 8.

"The Stalled Revolution." *World Press Review*. August 1988: 40.

Stenton, Doris Mary. *English Society in the Early Middle Ages*. Harmondsworth, Middlesex: Penguin Books, 1965.

Storm Across Georgia. London: Cassel, 1981.

"The 'Strongwomen' of South Asia." *World Press Review*. December 1994: 18–20.

Sturlason, Snorre. *Heimskringla, or The Lives of Norse Kings*. Trans. A. H. Smith. Editorial notes by Erling Monsen. New York: Dover Publications, 1990.

Suggs, Robert C. *The Island Civilizations of Polynesia*. New York: Mentor, 1960.

Sullivan, Richard E. *Heirs of the Roman Empire*. Ithaca: Cornell University Press, 1960.

Suny, Ronald Grigor. *The Making of the Georgian Nation*. Bloomington: Indiana University Press, in association with Hoover Institutions Press, Stanford University, 1988.

Szulc, Tad. "What Indira Gandhi Wants You To Know." *Parade*. 25 July 1982: 6–8.

Tanner, J. R., ed. *The Cambridge Medieval History,* Vol. 12. Cambridge: Cambridge University Press, 1967.

Tefft, Sheila. "Gandhi Murder Inquiry Released." *Christian Science Monitor*. 29 March 1989: 4.

"Thanksgiving 1991: Food for Thought." *Parade*. 24 November 1991: 11.

Thapar, Romila. *A History of India*. Vol. 1. London: Penguin Books, 1987.

Thompson, John M. *Revolutionary Russia, 1917*. New York: Charles Scribner's Sons, 1981.

"Throne Power." *World Press Review*. February 1988: 38.

Treaster, Joseph B. "Civilian Sworn In as Haiti's President." *New York Times*. 14 March 1990: A3.

Trevor-Roper, Hugh. *The Golden Age of Europe*. New York: Bonanza/Crown Publishers, 1987.

Trotta, Dan. "Chamorro's Days Numbered in Nicaragua?" *Houston Chronicle*. 1 August 1993: 28A.

Troynt, Henri. *Catherine the Great*. Trans. Joan Pinkham. New York: Dutton, 1980.

Tuchman, Barbara W. *A Distant Mirror, The Calamitous 14th Century*. New York: Ballantine Books, 1978.

Uçok Un, Badriye. *Al-nisa' al-hakimat fi tarikh*. Trans. I. Daquqi. Baghdad: Matba'a al-Sa'dun, 1973.

Uglow, Jennifer S., ed. *International Dictionary of Women's Biography*. New York: Continuum, 1982.

"U.S. Warns Bosnian Serbs to Honor Accords." *New York Times*. 31 August 1997: 6.

Vansina, Jan. "Inner Africa." In Alvin M. Josephy, Jr., ed., *The Horizon History of Africa*. New York: American Heritage Publishing, McGraw-Hill, 1971.

Vasiliev, A. A. *History of the Byzantine Empire*. Madison: University of Wisconsin Press, 1952.

Waley, Arthur, trans. *The Book of Songs*. New York: Grove Press, 1960.

Walter, Greg. "Interview." *People*. November 1983: 20, 46.

"War of the Ladies." *World Press Review*. September 1998: 21.

Warner, Marina. *The Dragon Empress: Life and Times of Tz'u-hsi (1835–1908)*. New York: Atheneum Press, 1986.

Watts, A. E., trans. *The Metamorphoses of Ovid*. San Francisco: North Point Press, 1980.

Weber, Eugen. *France*. Cambridge: The Belknap Press of Harvard University, 1986.

West, John Anthony. *The Traveler's Key to Ancient Egypt*. New York: Alfred A. Knopf, 1985.

White, J. E. Manchip. *Ancient Egypt: Its Culture and History*. New York: Dover Publishing, 1970.

Whitelock, Dorothy. *The Pelican History of England*. Vol. 2, *The Beginnings of English Society*. Harmondsworth, Middlesex: Penguin Books, 1952, 1976.

Whittemore, Hank. "She Leads a Nation." *Parade Magazine*. 18 August 1991: 4–5.

"Who's News." *USA Weekend*. 2–4 March 1990: 2.

Who's Who in the World 1997. New Providence, RI: Marquis Who's Who/Reed Elsevier, 1996.

Williamson, Hugh R. *Catherine de Medici*. New York: Viking Press, 1973.

Wilson, David. *The Vikings and Their Origins*. London: Thames and Hudson, 1970.

Wilson, Robert Dick. *A Scientific Investigation of the Old Testament*. Rev. Edward J. Young. Chicago: Moody Press, 1959.

Windle, Janice Woods. *True Women*. New York: G. P. Putnam's Sons, 1993.

"Women in Politics." *World Press Review*. March 1988: 53.

"Women on the Run." *World Press Review*. February 1996: 38–39.

Wright, Donald R. *Oral Traditions from the Gambia*. Vol. 2. Athens: Ohio University Center for International Studies, 1980.

Wright, Ernest. *Biblical Archaeology*. Philadelphia: Westminster Press, 1957.

Young, John Edward. "Iceland's 'Chief of State' Needs Plenty of Cod and Imagination." *Christian Science Monitor*. 8 July 987: 25.

Zakin, Susan. "Woman Chief Blazing an Indian Trail." *Mother Jones*. September 1986: 8, 10.

Index

Absh Khatun (queen of Persia), 1

Abyssinia, xix, 205–206

Achaea, xviii
  13th–14th c., 187, 268, 281
  co-ruler of, 187

Ada (queen of Caria), 1–2

Adame, Mama (ruler of Niumi Bato), 2

Addagoppe of Harran, Priestess (regent of Babylon), 3–4

Adela (countess and regent of Blois and Chartres), 4

Adelaide, Queen of Italy (regent of German Empire), 5–6

Adelaide of Salona, Countess (regent of Sicily), 6–7

Adele (co-ruler of Vendôme), 7

Aelfgifu of Northumbria (regent of Norway), 7–8

Aelfwyn (queen of Mercia), 8

Aelia (Placidia, Galla), 331

Aethelflaed (queen of Mercia), 8

Africa, xv–xvi, xxxv–xxxvi, xxxviii, xxxix, xlii–xliii. See also East Africa; West Africa; individual countries; individual tribes

Afua Koba, Asantehemaa (queen mother of Asante Empire), 9–10

Agnes de Dampierre, Baroness (ruler of Bourbon), 10

Agnes de Nevers, Countess (ruler of Nevers), 10–11

Agnes of Dunbar, Countess of March (ruler of Dunbar), 11

Agnes of Poitou, Duchess of Bavaria (regent for Holy Roman emperor), 11–12

Ahhotpe I (queen of Thebes), 12

Ahmose-Nofretari, Queen (co-ruler of Egypt), 12–13

Aisa Kili Ngirmaramma (Aissa Koli), 13–14

Aissa Koli (ruler of Kanuri empire of Bornu, West Africa), 13–14

Alaghai-bäki (Mongolian queen of the Ongüt, N. China), 14

Alam al-Malika, Al-hurra (ruler in Zubayd), 15

Albania, 382–383

Alexander (the Great), 2

Alexandra (empress of Russia), 16–17

Alexandra ("king" of the Maccabees), 15–16

Alice, Princess (regent of Antioch), 17

Aline Sitoe (queen of the Diola tribe, Casamance), 18–19

Alix of Anjou (ruler and regent of Brittany), 19

Alix of Vergy, Countess (ruler of Burgundy), 19

Altamsh (Radiyya, Sultana), 341–343

Amalsuntha, Queen (Amalswinthe), 20

Amalswinthe, Queen (regent of the Ostrogoths), 20

Amanishakhete, Queen (ruler of Kush in Meroë), 20–21

AmaRharhabe/Ngqika, xv, 305

Amina (queen of Zaria in Hausaland), 21–22

Amira al-umara, xlii

Ana de Sousa, Dona (Nzinga Mbandi), 308–310

Anatolia, xxxvii, 38, 228

Anches-en-Amen (Ankhesenamun), 22–23

Anga (Maham Anga), 237–238

Angola, xlii, 308–310, 349–350

Ankhesenamun, Queen (widow of Tutankhaten), 22–23

Ankhnesneferibre (queen of Egypt), 24

Ankyeaa Nyame (legendary queen in West Africa), 24

Anna Anachoutlou (queen of Trebizond), 24–25

Anna Dalassena (regent of Byzantine Empire), 25

Anna Leopoldovna (regent of Russia), 25–26

Anna of Savoy (regent of Byzantine Empire), 26–27

Anna Palaeologina, Despina (regent of Epirus), 27

Anna Palaeologina-Cantacuzena, Despina (regent of Epirus), 27

Anne, Duchess (ruler of Brittany), 28

Anne (queen of England and Scotland), 28–30

Anne (empress of Russia), 30–31

Anne-Marie-Louise d'Orléans (ruler of Auvergne), 31

Anne of Austria (queen regent of France, governor of Brittany), 31–32

Anne of England (regent of the Dutch Republic), 32–33

Anne of France (defacto regent of France), 33

Antioch, xviii, xxxix
    12th c., 17–18, 103–105
    13th–14th c., 83, 233–234
    co-ruler of, 103–104
    regents of, 17–18, 233–234

Anula (queen of Ceylon), 34

Apumatec (queen of North American Indian tribe), 34

Aquino, María Corazon (President of the Philippines), xliv, 34–36

Aquitaine, xix, 125–127

Arabia, xvi, 352, 428

Aragon, xxviii, 181, 205, 328

Arborea, 14th c., 127

Argentina, xvi, 326–327

Armenia, xvi, 138

Armenia, Lesser, xvi, 427–428

Arsinde, Countess (ruler of Carcassone), 36

Arsinoë II (queen of Thrace, Macedonia, Egypt, co-ruler of Egypt), xxxvii, 37–38

Artemisia I, Queen (ruler of Halicarnassus and Cos), 38

Artemisia II (Ruler of Caria), 38–39

Artois, xx, 199–200, 238, 251

Arts, xlv, 168, 184, 254, 331

'Arwa Bint Ahmad al-Sulayhiyya (Shi'ite queen and ruler of Yemen), 39–40

Asa (queen of Norway), 40

Asante Empire, xv, xxxix, xl
    17th–18th c., 24, 42–43
    19th–20th c., 9–10, 417–420

Asantehemaa, 9, 417

Asantehene, 9, 417

Ashanti Empire. *See* Asante Empire

Asia, Central, xxxvii, 173. *See also* Mongolian rulers

Asma Bint Shihab al-Sulayhiyya (Shi'ite queen and co-ruler of Yemen), 41

Assyria, xvi
    regents of, 300, 359

Atabeks, 1

Athaliah (queen of Judah), xl, 41–42

Atjeh, xxiii, 175, 215, 306, 377

August, augusta, 387

Augusta Theodora (Theodora), 389–390

Aung San Suu Kyi, xliv

Austrasia, xix, 68, 168
    regent of, 334

Austria, xvi, 245, 266

Auvergne, xx, 31, 268

Awura Pokou (queen of Baule tribe), xxxv, 42

Axum, xvi, 46–47

Āzarmēdukht (Sasanid queen of Persia), 43

Azna Kingdom, xv, 354

Az-Zabbā (Zenobia), 432

Babito dynasty, xxxvi, 307

Babylon, xvi
    regent in, 3–4

Bāī. *See* Lakshmi Bāī; Tara Bāī; Udham Bāī

Bailli, 187

Bailor-Caulker, Honoraria (Shenge tribal chief), xlii, 45

Bakwa (Turunku Bakwa), xxxv, 399–400

Balkis, Queen (ruler of Axum), 46–47

Balthild (regent of Neustria), 48

Bandaranaike, Sirimavo (prime minister of Sri Lanka), xliii, 48–49

Bangladesh, xvi, xliii, 412–413, 433–434

Baranamtarra (queen of Lagash), xxxvii

Barbados, xvi, 50–51

Barbara, Agatha (president of Malta), 49–50

Barrow, Ruth Nita (governor-general of Barbados), 50–51

BaTlokwa, xv, 244

Baule, xv, xxxv, 42–43

Bavaria, xxi, 189

Bazao (Turunku Bakwa), xxxv, 399–400

Bazao-Turunku (Turunku Bakwa), xxxv, 399–400

Beatrice (regent of Tuscany), 51

Beatrice, Countess (regent of Edessa), 52

Beatrice (nominal ruler in Portugal), 52

Beatrice, Countess (ruler of Provence), 52–53

Béatrix de Bourgogne (baroness of Bourbon), 53

Béatrix Wilhelmina Armgard (queen of The Netherlands), xlv, 53–54

Bedouins, xlii, 284

Beirut, xviii, 140, 180

Belgium, xvi
    6th c., 150
    13th–15th c., 202–203, 247, 254
    18th c., 261

Belize, xvi, 156–157

Bendjou, Empress (joint ruler of Mali), xxxviii, 54–55, 216

Berbers, xv, xlii, 214, 430

Berenice (co-ruler of Caesarea Paneas and Tiberias in Judaea), 55–56

Berenice III, Queen (co-ruler, ruler of Egypt), 56–57

Berenice IV (ruler of Egypt), 57

Bergmann-Pohl, Sabine (president of parliament of German Democratic Republic), 57–58

Bhutto, Benazir (prime minister of Pakistan), xliii, 58–61

Bianca, Queen (vicar of Sicily), 61

Bianca Maria, Duchess (regent of Milan), 61

Biblical persons, 41–42, 72, 113–114

Bilqis (Balkis), 46–47

Bin (Min), 291–292

Bjerregaard, Ritt (premier of Denmark), 62–63

Black Agnes (Agnes of Dunbar), 11

Black Meg (Margaret II), 246–247

Blanca, Doña (queen of Navarre), 63

Blanche of Castile (regent of France), 64

Blois, xx, 4–5, 196, 255, 268

Bloody Mary (Mary I), 274–275

Boadicea (Boudicca), 66

Bohemia, xviii, 119, 234, 266
    regents of, 119, 234

Bolivia, xvi, 380–381

Bona of Savoy (regent of Milan), 64

Bonaparte, Elisa (Elisa Bonaparte), 127–129

Bone rank, 90–91

Bōrān (Sasanid queen of Persia), 65

Boraqchin, Khatum (regent of Mongolian khanate), 65

Bosnian Serb Republic, xvi, 332–333

Boudicca (queen of the Iceni), 66

Boulogne, xx
    12th c., 175, 239, 267
    13th c., 175, 240, 267–268

Bourbon, xx, 10, 53, 238

Bourbonnais, 374–375

Brabant, xvi, 203, 267–268

Brazil, xvii, 179, 257
    regent of, 179

Brigantia, xxi, 66–67, 73

Brigantia (legendary queen of the Brigantes), 66–67

Brigid, Saint (Brigantia), 66

Brittany, xx
    12th–14th c., 19, 105, 197
    15th–17th c., 28, 31–32, 97

Brundtland, Gro Harlem (prime minster of Norway), xlv, 67–68

Brunhilde (queen regent for Austrasia and Burgundy), xl, 68–69

Buddhism, 173, 296, 370

Buganda, xxxvi

Bulgaria, xvii, 175–176

Bunyoro dynasty, xv, 307

Burgundy, xx, xxvi, 19, 68–69, 273

Burma, xvii, xliv, 356

Burundi, xvii, xliii, 218–219

Busignani, Patricia (co-captain-regent of San Marino), 70

Byzantine Empire, xvii
    5th–6th c., 20, 142, 337, 387–388
    8th–9th c., 176–178, 385, 388–390
    10th c., 165–166, 314–315, 391
    11th c., 25, 140–141, 272–273, 389–390, 434–435
    12th–14th c., 26, 27, 83–84, 145, 276–277
    co-rulers of, 142, 145, 165–166, 176–177
    regents of, 25, 26–27, 276–277, 337, 385, 388–389, 391

Caesarea Paneas, 55

Cahina (Kahina, Al-), xlii, 214

Cairo, 366–367

Cambodia, xvii, 221–222, 286

Cambrai, Treaty of (1529), 232, 250

Campbell, Kim (prime minister of Canada), 71–72

Canada, xvii, xlv, 71–72, 355–356

Candace, as name, 20, 21, 72

Candace (queen of Ethiopia and Meroë), 72–73

Capetian rulers, 199, 200, 238

Cappadocia, xvii, 228

Captains-regent, 70, 84, 325, 345

Carcassone, xx, 36, 138

Caria, xvii, 1–2, 38–39

Caribbean, 50–51, 86–88, 322–324, 413

Carinthia, xxi, 245

Carthage, xvii, 116, 214

Cartimandua, Queen (ruler of Brigantia), 73

Casamance, 18–19

Castile and León, xxviii, 180–181, 205, 405

Catalinda d'Albret (Queen and co-ruler of Navarre), 73–74

Caterina Sforza (effective ruler of Forli and Imola), 74–75

Catherine, Countess (ruler of Vendôme), 75

Catherine I (empress of Russia), 76–77

Catherine II the Great (empress of Russia), 77–79

Catherine Cornaro (regent ruler of Jerusalem on Cyprus), 79–80, 88

Catherine de Foix (Catalinda d'Albret), 73–74

Catherine de Médicis (regent of France), xliii, 80–82

Catherine of Aragon (regent of England), 82

Catherine of Braganza (regent of Portugal), 83

Catherine of Valois (titular Byzantine empress, ruler), 83–84

Caucasus, 378–379

Ceccoli, Edda (co-captain-regent of San Marino), 84

Celsine, 73

Central African Republic, xvii, 118
Ceylon. *See* Sri Lanka
Chamorro, Violeta Barrios de (president of
    Nicaragua), 84–86
Champagne, xx, 204
Charlemagne (emperor of the West), 178
Charles V (Holy Roman emperor), 202, 205,
    231, 250
Charles, Mary Eugenia (prime minister of
    Dominica), 86–88
Charlotte (queen of kingdom of Jerusalem on
    Cyprus), 88
Charlotte, Grand Duchess (ruler of
    Luxembourg), 88–89
Chartres, xx, 4–5
Chehrzād (Homāy), 171
Cheng-Chun, Empress (de facto co-ruler of
    China), 89–90
Cherokees, xliv, 241–243, 425–426
Childbearing, xlv
China, xvii, xxxix, xlii
    1st millenium B.C., 321
    2nd–1st c. B.C., 89–90, 234–235
    1st c., 89–90, 397, 398–399
    2nd c., 229, 381
    7th c., 415
    11th–13th c., 373–374, 374, 425
    19th c., 95, 400–401
    20th c., xliv, 96, 370–371
    co-rulers of, 89–90, 321
    dowager empresses of, xxxix, 234–235,
        397
    regents of, 229, 234–235, 318, 373–374,
        381, 397, 400–401, 415, 425
    See also Mongolian rulers
China, People's Republic of, xliv, 370–371
Chindók Yówang (queen of Kingdom of Silla),
    90–91
Chinsóng Yówang (queen of Silla), 91–92
Chosōn, xxiv
    regents of, 291–292, 296
Christianity, 234, 432
Christina (queen of Sweden), 92–93
Christine of France, Duchess (regent of
    Savoy), 93
Cicilia (Lesser Armenia), 427–428
Çiller, Tansu (prime minister of Turkey), 94–95
Cixi (empress of China), 95–96, 400–401
Claude (duchess of Brittany), 97
Claudine (titular sovereign of Monaco), 97
Cleopatra I (co-ruler, regent of Egypt),
    97–98
Cleopatra II (co-ruler and ruler of Upper
    Egypt), xxxvii, 98
Cleopatra III (co-ruler of Egypt), xxxvii, 99
Cleopatra VI Tryphaena (co-ruler of Egypt),
    99

Cleopatra VII (queen of Egypt), 99–102
Cleopatra Berenice (Berenice III), 56–57
Cleopatra of Cyrene (ruler of Cyrene),
    102–103
Cleopatra Selene (Cleopatra of Cyrene),
    102–103
Cleopatra Thea (ruler of Seleucid Empire),
    103
Colonialism, 418–419, 420, 423
    British, in Africa, 159, 418–419, 420, 423
    British, in India, 163–164, 197–198, 227
    French, in Africa, 18–19, 343–345, 354
    French, in Polynesia, 334–335, 338–339,
        407
    Portuguese, in Africa, 290–291
    U.S., in Hawaii, 230
Columbus, Christopher, 182
Congo, 349–350. *See also* Kongo
Constance (co-ruler of Antioch), 103–105
Constance, Duchess (co-ruler of Brittany),
    105
Constance (12th c. queen of Sicily), 106
Constance (13th c. queen of Sicily, 107
Co-rulers, xxxvi, xxxvii, xxxviii. *See also*
    under individual countries
Cos, xxii, 38
Creek Indians, 276
Crescentii (Marozia Crescentii), 271
Cresson, Edith (prime minister of France),
    108–109
Cristina, Queen of Spain (Maria Christina I of
    Naples), 263
Croatia, 129–130, 264–265
    regent of, 129–130
Crusader states, xviii
Crusades, xxxix, 4, 125, 140
Cyprus, xviii, xxxix
    13th–15th c., 79–80, 88, 186–187,
        331–332
    regent of, 331–332
Cyrene, xviii, 102–103, 329–330
Czechoslovakia, xviii

Da Lourdes-Pintasilgo, María (prime minister
    of Portugal), 111
Dahiya al-Kahina (al-Kahina), xlii, 214
Dahomey, 9
Damascus, 352
Daura, xv, 112
Daura, Queen of (ruler of Daura state,
    founder of Hausa states), 112
Dawlat Khatun (ruler of Luristan), 113
Deborah, Judge (ruler of Israel), 113–114
Deidameia, Queen (ruler of Epirus), 115
Deification of royalty, 37–38, 222, 336, 430
Delhi, xxii, 341–343
Denmark, xviii, 62–63, 245–246, 254–255

Diane of Poitiers, Duchess (de facto co-ruler of France), 115–116
Didda, Queen (regent of Kashmir), 116
Dido (queen of Phoenicians), 116–117
Diodorus Siculus, xxxvi, 359
Diola, xv, 18–19
Divine right of royalty, xxxvi, xxxvii, xxxviii, xxxix, xliv
Divinity of royalty, 37–38, 222, 336, 430
Dola (queen of Itsekiri kingdom in Nigeria), 118
Dominica, xviii, 86–88
Domitien, Élisabeth (prime minister of the Central African Republic), xliii, 118
Doquz-khatun (daughter-in-law of Jenghiz-khan), xl
Drahomira, Queen (regent of Bohemia), xli, 119
Dreifuss, Ruth (president of Switzerland), 120
Dreux, xx, 194, 256
Dunbar, 11
Durgavati, Rani (queen of Gondwana), xli, 120–121
Dutch Republic. See Netherlands, The
Dzeliwe Shongwe (queen regent of Swaziland), 121–122

East Africa, xxxvi
    10th–17th c., 205–206, 307, 325
    18th–19th c., 290–291, 308
Ebesjun, Khatun (regent of Turkestan), 123
Edessa, xviii, 52
Edweso, 419–420
Egypt, xviii, xxxvi–xxxvii, xli
    25th c. B.C., 167, 217–218, 303
    18th–15th c. B.C., 12–13, 161–163, 302
    14th–13th c. B.C., 22–23, 123–124, 393–394, 400
    8th–6th c. B.C., 24, 294–295
    4th–3rd c. B.C., 37–38, 290
    2nd–1st c. B.C., 56–57, 97 -102
    11th–13th c., 358–359, 366–367
    co-rulers of, 12–13, 37–38, 56–57, 97–99, 123–124, 217–218
    regents of, 12, 97–98, 358–359, 366–367, 393–394
Eji (co-ruler of Egypt), 123–124
Eleanor (queen of Navarre), 124–125
Eleanor of Aquitaine (duchess of Aquitaine, countess of Poitiers, queen of France and England, regent of England), 125–127
Eleanor of Arborea (ruler of Arborea), 127
Eligifu (regent of Norway), 7–8
Elisa Bonaparte (duchess of Tuscany), 127–129
Elissa (Dido), 116–117

Elizabeth, Queen (regent of Hungary and Croatia), 129–130
Elizabeth, Queen (ruler of Hungary), 130–131
Elizabeth I (queen of England), xliii, xlv, 131–132
Elizabeth I (tsarina of Russia), xli, 132–133
Elizabeth II (queen of Great Britain), 134–135
Elizabeth of Görlitz (co-ruler, ruler of Luxembourg), 135–136
Elizabeth of Luxembourg (Elizabeth of Görlitz), 135–136
Elizabeth of Poland, Queen of Hungary (regent of Poland), 136–137
Emma, Queen (regent of The Netherlands), 137
England, xxi, xliii
    1st c., 66, 73
    7th–11th c., 7–9, 160, 357
    12th c., 125–126, 239, 280–281
    14th–15th c., 11, 247–248
    16th c., 82, 131–132, 157–158, 274–275
    17th c., 132, 275–276
    18th–19th c., 28–30, 407–408
    20th c., 134–135, 383–385
    regents of, 82, 126–127, 247–248, 280–281
Epirus, xix, 115
    regents of, 27
Erato (queen of Kingdom of Armenia), 138
Ermengarde, Countess (ruler of Carcassonne), 138
Ermengarde, Viscountess (ruler of Narbonne), 139
Ermensinde, Countess (ruler of Luxembourg), 139
Esat, Esato (Judith), 205–206
Eschiva of Ibelin, Lady (queen of Beirut), 140
Ethelfleda (Aethelflaed), 8–9
Ethiopia, xix, 72, 205–206, 289, 377–378, 431
    regent of, 289
Etruria, xxiii, 235
Eudocia Macrembolitissa, Empress (regent, co-ruler of Byzantine Empire), 140–141
Eudoxia, Augusta (de facto co-ruler of Eastern Roman Empire), 142
Eugénie-Marie, Empress (regent of France), 143–144
Euphrosine, Countess (ruler of Vendôme), 144–145
Euphrosyne, Empress (de facto co-ruler of Byzantine Empire), 145
European unity, 20th c., 63, 67, 89, 255

Falasha, 206

Fatima, as name, xxxvi
Fatima, Sultana (ruler of the Maldive Islands), 147
Fatima (queen of Zanzibar), 147–148
Fatwa, 215, 306, 377
Finnbogadóttir, Vigdis (president of Iceland), xliv, 148–150
Flanders, xvi, 202–203, 246, 253–254, 273
Foix, xx, 180
Forli, xxiii, 74–75
France, xix–xx, xxxix
  7th c., 48, 68
  9th–10th c., 36, 279
  11th c., 4–5, 7, 138, 144–145
  12th c., 10–11, 105, 125–127, 139, 144–145, 175, 239, 267
  13th c., 10, 19, 52, 53, 64, 196, 204, 238–239, 255, 267–268, 425
  14th c., 53, 75, 186, 194, 196–197, 199–200, 203, 204, 238, 256
  15th c., 28, 33, 75, 180, 186, 187–188, 203, 273
  16th c., 28, 80–82, 97, 115–116, 166–167, 231–232, 374–375
  17th c., 31–32, 93, 196, 268, 269, 303
  19th c., 143–144, 171–172, 270–271
  20th c., 108–109
  co-rulers of, 7, 105–106, 115–116, 187–188, 203
  regents of, 4–5, 19, 31–32, 33, 48, 64, 80–82, 93, 143–144, 186, 196–197, 231–232, 269, 270–271, 282
Frankish rulers, xix
  6th–8th c., 68–69, 150–152, 168, 334
  13th–14th c., 187, 249
  as regents, 68–69, 168, 249, 334
Fredegund, Queen (regent of Neustria), xl, 69, 150–152

Galla Placidia (Placidia, Galla), 331
Gambia, The, xv, 2
Gandhi, Indira (prime minister of India), xliii, 153–155
Gelderland, xvi, 254
Gemmei-tennō (empress of Japan), 155–156
Genshō-tennō (empress of Japan), 156
Georgia, xxi
  11th–13th c., 272–273, 348–349, 378–379
  co-rulers of, 348–349, 378–379
  regent of, 272–273
Germany, xxi
  10th–12th c., 5–6, 106, 279, 391–392
  20th c., 57–58
  regents of, 5–6, 106, 279, 391–392
Ghaliyya al-Wahhabiyya (Bedouin generalissimo), xlii

Ghana, 9–10, 42–43
Gikuyu, xxxv
Giovanna I (Joanna I), 200–201
Giovanna II (Joanna II), 201–202
Giovanna III (Juana la Loca), 205
God's Wife, xxxvi, 13, 394
Gondwana, xxii, 120
Gordon, Minita (governor-general of Belize), 156–157
Go-Sakuramachi-tennō (empress of Japan), 157
Governors-general, 50–51, 156–157, 250–252, 261, 355–356
Great Britain. *See* England; Scotland
Greece, xxii
  5th c. B.C., 38
  4th c., 315–316
  12th–14th c., 187, 268, 281
  20th c., 314
  regents in, 314, 315–316
Grey, Lady Jane (queen of England), 157–158
Grimaldi family, 97
Griots, 2
Guastalla, xxiii, 324
Gulama, Madame (Mende chieftain in Sierra Leone), xlii, 158–159
Guyana, xxii, 191–192
Gwamile Mdluli, Queen (regent of Swaziland), 159
Gyda (queen of English jarldom), 160

Haile Selassie, 378, 431
Hainault, xxvi, 189, 246
Haiti, xxii, 322–324, 413
Hallicarnassus, xxii, 1–2, 38, 39
Hapsburg Empire, xxii, 266
Hatasu (Hatshepsut), 161–163
Hatshepsut (queen, pharaoh of Egypt), xli, 161–163
Hatti, xxxvii
Hausa, xvi, xxxv, 21–22, 112, 354
Hawaii, xxii, 213, 230–231
  co-ruler of, 213
Hazrat Mahal, Begum (regent of Oudh), xli, 163–164
Hedwig (Jadwiga), 190–191
Hedwig, Saint (duchess of Silesia), 164–165
Helen Glinski (Yelena Glinskaya), 421–422
Helena Lecapena (co-ruler of Eastern Roman Empire), 165–166
Henriette de Cleves, Duchess (ruler of Nevers), 166–167
Henry VIII (king of England), 82, 231, 274
Hereditary blood lines, 90
Herodotus (Greek historian), 3, 38, 217, 300, 303, 395, 396
Hetepheres I (queen mother of Egypt), 167

Himiko (Pimiku), 330
Himnechildis, Queen (guardian, regent of Austrasia), 168
Hind al-Hīrah, Queen (regent of kingdom of Lakhm), 168
Hinematioro (chieftainess of Ngati Porou), 168–169
Hittites, xxii, 336–337
Hodierna of Jerusalem, Countess (regent of Tripoli), 169–170
Hoho (South African Khoi chieftainess), 170
Holland. *See* Netherlands, The
Holy Roman Empire, xxvi, xxvii
    regent of, 11–12
Homage, practices of, xxxviii, 54, 216
Homāy (traditional queen of Persia), 171
Hortense de Beauharnais, Queen (regent of Holland), 171–173
Hottentot, 170
Hsiao-shih, Queen (regent of Khita), 173
Hu, Queen (ruler of the Toba in Central Asia), 173
Hungary, xxii, 129–130, 264–265, 266
    regent of, 129–130
Hurra, al-, 15, 39, 41

Ibn Battuta, xxxvii, xxxviii, 14, 54, 217, 342
Iceland, xxii, xlv, 148–149
Iceni, xxi, 66
Ide d'Alsace (countess of Boulogne), 175
Ilansura, xxv, 219
Illyria, xxii, 382–383
Imola, xxiii, 74–75
'Inayat Shah Zakiyyat al-Din Shah (sultana of Atjeh), 175
India, xxii–xxiii, xli–xlii, xliii
    2nd c. B.C., 321
    4th–5th c., 335
    13th–16th c., 120–121, 237, 341–343
    17th–18th c., 306–307, 380, 403
    19th c., 163–164, 197–198, 227–228
    20th c., 153–155, 193, 320
    co-ruler of, 403
    regents of, 163–164, 197–198, 227–228, 237, 335
Indonesia, xxiii, 175, 215, 306, 377, 398
Indzhova, Renata (interim prime minister of Bulgaria), 175–176
Inheritance, xxxvi
Iran, xxiii
Iraq, 392–393
Ireland, xxiii, 285–286, 346–348
Irene, Empress (co-ruler, emperor of Byzantine Empire), xl, 176–178
Irene Godunova, Tsaritsa (ruler of Russia), 178

Irene Palaeologina, Empress (ruler of the Empire of Trebizond), 178–179
Isabel (Perón, Isabel), 326–327
Isabel, Princess (regent of Brazilian Empire), 179
Isabella (queen of Beirut), 180
Isabella, Countess (ruler of Foix), 180
Isabella (Zabel), 427–428
Isabella I the Catholic (queen of Castile, León, and Spain), 180–182
Isabella II (queen of Spain), 182–183
Isabella II (Yolanda), 423–424
Isabella Clara Eugenia of Austria (co-ruler and governor of the Spanish Netherlands), 183–184
Isabella d'Este, Marquessa (regent of Mantua), 184
Isabella Farnesio of Parma (queen and de facto co-ruler of Spain), 185
Isabella of Bavaria (regent of France), 186
Isabella of Cyprus (regent of Jerusalem), 186–187
Isabelle, Princess (co-ruler of Achaea), 187
Isabelle, Duchess (co-ruler of Lorraine), 187–188
Isato (Judith), 205–206
Israel, xxiii
    13th–12th c. B.C., 113–114
    8th c. B.C., 352
    20th c., 287–288
Italy, xxiii
    6th–7th c., 20, 386–387
    10th–11th c., 5, 51, 271, 282–283
    13th–14th c., 127, 200–201, 424
    15th c., 61–62, 64–65, 74–75, 184, 201–202
    16th–17th c., 184, 196–197, 231–232, 409
    19th c., 127–128, 143–144, 235, 236, 270–271, 324
    co-ruler of, 282–283
    regent of, 6–7, 20, 51, 61–62, 184, 235, 236, 251–252, 386–387
Itsekiri Kingdom, xv, 118
Ivory Coast, 9–10, 42–43

Jacoba, Countess (Jacqueline), 189
Jacqueline, Countess (ruler of Holland), 189
Jadwiga ("maiden king" of Poland), xxxviii, 190–191
Jagan, Janet (prime minister, president of Guyana), 191–193
James, Evelyn (president of Southern Paiutes), xliv
Jammeh, 2
Jane (Grey, Lady Jane), 157–158
Jane (Joanna I), 200–201

Japan, xxiv, xxxviii
  2nd–3rd c., 198, 330
  6th–7th c., 199, 219–220, 373
  8th c., 155–156, 220–221
  17th–18th c., 157, 297
  regent of, 198
  on women rulers, 221
Jarl, 160
Java, xxiii, 398
Jayaram, Jayalalitha (chief of Tamil Nadu), 193–194
Jeanne I, Countess (ruler of Dreux), 194
Jeanne I, Countess (Joan I), 199–200
Jeanne I, Countess of Champagne (Juana I), 204
Jeanne II, Countess (ruler of Dreux), 194
Jeanne II, Countess (Joan II), 200
Jeanne II (Juana II), 204
Jeanne d'Albret (queen of Navarre), 195–196
Jeanne de Castile (co-ruler of Vendôme), 196
Jeanne de Chatillon, Countess (ruler of Blois), 196
Jeanne de Nemours, Duchess (regent of Savoy), 196–197
Jeanne de Penthièvre, Duchess (ruler of Brittany), 197
Jenghiz-khan, xl, xli, 14, 123, 240, 313, 396–397
Jerusalem, xviii, xxxix
  12th c., 6–7, 288–289, 362–363
  13th c., 186–187, 267, 331–332, 423–424
  15th c., 79–80, 88
  regents of, 79–80, 186–187, 267, 331–332
Jews, Ethiopian, 206
Jhānsi, xxii, 227
Jindan, Rani (regent of the Sikh kingdom of the Punjab), 197–198
Jinga (Nzinga Mbandi), 308–310
Jingoism, 310
Jingō-kōgū, Empress (regent of Japan), 198–199
Jitō-tennō, Empress (ruler of Japan), 199
Joan, Countess of Champagne (queen of Navarre), 204
Joan I, Countess (Capetian ruler of Artois), 199
Joan II, Countess (Capetian ruler of Artois), 200
Joan II (Juana II), 204–205
Joan III (Jeanne d'Albret), 195
Joanna I, Countess of Provence (queen of Naples), 200–201
Joanna II (queen of Naples), 201–202
Joanna III (Juana la Loca), 205
Joanna of Austria (regent of Portugal), 202
Jodit (Judith), 205–206
Johanna, Countess (ruler of Flanders), 202–203

Johanna, Duchess (ruler of Brabant), 203
Joint rule. *See* Co-rulers
Jolanthe, Duchess (co-ruler of Lorraine), 203
Juana I (queen of Navarre), 204
Juana II (queen of Navarre), 204–205
Juana III (Jeanne d'Albret), 195
Juana la Loca (queen of Castile, León, Aragon, Naples, Sicily), 205
Judah (Judaea), xxiii, 15–16, 41–42, 55–56, 352
Judge-rulers, 113–114
Judith (queen of the Falasha Agaw of Abyssinia), 205–206
Judith (Zauditu), 431–432
Julia Avita Mammaea, Augusta (regent of the Roman Empire), 207
Julia Berenice (Berenice), 55–56
Julia Domna, Empress (regent of the Roman Empire), 207–208
Julia Maesa, Augusta (de facto regent of Roman Empire), 208–209
Juliana (queen of The Netherlands), 209–210
Julius Caesar (Roman general), 100–101
Jumper, Betty Mae (chief of Seminole Nation), xliv, 210–211

Kaahumanu, Queen (co-ruler of Hawaii), 12, 213–214
Kahina, Al- (priestess-queen of North African Berbers), xlii, 214
Kalyānavati (queen of Sri Lanka), 215
Kamalat Shah, Zaynt al-Din (sultana of Atjeh in Indonesia), 215
Kanal-Ikal, Lady (Maya "King" of Palenque), xxxviii, 215–216
Kanem-Bornu, 13
Kanuri empire, xv, 13–14
Kara-Khitai Empire, xxix, 379–380, 422
Karakorum, 313–314
Kashmir, xxii, 116, 372
  regent of, 372
Kasimiera-Daniute Prunskiene (Prunskiene, Kazimiera-Daniute), 335
Kassi (empress of Mali), 54, 216–217
Khadija (sultana of the Maldives), 217
Khatuns, xxxvii
Khentkaues (co-ruler of Egypt), 216–218
Khita, xxv, 173
Khoi, xv, 170
Khutba, 15, 39, 41, 225, 355, 358, 367, 430
Kiev, 314
Kinigi, Sylvie (prime minister of Burundi), xliii, 218–219
Kipchak, xxv, 65
Kirman, 224
Kirum, Queen (mayor of Khaya-Sumu's city in Ilansura), 219

Kish, Kingdom of, xvi, 222
Kitara, xxxix
Kōgō, Empress (regent of Japan), 198
Kōgyoku-tennō, Empress (ruler of Japan),
    219–220
Kōken-tennō, Empress (ruler of Japan),
    220–221
Kololo, xv, 240
Kongo, xv, 293–294
Korea, xxiv, xxxviii
    3rd c., 198
    7th–9th c., 90–92, 369–370
    16th–19th c., 291–292, 296
    regent of, 296
Kossamak, Queen (joint ruler of Cambodia),
    221–222
Kpa Mende, xv, 422–423
Ku-Baba, Queen (founder of dynasty of Kish
    in Sumeria), 222
Kumaratunga, Chandrika (prime minister,
    president of Sri Lanka), xliii, 49,
    223–224
Kumasi, xv, 24
Kush, xxiv, 20–21
Kutlugh Khatun (queen of Kirman, Persia),
    224

Ladies' Peace (Treaty of Cambrai, 1529),
    232, 250
Lagash, xxiv, 357
Lakhm, xxiv, 168
Lakshmi Bāī, Rani (regent ruler of Jhānsi),
    xli, 227–228
Laodicé (queen of Cappadocia), 228
Latin Empire, xvii, xxvii
    regent of, 424
Legendary rulers, 24, 66, 399
León, xxviii, 353, 405
León and Castile, xxviii, 180–181, 205, 405
Leonor (Eleanor), 124–125
Leonora Telles, Queen (regent of Portugal),
    228–229
Liang, Empress (regent in China), 229
Liberia, xxiv, xliii, 243, 327–328
Libya, 329–330
Lilavati, Queen (ruler of Sinhala Kingdom,
    Ceylon), 229–230
Liliuokalani, Queen (ruler of Hawaii), xlv,
    230–231
Lithuania, 335
Lombards, xxiii
    regent of, 386–387
Lorraine, xx, 187–188, 203, 303
Louise de Savoy, Duchess (regent of France),
    231–232
Louise Hippolyte, Princess (titular ruler of
    Monaco), 232

Lourdes-Pintasilgo (da Lourdes-Pintasilgo,
    Maria), 111
Lovedu, xv, xxxvi, 295–296
Lucca, xxiii, 127, 235
Lucia of Antioch, Princess (titular ruler of
    Tripoli), 232–233
Lucienne, Princess (regent of Antioch),
    233–234
Ludmila (regent of Bohemia), xli, 234
Lü Hou, Empress (regent of China), 234–235
Luisa (regent of Etruria, duchess of Lucca),
    235
Luisa María de Guzmán (regent of Portugal),
    236
Luise-Marie, Duchess (regent of Parma and
    Piacenza), 236
Lunda, xv, 349–350
Luristan, xxiii, 113
Luxembourg, xxv
    13th–18th c., 135–136, 139, 266, 273
    20th c., 88–89, 258
    co-ruler of, 135–136

Maccabees, xxiii, 15–16
Macedonia, xxv, 37, 315–316, 387–388
    regent of, 315–316
Madagascar, xxv, 343–345, 346
Madlebe, xv, xlii, 436
Magajiva, defined, 112
Magical powers, xxxv, xlii
Maham Anga (de facto regent of Mughal
    Empire), 237–238
Mahaut, Countess (Capetian ruler of Artois),
    238
Mahaut I, Dame (ruler of Bourbon),
    238
Mahaut II de Dampierre, Countess (ruler of
    Bourbon, ruler of Nevers), 238–239
Mahaut de Boulogne, Countess (ruler of
    Boulogne), 239
Mahaut de Cortenay, Countess (ruler of
    Nevers), 239
Mahaut de Dammartin, Countess (ruler of
    Boulogne), 240
Makeda (Balkis), 46–47
Maldive Islands, xxv, 147, 217, 297
Mali, xv, xxxviii, 54–55, 216, 243
    co-ruler of, 54–55
Malika Iltutmish (Radiyya, Sultana), 341–343
Malta, xxv, 49–50
Mameluks, Mamluks, 15, 140, 341
Mammaea (Julia Avita Mammaea), 207
Mamochisane (queen of the Kololo in
    Zambia), 240
Mandughai, Khatun (regent of Mongolia), xli,
    240–241
Mani, xv, 243

Mankiller, Wilma (chief of Cherokee Nation), xliv, 241–243
Manneh, 2
Mansa, defined, 2, 243
Mansarico (Mani warrior queen in west Africa), 243
Mantantisi (queen regent of the baTlokwa in South Africa), 244
Mantua, xxiii, 184
Mantuab (Mentewab), 289
Maori, xxvi, 168–169
Marāthā State, xxii, 380
Margaret (duchess of Carinthia, countess of Tirol), 245
Margaret, Queen of Denmark and Norway (regent of Sweden), 245–246
Margaret I (Margareta), 253–254
Margaret II, Countess (ruler of Flanders, Hainault), 246–247
Margaret III, Countess (ruler of Belgium), 247
Margaret of Anjou, Queen (Lancastrian leader, acting regent of England), 247–249
Margaret of Antioch-Lusignan (regent of Tyre), 249
Margaret of Austria, Duchess of Savoy (regent of The Netherlands), 249–250
Margaret of Austria, Duchess of Parma (governor general of The Netherlands), 250–251
Margaret of Brabant, Countess (Burgundian ruler of Artois), 251
Margaret of Flanders (Margaret III), 247
Margaret of Navarre, Queen (regent of Sicily), 251–252
Margaret of Norway (child queen of Scotland), 252
Margaret Tudor, Queen (regent of Scotland), 253
Margareta, Countess (ruler of Flanders), 253–254
Margaretha (guardian for Otto II the Lame), 254
Margrethe II (queen of Denmark), xlv, 254–255
Marguerite II (Margaret II), 246–247
Marguerite, Countess (ruler of Blois), 255
Marguerite de Thouars (joint ruler of Dreux), 256
Mari, xxv, 219, 360
    regent of, 360
Maria (queen of Sicily), 256
María I of Braganza (queen of Portugal), 256–257
Maria II da Gloria (queen of Portugal), 257–258

Maria Adélaïde (grand duchess of the Grand Duchy of Luxembourg), 258
María Ana Victoria of Spain, Queen (regent of Portugal), 259
Maria Anna of Austria, Queen (regent of Spain), 259–260
Maria Carolina, Queen (de facto ruler of Naples and Sicily), 260–261
Maria Christina, Duchess (governor general of Austrian Netherlands), 261–262
Maria Christina of Austria, Queen (regent of Spain), 262
María Christina I of Naples, Queen (regent of Spain), 263
María de las Mercedes (queen infanta of Spain), 263–264
María Estela Martínez de Perón (Perón, Isabel), 326–327
Maria of Anjou ("king" of Hungary, queen of Croatia), 264–265
Maria of Austria, dowager queen of Hungary (governor of The Netherlands), 265
Maria Theresa (empress of Hapsburg Empire, queen of Bohemia and Hungary), 266
Marie, Countess (ruler of Boulogne), 267
Marie (regent of Jerusalem), 267
Marie, Countess (ruler of Brabant), 267
Marie de Bourbon, Princess (ruler of Achaea), 268
Marie de Bourbon Montpensier, Duchess (ruler of Auvergne), 268
Marie de Chatillon, Countess (ruler of Blois), 268
Marie de Médicis (regent, de facto ruler of France, governor of Normandy), 269
Marie d'Savoy-Nemours (Jeanne de Nemours), 196–197
Marie Antoinette (wife of Louis XVI of France), 260, 266
Marie-Louise (regent of France, duchess of Parma), 270–271
Marija (Maria of Anjou), 264–265
Mark Antony (Roman triumvir and general), 99, 101–102
Marozia Crescentii (ruler of Rome), 271
Marquesas Islands, xxv, 407
Marriage, consanguineous, xxxvi, xxxvii, 12, 37, 38, 98, 171, 302
Martha, Queen Mother (de facto ruler of Russia), 272
Mary, Queen (regent of Georgia), 272–273
Mary, Duchess (ruler of Burgundy and Luxembourg), 273
Mary I (queen of England), 274–275
Mary II (queen of England), 275–276
Mary Bosomworth, Princess (ruler of North American islands), 276

Mary of Antioch, Empress (regent of Byzantine Empire), 276–277
Mary of Guise, Queen (regent of Scotland), 277–278
Mary of Lorraine (Mary of Guise), 277–278
Mary Stuart (queen of Scots), 278–279
Massagetae, xxiii, 395–396
Matamba, xv, 308, 308–310
Mathilde, Countess (ruler of Nevers), 279
Matilda, Abbess (regent of Germany), 279
Matilda (uncrowned queen, regent of England, duchess of Normandy), 280–281
Matilda, Princess (ruler of Achaea), 281
Matilda of Flanders, Duchess (regent of Normandy), 282
Matilda of Tuscany, Duchess (co-ruler, ruler of central Italy), xxxviii, 282–283
Matriarchy, xxxv, xxxvi
Matrilineal succession, xxxvi, 22, 167, 242
Matrilocality, xxxvi
Maud, Empress (Mahaut de Boulogne), 239
Maud, Empress (Matilda), 239, 280–281
Mavia (queen of the Saracens), xlii, 284
Mawa (leader of Zulu political refugees), 284
Mawia, Queen of Syria (Mavia), xlii, 284
Maya, xxv, xxxviii
   6th–7th c., 215–216, 411–412, 429–430
   19th c., 404
   regent of, 411–412
Mbandi, Nzinga (Angolan queen), xl, xlii
Mbundu, xv, 308
McAleese, Mary, 285–286
Medici, de', family, 74–75, 80–82, 269, 409
Mehr-n-Nesā (Nūr Jahān), 306–307
Mehrunissa (Nūr Jahān), 306–307
Mei (queen of Cambodia), 286
Meir, Golda (premier of Israel), 287–288
Meisho (Myouo-tennō), 297
Melisende (queen of Jerusalem), 288–289
Mende, xv, xlii, 243
Mentewab, Empress (regent of Ethiopia), 289
Mercia, xxi, 8–9
Meroë, 20–21, 72
Merovingians, xl, 68–69
Meryit-Net, Queen (ruler of Egypt), 290
Mesopotamia, xxv, 103, 222, 428–429
Mexican Empire, 143
Mexico, 143, 215–216, 404, 411–412, 429–430
Mfalma Fatima (ruler of Pate in East Africa), 290–291
Mi Cō Ū (Saw), 356–357
Mihn-un-Nisa (Nūr Jahān), 306–307
Milan, xxiii, 61–62, 64–65
Min, Queen (regent ruler of Yi Dynasty in Korea), 291–292

Mkabayi (Mnkabayi), 292–293
Mnkabayi (regent ruler of the Zulus), 292–293
Mo-ki-lien, Khatun of (regent of Mongolia), 293
Monaco, xxv, 97, 232
Mongolian rulers, xxv, xxxvii–xxxviii, xl–xli
   8th–10th c., 293, 362
   13th c., 14–15, 65, 224–225, 313–314, 316–317, 319, 396–397, 428
   14th–15th c., 240–241, 355, 392–393
   as regents, 65, 173, 240–241, 293, 313–314, 316–317, 362, 379–380, 396–397, 422
Morocco, xxv, 430
Mossi, xxxviii
Mother of the King of Kongo, Queen (ruler of Mpemba Kazi), 293–294
Motherhood, xlv
Mothers-in-law, xxxix
Mout (queen of the Sudan), 294–295
Mpemba Kazi, 293–294
Mughal Empire, xxiii, 121, 237, 380, 403
Mujaji, defined, xxxvi, 295
Mujaji I, II, III, IV (rain queen of the Lovedu), 295–296
Munjōng, Queen Dowager (regent of Chosōn Dynasty in Korea), 296
Muslims, xxxvii–xxxviii
   11th–12th c., 39, 430
   13th c., 15, 225, 341–343, 358
   14th c., 147, 216, 355
   17th c., 175, 215, 306
   20th c., 59
Myanmar. *See* Burma
Myōjō-tennō (empress of Japan), 296
Myōsho (Myōjō-tennō), 296
Myriam (sultana of the Maldive Islands), 297
Myrtale (Olympias), 315–316

Nandi (queen mother of the Zulus), 299
Naples, xxiii–xxiv, 200–202, 205, 260–261
Napoleon Bonaparte (emperor of the French), 127–128, 171, 270, 324
Naqi'a (regent of Assyria), 300
Narbonne, xx, 139
Naryshkina, Natalya Kirillovna, Queen-mother (de facto ruler of Russia), 301
Native American tribal rulers, xxv, xliv
   17th–18th c., 34, 276, 399
   20th c., 210, 241–243, 425–426
Navajos, xliv
Navarre, xxviii
   13th–14th c., 204–205
   15th–16th c., 63, 73–74, 124, 195
Ndebele, xvi, 264
Ndongo, xvi, 303, 308

Nefertiti (queen of Egypt), 123
Nefrusobek (last queen of the Theban Twelfth Dynasty, Egypt), 302
Nehru, Jawaharlal, 143, 320
Netherlands, The, xxvi
    13th–15th c., 189, 254
    16th–17th c., 183–184, 249–251, 265
    18th c., 32–33, 261–262, 266
    19th c., 137, 171–173, 414
    20th c., 53–54, 209–210, 414–415
    co-ruler in, 183–184
    regents in, 32–33, 137, 171–173, 249–250
    under Austrian rule, 261–262
    under Spanish rule, 183–184, 250–251, 260
Neustria, xix, 48, 69, 150–152, 334
    regent of, 334
Nevers, xx
    10th–12th c., 10–11, 239, 279
    13th c., 238–239, 425
    16th–17th c., 166–167
New Zealand, xxvi, xliv, 168–169, 360–361, 394–395
Ngati Porou, 168–169
Ngola, defined, 308
Ngoni, xvi, 308
Nicaragua, xxvi, 84–86
Nicole, Duchess (ruler of Lorraine), 303
Niger, 112, 354
Nigeria, 21–22, 112, 118, 399
Nitocris (Egyptian adoratarice), 24
Nitocris (Addagoppe of Harran), 3
Nitocris (Naqi'a), 300
Nitocris (queen of Egypt), 303
Njinga Oande (Nzinga Mbandi), 308–310
Nobel Peace Prize, xliv
Normandy, xx, 269, 281, 282
North Africa. *See* Berbers
Norway, xxvi, 7–8, 40, 67–68, 246
    regent of, 7–8
Ntombe Twala (queen regent, queen mother of Swaziland), 304–305
Ntsusa (chief of the South African amaRharhabe/Ngqika), 305
Nur al'Alam Nakiyyat al-Din Shah (sultana of Atjeh in Indonesia), 306
Nūr Jahān, Empress (de facto ruler of India), xli, 306–307
Nyakaima, Queen (founder of Bunyoro or Babito dynasty), 307
Nyamazana (queen of the Ngoni in east Africa), 308
Nysa (Laodicé), 228
Nzinga Mbandi (queen of the Mbundu in kingdoms of Ndongo and Matamba), 308–311
Oberea (Purea), 338–339

Oelun-eke (mother of Jenghiz-khan), xl
Oghul Qamish, Empress (regent of Karakorum), 313–314
Olga, Queen (regent of Greece), 314
Olga, Saint (princess, regent of Kiev), 314–315
Olympias (queen regent of Macedonia), 315–316
Öngüt, 14–15
Oral history, 2, 24
Orghana, Princess (regent of the Mongolian khanate of Jagatai), 316–317
Ostrevant, xxi, 189
Ostrogoths, xxvii, 20
Otaheiti. *See* Tahiti
Oudh, xxii, 163–164

Padishah Khatun (queen of Kirman, Persia), 319
Pagan, xvii, 356
Paiutes, Southern, xliv
Pakistan, xxvi, xliii, 58–61, 351
    co-ruler of, 351
Palenque, xxxviii, 215–216, 429–430
Palmyra, xxvi, 432
Pandit, Vijaya Lakshmi (president of United Nations General Assembly), 320–321
Pāndya, xxii, 321
Pāndyan Queen (ruler in South India), 321
Pao-Ssŭ, Queen (possible co-ruler of Chou), 321
Parliaments, xlv. *See also* Prime ministers
Parma, xxiv, 236, 271
Parysatis, Queen (regent of Persia), 321–322
Pascal-Trouillot, Ertha (provisional president of Haiti), 322–324
Pate, xxvi, xxxvi, 290–291
Pauline, Princess (ruler of Guastalla), 324
Pedini-Angelini, Maria Lea (co-captain-regent of San Marino), 325
Pemba, xxvi, 325
Pemba, Queen of (ruler of Pemba), 325
Perón, Isabel (president of Argentina), 326–327
Perry, Ruth (president of Liberia), xliii, 327–328
Persia, xxiii
    7th–5th c. B.C., 171, 321–322, 395–396
    7th c., 43, 65
    13th–14th c., 1–2, 113, 224–225, 319, 355
    regent in, 321–322
Peter I (czar of Russia), 76, 132, 301, 368–369
Petronilla (queen of Aragon), 328–329
Pheretima (queen of Cyrene), 329–330
Philippines, The, xxvi, 34–36

Phoenicians, 116
Phwā Cō (Saw), 356
Piacenza, xxiv, 236
Pimiku, Queen (first known ruler of Japan), 330
Piombino, xxiv, 127
Placidia, Galla, Augusta (regent of the Western Roman Empire), 331
Plaisance of Antioch, Queen (regent of Cyprus and Jerusalem), 331–332
Plavsic, Biljana (president of the Bosnian Serb Republic), 332–333
Plectrudis, Queen (regent of Austrasia and Neustria), 334
Poitiers, xxi, 125–127
Pokou, Aura (Awura Pokou), 42–43
Poland, xxvi, xxxviii, 136–137, 164, 190–191, 371–372
    regent in, 136–137
Polyandry, xxxv, xxxvi
Polygamy, xxxvi
Polynesian tribes, 168–169, 334–335, 351–352, 407
Polyxena (Olympias), 315–316
Pomare, as name, xxxvi
Pomare IV, Queen (ruler on Tonga), 334
Pomare V, Queen (ruler on Tahiti), 334–335
Portugal, xxvii
    12th–14th c., 52, 228–229, 381–382
    16th–17th c., 202, 236, 308–310, 325
    18th–20th c., 83, 111, 256–257, 257–258, 259
    regents of, 83, 202, 228–229, 236, 259, 381–382
Prabhāvatī Gupta (regent of the kingdom of the Vākātakas), 335
Premierships. See Prime ministers
Presidents, xliv
    African, 327–328
    Asian, 34–36, 223–224
    Caribbean, 322–324
    Central American, 84–86
    European, 49–50, 120, 148–149, 285–286, 332–333, 346–348
    South American, 192–193, 326–327, 380–381
    United Nations, 320
Priestesses, xxxvii, 3, 214
Prime ministers, xliii–xliv
    African, 118, 218–219, 405–406
    Asian, 48, 58–61, 223–224, 412–413, 433–434
    Caribbean, 86–88, 413
    European, 67–68, 94, 108–109, 111, 175–176, 335, 371, 383–385
    Indian, 153–155
    New Zealand, 360–361

North American, 71–72
    South American, 192
Princesses, xxxvii, xxxix
Provence, xxi, 52, 200
Prunskiene, Kazimiera-Daniute (prime minister of Lithuania), 335
Pu-abi, Queen (co-ruler of Ur), 446
Puduhepa, Queen (co-ruler of the Hittites), 336–337
Pulcheria, Augusta (regent of the Eastern Empire), 337
Punjab, xxiii, 197–198
Purea (queen of the Landward Teva of Tahiti), 338–339
Pu-su-wan (Ye-lü Shih), 422

Queen infantas, 263
Queen-mothers, xxxix, 9, 41, 304, 417
Queens. See Candace
Queen-sisters, xxxix

Radiyya, Sultana (Muslim queen of Delhi), 341–343
Rainmakers, 295–296
Ranavalona I, Queen (titular ruler of Kingdom of Madagascar), 343–344
Ranavalona II (queen of Madagascar), 344
Ranavalona III (queen of Madagascar), 345
Rani of Tulsipur (India), xli–xlii
Ranocchini, Gloriana (co-captain-regent of San Marino), 345
Rasoherina (queen of Madagascar), 346
Rasputin, Grigory Yefimovich, 16
Razia Iltutmish (Radiyya, Sultana), 341–343
Regents, xl. See also under individual countries
Religious plurality, 199, 286
Religious practices. See Buddhism; Christianity; Muslims
Religious strife, 119, 195, 206, 250, 274, 277–278
Robinson, Mary (president of Ireland), xlv, 346–348
Roman Empire, xxvii, 73, 99–103, 207–208
    regents of, 207–208
Roman Empire, Eastern. See Byzantine Empire
Roman Empire, Western, regents of, 20, 331
Rome, xxiv, 271
Russia, xxvii
    10th c., 165, 314–315
    16th c., 178, 421
    17th c., 272, 301, 368–369
    18th c., 25–26, 30–31, 76–79, 132–133
    20th c., 16–17
    Europeanization of, 78–79, 133, 368
    regents of, 25–26, 314–315, 368–369, 421

Russudan, Queen (ruler, co-ruler of
Georgia), 348–349
Rwanda, xxvii, xliii, 405–406
Rweej (queen of the Lunda), 349–350

Sada Kaur, Rani (de facto co-ruler of
Śukerchakīās), 351
Saimei-tennō (Kogyoku-tennō), 219–220
Salic law, xxxix, 182, 263
Salome Alexandra (Alexandra), 15–16
Salote Tupou III, Queen (ruler of Tonga),
351–352
Sammuramat (Shammu-ramat), 359
Samsia, Queen (ruler of southern Arabia),
352–353
San Marino, xxvii, 70, 84, 325, 345
Sancha, Queen (titular ruler of León),
353
Sande Bush (female society), xlii–xliii,
158–159, 423
Saracens, xxvii, xlii, 284
Sardinia, xxiv, 127, 197
Sarraounia (sorceress-queen of the Azna
Kingdom), 354
Sasanid Empire, xxiii, 43, 65
Sati Beg (Il-Khanid sultana of Persia), 355
Sauvé, Jeanne Mathilde (governor-general of
Canada), 355–356
Savoy, xxvii, 93, 196
Saw, Chief Queen (virtual ruler of Pagan),
356–357
Saxons, West, xxi, 357
Scotland, xxii, 29, 252, 253, 277–279
regents of, 253, 277–278
Seaxburh (queen of the kingdom of Wessex),
357
Sebekkare (Nefrusobek), 302
Sebeknefru (Nefrusobek), 302
Seleucid Empire, xxvii, 103
Seminoles, xliv, 210–211
Semiramis (Shammu-ramat), 359–360
Senegal, xlii, 18–19
Serbia, 332–333
Sforza family, 61, 64, 74
Shagshag, Queen (administrator in Lagash),
357
Shajar Al Durr, Queen (regent of Egypt),
358–359
Shamiran (Shammu-ramat), 359–360
Shammu-ramat, Queen (regent of New
Assyrian Empire), 359–360
Sheba (Balkis), 46–47
Sheherezade (Homāy), 171
Shenge, xvi, xlii, 45
Shibtu, Queen (regent of Mari), 360
Shipley, Jenny (prime minister of New
Zealand), xliv, 360–362

Shōtoku-tennō (Kōken-tennō), 220–221
Shubad (Pu-abi), 336
Shu-lü shih, Khatum (regent of Turkish
Mongolia), 362
Sibylla (queen of Jerusalem), 362–363
Sibylle, Princess (ruler of Tripoli), 363–364
Sicily, xxiv
12th c., 6–7, 106, 251–252
13th–15th c., 61, 107, 256
16th–18th c., 197, 205, 261
Sierra Leone, xxvii, xlii, 45, 158–159, 243,
422–423
Silesia, xxi, 164
Silla, xxiv, 90–92, 369–370
Singa (Nzinga Mbandi), 308–310
Sinqobile Bahle Mabhena (chief of Ndebele
tribe in Zimbabwe), 364
Sirikit, Queen (regent of Thailand),
364–366
Sirimavo (Bandaranaike, Sirimavo), 48–49
Sitoe, Aline (Aline Sitoe), xlii, 18–19
Sitre-meryetamun Tawosret (Twosret),
400
Sitt al-Mulk, Fatimid Queen of Cairo (regent
of Cairo), 367–368
Sivali, Queen (ruler of Ceylon), 367
Skemiophris (Nefrusobek), 302
Slavery
7th c., 48
17th c., 308, 309, 310
19th c., 179, 419
20th c., 45
Sobekneferu (Nefrusobek), 302
Sofya Alekseyevna (regent of Russia),
368–369
Solomon, King, 46, 47, 206
Sóndók Yówang (queen of Silla), 369–370
Sonko, 2
Soong Ch'ing-ling, Madame (acting head of
state, The People's Republic of China),
xliv, 370–371
Sorceresses, 354
Sorqhaqtani (daughter-in-law of Jenghiz-
khan), xl
South Africa, xxxvi, xlii
18th c., 170, 292–293, 305
19th c., 244, 295–296
20th c., 295–296, 436
regents in, 244
Spain, xxviii
11th–14th c., 204–205, 328, 353, 405
15th c., 63, 73–74, 124, 180–182
16th–18th c., 185, 195, 205, 259–260
19th c., 182–183, 262, 263–264
co-rulers in, 73–74, 185
regents of, 259–260, 262–263
Spray of Pearls (Shajar Al Durr), 358–359

Sri Lanka, xxviii, xliii
   1st c. B.C., 34
   1st c., 367
   13th c., 215, 229–230
   20th c., 48–49, 223–224
Stratonicé (Olympias), 315–316
Succession, right of, xxxvii, xxxviii–xxxix
   African, 2, 431
   Egyptian, 22, 167, 302
   European, 182, 254, 263
   Korean, 90–91
   matrilineal, 22, 167, 242
Suchocka, Hanna (prime minister of Poland),
   371–372
Sudan, xix, xxxix, 294–295, 307
Sugandha, Queen (regent of Kashmir),
   372–373
Suiko-tennō, Empress (ruler of Japan), 373
Sultana, 217
Sumatra, 175, 377
Sumeria, xxix, xxxvii, 222, 336, 357
   co-ruler in, 336
Sung, Empress (11th c. regent of China),
   373–374
Sung, Empress (13th c. regent of China),
   374
Sung (Soong Ch'ing-ling, Madame), 370–371
Susanne de Bourbon, Duchess (ruler of
   Bourbonnais), 374–375
Swaziland, xxviii, xxxix
   regents of, 121–122, 159, 304
Sweden, xxviii, 92–93, 245–246, 404
   regent of, 245–246
Switzerland, xxviii, 120
Syria, xxvi
   1st c. B.C., 15
   3rd–6th c., 168, 432–433
   12th–13th c., 52, 140, 249
   regents in, 52, 168

Tadj al-'Alam Safiyyat al-Din Shah (sultana of
   Atjeh in Indonesia), 377
Tahiti, xxviii, xxxvi, 334–335, 338–339
Taiohae, xxv, 407
Taitu, Empress (de facto ruler of Ethiopia),
   377–378
Takano-tennō (Kōken), 220–221
Tamara, Queen (co-ruler and "king" of
   Karthalinia, Georgia), 378–379, 390
Tamil Nadu, xxiii, 193
Tamils, 321
Ta-pu-yen, Queen (regent of Kara-Khitai
   Empire), 379–380
Tara Bāī, Empress (ruler of the Marāthā State
   of the Deccan), 380
Tausert (Twosret), 400
Tawannanna, defined, xxxvii

Tejada, Lidia Gueiler (president of Bolivia),
   380–381
Telles, Leonora (Leonora Telles), 228–229
Teng, Empress (regent of China), 381
Teresa of Castile, Countess (regent of
   Portugal), 381–382
Teuta (queen of Illyria), 382–383
Thailand, xxviii
   regent of, 364–366
Thamar (Tamara), 378–379
Thatcher, Margaret (prime minister of Great
   Britain), 383–385
Thebes, 12
Thecla (co-regent of Byzantine Empire), 385
Theodolinda, Queen (ruler, regent of
   Lombards), 386–387
Theodora, Empress (de facto co-ruler of
   Macedonian Dynasty, Byzantium),
   387–388
Theodora, Empress (regent of Eastern Roman
   Empire), 388–389
Theodora, Empress (ruler of Byzantine
   Empire), 389–390, 435
Theodora, Queen (ruler of the Empire of
   Trebizond), 390
Theophano, Empress (regent of Byzantine
   Empire), 391
Theophano (regent of Germany), 391–392
Thrace, 37
Tindu (Mongol queen of Iraq), 392–393
Tirol, xxi, 245
Tiy, Queen (de facto regent-ruler of Egypt),
   393–394
Tizard, Dame Catherine (governor-general of
   New Zealand), xliv, 394–395
Tlokwa, 244
Toba, xxviii, 173
Togo, 9
Toleration, Edict of, xliii, 81
Tomyris (queen of the Massagetae), xli,
   395–396
Tonga, xxviii, xxxvi, 334, 351–352
Töregene, Khatun (regent of Outer
   Mongolia), 396–397
Tou Hsien, Empress (regent of China),
   397
Trabzon. See Trebizond, Empire of
Traditional teachings, crafts, 365, 373,
   426
Trapezus. See Trebizond, Empire of
Trebizond, Empire of, xxviii, 24–25,
   178–179, 390
Tree of Pearls (Shajar Al Durr), 358–359
Tribhuvana, Queen (Majapahit ruler of Java),
   398
Trieu Au (ruler of Vietnamese hill-people),
   398

Tripoli (Lebanon), xviii, 169–170, 232, 233, 363–364
  regent of, 169–170
Trung Nhi and Trung Trac (co-queens of Vietnam), xlii, 398–399
Tuckabatchee, Queen of (legendary queen of Tuckabatchee Creek), 399
Turakina (Töregene), 396–397
Turkan Khatun (Kutlugh Khatun), 224
Turkestan, xxviii, 123, 379–380, 422
  regents of, 123, 379–380, 422
Turkey, xxix
  13th c. B.C., 336–337
  4th c. B.C., 39
  8th c., 293
  13th c., 390, 427–428
  14th c., 24–25, 178–179
  20th c., 94
  co-ruler, regent of, 336–337
Turko-Mongols, xl, 362, 379–380
  regent of, 293
Turunku Bakwa, Queen (founder and ruler of Zaria), xxxv, 399–400
Tuscany, xxiv, 51, 127, 282–283
Twosret, "King" (last ruler of Nineteenth Dynasty, Egypt), 400
Tyre, xviii, 249
Tz'u-an, Queen (regent of China), 400–401
Tz'u-hsi (Cixi), 95–96, 400–401

Udham Bāī, Queen (de facto co-ruler of Mughal India), 403–404
Uicab, María ("queen" of Tulum), 404
Ulrica Eleanora (queen of Sweden), 404–405
United Nations, 320
United States. See Native American tribal rulers
Ur, xxix, xxxvii, 336
Urbino, xxiv, 409
Urraca, Doña, Queen (ruler of León and Castile united), 405
Uwilingiyimana, Agathe (prime minister of Rwanda), xliii, 404–406
Vaekehu, Queen (ruler of the Taiohae tribe), 407
Vākātakas, xxiii, 335
Vendôme, xxi, 7, 75, 144–145, 196
Victoria (queen of Great Britain and Ireland), 407–409
Vietnam, xxix, xlii, 398
  co-rulers in, 398–399
Vigdis (Finnbogadottir, Vigdis), xliv, 148–150
Vittoria, Duchess (ruler of Urbino), 409

Wac-Chanil-Ahau, Lady, Maya Queen (regent of Naranjo), xxxviii, 411–412
Waizero (Zauditu), 431–432

Wajed, Hasina (prime minister of Bangladesh), xliii, 412–413
Wang (Cheng-Chun), 89–90
Wenceslas (king of Bohemia), 119, 234
Werleigh, Claudette (prime minister of Haiti), 413
Wessex, xxi, 357
West Africa, xxxv
  10th–13th c., 2–3, 112
  15th–16th c., 13–14, 21–22, 243
  17th–18th c., 24, 42, 308–310
  19th c., 354, 417–420
  20th c., 18–19, 45, 327–328, 419–420
Wilhelmina, Queen (ruler of The Netherlands), 414–415
William I (the Conqueror) (king of England), 5
Women's leadership training, xlii–xliii, 158–159, 423
Women's status, rights, 60, 87, 118, 144, 172, 387
Wu Hou (Wu Chao), Empress (ruler, regent of China), xxxix, xl, 415–416

Yaa Akyaa, Asantehemaa (queen-mother of Asante Empire), xxxix, xli, 417–419
Yaa Asantewaa, Edwesohemaa (queen mother of the Edweso tribe of the Asante), 419–420
Yamato-hime-mikoto (Pimiku), 330
Yametsu-hime (Pimiku), 330
Yehudit (Judith), 205–206
Yelena Glinskaya, Grand Princess (regent of Russia), 421–422
Ye-lü Shih (regent of Kara Khitai), 422
Yemen, xxix, 15, 39–40, 41, 46–47
  co-ruler of, 41
Yoko, Madame (ruler of the Kpa Mende Confederacy in Sierra Leone), 422–423
Yolanda (titular queen of Jerusalem), 423–424
Yolande, Empress (regent of Latin Empire), 424
Yolande de Bourgogne, Countess (ruler of Nevers), 425
Yüan Yu (regent of Sung Dynasty, China), 425
Ywahoo, Dhyani (Cherokee Nation clan chief), xliv, 425–426

Zabel, Queen (ruler of Lesser Armenia), 427–428
Zabibi, Queen (ruler of Arabian state), 428–429
Zac-Kuk, Lady ("king" and co-ruler of the Mayas of Palenque), xxxviii, 429–430
Zainab al-Nafzawiyya (Berber queen of Morocco), 430–431

Zambia, 240, 349–350
Zanzibar, xxix, xxxvi, 147–148
Zaria, xvi, xxxv, 21–22, 399
Zauditu, Empress (titular ruler of Ethiopia), 431–432
Zeeland, xxvi, 189
Zenobia, Queen (ruler of Palmyra, Syria), 432–433
Zhinga (Nzinga Mbandi), 308–310
Zia, Begum Khaleda (prime minister of Bangladesh), xliii, 433-434

Zimbabwe, 47, 308, 364
Zoë (empress of Byzantine Empire), 389, 434–436
Zubayd, xxix, 15
Zulu, xvi, 284, 292–293, 299
    regent of, 292–293
Zungu, Dr. Sibongile (chief of the South African Madlebe tribe), xlii, 436
Zutphen, xvi, 254

Guida M. Jackson holds a doctorate in comparative literature and has served as a lecturer in the English Foundations department at the University of Houston. A published novelist and playwright, she has also written two nonfiction books, a dozen short stories, and over one hundred articles.

Dr. Jackson has devoted more than 15 years to her research for this book, aided by her specialization in Third World literature and by her experiences and contacts around the world.